8th Workshop on Computational Approaches to Subjectivity, Sentiment and Social Media Analysis (WASSA 2017)

Copenhagen, Denmark
8 September 2017

ISBN: 978-1-5108-4755-2

EMNLP 2017

8th Workshop on Computational Approaches to Subjectivity, Sentiment and Social Media Analysis
WASSA 2017

Proceedings of the Workshop

September 8, 2017
Copenhagen, Denmark

Introduction

The word for 2016 was "post-truth", marking the fact that in the era of Social Media and citizen-created or reported news, the border between facts and speculation, verifiable reality and opinions has become blurred. The phenomenon of fake news has created an avalanche of public and private action, from big companies to universities and individual researchers, with the goal to find mechanisms through which this type of news can be identified (automatically).

In this context, too (or even more), detecting and analyzing opinions, arguments, stance as well as detecting the emotional effect that facts (whether truthful or not) can have on the public has become of paramount importance.

WASSA 2017 was organized in conjunction to the Conference on Empirical Methods in Natural Language Processing on September 8th, 2017, in Copenhagen, Denmark.

For this year's edition of WASSA, we received a total of 41 submissions for the main workshop, from universities and research centers all over the world, out of which 10 were accepted as long and another 5 as short papers. The main topics of the accepted papers are related to stance detection, argument mining and beyond sentiment analysic challenges, such as irony detection or linking emotions to needs and values - e.g. psychometrics.

Apart from that, for the first time, we presented a shared task on automatically detecting intensity of emotion felt by the speaker of a tweet: WASSA-2017 Shared Task on Emotion Intensity. Twenty-two teams participated in the shared task, with results that showcase the latest developments in the theoretical and applied areas of Sentiment Analysis and Opinion Mining.

We would like to thank the EMNLP 2017 Organizers and Workshop Chairs for the help and support, to the Program Committee members and the external reviewers for the time and effort spent assessing the papers. We would like to extend our thanks to our invited speakers – Dr. Iryna Gurevych, Aditya Joshi and Dr. Viktor Pekar - for accepting to deliver the keynote talks, opening new horizons for research and applications of Sentiment Analysis.

Alexandra Balahur, Saif M. Mohammad and Erik van der Goot

WASSA 2017 Chairs

Organizers:

Alexandra Balahur, European Commission Joint Research Centre

Saif M. Mohammad, National Research Council Canada

Erik van der Goot, European Commission Joint Research Centre

Program Committee:

Sabine Bergler - Concordia University, Canada

Felipe Bravo - University of Waikato, New Zealand

Nicoletta Calzolari - CNR Pisa, Italy

Erik Cambria - University of Stirling, U.K.

Fermin Cruz Mata - University of Seville, Spain

Montse Cuadros - Vicomtech, Spain

Lingjia Deng - University of Pittsburg, U.S.A.

Michael Gamon – Microsoft, U.S.A.

Veronique Hoste - University of Ghent, Belgium

Carlos Iglesias - Universidad Politecnica de Madrid, Spain

Ruben Izquierdo Bevia – Nuance, Spain

Aditya Joshi - IITB-Monash Research Academy, India

Manfred Klenner, University of Zuerich, Switzerland

Roman Klinger, University of Stuttgart, Germany

Emiel Krahmer - University of Tilburg, The Netherlands

Isa Maks - Vrije Universiteit Amsterdam, The Netherlands

Maite Martin Valdivia – University of Jaen, Spain

Karo Moilanen - University of Oxford, U.K.

Günter Neumann - DFKI, Germany

Malvina Nissim - University of Groeningen, The Netherlands

Constantin Orasan - University of Wolverhampton, U.K.

Viviana Patti - University of Torino, Italy

Viktor Pekar - University of Wolverhampton, U.K.

Jose-Manuel Perea-Ortega – University of Extremadura, Spain

Daniel Preotiuc-Pietro - University of Pennsylvania, U.S.A.

Paolo Rosso - Technical University of Valencia, Spain

Josef Steinberger - West Bohemia University Prague, The Czech Republic

Mike Thelwall - University of Wolverhampton, U.K

Mariët Theune - University of Twente, The Netherlands

Dan Tufis - RACAI, Romania

Alfonso Ureña - University of Jaén, Spain

Tony Veale - University College Dublin, Ireland

Michael Wiegand - Saarland University, Germany

Taras Zagibalov - Brantwatch, U.K.

Invited Speakers:

Dr. Iryna Gurevych - University of Darmstadt, Germany
Dr. Viktor Pekar - University of Birmingham, U.K.
Aditya Joshi - IIIT Hyderabad, India

Table of Contents

Friday, September 8, 2017

08:30–08:40   **Opening Remarks**

08:40–10:30   **Session 1: Irony, stance and negotiating interpersonal meaning**

08:40–09:15   *Detecting Sarcasm Using Different Forms Of Incongruity*
Aditya Joshi

09:15–09:40   *Assessing State-of-the-Art Sentiment Models on State-of-the-Art Sentiment Datasets*
Jeremy Barnes, Roman Klinger and Sabine Schulte im Walde

09:40–10:05   *Annotation, Modelling and Analysis of Fine-Grained Emotions on a Stance and Sentiment Detection Corpus*
Hendrik Schuff, Jeremy Barnes, Julian Mohme, Sebastian Padó and Roman Klinger

10:05–10:30   *Ranking Right-Wing Extremist Social Media Profiles by Similarity to Democratic and Extremist Groups*
Matthias Hartung, Roman Klinger, Franziska Schmidtke and Lars Vogel

10:30–11:00   *Coffee Break*

11:00–12:30   **Session 2: Emotion Intensity Task**

11:00–11:40   *WASSA-2017 Shared Task on Emotion Intensity*
Saif Mohammad and Felipe Bravo-Marquez

11:40–12:05   *IMS at EmoInt-2017: Emotion Intensity Prediction with Affective Norms, Automatically Extended Resources and Deep Learning*
Maximilian Köper, Evgeny Kim and Roman Klinger

12:05–12:30   *Prayas at EmoInt 2017: An Ensemble of Deep Neural Architectures for Emotion Intensity Prediction in Tweets*
Prayas Jain, Pranav Goel, Devang Kulshreshtha and Kaushal Kumar Shukla

12:30–14:00   *Lunch Break*

Friday, September 8, 2017 (continued)

xv

18:25–18:30   Closing remarks

Detecting Sarcasm Using Different Forms Of Incongruity

Aditya Joshi[1,2,3]

[1]Indian Institute of Technology Bombay, India, [2]Monash University, Australia
[3]IITB-Monash Research Academy, India
adityaj@cse.iitb.ac.in

Sarcasm is a form of verbal irony that is intended to express contempt or ridicule. Often quoted as a challenge to sentiment analysis, sarcasm involves use of words of positive or no polarity to convey negative sentiment. Incongruity has been observed to be at the heart of sarcasm understanding in humans. Our work in sarcasm detection identifies different forms of incongruity and employs different machine learning techniques to capture them. This talk will describe the approach, datasets and challenges in sarcasm detection using different forms of incongruity.

We identify two forms of incongruity: incongruity which can be understood based on the target text and common background knowledge, and incongruity which can be understood based on the target text and additional, specific context. The former involves use of sentiment-based features, word embeddings, and topic models. The latter involves creation of author's historical context based on their historical data, and creation of conversational context for sarcasm detection of dialogue.

1

Proceedings of the 8th Workshop on Computational Approaches to Subjectivity, Sentiment and Social Media Analysis, page 1
Copenhagen, Denmark, September 7–11, 2017. ©2017 Association for Computational Linguistics

Assessing State-of-the-Art Sentiment Models on State-of-the-Art Sentiment Datasets

Jeremy Barnes, Roman Klinger, and **Sabine Schulte im Walde**
Institut für Maschinelle Sprachverarbeitung
University of Stuttgart
Pfaffenwaldring 5b, 70569 Stuttgart, Germany
{barnesjy,klinger,schulte}@ims.uni-stuttgart.de

Abstract

There has been a good amount of progress in sentiment analysis over the past 10 years, including the proposal of new methods and the creation of benchmark datasets. In some papers, however, there is a tendency to compare models only on one or two datasets, either because of time restraints or because the model is tailored to a specific task. Accordingly, it is hard to understand how well a certain model generalizes across different tasks and datasets. In this paper, we contribute to this situation by comparing several models on six different benchmarks, which belong to different domains and additionally have different levels of granularity (binary, 3-class, 4-class and 5-class). We show that Bi-LSTMs perform well across datasets and that both LSTMs and Bi-LSTMs are particularly good at fine-grained sentiment tasks (*i. e.*, with more than two classes). Incorporating sentiment information into word embeddings during training gives good results for datasets that are lexically similar to the training data. With our experiments, we contribute to a better understanding of the performance of different model architectures on different data sets. Consequently, we detect novel state-of-the-art results on the *SenTube* datasets.

1 Introduction

The task of analyzing private states expressed by an author in text, such as sentiment, emotion or affect, can give us access to a wealth of hidden information to analyze product reviews (Liu et al., 2005), political views (Speriosu et al., 2011), or to identify potentially dangerous activity on the Internet (Forsyth and Martell, 2007). The first approaches in this field of research depended on the use of words at a symbolic level (unigrams, bigrams, bag-of-words features), where generalizing to new words was difficult (Pang et al., 2002; Riloff and Wiebe, 2003).

Current state-of-the-art methods rely on features extracted in an unsupervised manner, mainly through one of the existing pre-trained word embedding approaches (Collobert et al., 2011; Mikolov et al., 2013; Pennington et al., 2014). These approaches represent words as some function of their contexts, enabling machine learning algorithms to generalize over tokens that have similar representations, arguably giving them an advantage over previous symbolic approaches.

In order to evaluate state-of-the-art models (both symbolic and embedding-based), different datasets are used. However, it is not clear that a model that performs well on one certain dataset will transfer well to other datasets with different properties. The work we describe in this paper aims at discovering if there are certain models that generally perform better or if there are certain models that are better adapted to certain kinds of datasets. Ultimately, the goal of this paper is to contribute to the current situation by supporting the choice of a method for novel domains and datasets, based on properties of the task at hand.

Our main contributions are, therefore, comparing seven approaches to sentiment analysis on six benchmark datasets[1]. We show that

- bidirectional LSTMs perform well across datasets,
- both LSTMs and bidirectional LSTMs are particularly good at fine-grained sentiment tasks,
- and embeddings trained jointly for semantics

---

[1] The code and embeddings for the best models are available at http://www.ims.uni-stuttgart.de/data/sota_sentiment

Proceedings of the 8th Workshop on Computational Approaches to Subjectivity, Sentiment and Social Media Analysis, pages 2–12
Copenhagen, Denmark, September 7–11, 2017. ©2017 Association for Computational Linguistics

and sentiment perform well on datasets that are similar to the training data.

2   Related Work

This section discusses three approaches to sentiment analysis and then describes in detail benchmark datasets which will be used in the experiments.

2.1   Approaches

To analyze the performance of state-of-the-art methods across datasets, we experiment with three approaches to sentiment analysis: (1) updating pre-trained word embeddings using a neural classifier and labeled data, (2) updating pre-trained word embeddings using a semantic lexicon, and (3) training word embeddings to jointly maximize a language model score and a sentiment score. Sections 2.1.1 to 2.1.3 discuss these three approaches. We focus on sentiment-related methods, however, where appropriate, we discuss general approaches which can be adapted to this use case in a straightforward manner as well.

2.1.1   Retrofitting to Semantic Lexicons

There have been several proposals to improve the quality of word embeddings using semantic lexicons. Yu and Dredze (2014) propose several methods which combine the CBOW architecture (Mikolov et al., 2013) and a second objective function which attempts to maximize the relations found within some semantic lexicon. They use both the Paraphrase Database (Ganitkevitch et al., 2013) and WordNet (Fellbaum, 1999) and test their models on language modeling and semantic similarity tasks. They report that their method leads to an improvement on both tasks.

Kiela et al. (2015) aim to improve embeddings by augmenting the context of a given word while training a skip-gram model (Mikolov et al., 2013). They sample extra context words, taken either from a thesaurus or association data, and incorporate this into the context of the word for each update. The evaluation is both intrinsical, on word similarity and relatedness tasks, as well as extrinsical on TOEFL synonym and document classification tasks. The augmentation strategy improves the word vectors on all tasks.

Faruqui et al. (2015) propose a method to refine word vectors by using relational information from semantic lexicons (we will refer to this method

in this paper as RETROFIT). They require a vocabulary $V = \{w_1, \ldots, w_n\}$, its word embeddings matrix $\hat{Q} = \{\hat{q}_1, \ldots, \hat{q}_n\}$, where each $\hat{q}_i$ is one vector for one word w_i and an ontology Ω, which they represent as an undirected graph (V, E) with one vertex for each word type and edges $(w_i, w_j) \in E \subseteq V \times V$. They attempt to learn the matrix $Q = \{q_1, \ldots, q_n\}$, such that q_i is similar to both $\hat{q}_i$ and $q_j \forall j$ for $(i, j) \in E$. Therefore, the objective function to minimize is

$$\Psi(Q) = \sum_{i=1}^{n} \left[\alpha_i ||q_i - \hat{q}_i||^2 + \sum_{(i,j) \in E} \beta_{i,j} ||q_i - q_j||^2 \right],$$

where α and β control the relative strengths of associations.

They use the XL version of the Paraphrase Database (PPDB-XL) dataset (Ganitkevitch et al., 2013), which is a dataset of paraphrases as the semantic lexicon, to improve the original vectors. This dataset includes 8 million lexical paraphrases collected from bilingual corpora, where words in language A are considered paraphrases if they are consistently translated to the same word in language B. They then test on the Stanford Sentiment Treebank (Socher et al., 2013). They train an L2-regularized logistic regression classifier on the average of the word embeddings for a text and find improvements after retrofitting.

All above approaches show improvements over previous word embedding approaches (Mnih and Teh, 2012; Yu and Dredze, 2014; Xu et al., 2014) on this data set.

2.1.2   Joint Training

Maas et al. (2011) were the first to jointly train semantic and sentiment word vectors. In order to capture semantic similarities, they propose a probabilistic model using a continuous mixture model over words, similar to Latent Dirichlet Allocation (LDA, Blei et al., 2003). To capture sentiment information, they include a sentiment term which uses logistic regression to predict the sentiment of a document. The full objective function is a combination of the semantic and sentiment objectives. They test their model on several sentiment and subjectivity benchmarks. Their results indicate that including the sentiment information during training actually leads to decreased performance.

Tang et al. (2014) take the joint training approach and simultaneously incorporate syntactic[2]

---

[2] We use the authors' terminology here, but make no as-

and sentiment information into their word embeddings (we refer to this method as JOINT). They extend the word embedding approach of Collobert et al. (2011), who use a neural network to predict whether an n-gram is a true n-gram or a "corrupted" version. They use the hinge-loss

$$\text{loss}_{\text{cw}}(t, t^r) = \max(0, 1 - f^{cw}(t) + f^{cw}(t^r)) \tag{1}$$

and backpropagate the error to the corresponding word embeddings. Here, t is the original n-gram, t^r is the corrupted n-gram and f^{cw} is the language model score. Tang et al. (2014) add a sentiment hinge loss to the Collobert and Weston model, as

$$\text{loss}_{s}(t, t^r) = \max(0, 1 - \delta_s(t)f_1^s(t) + \delta_s(t)f_1^s(t^r)), \tag{2}$$

where f_1^s is the predicted negative score and $\delta_s(t)$ is an indicator function that reflects the sentiment of a sentence. $\delta_s(t)$ is 1 if the true sentiment is positive and -1 if it is negative. They then use a weighted sum of both scores to create their sentiment embeddings:

$$\text{loss}_{\text{combined}}(t, t^r) = \alpha \cdot \text{loss}_{\text{cw}}(t, t^r) + (1 - \alpha) \cdot \text{loss}_{s}(t, t^r). \tag{3}$$

This requires sentiment-annotated data for training both the syntactic and sentiment losses, which they acquire by collecting tweets associated with certain emoticons. In this way, they are able to simultaneously incorporate sentiment and semantic information relevant to their task. They test their approach on the SemEval 2013 twitter dataset (Nakov et al., 2013), changing the task from three-class to binary classification, and find that they outperform other approaches.

Overall, the joint approach shows promise for tasks with a large amount of distantly-labeled data.

2.1.3 Supervised training

The most common approach to sentiment analysis is to use pre-trained word embeddings in combination with a supervised classifier. In this framework, the word embedding algorithm acts as a feature extractor for classification.

Recurrent neural networks (RNNs), such as the LONG SHORT-TERM MEMORY network (LSTM) (Hochreiter and Schmidhuber, 1997) or the GATED

RECURRENT UNITS (GRUs) (Chung et al., 2014), are a variant of a feed-forward network which includes a memory state capable of learning long distance dependencies. In various forms, they have proven useful for text classification tasks (Tai et al., 2015; Tang et al., 2016). Socher et al. (2013) and Tai et al. (2015) use Glove vectors (Pennington et al., 2014) in combination with a recurrent neural networks and train on the Stanford Sentiment Treebank (Socher et al., 2013). Since this dataset is annotated for sentiment at each node of a parse tree, they train and test on these annotated phrases.

Both Socher et al. (2013) and Tai et al. (2015) also propose various RNNs which are able to take better advantage of the labeled nodes and which achieve better results than standard RNNs. However, these models require annotated parse trees, which are not necessarily available for other datasets.

CONVOLUTIONAL NEURAL NETWORKS (CNN) have proven effective for text classification (dos Santos and Gatti, 2014; Kim, 2014; Flekova and Gurevych, 2016). Kim (2014) use skipgram vectors (Mikolov et al., 2013) as input to a variety of Convolutional Neural Networks and test on seven datasets, including the Stanford Sentiment Treebank (Socher et al., 2013). The best performing setup across datasets is a single layer CNN which updates the original skipgram vectors during training.

Overall, these approaches currently achieve state-of-the-art results on many datasets, but they have not been compared to retrofitting or joint training approaches.

2.2 Datasets

We choose to evaluate the approaches presented in Section 2.1 on a number of different datasets from different domains, which also have differing levels of granularity of class labels. The Stanford Sentiment Treebank and SemEval 2013 shared-task dataset have already been used as benchmarks for some of the approaches mentioned in Section 2.1. Table 1 shows which approaches have been tested on which datasets and Table 2 gives an overview of the statistics for each dataset.

2.2.1 Stanford Sentiment

The Stanford Sentiment Treebank (*SST-fine*) (Socher et al., 2013) is a dataset of movie reviews which was annotated for 5 levels of sentiment: strong negative, negative, neutral, positive, and

---

sumptions that the distributional representation encodes information directly pertaining to syntax.

	Train	Dev.	Test	Number of Labels	Avg. Sentence Length	Vocabulary Size
SST-fine	8,544	1,101	2,210	5	19.53	19,500
SST-binary	6,920	872	1,821	2	19.67	17,539
OpeNER	2,780	186	743	4	4.28	2,447
SenTube-A	3,381	225	903	2	28.54	18,569
SenTube-T	4,997	333	1,334	2	28.73	20,276
SemEval	6,021	890	2,376	3	22.40	21,163

Table 2: Statistics of datasets. Train, Dev., and Test refer to the number of examples for each subsection of a dataset. The number of labels corresponds to the annotation scheme, where: two is positive and negative; three is positive, neutral, negative; four is strong positive, positive, negative, strong negative; five is strong positive, positive, neutral, negative, strong negative.

	BOW	AVE	RETROFIT	JOINT	LSTM	BILSTM	CNN
SST-fine					+	+	+
SST-binary		+	+		+	+	+
OpeNER	+						
SenTube-A	+						
SenTube-T	+						
SemEval				+			

Table 1: Mapping of previous state-of-the-art methods to previous evaluations on state-of-the-art data sets. An + indicates that we are aware of a publication which reports on this combination and a – indicates our assumption that no reported results are available.

strong positive. It is annotated both at the clause level, where each node in a binary tree is given a sentiment score, as well as at sentence level. We use the standard split of 8544/1102/2210 for training, validation and testing. In order to compare with Faruqui et al. (2015), we also adapt the dataset to the task of binary sentiment analysis, where strong negative and negative are mapped to one label, and strong positive and positive are mapped to another label, and the neutral examples are dropped. This leads to a slightly different split of 6920/872/1821 (we refer to this dataset as *SST-binary*).

2.2.2 OpeNER

The *OpeNER* dataset (Agerri et al., 2013) is a dataset of hotel reviews in which each review is annotated for opinions. An opinion includes sentiment holders, targets, and phrases, of which only the sentiment phrase is obligatory. Additionally, sentiment phrases are annotated for four levels of sentiment: strong negative, negative, positive and strong positive. We use a split of 2780/186/734 examples.

2.2.3 Sentube Datasets

The SenTube datasets (Uryupina et al., 2014) are texts that are taken from YouTube comments regarding automobiles and tablets. These comments are normally directed towards a commercial or a video that contains information about the product. We take only those comments that have some polarity towards the target product in the video. For the automobile dataset (*SenTube-A*), this gives a 3381/225/903 training, validation, and test split. For the tablets dataset (*SenTube-T*) the splits are 4997/333/1334. These are annotated for positive, negative, and neutral sentiment.

2.2.4 Semeval 2013

The SemEval 2013 Twitter dataset (*SemEval*) (Nakov et al., 2013) is a dataset that contains tweets collected for the 2013 SemEval shared task B. Each tweet was annotated for three levels of sentiment: positive, negative, or neutral. There were originally 9684/1654/3813 tweets annotated, but when we downloaded the dataset, we were only able to download 6021/890/2376 due to many of the tweets no longer being available.

3 Experimental Setup

We compare seven approaches, five of which fall into the categories mentioned in Section 2, as well as two baselines. The models and parameters are described in Section 3.1. We test these models on the benchmark datasets mentioned in Section 2.2.

3.1 Models

3.1.1 Baselines

We compare our models against two baselines. First, we train an L2-regularized logistic regression on a bag-of-words representation (BOW) of the training examples, where each example is represented as a vector of size n, with $n = |V|$ and V the vocabulary. This is a standard baseline for text classification.

Our second baseline is an L2-regularized logistic regression classifier trained on the average of the word vectors in the training example (AVE). We train word embeddings using the skip-gram with negative sampling algorithm (Mikolov et al., 2013) on a 2016 Wikipedia dump, using 50-, 100-, 200-, and 600-dimensional vectors, a window size of 10, 5 negative samples, and we set the subsampling parameter to 10^{-4}. Additionally, we use the publicly available 300-dimensional GoogleNews vectors[3] in order to compare to previous work.

3.1.2 Retrofitting

We apply the approach by Faruqui et al. (2015) and make use of the code[4] released in combination with the PPDB-XL lexicon, as this gave the best results for sentiment analysis in their experiments. We train for 10 iterations. Following the authors' setup, for testing we train an L2-regularized logistic regression classifier on the average word embeddings for a phrase (RETROFIT).

3.1.3 Joint Training

For the joint method, we use the 50-dimensional sentiment embeddings provided by Tang et al. (2014). Additionally, we create 100-, 200-, and 300-dimensional embeddings using the code that is publicly available[5]. We use the same hyperparameters as Tang et al. (2014): five million positive and negative tweets crawled using hashtags as proxies for sentiment, a 20-dimensional hidden layer, and a window size of three. Following the authors' setup, we concatenate the maximum, minimum and average vectors of the word embeddings for each phrase. We then train a linear SVM on these representations (JOINT).

3.1.4 Supervised Training

We implement a standard LSTM which has an embedding layer that maps the input to a 50-, 100-, 200-, 300-, or 600-dimensional vector, depending on the embeddings used to initialize the layer. These vectors then pass to an LSTM layer. We feed the final hidden state to a standard fully-connected 50-dimensional dense layer and then to a softmax layer, which gives us a probability distribution over our classes. As a regularizer, we use a dropout (Srivastava et al., 2014) of 0.5 before the LSTM layer.

The BIDIRECTIONAL LSTM (BiLSTM) has the same architecture as the normal LSTM, but includes an additional layer which runs from the end of the text to the front. This approach has led to state-of-the-art results for POS-tagging (Plank et al., 2016), dependency parsing (Kiperwasser and Goldberg, 2016) and text classification (Zhou et al., 2016), among others. We use the same parameters as the LSTM, but concatenate the two hidden layers before passing them to the dense layer[6].

We also train a simple one-layer CNN with one convolutional layer on top of pre-trained word embeddings. The first layer is an embeddings layer that maps the input of length n (padded when needed) to an $n \times R$ dimensional matrix, where R is the dimensionality of the word embeddings. The embedding matrix is then convoluted with filter sizes of 2, 3, and 4, followed by a pooling layer of length 2. This is then fed to a fully connected dense layer with ReLU activations (Nair and Hinton, 2010) and finally to the softmax layer. We again use dropout (0.5), this time before and after the convolutional layers.

For all neural models, we initialize our word representations with the skip-gram algorithm with negative sampling (Mikolov et al., 2013). For the 300-dimensional vectors, we use the publicly available GoogleNews vectors. For the other dimensions (50, 100, 200, 600), we create skip-gram vectors with a window size of 10, 5 negative samples and run 5 iterations. For out-of-vocabulary words, we use vectors initialized randomly between -0.25 and 0.25 to approximate the variance of the pre-trained vectors. We train our models using ADAM (Kingma and Ba, 2014) and a minibatch size of 32

---

[3] https://code.google.com/archive/p/word2vec/

[4] https://github.com/mfaruqui/retrofitting

[5] http://ir.hit.edu.cn/~dytang

[6] For the neural models on the *SST-fine* and *SST-binary* datasets, we do not achieve results as high as Tai et al. (2015) and Kim (2014), because we train our models only on sentence representations, not on the labeled phrase representations. We do this to be able to compare across datasets.

and tune the hidden layer dimension and number of training epochs on the validation set.

4 Results

Table 3 shows the results for the seven models across all datasets, as well as the macro-averaged results. We visualize them in Figure 3. We performed random approximation tests (Yeh, 2000) using the *sigf* package (Padó, 2006) with 10,000 iterations to determine the statistical significance of differences between models. Since the reported accuracies for the neural models are the means over five runs, we cannot use this technique in a straightforward manner. Therefore, we perform the random approximation tests between the runs[7] and consider the models statistically different if a majority (at least 3) of the runs are statistically different ($p < 0.01$, which corresponds to $p < 0.05$ with Bonferroni correction for 5 hypotheses). The results of statistical testing are summarized in Table 2.

Obviously, BOW continues to be a strong baseline: Though it never provides the best result on a dataset, it gives better results than AVE on *OpeNER*, *SenTube-T*, and *SemEval*. Surprisingly, it also performs better than JOINT on the same sets except for *SenTube-T*. Similarly, it outperforms RETROFIT on *SenTube-T* and *SemEval*.

RETROFIT performs better than CNN on *SST-fine* and JOINT on *SST-fine*, *SST-binary*, and *OpeNER*. It also improves the results of AVE across all datasets but *SenTube-A* and *SemEval* datasets.

Although JOINT does not perform well across datasets and, in fact, does not surpass the baselines on some datasets, it does lead to good results on *SemEval* and to state-of-the-art results on *SenTube-A* and *SenTube-T*.

Similarly to RETROFIT, CNN does not outperform any of the other methods on any dataset. As said, this method does not beat the baseline on *SST-fine*, *SenTube-A*, and *SenTube-T*. However, it outperforms the AVE baseline on *SST-binary* and *OpeNER*.

The best models are LSTM and BiLSTM. The best overall model is BiLSTM, which outperforms the other models on half of the tasks (*SST-fine*,

Opener, and *SemEval*) and consistently beats the baseline. This is in line with other research (Plank et al., 2016; Kiperwasser and Goldberg, 2016; Zhou et al., 2016), which suggests that this model is very robust across tasks as well as datasets. The differences in performance between LSTM and BiLSTM, however, are only significant (p < 0.01) on the *SemEval* dataset.

We also see that the difference in performance between the two LSTM models and the others is larger on datasets with fine-grained labels (BiLSTM 45.6 and LSTM 45.3 vs. an average of 40 for all others on the *SST-fine* and BiLSTM 83 and LSTM 83.1 vs. an average of 76.5 on *OpeNER*). These differences between the LSTM models and other models are statistically significant, except for the difference between BiLSTM and CNN at 50 dimensions on the *OpeNER* dataset.

Our analysis of different dimensionalities as input for the classification models reveals that, typically, the higher dimensional vectors (300 or 600) outperform lower dimensions. The only differences are in JOINT for *SenTube-T* and *SemEval* and LSTM for *SenTube-A* and AVE on all datasets except *OpeNER*.

5 Discussion

While approaches that average the word embeddings for a sentence are comparable to state-of-the-art results (Iyyer et al., 2015), AVE and RETROFIT do not perform particularly well. This is likely due to the fact that logistic regression lacks the non-linearities which Iyyer et al. (2015) found helped, especially at deeper layers. Averaging all of the embeddings for longer phrases also seems to lead to representations that do not contain enough information for the classifier.

We also experimented with using large sentiment lexicons as the semantic lexicon for retrofitting, but found that this hurt the representation more than it helped. We believe this is because there are not enough kinds of relationships to exploit the graph structure and by trying to collapse all words towards either a positive or negative center, too much information is lost.

We expected that JOINT would perform well on *SemEval*, given that it was designed for this task, but it was surprising that it performed so well on the *SenTube* datasets. It might be due to the fact that comments for these three datasets are comparably informal and make use of emoticons and Internet

---

[7]We compare the results from the first run of model A with the first run of model B, then the second from A with the second from B, an so forth. An alternative would have been to use a t-test, which is common in such setting. However, we opted against this as the independence assumptions for such test do not hold.

	Model	Dim.	SST-fine	SST-binary	OpeNER	SenTube-A	SenTube-T	SemEval	Macro-Avg.
Baselines	BOW		40.3	80.7	77.1[4]	60.6[5]	66.0[5]	65.5	65.0
	AVE	50	38.9	74.1	59.5	62.0	61.7	58.1	59.0
		100	39.7	76.7	67.2	61.5	61.8	58.8	60.9
		200	40.7	78.2	69.3	60.6	62.8	61.1	62.1
		300	41.6	80.3[3]	76.3	61.5	64.3	63.6	64.6
		600	40.6	79.1	77.0	56.4	62.9	61.8	63.0
State-of-the-Art Methods	RETROFIT	50	39.2	75.3	63.9	60.6	62.3	58.1	59.9
		100	39.7	76.7	70.0	61.4	62.8	59.5	61.7
		200	41.8	78.3	73.5	60.0	63.2	61.2	63.0
		300	42.2	81.2[3]	75.9	61.7	63.6	61.8	64.4
		600	42.9	81.1	78.3	60.0	65.5	62.4	65.0
	JOINT	50	35.8	70.6	72.9	65.1	**68.1**	66.8[6]	63.2
		100	34.3	70.8	67.0	64.3	66.4	60.1	60.5
		200	33.7	72.3	68.6	**66.2**	66.6	58.4	61.0
		300	36.0	71.6	70.1	64.7	67.6	60.8	61.8
		600	36.9	74.0	75.8	63.7	64.2	60.9	62.6
	LSTM	50	43.3 (1.0)	80.5 (0.4)	81.1 (0.4)	58.9 (0.8)	63.4 (3.1)	63.9 (1.7)	65.2 (1.2)
		100	44.1 (0.8)	79.5 (0.6)	82.4 (0.5)	58.9 (1.1)	63.1 (0.4)	67.3 (1.1)	65.9 (0.7)
		200	44.1 (1.6)	80.9 (0.6)	82.0 (0.6)	58.6 (0.6)	65.2 (1.6)	66.8 (1.3)	66.3 (1.1)
		300	45.3[1] (1.9)	81.7[1] (0.7)	82.3 (0.6)	57.4 (1.3)	63.6 (0.7)	67.6 (0.6)	66.3 (1.0)
		600	44.5 (1.4)	**83.1** (0.9)	81.2 (0.8)	57.4 (1.1)	65.7 (1.2)	67.5 (0.7)	66.5 (1)
	BILSTM	50	43.6 (1.2)	82.9 (0.7)	79.2 (0.8)	59.5 (1.1)	65.6 (1.2)	64.3 (1.2)	65.9 (1.0)
		100	43.8 (1.1)	79.8 (1.0)	82.4 (0.6)	58.6 (0.8)	66.4 (1.4)	65.2 (0.6)	66.0 (0.9)
		200	44.0 (0.9)	80.1 (0.6)	81.7 (0.5)	58.9 (0.3)	63.3 (1.0)	66.4 (0.3)	65.7 (0.6)
		300	**45.6**[1] (1.6)	82.6[1] (0.7)	**82.5** (0.6)	59.3 (1.0)	66.2 (1.5)	65.1 (0.9)	**66.9** (1.1)
		600	43.2 (1.1)	83 (0.4)	81.5 (0.5)	59.2 (1.6)	66.4 (1.1)	**68.5** (0.7)	**66.9** (0.9)
	CNN	50	39.9 (0.7)	81.7 (0.3)	80.0 (0.9)	55.2 (0.7)	57.4 (3.1)	65.7 (1.0)	63.3 (1.1)
		100	40.1 (1.0)	81.6 (0.5)	79.5 (0.9)	56.0 (2.2)	61.5 (1.1)	64.2 (0.8)	63.8 (1.1)
		200	39.1 (1.1)	80.7 (0.4)	79.8 (0.7)	56.3 (1.8)	64.1 (1.1)	65.3 (0.8)	64.2 (1.0)
		300	39.8[2] (0.7)	81.3[2] (1.1)	80.3 (0.9)	57.3 (0.5)	62.1 (1.0)	63.5 (1.3)	64.0 (0.9)
		600	40.7 (2.6)	82.7 (1.2)	79.2 (1.4)	56.6 (0.6)	61.3 (2)	65.9 (1.8)	64.4 (1.5)

Table 3: Accuracy on the test sets. For all neural models we perform 5 runs and show the mean and standard deviation. The best results for each dataset is given in **bold** and results that have been previously reported are highlighted. All results derive from our reimplementation of the methods. We describe significance values in the text and appendix. Footnotes refer to the work where a method was previously tested on a specific dataset, although not necessarily with the same results: [1] Tai et al. (2015) [2] Kim (2014) [3] Faruqui et al. (2015) [4] Lambert (2015) [5] Uryupina et al. (2014) [6] Tang et al. (2014).

jargon. We performed a short analysis of datasets (shown in Table 4), where we take frequency of emoticons usage as an indirect indicator of informal speech and found that, indeed, the frequency of emoticons in the *SemEval* and *SenTube* datasets diverges significantly from the other datasets. The fact that JOINT is distantly trained on similar data gives it an advantage over other models on these datasets. This leads us to believe that this approach would transfer well to novel sentiment analysis tasks with similar properties.

The fact that CNN performs much better on *OpeNER* may be due to the smaller size of the phrases (an average of 4.28 vs. 20+ for other datasets), however, further analyses to prove this are needed.

The good results that both LSTM models achieved on the more fine-grained sentiment datasets (*SST-fine* and *OpeNER*) seem to indicate that LSTMs are able to learn dependencies that help to differentiate strong and weak versions of sentiment better than other models. This is supported by the confusion matrices shown in Figure 1. This makes them natural candidates for fine-grained sentiment analysis tasks.

LSTM perfoms better than BILSTM on two datasets but these differences are not statistically significant.

The effect of the dimensionality of the input for the classification models suggests that larger

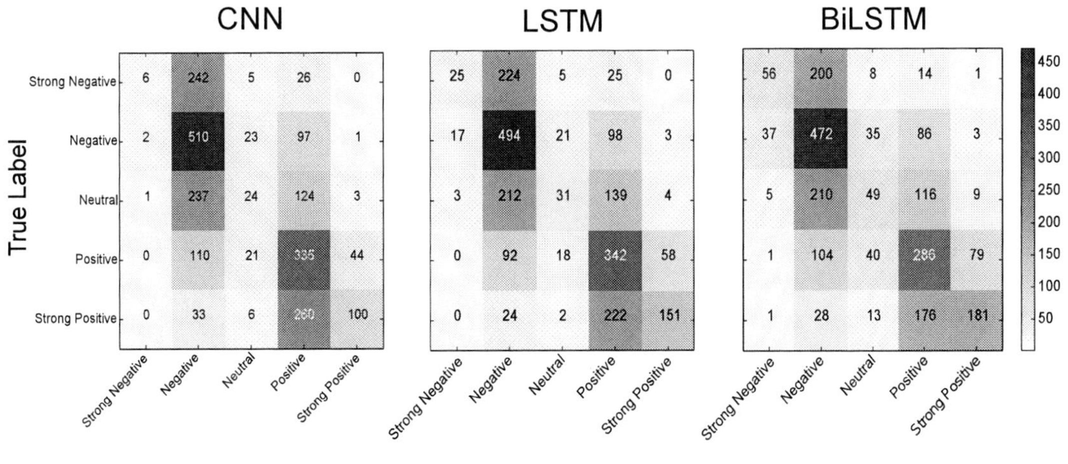

Figure 1: Confusion matrices of CNN, LSTM, and BiLSTM on *SST-fine* dataset. We can see that both LSTM and BiLSTM perform much better than CNN on strong negative, neutral, and strong positive classes.

χ^2 with SemEval	χ^2	p-value
SST-fine	19.408	0.002
SST-binary	19.408	0.002
OpeNER	19.408	0.002
SenTube-A	9.305	0.097
SenTube-T	7.377	0.194

Table 4: χ^2 statistics comparing the frequency of the following emoticons over the different datasets, :), :(, :-), :-(, :D, =). The difference in frequency of emoticons between the SemEval and SenTube datasets is not significant ($p > 0.05$), while for SST and OpeNER it is ($p < 0.05$).

dimensionalities tend to perform better. This seems particularly true for RETROFIT, which continues gaining performance even at 600 dimensions. Most other approaches perform slightly better at 600 dimensions, but AVE consistently performs worse at 600 than at 300.

6 Conclusions

The goal of this paper has been to discover which models perform better across different datasets. We compared state-of-the-art models (both symbolic and embedding-based) on six benchmark datasets with different characteristics and showed that Bi-LSTMs perform well across datasets and that both LSTMs and Bi-LSTMs are particularly good at fine-grained sentiment tasks. Additionally, incorporating sentiment information into word embeddings during training gives good results for datasets that are lexically similar to the training data. Finally, we reported a new state of the art on the *SenTube* datasets.

Acknowledgments

We thank Sebastian Padó for fruitful discussions. Thanks to Diego Frassinelli for help with the statistical tests. This work has been partially supported by the DFG Collaborative Research Centre SFB 732.

References

Rodrigo Agerri, Montse Cuadros, Sean Gaines, and German Rigau. 2013. OpeNER: Open polarity enhanced named entity recognition. In *Sociedad Española para el Procesamiento del Lenguaje Natural*, volume 51.

David M. Blei, Andrew Y. Ng, and Michael I. Jordan. 2003. Latent dirichlet allocation. *Journal of Machine Learning Research*, 3:993–1022.

Junyoung Chung, Çaglar Gülçehre, KyungHyun Cho, and Yoshua Bengio. 2014. Empirical evaluation of gated recurrent neural networks on sequence modeling. *CoRR*, abs/1412.3555.

Ronan Collobert, Jason Weston, Léon Bottou, Michael Karlen, Koray Kavukcuoglu, and Pavel Kuksa. 2011. Natural language processing (almost) from scratch. *Journal of Machine Learning Research*, 12:2493–2537.

Manaal Faruqui, Jesse Dodge, Sujay Kumar Jauhar, Chris Dyer, Eduard Hovy, and Noah A. Smith. 2015.

	BOW	AVE	RETROFIT	JOINT	LSTM	BILSTM	CNN
BOW		*SST-fine* *SenTube-A* *SenTube-T* *SemEval*	*SST-fine* *OpeNER* *SenTube-A* *SemEval*	*SST-fine* *SST-binary* *OpeNER* *SenTube-A* *SenTube-T* *SemEval*	*SST-fine* *SST-binary* *OpeNER* *SemEval*	*SST-fine* *SST-binary* *OpeNER* *SemEval*	*SST-binary* *OpeNER* *SenTube-A* *SenTube-T*
AVE	3		*SST-fine* *SST-binary* *SenTube-A* *SenTube-T*	*SST-fine* *SST-binary* *OpeNER* *SenTube-A* *SenTube-T* *SemEval*	*SST-fine* *SST-binary* *OpeNER* *SenTube-A* *SenTube-T* *SemEval*	*SST-fine* *SST-binary* *OpeNER* *SenTube-A* *SemEval*	*SST-fine* *SST-binary* *OpeNER* *SenTube-A* *SemEval*
RETROFIT	3	3		*SST-fine* *SST-binary* *OpeNER* *SenTube-A* *SenTube-T* *SemEval*	*SST-fine* *SST-binary* *OpeNER* *SenTube-A* *SemEval*	*SST-fine* *SST-binary* *OpeNER* *SenTube-A* *SemEval*	*SST-fine* *SST-binary* *SenTube-A* *SemEval*
JOINT	3	3	3		*SST-fine* *SST-binary* *OpeNER* *SenTube-A* *SenTube-T*	*SST-fine* *SST-binary* *OpeNER* *SenTube-A* *SenTube-T* *SemEval*	*SST-fine* *SST-binary* *OpeNER* *SenTube-A* *SenTube-T* *SemEval*
LSTM	4	5	4	3		*SemEval*	*SST-fine* *OpeNER* *SenTube-A* *SenTube-T* *SemEval*
BILSTM	4	5	5	4	1		*SST-fine* *OpeNER* *SenTube-A* *SenTube-T* *SemEval*
CNN	2	3	2	3	0	0	

Figure 2: Results of the statistical analysis described in Section 3 for the best performing dimension of embeddings, where applicable. Datasets where there is a statistical difference (above diagonal) and number of datasets where a model on the Y axis is statistically better than a model on the X axis (below diagonal).

Retrofitting word vectors to semantic lexicons. In *Proceedings of the 2015 Conference of the North American Chapter of the Association for Computational Linguistics: Human Language Technologies*.

Cristine Fellbaum. 1999. Wordnet. Wiley Online Library.

Lucie Flekova and Iryna Gurevych. 2016. Supersense embeddings: A unified model for supersense interpretation, prediction, and utilization. In *Proceedings of the 54th Annual Meeting of the Association for Computational Linguistics (ACL)*.

Eric N. Forsyth and Craig H. Martell. 2007. Lexical and discourse analysis of online chat dialogue. In *Proceedings of the First IEEE International Conference on Semantic Computing (ICSC 2007)*.

Juri Ganitkevitch, Benjamin Van Durme, and Chris Callison-Burch. 2013. Ppdb: The paraphrase database. In *Proceedings of the 2013 Conference of the North American Chapter of the Association for Computational Linguistics: Human Language Technologies*.

Sepp Hochreiter and Jürgen Schmidhuber. 1997. Long short-term memory. *Neural computation*, 9(8):1735–1780.

Mohit Iyyer, Varun Manjunatha, Jordan Boyd-Graber, and Hal Daume III. 2015. Deep unordered composition rivals syntactic methods for text classification. In *Proceedings of the 53rd Annual Meeting of the Association for Computational Linguistics and the 7th International Joint Conference on Natural Language Processing (Volume 1: Long Papers)*.

Douwe Kiela, Felix Hill, and Stephen Clark. 2015. Specializing word embeddings for similarity or relatedness. In *Proceedings of the 2015 Conference on Empirical Methods in Natural Language Processing*.

Yoon Kim. 2014. Convolutional neural networks for sentence classification. In *Proceedings of the 2014*

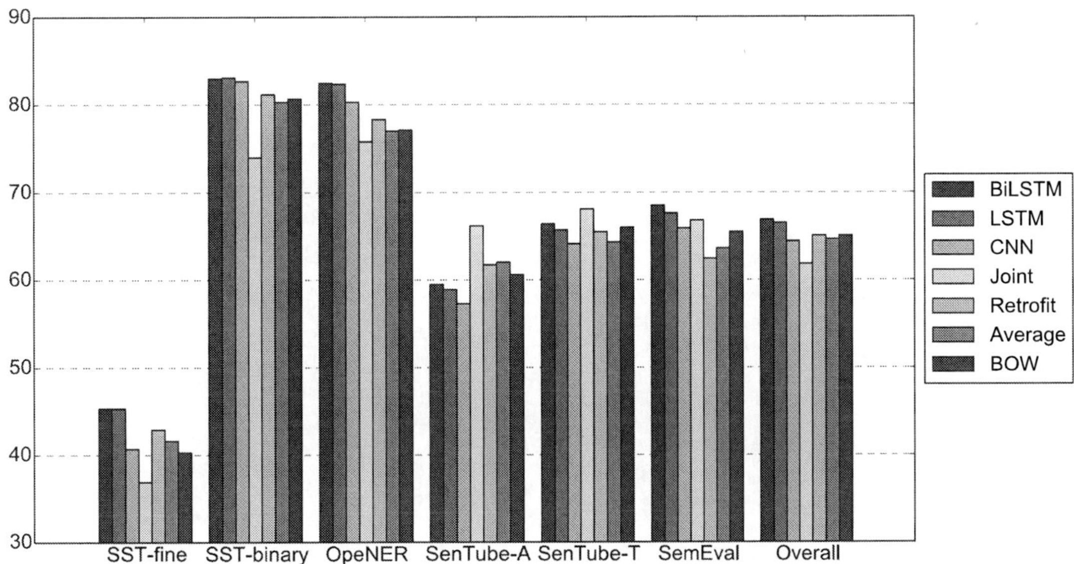

Figure 3: Maximum accuracy scores in percent for each model on the datasets. LSTM and BiLSTM outperform other models on tasks with more than two labels (*SST-fine*, *OpeNER*, and *SemEval*). BOW peforms well against more powerful models. JOINT performs well on social media (*SenTube-A*, *SenTube-T*, and *SemEval*), but poorly on other tasks.

Conference on Empirical Methods in Natural Language Processing (EMNLP).

Diederik Kingma and Jimmy Ba. 2014. Adam: A method for stochastic optimization. In *Proceedings of the 3rd International Conference on Learning Representations (ICLR).*

Eliyahu Kiperwasser and Yoav Goldberg. 2016. Simple and accurate dependency parsing using bidirectional LSTM feature representations. *Transactions of the Association for Computational Linguistics,* 4:313–327.

Patrik Lambert. 2015. Aspect-level cross-lingual sentiment classification with constrained SMT. In *Proceedings of the 53rd Annual Meeting of the Association for Computational Linguistics (ACL).*

Bing Liu, Minqing Hu, and Junsheng Cheng. 2005. Opinion Observer: Analyzing and comparing opinions on the web. In *Proceedings of the 14th international World Wide Web conference (WWW-2005).*

Andrew L. Maas, Raymond E. Daly, Peter T. Pham, Dan Huang, Andrew Y. Ng, and Christopher Potts. 2011. Learning word vectors for sentiment analysis. In *Proceedings of the 49th Annual Meeting of the Association for Computational Linguistics: Human Language Technologies.*

Tomas Mikolov, Greg Corrado, Kai Chen, and Jeffrey Dean. 2013. Efficient estimation of word representations in vector space. In *Proceedings of the Inter-*

national Conference on Learning Representations (ICLR 2013).

Andriy Mnih and Yee Whye Teh. 2012. A fast and simple algorithm for training neural probabilistic language models. In *Proceedings of the 2012 International Conference on Machine Learning (ICML).*

Vinod Nair and Geoffrey E. Hinton. 2010. Rectified linear units improve restricted boltzmann machines. In *Proceedings of the 2010 International Conference on Machine Learning (ICML).*

Preslav Nakov, Sara Rosenthal, Zornitsa Kozareva, Veselin Stoyanov, Alan Ritter, and Theresa Wilson. 2013. Semeval-2013 task 2: Sentiment analysis in twitter. In *Second Joint Conference on Lexical and Computational Semantics (*SEM), Volume 2: Proceedings of the Seventh International Workshop on Semantic Evaluation (SemEval 2013).*

Sebastian Padó. 2006. User's guide to `sigf`: Significance testing by approximate randomisation. `https://nlpado.de/~sebastian/software/sigf.shtml`.

Bo Pang, Lillian Lee, and Shivakumar Vaithyanathan. 2002. Thumbs up?: Sentiment classification using machine learning techniques. In *Proceedings of the ACL-02 Conference on Empirical Methods in Natural Language Processing - Volume 10.*

Jeffrey Pennington, Richard Socher, and Christopher Manning. 2014. Glove: Global vectors for word representation. In *Proceedings of the 2014 Conference on Empirical Methods in Natural Language Processing (EMNLP)*.

Barbara Plank, Anders Søgaard, and Yoav Goldberg. 2016. Multilingual part-of-speech tagging with bidirectional long short-term memory models and auxiliary loss. In *Proceedings of the 54th Annual Meeting of the Association for Computational Linguistics (ACL)*.

Ellen Riloff and Janyce Wiebe. 2003. Learning extraction patterns for subjective expressions. In *Proceedings of the 2003 Conference on Empirical Methods in Natural Language Processing (EMNLP-03)*.

Cicero dos Santos and Maira Gatti. 2014. Deep convolutional neural networks for sentiment analysis of short texts. In *Proceedings of COLING 2014, the 25th International Conference on Computational Linguistics: Technical Papers*, pages 69–78.

Richard Socher, Alex Perelygin, Jy Wu, Jason Chuang, Chris Manning, Andrew Ng, and Chris Potts. 2013. Recursive deep models for semantic compositionality over a sentiment treebank. In *Proceedings of the 2013 Conference on Empirical Methods in Natural Language Processing (EMNLP 2013)*.

Michael Speriosu, Nikita Sudan, Sid Upadhyay, and Jason Baldridge. 2011. Twitter polarity classification with label propagation over lexical links and the follower graph. In *Unsupervised Learning in NLP*.

Nitish Srivastava, Geoffrey Hinton, Alex Krizhevsky, and Ruslan Salakhutdinov. 2014. Dropout: A simple way to prevent neural networks from overfitting. *Journal of Machine Learning Research*, 15:1929–1958.

Kai Sheng Tai, Richard Socher, and Christopher D Manning. 2015. Improved semantic representations From tree-structured long short-term memory networks. In *Proceedings of the 53rd Annual Meeting of the Association for Computational Linguistics (ACL)*.

Duyu Tang, Bing Qin, Xiaocheng Feng, and Ting Liu. 2016. Effective LSTMs for target-dependent sentiment classification. In *Proceedings of COLING 2016, the 26th International Conference on Computational Linguistics: Technical Papers*.

Duyu Tang, Furu Wei, Nan Yang, Ming Zhou, Ting Liu, and Bing Qin. 2014. Learning sentiment-specific word embedding for twitter sentiment classification. In *Proceedings of the 52nd Annual Meeting of the Association for Computational Linguistics (ACL)*.

Olga Uryupina, Barbara Plank, Aliaksei Severyn, Agata Rotondi, and Alessandro Moschitti. 2014. Sentube: A corpus for sentiment analysis on youtube social media. In *Proceedings of the Ninth International Conference on Language Resources and Evaluation (LREC'14)*.

Chang Xu, Yalong Bai, Jiang Bian, Bin Gao, Gang Wang, Xiaoguang Liu, and Tie-Yan Liu. 2014. Rc-net: A general framework for incorporating knowledge into word representations. In *Proceedings of the 23rd ACM International Conference on Conference on Information and Knowledge Management*.

Alexander Yeh. 2000. More accurate tests for the statistical significance of result differences. In *Proceedings of the 18th Conference on Computational Linguistics - Volume 2*.

Mo Yu and Mark Dredze. 2014. Improving lexical embeddings with semantic knowledge. In *Proceedings of the 52nd Annual Meeting of the Association for Computational Linguistics (Volume 2: Short Papers)*.

Peng Zhou, Zhenyu Qi, Suncong Zheng, Jiaming Xu, Hongyun Bao, and Bo Xu. 2016. Text classification improved by integrating bidirectional LSTM with two-dimensional max pooling. In *Proceedings of COLING 2016, the 26th International Conference on Computational Linguistics: Technical Papers*.

Annotation, Modelling and Analysis of Fine-Grained Emotions on a Stance and Sentiment Detection Corpus

Hendrik Schuff, Jeremy Barnes, Julian Mohme, Sebastian Padó, and **Roman Klinger**[*]
Institut für Maschinelle Sprachverarbeitung
University of Stuttgart
Pfaffenwaldring 5b, 70569 Stuttgart, Germany
`{firstname,lastname}@ims.uni-stuttgart.de`

Abstract

There is a rich variety of data sets for sentiment analysis (*viz.*, polarity and subjectivity classification). For the more challenging task of detecting discrete emotions following the definitions of Ekman and Plutchik, however, there are much fewer data sets, and notably no resources for the social media domain. This paper contributes to closing this gap by extending the SemEval 2016 stance and sentiment dataset with emotion annotation. We (a) analyse annotation reliability and annotation merging; (b) investigate the relation between emotion annotation and the other annotation layers (stance, sentiment); (c) report modelling results as a baseline for future work.

1 Introduction

Emotion recognition is a research area in natural language processing concerned with associating words, phrases or documents with predefined emotions from psychological models. *Discrete emotion recognition* assigns categorial emotions (Ekman, 1999; Plutchik, 2001), namely *Anger, Anticipation, Disgust, Fear, Joy, Sadness, Surprise* und *Trust*. Compared to the very active area of sentiment analysis, whose goal is to recognize the polarity of text (*e. g.*, positive, negative, neutral, mixed), few resources are available for discrete emotion analysis.

Emotion analysis has been applied to several domains, including tales (Alm et al., 2005), blogs (Aman and Szpakowicz, 2007) and microblogs (Dodds et al., 2011). The latter in particular provides a major data source in the form of user messages from platforms such as Twitter (Costa et al.,

2014) which contain semi-structured information (hashtags, emoticons, emojis) that can be used as weak supervision for training classifiers (Suttles and Ide, 2013). The classifier then learns the association of all other words in the message with the "self-labeled" emotion (Wang et al., 2012).

While this approach provides a practically feasible approximation of emotions, there is no publicly available, manually vetted data set for Twitter emotions that would support accurate and comparable evaluations. In addition, it has been shown that distant annotation is conceptually different from manual annotation for sentiment and emotion (Purver and Battersby, 2012).

With this paper, we contribute manual emotion annotation for a publicly available Twitter data set. We annotate the SemEval 2016 Stance Data set (Mohammad et al., 2016) which provides sentiment and stance information and is popular in the research community (Augenstein et al., 2016; Wei et al., 2016; Dias and Becker, 2016; Ebrahimi et al., 2016). It therefore enables further research on the relations between sentiment, emotions, and stances. For instance, if the distribution of subclasses of positive or negative emotions is different for *against* and *in-favor*, emotion-based features could contribute to stance detection.

An additional feature of our resource is that we do not only provide a "majority annotation" as is usual. We do define a well-performing aggregated annotation, but additionally provide the *individual labels* of each of our six annotators. This enables further research on differences in the perception of emotions.

2 Background and Related Work

For a review of the fundaments of emotion and sentiment and the differences between these concepts, we refer the reader to Munezero et al. (2014).

---

[*]We thank Marcus Hepting, Chris Krauter, Jonas Vogelsang, Gisela Kollotzek for annotation and discussion.

Proceedings of the 8th Workshop on Computational Approaches to Subjectivity, Sentiment and Social Media Analysis, pages 13–23
Copenhagen, Denmark, September 7–11, 2017. ©2017 Association for Computational Linguistics

Name	Granularity	Annotation	Size	Topic	Source
STS-test	tweet	1	498	General	Go et al. (2009)
SemEval 2013	tweet	2	15,196	General	Nakov et al. (2013)
Healthcare Reform	tweet	2	2,516	Politics	Speriosu et al. (2011)
Obama-McCain Debate	tweet	3	3,238	Politics	Shamma et al. (2009)
Dialogue Earth-WA	tweet	4	4,490	Weather	Cavender-Bares (2011)
Dialogue Earth-WB	tweet	4	8,850	Weather	Busch (2011)
Dialogue Earth-GASP	tweet	4	12,770	Gas prices	Busch (2012)
STS-GOLD	entity/tweet	5	2,205	General	Hassan Saif and Alani (2013)
SemEval 2016	topics/tweets	6	4,870	5 topics	Mohammad et al. (2016)
Sentiment Strength	tweet	7	4,242	General	Thelwall et al. (2012)
ISEAR	descriptions	8	7,666	Emotional Events	Scherer and Wallbott (1997)
Tales	sentences	9	1,580	Grim's Fairytales	Alm et al. (2005)
Blogs	blogs	10	173	General	Aman and Szpakowicz (2007)
SemEval 2017	headlines	11	1,250	General	Strapparava and Mihalcea (2007)
WASSA EmoInt 2017	tweets	12	7,102	General	Mohammad and Bravo-Marquez (2017)
Electoral Tweets	tweets	13	965	Elections	Mohammad et al. (2015)

Table 1: A selection of resources for sentiment analysis (on Twitter, 1–7) and emotion analysis (in general, 8–12). Annotation refers to the following annotation schemes: [1] positive-negative, [2] positive-negative-neutral, [3] positive-negative-mixed-other, [4] positive-negative-netural-unrelated-can't tell, [5] positive-negative-neutral-mixed-other, [6] for-against, [7] positive and negative strength (range), [8] joy, fear, anger, sadness, disgust, shame, guilt, [9] angry, disgusted, fearful, happy, sad, positively surprised, negatively surprised, [10] happiness, sadness, anger, disgust, surprise, fear, mixed, [11] anger, disgust, fear, joy, sadness, surprise, [12] anger, fear, joy, sadness, [13] positive, negative, mixed, intensity, trust, fear, surprise, disgust, anger, anticipation, joy, roles, style, purpose (number denotes subset in corpus with emotion annotations)

For sentiment analysis, a large number of annotated data sets exists. These include review texts from different domains, for instance from Amazon and other shopping sites (Hu and Liu, 2004; Ding et al., 2008; Toprak et al., 2010; Lakkaraju et al., 2011), restaurants (Ganu et al., 2009), news articles (Wiebe et al., 2005), blogs (Kessler et al., 2010), as well as microposts on Twitter. For the latter, shown in the upper half of Table 1, there are general corpora (Nakov et al., 2013; Spina et al., 2012; Thelwall et al., 2012) as well as ones focused on very specific subdomains, for instance on Obama-McCain Debates (Shamma et al., 2009), Health Care Reforms (Speriosu et al., 2011). A popular example for a manually annotated corpus for sentiment, which includes stance annotation for a set of topics is the SemEval 2016 data set (Mohammad et al., 2016).

For emotion analysis, the set of annotated resources is smaller (compare the lower half of Table 1). A very early resource is the ISEAR data set (Scherer and Wallbott, 1997) which contains descriptions of emotional events. While motivated by psychological research, it was later repurposed for computational research. The first data set developed specifically for computational research was the tales corpus by Alm et al. (2005). Aman and Sz-

pakowicz (2007) published a corpus of blog posts. In the context of SemEval, Strapparava and Mihalcea (2007) annotated news headlines.

A notable gap is the unavailability of a publicly available set of microposts (*e. g.*, tweets) with emotion labels. To the best of our knowledge, there are only three previous approaches to labeling tweets with discrete emotion labels. One is the recent data set on for emotion intensity estimation, a shared task aiming at the development of a regression model. The goal is not to predict the emotion class, but a distribution over their intensities, and the set of emotions is limited to *fear*, *sadness*, *anger*, and *joy* (Mohammad and Bravo-Marquez, 2017).

Most similar to our work is a study by Roberts et al. (2012) which annotated 7,000 tweets manually for 7 emotions (anger, disgust, fear, joy, love, sadness and surprise). They chose 14 topics which they believe should elicit emotional tweets and collect hashtags to help identify tweets that are on these topics. After several iterations, the annotators reached $\kappa = 0.67$ inter-annotator agreement on 500 tweets. Unfortunately, the data appear not to be available any more. An additional limitation of that dataset was that 5,000 of the 7,000 tweets were annotated by one annotator only. In contrast, we provide several annotations for each tweet.

Emotion	\multicolumn{5}{c}{Label count for threshold t}
	0.0	0.33	0.5	0.66	0.99
Anger	2,902	2,238	1,388	1,315	578
Anticipation	2,700	1,656	739	677	199
Disgust	2,183	1,199	440	404	106
Fear	1,840	895	274	246	68
Joy	2,067	1,384	815	764	402
Sadness	2,644	1,389	414	343	78
Surprise	1,108	489	177	156	33
Trust	1,713	984	520	487	213

Table 2: Corpus Statistics. The threshold t measures that a fraction of more than t annotators labeled the respective emotion (*e. g.*, t=0.0: at least one annotator t=0.99: all annotators). Overall number of tweets: 4,868.

Mohammad et al. (2015) annotated electoral tweets for sentiment, intensity, semantic roles, style, purpose and emotions. This is the only available corpus similar to our work we are aware of. However, the focus of this work was not emotion annotation in contrast to ours. In addition, we publish the data of all annotators.

3 Corpus Annotation and Analysis

3.1 Annotation Procedure

As motivated above, we re-annotate the extended SemEval 2016 Stance Data set (Mohammad et al., 2016) which consists of 4,870 tweets (a subset of which was used in the SemEval competition). For a discussion of the differences of these data sets, we refer to Mohammad et al. (2017). We omit two tweets with special characters, which leads to an overall set of 4,868 tweets used in our corpus.[1]

We frame annotation as a multi-label classification task at the tweet level. The tweets were annotated by a group of six independent annotators, with a minimum number of three annotations for each tweet (696 tweets were labeled by 6 annotators, 703 by 5 annotators, 2,776 by 4 annotators and 693 by 3 annotators). All annotators were undergraduate students of media computer science and between the age of 20 and 30. Only one annotator is female. All students are German native speak-

Emotion	\multicolumn{2}{c}{Cohen's κ}
	Min	Max
Anger	0.28	0.49
Anticipation	0.11	0.39
Disgust	0.06	0.30
Fear	0.08	0.25
Joy	0.30	0.52
Sadness	0.04	0.30
Surprise	0.09	0.33
Trust	0.29	0.57

Table 3: Kappa Statistics for all pairs of annotators.

ers and have college-level proficiency in English. To train the annotators on the task, we performed two training iterations based on 50 randomly selected tweets from the SemEval 2016 Task 4 corpus (Nakov et al., 2016). After each iteration, we discussed annotation differences (informally) in face-to-face meetings.

For the final annotation, tweets were presented to the annotators in a web interface which paired a tweet with a set of binary check boxes, one for each emotion. Taggers could annotate any set of emotions. Each annotator was assigned with 5/7 of the corpus with equally-sized overlap of instances based on an offset shift. Not all annotators finished their task.[2]

3.2 Emotion Annotation Reliability and Aggregated Annotation

Our annotation represents a middle ground between traditional linguistic "expert" annotation and crowdsourcing: We assume that intuitions about emotions diverge more than for linguistic structures. At the same time, we feel that there is information in the individual annotations beyond the simple "majority vote" computed by most crowdsourcing studies. In this section, we analyse the annotations intrinsically; a modelling-based evaluation follows in Section 5.

Our first analysis, shown in Table 2, compares annotation strata with different agreement. For example, the column labeled 0.0 lists the frequencies of emotion labels assigned by at least one annotator, a *high recall* annotation. In contrast, the column labeled 0.99 lists frequencies for emotion labels that all annotators agreed on. This represents a *high*

---

[1]Our annotations and original tweets are available at `http://www.ims.uni-stuttgart.de/data/ssec` and `http://alt.qcri.org/semeval2016/task6/data/uploads/stancedataset.zip`, see also `http://alt.qcri.org/semeval2016/task6`.

[2]Initially, we recruited seven annotators. One annotator dropped out; we do not publish their data.

		Emotions								Sentiment			Stance		
		Anger	Anticipation	Disgust	Fear	Joy	Sadness	Surprise	Trust	Positive	Negative	Neutral	In Favor	Against	None
Emotion	Anger	**2902**	1437	1983	1339	774	2065	711	640	275	2534	93	630	1628	644
	Anticipation	0.55	**2700**	1016	1029	1330	1369	482	1234	1094	1445	161	772	1291	637
	Disgust	19.05	0.52	**2183**	1024	512	1628	526	404	126	2008	49	429	1291	463
	Fear	2.51	1.03	2.02	**1840**	466	1445	407	497	306	1445	89	448	982	410
	Joy	0.19	1.88	0.22	0.30	**2067**	682	438	1101	1206	750	111	596	952	519
	Sadness	5.91	0.72	4.82	5.58	0.21	**2644**	664	613	345	2171	128	604	1429	611
	Surprise	1.28	0.54	1.15	0.94	0.86	1.34	**1108**	222	219	801	88	257	521	330
	Trust	0.24	2.97	0.24	0.55	4.08	0.31	0.38	**1713**	1082	558	73	500	860	353
Sent.	Positive	0.06	2.75	0.06	0.30	10.94	0.13	0.46	10.53	**1524**	0	0	485	673	366
	Negative	20.3	0.42	18.61	3.32	0.13	7.27	1.79	0.13	0.0	**3032**	0	622	1665	745
	Neutral	0.26	0.85	0.21	0.64	0.73	0.56	1.36	0.54	0.0	0.0	**312**	97	71	144
Stance	In Favor	0.67	1.61	0.60	0.97	1.46	0.80	0.90	1.44	1.70	0.56	1.41	**1204**	0	0
	Against	1.94	0.86	2.03	1.28	0.79	1.49	0.88	1.05	0.73	1.79	0.28	0.0	**2409**	0
	None	0.63	0.77	0.64	0.74	0.94	0.74	1.30	0.65	0.87	0.85	2.66	0.0	0.0	**1255**

Table 4: Tweet Counts (above diagonal) and odds ratio (below diagonal) for cooccurring annotations for all classes in the corpus (emotions based on aggregated annotation, $t=0.0$).

precision annotation. The other levels represent intermediate precision-recall trade-offs.

These numbers confirm that emotion labeling is a somewhat subjective task: only a small subset of the emotions labeled by at least one annotator ($t=0.0$) is labeled by most ($t=0.66$) or all of them ($t=0.99$). Interestingly, the exact percentage varies substantially by emotion, between 2 % for *sadness* and 20 % for *anger*.

Many of these disagreements stem from tweets that are genuinely difficult to categorize emotionally, like

> *That moment when Canadians realised global warming doesn't equal a tropical vacation*

for which one annotator chose *anger* and *sadness*, while one annotator chose surprise. Arguably, both annotations capture aspects of the meaning. Similarly, the tweet

> *2 pretty sisters are dancing with cancered kid*

(a reference to an online video) is marked as *fear* and *sadness* by one annotator and with *joy* and *sadness* by another. Naturally, not all differences arise from justified annotations. For instance the tweet

> *#BIBLE = Big Irrelevant Book of Lies and Exaggerations*

has been labeled by two annotators with the emotion *trust*, presumably because of the word *bible*. This appears to be a classical oversight error, where the tweet is labeled on the basis of the first spotted keyword, without substantially studying its content.

To quantify these observations, we follow general practice and compute a chance-corrected measure of inter-annotator agreement. Table 3 shows the minimum and maximum Cohen's κ values for pairs of annotators, computed on the intersection of instances annotated by either annotator within each pair. We obtain relatively high κ values of *anger*, *joy*, and *trust*, but lower values for the other emotions.

These small κ values could be interpreted as indicators of problems with reliability. However, κ is notoriously difficult to interpret, and a number of studies have pointed out the influence of marginal frequencies (Cicchetti and Feinstein, 1990): In the presence of skewed marginals (and most of our emotion labels are quite rare, *cf.* Table 2), the expected agreement (referred to as $P(E)$ in contrast to $P(A)$ for the empirical agreement) is quite high. This makes it hard to obtain high κ values; thus, low κ values do not necessarily indicate unreliable annotation.

To avoid these methodological problems, we assess the usefulness of our annotation extrinsically by comparing the performance of computational models for different values of t. In a nutshell, these experiments will show best results $t=0.0$, *i. e.*, the

		Emotions								Sentiment			Stance		
		Anger	Anticipation	Disgust	Fear	Joy	Sadness	Surprise	Trust	Positive	Negative	Neutral	In Favor	Against	None
Emotion	Anger	**1388**	53	334	87	37	195	63	12	28	1353	7	272	840	276
	Anticipation	0.16	**739**	16	42	218	14	2	182	445	253	41	258	333	148
	Disgust	10.09	0.19	**440**	39	11	72	26	2	1	439	0	67	289	84
	Fear	1.18	1.01	1.74	**274**	4	58	9	13	26	241	7	83	116	75
	Joy	0.10	2.48	0.12	0.07	**815**	7	9	196	658	142	15	263	304	248
	Sadness	2.43	0.18	2.34	3.20	0.08	**414**	14	3	28	377	9	102	216	96
	Surprise	1.40	0.06	1.78	0.89	0.26	0.92	**177**	0	16	145	16	46	76	55
	Trust	0.05	3.66	0.03	0.40	3.64	0.06	0.0	**520**	462	43	15	142	337	41
Sent.	Positive	0.03	4.28	0.0	0.22	15.42	0.14	0.21	24.65	**1524**	0	0	485	673	366
	Negative	41.47	0.25	310.67	4.72	0.08	6.90	2.83	0.04	0.0	**3032**	0	622	1665	745
	Neutral	0.05	0.84	0.0	0.37	0.24	0.30	1.48	0.41	0.0	0.0	**312**	97	71	144
Stance	In Favor	0.67	1.80	0.52	1.35	1.58	0.99	1.07	1.16	1.70	0.56	1.41	**1204**	0	0
	Against	1.87	0.81	2.08	0.74	0.55	1.12	0.76	2.02	0.73	1.79	0.28	0.0	**2409**	0
	None	0.63	0.68	0.66	1.09	1.32	0.86	1.31	0.22	0.87	0.85	2.66	0.0	0.0	**1255**

Table 5: Tweet Counts (above diagonal) and odds ratio (below diagonal) for cooccurring annotations for all classes in the corpus (emotions based on majority annotation, t=0.5).

high-recall annotation (see Section 5 for details). We therefore define t=0.0 as our *aggregated annotation*. For comparison, we also consider t=0.5, which corresponds to the *majority annotation* as generally adopted in crowdsourcing studies.

3.3 Distribution of Emotions

As shown in Table 2, nearly 60 % of the overall tweet set are annotated with *anger* by at least one annotator. This is the predominant emotion class, followed by *anticipation* and *sadness*. This distribution is comparably uncommon and originates from the selection of tweets in SemEval as a stance data set. However, while *anger* clearly dominates in the aggregated annotation, its predominance weakens for the more precision-oriented data sets. For t=0.99, *joy* becomes the second most frequent emotion. In uniform samples from Twitter, joy typically dominates the distribution of emotions (Klinger, 2017). It remains a question for future work how to reconciliate these observations.

3.4 Emotion vs. other Annotation Layers

Table 4 shows the number of cooccurring label pairs (above the diagonal) and the odds ratios (below the diagonal) for emotion, stance, and sentiment annotations on the whole corpus for our aggregated annotation (t=0.0). Odds ratio is

$$\text{R(A:B)} = \frac{P(A)(1 - P(B))}{P(B)(1 - P(A))},$$

where $P(A)$ is the probability that both labels (at row and column in the table) hold for a tweet and $P(B)$ is the probability that only one holds. A ratio of x means that the joint labeling is x times more likely than the independent labeling. Table 5 shows the same numbers for the majority annotation, t=0.5.

We first analyze the relationship between emotions and sentiment polarity in Table 4. For many emotions, the polarity is as expected: *Joy* and *trust* occur predominantly with positive sentiment, and *anger, disgust, fear* and *sadness* with negative sentiment. The emotions *anticipation* and *surprise* are, in comparison, most balanced between polarities, however with a majority for positive sentiment in anticipation and a negative sentiment for surprise. For most emotions there is also a non-negligible number of tweets with the sentiment opposite to a common expectation. For example, *anger* occurs 28 times with positive sentiment, mainly tweets which call for (positive) change regarding a controversial topic, for instance

Lets take back our country! Whos with me? No more Democrats!2016

Why criticise religions? If a path is not your own. Don't be pretentious. And get down from your throne.

Conversely, more than 15 % of the *joy* tweets carry negative sentiment. These are often cases in which either the emotion annotator or the sentiment annotator assumed some non-literal meaning to be associated with the text (mainly irony), for instance

> *Global Warming! Global Warming!*
> *Global Warming! Oh wait, it's summer.*
>
> *I love the smell of Hillary in the*
> *morning. It smells like Republican*
> *Victory.*

Disgust occurs almost exclusively with negative sentiment.

For the majority annotation (Table 5), the number of annotations is smaller. However, the average size of the odds ratios increase (from 1.96 for $t=0.0$ to 5.39 for $t=0.5$).

A drastic example is *disgust* in combination with negative sentiment, the predominant combination. *Disgust* is only labeled once with positive sentiment in the $t=0.5$ annotation:

> *#WeNeedFeminism because*
> *#NoMeansNo it doesnt mean yes, it*
> *doesnt mean try harder!*

Similarly, the odds ratio for the combination *anger* and negative sentiment nearly doubles from 20.3 for $t=0.0$ to 41.47 for $t=0.5$. These numbers are an effect of the majority annotation having a higher precision in contrast to more "noisy" aggregation of all annotations ($t=0.0$).

Regarding the relationship between emotions and stance, most odds ratios are relatively close to 1, indicating the absence of very strong correlations. Nevertheless, the "Against" stance is associated with a number of negative emotions (*anger, disgust, sadness*, the "In Favor" stance with *joy, trust*, and *anticipation*, and "None" with an absence of all emotions except *surprise*.

4 Models

We apply six standard models to provide baseline results for our corpus: Maximum Entropy (MAXENT), Support Vector Machines (SVM), a Long-Short Term Memory Network (LSTM), a Bidirectional LSTM (BI-LSTM), and a Convolutional Neural Network (CNN).

MaxEnt and **SVM** classify each tweet separately based on a bag-of-words. For the first, the linear separator is estimated based on log-likelihood optimization with an L2 prior. For the second, the optimization follows a max-margin strategy.

LSTM (Hochreiter and Schmidhuber, 1997) is a recurrent neural network architecture which includes a memory state capable of learning long distance dependencies. In various forms, they have proven useful for text classification tasks (Tai et al., 2015; Tang et al., 2016). We implement a standard LSTM which has an embedding layer that maps the input (padded when needed) to a 300 dimensional vector. These vectors then pass to a 175 dimensional LSTM layer. We feed the final hidden state to a fully-connected 50-dimensional dense layer and use sigmoid to gate our 8 output neurons. As a regularizer, we use a dropout (Srivastava et al., 2014) of 0.5 before the LSTM layer.

Bi-LSTM has the same architecture as the normal LSTM, but includes an additional layer with a reverse direction. This approach has produced state-of-the-art results for POS-tagging (Plank et al., 2016), dependency parsing (Kiperwasser and Goldberg, 2016) and text classification (Zhou et al., 2016), among others. We use the same parameters as the LSTM, but concatenate the two hidden layers before passing them to the dense layer.

CNN has proven remarkably effective for text classification (Kim, 2014; dos Santos and Gatti, 2014; Flekova and Gurevych, 2016) . We train a simple one-layer CNN with one convolutional layer on top of pre-trained word embeddings, following Kim (2014). The first layer is an embeddings layer that maps the input of length n (padded when needed) to an n x 300 dimensional matrix. The embedding matrix is then convoluted with filter sizes of 2, 3, and 4, followed by a pooling layer of length 2. This is then fed to a fully connected dense layer with ReLu activations and finally to the 8 output neurons, which are gated with the sigmoid function. We again use dropout (0.5), this time before and after the convolutional layers.

For all neural models, we initialize our word representations with the skip-gram algorithm with negative sampling (Mikolov et al., 2013), trained on nearly 8 million tokens taken from tweets collected using various hashtags. We create 300-dimensional vectors with window size 5, 15 negative samples and run 5 iterations. For OOV words, we use a vector initialized randomly between -0.25 and 0.25 to approximate the variance of the pretrained vectors. We train our models using ADAM (Kingma and Ba, 2015) and a minibatch size of 32. We set 10 % of

| | Linear | | | | | | Neural | | | | | | | | |
| | MaxEnt | | | SVM | | | LSTM | | | Bi-LSTM | | | CNN | | |
Emotion	P	R	F_1	P	R	F_1	P	R	F_1	P	R	F_1	P	R	F_1
Anger	76	72	74	76	69	72	76 (1.7)	77 (5.3)	76 (1.9)	77 (0.8)	77 (2.7)	**77** (1.3)	77 (0.8)	77 (2.7)	**77** (1.3)
Anticipation	72	61	66	70	60	64	68 (1.8)	68 (8.9)	67 (3.5)	70 (1.2)	66 (3.6)	**68** (1.6)	68 (1.2)	60 (0.8)	64 (0.5)
Disgust	62	47	54	59	53	56	64 (3.2)	68 (8.7)	**65** (2.5)	61 (1.4)	64 (4.6)	63 (1.7)	62 (0.6)	61 (3.9)	62 (1.9)
Fear	57	31	40	55	40	46	51 (3.5)	48 (8.5)	**49** (4.6)	58 (1.6)	43 (6.3)	**49** (3.8)	53 (1.7)	46 (6.2)	**49** (3.9)
Joy	55	50	52	52	52	52	56 (5.9)	41 (8.3)	46 (4.8)	54 (2.9)	59 (10.5)	**56** (4.8)	54 (1.7)	56 (5.6)	55 (2.3)
Sadness	65	65	65	64	60	62	60 (2.5)	77 (11.1)	**67** (3.9)	62 (0.6)	72 (7.5)	**67** (3.2)	63 (0.9)	72 (0.3)	**67** (0.5)
Surprise	62	15	24	46	22	30	40 (4.4)	17 (10.4)	21 (8.7)	42 (2.9)	20 (3.2)	27 (2.5)	36 (3.7)	24 (6.3)	**28** (5.0)
Trust	62	38	47	57	45	50	57 (6.1)	49 (12.3)	**51** (5.9)	59 (2.5)	44 (4.1)	50 (2.5)	53 (0.6)	49 (6.6)	50 (3.3)
Micro-Avg.	66	52	58	63	53	58	62 (0.9)	60 (1.9)	61 (0.7)	64 (0.3)	60 (2.4)	**62** (1.2)	62 (0.6)	59 (2.0)	60 (1.0)

Results for Threshold $t = 0.0$ for standard models

Table 6: Results of linear and neural models for labels from the aggregated annotation (t=0.0). For the neural models, we report the average of five runs and standard deviation in brackets. Best F_1 for each emotion shown in boldface.

the training data aside to tune the hyperparameters for each model (hidden dimension size, dropout rate, and number of training epochs).

5 Results

Table 6 shows the results for our canonical annotation aggregation with t=0.0 (aggregated annotation) for our models. The two linear classifiers (trained as MaxEnt and SVM) show comparable results, with an overall micro-average F_1 of 58 %. All neural network approaches show a higher performance of at least 2 percentage points (3 pp for LSTM, 4 pp for Bi-LSTM, 2 pp for CNN). Bi-LSTM also obtains the best F-Score for 5 of the 8 emotions (4 out of 8 for LSTM and CNN). We conclude that the Bi-LSTM shows the best results of all our models. Our discussion focuses on this model.

The performance clearly differs between emotion classes. Recall from Section 3.2 that *anger, joy* and *trust* showed much higher agreement numbers than the other annotations. There is however just a mild correlation between reliability and modeling performance. *Anger* is indeed modelled very well: it shows the best prediction performance with a similar precision and recall on all models. We ascribe this to it being the most frequent emotion class. In contrast, *joy* and *trust* show only middling performance, while we see relatively good results for *anticipation* and *sadness* even though there was considerable disagreement between annotators. We

find the overall worst results for *surprise*. This is not surprising, *surprise* being a scarce label with also very low agreement. This might point towards underlying problems in the definition of *surprise* as an emotion. Some authors have split this class into positive and negative surprise in an attempt to avoid this (Alm et al., 2005).

We finally come to our justification for choosing t=0.0 as our aggregated annotation. Table 7 shows results for the best model (Bi-LSTM) on the datasets for different thresholds. We see a clear downward monotone trend: The higher the threshold, the lower the F_1 measures. We obtain the best results, both for individual emotions and at the average level, for t=0.0. This is at least partially counterintuitive – we would have expected a dataset with "more consensual" annotation to yield better models – or at least models with higher precision. This is not the case. Our interpretation is that frequency effects outweigh any other considerations: As Table 2 shows, the amount of labeled data points drops sharply with higher thresholds: even between t=0.0 and t=0.33, on average half of the labels are lost. This interpretation is supported by the behavior of the individual emotions: for emotions where the data sets shrink gradually (*anger, joy*), performance drops gradually, while it dips sharply for emotions where the data sets shrink fast (*disgust, fear*). Somewhat surprisingly, therefore, we conclude that t=0.0 appears to be the

| | Results of BiLSTM for different voting thresholds t | | | | | | | | | | | | | | |
| | 0.0 | | | 0.33 | | | 0.5 | | | 0.66 | | | 0.99 | | |
Emotion	P	R	F_1	P	R	F_1	P	R	F_1	P	R	F_1	P	R	F_1
Anger	77	76	77	64	71	68	52	45	48	47	51	49	34	14	20
	(1.3)	(4.8)	(1.9)	(1.7)	(3.8)	(1.5)	(0.6)	(7.8)	(4.8)	(1.5)	(6.7)	(2.6)	(5.2)	(2.6)	(2.4)
Anticipation	70	66	68	60	43	50	42	23	29	37	20	25	11	12	11
	(1.2)	(3.6)	(1.6)	(2.3)	(5.6)	(3.4)	(5.9)	(4.4)	(2.8)	(4.1)	(7.6)	(6.0)	(3.3)	(2.9)	(1.9)
Disgust	61	64	63	48	38	42	34	13	18	24	8	11	11	2	3
	(1.4)	(4.6)	(1.7)	(1.5)	(4.4)	(2.6)	(4.9)	(2.7)	(3.5)	(6.2)	(2.7)	(3.7)	(10.7)	(2.0)	(3.4)
Fear	58	43	49	34	22	26	18	15	13	11	14	11	1	6	1
	(1.6)	(6.3)	(3.8)	(3.2)	(5.9)	(4.6)	(8.1)	(10.5)	(5.3)	(5.0)	(10.5)	(7.9)	(1.3)	(11.7)	(2.3)
Joy	54	59	56	56	41	47	53	37	43	54	34	41	64	27	35
	(2.9)	(10.5)	(4.8)	(2.8)	(6.3)	(3.6)	(4.3)	(3.6)	(1.6)	(7.1)	(4.2)	(2.1)	(14.9)	(9.6)	(6.8)
Sadness	62	72	67	42	47	44	16	24	19	15	19	16	3	6	4
	(0.6)	(7.5)	(3.2)	(1.4)	(6.2)	(2.1)	(2.1)	(6.0)	(2.0)	(2.3)	(7.6)	(3.0)	(2.0)	(2.9)	(1.9)
Surprise	42	20	27	31	20	23	12	20	13	12	12	12	0	0	0
	(2.9)	(3.2)	(2.5)	(6.8)	(7.5)	(3.2)	(2.3)	(8.9)	(2.1)	(1.3)	(2.6)	(1.7)	(0.0)	(0.0)	(0.0)
Trust	59	44	50	66	31	42	60	24	34	59	23	33	35	14	18
	(2.5)	(4.1)	(2.5)	(3.4)	(2.7)	(2.3)	(4.6)	(7.1)	(7.1)	(3.5)	(6.8)	(6.8)	(7.4)	(11.2)	(9.7)
Micro-Avg.	64	60	62	53	44	48	38	30	33	38	29	33	21	14	17
	(0.3)	(2.4)	(1.2)	(1.8)	(1.8)	(0.6)	(2.2)	(3.3)	(2.4)	(1.8)	(4.1)	(2.9)	(4.2)	(3.1)	(3.2)

Table 7: Results of the BiLSTM for different voting thresholds. We report average results for each emotion over 5 runs (standard deviations are included in parenthesis).

most useful datasets from a computational modeling perspective.

In terms of how to deal with diverging annotations, we believe that this result bolsters our general approach to pay attention to individual annotators' labels rather than just majority votes: if the individual labels were predominantly noisy, we would not expect to see relatively high F_1 scores.

6 Conclusion and Future Work

With this paper, we publish the first manual emotion annotation for a publicly available micropost corpus. The resource we chose to annotate already provides stance and sentiment information. We analyzed the relationships among emotion classes and between emotions and the other annotation layers.

In addition to the data set, we implemented well-known standard models which are established for sentiment and polarity prediction for emotion classification. The BI-LSTM model outperforms all other approaches by up to 4 points F_1 on average compared to linear classifiers.

Inter-annotator analysis showed a limited agreement between the annotators – the task is, at least to some degree, driven by subjective opinions. We found, however, that this is not necessarily a problem: Our models perform best on a *high-recall aggregate annotation* which includes all labels assigned by at least one annotator. Thus, we believe that the individual labels have value and are not, like generally assumed in crowdsourcing, noisy inputs suitable only as input for majority voting.

In this vein, we publish all individual annotations. This enables further research on other methods of defining consensus annotations which may be more appropriate for specific downstream tasks. More generally, we will make all annotations, resources and model implementations publicly available.

References

Cecilia Ovesdotter Alm, Dan Roth, and Richard Sproat. 2005. Emotions from text: Machine learning for text-based emotion prediction. In *Proceedings of Human Language Technology Conference and Conference on Empirical Methods in Natural Language Processing*, pages 579–586, Vancouver, BC, Canada.

Saima Aman and Stan Szpakowicz. 2007. Identifying expressions of emotion in text. In *Text, Speech and Dialogue: 10th International Conference, TSD 2007, Pilsen, Czech Republic, September 3-7, 2007. Proceedings*, pages 196–205. Springer.

Isabelle Augenstein, Andreas Vlachos, and Kalina Bontcheva. 2016. USFD at semeval-2016 task 6: Any-target stance detection on twitter with autoencoders. In *Proceedings of the 10th International Workshop on Semantic Evaluation (SemEval-2016)*, pages 389–393, San Diego, California.

Sarah Busch. 2011. Capturing mood about daily weather from twitter posts. http://www.dialogueearth.org/2011/09/29/capturing-mood-about-daily-weather-from-twitter-posts.

Sarah Busch. 2012. Tracking the mood about gas prices on twitter: A case study. http://www.dialogueearth.org/2012/01/25/tracking-the-mood-about-gas-prices-on-twitter-a-case-study.

Kent Cavender-Bares. 2011. Preparing to extract weather mood from tweets. http://www.dialogueearth.org/2011/03/03/preparing-to-extract-weather-mood-from-tweets.

Domenic V. Cicchetti and Alvan R. Feinstein. 1990. High agreement but low kappa: II. resolving the paradoxes. *Journal of clinical epidemiology*, 43:551–558.

Joana Costa, Catarina Silva, Mario Antunes, and Bernardete Ribeiro. 2014. Concept drift awareness in twitter streams. In *13th International Conference on Machine Learning and Applications*, pages 294–299.

Marcelo Dias and Karin Becker. 2016. INF-UFRGS-OPINION-MINING at SemEval-2016 task 6: Automatic generation of a training corpus for unsupervised identification of stance in tweets. In *Proceedings of the 10th International Workshop on Semantic Evaluation (SemEval-2016)*, pages 378–383, San Diego, California.

Xiaowen Ding, Bing Liu, and Philip S. Yu. 2008. A holistic lexicon-based approach to opinion mining. In *WSDM '08 Proceedings of the 2008 International Conference on Web Search and Data Mining*, pages 213–239, Palo Alto, California, USA.

Peter S. Dodds, Kameron D. Harris, Isabel M. Kloumann, Catherine A. Bliss, and Christopher M. Danforth. 2011. Temporal patterns of happiness and information in a global social network: Hedonometrics and twitter. *PloS one*, 6(12).

Javid Ebrahimi, Dejing Dou, and Daniel Lowd. 2016. Weakly supervised tweet stance classification by relational bootstrapping. In *Proceedings of the 2016 Conference on Empirical Methods in Natural Language Processing*, pages 1012–1017, Austin, Texas.

Paul Ekman. 1999. Basic emotions. In M Dalgleish, T; Power, editor, *Handbook of Cognition and Emotion*. John Wiley & Sons, Sussex, UK.

Lucie Flekova and Iryna Gurevych. 2016. Supersense embeddings: A unified model for supersense interpretation, prediction, and utilization. In *Proceedings of the 54th Annual Meeting of the Association for Computational Linguistics (Volume 1: Long Papers)*, pages 2029–2041, Berlin, Germany.

Gayatree Ganu, Noemie Elhadad, and Amélie Marian. 2009. Beyond the stars: Improving rating predictions using review text content. In *International Workshop on the Web and Databases (WebDB 2009)*, Providence, Rhode Island, USA.

Alec Go, Richa Bhayani, and Lei Huang. 2009. Twitter sentiment classification using distant supervision. Technical report, Stanford.

Yulan He Hassan Saif, Miriam Fernandez and Harith Alani. 2013. Evaluation Datasets for Twitter Sentiment Analysis: A survey and a new dataset, the STS-Gold. In *Proceedings of the First International Workshop on Emotion and Sentiment in Social and Expressive Media: approaches and perspectives from AI (ESSEM 2013)*, pages 9–21, Turin, Italy.

Sepp Hochreiter and Jürgen Schmidhuber. 1997. Long short-term memory. *Neural Computation*, 9(8):1735–1780.

Minqing Hu and Bing Liu. 2004. Mining and summarizing customer reviews. In *KDD '04 Proceedings of the tenth ACM SIGKDD international conference on Knowledge discovery and data mining*, pages 168–177, Seattle, WA, USA.

Jason S. Kessler, Miriam Eckert, Lyndsie Clark, and Nicolas Nicolov. 2010. The 2010 ICWSM JDPA Sentiment Corpus for the Automotive Domain. In *Proc. of the 4th International AAAI Conference on Weblogs and Social Media Data Workshop Challenge (ICWSM-DWC)*.

Yoon Kim. 2014. Convolutional neural networks for sentence classification. In *Proceedings of the 2014 Conference on Empirical Methods in Natural Language Processing (EMNLP)*, pages 1746–1751, Doha, Qatar.

Diederik Kingma and Jimmy Ba. 2015. Adam: A method for stochastic optimization. In *Proceedings of International Conference on Learning Representations*, San Diego, CA, USA.

Eliyahu Kiperwasser and Yoav Goldberg. 2016. Simple and accurate dependency parsing using bidirectional LSTM feature representations. *Transactions of the Association for Computational Linguistics*, 4:313–327.

Roman Klinger. 2017. Does optical character recognition and caption generation improve emotion detection in microblog posts? In *Natural Language Processing and Information Systems: 22nd International Conference on Applications of Natural Language to Information Systems, NLDB 2017, Liège, Belgium, June 21-23, 2017, Proceedings*, pages 313–319, Cham. Springer International Publishing.

Himabindu Lakkaraju, Chiranjib Bhattacharyya, Indrajit Bhattacharya, and Srujana Merugu. 2011. Exploiting coherence for the simultaneous discovery of latent facets and associated sentiments. In *Proceedings of the 2011 SIAM International Conference on Data Mining*, pages 498–509, Mesa, Arizona, USA.

Tomas Mikolov, Greg Corrado, Kai Chen, and Jeffrey Dean. 2013. Efficient estimation of word representations in vector space. In *Proceedings of International Conference on Learning Representations*, Scottsdale, AZ, USA.

Saif Mohammad and Felipe Bravo-Marquez. 2017. WASSA-2017 shared task on emotion intensity. In *Proceedings of WASSA at EMNLP*, Copenhagen, Denmark.

Saif Mohammad, Svetlana Kiritchenko, Parinaz Sobhani, Xiaodan Zhu, and Colin Cherry. 2016. SemEval-2016 Task 6: Detecting stance in tweets. In *Proceedings of the 10th International Workshop on Semantic Evaluation (SemEval-2016)*, pages 31–41, San Diego, California.

Saif M. Mohammad, Parinaz Sobhani, and Svetlana Kiritchenko. 2017. Stance and sentiment in tweets. *Special Section of the ACM Transactions on Internet Technology on Argumentation in Social Media*, 17(3).

Saif M. Mohammad, Xiaodan Zhu, Svetlana Kiritchenko, and Joel Martin. 2015. Sentiment, emotion, purpose, and style in electoral tweets. *Information Processing & Management*, 51(4):480 – 499.

Myriam Munezero, Calkin Suero Montero, Erkki Sutinen, and John Pajunen. 2014. Are they different? Affect, feeling, emotion, sentiment, and opinion detection in text. *IEEE Transactions on Affective Computing*, 5(2):101–111.

Preslav Nakov, Alan Ritter, Sara Rosenthal, Veselin Stoyanov, and Fabrizio Sebastiani. 2016. SemEval-2016 task 4: Sentiment analysis in Twitter. In *Proceedings of the 10th International Workshop on Semantic Evaluation*, SemEval '16, San Diego, California. Association for Computational Linguistics.

Preslav Nakov, Sara Rosenthal, Zornitsa Kozareva, Veselin Stoyanov, Alan Ritter, and Theresa Wilson. 2013. SemEval-2013 Task 2: Sentiment analysis in twitter. In *Second Joint Conference on Lexical and Computational Semantics (*SEM), Volume 2: Proceedings of the Seventh International Workshop on Semantic Evaluation (SemEval 2013)*, pages 312–320, Atlanta, Georgia, USA.

Barbara Plank, Anders Søgaard, and Yoav Goldberg. 2016. Multilingual part-of-speech tagging with bidirectional long short-term memory models and auxiliary loss. In *Proceedings of the 54th Annual Meeting of the Association for Computational Linguistics (Volume 2: Short Papers)*, pages 412–418, Berlin, Germany.

Robert Plutchik. 2001. The nature of emotions. *American Scientist*, 89(July–August):344–350.

Matthew Purver and Stuart Battersby. 2012. Experimenting with distant supervision for emotion classification. In *Proceedings of the 13th Conference of the European Chapter of the Association for Computational Linguistics*, pages 482–491, Avignon, France.

Kirk Roberts, Michael A. Roach, Joseph Johnson, Josh Guthrie, and Sanda M. Harabagiu. 2012. Empatweet: Annotating and detecting emotions on twitter. In *Proceedings of the Eighth International Conference on Language Resources and Evaluation (LREC-2012)*, pages 3806–3813, Istanbul, Turkey.

Cicero dos Santos and Maira Gatti. 2014. Deep convolutional neural networks for sentiment analysis of short texts. In *Proceedings of COLING 2014, the 25th International Conference on Computational Linguistics: Technical Papers*, pages 69–78, Dublin, Ireland.

Klaus Scherer and Harald Wallbott. 1997. The ISEAR questionnaire and codebook. Geneva Emotion Research Group.

David A. Shamma, Lyndon Kennedy, and Elizabeth F. Churchill. 2009. Tweet the debates: Understanding community annotation of uncollected sources. In *Proceedings of the First SIGMM Workshop on Social Media*, pages 3–10, Beijing, China.

Michael Speriosu, Nikita Sudan, Sid Upadhyay, and Jason Baldridge. 2011. Twitter polarity classification with label propagation over lexical links and the follower graph. In *Proceedings of the First workshop on Unsupervised Learning in NLP*, pages 53–63, Edinburgh, Scotland.

Damiano Spina, Edgar Meij, Maarten de Rijke, Andrei Oghina, Minh Thuong Bui, and Mathias Breuss. 2012. Identifying entity aspects in microblog posts. In *Proceedings of the 35th International ACM SIGIR Conference on Research and Development in Information Retrieval*, pages 1089–1090, New York, NY, USA. ACM.

Nitish Srivastava, Geoffrey Hinton, Alex Krizhevsky, and Ruslan Salakhutdinov. 2014. Dropout: A simple way to prevent neural networks from overfitting. *Journal of Machine Learning Research*, 15:1929–1958.

Carlo Strapparava and Rada Mihalcea. 2007. SemEval-2007 Task 14: Affective Text. In *Proceedings of the Fourth International Workshop on Semantic Evaluations (SemEval-2007)*, pages 70–74, Prague, Czech Republic.

Jared Suttles and Nancy Ide. 2013. Distant supervision for emotion classification with discrete binary values. In *Computational Linguistics and Intelligent Text Processing: 14th International Conference, CICLing 2013, Samos, Greece, March 24-30, 2013, Proceedings, Part II*, pages 121–136, Berlin, Heidelberg. Springer Berlin Heidelberg.

Kai Sheng Tai, Richard Socher, and Christopher D. Manning. 2015. Improved semantic representations from tree-structured long short-term memory networks. In *Proceedings of the 53rd Annual Meeting of the Association for Computational Linguistics and the 7th International Joint Conference on Natural Language Processing (Volume 1: Long Papers)*, pages 1556–1566, Beijing, China.

Duyu Tang, Bing Qin, Xiaocheng Feng, and Ting Liu. 2016. Effective LSTMs for target-dependent sentiment classification. In *Proceedings of COLING*

2016, the 26th International Conference on Computational Linguistics: Technical Papers*, pages 3298–3307, Osaka, Japan.

Mike Thelwall, Kevan Buckley, and Georgios Paltoglou. 2012. Sentiment strength detection for the social web. *Journal of the American Society for Information Science Technology*, 63(1):163–173.

Cigdem Toprak, Niklas Jakob, and Iryna Gurevych. 2010. Sentence and expression level annotation of opinions in user-generated discourse. In *Proceedings of the 48th Annual Meeting of the Association for Computational Linguistics*, pages 575–584, Uppsala, Sweden.

Wenbo Wang, Lu Chen, Krishnaprasad Thirunarayan, and Amit P. Sheth. 2012. Harnessing twitter "big data" for automatic emotion identification. In *2012 ASE/IEEE International Conference on Social Computing and 2012 ASE/IEEE International Conference on Privacy, Security, Risk and Trust*, pages 587–592, Washington, DC, USA.

Wan Wei, Xiao Zhang, Xuqin Liu, Wei Chen, and Tengjiao Wang. 2016. pkudblab at SemEval-2016 Task 6: A specific convolutional neural network system for effective stance detection. In *Proceedings of the 10th International Workshop on Semantic Evaluation (SemEval-2016)*, pages 384–388, San Diego, California.

Janyce Wiebe, Theresa Wilson, and Claire Cardie. 2005. Annotating expressions of opinions and emotions in language. *Language Resources and Evaluation*, 39(2-3).

Peng Zhou, Zhenyu Qi, Suncong Zheng, Jiaming Xu, Hongyun Bao, and Bo Xu. 2016. Text classification improved by integrating bidirectional LSTM with two-dimensional max pooling. In *Proceedings of COLING 2016, the 26th International Conference on Computational Linguistics: Technical Papers*, pages 3485–3495, Osaka, Japan.

Ranking Right-Wing Extremist Social Media Profiles by Similarity to Democratic and Extremist Groups

Matthias Hartung
CITEC, Bielefeld University

Roman Klinger
IMS, University of Stuttgart

Franziska Schmidtke and **Lars Vogel**
Kompetenzzentrum Rechtsextremismus
Friedrich-Schiller-Universität Jena

```
mhartung@cit-ec.uni-bielefeld.de
klinger@ims.uni-stuttgart.de
{franziska.schmidtke, lars.vogel}@uni-jena.de
```


Abstract

Social media are used by an increasing number of political actors. A small subset of these is interested in pursuing extremist motives such as mobilization, recruiting or radicalization activities. In order to counteract these trends, online providers and state institutions reinforce their monitoring efforts, mostly relying on manual workflows. We propose a machine learning approach to support manual attempts towards identifying right-wing extremist content in German Twitter profiles. Based on a fine-grained conceptualization of right-wing extremism, we frame the task as ranking each individual profile on a continuum spanning different degrees of right-wing extremism, based on a nearest neighbour approach. A quantitative evaluation reveals that our ranking model yields robust performance (up to 0.81 F_1 score) when being used for predicting discrete class labels. At the same time, the model provides plausible continuous ranking scores for a small sample of borderline cases at the division of right-wing extremism and New Right political movements.

1 Introduction

Recent years have seen a dramatic rise in importance of social media as communication channels for political discourse (Parmelee and Bichars, 2013). Political actors use social platforms to engage directly with potential voters and supporter networks in order to shape public discussions, in-duce viral social trends, or spread political ideas and programmes for which they seek support.

With regard to extremist political actors and parties, a major current focus is on recruiting and radicalizing potential activists in social media. For instance, the American white nationalist movements have been able to attract a 600 % increase of followers on Twitter since 2012 (Berger, 2016). Twitter is comparably under-moderated in comparison to other platforms and therefore constitutes a predestinated channel for such activities (Blanquart and Cook, 2013).

State institutions, platform providers or companies spend growing efforts into monitoring extremist activities in social media. Extremism monitoring aims at detecting *who* is active (possibly separating opinion leaders from adopters, and discovering dynamics of network evolution), *what* they say (identifying prominent topics and possibly hate speech or fake news), and *which purpose* they pursue (revealing strategic objectives such as mobilization or recruiting). Currently, these goals are mostly pursued in time-consuming manual work. For instance, the Amadeu Antonio foundation, a non-governmental organization countering right-wing extremism in Germany, conducts an annual report that relies on a "qualitative method" (Amadeu-Antonio-Stiftung, 2016). Furthermore, the Anti Defamation League issued a report on anti-semitic harassment on Twitter, based on manually reviewed 2.6 million Tweets (ADL, 2016).

In this paper, we propose an approach to support the first of the above-mentioned aspects, *i. e.*, the identification of extremist users in Twitter. In particular, we aim at detecting potential right-wing extremist content in German Twitter profiles, based

Proceedings of the 8th Workshop on Computational Approaches to Subjectivity, Sentiment and Social Media Analysis, pages 24–33
Copenhagen, Denmark, September 7–11, 2017. ©2017 Association for Computational Linguistics

on lexical information and patterns of emotion underlying language use (cf. Ghazi et al., 2010; Suttles and Ide, 2013; Wang et al., 2012). Contrary to previous work (Hartung et al., 2017), we phrase the problem as ranking between manually selected groups of Twitter profiles which constitute seeds of right-wing extremists and non-extremist users. We show that our ranking model achieves robust performance in discrete binary categorizations, while also being capable of predicting plausible continuous ranking scores for a sample of borderline cases which specifically address the notoriously hard delimitation of right-wing extremism from New Right political movements in Germany and Europe. This lazy machine learning approach outperforms the eager method proposed in previous work on the same data set (Hartung et al., 2017).

2 Background and Related Work

Background. Right-wing extremism is an ideology of asymmetric quality of social groups, defined by race, ethnicity or nationality, and a related authoritarian concept of society. It encompasses aggressive behavior and the underlying attitudes of *xenophobia, racism, anti-Semitism, social Darwinism,* as well as *national chauvinism, glorification of the historical national socialism* and *support for dictatorship* (Stöss, 2010).

When transforming this concept into patterns used in Twitter communication, certain domain-specific contextual opportunities and restrictions have to be considered. First, Tweets are motivated by latent attitudes, but they are manifest communicative behavior. The transformation of attitudes into behavior is, however, conditional. While attitudes are usually revealed in the secrecy of anonymous interviews, Twitter requires to display attitudes in public. This may lead to strategies of camouflage and the use of codes. Second, these attitudes are revealed by commenting on particular topics requiring that their changing saliency over time must be considered. Third, expressing some of these attitudes publicly in a particular manner can become relevant to criminal law. Thus, especially the glorification of national socialism is not suited to serve as a distinctive criterion, since its public expression in a non-subtle manner is avoided by Twitter users. Finally, research has repeatedly demonstrated that *some* of the attitudes mentioned above (*e. g.*, xenophobia) are widespread among the German population (Best et al., 2016; Zick et al.,

2016), whereas right-wing extremism is defined by adopting *all* or at least a *majority* of these attitudes.

Related Work. There is only limited work with a focus on right-wing extremism detection. However, other forms of extremism have been the subject of research. As an early example, Ting et al. (2013) aim at identification of hate groups on Facebook. They build automatic classifiers based on social network structure properties and keywords. While this work focuses on detection of groups, Scanlon and Gerber (2014) deal with specific events of interaction, namely the recruitment of individuals on specific extremist's websites. Their domain are Western Jihadists. In contrast, Ashcroft et al. (2015) identify specific messages from Twitter. Similarly, Wei et al. (2016) identify Jihadist-related conversations.

Recently, the identification of Twitter users displaying different traits or attitudes of extremism has gained growing attention. For instance, Ferrara et al. (2016) identify ISIS members among Twitter users, while Kaati et al. (2015) focus on multipliers of Jihadism on Twitter. In very recent work, Wei and Singh (2017) present an approach to detecting Jihadism on Twitter both at the level of user profiles and individual Tweets, using a graph-based approach. The only approach towards automated detection of right-wing extremist users on Twitter we are aware of is our previous work (Hartung et al., 2017).

As a common assumption, all of the latter models rely on discrete output spaces; more specifically, they frame the profile identification task as a binary classification problem. In this paper, we argue that this assumption is overly simplistic as (i) it obscures the complexity of the spectrum of political attitudes, and (ii) it is unable to capture different degrees of radicalization. Therefore, we propose a ranking approach which is capable of projecting user profiles to a continuous range spanning different degrees of similarity to known (groups of) right-wing extremist or non-extremist users.

Extremism detection can also be seen as special case of profiling users of social network platforms in a more general way, *e. g.*, classification of personality traits (Golbeck et al., 2011; Quercia et al., 2011). Such approaches can be seen as extensions to sentiment analysis in general (Liu, 2015). More recently, there is a growing interest in particular aspects such as hate speech (Schmidt and Wiegand, 2017; Waseem and Hovy, 2016), racism (Waseem,

2016), violence or threat detection (C. Basave et al., 2013; Wester et al., 2016).

3 Profile Ranking

Right-wing extremism is defined by adopting all or at least a majority of the attitudes mentioned in Section 2. It is, accordingly, appropriate to investigate entire Twitter profiles rather than individual Tweets. We frame the task of detecting right-wing extremism in Twitter as ranking of user profiles according to their relative proximity to (groups of) other users in high-dimensional vector space.

3.1 Conceptualizing the Dimensions of Right-Wing Extremism

Our approach is based on the general assumption that linguistic variables serve as informative predictors of user's underlying attitudes. We mainly focus on the vocabulary and certain semantic patterns the use of which may be considered as communicative behavior that is motivated by the ideology of right-wing extremism. In the following, we justify this choice by a more thorough description of the conceptual dimensions of right-wing extremism (as introduced in Section 2) and highlight presumable links to linguistic behavior.

National-chauvinism. Migration is currently the most salient topic of German right-wing extremism, touching upon the attitudes of *national-chauvinism* combined with *xenophobia.* In the view of right-wing extremists, migration is perceived as a threat to the homogeneity of the superior German nation (in-group) by migrants from inferior nations (out-group). National-chauvinism expresses the presumed superiority and demanded homogeneity of the in-group, while xenophobia encompasses the imagined inferiority of the out-group and its potential threat to the in-group. Relevant words and hashtags may be "Rapefugees" or "Invasoren" ("invaders"), for instance.

Racism. Although related to national-chauvinism and xenophobia, *racism* is distinct, since it defines the in- and out-group in terms of race rather than nationality. Racism becomes especially obvious with references to the physical appearance of out- and in-group members, as expressed by, *e. g.,* "Neger" ("nigger"), #whitepower or #whiteresistance.

Social Darwinism builds upon racism, but claims that fight either between or within races is an unavoidable means to leverage the survival of the strongest race. Violence is legitimated as a basic law of society and any deviation from violence, *e. g.,* by peaceful agreement, is considered to undermine the chances for survival and is thus illegitimate. The imagined homogeneity and purity of the own race needs to be defended; hence, political opponents and other people who are perceived as not fitting are considered as enemies who can be fought without any reservation. Indicative are thus words and semantic structures which aggressively offend the opponents as enemies refusing any agreement with them, *e. g.,* "Abschaumpresse" ("scum press"), "Volksverräter" ("betrayer of the nation"). Expressions conveying negative emotions such as anger or disgust when referring to opponents may be indicative as well.

Democracy vs. dictatorship. In turn, democracy is considered as weakening the in-group by substituting violent struggle by peaceful competition, negotiation and acceptance of universal rights. Instead, *dictatorship* is favored, since given the homogeneity of the nation or the race, political parties and their competition is considered needless. In the current debate on migration, the rejection of democracy has been fused with conspiracy theories. Indicative for the rejection of democracy and accompanying conspiracy theories are vocabulary like "Lügenpresse" ("lying press"), "Gehirnwäsche" ("brainwash"), or #stopislam.

National socialism. The glorification of the historical *national socialism* by explicitly referring to its symbols or the denial of the Holocaust is relevant to German criminal law. However, using legal references to national socialism or symbolic codes can circumvent this restriction. Indicative are words and number codes like "Heil", 18 or 88 (one and eight representing the letters A and H, respectively, thus abbreviating "Heil Hitler" or "Adolf Hitler").

Additionally, indications of behavior clearly associated to right-wing extremist organizations or parties can be used to classify the profiles. Indicative are therefore expressions of approval, affinity of even membership in such organizations, for instance by following them, or posting hashtags in an affirmative manner such as #NPD, #DritteWeg, #Die Rechte (all referring to German right-wing extremist parties).

3.2 Features

In this section, we describe how the previously discussed dimensions of right-wing extremism are incorporated as features into our ranking model.

Lexical Features. We create a *bag-of-words frequency profile* of all tokens (unigrams and bigrams) used by an author in the entirety of all messages in their profile after stopword filtering. This frequency profile is able to capture lexical expressions described in the previous section. Twitter-specific vocabulary such as "RT" (indicating re-tweets) or short links (URLs referring to websites external to Twitter) are filtered; however, hashtags and references to other Twitter users (*e. g.*, @NPD) are kept in the lexical profile.

Emotion Features. Similarly to previous research on emotion detection on Twitter (Ghazi et al., 2010; Suttles and Ide, 2013; Wang et al., 2012), we estimate a single-label classification model for various emotion categories, *viz.*, anger, disgust, fear, joy, love, sadness, shame, surprise, trust (motivated by fundamental emotions (Ekman, 1970; Plutchik, 2001)) on a subsample of approx. 1.2 Million English and German Tweets from March 2016 until November 2016. All English Tweets are machine translated to German via Google translate[1] to receive a more comprehensive training set. We use a weak supervision approach by utilizing the emotion hashtags (which are disregarded during training). As features in our downstream ranking model, we use confidence scores derived from the single-label classification model (capturing the most prominent emotions and the proportion of emotionally charged Tweets per user profile).

Pro/Con Features. We use lexico-syntactic patterns encoding shallow argumentation patterns to capture the main political goals or motives to be conveyed by an author in their messages:

```
gegen ... <NOUN>
against ... <NOUN>

<NOUN> ... statt ... <NOUN>
<NOUN> ... instead of ... <NOUN>
```

As a fundament to apply these rules, noun detection is performed with regular expressions for capitalization, which works well in German, instead of incorporating a full-fledged (and slower) part-of-speech tagger. An arbitrary number of intermediate tokens is accepted between the prepositional cue and the closest subsequent noun denoting the objective of support or disaffirmation.

The following examples[2] illustrate these patterns (pro and con objectives in boldface):

(1)   a.   *#Muslimefürfrieden bringen Antwort auf die Broschüre der AfD in die Öffentlichkeit:* **Aufklärung** *statt* **Hetze**...

       b.   *#Muslimefürfrieden publicly reply to AfD brochure:* **awareness** *rather than* **agitation**

(2)   a.   *Demo gegen* **Abschiebung***: In Erfurt demonstrierten am 25. Januar etwa 200 Menschen gegen die* **Abschiebungen** *der R...*

       b.   *Demonstration against* **deportation***: On January 25, 200 people demonstrated in Erfurt against the* **deportations** *of...*

Social Identity Features. Based on the assumption that collective identities are constructed by means of discursive appropriation of particular entities of the real world, we apply another shallow lexico-syntactic pattern in order to detect such entities that are recurrently used in appropriation contexts:

```
unser_ ... <NOUN>
our_ ... <NOUN>
```

In this pattern, all morphological variants of the lexical cue are considered (*e. g.*, *unsere*, *unseren*), as indicated by the _ symbol. The following example illustrates this pattern:

(3)   a.   *RT @... Das war klar, es sind Muslime, sie wollen nur Teilhabe an unserem* **Wohlstand** *haben, ansonsten verachten sie uns...*

       b.   *RT @... Obviously, they are muslims, they only want to participate in our* **wealth***, apart from that they scorn us...*

Both pro/con features and social identity features are primarily intended to capture aspects of

---

[2] In all examples throughout this paper, original German Tweets are presented in (a.), with our translation to English given in (b.), respectively.

national-chauvinism and social darwinism (*cf.* Section 3.1).

Transformation of Feature Values. After extracting the previously described features, the resulting feature vector describing each profile is transformed by following the tf·idf scheme (Manning et al., 2008). This is a standard approach in information retrieval to increase the relative impact of features that are (i) prominent in the respective profile and (ii) bear high discriminative power in the sense that they occur in a relatively small proportion of all profiles in the data.

3.3 Ranking Model

Our approach in this work can be seen as a generalization of nearest neighbour classification in a vector space framework (Manning et al., 2008): Twitter profiles are represented as points in a high-dimensional vector space using the features described in Section 3.2. Assuming a set of seed profiles that are labeled with one of the categories *right-wing extremist* (R) or *non-extremist* (N), the task is to rank an unseen profile $\vec{x}$ on a continuous scale spanning the range from right-wing extremist to non-extremist (N) content. Profiles are ranked according to their similarity to groups of nearest neighbours in the seed profiles.

We define centroids of non-extremist and right-wing nearest neighbours of $\vec{x}$, namely $C_N(\vec{x})$ and $C_R(\vec{x})$, respectively, as

$$C_N(\vec{x}) = \frac{1}{|N_k(\vec{x})|} \sum_{\vec{x'} \in N_k(\vec{x})} \vec{x'} \qquad (1)$$

$$C_R(\vec{x}) = \frac{1}{|R_\ell(\vec{x})|} \sum_{\vec{x'} \in R_\ell(\vec{x})} \vec{x'}, \qquad (2)$$

where $N_k(\vec{x})$ and $R_\ell(\vec{x})$ denote the sets of the k and ℓ nearest neighbours of $\vec{x}$ in the respective class in the training data. Then, the ranking score of the model is determined as the relative similarity of $\vec{x}$ to each centroid:

$$\text{score}(\vec{x}) = \text{sim}(\vec{x}, C_N(\vec{x})) - \text{sim}(\vec{x}, C_R(\vec{x})) \qquad (3)$$

With sim being instantiated as cosine similarity, this score ranges from -1 ($\vec{x}$ maximally similar to right-wing groups) to $+1$ ($\vec{x}$ maximally similar to non-extremist groups); borderline cases between both categories are expected to center around 0 (indicating equidistance of $\vec{x}$ to both groups). Setting $k{=}1$ and $\ell{=}1$ renders the model an instance of nearest neighbour ranking.

4 Evaluation

4.1 Data Set

In our experiments, we use the data set previously discussed in Hartung et al. (2017). Annotations are provided by domain experts at the level of individual user profiles. These annotations comprise a set of 37 *seed profiles* of political actors from the German federal state Thuringia. They are split into 20 profiles labeled as right-wing and 17 non-extremist ones. Right-wing seed profiles contain organizations as well as leading individuals within the formal and informal extremist scene as documented by Quent et al. (2016). Non-extremist seed profiles contain political actors of the governing parties and single-issue associations (*e. g.*, nature conservation, social equality) (Quent et al., 2016).

In five other user profiles, the annotators were unable to reach a consensus on whether to classify the user as R or N. The latter profiles were kept in the data set as unlabeled *differential profiles*.

The test set comprises 100 randomly sampled profiles from followers of the seed users which have been annotated as being members of the R or N category.

4.2 Experiments and Results

4.2.1 Discrete Decoding

Given that ground truth annotations in the testing data are only available in terms of discrete labels (rather than continuous scores; cf. Section 4.1), the ranking model is evaluated in a discrete setting, using the following indicator function as a decision rule that is applied to the model score as given in Equation (3):

$$\text{class}(\vec{x}) = \begin{cases} R, & \text{score}(\vec{x}) < 0 \\ N, & \text{score}(\vec{x}) > 0 \\ \text{None}, & \text{otherwise} \end{cases} \qquad (4)$$

Note that discrete decoding can be applied in a *balanced* and *unbalanced* manner by setting the k and ℓ parameters in Equations (1) and (2) to the same or different numbers (thus considering nearest neighbour centroids of equal or different sizes).

Baseline Classifier. As a baseline classification model for comparison, we train a support vector machine (Cortes and Vapnik, 1995) with a linear kernel on the seed profiles (comprising 45,747 Tweets in total, among them 15,911 of category

	Entire sub-sample			Profiles $>$100 Tweets		
	P	R	F_1	P	R	F_1
discrete decoding unbalanced (k=4, ℓ=5)	0.56	0.79	0.65	0.79	0.85	0.81
discrete decoding balanced (k=10, ℓ=10)	0.55	0.65	0.59	0.80	0.62	0.70
discrete decoding balanced (k=1, ℓ=1)	0.44	0.63	0.52	0.69	0.69	0.69
Classification (Hartung et al., 2017)	0.25	0.95	0.40	0.32	0.92	0.47
Baseline	0.19	1.00	0.32	0.21	1.00	0.35

Table 1: Performance of the ranking model on the test set when being applied in a discrete decoding scenario, compared to a binary SVM classifier and a one-class baseline. Parameters k and ℓ in discrete decoding indicate the number of nearest neighbours in the centroids (cf. Equations 1 and 2).

R and 29,836 of category N) with all features described in Section 3.2. This implementation corresponds to our previous approach (Hartung et al., 2017).

Results. The results of this experiment can be seen in Table 1. We compare three variants of our ranking model in the previously described discrete decoding setting, the classification model and a baseline assigning all profiles to category R.

All models perform well above the baseline. While the classification model has a strong tendency towards recall, the ranking model generally offers a more harmonic precision-recall trade-off. Comparing the balanced and unbalanced model variants, we observe that our ranking approach generally benefits from larger centroids (thus preferring group similarities over individual ones), while the best performance can be obtained by choosing the k and ℓ parameters independently of one another (k=4, ℓ=5).

As can be seen from the right-most column of Table 1, reducing the test set to a subsample of profiles with at least 100 Tweets each (62 profiles remaining) leads to an additional performance increase up to an F_1 score of 0.81 in unbalanced discrete decoding.

All differences of the ranking models as reported in Table 1 are statistically significant over the baseline and the classifier according to an approximate randomization test (Yeh, 2000) at significance levels of $p < 0.05$ or smaller.

Discussion. In Figure 1 we explore the parameter space for different values of k and ℓ in unbalanced discrete decoding. While analyzing the variation in one parameter, the other one is fixed to its global optimum (k=4 and ℓ=5, respectively). For comparison, the dashed line indicates the performance of the nearest neighbour approach (i. e., setting k=1 and ℓ=1) in terms of F_1 score.

As a general pattern, increasing the number of non-extremist neighbours in unbalanced discrete decoding fosters recall, while increasing the number of right-wing extremist neighbours fosters precision. Having said that, we also observe that the nearest neighbour approach generally yields robust performance which can be outperformed only in very few configurations throughout the parameter space. Apparently, in these configurations the model based on centroids of nearest neighbours is more effective in abstracting from outliers or borderline cases that might otherwise blur the decision boundary.

Figure 1 also illustrates that k and ℓ cannot be set to arbitrary large values without taking a considerable loss in performance. This indicates that, apart from abstracting from outliers, it is also crucial that the centroids are, to some degree, specific for the particular instance to be categorized, rather than a mere class prototype.

4.2.2 Continuous Ranking

In order to evaluate the plausibility of the ranking model scores in the absence of ground truth ranking annotations, we analyze the model predictions on the differential profiles for which no consensus regarding their category membership could be reached among the expert annotators (cf. Section 4.1). Being related to some New Right German political movements, which are notoriously hard to be delimited from right-wing extremist political

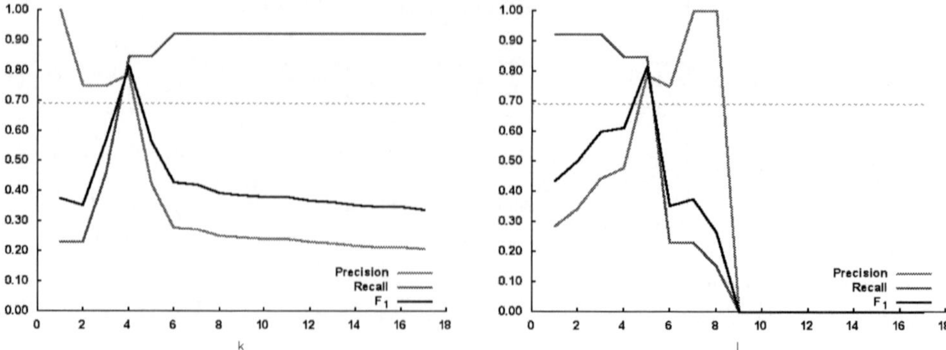

(a) Increasing k (number of non-extremist neighbours) for a fixed optimal value of ℓ=5

(b) Increasing ℓ (number of right-wing extremist neighbours) for a fixed optimal value of k=4

Figure 1: Exploration of the parameter space of k and ℓ on restricted test set (only profiles $>$100 Tweets). The dashed line indicates the performance of the nearest neighbour approach (*i. e.*, setting k=1 and ℓ=1)

actors, these cases are of particular interest from a social science perspective (*cf.* Zick et al., 2016). Due to their borderline character, we expect the ranking model to produce scores close to 0 for all these profiles.

Results. Figure 2 plots the profiles analyzed here on a continuous scale according to their predicted model score. We rely on the parameter settings which yielded best performance in the previous experiment (*i. e.*, k=4 and ℓ=5)[3]. As expected, all profiles are located closely around 0, which indicates that their predicted relative distance to extremist and non-extremist groups is almost equal. Despite the small sample size underlying this analysis, we consider this result as preliminary evidence of the plausibility of the ranking model on a selection of inherently difficult cases.

Discussion. Each data point in Figure 2 carries two types of information, viz. their position on the R–N spectrum according to the ranking model, and its category label as assigned by the baseline classifier. The latter is indicated in terms of crosses (denoting category N) and circles (category R). Comparing the predictions of both models, we find that they are in agreement in most of the cases. An interesting divergence concerns the case of a prominent member of a New Right German policitical party (explicitly marked by the arrow in Figure 2), who is categorized as R by the classifier, while being projected to the N range of the spectrum by the ranking model. We argue that this finding sheds light on the different methodological underpinnings of the models compared here: Apparently, this profile is sharing many properties with other non-extremist profiles, while the classifier still identifies a critical number of individual features which are taken as evidence in favour of an extremist profile. From our perspective, this finding reflects quite well the observed communicative strategies of the respective political party. Future work should be invested to corroborate this hypothesis.

4.3 Feature Analysis

Table 2 shows the impact of the individual feature groups as described in Section 3.2 in the ranking model when being used in isolation. In this analysis, Pro/Con features and Social Identity features are combined into one group (Pattern features).

We observe that all feature groups are effective to some degree: Emotion features tend to foster recall; pattern features may provide high precision, but suffer from low coverage due to their inherent sparsity. However, there is low complementarity between these feature groups, as the overall performance of the model (*cf.* Table 1) is clearly dominated by the lexical features.[4]

A preliminary analysis of the individual contributions of the emotion and pattern features according to their relative tf·idf weights per class shows that they are conceptually meaningful despite being superseded by other lexical features:

---

[3]However, the results reported in Figure 2 are largely stable with regard to the relative positions of the profiles to each other, despite some variation in the absolute values of the predicted model scores.

[4]A similar result has been found by Wester et al. (2016) for threat detection in social media.

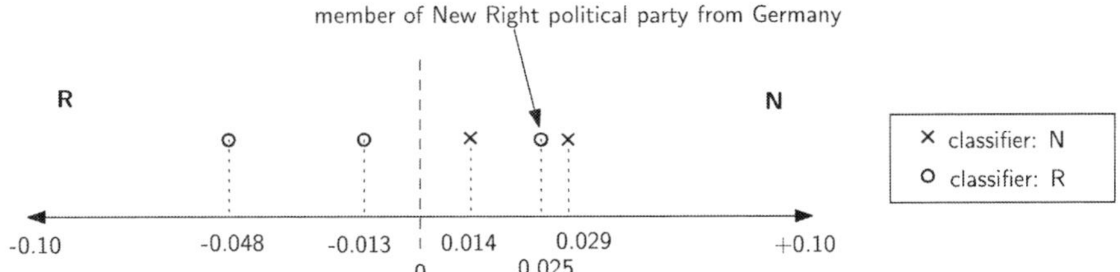

Figure 2: Continuous ranking of differential profiles (*cf.* Section 4.1). Position on the scale indicates the ranking score as given in Equation (3), based on optimal parameters k=4 and ℓ=5. The marked data point is assigned different categories by ranking and classification models (*cf.* discussion in Section 4.2.2).

	Lexical Features			Emotion Features			Pattern Features		
	P	R	F$_1$	P	R	F$_1$	P	R	F$_1$
discrete decoding unbalanced (k=4, ℓ=5)	0.79	0.85	0.81	0.38	0.62	0.47	1.00	0.08	0.14
discrete decoding balanced (k=10, ℓ=10)	0.80	0.62	0.70	0.20	0.38	0.26	0.00	0.00	0.00
discrete decoding balanced (k=1, ℓ=1)	0.69	0.69	0.69	0.48	0.85	0.61	0.63	0.38	0.48

Table 2: Results of analyzing the impact of individual feature groups in the ranking model when being used in isolation (on test set)

First, higher degrees of emotion in language use are clearly associated with category R profiles. Individual emotions most strongly associated with one of the categories are surprise, trust and disgust (for right-wing extremists), and love and sadness (for non-extremist users). Second, the most highly weighted pattern features for category R are GEGEN_Masseneinwanderung ('mass immigration'), UNSER_Politiker ('politicians'), UNSER_Fahne ('banner'), GEGEN_Syrien ('Syria') and GEGEN_Merkel, whereas UNSER_Land ('country'), GEGEN_Rechts ('Right-wing'), GEGEN_Gebietsreform ('territorial reform'), PRO_Aufklärung ('information') and UNSER_Jugendkandidat*innen ('youth contestants') are the most indicative patterns of category N.

5 Conclusions and Outlook

In this paper, we have presented a ranking model to identify Twitter profiles which display traits or attitudes of right-wing extremism. Our work is motivated by the goal of supporting human experts in their monitoring activities which are currently carried out purely manually.

Similarly to standard nearest-neighbour classification approaches, the model is based on estimating the relative proximity of an unseen profile to a limited number of manually annotated groups of seed profiles in high-dimensional vector space. We apply this model in the two settings of discrete decoding and continuous ranking. Our evaluation shows a significant advantage of the ranking model over a binary classification approach (Hartung et al., 2017). At the same time, the ranking model is found to deliver plausible predictions for a sample of borderline cases which specifically address actors from New Right political movements in Germany, whose categorization as right-wing extremists is currently debated in the social sciences (*cf.* Zick et al., 2016).

The latter finding clearly deserves a more thorough investigation based on a larger sample of cases, which we would like to address in future work. Additionally, we aim at developing this method further into a learning-to-rank approach in order to enable the comparison of profiles based on weighted properties. Finally, we propose the development of features that are based on deeper methods of natural language analysis in order to be able to address more fine-grained aspects in the conceptualization of right-wing extremism.

References

ADL. 2016. Anti-Semitic Targeting of Journalists during the 2016 Presidential Campaign. A Report from ADL's Task Force on Harassment and Journalism. `http://www.adl.org/assets/pdf/press-center/CR_4862_Journalism-Task-Force_v2.pdf`.

Amadeu-Antonio-Stiftung. 2016. Rechtsextreme und menschenverachtende Phänomene im Social Web. `https://www.amadeu-antonio-stiftung.de/w/files/pdfs/monitoringbericht-2015.pdf`.

M. Ashcroft, A. Fisher, L. Kaati, E. Omer, and N. Prucha. 2015. Detecting Jihadist Messages on Twitter. In *Proc. of EISIC*. https://doi.org/10.1109/EISIC.2015.27.

J.M. Berger. 2016. Nazis vs. ISIS on Twitter. A Comparative Study of White Nationalist and ISIS Online Social Media Networks. Technical report, Center for Cyber and Homeland Security, George Washington University, Washington, D.C.

H. Best, St. Niehoff, A. Salheiser, and L. Vogel. 2016. Gemischte Gefühle. Thüringen nach der "Flüchtlingskrise". Ergebnisse des Thüringen-Monitors. `http://www.thueringen.de/mam/th1/tsk/thuringen-monitor_2016_mit_anhang.pdf`.

G. Blanquart and D. Cook. 2013. Twitter Influence and Cumulative Perceptions of Extremist Support. A Case Study of Geert Wilders. In *Proc. of ACTC*.

A. Elizabeth C. Basave, Y. He, K. Liu, and J. Zhao. 2013. A Weakly Supervised Bayesian Model for Violence Detection in Social Media. In *Proceedings of the JCNLP*.

C. Cortes and V. Vapnik. 1995. Support-Vector Networks. *Machine Learning* 20:273–297.

P. Ekman. 1970. Universal Facial Expressions of Emotion. *California Mental Health Research Digest* 8(4):151–158.

E. Ferrara, W.-Q. Wang, O. Varol, A. Flammini, and A. Galstyan. 2016. Predicting Online Extremism, Content Adopters, and Interaction Reciprocity. *arxiv:* `https://arxiv.org/abs/1605.00659`.

D. Ghazi, D. Inkpen, and St. Szpakowicz. 2010. Hierarchical versus Flat Classification of Emotions in Text. In *NAACL HLT Workshop on Computational Approaches to Analysis and Generation of Emotion in Text*.

J. Golbeck, C. Robles, M. Edmondson, and K. Turner. 2011. Predicting Personality from Twitter. In *IEEE Int. Conference on Privacy, Security, Risk and Trust and IEEE Int. Conference on Social Computing*.

M. Hartung, R. Klinger, F. Schmidtke, and L. Vogel. 2017. Identifying Right-Wing Extremism in German Twitter Profiles: a Classification Approach. In F. Frascinar, A. Ittoo, L.M. Nguyen, and E. Métais, editors, *Natural Language Processing and Information Systems*, Springer, volume 10260 of *LNCS*, pages 320–325.

L. Kaati, E. Omer, N. Prucha, and A. Shrestha. 2015. Detecting Multipliers of Jihadism on Twitter. In *IEEE Int. Conference on Data Mining Workshop (ICDMW)*.

B. Liu. 2015. *Sentiment Analysis. Mining Opinions, Sentiments, and Emotions*. Cambridge University Press.

Ch. D. Manning, P. Raghavan, and H. Schütze. 2008. *Introduction to Information Retrieval*. Cambridge University Press.

J.H. Parmelee and S.L. Bichars. 2013. *Politics and the Twitter Revolution*. Lexington Books, Landham, MD.

R. Plutchik. 2001. The Nature of Emotions. *American Scientist* .

M. Quent, A. Salheiser, and F. Schmidtke. 2016. Gefährdungen der demokratischen Kultur in Thüringen. `http://www.denkbunt-thueringen.de/wp-content/uploads/2016/02/Gef%C3%A4hrdungsanalyse.pdf`.

D. Quercia, M. Kosinski, D. Stillwell, and J. Crowcroft. 2011. Our Twitter Profiles, Our Selves: Predicting Personality with Twitter. In *IEEE Int. Conference on Privacy, Security, Risk and Trust and IEEE Int. Conference on Social Computing*.

J. R. Scanlon and M. S. Gerber. 2014. Automatic detection of cyber-recruitment by violent extremists. *Security Informatics* 3(1):5.

A. Schmidt and M. Wiegand. 2017. A Survey on Hate Speech Detection using Natural Language Processing. In *Proceedings of the Fifth International Workshop on Natural Language Processing for Social Media*. Association for Computational Linguistics, Valencia, Spain, pages 1–10.

R. Stöss. 2010. *Rechtsextremismus im Wandel*. Friedrich-Ebert-Stiftung, Berlin.

J. Suttles and N. Ide. 2013. *Distant Supervision for Emotion Classification with Discrete Binary Values*, Springer, Berlin, Heidelberg.

I-H. Ting, H.-M. Chi, J.-S. Wu, and S.-L. Wang. 2013. *An Approach for Hate Groups Detection in Facebook*, Springer Netherlands.

W. Wang, L. Chen, K. Thirunarayan, and A. P. Sheth. 2012. Harnessing Twitter "Big Data" for Automatic Emotion Identification. In *IEEE Int. Conference on Privacy, Security, Risk and Trust and IEEE Int. Conference on Social Computing*.

Z. Waseem. 2016. Are You a Racist or Am I Seeing Things? Annotator Influence on Hate Speech Detection on Twitter. In *Proceedings of the First Workshop on NLP and Computational Social Science*. Austin, Texas.

Z. Waseem and D. Hovy. 2016. Hateful Symbols or Hateful People? Predictive Features for Hate Speech Detection on Twitter. In *Proceedings of the NAACL Student Research Workshop*.

Y. Wei and L. Singh. 2017. Using Network Flows to Identify Users Sharing Extremist Content on Social Media. In *Proceedings of PAKDD 2017*, Springer, volume 10234 of *LNAI*, pages 330–342.

Y. Wei, L. Singh, and S. Martin. 2016. Identification of Extremism on Twitter. In *Int. Conference on Advances in Social Networks Analysis and Mining*.

A. Wester, L. Øvrelid, E. Velldal, and H. L. Hammer. 2016. Threat Detection in Online Discussions. In *Proceedings of the 7th Workshop on Computational Approaches to Subjectivity, Sentiment and Social Media Analysis*.

A. Yeh. 2000. More Accurate Tests for the Statistical Significance of Result Differences. In *Proceedings of COLING*.

A. Zick, B. Küpper, D. Krause, R. Melzer, and W. Berghan, editors. 2016. *Gespaltene Mitte – Feindselige Zustände. Rechtsextreme Einstellungen in Deutschland 2016*. Dietz.

WASSA-2017 Shared Task on Emotion Intensity

Saif M. Mohammad
Information and Communications Technologies
National Research Council Canada
Ottawa, Canada
saif.mohammad@nrc-cnrc.gc.ca

Felipe Bravo-Marquez
Department of Computer Science
The University of Waikato
Hamilton, New Zealand
felipe.bravo@waikato.ac.nz

Abstract

We present the first shared task on detecting the intensity of emotion felt by the speaker of a tweet. We create the first datasets of tweets annotated for anger, fear, joy, and sadness intensities using a technique called best–worst scaling (BWS). We show that the annotations lead to reliable fine-grained intensity scores (rankings of tweets by intensity). The data was partitioned into training, development, and test sets for the competition. Twenty-two teams participated in the shared task, with the best system obtaining a Pearson correlation of 0.747 with the gold intensity scores. We summarize the machine learning setups, resources, and tools used by the participating teams, with a focus on the techniques and resources that are particularly useful for the task. The emotion intensity dataset and the shared task are helping improve our understanding of how we convey more or less intense emotions through language.

1 Introduction

We use language to communicate not only the emotion we are feeling but also the intensity of the emotion. For example, our utterances can convey that we are very angry, slightly sad, absolutely elated, etc. Here, *intensity* refers to the degree or amount of an emotion such as anger or sadness.[1] Automatically determining the intensity of emotion felt by the speaker has applications in commerce, public health, intelligence gathering, and social welfare.

Twitter has a large and diverse user base which entails rich textual content, including nonstandard language such as emoticons, emojis, creatively spelled words (*happee*), and hashtagged words (*#luvumom*). Tweets are often used to convey one's emotion, opinion, and stance (Mohammad et al., 2017). Thus, automatically detecting emotion intensities in tweets is especially beneficial in applications such as tracking brand and product perception, tracking support for issues and policies, tracking public health and well-being, and disaster/crisis management. Here, for the first time, we present a shared task on automatically detecting intensity of emotion felt by the speaker of a tweet: WASSA-2017 Shared Task on Emotion Intensity.[2]

Specifically, given a tweet and an emotion X, the goal is to determine the intensity or degree of emotion X felt by the speaker—a real-valued score between 0 and 1.[3] A score of 1 means that the speaker feels the highest amount of emotion X. A score of 0 means that the speaker feels the lowest amount of emotion X. We first ask human annotators to infer this intensity of emotion from a tweet. Later, automatic algorithms are tested to determine the extent to which they can replicate human annotations. Note that often a tweet does not explicitly state that the speaker is experiencing a particular emotion, but the intensity of emotion felt by the speaker can be inferred nonetheless. Sometimes a tweet is sarcastic or it conveys the emotions of a different entity, yet the annotators (and automatic algorithms) are to infer, based on the tweet, the extent to which the speaker is likely feeling a particular emotion.

---

[1] Intensity should not be confused with *arousal*, which refers to activation–deactivation dimension—the extent to which an emotion is calming or exciting.

[2] http://saifmohammad.com/WebPages/EmotionIntensity-SharedTask.html

[3] Identifying intensity of emotion evoked in the reader, or intensity of emotion felt by an entity mentioned in the tweet, are also useful tasks, and left for future work.

Proceedings of the 8th Workshop on Computational Approaches to Subjectivity, Sentiment and Social Media Analysis, pages 34–49
Copenhagen, Denmark, September 7–11, 2017. ©2017 Association for Computational Linguistics

In order to provide labeled training, development, and test sets for this shared task, we needed to annotate instances for *degree* of affect. This is a substantially more difficult undertaking than annotating only for the broad affect class: respondents are presented with greater cognitive load and it is particularly hard to ensure consistency (both across responses by different annotators and within the responses produced by an individual annotator). Thus, we used a technique called *Best–Worst Scaling (BWS)*, also sometimes referred to as *Maximum Difference Scaling (MaxDiff)*. It is an annotation scheme that addresses the limitations of traditional rating scales (Louviere, 1991; Louviere et al., 2015; Kiritchenko and Mohammad, 2016, 2017). We used BWS to create the *Tweet Emotion Intensity Dataset*, which currently includes four sets of tweets annotated for intensity of anger, fear, joy, and sadness, respectively (Mohammad and Bravo-Marquez, 2017). These are the first datasets of their kind.

The competition is organized on a CodaLab website, where participants can upload their submissions, and the leaderboard reports the results.[4] Twenty-two teams participated in the 2017 iteration of the competition. The best performing system, *Prayas*, obtained a Pearson correlation of 0.747 with the gold annotations. Seven teams obtained scores higher than the score obtained by a competitive SVM-based benchmark system (0.66), which we had released at the start of the competition.[5] Low-dimensional (dense) distributed representations of words (word embeddings) and sentences (sentence vectors), along with presence of affect–associated words (derived from affect lexicons) were the most commonly used features. Neural network were the most commonly used machine learning architecture. They were used for learning tweet representations as well as for fitting regression functions. Support vector machines (SVMs) were the second most popular regression algorithm. Keras and Tensor-Flow were some of the most widely used libraries.

The top performing systems used ensembles of models trained on dense distributed representations of the tweets as well as features drawn from affect lexicons. They also made use of a substantially larger number of affect lexicons than systems that did not perform as well.

The emotion intensity dataset and the corresponding shared task are helping improve our understanding of how we convey more or less intense emotions through language. The task also adds a dimensional nature to model of basic emotions, which has traditionally been viewed as categorical (joy or no joy, fear or no fear, etc.). On going work with annotations on the same data for valence , arousal, and dominance aims to better understand the relationships between the circumplex model of emotions (Russell, 2003) and the categorical model of emotions (Ekman, 1992; Plutchik, 1980). Even though the 2017 WASSA shared task has concluded, the CodaLab competition website is kept open. Thus new and improved systems can continually be tested. The best results obtained by any system on the 2017 test set can be found on the CodaLab leaderboard.

The rest of the paper is organized as follows. We begin with related work and a brief background on best–worst scaling (Section 2). In Section 3, we describe how we collected and annotated the tweets for emotion intensity. We also present experiments to determine the quality of the annotations. Section 4 presents details of the shared task setup. In Section 5, we present a competitive SVM-based baseline that uses a number of common text classification features. We describe ablation experiments to determine the impact of different feature types on regression performance. In Section 6, we present the results obtained by the participating systems and summarize their machine learning setups. Finally, we present conclusions and future directions. All of the data, annotation questionnaires, evaluation scripts, regression code, and interactive visualizations of the data are made freely available on the shared task website.[2]

2 Related Work

2.1 Emotion Annotation

Psychologists have argued that some emotions are more basic than others (Ekman, 1992; Plutchik, 1980; Parrot, 2001; Frijda, 1988). However, they disagree on which emotions (and how many) should be classified as basic emotions—some propose 6, some 8, some 20, and so on. Thus, most efforts in automatic emotion detection have focused on a handful of emotions, especially since manually annotating text for a large number of emotions is arduous. Apart from these categorical models of emotions, certain dimensional models of emotion

---

[4]https://competitions.codalab.org/competitions/16380
[5]https://github.com/felipebravom/AffectiveTweets

have also been proposed. The most popular among them, Russell's circumplex model, asserts that all emotions are made up of two core dimensions: valence and arousal (Russell, 2003). We created datasets for four emotions that are the most common amongst the many proposals for basic emotions: anger, fear, joy, and sadness. However, we have also begun work on other affect categories, as well as on valence and arousal.

The vast majority of emotion annotation work provides discrete binary labels to the text instances (joy–nojoy, fear–nofear, and so on) (Alm et al., 2005; Aman and Szpakowicz, 2007; Brooks et al., 2013; Neviarouskaya et al., 2009; Bollen et al., 2009). The only annotation effort that provided scores for degree of emotion is by Strapparava and Mihalcea (2007) as part of one of the SemEval-2007 shared task. Annotators were given newspaper headlines and asked to provide scores between 0 and 100 via slide bars in a web interface. It is difficult for humans to provide direct scores at such fine granularity. A common problem is inconsistency in annotations. One annotator might assign a score of 79 to a piece of text, whereas another annotator may assign a score of 62 to the same text. It is also common that the same annotator assigns different scores to the same text instance at different points in time. Further, annotators often have a bias towards different parts of the scale, known as *scale region bias*.

2.2 Best–Worst Scaling

Best–Worst Scaling (BWS) was developed by Louviere (1991), building on some ground-breaking research in the 1960s in mathematical psychology and psychophysics by Anthony A. J. Marley and Duncan Luce. Annotators are given n items (an n-tuple, where $n > 1$ and commonly $n = 4$). They are asked which item is the *best* (highest in terms of the property of interest) and which is the *worst* (lowest in terms of the property of interest). When working on 4-tuples, best–worst annotations are particularly efficient because each best and worst annotation will reveal the order of five of the six item pairs. For example, for a 4-tuple with items A, B, C, and D, if A is the best, and D is the worst, then A > B, A > C, A > D, B > D, and C > D.

BWS annotations for a set of 4-tuples can be easily converted into real-valued scores of association between the items and the property of interest (Orme, 2009; Flynn and Marley, 2014). It has

Emotion	Thes. Category	Head Word
anger	900	resentment
fear	860	fear
joy	836	cheerfulness
sadness	837	dejection

Table 1: Categories from the Roget's Thesaurus whose words were taken to be the query terms.

been empirically shown that annotations for $2N$ 4-tuples is sufficient for obtaining reliable scores (where N is the number of items) (Louviere, 1991; Kiritchenko and Mohammad, 2016).[6]

Kiritchenko and Mohammad (2017) show through empirical experiments that BWS produces more reliable fine-grained scores than scores obtained using rating scales. Within the NLP community, Best–Worst Scaling (BWS) has thus far been used only to annotate words: for example, for creating datasets for relational similarity (Jurgens et al., 2012), word-sense disambiguation (Jurgens, 2013), word–sentiment intensity (Kiritchenko et al., 2014), and phrase sentiment composition (Kiritchenko and Mohammad, 2016). However, we use BWS to annotate whole tweets for intensity of emotion.

3 Data

Mohammad and Bravo-Marquez (2017) describe how the *Tweet Emotion Intensity Dataset* was created. We summarize below the approach used and the key properties of the dataset. Not included in this summary are: (a) experiments showing marked similarities between emotion pairs in terms of how they manifest in language, (b) how training data for one emotion can be used to improve prediction performance for a different emotion, and (c) an analysis of the impact of hashtag words on emotion intensities.

For each emotion X, we select 50 to 100 terms that are associated with that emotion at different intensity levels. For example, for the anger dataset, we use the terms: *angry, mad, frustrated, annoyed, peeved, irritated, miffed, fury, antagonism,* and so on. For the sadness dataset, we use the terms: *sad, devastated, sullen, down, crying, dejected, heartbroken, grief, weeping,* and so on. We will refer to these terms as the *query terms*.

We identified the query words for an emotion

---

[6]At its limit, when $n = 2$, BWS becomes a *paired comparison* (Thurstone, 1927; David, 1963), but then a much larger set of tuples need to be annotated (closer to N^2).

by first searching the *Roget's Thesaurus* to find categories that had the focus emotion word (or a close synonym) as the head word.[7] The categories chosen for each head word are shown in Table 1. We chose all single-word entries listed within these categories to be the query terms for the corresponding focus emotion.[8] Starting November 22, 2016, and continuing for three weeks, we polled the Twitter API for tweets that included the query terms. We discarded retweets (tweets that start with RT) and tweets with urls. We created a subset of the remaining tweets by:

- selecting at most 50 tweets per query term.

- selecting at most 1 tweet for every tweeter–query term combination.

Thus, the *master set of tweets* is not heavily skewed towards some tweeters or query terms.

To study the impact of emotion word hashtags on the intensity of the whole tweet, we identified tweets that had a query term in hashtag form towards the end of the tweet—specifically, within the trailing portion of the tweet made up solely of hashtagged words. We created copies of these tweets and then removed the hashtag query terms from the copies. The updated tweets were then added to the master set. Finally, our master set of 7,097 tweets includes:

1. *Hashtag Query Term Tweets (HQT Tweets)*: 1030 tweets with a query term in the form of a hashtag (#<query term>) in the trailing portion of the tweet;

2. *No Query Term Tweets (NQT Tweets)*: 1030 tweets that are copies of '1', but with the hashtagged query term removed;

3. *Query Term Tweets (QT Tweets)*: 5037 tweets that include:
a. tweets that contain a query term in the form of a word (no #<query term>)
b. tweets with a query term in hashtag form followed by at least one non-hashtag word.

The master set of tweets was then manually annotated for intensity of emotion. Table 3 shows a breakdown by emotion.

3.1 Annotating with Best–Worst Scaling

We followed the procedure described in Kiritchenko and Mohammad (2016) to obtain BWS annotations. For each emotion, the annotators were presented with four tweets at a time (4-tuples) and asked to select the speakers of the tweets with the highest and lowest emotion intensity. $2 \times N$ (where N is the number of tweets in the emotion set) distinct 4-tuples were randomly generated in such a manner that each item is seen in eight different 4-tuples, and no pair of items occurs in more than one 4-tuple. We refer to this as *random maximum-diversity selection (RMDS)*. RMDS maximizes the number of unique items that each item co-occurs with in the 4-tuples. After BWS annotations, this in turn leads to direct comparative ranking information for the maximum number of pairs of items.[9]

It is desirable for an item to occur in sets of 4-tuples such that the the maximum intensities in those 4-tuples are spread across the range from low intensity to high intensity, as then the proportion of times an item is chosen as the best is indicative of its intensity score. Similarly, it is desirable for an item to occur in sets of 4-tuples such that the minimum intensities are spread from low to high intensity. However, since the intensities of items are not known before the annotations, RMDS is used.

Every 4-tuple was annotated by three independent annotators.[10] The questionnaires used were developed through internal discussions and pilot annotations. (See the Appendix (8.1) for a sample questionnaire. All questionnaires are also available on the task website.)

The 4-tuples of tweets were uploaded on the crowdsourcing platform, CrowdFlower. About 5% of the data was annotated internally beforehand (by the authors). These questions are referred to as gold questions. The gold questions are interspersed with other questions. If one gets a gold

---

[7]The *Roget's Thesaurus* groups words into about 1000 categories, each containing on average about 100 closely related words. The head word is the word that best represents the meaning of the words within that category.

[8]The full list of query terms is available on request.

[9]In combinatorial mathematics, *balanced incomplete block design* refers to creating blocks (or tuples) of a handful items from a set of N items such that each item occurs in the same number of blocks (say x) and each pair of distinct items occurs in the same number of blocks (say y), where x and y are integers ge 1 (Yates, 1936). The set of tuples we create have similar properties, except that since we create only $2N$ tuples, pairs of distinct items either never occur together in a 4-tuple or they occur in exactly one 4-tuple.

[10]Kiritchenko and Mohammad (2016) showed that using just three annotations per 4-tuple produces highly reliable results. Note that since each tweet is seen in eight different 4-tuples, we obtain $8 \times 3 = 24$ judgments over each tweet.

question wrong, they are immediately notified of it. If one's accuracy on the gold questions falls below 70%, they are refused further annotation, and all of their annotations are discarded. This serves as a mechanism to avoid malicious annotations.[11]

The BWS responses were translated into scores by a simple calculation (Orme, 2009; Flynn and Marley, 2014): For each item t, the score is the percentage of times the t was chosen as having the most intensity minus the percentage of times t was chosen as having the least intensity.[12]

$$intensity(t) = \%most(t) - \%least(t) \qquad (1)$$

Since intensity of emotion is a unipolar scale, we linearly transformed the the -100 to 100 scores to scores in the range 0 to 1.

3.2 Reliability of Annotations

A useful measure of quality is reproducibility of the end result—if repeated independent manual annotations from multiple respondents result in similar intensity rankings (and scores), then one can be confident that the scores capture the true emotion intensities. To assess this reproducibility, we calculate average *split-half reliability (SHR)*, a commonly used approach to determine consistency (Kuder and Richardson, 1937; Cronbach, 1946). The intuition behind SHR is as follows. All annotations for an item (in our case, tuples) are randomly split into two halves. Two sets of scores are produced independently from the two halves. Then the correlation between the two sets of scores is calculated. If the annotations are of good quality, then the correlation between the two halves will be high.

Since each tuple in this dataset was annotated by three annotators (odd number), we calculate SHR by randomly placing one or two annotations per tuple in one bin and the remaining (two or one) annotations for the tuple in another bin. Then two sets of intensity scores (and rankings) are calculated from the annotations in each of the two bins.

Emotion	Spearman	Pearson
anger	0.779	0.797
fear	0.845	0.850
joy	0.881	0.882
sadness	0.847	0.847

Table 2: Split-half reliabilities (as measured by Pearson correlation and Spearman rank correlation) for the anger, fear, joy, and sadness tweets in the Tweet Emotion Intensity Dataset.

The process is repeated 100 times and the correlations across the two sets of rankings and intensity scores are averaged. Table 2 shows the split-half reliabilities for the anger, fear, joy, and sadness tweets in the *Tweet Emotion Intensity Dataset*.[13] Observe that for fear, joy, and sadness datasets, both the Pearson correlations and the Spearman rank correlations lie between 0.84 and 0.88, indicating a high degree of reproducibility. However, the correlations are slightly lower for anger indicating that it is relative more difficult to ascertain the degrees of anger of speakers from their tweets. Note that SHR indicates the quality of annotations obtained when using only half the number of annotations. The correlations obtained when repeating the experiment with three annotations for each 4-tuple is expected to be even higher. Thus the numbers shown in Table 2 are a lower bound on the quality of annotations obtained with three annotations per 4-tuple.

4 Task Setup

4.1 The Task

Given a tweet and an emotion X, automatic systems have to determine the intensity or degree of emotion X felt by the speaker—a real-valued score between 0 and 1. A score of 1 means that the speaker feels the highest amount of emotion X. A score of 0 means that the speaker feels the lowest amount of emotion X. The competition is organized on a CodaLab website, where participants can upload their submissions, and the leaderboard reports the results.[14]

---

[11]In case more than one item can be reasonably chosen as the best (or worst) item, then more than one acceptable gold answers are provided. The goal with the gold annotations is to identify clearly poor or malicious annotators. In case where two items are close in intensity, we want the crowd of annotators to indicate, through their BWS annotations, the relative ranking of the items.

[12]Kiritchenko and Mohammad (2016) provide code for generating tuples from items using RMDS, as well as code for generating scores from BWS annotations: http://saifmohammad.com/WebPages/BestWorst.html

[13]Past work has found the SHR for sentiment intensity annotations for words, with 8 annotations per tuple, to be 0.98 (Kiritchenko et al., 2014). In contrast, here SHR is calculated from 3 annotations, for emotions, and from whole sentences. SHR determined from a smaller number of annotations and on more complex annotation tasks are expected to be lower.

[14]https://competitions.codalab.org/competitions/16380

Emotion	Train	Dev.	Test	All
anger	857	84	760	1701
fear	1147	110	995	2252
joy	823	74	714	1611
sadness	786	74	673	1533
All	3613	342	3142	7097

Table 3: The number of instances in the Tweet Emotion Intensity dataset.

4.2 Training, development, and test sets

The *Tweet Emotion Intensity Dataset* is partitioned into training, development, and test sets for machine learning experiments (see Table 3). For each emotion, we chose to include about 50% of the tweets in the training set, about 5% in the development set, and about 45% in the test set. Further, we ensured that an No-Query-Term (NQT) tweet is in the same partition as the Hashtag-Query-Term (HQT) tweet it was created from.

The training and development sets were made available more than two months before the two-week official evaluation period. Participants were told that the development set could be used to tune ones system and also to test making a submission on CodaLab. Gold intensity scores for the development set were released two weeks before the evaluation period, and participants were free to train their systems on the combined training and development sets, and apply this model to the test set. The test set was released at the start of the evaluation period.

4.3 Resources

Participants were free to use lists of manually created and/or automatically generated word–emotion and word–sentiment association lexicons.[15] Participants were free to build a system from scratch or use any available software packages and resources, as long as they are not against the spirit of fair competition. In order to assist testing of ideas, we also provided a baseline Weka system for determining emotion intensity, that participants can build on directly or use to determine the usefulness of different features.[16] We describe the baseline system in the next section.

---

[15] A large number of sentiment and emotion lexicons created at NRC are available here: http://saifmohammad.com/WebPages/lexicons.html

[16] https://github.com/felipebravom/AffectiveTweets

4.4 Official Submission to the Shared Task

System submissions were required to have the same format as used in the training and test sets. Each line in the file should include:

id[tab]tweet[tab]emotion[tab]score

Each team was allowed to make as many as ten submissions during the evaluation period. However, they were told in advance that only the final submission would be considered as the official submission to the competition.

Once the evaluation period concluded, we released the gold labels and participants were able to determine results on various system variants that they may have developed. We encouraged participants to report results on all of their systems (or system variants) in the system-description paper that they write. However, they were asked to clearly indicate the result of their official submission.

During the evaluation period, the CodaLab leaderboard was hidden from participants—so they were unable see the results of their submissions on the test set until the leaderboard was subsequently made public. Participants were, however, able to immediately see any warnings or errors that their submission may have triggered.

4.5 Evaluation

For each emotion, systems were evaluated by calculating the Pearson Correlation Coefficient of the system predictions with the gold ratings. Pearson coefficient, which measures linear correlations between two variables, produces scores from -1 (perfectly inversely correlated) to 1 (perfectly correlated). A score of 0 indicates no correlation. The correlation scores across all four emotions was averaged to determine the bottom-line competition metric by which the submissions were ranked.

In addition to the bottom-line competition metric described above, the following additional metrics were also provided:

- Spearman Rank Coefficient of the submission with the gold scores of the test data.
  Motivation: Spearman Rank Coefficient considers only how similar the two sets of ranking are. The differences in scores between adjacently ranked instance pairs is ignored. On the one hand this has been argued to alleviate some biases in Pearson, but on the other hand it can ignore relevant information.

- Correlation scores (Pearson and Spearman) over a subset of the testset formed by taking instances with gold intensity scores ≥ 0.5.

  Motivation: In some applications, only those instances that are moderately or strongly emotional are relevant. Here it may be much more important for a system to correctly determine emotion intensities of instances in the higher range of the scale as compared to correctly determine emotion intensities in the lower range of the scale.

Results with Spearman rank coefficient were largely inline with those obtained using Pearson coefficient, and so in the rest of the paper we report only the latter. However, the CodaLab leaderboard and the official results posted on the task website show both metrics. The official evaluation script (which calculates correlations using both metrics and also acts as a format checker) was made available along with the training and development data well in advance. Participants were able to use it to monitor progress of their system by cross-validation on the training set or testing on the development set. The script was also uploaded on the CodaLab competition website so that the system evaluates submissions automatically and updates the leaderboard.

5 Baseline System for Automatically Determining Tweet Emotion Intensity

5.1 System

We implemented a package called AffectiveTweets (Mohammad and Bravo-Marquez, 2017) for the Weka machine learning workbench (Hall et al., 2009). It provides a collection of filters for extracting features from tweets for sentiment classification and other related tasks. These include features used in Kiritchenko et al. (2014) and Mohammad et al. (2017).[17] We use the AffectiveTweets package for calculating feature vectors from our emotion-intensity-labeled tweets and train Weka regression models on this transformed data. The regression model used is an L_2-regularized L_2-loss SVM regression model with the regularization parameter C set to 1,

implemented in LIBLINEAR[18]. The system uses the following features:[19]

a. Word N-grams (WN): presence or absence of word n-grams from $n = 1$ to $n = 4$.

b. Character N-grams (CN): presence or absence of character n-grams from $n = 3$ to $n = 5$.

c. Word Embeddings (WE): an average of the word embeddings of all the words in a tweet. We calculate individual word embeddings using the negative sampling skip-gram model implemented in *Word2Vec* (Mikolov et al., 2013). Word vectors are trained from ten million English tweets taken from the Edinburgh Twitter Corpus (Petrović et al., 2010). We set *Word2Vec* parameters: window size: 5; number of dimensions: 400.[20]

d. Affect Lexicons (L): we use the lexicons shown in Table 4 by aggregating the information for all the words in a tweet. If the lexicon provides nominal association labels (e.g, positive, anger, etc.), then the number of words in the tweet matching each class are counted. If the lexicon provides numerical scores, the individual scores for each class are summed. and whether the affective associations provided are nominal or numeric.

5.2 Experiments

We developed the baseline system by learning models from each of the *Tweet Emotion Intensity Dataset* training sets and applying them to the corresponding development sets. Once the system parameters were frozen, the system learned new models from the combined training and development corpora. This model was applied to the test sets. Table 5 shows the results obtained on the test sets using various features, individually and in combination. The last column 'avg.' shows the macro-average of the correlations for all of the emotions.

Using just character or just word n-grams leads to results around 0.48, suggesting that they are reasonably good indicators of emotion intensity by themselves. (Guessing the intensity scores at random between 0 and 1 is expected to get correlations close to 0.) Word embeddings produces statistically significant improvement over the ngrams (avg. r = 0.55).[21] Using features drawn from af-

---

[17]Kiritchenko et al. (2014) describes the NRC-Canada system which ranked first in three sentiment shared tasks: SemEval-2013 Task 2, SemEval-2014 Task 9, and SemEval-2014 Task 4. Mohammad et al. (2017) describes a stance-detection system that outperformed submissions from all 19 teams that participated in SemEval-2016 Task 6.

[18]http://www.csie.ntu.edu.tw/~cjlin/liblinear/

[19]See Appendix (A.3) for further implementation details.

[20]Optimized for the task of word–emotion classification on an independent dataset (Bravo-Marquez et al., 2016).

[21]We used the Wilcoxon signed-rank test at 0.05 significance level calculated from ten random partitions of the data, for all the significance tests reported in this paper.

	Twitter	Annotation	Scope	Label
AFINN (Nielsen, 2011)	Yes	Manual	Sentiment	Numeric
BingLiu (Hu and Liu, 2004)	No	Manual	Sentiment	Nominal
MPQA (Wilson et al., 2005)	No	Manual	Sentiment	Nominal
NRC Affect Intensity Lexicon (NRC-Aff-Int) (Mohammad, 2017)	Yes	Manual	Emotions	Numeric
NRC Word-Emotion Assn. Lexicon (NRC-EmoLex) (Mohammad and Turney, 2013)	No	Manual	Emotions	Nominal
NRC10 Expanded (NRC10E) (Bravo-Marquez et al., 2016)	Yes	Automatic	Emotions	Numeric
NRC Hashtag Emotion Association Lexicon (NRC-Hash-Emo) (Mohammad, 2012a; Mohammad and Kiritchenko, 2015)	Yes	Automatic	Emotions	Numeric
NRC Hashtag Sentiment Lexicon (NRC-Hash-Sent) (Mohammad et al., 2013)	Yes	Automatic	Sentiment	Numeric
Sentiment140 (Mohammad et al., 2013)	Yes	Automatic	Sentiment	Numeric
SentiWordNet (Esuli and Sebastiani, 2006)	No	Automatic	Sentiment	Numeric
SentiStrength (Thelwall et al., 2012)	Yes	Manual	Sentiment	Numeric

Table 4: Affect lexicons used in our experiments.

fect lexicons produces results ranging from avg. r = 0.19 with SentiWordNet to avg. r = 0.53 with NRC-Hash-Emo. Combining all the lexicons leads to statistically significant improvement over individual lexicons (avg. r = 0.63). Combining the different kinds of features leads to even higher scores, with the best overall result obtained using word embedding and lexicon features (avg. r = 0.66).[22] The feature space formed by all the lexicons together is the strongest single feature category. The results also show that some features such as character ngrams are redundant in the presence of certain other features.

Among the lexicons, NRC-Hash-Emo is the most predictive single lexicon. Lexicons that include Twitter-specific entries, lexicons that include intensity scores, and lexicons that label emotions and not just sentiment, tend to be more predictive on this task–dataset combination. NRC-Aff-Int has real-valued fine-grained word–emotion association scores for all the words in NRC-EmoLex that were marked as being associated with anger, fear, joy, and sadness.[23] Improvement in scores obtained using NRC-Aff-Int over the scores obtained using NRC-EmoLex also show that using fine intensity scores of word-emotion association are beneficial for tweet-level emotion intensity detection. The correlations for anger, fear, and joy are similar (around 0.65), but the correlation for sadness is markedly higher (0.71). We can observe from Table 5 that this boost in performance for sadness is to some extent due to word embeddings, but is more so due to lexicon features, especially those from SentiStrength. SentiStrength focuses solely on positive and negative classes, but provides numeric scores for each.

To assess performance in the moderate-to-high range of the intensity scale, we calculated correla-

	Pearson correlation r				
	anger	fear	joy	sad.	avg.
Individual feature sets					
word ngrams (WN)	0.42	0.49	0.52	0.49	0.48
char. ngrams (CN)	0.50	0.48	0.45	0.49	0.48
word embeds. (WE)	0.48	0.54	0.57	0.60	0.55
all lexicons (L)	**0.62**	**0.60**	**0.60**	**0.68**	**0.63**
Individual Lexicons					
AFINN	0.48	0.27	0.40	0.28	0.36
BingLiu	0.33	0.31	0.37	0.23	0.31
MPQA	0.18	0.20	0.28	0.12	0.20
NRC-Aff-Int	0.24	0.28	0.37	0.32	0.30
NRC-EmoLex	0.18	0.26	0.36	0.23	0.26
NRC10E	0.35	0.34	0.43	0.37	0.37
NRC-Hash-Emo	**0.55**	**0.55**	**0.46**	0.54	**0.53**
NRC-Hash-Sent	0.33	0.24	0.41	0.39	0.34
Sentiment140	0.33	0.41	0.40	0.48	0.41
SentiWordNet	0.14	0.19	0.26	0.16	0.19
SentiStrength	0.43	0.34	**0.46**	**0.61**	0.46
Combinations					
WN + CN + WE	0.50	0.48	0.45	0.49	0.48
WN + CN + L	0.61	0.61	0.61	0.63	0.61
WE + L	**0.64**	0.63	**0.65**	**0.71**	**0.66**
WN + WE + L	0.63	**0.65**	**0.65**	0.65	0.65
CN + WE + L	0.61	0.61	0.62	0.63	0.62
WN + CN + WE + L	0.61	0.61	0.61	0.63	0.62
Over the subset of test set where intensity ≥ 0.5					
WN + WE + L	0.51	0.51	0.40	0.49	0.47

Table 5: Pearson correlations (r) of emotion intensity predictions with gold scores. Best results for each column are shown in bold: highest score by a feature set, highest score using a single lexicon, and highest score using feature set combinations.

tion scores over a subset of the test data formed by taking only those instances with gold emotion intensity scores ≥ 0.5. The last row in Table 5 shows the results. We observe that the correlation scores are in general lower here in the 0.5 to 1 range of intensity scores than in the experiments over the full intensity range. This is simply because this is a harder task as now the systems do not benefit by making coarse distinctions over whether a tweet is in the lower range or in the higher range.

---

[22]The increase from 0.63 to 0.66 is statistically significant.

[23]http://saifmohammad.com/WebPages/AffectIntensity.htm

6 Official System Submissions to the Shared Task

Twenty-two teams made submissions to the shared task. In the subsections below we present the results and summarize the approaches and resources used by the participating systems.

6.1 Results

Table 6 shows the Pearson correlations (r) and ranks (in brackets) obtained by the systems on the full test sets. The bottom-line competition metric, 'r avg.', is the average of Pearson correlations obtained for each of the four emotions. (The task website shows Spearman rank coefficient as well. Those scores are close in value to the Pearson correlations, and most teams rank the same by either metric.) The top ranking system, *Prayas*, obtained an *r avg.* of 0.747. It obtains slightly better correlations for joy and anger (around 0.76) than for fear and sadness (around 0.73). *IMS*, which ranked second overall, obtained slightly higher correlation on anger, but lower scores than *Prayas* on the other emotions. The top 12 teams all obtain their best correlation on anger as opposed to any of the other three emotions. They obtain lowest correlations on fear and sadness. Seven teams obtained scores higher than that obtained by the publicly available benchmark system (r avg. = 0.66).

Table 7 shows the Pearson correlations (r) and ranks (in brackets) obtained by the systems on those instances in the test set with intensity scores ≥ 0.5. *Prayas* obtains the best results here too with r avg. = 0.571. *SeerNet*, which ranked third on the full test set, ranks second on this subset. As found in the baseline results, system results on this subset overall are lower than than on the full test set. Most systems perform best on the joy data and worst on the sadness data.

6.2 Machine Learning Setups

Systems followed a supervised learning approach in which tweets were mapped into feature vectors that were then used for training regression models.

Features were drawn both from the training data as well as from external resources such as large tweet corpora and affect lexicons. Table 8 lists the feature types (resources) used by the teams. (To save space, team names are abbreviated to just their rank on the full test set (as shown in Table 6).) Commonly used features included word embeddings and sentence repre-

sentations learned using neural networks (sentence embeddings). Some of the word embeddings models used were Glove (SeerNet, UWaterloo, YZU NLP), Word2Vec (SeerNet), and Word Vector Emoji Vectors (SeerNet). The models used for learning sentence embeddings included LSTM (Prayas, IITP), CNN (SGNLP), LSTM–CNN combinations (IMS, YMU-HPCC), bi-directional versions (YZU NLP), and augmented LSTMs models with attention layers (Todai). High-dimensional sparse representations such as word n-grams or character n-grams were rarely used. Affect lexicons were also widely used, especially by the top eight teams. Some teams built their own affect lexicons from additional data (IMS, XRCE).

The regression algorithms applied to the feature vectors included SVM regression or SVR (IITP, Code Wizards, NUIG, H.Niemstov), Neural Networks (Todai, YZU NLP, SGNLP), Random Forest (IMS, SeerNet, XRCE), Gradient Boosting (UWaterLoo, PLN PUCRS), AdaBoost (SeerNet), and Least Square Regression (UWaterloo). Table 9 provides the full list.

Some teams followed a popular deep learning trend wherein the feature representation and the prediction model are trained in conjunction. In those systems, the regression algorithm corresponds to the output layer of the neural network (YZU NLP, SGNLP, Todai).

Many libraries and tools were used for implementing the systems. The high-level neural networks API library *Keras* was the most widely used off-the-shelf package. It is written in Python and runs on top of either *TensorFlow* or *Theano*. *TensorFlow* and *Sci-kit learn* were also popular (also Python libraries).[24] Our AffectiveTweets Weka baseline package was used by five participating teams, including the teams that ranked first, second, and third. The full list of tools and libraries used by the teams is shown in Table 10.

In the subsections below, we briefly summarize the three top-ranking systems. The Appendix (8.3) provides participant-provided summaries about each system. See system description papers for detailed descriptions.

---

[24]TensorFlow provides implementations of a number of machine learning algorithms, including deep learning ones such as CNNs and LSTMs.

Team Name	r avg. (rank)	r fear (rank)	r joy (rank)	r sadness (rank)	r anger (rank)
1. Prayas	0.747 (1)	0.732 (1)	0.762 (1)	0.732 (1)	0.765 (2)
2. IMS	0.722 (2)	0.705 (2)	0.726 (2)	0.690 (4)	0.767 (1)
3. SeerNet	0.708 (3)	0.676 (4)	0.698 (6)	0.715 (2)	0.745 (3)
4. UWaterloo	0.685 (4)	0.643 (8)	0.699 (5)	0.693 (3)	0.703 (7)
5. IITP	0.682 (5)	0.649 (7)	0.713 (4)	0.657 (7)	0.709 (5)
6. YZU NLP	0.677 (6)	0.666 (5)	0.677 (8)	0.658 (6)	0.709 (5)
7. YNU-HPCC	0.671 (7)	0.661 (6)	0.697 (7)	0.599 (9)	0.729 (4)
8. TextMining	0.649 (8)	0.604 (10)	0.663 (9)	0.660 (5)	0.668 (10)
9. XRCE	0.638 (9)	0.629 (9)	0.657 (10)	0.594 (10)	0.672 (8)
10. LIPN	0.619 (10)	0.58 (11)	0.639 (11)	0.583 (11)	0.676 (8)
11. DMGroup	0.571 (11)	0.55 (12)	0.576 (12)	0.556 (12)	0.603 (11)
12. Code Wizards	0.527 (12)	0.465 (16)	0.534 (15)	0.532 (14)	0.578 (13)
13. Todai	0.522 (13)	0.470 (15)	0.561 (13)	0.537 (13)	0.520 (16)
14. SGNLP	0.494 (14)	0.486 (14)	0.512 (16)	0.429 (18)	0.550 (14)
15. NUIG	0.494 (14)	0.680 (3)	0.717 (3)	0.625 (8)	-0.047 (21)
16. PLN PUCRS	0.483 (16)	0.508 (13)	0.460 (19)	0.425 (19)	0.541 (15)
17. H.Niemtsov	0.468 (17)	0.412 (17)	0.511 (17)	0.437 (17)	0.513 (17)
18. Tecnolengua	0.442 (18)	0.373 (18)	0.488 (18)	0.439 (16)	0.469 (18)
19. GradAscent	0.426 (19)	0.356 (19)	0.543 (14)	0.226 (20)	0.579 (12)
20. SHEF/CNN	0.291 (20)	0.277 (20)	0.109 (20)	0.517 (15)	0.259 (19)
21. deepCybErNet	0.076 (21)	0.176 (21)	0.023 (21)	-0.019 (21)	0.124 (20)
Late submission					
∗ SiTAKA	0.631	0.626	0.619	0.593	0.685

Table 6: Official Competition Metric: Pearson correlations (r) and ranks (in brackets) obtained by the systems on the full test sets. The bottom-line competition metric, 'r avg.', is the average of Pearson correlations obtained for each of the four emotions.

Team Name	r avg. (rank)	r fear (rank)	r joy (rank)	r sadness (rank)	r anger (rank)
1. Prayas	0.571 (1)	0.605 (1)	0.621 (1)	0.500 (2)	0.557 (2)
3. SeerNet	0.547 (2)	0.529 (5)	0.551 (7)	0.551 (1)	0.556 (3)
4. UWaterloo	0.520 (3)	0.499 (9)	0.562 (4)	0.480 (3)	0.538 (4)
6. YZU NLP	0.516 (4)	0.544 (3)	0.552 (5)	0.471 (5)	0.495 (7)
2. IMS	0.514 (5)	0.519 (7)	0.552 (5)	0.415 (7)	0.570 (1)
5. IITP	0.505 (6)	0.525 (6)	0.575 (2)	0.406 (8)	0.513 (6)
7. YNU-HPCC	0.500 (7)	0.530 (4)	0.540 (8)	0.406 (8)	0.526 (5)
8. TextMining	0.486 (8)	0.480 (10)	0.513 (9)	0.472 (4)	0.477 (9)
9. XRCE	0.450 (9)	0.506 (8)	0.507 (10)	0.357 (14)	0.430 (12)
10. LIPN	0.446 (10)	0.435 (12)	0.496 (11)	0.366 (12)	0.489 (8)
11. DMGroup	0.432 (11)	0.456 (11)	0.483 (13)	0.329 (16)	0.462 (10)
15. NUIG	0.390 (12)	0.567 (2)	0.566 (3)	0.426 (6)	0.003 (21)
13. Todai	0.387 (13)	0.350 (15)	0.484 (12)	0.362 (13)	0.351 (17)
12. Code Wizards	0.380 (14)	0.344 (16)	0.422 (16)	0.318 (17)	0.437 (11)
14. SGNLP	0.373 (15)	0.386 (13)	0.390 (17)	0.330 (15)	0.387 (16)
19. GradAscent	0.367 (16)	0.245 (19)	0.457 (14)	0.376 (11)	0.392 (15)
17. H.Niemtsov	0.347 (17)	0.275 (17)	0.441 (15)	0.242 (18)	0.428 (13)
16. PLN PUCRS	0.313 (18)	0.361 (14)	0.315 (18)	0.155 (19)	0.424 (14)
20. SHEF/CNN	0.220 (19)	0.188 (21)	0.095 (20)	0.396 (10)	0.202 (20)
18. Tecnolengua	0.209 (20)	0.247 (18)	0.224 (19)	0.061 (20)	0.305 (18)
21. deepCybErNet	0.140 (21)	0.190 (20)	0.077 (21)	0.057 (21)	0.235 (19)
Late submission					
∗ SiTAKA	0.484	0.496	0.46	0.465	0.513

Table 7: Pearson correlations (r) and ranks (in brackets) obtained by the systems on a subset of the test set where gold scores ≥ 0.5

Features	1	2	3	4	5	6	7	8	9	*	10	11	12	13	14	15	16	17	18	19	20	21
N-grams				✓									✓									
CN													✓									
WN				✓									✓		✓							
Word Embeddings	✓	✓	✓	✓	✓	✓	✓	✓		✓			✓	✓	✓	✓				✓		
Glove			✓	✓	✓	✓	✓	✓		✓				✓		✓				✓		
Emoji Vectors			✓	✓																		
Word2Vec	✓	✓	✓	✓																		
Other								✓					✓		✓							
Sentence Embeddings																						
CNN	✓	✓				✓	✓	✓		✓					✓						✓	✓
LSTM	✓	✓			✓	✓	✓	✓						✓		✓				✓		
Other				✓										✓						✓	✓	
Affective Lexicons		✓	✓	✓	✓	✓		✓	✓				✓				✓	✓	✓			
AFINN	✓	✓	✓		✓			✓														
ANEW		✓																				
BingLiu	✓	✓	✓		✓			✓	✓													
Happy Ratings		✓																				
Lingmotif																			✓			
LIWC																	✓					
MPQA	✓	✓	✓		✓			✓														
NRC-Aff-Int	✓		✓	✓				✓														
NRC-EmoLex	✓	✓	✓	✓	✓			✓	✓													
NRC-Emoticon-Lex	✓		✓	✓				✓						✓								
NRC-Hash-Emo	✓	✓	✓	✓	✓			✓	✓													
NRC-Hash-Sent		✓	✓	✓	✓			✓														
NRC-Hashtag-Sent.	✓		✓	✓																		
NRC10E	✓	✓	✓					✓														
Sentiment140	✓	✓	✓	✓				✓														
SentiStrength		✓	✓					✓														
SentiWordNet	✓	✓	✓	✓	✓			✓														
Vader				✓																		
Word.Affect			✓																			
In-house lexicon	✓							✓								✓						
Linguistic Features								✓														
Dependency Parser								✓														

Table 8: Feature types (resources) used by the participating systems. Teams are indicated by their rank.

Regression	1	2	3	4	5	6	7	8	9	*	10	11	12	13	14	15	16	17	18	19	20	21
AdaBoost			✓																			
Gradient Boosting		✓	✓														✓					
Linear Regression			✓																			
Logistic Regression									✓										✓			
Neural Network	✓			✓		✓	✓	✓				✓	✓			✓				✓	✓	✓
Random Forest		✓	✓						✓													
SVM or SVR			✓	✓	✓								✓			✓	✓	✓		✓		
Ensemble	✓		✓										✓			✓				✓		

Table 9: Regression methods used by the participating systems. Teams are indicated by their rank.

Tools	1	2	3	4	5	6	7	8	9	*	10	11	12	13	14	15	16	17	18	19	20	21
AffectiveTweets-Weka	✓	✓	✓					✓												✓		
Gensim	✓			✓																		
Glove				✓		✓	✓	✓												✓		
Keras	✓	✓		✓	✓	✓	✓	✓					✓			✓				✓	✓	
LIBSVM																		✓				
NLTK				✓		✓																
Pandas	✓			✓													✓					
PyTorch																				✓		
Sci-kit learn	✓		✓	✓		✓							✓			✓	✓					
TensorFlow	✓			✓			✓	✓				✓	✓									
Theano								✓			✓											
TweetNLP		✓																				
TweeboParser														✓								
Tweetokenize			✓																			
Word2Vec	✓	✓		✓				✓														
XGBoost			✓	✓																		

Table 10: Tools and libraries used by the participating systems. Teams are indicated by their rank.

6.3 Prayas: Rank 1

The best performing system, *Prayas*, used an ensemble of three different models: The first is a feed-forward neural network whose input vector is formed by concatenating the average word embedding vector with the lexicon features vector provided by the AffectiveTweets package (Mohammad and Bravo-Marquez, 2017). These embeddings were trained on a collection of 400 million tweets (Godin et al., 2015). The network has four hidden layers and uses rectified linear units as activation functions. Dropout is used a regularization mechanisms and the output layer consists of a sigmoid neuron. The second model treats the problem as a multi-task learning problem with the labeling of the four emotion intensities as the four sub-tasks. Authors use the same neural network architecture as in the first model, but the weights of the first two network layers are shared across the four subtasks. The weights of the last two layers are independently optimized for each subtask. In the third model, the word embeddings of the words in a tweet are concatenated and fed into a deep learning architecture formed by LSTM, CNN, max pooling, fully connected layers. Several architectures based on these layers are explored. The final predictions are made by combining the first two models with three variations of the third model into an ensemble. A weighted average of the individual predictions is calculated using cross-validated performances as the relative weights. Experimental results show that the ensemble improves the performance of each individual model by at least two percentage points.

6.4 IMS: Rank 2

IMS applies a random forest regression model to a representation formed by concatenating three vectors: 1. a feature vector drawn from existing affect lexicons, 2. a feature vector drawn from expanded affect lexicons, and 3. the output of a neural network. The first vector is obtained using the lexicons implemented in the AffectiveTweets package. The second is based on an extended lexicons built from feed-forward neural networks trained on word embeddings. The gold training words are taken from existing affective norms and emotion lexicons: NRC Hashtag Emotion Lexicon (Mohammad, 2012b; Mohammad and Kiritchenko, 2015), affective norms from Warriner et al. (2013), Brysbaert et al. (2014), and ratings

for happiness from Dodds et al. (2011). The third vector is taken from the output of neural network that combines CNN and LSTM layers.

6.5 SeerNet: Rank 3

SeerNet creates an ensemble of various regression algorithms (e.g, SVR, AdaBoost, random forest, gradient boosting). Each regression model is trained on a representation formed by the affect lexicon features (including those provided by AffectiveTweets) and word embeddings. Authors also experiment with different word embeddings models: Glove, Word2Vec, and Emoji embeddings (Eisner et al., 2016).

7 Conclusions

We conducted the first shared task on detecting the intensity of emotion felt by the speaker of a tweet. We created the emotion intensity dataset using best–worst scaling and crowdsourcing. We created a benchmark regression system and conducted experiments to show that affect lexicons, especially those with fine word–emotion association scores, are useful in determining emotion intensity.

Twenty-two teams participated in the shared task, with the best system obtaining a Pearson correlation of 0.747 with the gold annotations on the test set. As in many other machine learning competitions, the top ranking systems used ensembles of multiple models (Prayas-rank1, SeerNet-rank3). IMS, which ranked second, used random forests, which are ensembles of multiple decision trees. The top eight systems also made use of a substantially larger number of affect lexicons to generate features than systems that did not perform as well. It is interesting to note that despite using deep learning techniques, training data, and large amounts of unlabeled data, the best systems are finding it beneficial to include features drawn from affect lexicons.

We have begun work on creating emotion intensity datasets for other emotion categories beyond anger, fear, sadness, and joy. We are also creating a dataset annotated for valence, arousal, and dominance. These annotations will be done for English, Spanish, and Arabic tweets. The datasets will be used in the upcoming SemEval-2018 Task #1: Affect in Tweets (Mohammad et al., 2018).[25]

---

[25] http://alt.qcri.org/semeval2018/

Acknowledgment

We thank Svetlana Kiritchenko and Tara Small for helpful discussions. We thank Samuel Larkin for help on collecting tweets.

References

Cecilia Ovesdotter Alm, Dan Roth, and Richard Sproat. 2005. Emotions from text: Machine learning for text-based emotion prediction. In *Proceedings of the Joint Conference on HLT–EMNLP*. Vancouver, Canada.

Saima Aman and Stan Szpakowicz. 2007. Identifying expressions of emotion in text. In *Text, Speech and Dialogue*, volume 4629 of *Lecture Notes in Computer Science*, pages 196–205.

Johan Bollen, Huina Mao, and Alberto Pepe. 2009. Modeling public mood and emotion: Twitter sentiment and socio-economic phenomena. In *Proceedings of the Fifth International Conference on Weblogs and Social Media*. pages 450–453.

Felipe Bravo-Marquez, Eibe Frank, Saif M. Mohammad, and Bernhard Pfahringer. 2016. Determining word–emotion associations from tweets by multi-label classification. In *Proceedings of the 2016 IEEE/WIC/ACM International Conference on Web Intelligence*. Omaha, NE, USA, pages 536–539.

Michael Brooks, Katie Kuksenok, Megan K Torkildson, Daniel Perry, John J Robinson, Taylor J Scott, Ona Anicello, Ariana Zukowski, and Harris. 2013. Statistical affect detection in collaborative chat. In *Proceedings of the 2013 conference on Computer supported cooperative work*. San Antonio, Texas, USA, pages 317–328.

Marc Brysbaert, Amy Beth Warriner, and Victor Kuperman. 2014. Concreteness ratings for 40 thousand generally known english word lemmas. *Behavior research methods* 46(3):904–911.

LJ Cronbach. 1946. A case study of the splithalf reliability coefficient. *Journal of educational psychology* 37(8):473.

Herbert Aron David. 1963. *The method of paired comparisons*. Hafner Publishing Company, New York.

Peter Sheridan Dodds, Kameron Decker Harris, Isabel M. Kloumann, Catherine A. Bliss, and Christopher M. Danforth. 2011. Temporal patterns of happiness and information in a global social network: Hedonometrics and Twitter. *PloS One* 6(12):e26752.

Ben Eisner, Tim Rocktäschel, Isabelle Augenstein, Matko Bosnjak, and Sebastian Riedel. 2016. emoji2vec: Learning emoji representations from their description. In *Proceedings of The Fourth International Workshop on Natural Language Processing for Social Media*. Association for Computational Linguistics, Austin, TX, USA, pages 48–54. http://aclweb.org/anthology/W16-6208.

Paul Ekman. 1992. An argument for basic emotions. *Cognition and Emotion* 6(3):169–200.

Andrea Esuli and Fabrizio Sebastiani. 2006. SENTIWORDNET: A publicly available lexical resource for opinion mining. In *Proceedings of the 5th Conference on Language Resources and Evaluation (LREC)*. Genoa, Italy, pages 417–422.

T. N. Flynn and A. A. J. Marley. 2014. Best-worst scaling: theory and methods. In Stephane Hess and Andrew Daly, editors, *Handbook of Choice Modelling*, Edward Elgar Publishing, pages 178–201.

Nico H Frijda. 1988. The laws of emotion. *American psychologist* 43(5):349.

Kevin Gimpel, Nathan Schneider, et al. 2011. Part-of-speech tagging for Twitter: Annotation, features, and experiments. In *Proceedings of the Annual Meeting of the Association for Computational Linguistics (ACL)*. Portland, OR, USA.

Fréderic Godin, Baptist Vandersmissen, Wesley De Neve, and Rik Van de Walle. 2015. Named entity recognition for twitter microposts using distributed word representations. *ACL-IJCNLP* 2015:146–153.

Mark Hall, Eibe Frank, Geoffrey Holmes, Bernhard Pfahringer, Peter Reutemann, and Ian H. Witten. 2009. The WEKA data mining software: An update. *SIGKDD Explor. Newsl.* 11(1):10–18. https://doi.org/10.1145/1656274.1656278.

Minqing Hu and Bing Liu. 2004. Mining and summarizing customer reviews. In *Proceedings of the tenth ACM SIGKDD international conference on Knowledge discovery and data mining*. ACM, New York, NY, USA, pages 168–177.

David Jurgens. 2013. Embracing ambiguity: A comparison of annotation methodologies for crowdsourcing word sense labels. In *Proceedings of the Annual Conference of the North American Chapter of the Association for Computational Linguistics*. Atlanta, GA, USA.

David Jurgens, Saif M. Mohammad, Peter Turney, and Keith Holyoak. 2012. Semeval-2012 task 2: Measuring degrees of relational similarity. In *Proceedings of the 6th International Workshop on Semantic Evaluation*. Montréal, Canada, pages 356–364.

Svetlana Kiritchenko and Saif M. Mohammad. 2016. Capturing reliable fine-grained sentiment associations by crowdsourcing and best–worst scaling. In *Proceedings of The 15th Annual Conference of the North American Chapter of the Association for Computational Linguistics: Human Language Technologies (NAACL)*. San Diego, California.

Svetlana Kiritchenko and Saif M. Mohammad. 2017. Best-worst scaling more reliable than rating scales: A case study on sentiment intensity annotation. In *Proceedings of The Annual Meeting of the Association for Computational Linguistics (ACL)*. Vancouver, Canada.

Svetlana Kiritchenko, Xiaodan Zhu, and Saif M. Mohammad. 2014. Sentiment analysis of short informal texts. *Journal of Artificial Intelligence Research (JAIR)* 50:723–762.

G Frederic Kuder and Marion W Richardson. 1937. The theory of the estimation of test reliability. *Psychometrika* 2(3):151–160.

Jordan J. Louviere. 1991. Best-worst scaling: A model for the largest difference judgments. Working Paper.

Jordan J. Louviere, Terry N. Flynn, and A. A. J. Marley. 2015. *Best-Worst Scaling: Theory, Methods and Applications*. Cambridge University Press.

Tomas Mikolov, Kai Chen, Greg Corrado, and Jeffrey Dean. 2013. Efficient estimation of word representations in vector space. In *Proceedings of Workshop at ICLR*.

Saif Mohammad. 2012a. #Emotional tweets. In *The First Joint Conference on Lexical and Computational Semantics (*SEM 2012)*. Montréal, Canada.

Saif M. Mohammad. 2012b. From once upon a time to happily ever after: Tracking emotions in mail and books. *Decision Support Systems* 53(4):730–741.

Saif M. Mohammad. 2017. Word affect intensities. *arXiv preprint arXiv:1704.08798* .

Saif M. Mohammad and Felipe Bravo-Marquez. 2017. Emotion intensities in tweets. In *Proceedings of the sixth joint conference on lexical and computational semantics (*Sem)*. Vancouver, Canada.

Saif M. Mohammad, Felipe Bravo-Marquez, Svetlana Kiritchenko, and Mohammad Salameh. 2018. Semeval-2018 Task 1: Affect in tweets. In *Proceedings of International Workshop on Semantic Evaluation (SemEval-2018)*.

Saif M. Mohammad and Svetlana Kiritchenko. 2015. Using hashtags to capture fine emotion categories from tweets. *Computational Intelligence* 31(2):301–326. https://doi.org/10.1111/coin.12024.

Saif M. Mohammad, Svetlana Kiritchenko, and Xiaodan Zhu. 2013. NRC-Canada: Building the state-of-the-art in sentiment analysis of tweets. In *Proceedings of the International Workshop on Semantic Evaluation*. Atlanta, GA, USA.

Saif M. Mohammad, Parinaz Sobhani, and Svetlana Kiritchenko. 2017. Stance and sentiment in tweets. *Special Section of the ACM Transactions on Internet Technology on Argumentation in Social Media* 17(3).

Saif M. Mohammad and Peter D. Turney. 2013. Crowdsourcing a word–emotion association lexicon. *Computational Intelligence* 29(3):436–465.

Alena Neviarouskaya, Helmut Prendinger, and Mitsuru Ishizuka. 2009. Compositionality principle in recognition of fine-grained emotions from text. In *Proceedings of the Proceedings of the Third International Conference on Weblogs and Social Media (ICWSM-09)*. San Jose, California, pages 278–281.

Finn Årup Nielsen. 2011. A new ANEW: Evaluation of a word list for sentiment analysis in microblogs. In *Proceedings of the ESWC Workshop on 'Making Sense of Microposts': Big things come in small packages*. Heraklion, Crete, pages 93–98.

Bryan Orme. 2009. Maxdiff analysis: Simple counting, individual-level logit, and HB. Sawtooth Software, Inc.

W Parrot. 2001. *Emotions in Social Psychology*. Psychology Press.

Saša Petrović, Miles Osborne, and Victor Lavrenko. 2010. The Edinburgh Twitter corpus. In *Proceedings of the NAACL HLT 2010 Workshop on Computational Linguistics in a World of Social Media*. Association for Computational Linguistics, Stroudsburg, PA, USA, pages 25–26.

Robert Plutchik. 1980. A general psychoevolutionary theory of emotion. *Emotion: Theory, research, and experience* 1(3):3–33.

James A Russell. 2003. Core affect and the psychological construction of emotion. *Psychological review* 110(1):145.

Carlo Strapparava and Rada Mihalcea. 2007. Semeval-2007 task 14: Affective text. In *Proceedings of SemEval-2007*. Prague, Czech Republic, pages 70–74.

Mike Thelwall, Kevan Buckley, and Georgios Paltoglou. 2012. Sentiment strength detection for the social web. *Journal of the American Society for Information Science and Technology* 63(1):163–173.

Louis L. Thurstone. 1927. A law of comparative judgment. *Psychological review* 34(4):273.

Amy Beth Warriner, Victor Kuperman, and Marc Brysbaert. 2013. Norms of valence, arousal, and dominance for 13,915 English lemmas. *Behavior Research Methods* 45(4):1191–1207.

Theresa Wilson, Janyce Wiebe, and Paul Hoffmann. 2005. Recognizing contextual polarity in phrase-level sentiment analysis. In *Proceedings of the Joint Conference on HLT and EMNLP*. Stroudsburg, PA, USA, pages 347–354.

Frank Yates. 1936. Incomplete randomized blocks. *Annals of Human Genetics* 7(2):121–140.

8　Appendix

8.1　Best–Worst Scaling Questionnaire used to Obtain Emotion Intensity Scores

The BWS questionnaire used for obtaining fear annotations is shown below.

Degree Of Fear In English Language Tweets

The scale of fear can range from not fearful at all (zero amount of fear) to extremely fearful. One can often infer the degree of fear felt or expressed by a person from what they say. The goal of this task is to determine this degree of fear. Since it is hard to give a numerical score indicating the degree of fear, we will give you four different tweets and ask you to indicate to us:

- Which of the four speakers is likely to be the MOST fearful, and

- Which of the four speakers is likely to be the LEAST fearful.

Important Notes

- This task is about fear levels of the speaker (and not about the fear of someone else mentioned or spoken to).

- If the answer could be either one of two or more speakers (i.e., they are likely to be equally fearful), then select any one of them as the answer.

- Most importantly, try not to over-think the answer. Let your instinct guide you.

EXAMPLE

Speaker 1: *Don't post my picture on FB #grrr*
Speaker 2: *If the teachers are this incompetent, I am afraid what the results will be.*
Speaker 3: *Results of medical test today #terrified*
Speaker 4: *Having to speak in front of so many people is making me nervous.*

Q1. Which of the four speakers is likely to be the MOST fearful?
– Multiple choice options: Speaker 1, 2, 3, 4 –
Ans: Speaker 3

Q2. Which of the four speakers is likely to be the LEAST fearful?
– Multiple choice options: Speaker 1, 2, 3, 4 –
Ans: Speaker 1

The questionnaires for other emotions are similar in structure. In a post-annotation survey, the respondents gave the task high scores for clarity of instruction (4.2/5) despite noting that the task itself requires some non-trivial amount of thought (3.5 out of 5 on ease of task).

8.2　An Interactive Visualization to Explore the Tweet Emotion Intensity Dataset

We created an interactive visualization to allow ease of exploration of the *Tweet Emotion Intensity Dataset*. This visualization was made public after the the official evaluation period had concluded – so participants in the shared task did not have access to it when building their system. It is worth noting that if one intends to evaluate their emotion intensity detection system on the *Tweet Emotion Intensity Dataset*, then as a matter of commonly-followed best practices, they should not use the visualization to explore the test data in the system development phase (until all the system parameters are frozen).

The visualization has three main components:

1. Tables showing the percentage of instances in each of the emotion partitions (train, dev, test). Hovering over a row shows the corresponding number of instances. Clicking on an emotion filters out data from all other emotions, in all visualization components. Similarly, one can click on just the train, dev, or test partitions to view information just for that data. Clicking again deselects the item.

2. A histogram of emotion intensity scores. A slider that one can use to view only those tweets within a certain score range.

3. The list of tweets, emotion label, and emotion intensity scores.

Notably, the three components are interconnected, such that clicking on an item in one component will filter information in all other components to show only the relevant details. For example, clicking on 'joy' in 'a' will cause 'b' to show the histogram for only the joy tweets, and 'c' to show only the 'joy' tweets. Similarly one can click on the test/dev/train set, a particular band of emotion intensity scores, or a particular tweet. Clicking again deselects the item. One can use filters in combination. For e.g., clicking on fear, test data, and setting the slider for the 0.5 to 1 range, shows information for only those fear–testdata instances with scores ≥ 0.5.

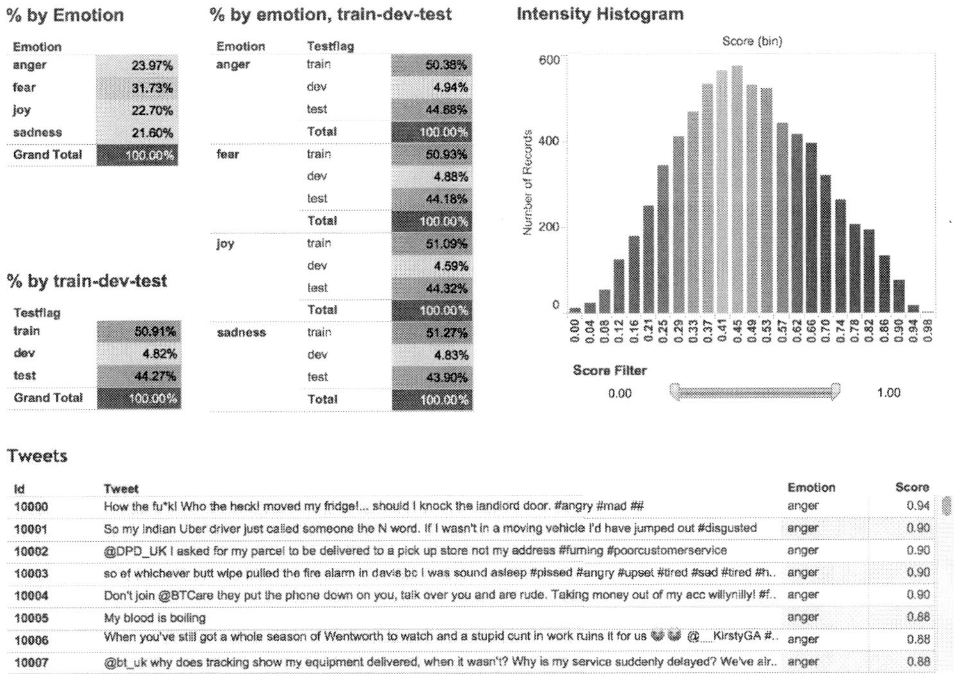

Figure 1: Screenshot of the interactive visualization to explore the Tweet Emotion Intensity Dataset. Available at: http://saifmohammad.com/WebPages/EmotionIntensity-SharedTask.html

8.3 AffectiveTweets Weka Package: Implementation Details

AffectiveTweets includes five filters for converting tweets into feature vectors that can be fed into the large collection of machine learning algorithms implemented within Weka. The package is installed using the *WekaPackageManager* and can be used from the Weka GUI or the command line interface. It uses the *TweetNLP* library (Gimpel et al., 2011) for tokenization and POS tagging. The filters are described as follows.

- *TweetToSparseFeatureVector* filter: calculates the following sparse features: word n-grams (adding a NEG prefix to words occurring in negated contexts), character n-grams (CN), POS tags, and Brown word clusters.[26]

- *TweetToLexiconFeatureVector* filter: calculates features from a fixed list of affective lexicons.

- *TweetToInputLexiconFeatureVector*: calculates features from any lexicon. The input lexicon can have multiple numeric or nominal word–affect associations. This filter allows users to experiment with their own lexicons.

- *TweetToSentiStrengthFeatureVector* filter: calculates positive and negative sentiment intensities for a tweet using the SentiStrength lexicon-based method (Thelwall et al., 2012)

- *TweetToEmbeddingsFeatureVector* filter: calculates a tweet-level feature representation using pre-trained word embeddings supporting the following aggregation schemes: average of word embeddings; addition of word embeddings; and concatenation of the first k word embeddings in the tweet. The package also provides *Word2Vec's* pre-trained word.[27]

Once the feature vectors are created, one can use any of the Weka regression or classification algorithms. Additional filters are under development.

---

[26]The scope of negation was determined by a simple heuristic: from the occurrence of a negator word up until a punctuation mark or end of sentence. We used a list of 28 negator words such as *no, not, won't* and *never*.

[27]https://code.google.com/archive/p/word2vec/

IMS at EmoInt-2017:
Emotion Intensity Prediction with Affective Norms, Automatically Extended Resources and Deep Learning

Maximilian Köper, Evgeny Kim and **Roman Klinger**
Institut für Maschinelle Sprachverarbeitung
Universität Stuttgart, Germany
{maximilian.koeper,evgeny.kim,roman.klinger}@ims.uni-stuttgart.de

Abstract

Our submission to the WASSA-2017 shared task on the prediction of emotion intensity in tweets is a supervised learning method with extended lexicons of affective norms. We combine three main information sources in a random forrest regressor, namely (1), manually created resources, (2) automatically extended lexicons, and (3) the output of a neural network (CNN-LSTM) for sentence regression. All three feature sets perform similarly well in isolation ($\approx$ .67 macro average Pearson correlation). The combination achieves .72 on the official test set (ranked 2nd out of 22 participants). Our analysis reveals that performance is increased by providing cross-emotional intensity predictions. The automatic extension of lexicon features benefit from domain specific embeddings. Complementary ratings for affective norms increase the impact of lexicon features. Our resources (ratings for 1.6 million twitter specific words) and our implementation is publicly available at http://www.ims.uni-stuttgart.de/data/ims_emoint.

1 Introduction

In natural language processing, emotion recognition is the task of associating words, phrases or documents with predefined emotions from psychological models. Typical discrete categories are those proposed by Ekman (Ekman, 1999) and Plutchik (Plutchik, 2001), namely *Anger, Anticipation, Disgust, Fear, Joy, Sadness, Surprise* und *Trust*. In contrast to sentiment analysis with its main task to recognize the polarity of text (*e. g.*, positive, negative, neutral, mixed), only a few resources and domains have been subject of analysis. Examples are, *e. g.*, tales (Alm et al., 2005), blogs (Aman and Szpakowicz, 2007), and as a very popular domain, microblogs on Twitter (Dodds et al., 2011). The latter in particular provides a large resource of data in the form of user messages (Costa et al., 2014). A common source of weak supervision for training classifiers are hashtags, emoticons, or emojis, which are interpreted as a weak form of author "self-labeling" (Suttles and Ide, 2013). The classifier then learns the association of all other words in the message with the emotion (Wang et al., 2012). An alternative to discrete models are continuous models that map emotions to an n-dimensional space with valence, arousal and dominance (VAD) being usual dimensions. Previous works that rely on the VAD-scheme focus mainly on extending and adapting the affective lexicons (Bestgen and Vincze, 2012; Turney and Littman, 2003), including to historical texts (Buechel et al., 2016), and on the prediction and extrapolation of affective ratings (Recchia and Louwerse, 2015a; Hollis et al., 2017).

The WASSA-2017 shared task on the prediction of emotion intensity in tweets (EmoInt) aims at combining discrete emotion classes with different levels of activation. Given a tweet and an emotion (*anger, fear, joy*, and *sadness*), the task requires to determine the intensity expressed regarding a particular emotion. This score can be seen as an approximation of the emotion intensity felt by the reader or expressed by the author. For a detailed task descriptions and background information on the data collection see Mohammad and Bravo-Marquez (2017).

2 System Description

In the following, we introduce all feature sets we experimented with. We start with an analysis and selection of features obtained from the baseline

Proceedings of the 8th Workshop on Computational Approaches to Subjectivity, Sentiment and Social Media Analysis, pages 50–57
Copenhagen, Denmark, September 7–11, 2017. ©2017 Association for Computational Linguistics

Rating	Top 4 words
Concreteness	fish, microphone, rope, toilet
Arousal	#attack, scare, attack, exciting
Dominance	#safe, #everydayhappy, courageous, #Amoved
Happiness	babygiggles, love, laughter, lovelysmile
Anger	soangry, comcastsucks, #soangry, #comcastsucks
Fear	#hyperventilation, #irrationalfear, aerophobia, #anxiety
Sadness	#greatloss, greatloss, sadsadsad, cryinggame
Joy	#peaceandharmony, #alwaysbethankful, positiveenergy, #youchoosehowtofeel

Table 1: Top four words for eight different rating types based on our automatically generated ratings.

system AffectiveTweets, explain how we extend resources to the domain of Twitter. Then, we explain our sentence regressor, which is based on deep learning and pre-trained word embeddings. Finally, we introduce two additional, manually defined features.

2.1 Baseline Features

The baseline system *AffectiveTweets*[1] which has been provided to participants together with the training and development data includes a huge variety of different features and configurations. The different feature types can be classified into a), *SparseFeatures*, which refer to word and character n-grams from tweets, b), *LexiconFeatures*, which are taken from several emotion and sentiment lists (we consider the *SentiStrength*-based feature to be part of this), and c), the *EmbeddingsFeature*, which comprise a tweet-level feature representation that can incorporate any pre-trained word embeddings.

2.2 Extending and Adding Norms

The baseline system builds on top of a variety of different lexical resources (Hu and Liu, 2004; Wilson et al., 2005; Svetlana Kiritchenko and Mohammad; Mohammad and Turney, 2013; Mohammad and Kiritchenko, 2015; Baccianella et al., 2010; Bravo-Marquez et al., 2016; Nielsen, 2011). Such

resources are naturally limited in coverage and often focus on words that are closely associated with a certain emotion or sentiment (*e. g.*, the word "hate" with the emotion *anger*).

At the same time, social media data is typically rich in lexical variations, and hence, tend to contain a great deal of out-of-vocabulary words. We address this with three separate approaches, namely by i) applying a supervised method to extend these lexicons to larger Twitter specific vocabulary ii), learning a new rating score for every word and not just highly associated terms and iii), including novel rating categories that provide complementary and potential useful information, such as valence, arousal, dominance and concreteness.

Several approaches have been proposed to combine distributional word representations with supervised machine learning methods to extend affective norms (Turney et al., 2011; Tsvetkov et al., 2014; Recchia and Louwerse, 2015b; Vankrunkelsven et al., 2015; Köper and Schulte im Walde, 2016; Sedoc et al., 2017). Köper and Schulte im Walde (2017) compared various supervised methods and showed that a feed forward neural network together with low dimensional distributed word representations (embeddings) obtained the highest correlation with human annotated ratings for concreteness.

Following these findings, we apply the same methodology. For a given emotion or norm we train a feed forward neural network with two hidden layers, each having 200 neurons. The input of the network is a single word representation (300 dimensions) and the output is one numerical value trained to correspond to the human annotated (gold) rating for the given input word. We apply the model to predict a rating score for every word representation in our distributional space (which includes the training data).

This method strongly depends on the underlying word representation. We therefore conduct multiple experiments using different word embeddings (shown in Section 4.2). We apply this procedure for 13 different lexicons using the following resources: *NRC Hashtag Emotion Lexicon* (Mohammad and Kiritchenko, 2015) containing ratings for $17k$ words with associations to *anger, anticipation, disgust, fear, joy, sadness, surprise* and *trust*. Additionally, we use the $14k$ ratings for *valence, arousal*, and *dominance* collected by Warriner et al. (2013). For *concreteness* we rely on the collection of $40k$ ratings from Brysbaert et al. (2014). Finally,

---

[1]https://github.com/felipebravom/AffectiveTweets

we use the $10k$ ratings for *happiness* from Dodds et al. (2011). These 13 ratings correspond to an automatic extension to 1.6 million word types with $\approx$ 21 million new word ratings. We map the ratings to an interval of $[0, 10]$. Table 1 shows the top words for eight ratings. For the emotion intensity prediction in our predictive model, we represent each rating with seven feature dimensions per tweet:

1. Average rating score across all words
2. Average rating score across all nouns
3. Average rating score across all adjectives
4. Average rating score across all verbs
5. Average rating score across all hashtags
6. Maximum rating score
7. Standard deviation of all rating scores

2.3 Tweet Regression

The tweet regression feature relies on the annotated training samples. We train a neural network based on word embeddings to predict the emotion intensity for each tweet.

Convolutional neural networks (CNNs), trained on top of pre-trained word vectors, have been shown to work well for sentence-level classification tasks (Kim, 2014). We apply a similar method here, combining CNNs and LSTMs (Hochreiter and Schmidhuber, 1997). The final architecture used by IMS is shown in Figure 1. Each tweet is represented by a matrix of size 50×300 (padded where necessary, embedding dimension is 300, the maximal token sequence in a tweet is set to 50). We apply dropout with a rate of 0.25. The matrix is then the input for a convolutional layer with a window size of 3, followed by a maxpooling layer (size 2) and an LSTM to predict a numerical output for each tweet.

This architecture captures sequential information in a compact way. For comparison, we conduct experiments using a variety of different architectures (shown in Section 4.3) including linear regression, multilayer perceptron (MLP), two stacked LSTMs and the proposed CNN-LSTM architecture.

2.4 Additional Features

In addition to regression and lexical features, we add two hand-crafted features. The first is a Boolean feature which holds if and only if an exclamation mark is present in the tweet. The second represents the overall number of tokens in the tweet.

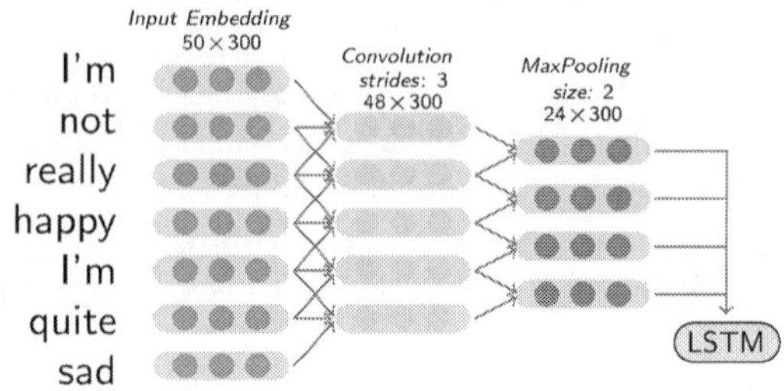

Figure 1: CNN-LSTM Architecture used for tweet regression.

3 Implementation Details

As a source for our in-domain embeddings, we use a corpus from 2016 retrieved with the Twitter streaming and rest APIs with emotion hashtags and popular general hashtags. It consists of $\approx$50 million tweets and $\approx$800 million tokens. After removing words with less than 10 occurrences, the resource contains 1.6 million word types. The 300 dimensional word representations are obtained with *word2vec*[2] (Mikolov et al., 2013). To study the impact of the training domain, we additionally conduct experiments with the public available *GoogleNews-vectors* that were trained on a 100b words corpus of news texts. Both word embeddings are used to extend the emotion lexicons (Section 2.2) as well as input embeddings in our tweet regression model (Section 2.3).

We use *TweetNLP*[3] (Owoputi et al., 2013) as tokenizer. In the case of observing only out-of-vocabulary words (no rating available) we set the score to the median value of the corresponding category.

The regressor based on the tweet text is implemented with *keras* (Chollet et al., 2015). We train one model for each of the four emotions separately. Furthermore, we provide the output of all four emotion-specific regression models in all emotion intensity prediction tasks.[4]

Finally, for the full system IMS, we combine features in a random forest classifier using *weka* (Witten et al., 1999). We use 800 trees (called *iterations* in Weka). We estimate one model for each of the four target emotions.

---

[2]Hyperparameters were set to window:5, min-count:10, neg-samples:15, dim:300, iteration:5.

[3]http://www.cs.cmu.edu/~ark/TweetNLP/

[4]To provide this feature for the within-emotion training data (*e. g.*, anger-regression output for anger training dataset), we split the training data into 20 folds – training on 19 and

Feature	Model	a	f	j	s	Avg
✓ Lexicons	✗ SVM	.62	.62	.62	.62	.62
	✓ RF	**.67**	**.69**	**.66**	**.66**	**.67**
✗ Sparse	✗ SVM	.58	.61	.63	.52	.58
	✗ RF	.53	.57	.61	.53	.56
✗ Embd.	✗ SVM	.48	.50	.55	.53	.51
	✗ RF	.53	.53	.61	.49	.54
✗ Comb	✗ SVM	.64	.64	.66	.64	.64
	✗ RF	.63	.64	.66	.63	.64

Table 2: Baseline features across training data using support vector machines (SVM) and random forest (RF). Pearson correlation based on 10-fold cross validation. The column names denote anger (a), fear (f), joy (j), sadness (s).

Feat	a	f	j	s	Avg
✓ Lexicons(=BL)	**.67**	.69	**.66**	.66	**.67**
✗ ACVH-Lexicons	.48	.45	.59	.35	.47
✗ Ext.News	.52	.52	.60	.44	.52
✓ Ext.Twitter	.65	**.69**	.65	**.68**	.67
✗ ACVH-Lexicons+BL	.66	.67	.67	.64	.66
✗ Ext.News+BL	.65	.66	.67	.64	.65
✓ Ext.Twitter+BL	**.68**	**.71**	**.68**	**.69**	**.69**

Table 3: Performance of lexicons and our automatically extended lexicons. Results are based on the random forest classifier. Top part compares performance of lexicon features in isolation. Ext.News and Ext.Twitter build on top of the baseline lexicons and the ACVH lexicons. The bottom part shows performance in combination with the original lexicons provided by the baseline (=BL).

4 Feature Subset Selection and Analysis

Feature selection and analysis was performed on annotated training and development data. All experiments were carried out using 10-fold cross validation. We report results following the official shared task evaluation measure to predict a value between 0 and 1, namely Pearson correlation for each emotion separately as well as a macro average over all emotions. Features that were finally used in IMS are marked with ✓ and respectively ✗ for features that were disregarded.

4.1 Baseline Feature Engineering

We start with feature engineering based solely on the baseline features (see Section 2.1). Table 2 shows our observation when exploring the different options from *AffectiveTweets* using default parameters. The embeddings (Embd.) are the recommended 400 dimensional Twitter embeddings available from the baseline system's homepage.

As we see in this table, an average performance of .67 is already obtained when relying only on a random forest in combination with the lexicon features. The other features, as well as the combination, result in inferior performance. In addition, the lexicon-based system is comparably simple with only 45 feature dimensions. We therefore only use the lexicon features from the baseline system.

4.2 Lexicons and Extended Lexicons

As a next feature, we explore various settings for the automatic extension of the lexicon features. Ta-

providing the predictions for the remaining.

ble 3 compares the baseline lexicon against the lexicons we add without extension (*ACVH-Lexicons*) as well as the automatically extended resources (*Ext.**). *ACVH-Lexicons* contains the unmodified ratings for arousal, concreteness, valency and happiness (ACVH), which were not part of the baseline system. For *Ext.** we present results based on underlying news (*Ext.News*) and Twitter (*Ext.Twitter*) embeddings. In addition we present results for each lexicon-feature in isolation, as well as in combination with the baseline lexicons (*Lexicons(=BL)*). It can be seen that the ACVH lexicons without automatic extension (*ACVH-Lexicons*) perform poorly and provide no performance gain when combined with the baseline (*ACVH-Lexicons+BL*). We assume that the poor coverage on Twitter data is the main reason. On the other hand, the automatically extended ratings perform well, and the choice of embeddings here has a high impact on the quality of the resulting ratings. In more detail, the in-domain embeddings (*Ext.Twitter*) create ratings that are extrinsically evaluated superior to the out-domain embeddings (*Ext.News*) with an average score .52 against .67.

The information of existing lexicons and extended norms is not redundant. The combination (*Ext.Twitter+BL*) increases average correlation across all four emotions by +.02 points, from .67 → .69..

To get a further understanding of the automatically extended norms, Figure 2 shows the evaluation performance of the thirteen extended norm

	anger	fear	joy	sadness	Avg
happiness (10.2k)	0.498	0.527	0.611	0.598	0.559
concreteness (39.9k)	0.317	0.308	0.399	0.385	0.352
dominance (13.9k)	0.499	0.555	0.546	0.568	0.542
valency (13.9k)	0.481	0.51	0.569	0.588	0.537
arousal (13.9k)	0.376	0.417	0.387	0.109	0.322
trust (1.6k)	0.301	0.292	0.31	0.208	0.278
surprise (6.0k)	0.286	0.311	0.331	0.282	0.302
sadness (2.5k)	0.381	0.353	0.316	0.528	0.395
joy (3.4k)	0.352	0.288	0.4	0.347	0.347
fear (3.8k)	0.318	0.516	0.338	0.346	0.38
disgust (5.3k)	0.476	0.334	0.433	0.346	0.397
anticipation (3.9k)	0.312	0.3	0.333	0.292	0.309
anger (5.6k)	0.502	0.315	0.416	0.366	0.4

Figure 2: Pearson's correlation of single rating categories (Y-Axis) on each target emotion (X-Axis). Numbers in brackets refer to training size used to extend the norms. Evaluation based on 10-fold cross validation using the full training data and random forest.

Feature	a	f	j	s	Avg
✗ Linear Reg. (BoW)	.48	.49	.44	.36	.44
✗ MLP (BoW)	.59	.64	.60	.56	.60
✗ Stacked LSTMs	.58	.66	.61	.61	.61
✓ CNN-LSTM	**.66**	**.68**	**.66**	**.65**	**.67**

Table 4: Comparing the performance of Tweet Regression Architectures.

categories separately. Especially the extended ratings from the new lexicons perform well: *happiness*, *dominance* and *valency*. However, we also see that the number of training samples might have a big impact, *e. g.*, the automatical ratings of joy are only trained on $3.4k$ samples while the size of the *happiness* training data is larger.

4.3 Tweet Regression Architectures

In addition to the CNN-LSTM architecture used in the final system (see Section 2.3), we experimented with different models for tweet regression. Table 4 shows results using various machine learning algorithms to directly predict the emotion intensity.

We use the in-domain Twitter embeddings as input. We observe that our architecture, introduced in Section 2.3, performs superior to other methods. Remarkable, the CNN-LSTM feature, as well

Feature Name	# Features
AffectiveTweets-Lexicons	45
Aut. Ext. Lexicons (Twitter)	91
Tweet Regression (CNN-LSTM)	4
Manual Features	2
Total	142

Table 5: Overview IMS full system, features, feature counts.

	a	f	j	s	Avg
Full IMS-Train	.71	.74	.71	.71	.72

Table 6: Final official system on training data (10 fold cross validation).

as our *Ext. Twitter* lexicons and the baseline *Lexicons(=BL)* obtain a score of $\approx .66$ when used in isolation.

4.4 Full System Combination

A combination of all features leads to the best performance, they provide complementary information. An overview is given in Table 5 and Table 6.

Another interesting observation is found with respect to the usage of cross-emotional intensity predictions: IMS trains a classifier for each emotion in isolation. Similarly, the tweet regression feature is trained emotion-wise but for each instance we also provide the intensity prediction from all other emotion models (therefore, 4 features). Without the cross-emotion information, we yield only a macro average across all emotions of .707 (vs. .719). Figure 3 shows how the emotion intensity predictions of these models correlate. It can be seen that *fear*, *sadness* and *anger* are slightly correlated while *joy* is negatively correlated with all three emotions. Interestingly, a combined model (*Comb*), which is trained on all emotions also leads to a high correlation for each emotion and especially *sadness*. Note that the classifier trained on all emotions (*Comb*) is not used by the final system IMS.

Finally, we want to mention that the impact of the two manual defined features is very little, we found that they increase performance on *joy* by $+.01$ and we therefore decided to keep them.

5 Official Results – Analysis Test Data

Table 7 shows the official results (Full IMS-Test) and the performance using only a subset of the

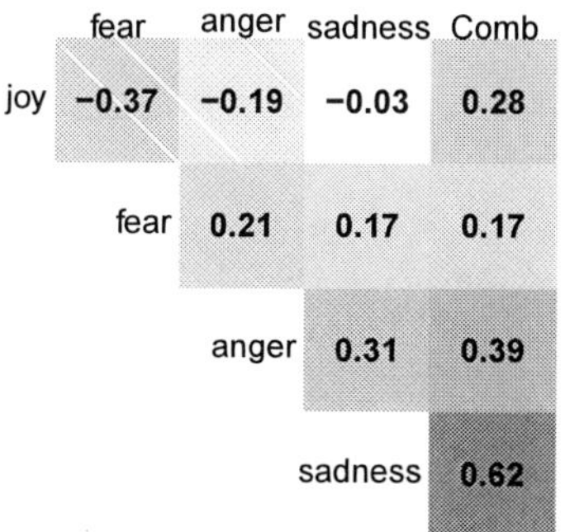

Figure 3: Pairwise Pearson correlation based on the output of our emotion-wise Tweet regression feature.

Feat	a	f	j	s	Avg
Lexicons(=BL)	.65	.66	.60	.70	.65
Ext.Twitter+BL	.68	.72	.66	.74	.70
CNN-LSTM+BL	.69	.69	.67	.76	.70
Full IMS-Test	.71	.73	.69	.77	.72
Best-Competitor	.73	.76	.73	.76	.75

Table 7: Overview IMS full and partial System performance on Test data.

entire features. For comparison, we also show the results of the best performing system (Best-Competitor). our baseline, using only the lexicon features and a random forest classifier obtains a competitive Pearson correlation of .65, which would have been ranked as the 8th best system.

Both of our core features, namely the extended resources, as well as the CNN-LSTM tweet regression architecture, increase performance by +.05 points when combined with the baseline lexicons (Lexicons(=BL)). Their performance is similar for *anger* and *joy*, but the ratings seem more useful for *fear*, and the regression more useful for *sadness*. The result of *Ext.Twitter+BL* with .70 would have ranked the 4th best system.

The final combination of all our features results in an increase of $\approx +.020$ correlation points. The performance of IMS on the test set without the two manually defined features is .719. Furthermore, we observe that our submission on the test data is on average very close to the estimated performance on the training data (both .72), but when looking at individual emotions our system is performing better on *sadness* and slightly worse on *fear*.

5.1 Error Analysis

Based on a manual inspection of individual tweets with a large gap between prediction and gold rating, we found that the model's prediction often depends on single words and ignores larger contexts. An example case with a high error for *fear* is:

> "*Most people never achieve their goals because they are afraid to fail.*"
> *(fear, G: .22, P: .55)*

Here, the gold emotion intensity for *fear* is comparably low, but our model predicts a high fear intensity. Similarly, in the tweet with high joy intensity

> "*Just died from laughter after seeing that.*"
> *(joy, G: .92, P: .50)*

our model predicts a low joy intensity.

Another challenge are modifications as in

> "*After this news Im supposed to be so damn happy and rejoicing but Im here like □*"
> *(joy, G: .07, P: .53)*

Here, the gold annotation is very low, but our model predicts a medium intensity for joy.

6 Conclusion

Our system IMS, submitted to the *EmoInt-2017* shared task, combines existing lexicons with automatically extended norms and a CNN-LSTM neural network based on embeddings. Our findings show that each of the three main components performs equally well, but the highest performance is achieved in combination. In addition, we found that extending existing emotion lexicons and affective norms improves performance over the original resources. We also showed that the impact of underlying word representation is important. In particular in-domain embeddings (trained on twitter data) perform superior to other embeddings. A particularly interesting observation is that providing cross-emotional intensity predictions benefits the performance.

7 Acknowledgement

The research was supported by the DFG Collaborative Research Centre SFB 732 and the German Ministry for Education and Research (BMBF) within the Center for Reflected Text Analytics (CRETA). We thank the anonymous reviewers for their comments and Jeremy Barnes for helpful suggestions.

References

Cecilia Ovesdotter Alm, Dan Roth, and Richard Sproat. 2005. Emotions from Text: Machine Learning for Text-based Emotion Prediction. In *Proceedings of HLT-EMNLP*, pages 579–586, Vancouver, BC.

Saima Aman and Stan Szpakowicz. 2007. Identifying expressions of emotion in text. In *Proceedings of TSD*, pages 196–205, Plzeň, Czech Republic.

Stefano Baccianella, Andrea Esuli, and Fabrizio Sebastiani. 2010. SentiWordNet 3.0: An Enhanced Lexical Resource for Sentiment Analysis and Opinion Mining. In *Proceedings of the International Conference on Language Resources and Evaluation, LREC 2010, 17-23 May 2010, Valletta, Malta*.

Yves Bestgen and Nadja Vincze. 2012. Checking and bootstrapping lexical norms by means of word similarity indexes. *Behavior research methods*, 44(4):998–1006.

Felipe Bravo-Marquez, Eibe Frank, Saif M. Mohammad, and Bernhard Pfahringer. 2016. Determining Word-Emotion Associations from Tweets by Multilabel Classification. In *2016 IEEE/WIC/ACM International Conference on Web Intelligence, WI 2016, Omaha, NE, USA, October 13-16, 2016*, pages 536–539.

Marc Brysbaert, AmyBeth Warriner, and Victor Kuperman. 2014. Concreteness Ratings for 40 Thousand Generally known English Word Lemmas. *Behavior Research Methods*, pages 904–911.

Sven Buechel, Johannes Hellrich, and Udo Hahn. 2016. Feelings from the PastAdapting Affective Lexicons for Historical Emotion Analysis. *LT4DH 2016*, page 54.

François Chollet et al. 2015. Keras. https://github.com/fchollet/keras.

Joana Costa, Catarina Silva, Mário Antunes, and Bernardete Ribeiro. 2014. Concept Drift Awareness in Twitter Streams. In *Proceedings of ICMLA*, pages 294–299, Detroit, MI.

Peter Sheridan Dodds, Kameron D. Harris, Isabel M. Kloumann, Catherine A. Bliss, and C. M. Danforth. 2011. Temporal Patterns of Happiness and Information in a Global Social Network: Hedonometrics and Twitter. Draft version. Available at http://arxiv.org/abs/1101.5120v3. Accessed October 24, 2011.

Paul Ekman. 1999. Basic emotions. In M Dalgleish, T; Power, editor, *Handbook of Cognition and Emotion*. John Wiley & Sons, Sussex, UK.

Sepp Hochreiter and Jürgen Schmidhuber. 1997. Long short-term memory. *Neural Comput.*, 9(8):1735–1780.

Geoff Hollis, Chris Westbury, and Lianne Lefsrud. 2017. Extrapolating human judgments from skip-gram vector representations of word meaning. *The Quarterly Journal of Experimental Psychology*, 70(8):1603–1619.

Minqing Hu and Bing Liu. 2004. Mining and summarizing customer reviews. In *Proceedings of the tenth ACM SIGKDD international conference on Knowledge discovery and data mining*, pages 168–177, New York, NY, USA. ACM.

Yoon Kim. 2014. Convolutional neural networks for sentence classification. In *Proceedings of the 2014 Conference on Empirical Methods in Natural Language Processing*, pages 1746–1751, Doha, Qatar.

Maximilian Köper and Sabine Schulte im Walde. 2016. Automatically Generated Affective Norms of Abstractness, Arousal, Imageability and Valence for 350000 German Lemmas. In *Proceedings of the 10th International Conference on Language Resources and Evaluation*, Portoro, Slovenia.

Maximilian Köper and Sabine Schulte im Walde. 2017. Improving Verb Metaphor Detection by Propagating Abstractness to Words, Phrases and Individual Senses. In *Proceedings of the 1st Workshop on Sense, Concept and Entity Representations and their Applications*, pages 24–30, Valencia, Spain.

Tomas Mikolov, Ilya Sutskever, Kai Chen, Greg S Corrado, and Jeff Dean. 2013. Distributed Representations of Words and Phrases and their Compositionality. In *Advances in Neural Information Processing Systems 26*, pages 3111–3119.

Saif Mohammad and Felipe Bravo-Marquez. 2017. WASSA-2017 Shared Task on Emotion Intensity. In *In Proceedings of the EMNLP 2017 Workshop on Computational Approaches to Subjectivity, Sentiment, and Social Media (WASSA)*, Copenhagen, Denmark.

Saif M. Mohammad and Svetlana Kiritchenko. 2015. Using Hashtags to Capture Fine Emotion Categories from Tweets. *Computational Intelligence*, 31(2):301–326.

Saif M. Mohammad and Peter D. Turney. 2013. Crowdsourcing a Word-Emotion Association Lexicon. 29(3):436–465.

Finn Årup Nielsen. 2011. A new ANEW: Evaluation of a Word List for Sentiment Analysis in Microblogs. In *Proceedings of the ESWC2011 Workshop on 'Making Sense of Microposts': Big things come in small packages, Heraklion, Crete, Greece, May 30, 2011*, pages 93–98.

Olutobi Owoputi, Chris Dyer, Kevin Gimpel, Nathan Schneider, and Noah A. Smith. 2013. Improved Part-of-Speech Tagging for Online Conversational Text with Word Clusters. In *In Proceedings of NAACL*, pages 380–390, Atlanta,GA, USA.

Robert Plutchik. 2001. The nature of emotions. *American Scientist*, 89(July–August):344–350.

Gabriel Recchia and Max M Louwerse. 2015a. Reproducing affective norms with lexical co-occurrence statistics: Predicting valence, arousal, and dominance. *The Quarterly Journal of Experimental Psychology*, 68(8):1584–1598.

Gabriel Recchia and Max M. Louwerse. 2015b. Reproducing Affective Norms with Lexical Co-occurrence Statistics: Predicting Valence, Arousal, and Dominance. *The Quarterly Journal of Experimental Psychology*, 68(8):1584–1598.

Joao Sedoc, Daniel Preotiuc-Pietro, and Lyle Ungar. 2017. Predicting Emotional Word Ratings using Distributional Representations and Signed Clustering. In *Proceedings of the 15th Conference of the European Chapter of the Association for Computational Linguistics*, EACL, Valencia, Spain.

Jared Suttles and Nancy Ide. 2013. Distant Supervision for Emotion Classification with Discrete Binary Values. In *Proceedings of CiCLing*, volume 7817 of *Lecture Notes in Computer Science*, pages 121–136. Springer.

Xiaodan Zhu Svetlana Kiritchenko and Saif M. Mohammad. Sentiment Analysis of Short Informal Texts. 50:723–762.

Yulia Tsvetkov, Leonid Boytsov, Anatole Gershman, Eric Nyberg, and Chris Dyer. 2014. Metaphor Detection with Cross-Lingual Model Transfer. In *Proceedings of the 52nd Annual Meeting of the Association for Computational Linguistics*, pages 248–258.

Peter Turney, Yair Neuman, Dan Assaf, and Yohai Cohen. 2011. Literal and Metaphorical Sense Identification through Concrete and Abstract Context. In *Proceedings of the Conference on Empirical Methods in Natural Language Processing*, pages 680–690, Edinburgh, UK.

Peter D Turney and Michael L Littman. 2003. Measuring Praise and Criticism: Inference of Semantic Orientation from Association. *ACM Transactions on Information Systems (TOIS)*, 21(4):315–346.

Hendrik Vankrunkelsven, Steven Verheyen, Simon De Deyne, and Gerrit Storms. 2015. Predicting Lexical Norms Using a Word Association Corpus. In *Proceedings of the 37th Annual Meeting of the Cognitive Science Society*, Pasadena, California, USA.

Wenbo Wang, Lu Chen, Krishnaprasad Thirunarayan, and Amit P. Sheth. 2012. Harnessing Twitter "Big Data" for Automatic Emotion Identification. In *Proceedings of SocialCom/PASSAT*, pages 587–592, Amsterdam, Netherlands.

Amy Beth Warriner, Victor Kuperman, and Marc Brysbaert. 2013. Norms of Valence, Arousal, and Dominance for 13,915 English Lemmas. *Behavior Research Methods*, 45(4):1191–1207.

Theresa Wilson, Janyce Wiebe, and Paul Hoffmann. 2005. Recognizing Contextual Polarity in Phrase-Level Sentiment Analysis. In *HLT/EMNLP 2005, Human Language Technology Conference and Conference on Empirical Methods in Natural Language Processing, Proceedings of the Conference, 6-8 October 2005, Vancouver, British Columbia, Canada*, pages 347–354.

Ian H. Witten, Eibe Frank, Len Trigg, Mark Hall, Geoffrey Holmes, and Sally Jo Cunningham. 1999. Weka: Practical Machine Learning Tools and Techniques with Java Implementations.

Prayas at EmoInt 2017: An Ensemble of Deep Neural Architectures for Emotion Intensity Prediction in Tweets

Pranav Goel*, Devang Kulshreshtha*, Prayas Jain and K.K. Shukla

Indian Institute of Technology (Banaras Hindu University) Varanasi, India
{pranav.goel.cse14, devang.kulshreshtha.cse14, prayas.jain.cse14, kkshkla.cse}@iitbu.ac.in
publication@emnlp2017.net

Abstract

The paper describes the best performing system for EmoInt - a shared task to predict the intensity of emotions in tweets. Intensity is a real valued score, between 0 and 1. The emotions are classified as - anger, fear, joy and sadness. We apply three different deep neural network based models, which approach the problem from essentially different directions. Our final performance quantified by an average pearson correlation score of 74.7 and an average spearman correlation score of 73.5 is obtained using an ensemble of the three models. We outperform the baseline model of the shared task by 9.9% and 9.4% pearson and spearman correlation scores respectively.

1 Introduction

EmoInt (Mohammad and Bravo-Marquez, 2017) is a shared task hosted by WASSA 2017, aiming to predict the emotion intensity in tweets. The emotion can be one out of anger, joy, fear and sadness. For each tweet, the emotion is known, and the task is to *predict the intensity of the corresponding emotion*, where intensity is a real valued score ranging from 0 to 1. This is different from most of the other tasks or systems in the domain of emotion detection/sentiment analysis which tend to focus on classifying the tweets or text into different categories.

For example, given the tweet - 'I hate my lawn mower. If it had a soul, I'd condemn it to the fiery pits of Hell.' and the corresponding emotion - 'anger', the system has to predict a value for how intensely this emotion is felt by the author of the tweet which is as close as possible to the gold label intensity (0.833 in this case).

The systems built for this task are useful across various NLP applications, but perhaps most obviously in complementing sentiment analysis systems. For example, the degree of anger expressed in a grievance can be used to decide its priority of being addressed, and the intensity of joy can help decide which reviews to project when publicizing a product.

Our submitted system is an ensemble of three broad sets of approaches combined using a weighted average of the separate predictions (section 3). All the approaches rely on representing the input tweet as a word vector using the word2vec approach (Mikolov et al., 2013), and using neural network based architectures to finally give the intensity score for the tweet of the given emotion X (please note that we already know the emotion of the tweet in this task).

The shared task organizers provided the training and a small development dataset for building our systems, and then a period of about 2 weeks was given for submitting our predictions on a blind test set.[1]

The rest of the paper is structured as follows. Section 2 discusses in brief the dataset for the task. Section 3 explains the various approaches used by our ensemble model, the kind of experiments we carried out along with the details of the parameters which gave optimal results on cross validation, and the way we combined the predictions. Section 4 explains how the system is evaluated and Section 5 states the results we achieved and discusses the various implications of those results. We conclude our work in Section 6.

---

* these authors have equal contributions to the paper

[1]http://saifmohammad.com/WebPages/EmotionIntensity-SharedTask.html

Proceedings of the 8th Workshop on Computational Approaches to Subjectivity, Sentiment and Social Media Analysis, pages 58–65
Copenhagen, Denmark, September 7–11, 2017. ©2017 Association for Computational Linguistics

2   Data

We used the dataset provided within the shared task for training our system. No other external datasets were used in training. The data files include the tweet id, the tweet, the emotion of the tweet and the emotion intensity (for training and dev sets). Test set's gold labels were given only after the evaluation period.

There are around 800-1100 tweets in the training set, 70-110 in the development set, and around 700-1000 in the test set (across all the emotions). The complete details of the dataset can be found in (Mohammad and Bravo-Marquez, 2017).

3   Proposed System

Our system is an ensemble of three sets of approaches. We describe the individual approaches, followed by the ensemble process. We mention the parameters for the optimal variants of each approach and the architecture based decisions or parameters that were varied to provide an insight into the scope of our experiments. The parameters were chosen so that they maximize the Pearson-correlation between the predicted and actual scores on the K-fold cross-validation. The evaluation method used to select the optimal variants is explained in section 4.

A bird's eye view of the various architectures is shown in Figure 1.

3.1   Approach 1: Feed-forward neural network

Feed forward neural networks have proven to be highly successful in classification and real value prediction based tasks across a variety of domains, including NLP applications ((Bengio et al., 2003), (Collobert et al., 2011)). (Deep) Neural networks have given state-of-the-art results in sentiment analysis (Tang et al., 2014) which is closely related to our task. Here we detail the architecture of our network -

Input features: Each tweet is represented as a 443 dimensional vector by concatenating two different feature vectors obtained as follows -

1. Word2Vec (Mikolov et al., 2013) representation of the tweet using publicly available embeddings (Godin et al., 2015) which were trained on 400 million tweets for the ACL W-NUT 2015 shared task (Baldwin et al., 2015). We chose it over other available pre-trained

tweet based embeddings as it is trained on a large dataset and we also prefer its high dimensionality of 400. The vector for each word is *averaged* to get a 400 dimensional representation of the tweet.

2. TweetToLexiconFeatureVector is a filter in the AffectiveTweets[2] (Mohammad and Bravo-Marquez, 2017) package for converting tweets into numeric 43-dimensional vectors that can be used directly as features in our machine learning system. The filter calculates the features from the tweet using several lexicons:

   (a) MPQA Subjectivity Lexicon: Calculates the number of positive and negative words from the lexicon (Wilson et al., 2005)

   (b) Bing-Lui: Calculates the number of positive and negative words from the lexicon (Bauman et al., 2017)

   (c) AFINN: Wordlist-based approach for calculating positive and negative sentiment scores from the lexicon(Nielsen, 2011)

   (d) Sentiment140: Calculates positive and negative sentiment score provided by the lexicon in which tweets are annotated by lexicons (Mohammad and Turney, 2013)

   (e) NRC Hashtag Sentiment lexicon: Uses same lexicon as Sentiment 140 but here tweets with only emotional hashtags are considered during training.

   (f) NRC-10 Expanded: Emotional associations of words matching the Twitter specific expansion of the lexicon(Bravo-Marquez et al., 2016) are added to give the vale of this feature.

   (g) NRC Hashtag Emotion Association Lexicon: Emotional associations of words of the lexicon(Mohammad and Kiritchenko, 2015) are added to give the vale of this feature.

   (h) SentiWordNet: Calculates positive and negative sentiment score using SentiWordNet(Baccianella et al., 2010)

   (i) Emoticons: Calculates sentiment scores using word associations provided by

---

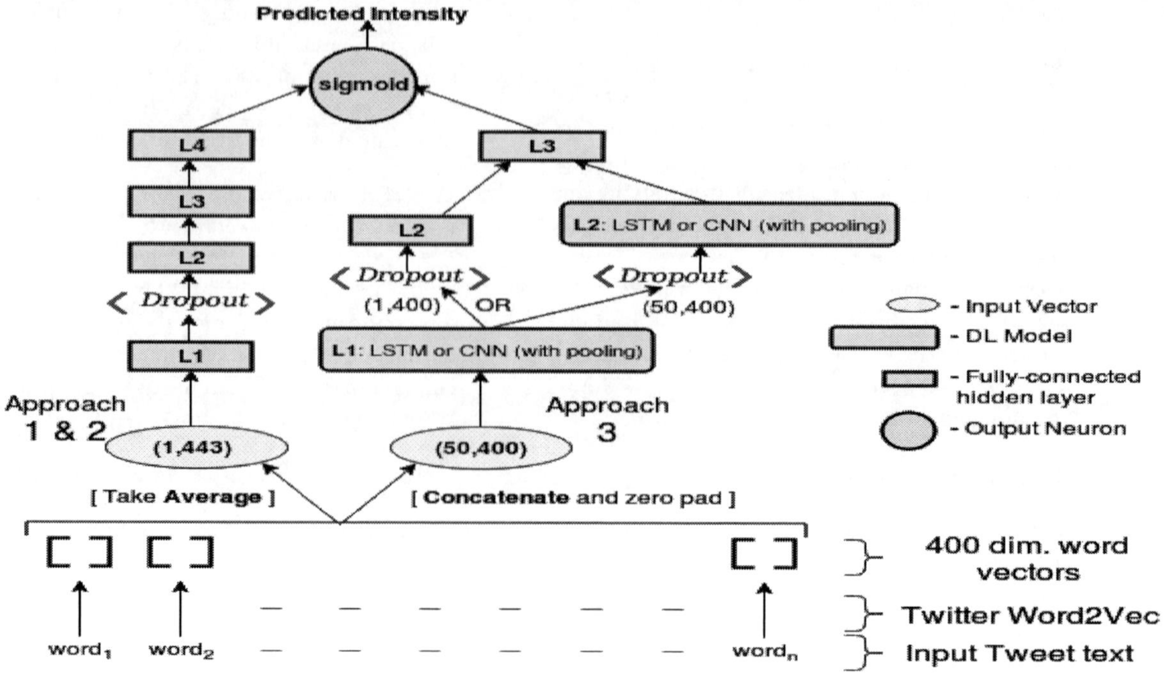

Figure 1: The architecture of our various approaches

emoticons from the lexicon(Nielsen, 2011)

(j) Negations: This feature simply count the number of negating words in the tweet.

Network Architecture: The input layer passes the 443 dimensional vector into 4 subsequent hidden layers ($L1, L2, L3, L4$) (the left half of Figure 1). We use Rectified Linear Unit ('relu') (Maas et al., 2013) as an activation function for each of the hidden layers (chosen as per the cross validation performance described in section 4). $L1$ is followed by *dropout* (Srivastava et al., 2014) to avoid over-fitting and co-adaption of features. The number of hidden units in $L1 - L4$ and value of dropout (p) was varied, and the optimal settings were decided as per the cross validation performance for each emotion separately. The chosen values are mentioned in Table 1. $L4$ is followed by a single sigmoid neuron which predicts the intensity of the emotion between 0 to 1.

Training: The network parameters are learned by directly minimizing the negative of the Pearson-correlation (as it is a differentiable function) between actual and predicted intensities. We optimize the above function by back-propagating through layers via Mini-batch Gradient Descent.

Parameter/ Emotion	L1	p	L2	L3	L4
Anger	300	0.5	125	50	25
Fear	300	0.5	150	50	25
Joy	300	0.5	100	50	25
Sadness	300	0.5	125	50	25

Table 1: Network parameters for Approach 1

We use a batch size of 8, 30 training epochs and Adam optimization algorithm (Kingma and Ba, 2014) with the parameters set as $\alpha = 0.001, \beta_1 = 0.9, \beta_2 = 0.999$ and $\epsilon = 10^{-9}$.

3.2 Approach 2: Multitask Deep Learning

Multitask learning using deep neural network via shared layers has become quite popular and successful as exploited in, for example (Collobert and Weston, 2008), and has been the focus of many cross lingual models like (Huang et al., 2013). (Collobert and Weston, 2008) described a single unified architecture for performing a variety of NLP tasks: named entity recognition, semantic similarity, part-of-speech tagging, etc. In this approach, we attempt to use the idea of multitask learning to explore the notion of generalized or shared learning across the different emotions.

Parameter/ Emotion	L1 (shared)	p	L2 (shared)	L3	L4
Anger(a)	300	0.3	150	50	20
Fear(b)	300	0.3	150	75	25
Joy(c)	300	0.3	150	50	15
Sadness(d)	300	0.3	150	50	20

Table 2: Network parameters for Approach 2

Input features: The input features are same as Approach 1 and same for all the 4 subtasks. We treat the 4 emotions as different subtasks to apply deep multi-task learning.

Network Architecture: The overall architecture can still be realized using the left side of figure 1. The network's initial layers are shared across multiple emotions with an objective to increase the generalization whereas the individual top layers can be seen as learning emotion specific features. Specifically, the system consists of two hidden layers ($L1$ & $L2$) shared between 4 regressors, while the last two layers ($L3$ & $L4$) are allowed to be different across the different subtasks (L3a, L3b, L3c, L3d and the same for L4). The model can be thought of as an input vector for the tweet going into the exact same two hidden layers regardless of the subtask, but then going into different layers (at the 3rd and 4th level) with the output from L4 going into their respective output neurons. The parameters (number of neurons in the shared as well as the non shared layers along with the dropout rate p) for each emotion are given in Table 2. Note that these parameters are optimized using cross validation (section 4).

Training: We use the same settings as in Approach 1 with respect to the cost function, optimization algorithm, update rule, learning rate, epochs, etc.
We train the network for 4 cycles at every epoch. During the 1st cycle, we train the model for anger, where the input will pass through L1, L2, L3a, L4a and finally the corresponding output neuron. The network is similarly trained for fear, joy and sadness during the 2nd, 3rd and 4th cycles respectively. Learning parameters this way ensures additional training examples for the initial layers (L1, L2) so that they may generalize well to learn task-independent representations while the higher layers (L3, L4) put pressure on the parameters to

learn more task-specific representations.

3.3 Approach 3: Sequence Modeling using CNNs and LSTMs

Using Recurrent Neural Networks (RNN) has become a very common technique for various NLP based tasks like language modeling (Mikolov et al., 2010). Their time step based sequentially connected structure is intuitive to use for sequential data such as sentences. Long-short term memory (LSTM) (Hochreiter and Schmidhuber, 1997) architecture is an advanced version of RNN that uses various gates to control the vanishing gradient problem (among other obstacles) that arise during the training of RNNs, and has found resounding success in a host of applications ((Graves and Jaitly, 2014), (Graves and Schmidhuber, 2005)). Convolutional Neural Network (CNN) is also a popular neural network based architecture, and has been successful in the NLP domain in various tasks ((Lee and Dernoncourt, 2016), (Kim, 2014)). Combining these architectures has also been found to be quite successful as in (Zhou et al., 2015) Both these architecture expect a sequence of vectors as input to operate on.
We describe how we use these deep learning models, which play a dominant role in our final ensemble system -

Input features: We again use the word2vec embeddings trained on twitter tweets ((Godin et al., 2015)) to represent the words in a tweet as 400 dimensional vectors, ignoring the words not found. These embeddings are ideal for representing tweets as they have been trained on a very large amount of tweets. Instead of averaging the word vectors as in our first two approaches, we *concatenate* them. Since length of different tweets can vary, we fix the length of each concatenated representation as 50 (since the maximum tweet length across the training and development data is 46 according to our analysis and we do not want to miss out on any information in the already short tweet) by performing zero padding. For datasets where a tweet may have length greater than 50, the number has to be tuned accordingly. Padding of zero vectors is done to make the representation of every tweet as a (50,400) vector. These representations are then fed to a host of architectures, whose general representation is given in the figure 1.

Parameter/ Emotion	L1	p	L2	L3
Anger (1)	CNN (250,Max)	0	125	50
Anger (2)	CNN (256,Avg)	0	100	-
Anger (3)	LSTM (300)	0	CNN (200,Avg)	100
Fear (1)	LSTM (256)	.2	CNN (150,Avg)	100
Fear (2)	CNN (250,Max)	0	125	50
Fear (3)	LSTM (250)	.2	CNN (120,Avg)	50
Joy (1)	CNN (256,Max)	0	100	-
Joy (2)	LSTM (300)	0	CNN (200,Avg)	100
Joy (3)	LSTM (300)	.2	CNN (200,Avg)	100
Sadness(1)	CNN (250,Max,)	0	125	50
Sadness(2)	CNN (250,Max)	.2	125	50
Sadness(3)	CNN (256,Max)	0	100	-

Table 3: Network Parameters for the 3 best models built according to Approach 3 (Ranked as per the cross validation scores ; The numbers in the Layer (L) columns represent the output dimensionality of that layer ; Max and Avg refer to the type of pooling)

Network Architecture: As shown in figure 1, the concatenated vector representation of the tweet is first fed to a **LSTM** or **CNN** and then some fully connected (dense) hidden layers. The representation learned in the last hidden layer is fed to a single sigmoid neuron which gives us the intensity of the emotion (as in the previous 2 approaches). We tried many variations of the different parameters involved in constructing this model (keeping all others fixed while one is varied) to come up with several architectures but show the parameters for only the three top performing ones (as per cross validation) for each emotion in Table 3. The variations we tried include -
i) using only LSTM/CNN plus fully connected layers, and also the combination of these architectures with the initial LSTM's output for each word

fed to a CNN, or vice versa.
ii) Using Simple RNN, Bidirectional LSTM ((Schuster and Paliwal, 1997), (Godin et al., 2015)), Gated Recurrent Units (GRU) (Cho et al., 2014) instead of LSTM.
iii) Using (global) max pooling versus (global) average pooling for CNNs.
iv) Using dropout (Srivastava et al., 2014). Note that a dropout layer was added after pooling layer for a CNN, while the same dropout rate was set for both matrices involved in the standard definition in case of LSTM (Zaremba et al., 2014).
v) Using different number of neurons for CNN/LSTM/fully connected hidden layers. (usually starting from 300 or 256, and halving the number of neurons as we went deeper)
vi) Using different number of fully connected hidden layers (0,1 or 2 in between the LSTM/CNN layer and sigmoid neuron).

In every case, 'relu' activation function was used in the hidden dense layers (except the last neuron which uses sigmoid). Dropout, if applied was always set to 0.2 (we also experimented with 0.1,0.3,0.4 and 0.5 as the dropout rate). Also, the filter height used for CNNs was always set to 3, and striding length for convolution was always 1.

Training: The network parameters are learned by minimizing the Mean Absolute Error between the actual and predicted values of emotion intensity. We optimize this loss function by back-propagating through layers via Mini-batch Gradient descent, with batch size of 8, 15 training epochs and Adam optimization algorithm (Kingma and Ba, 2014) with the same parameters as mentioned in Approach 1.

The deep learning based models in all the above approaches were implemented in Python using Keras library (Chollet et al., 2015).

3.4 Bringing it all together: The submitted ensemble system

As described above, we now have 5 models to combine - 1 each out of Approach 1 and 2, and 3 from Approach 3. We take a weighted average of the predictions from each of the system to form our final submission. The weights are informed from the results from cross validation (the CV score as explained in section 4), and are as follows - 1 for Approach 1, 3 for Approach 2, 3 each for the two best systems from approach 3 (which

Approach	Average		Anger		Fear		Joy		Sadness	
	CV	Test	CV	Test	CV	Test	CV	Test	CV	Test
Feed Forward NN	69.75	69.58	66.22	67.88	72.71	72.42	72.08	68.26	67.99	69.77
Multitask DL	66.30	66.20	63.73	64.49	68.07	67.74	66.80	65.37	66.65	67.22
CNN+LSTM Seq. Modeling	70.70	71.79	69.22	70.15	72.08	72.95	73.22	69.14	68.29	74.93
CNN+LSTM Seq. Modeling	70.25	72.15	69.08	69.86	70.95	73.27	72.93	69.86	68.04	75.6
CNN+LSTM Seq. Modeling	70.03	71.81	68.90	69.71	70.67	72.92	72.81	69.57	67.74	75.06
Ensemble Model	**75.26**	**74.70**	**72.94**	**73.2**	**76.78**	**76.20**	**74.42**	**73.20**	**76.90**	**76.50**
Baseline	61.10	64.8	60.50	63.9	57.40	65.2	70.30	65.4	56.20	64.8

Table 4: Results

are very close in performance as can be seen in Table 4), and 2 for the 3rd best system in approach 3. Our ensemble model improves the performance by at least 2% over any of our individual models (Table 4).

4 Evaluation

Cross Validation (CV): We combined the training and development sets, trained on 80% of this set while predicting on the remaining 20%, and repeated this seven times (for each emotion separately). The average of these was used as the CV score to evaluate our models. The metric used for evaluating performance was Pearson Correlation.

Test: The optimal setting for each model was decided using the CV score (Table 4). Then these chosen models (as described in Table 1,2 and 3) were used to generate predicted intensities on the test set, by training on the *full training and development sets combined*. Again an average of seven runs was taken. The predictions for the final ensemble model are generated using a weighted average of the individual predictions as described in section 3.4.

5 Results and Discussion

We compare the results achieved by our individual approaches, the submitted ensemble system and the WEKA Baseline system which is the official baseline model for this task (Mohammad and Bravo-Marquez, 2017) in Table 4. For brevity, we only show the Pearson Correlation scores on the test set (although the Spearman correlation scores show similar trends). We discuss the major takeaways from these results -

1. Our submitted ensemble model achieves an average (or overall) score of 75.26% and 74.70%, which beats the baseline model by about 14% and 10% on cross validation and test sets respectively. The improvement points to the potential of deep learning based models over the simpler lexicon based approaches. These are also the best scores among all participating systems in the shared task (according to the public leaderboard [3]).

2. The ensemble model achieves about 3-5% improvement over the average scores, and offers significant improvement in performance across all the emotions, which indicates that the approaches do complement each other quite well.

3. Approach 2 (Multitask DL) achieves the lowest scores among the three sets of approaches. Among Approach 1 (Feed Forward NN) and Approach 3 (CNN+LSTM Seq. Modeling), approach 3 has a best test score of 72.15 compared to approach 1's 69.58, which is a significant improvement and points to sequential models like LSTMs and CNNs being a better choice over feed forward neural networks.

---

[3]https://competitions.codalab.org/competitions/16380#results

4. Among the individual emotions, our ensemble model gives the best performance for 'Sadness', followed very closely by 'Fear', then 'Joy' and finally 'Anger'.

6 Conclusion and Future Work

In this paper, we propose a deep learning framework to predict the intensity of the emotion in tweets exhibiting that emotion. The proposed approach is based on an ensemble of Feed-Forward Neural Networks, Multi-Task Deep Learning and Sequence Modeling using CNNs and LSTMs, allowing us to explore the different directions a neural network based methodology can take. Each individual approach is described in detail with a view of making our experiments replicable. The optimal parameters are mentioned, along with our method of bringing the approaches together. Our submitted system beats the baseline system by about 10% on the test set.

Although our model achieves state-of-the-art results, there is definite room for improvement. In the future, we would like to experiment with hand-crafted features in addition to word-vectors and lexicon features. We would also experiment with other filters provided in AffectiveTweets package (Mohammad and Bravo-Marquez, 2017) such as TweetToSentiStrengthFeatureVector, TweetNLP-Tokenizer etc. Another very interesting idea would be to try better ways of 'ensembling' the different models and analyze how each system or approach complements the other.

References

Stefano Baccianella, Andrea Esuli, and Fabrizio Sebastiani. 2010. Sentiwordnet 3.0: An enhanced lexical resource for sentiment analysis and opinion mining. In *LREC*. volume 10, pages 2200–2204.

Timothy Baldwin, Marie Catherine De Marneffe, Bo Han, Young-Bum Kim, Alan Ritter, and Wei Xu. 2015. Shared tasks of the 2015 workshop on noisy user-generated text: Twitter lexical normalization and named entity recognition. In *Proceedings of the Workshop on Noisy User-generated Text (WNUT 2015), Beijing, China*.

Konstantin Bauman, Bing Liu, and Alexander Tuzhilin. 2017. Aspect based recommendations: Recommending items with the most valuable aspects based on user reviews .

Yoshua Bengio, Réjean Ducharme, Pascal Vincent, and Christian Jauvin. 2003. A neural probabilistic language model. *Journal of machine learning research* 3(Feb):1137–1155.

Felipe Bravo-Marquez, Eibe Frank, Saif M Mohammad, and Bernhard Pfahringer. 2016. Determining word-emotion associations from tweets by multilabel classification. In *Web Intelligence (WI), 2016 IEEE/WIC/ACM International Conference on*. IEEE, pages 536–539.

Kyunghyun Cho, Bart Van Merriënboer, Dzmitry Bahdanau, and Yoshua Bengio. 2014. On the properties of neural machine translation: Encoder-decoder approaches. *arXiv preprint arXiv:1409.1259* .

François Chollet et al. 2015. Keras. https://github.com/fchollet/keras.

Ronan Collobert and Jason Weston. 2008. A unified architecture for natural language processing: Deep neural networks with multitask learning. In *Proceedings of the 25th international conference on Machine learning*. ACM, pages 160–167.

Ronan Collobert, Jason Weston, Léon Bottou, Michael Karlen, Koray Kavukcuoglu, and Pavel Kuksa. 2011. Natural language processing (almost) from scratch. *Journal of Machine Learning Research* 12(Aug):2493–2537.

Fréderic Godin, Baptist Vandersmissen, Wesley De Neve, and Rik Van de Walle. 2015. Multimedia lab@ acl w-nut ner shared task: named entity recognition for twitter microposts using distributed word representations. *ACL-IJCNLP* 2015:146–153.

Alex Graves and Navdeep Jaitly. 2014. Towards end-to-end speech recognition with recurrent neural networks. In *ICML*. volume 14, pages 1764–1772.

Alex Graves and Jürgen Schmidhuber. 2005. Framewise phoneme classification with bidirectional lstm and other neural network architectures. *Neural Networks* 18(5):602–610.

Sepp Hochreiter and Jürgen Schmidhuber. 1997. Long short-term memory. *Neural computation* 9(8):1735–1780.

Jui-Ting Huang, Jinyu Li, Dong Yu, Li Deng, and Yifan Gong. 2013. Cross-language knowledge transfer using multilingual deep neural network with shared hidden layers. In *Acoustics, Speech and Signal Processing (ICASSP), 2013 IEEE International Conference on*. IEEE, pages 7304–7308.

Yoon Kim. 2014. Convolutional neural networks for sentence classification. *arXiv preprint arXiv:1408.5882* .

Diederik Kingma and Jimmy Ba. 2014. Adam: A method for stochastic optimization. *arXiv preprint arXiv:1412.6980* .

Ji Young Lee and Franck Dernoncourt. 2016. Sequential short-text classification with recurrent and convolutional neural networks. *arXiv preprint arXiv:1603.03827* .

Andrew L Maas, Awni Y Hannun, and Andrew Y Ng. 2013. Rectifier nonlinearities improve neural network acoustic models. In *Proc. ICML*. volume 30.

Tomas Mikolov, Kai Chen, Greg Corrado, and Jeffrey Dean. 2013. Efficient estimation of word representations in vector space. *arXiv preprint arXiv:1301.3781* .

Tomas Mikolov, Martin Karafiát, Lukas Burget, Jan Cernockỳ, and Sanjeev Khudanpur. 2010. Recurrent neural network based language model. In *Interspeech*. volume 2, page 3.

Saif M. Mohammad and Felipe Bravo-Marquez. 2017. WASSA-2017 shared task on emotion intensity. In *Proceedings of the Workshop on Computational Approaches to Subjectivity, Sentiment and Social Media Analysis (WASSA)*. Copenhagen, Denmark.

Saif M Mohammad and Svetlana Kiritchenko. 2015. Using hashtags to capture fine emotion categories from tweets. *Computational Intelligence* 31(2):301–326.

Saif M. Mohammad and Peter D. Turney. 2013. Crowdsourcing a word-emotion association lexicon 29(3):436–465.

Finn Årup Nielsen. 2011. A new anew: Evaluation of a word list for sentiment analysis in microblogs. *arXiv preprint arXiv:1103.2903* .

Mike Schuster and Kuldip K Paliwal. 1997. Bidirectional recurrent neural networks. *IEEE Transactions on Signal Processing* 45(11):2673–2681.

Nitish Srivastava, Geoffrey Hinton, Alex Krizhevsky, Ilya Sutskever, and Ruslan Salakhutdinov. 2014. Dropout: A simple way to prevent neural networks from overfitting. *The Journal of Machine Learning Research* 15(1):1929–1958.

Duyu Tang, Furu Wei, Bing Qin, Ting Liu, and Ming Zhou. 2014. Coooolll: A deep learning system for twitter sentiment classification. In *Proceedings of the 8th International Workshop on Semantic Evaluation (SemEval 2014)*. pages 208–212.

Theresa Wilson, Janyce Wiebe, and Paul Hoffmann. 2005. Recognizing contextual polarity in phrase-level sentiment analysis. In *Proceedings of the conference on human language technology and empirical methods in natural language processing*. Association for Computational Linguistics, pages 347–354.

Wojciech Zaremba, Ilya Sutskever, and Oriol Vinyals. 2014. Recurrent neural network regularization. *arXiv preprint arXiv:1409.2329* .

Chunting Zhou, Chonglin Sun, Zhiyuan Liu, and Francis Lau. 2015. A c-lstm neural network for text classification. *arXiv preprint arXiv:1511.08630* .

Latest News in Computational Argumentation: Surfing on the Deep Learning Wave, Scuba Diving in the Abyss of Fundamental Questions

Iryna Gurevych

gurevych@ukp.informatik.tu-darmstadt.de

1 Abstract of talk

Mining arguments from natural language texts, parsing argumentative structures, and assessing argument quality are among the recent challenges tackled in computational argumentation. While advanced deep learning models provide state-of-the-art performance in many of these tasks, much attention is also paid to the underlying fundamental questions. How are arguments expressed in natural language across genres and domains? What is the essence of an argument's claim? Can we reliably annotate convincingness of an argument? How can we approach logic and common-sense reasoning in argumentation? This talk highlights some recent advances in computational argumentation and shows why researchers must be both "surfers" and "scuba divers".

Proceedings of the 8th Workshop on Computational Approaches to Subjectivity, Sentiment and Social Media Analysis, page 66
Copenhagen, Denmark, September 7–11, 2017. ©2017 Association for Computational Linguistics

Towards Syntactic Iberian Polarity Classification [*]

David Vilares[♠†], **Marcos Garcia**[♠‡], **Miguel A. Alonso**[♠†], **Carlos Gómez-Rodríguez**[♣♠†]

Universidade da Coruña
♣FASTPARSE Lab, ♠LyS Group
† Departamento de Computación, Campus de Elviña
‡Departamento de Letras, Campus da Zapateira
15701, A Coruña, Spain
`david.vilares@udc.es,marcos.garcia.gonzalez@udc.es`
`miguel.alonso@udc.es,carlos.gomez@udc.es`

Abstract

Lexicon-based methods using syntactic rules for polarity classification rely on parsers that are dependent on the language and on treebank guidelines. Thus, rules are also dependent and require adaptation, especially in multilingual scenarios. We tackle this challenge in the context of the Iberian Peninsula, releasing the first symbolic syntax-based Iberian system with rules shared across five official languages: Basque, Catalan, Galician, Portuguese and Spanish. The model is made available.[1]

1 Introduction

Finding the scope of linguistic phenomena in natural language processing (NLP) is a core utility of parsing. In sentiment analysis (SA), it is used to address structures that play a role in polarity classification, both in supervised (Socher et al., 2013) and symbolic (Vilares et al.) models. In the latter case, these are mostly monolingual and dependent on the annotation of the training treebank, and so the rules are annotation-dependent too. Advances in NLP make it now possible to overcome such issues. We present a model that analyzes five official languages in the Iberian Peninsula: Basque (*eu*), Catalan (*ca*), Galician (*gl*), Portuguese (*pt*) and Spanish (*es*). We rely on three premises:

1. Syntactic structures can be defined in a universal way (Nivre et al., 2015).

2. Training a single model for multilingual parsing is feasible (Ammar et al., 2016).

3. We can define universal rules for various phenomena, if 1 is assured (Vilares et al., 2017).

Based on those, we: (a) combine existing subjectivity lexica, (b) train an *Iberian* tagger and parser, and (c) define a set of Iberian syntax-based rules. The main contributions of the paper are:

1. A single set of syntactic rules to handle linguistic phenomena across five Iberian languages from different families.

2. The first end-to-end multilingual syntax-based SA system that analyzes five official languages of the Iberian Peninsula. This is also the first evaluation for SA that provides results for some of them.

2 Related work

Polarity classification has been addressed through machine learning (Mohammad et al., 2013; Socher et al., 2013; Vo and Zhang, 2016), and lexicon-based models (Turney, 2002). Most of the research involves English texts, although studies can be found for other languages such as Chinese (Chen and Chen, 2016) or Arabic (Shoukry and Rafea, 2012).

For the official languages in the Iberian Peninsula, much of the literature has focused on Spanish. Brooke et al. (2009) proposed a lexicon-based SA system that defines rules at the lexical level to handle negation, intensification or adversative subordinate clauses. They followed a cross-lingual approach, adapting their English method (Taboada et al., 2011) to obtain the semantic orientation (SO) of Spanish texts. Vilares et al. created a syntactic rule-based system, by making an interpretation of Brooke et al.'s system, but limited to AnCora trees (Taulé et al., 2008). Martínez-Cámara et al. (2011) were one of the first to report a wide set of experiments on a number of

---

[*] DV was funded by MECD (FPU13/01180). MG is funded by a *Juan de la Cierva* grant (FJCI-2014-22853). CGR has received funding from the ERC, under the European Union's Horizon 2020 research and innovation programme (FASTPARSE, grant agreement No 714150). This research was supported by MINECO (FFI2014-51978-C2).

[1] The resources used in this work have been integrated as a part of `https://github.com/aghie/uuusa`

Proceedings of the 8th Workshop on Computational Approaches to Subjectivity, Sentiment and Social Media Analysis, pages 67–73
Copenhagen, Denmark, September 7–11, 2017. ©2017 Association for Computational Linguistics

bag-of-words supervised classifiers. The TASS workshop on sentiment analysis focused on Spanish language (Villena-Román et al., 2013) annually proposes different challenges related to polarity classification, and a number of approaches have used its framework to build their Spanish systems, most of them based on supervised learning (Saralegi and San Vicente, 2013; Gamallo et al., 2013; Hurtado et al., 2015; Vilares et al., 2015).

Sentiment analysis for Portuguese has also attracted the interest of the research community. Silva et al. (2009) presented a system for detection of opinions about Portuguese politicians. Souza et al. (2011) built a lexicon for Brazilian Portuguese exploring different techniques (e.g. translation and thesaurus-based approaches) and available resources. Souza and Vieira (2012) carried out a study of Twitter data, exploring preprocessing techniques, subjectivity data and negation approaches. They concluded that those have a small impact on the polarity classification of tweets. Balage Filho et al. (2013) evaluate the quality of the Brazilian LIWC dictionary (Pennebaker et al., 2001) for SA, comparing it with existing lexica for this language.

For Basque, Catalan and Galician, literature is scarce. Cruz et al. (2014) introduce a method to create multiple layered lexicons for different languages including co-official languages in Spain. San Vicente and Saralegi (2016) explore different ways to create lexicons, and apply them to the Basque case. They report an evaluation on a Basque dataset intended for polarity classification. Bosco et al. (2016) discuss the collection of data for the Catalan Elections and design an annotation scheme to apply SA techniques, but the dataset is still not available. With respect to Galician, in this article we will present the first published results for this language.

3 SISA: Syntactic Iberian SA

3.1 Preliminaries

Vilares et al. (2017) propose a formalism to define *compositional operations*. Given a dependency tree for a text, a compositional operation defines how a node in the tree modifies the semantic orientation (SO) of a branch or node, based on elements such as the word form, part-of-speech (PoS) tag or dependency type, without limitations in terms of its location inside such tree. They released an implementation, where an ar-

Tag	es	pt	ca	eu	gl
ADJ	2,045	1,865	1,686	1,757	2,002
NOUN	1,323	1,183	1,168	1,211	1,270
ADV	594	570	533	535	599
VERB	739	688	689	563	723

Table 1: Size of the SFU (single words) lexica.

bitrary number of practical compositional operations can be defined. The system queues and propagates them through the tree, until the moment they must be dequeued and applied to their target. The authors showed how the same set of operations, defined to work under the Universal Treebank (UT) guidelines (McDonald et al., 2013), can be shared across languages, but they do not explore how to create a single pipeline for analyzing many languages. This paper explores that path in the context of Iberian Peninsula, presenting an unified syntactic Iberian SA model (SISA).

We below present how to build SISA, from the bottom (subjectivity lexica, tagging and dependency parsing) to the top levels (application of compositional operations to compute the final SO).

3.2 Subjectivity Lexica

SISA needs multilingual polarity lexica in order to predict the sentiment of a text. We used two sets of monolingual lexica as our starting points:

1. *Spanish SFU lexicon* (Brooke et al., 2009): It contains SO's for subjective words that range from 1 to 5 for positive and negative terms. We translated it to *ca, eu, gl* and *pt* using *apertium* (Forcada et al., 2011). We removed the unknown words and obtained the numbers in Table 1.[2]

2. *ML-Senticon* (Cruz et al., 2014): Multi-layered lexica (not available for *pt*) with SO's where each layer contains a larger number of terms, but less trustable. We used the seventh layer for each language. As *eu, ca* and *gl* files have the same PoS-tag for adverbs and adjectives, they were automatically classified using monolingual tools (Agerri et al., 2014; Padró and Stanilovsky, 2012; Garcia and Gamallo, 2015) (Table 2 contains the statistics). SO's (originally from 0 to 1) were linearly transformed to the scale of the SFU lexicon.

The SFU and ML-Senticon lexica for each language were combined to obtain larger monolingual resources, and these were in turn combined

---

[2]We used the original *apertium* outputs, except for the *pt* and *gl* lexica (manually reviewed by a linguist).

Tag	es	ca	eu	gl
ADJ	2,558	1,619	22	1,530
NOUN	2,094	1,535	1,365	579
ADV	117	23	3	26
VERB	603	500	272	144

Table 2: Size of the resulting ML-Senticon lexica.

Tag	es	pt	ca	eu	gl	Iberian
ADJ	3,775	1,865	2,704	1,529	2,990	9,385
NOUN	3,079	1,183	2,377	2,392	1,684	8,733
ADV	665	570	545	485	612	1,891
VERB	1,177	688	1,034	728	801	2,998

Table 3: Size of the final lexica.

into a common Iberian lexicon (see Table 3). When merging lexica, we must consider that:

1. In monolingual mergings, the same word can have different SO's. E.g., the Catalan adjective 'abandonat' (*abandoned*) has -1.875 and -3 in ML-Senticon and SFU, respectively.

2. When combining lexica of different languages, the same word form might have different meanings (and SOs) in each language. Merging them in a multilingual resource could be problematic. For example, the adjective 'espantoso' has a value of -4.1075 in the combined *es* lexicon (*frightening*), and of -3.125 in the *gl* one (*frightening*), while the same word in the *pt* data (*astonishing*) has a positive value of 5. Note, however, that even if they could be considered very similar from a lexical or morphological perspective, many phonological false friends have different spellings in each language (such as the negative 'vessar' (*to spill*) in *ca* and the positive 'besar' (*to kiss*) in *es*), so these cases end up not being a frequent problem (only 0.36% of the words have both positive and negative polarity in the monolingual lexica).

These two problems were tackled by averaging the polarities of words with the same form. Thus, the first monolingual mergings produced a balanced SO (e.g., 'abandonat' has -2.4375 in the combined *ca* lexicon), while in the subsequent multilingual fusion, contradictory false friends have a final value close to *no polarity* (e.g., 'espantoso', with a SO of -0.7 in the Iberian lexicon). The impact of these mergings is analyzed in §4.

3.3 PoS-tagging and dependency parsing

For the compositional operations to be triggered, we first need to do the tagging and the dependency parse for a sentence. To do so, we trained an Iberian PoS-tagger and parser, i.e. single modules that can analyze Iberian languages without applying any language identification tool. Multilingual taggers and parsers can be trained following approaches based on (Vilares et al., 2016; Ammar et al., 2016). We are relying on the Universal Dependency (UD) guidelines (Nivre et al., 2015) to train these tools, since they provide corpora for all languages studied in this paper.

For the Iberian tagger we relied on Toutanova and Manning (2000), obtaining the following accuracies (%) in the monolingual UD test sets: *pt* (95.96), *es* (94.37), *ca* (97.41), *eu* (93.88) and *gl* (94.09). For the Iberian parser we used the approach by Vilares et al. (2016), whose performance (LAS/UAS)[3] on the same UD test sets was: *pt* (78.78/84.50), *es* (80.20/85.23), *cat* (84.01/88.08), *eu* (62.01/71.64)[4] and *gl* (75.65/82.11).

3.4 Compositional operations

For a detailed explanation of compositional operations, we encourage the reader to consult Vilares et al. (2017), but we here include an overview as part of SISA. Briefly, a compositional operation is tuple $o = (\tau, C, \delta, \pi, S)$ such that:

- $\tau : \mathbb{R} \to \mathbb{R}$ is a transformation function to apply on the semantic orientation of nodes, where τ can be $weighting_\beta(SO) = SO \times (1 + \beta)$ or $shift_\alpha(SO) = \begin{cases} SO - \alpha & \text{if } SO \geqq 0 \\ SO + \alpha & \text{if } SO < 0 \end{cases}$,

- $C : V \to \{true, false\}$ is a predicate that determines whether a node in the tree will trigger the operation, based on word forms, PoS-tags and dependency types,

- $\delta \in \mathbb{N}$ is a number of levels that we need to ascend in the tree to calculate the scope of o, i.e., the nodes of T whose SO is affected by the transformation function τ,

- π is a priority used to break ties when several operations coincide on a given node, and

- S is a scope function that will be used to determine the nodes affected by the operation.

---

[3]LAS/UAS: The percentage of arcs where both the head and dependency type / the head are correct.

[4]The parsing results for Basque (with a high proportion of non-projective trees) were worse than expected. However, the parser trained based on the method by Vilares et al. (2016) automatically selected a projective algorithm for training, as the average prevalence of non-projectivity across our five Iberian languages is low. We hypothesize that this is the main reason of the lower performance for this language.

We adapt the UT operations used by Vilares et al. (2017) to the UD style to handle, which are now described:

1. *Intensification*: It diminishes or amplifies the SO of a word or a phrase. It operates from adjectives or adverbs modifying the SO of the head structure they depend on: e.g., the SO of 'grande' (*big*, in *es*) increases from 1.87 to 2.34 if a word such as 'muy' (*very*) depends on it and its labeled with the dependency type *advmod*. Formally, for $o_{intensification}$, $\tau = weight_\beta(SO)$, $C = w \in$ intensifiers $\wedge$ $t \in \{ADV,ADJ\} \wedge d \in \{advmod,amod,nmod\}$, $\delta = 1$, $\pi = 3$ and $S = \{target\ node,\ b(advmod),\ b(amod)\}$, where $b(x)$ indicates that the scope is the first branch at the target level whose dependency type is x. β is extracted from a lexicon with *booster* values (in this work obtained from SFU, where 'muy' has a *booster* value of 0.25).

2. *Subordinate adversative clauses*: This rule is designed for dealing with structures coordinated by adversative conjunctions (such as *but*), which usually involve opposite polarities between the two joint elements (e.g., "good but expensive"). Here, the SO of the first element is multiplied by $1 - 0.25$, so its polarity decreases. Formally, $\tau = weight_{-0.25}(SO)$, $C = w \in$ adversatives $\wedge$ $t \in \{CONJ,SCONJ\} \wedge d \in \{cc,advmod,mark\}$, $\delta = 1$, $\pi = 1$ and $S = \{subjl\}$. *Subjl* indicates that the scope is the first left branch with SO $! = 0$ at the target level.

3. *Negation*: In most cases, negative adverbs shift the polarity of the structures they depend on ("It is nice" *versus* "It is not nice"). In order to handle these cases, the present rule shifts the polarity of the head structures of a negative adverb by α (where $\alpha = 4$, in our experiments). In the previous example, the polarity of "nice" would drop from 3.5 to -0.5 if affected by the rule. Formally, for $o_{negation}$, $\tau = shift_4(SO)$, $C = w \in$ negators $\wedge$ $d \in \{neg,advmod\}$, $\delta = 1$, $\pi = 2$ and $S = \{target\ node,\ b(root),\ b(cop),\ b(nsubj),\ subjr,\ all\}$. *Subjr* indicates that the scope is the first branch with SO $! = 0$ and *all* indicates to apply negation at the target level as a backoff option, if none of the previous scopes matched.

4. *'If' irrealis*: In conditional statements, a SA system may obtain an incorrect polarity due to the presence of polarity words which actually do not reflect a real situation ("This is good" *vs* "If this is good"). This rule attempts to better analyze these structures by shifting the polarity (here, multiplied by -1) if a conditional conjunction depends on it. Formally, for $o_{irrealis}$, $\tau = weight_{-1}(SO)$, $C = w \in$ irrealis $\wedge d \in \{mark,advmod,cc\}$, $\delta = 1$, $\pi = 3$ and $S = \{target\ node,\ subjr\}$.

4 Evaluation

This section presents the results of the experiments we carried out with our system using both the monolingual and the multilingual lexica, compared to the performance of a supervised classifier for three of the five analyzed languages.

4.1 Testing corpora

• *Spanish SFU* (Brooke et al., 2009): A set of 400 long reviews (200 positive, 200 negative) from different domains such as movies, music, computers or washing machines.

• *Portuguese SentiCorpus-PT 0.1* (Carvalho et al., 2011): A collection of comments from the Portuguese newspaper *Público* with polarity annotation at the entity level. As our system assigns the polarity at the sentence level, we selected the SentiCorpus sentences with (a) only one SO and (b) with > 1 SO iff all of them were the same, generating a corpus with $2,086$ (from $2,604$) sentences.

• *Basque Opinion Dataset* (San Vicente and Saralegi, 2016): Two small corpora in Basque containing news articles and reviews (music and movie domains). We merged them to create a larger dataset, containing a total of 224 reviews.

In addition, due to the lack of available sentence- or document-level corpora for Catalan or Galician, we opted for synthetic corpora:

• *Synthetic Catalan SFU*: An automatically translated version to *ca* of the Spanish SFU, with 5% of the words from the original corpus considered as unknown by the translation tool.

• *Synthetic Galician SFU*: An automatically translated version to *gl* of the Spanish SFU ($\approx$ 6.4% of the words not translated).

4.2 Experiments

We performed different experiments on binary polarity classification for knowing (a) the accuracy of the system, (b) the impact of the merged resources, and (c) the impact of the universal rules in monolingual and multilingual settings:

Lg	SL-O	SL+O	ML-O	ML+O	LKit
es	60.00	75.75	63.75	**76.50**	58.75
ca	54.00	57.50	58.25	**73.00**	—
gl	60.75	**73.00**	60.00	70.00	50.25
eu	62.95	69.20	65.63	**72.32**	—
pt	60.50	**67.35**	57.29	65.01	60.55

Table 4: Results of the different tests. In *LKit* we only evaluated the positive and negative results (it also classifies sentences with no polarity).

1. *SL-O*: Single lexica, no operations (baseline).
2. *ML-O*: Multilingual lexica, no operations.
3. *SL+O*: Single lexica with universal operations.
4. *ML+O*: Multilingual lexica with universal operations.

The performance of our system was compared to LinguaKit (*LKit*), an open-source toolkit which performs supervised sentiment analysis in several languages (Gamallo et al., 2013; Gamallo and Garcia, 2017).

Table 4 shows the results of each of these models on the different corpora. The baseline (*SL-O*) obtained values between 54% (*ca*) and 62.95% (*eu*), results that are in line to those obtained by the supervised model.[5] As we are not aware of available SA tools for *ca*, we could not compare our results with other systems. For Basque, San Vicente and Saralegi (2016) evaluated several lexica (both automatically translated and extracted, as well as with human annotation) in the same dataset used in this paper. They used a simple average polarity ratio classifier, which is similar to our baseline. Even if the lexica are different, their results are very similar to our *SL-O* system (63% *vs* 62, 95%), and they also show that manually reviewing the lexica can boost the accuracy by up to 13%.

The central columns of Table 4 show the results of using universal rules and a merged lexicon in the same datasets. In *gl* and *pt* the best values were obtained using individual lexica together with syntactic rules, while the Iberian system achieved the best results in the other languages.

Table 5 summarizes the impact that the rules have in both the monolingual and the multilingual setting, as well as the differences in performance due to the fusion process. Concerning the rules (columns 2 and 3), the results show that using the same set of universal rules improves the performance of the classifier in all the languages and settings. Their impact varies between 3.5 percentage

Lg	O(SL)	O(ML)	ML(-O)	ML(+O)
es	15.75	12.75	3.75	0.75
ca	3.50	14.75	4.25	15.5
gl	12.25	10.00	-0.75	-3.00
eu	6.25	6.69	2.68	3.12
pt	6.85	7.72	-3.21	-2.34

Table 5: Impact of the operations (O) with mono (SL) and multilingual lexica (ML) and of the ML with (+O) and without operations (-O).

points (*ca*) and more than 15 (*es*) and, for each language, the rules provide a similar effect in monolingual and multilingual lexica (except for *ca*, with much higher values in the ML scenario).

The fusion of the different lexica had different results (columns 4 and 5 of Table 5): in *gl* and *pt*, it had a negative impact (between -0.75% and -3.21%) while in the other three the ML setting achieved better values (between 0.75 and 15.5 points, again with huge differences in *ca*). On average, using multilingual lexica had a positive impact of 1.3 (-O) and 2.8 points (+O). As mentioned, *ca* has a different behaviour: the gain from rules when using monolingual lexica is about 3.50 points (lower than other languages), and the benefit of the ML lexicon without syntactic rules is of 4.25 points. However, when combining both the universal rules and the ML lexicon its performance increases $\approx$ 15 points, turning out that the combination of these two factors is decisive.

In sum, the results of the experiments indicate that syntactic rules defined by means of a harmonized annotation can be used in several languages with positive results. Furthermore, the merging of monolingual lexica (some of them automatically translated) can be applied to perform multilingual SA with little impact in performance when compared to language-dependent systems.

5 Conclusions and current work

We built a single symbolic syntactic system for polarity classification that analyzes five official languages of the Iberian peninsula. With little effort we obtain robust results for many languages. As current work, we are working on texts harder to parse and low-resource languages: we developed a Galician corpus of manually labeled tweets, where SISA obtains between 62% and 65% accuracy for different settings,[6] and plan to incorporate Kong et al. (2014) parser to improve its performance.

---

[5] LinguaKit was intended for tweets (not long texts).

[6] This corpus is available at `http://grupolys.org/software/CHIOS-SISA/`

References

R. Agerri, J. Bermudez, and G. Rigau. 2014. IXA pipeline: Efficient and Ready to Use Multilingual NLP tools. In *Proceedings of the 9th edition of the Language Resources and Evaluation Conference (LREC 2014)*, pages 3823–3828.

Waleed Ammar, George Mulcaire, Miguel Ballesteros, Chris Dyer, and Noah Smith. 2016. Many languages, one parser. *Transactions of the Association for Computational Linguistics*, 4:431–444.

P. P. Balage Filho, T. AS Pardo, and S. M. Aluísio. 2013. An evaluation of the Brazilian Portuguese LIWC dictionary for sentiment analysis. In *Proceedings of the 9th Brazilian Symposium in Information and Human Language Technology (STIL)*, pages 215–219.

C. Bosco, M. Lai, V. Patti, F. M. Rangel Pardo, and P Rosso. 2016. Tweeting in the debate about catalan elections. In *Proceedings of the Tenth International Conference on Language Resources and Evaluation (LREC 2016). Emotion and Sentiment Analysis Workshop.*, pages 67–70.

J. Brooke, M. Tofiloski, and M. Taboada. 2009. Cross-Linguistic Sentiment Analysis: From English to Spanish. In *Proceedings of RANLP 2009, Recent Advances in Natural Language Processing*, pages 50–54, Bovorets, Bulgaria.

P. Carvalho, L. Sarmento, J. Teixeira, and M. J. Silva. 2011. Liars and saviors in a sentiment annotated corpus of comments to political debates. In *Proceedings of the 49th Annual Meeting of the Association for Computational Linguistics: Human Language Technologies: short papers-Volume 2*, pages 564–568. Association for Computational Linguistics.

H. Chen and H. Chen. 2016. Implicit Polarity and Implicit Aspect Recognition in Opinion Mining. In *The 54th Annual Meeting of the Association for Computational Linguistics*, pages 20–25.

F. L Cruz, J. A Troyano, B. Pontes, and F. J. Ortega. 2014. ML-SentiCon: Un lexicón multilingüe de polaridades semánticas a nivel de lemas. *Procesamiento del Lenguaje Natural*, 53:113–120.

M. L Forcada, M. Ginestí-Rosell, J. Nordfalk, J. O'Regan, S. Ortiz-Rojas, J. A. Pérez-Ortiz, F. Sánchez-Martínez, G. Ramírez-Sánchez, and F. M. Tyers. 2011. Apertium: a free/open-source platform for rule-based machine translation. *Machine translation*, 25(2):127–144.

P. Gamallo and M. Garcia. 2017. LinguaKit: uma ferramenta multilingue para a análise linguística e a extração de informação. *Linguamática*, 9(1):19–28.

P. Gamallo, M. García, and S. Fernández Lanza. 2013. TASS: A Naive-Bayes strategy for sentiment analysis on Spanish tweets. In *XXIX Congreso de la Sociedad Española de Procesamiento de Lenguaje Natural (SEPLN 2013). TASS 2013 - Workshop on Sentiment Analysis at SEPLN 2013*, pages 126–132, Madrid, Spain.

M. Garcia and P. Gamallo. 2015. Yet Another Suite of Multilingual NLP Tools. In *Languages, Applications and Technologies. Communications in Computer and Information Science*, volume 563, pages 65–75. Springer.

L. F. Hurtado, F. Pla, and D. Buscaldi. 2015. ELiRF-UPV en TASS 2015: Análisis de Sentimientos en Twitter. In *Proceedings of TASS 2015: Workshop on Sentiment Analysis at SEPLN*, pages 35–40.

L. Kong, N. Schneider, S. Swayamdipta, A. Bhatia, C. Dyer, and N. A. Smith. 2014. A Dependency Parser for Tweets. In *Proceedings of the 2014 Conference on Empirical Methods in Natural Language Processing (EMNLP)*, pages 1001–1012, Doha, Qatar. ACL.

Eugenio Martínez-Cámara, M Teresa Martín-Valdivia, and L Alfonso Ureña-López. 2011. Opinion classification techniques applied to a spanish corpus. In *International Conference on Application of Natural Language to Information Systems*, pages 169–176. Springer.

R. T McDonald, J. Nivre, Y. Quirmbach-Brundage, Y. Goldberg, D. Das, K. Ganchev, K. B. Hall, S. Petrov, H. Zhang, O. Täckström, et al. 2013. Universal Dependency Annotation for Multilingual Parsing. In *Proceedings of the 51st Annual Meeting of the Association for Computational Linguistics*, pages 92–97. Association for Computational Linguistics.

S. M Mohammad, S. Kiritchenko, and X. Zhu. 2013. NRC-Canada: Building the State-of-the-Art in Sentiment Analysis of Tweets. In *Proceedings of the seventh international workshop on Semantic Evaluation Exercises (SemEval-2013)*, Atlanta, Georgia, USA.

J. Nivre, Ž. Agić, M. J. Aranzabe, M. Asahara, A. Atutxa, M. Ballesteros, J. Bauer, K. Bengoetxea, R. A. Bhat, C. Bosco, et al. 2015. Universal dependencies 1.2.

L. Padró and E. Stanilovsky. 2012. Freeling 3.0: Towards wider multilinguality. In *Proceedings of the 8th edition of the Language Resources and Evaluation Conference (LREC 2012)*, Istambul.

J. W. Pennebaker, M. E. Francis, and R. J. Booth. 2001. Linguistic inquiry and word count: LIWC 2001. *Mahway: Lawrence Erlbaum Associates*, page 71.

I. San Vicente and X. Saralegi. 2016. Polarity lexicon building: to what extent is the manual effort worth? In *Proceedings of the Tenth International Conference on Language Resources and Evaluation (LREC 2016)*, Paris, France. European Language Resources Association (ELRA).

X. Saralegi and I. San Vicente. 2013. Elhuyar at tass 2013. In *Proceedings of the Workshop on Sentiment Analysis at SEPLN (TASS 2013)*, pages 143–150.

A. Shoukry and A. Rafea. 2012. Sentence-level Arabic sentiment analysis. In *Collaboration Technologies and Systems (CTS), 2012 International Conference on*, pages 546–550. IEEE.

M. J Silva, P. Carvalho, L. Sarmento, E. de Oliveira, and P. Magalhaes. 2009. The design of OPTIMISM, an opinion mining system for Portuguese politics. *New trends in artificial intelligence: Proceedings of EPIA*, pages 12–15.

R. Socher, A. Perelygin, J. Wu, J. Chuang, C. D Manning, A. Ng, and C. Potts. 2013. Recursive Deep Models for Semantic Compositionality Over a Sentiment Treebank. In *EMNLP 2013. 2013 Conference on Empirical Methods in Natural Language Processing. Proceedings of the Conference*, pages 1631–1642, Seattle, Washington, USA. ACL.

M. Souza and R. Vieira. 2012. Sentiment analysis on twitter data for portuguese language. In *International Conference on Computational Processing of the Portuguese Language*, pages 241–247. Springer.

M. Souza, R. Vieira, D. Busetti, R. Chishman, I. M. Alves, and Others. 2011. Construction of a portuguese opinion lexicon from multiple resources. In *8th Brazilian Symposium in Information and Human Language Technology*, pages 59–66.

M. Taboada, J. Brooke, M. Tofiloski, K. Voll, and M. Stede. 2011. Lexicon-based methods for sentiment analysis. *Computational Linguistics*, 37(2):267–307.

M. Taulé, M. A. Martí, and M. Recasens. 2008. AnCora: Multilevel Annotated Corpora for Catalan and Spanish. In *Proceedings of the Sixth International Conference on Language Resources and Evaluation (LREC'08)*, pages 96–101, Marrakech, Morocco.

K. Toutanova and C. D. Manning. 2000. Enriching the knowledge sources used in a maximum entropy part-of-speech tagger. In *Proceedings of the 2000 Joint SIGDAT conference on Empirical methods in natural language processing and very large corpora: held in conjunction with the 38th Annual Meeting of the Association for Computational Linguistics-Volume 13*, pages 63–70.

P. D. Turney. 2002. Thumbs up or thumbs down?: semantic orientation applied to unsupervised classification of reviews. In *Proceedings of the 40th Annual Meeting on Association for Computational Linguistics*, ACL '02, pages 417–424, Stroudsburg, PA, USA. ACL.

D. Vilares, M. A. Alonso, and C. Gómez-Rodríguez. A syntactic approach for opinion mining on Spanish reviews. *Natural Language Engineering*, 21(01):139–163.

D. Vilares, M. A. Alonso, and C. Gómez-Rodríguez. 2015. On the usefulness of lexical and syntactic processing in polarity classification of Twitter messages. *Journal of the Association for Information Science and Technology*, 66(9):1799–1816.

D. Vilares, C. Gómez-Rodríguez, and M. A. Alonso. 2016. One model, two languages: training bilingual parsers with harmonized treebanks. In *Proceedings of the 54th Annual Meeting of the Association for Computational Linguistics (Volume 2: Short Papers)*, pages 425–431, Berlin, Germany. Association for Computational Linguistics.

David Vilares, Carlos Gómez-Rodríguez, and Miguel A. Alonso. 2017. Universal, unsupervised (rule-based), uncovered sentiment analysis. *Knowledge-Based Systems*, 118:45–55.

J. Villena-Román, S. Lana-Serrano, E. Martínez-Cámara, and J C González C. 2013. TASS - Worshop on Sentiment Analysis at SEPLN. *Procesamiento de Lenguaje Natural*, 50:37–44.

D. T. Vo and Y. Zhang. 2016. Don't count, predict! an automatic approach to learning sentiment lexicons for short text. In *Proceedings of the 54th Annual Meeting of the Association for Computational Linguistics (Volume 2: Short Papers)*, pages 219–224, Berlin, Germany. Association for Computational Linguistics.

Toward Stance Classification Based on Claim Microstructures

Filip Boltužić and **Jan Šnajder**
University of Zagreb, Faculty of Electrical Engineering and Computing
Text Analysis and Knowledge Engineering Lab
Unska 3, 10000 Zagreb, Croatia
{filip.boltuzic, jan.snajder}@fer.hr

Abstract

Claims are the building blocks of arguments and the reasons underpinning opinions, thus analyzing claims is important for both argumentation mining and opinion mining. We propose a framework for representing claims as *microstructures*, which express the beliefs, judgments, and policies about the relations between domain-specific concepts. In a proof-of-concept study, we manually build microstructures for over 800 claims extracted from an online debate. We test the so-obtained microstructures on the task of claim stance classification, achieving considerable improvements over text-based baselines.

1 Introduction

In online discussions, users express their opinions using more or less well structured arguments. The building blocks of these arguments are *claims*: statements that are in dispute and that we are trying to support with reason Govier (2013). Claims can support or attack other claims, giving rise to complex argumentative structures. Thus, the ability to identify and analyze claims in text is a crucial part of argumentation mining (Moens, 2014; Lippi and Torroni, 2016). Outside the realm of well-structured argumentation, the ability to analyze claims is crucial for tasks such as stance classification (Anand et al., 2011; Hasan and Ng, 2013; Mohammad et al., 2016) and fine-grained opinion analysis (Stoyanov and Cardie, 2008; Yang and Cardie, 2013), as well as the converging task of argument-based opinion mining (Clos et al., 2014; Boltužić and Šnajder, 2014), which aims to uncover the reasons underpinning the opinions.

Previous research has tackled the claim detection task for diverse domains, including legal documents (Palau and Moens, 2009), microtexts (Peldszus and Stede, 2015), Wikipedia articles (Aharoni et al., 2014; Levy et al., 2014; Rinott et al., 2015), student essays (Stab and Gurevych, 2017), and user-generated web discourse (Habernal and Gurevych, 2015). Boltužić and Šnajder (2015) addressed the task of identifying prominent claims in online debates, while Boltužić and Šnajder (2016) analyzed the implicit premises between two claims. Recently, Bar-Haim et al. (2017) introduced the claim stance classification task, where classification is done at the claim rather than document level.

In this paper, we address the task of claim analysis from a different angle. While prior work has dealt with claims as textual fragments, we study the possibility of a more precise, domain-specific analysis of claims based on their internal logical structure. The work closest to ours is that of Wyner and Van Engers (2010) and Wyner et al. (2016), who explored normalizing claims from the policy making domain by translating them to Attempto Controlled English (Fuchs et al., 2008), and then mapping them to propositions. In contrast, we propose a framework for representing claims as *microstructures*: structures expressing the relations between the domain-specific concepts, reflecting the beliefs, value judgments, or desired policies of the claim author. We present a preliminary proof-of-concept study, where we use the proposed framework to manually create microstructures for over eight hundred claims extracted from an online debate.

We envisage that claim microstructures could play an important role in a variety of opinion mining and argument mining tasks, including stance classification, extraction of argumentative structures, analysis of implicit premises, fine-grained opinion mining, identifying prominent claims, and claim matching. To demonstrate the viability of claim microstructures for a downstream task, we look into supervised claim stance classification

Proceedings of the 8th Workshop on Computational Approaches to Subjectivity, Sentiment and Social Media Analysis, pages 74–80
Copenhagen, Denmark, September 7–11, 2017. ©2017 Association for Computational Linguistics

and show that, even with a simple encoding of microstructures as features, we get substantial improvements on this task over text-based baselines.

The contribution of our work may be summed up as follows: (1) we investigate the feasibility of using microstructures for representing claims, (2) we demonstrate the use of microstructures for stance classification, and (3) to promote further research, we make available the dataset annotated with claim paraphrases and microstructures.[1]

2 Claim Microstructures

We introduce a framework for representing claims from text using logical *microstructures* whose purpose is to capture the gist of a claim. The initial motivation came from the analysis of our dataset (cf. Section 4), which revealed that a large majority of claims can be conceived of as expressing *relations* between *concepts* using a certain *modality*. Figure 1 shows a claim microstructure bringing together these three elements.

Relations. Many claims can be represented as expressing a relation between two concepts. For example, on the topic of gay rights, the relations may be 'promotes(GayMarriage, Depopulation)' or 'purpose(Love, Procreation)'. There are also comparably fewer claims that can be expressed via higher-order relations, e.g., 'entails(Constitution, allow(State, GayMarriage)))'. Each relation can be negated, e.g., '¬promotes(GayMarriage, Depopulation)' expresses that gay marriage does not cause depopulation.

Concepts. The relations are established between concepts, expressed by noun phrases. For ease of access, these can be arranged into a small, domain-specific taxonomy of concepts. For instance, "gay marriage", "heterosexual marriage", and "religious marriage" all belong under the concept of "marriage". The taxonomic relations could also be useful for later computational processing. Unlike relations, concepts are domain dependent and need to be defined for each new topic.

Modalities. We furthermore observed that the claims express different *modalities*, which can roughly be categorized into *beliefs*, *value judgments*, and *policies*. We formalize this via unary relations 'believes', 'approves', and 'desires', corresponding to beliefs (factual, religious,

[1] http://takelab.fer.hr/claim-micro

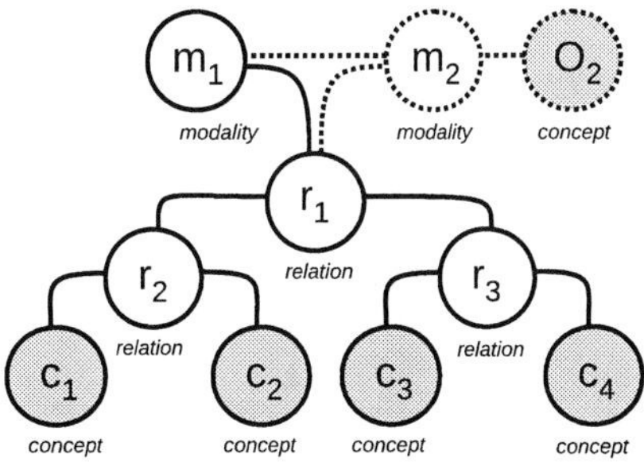

Figure 1: Claim microstructure (2nd-order).

and opinion-based), positive value judgment, and desired policy (desired state of affairs), respectively. The three modalities act as a wrapper on the propositional content of the claim, effectively modulating what is being claimed. For instance, 'believes(purpose(Love, Procreation))' expresses the belief that love serves procreation, while 'desires(¬allow(State, GayMarriage))' expresses the wish for the state not to allow gay marriages. Finally, we observed that in a fair number of cases the claims are supported by a reference to a second opinion holder (e.g., the Bible, the state). We represent this by introducing one additional modality layer with the opinion holder as an additional modifier. For instance, 'believes(believes[State](promotes(Marriage, Advancement)))' corresponds to the belief that the state believes gay marriages lead to an advancement. By convention, the opinion holder of the first modality is always the author of the post.

Let $\mathcal{R}$, $\mathcal{C}$, and $\mathcal{M}$ denote the set of relations, concepts, and modalities, respectively. Formally, we define a claim microstructure as a quadruple (m_1, m_2, o_2, r), where $m_1 \in \mathcal{M}$ and (optionally) $m_2 \in \mathcal{M} \cup \{\epsilon\}$ are the modalities, $o_2 \in \mathcal{C} \cup \{\epsilon\}$ is the (optional) second opinion holder, and $r = (t, c_1, c_2) \in \mathcal{R}$ is the (possibly higher-order) relation between two concepts or relations $c_1, c_2 \in \mathcal{C} \cup \mathcal{R}$, conveyed by the relation type t. Table 1 defines the relation types used in this work.

It should be noted that, unlike Aharoni et al. (2014), who consider as claims only the statements that directly support or contest the debating topic, we consider all statements with propositional content. For example, in the context of gay rights, 'belief(purpose(Life, Love))' is a valid claim in our framework, although it does not support nor contest the topic, i.e., the stance of that claim is neutral.

Relation	Definition
promotes(A, B)	Promoting agent A promotes, fosters, leads, increases likelihood, boosts B.
suppress(A, B)	Suppressing agent A suppresses, decreases likelihood, puts down, vanquishes B
allow(A, B)	Principle A allows, approves, licenses state of affairs B
entails(A, B)	State of affairs A, necessarily, per definition or causally, makes B true.
contradicts(A, B)	State of affairs A, necessarily, per definition or causally, makes B false.
purpose(A, B)	The purpose of A is B.
equal(A, B)	State of affairs A is equal to state of affairs B.
has(A, B)	A has the properties affected by the existence of B.

Table 1: Relations types in claim microstructures.

3   Data Annotation

We adopted the dataset of Hasan and Ng (2014), which contains user posts from online two-sided debates on a number of topics. For reasons of feasibility, in this study we consider only one topic: "Gay rights". We sampled 100 posts (50 for and 50 against) from this topic. The manual annotation was carried out in two steps. In the first step, the annotators segmented out the individual claims from user posts and paraphrased them into well-articulated claims. In the second step, the annotators translated each paraphrased claim into the corresponding logical microstructure.

While in principle the claim microstructures could have been built directly from segments, we chose to introduce the additional step of claim paraphrasing for three reasons. First, we assumed that paraphrasing would help in identifying the segments corresponding to individual claims, since paraphrasing demonstrates understanding. In that respect, our work is similar to that of Wyner and Van Engers (2010), who used a controlled language for paraphrasing the claims. Second, we assumed that paraphrases will make overt the logical structure of claims, making their translation into microstructures easier. Lastly, we assumed that paraphrases could help in identifying the prominent concepts for the domain-specific taxonomy.

3.1   Claim Segments and Paraphrases

The purpose of the this step was to extract claim segments from user posts, thus separating argumentative from non-argumentative content, and to paraphrase the claims into simple, well-articulated statements. This obviously involves two non-trivial tasks: segmentation and paraphrasing. Arguably, there are many ways in which a post can be segmented into claims, and even more ways in which each segment could be paraphrased. We hypothesize that much of this ambiguity can be reduced by considering these two tasks jointly, and by adopting certain paraphrasing principles aimed at obtaining *simplifying paraphrases* – paraphrases that expresses the essence of the claims devoid of superfluous words and phrases. To this end, we adopted the following nine paraphrasing principles: (1) **Argumentativeness** – Only argumentative text should be paraphrased; (2) **Atomicity** – A claim should convey a single thought; (3) **Authority** – Experts in claims from expert opinion should be made explicit in the paraphrase; (4) **Brevity** – Paraphrases should keep only the relevant argumentative content; (5) **Canonicity** – Canonical terms and phrases are preferred over idiomatic language; (6) **Contextuality** – Claims should be paraphrased by considering their local and topical context as well as their context; (7) **Declarativity** – paraphrases should be in declarative form, and (8) **Dereferencing** – Pronouns and nominal references should be resolved; and (9) **Explicitness** – Only explicitly stated information should be paraphrased, and not whatever might be implied by the claim.

The annotation was carried out by one trained annotator and took 25 hours. The 100 user posts yielded 920 claim segments and the same number of paraphrases. Table 2 gives an example. Note that generally the claim segments may overlap, though this is not the case in this example. Overall, the segments covered 79.6% of the text, while the remaining 20.4% may be considered non-argumentative.

3.2   Claim Microstructures

In the second step, we asked two annotators (A1 and A2) to translate each of the 920 paraphrases into claim microstructures. The annotators were provided with a domain-specific taxonomy on "Gay rights", compiled based on a manual analysis of claim paraphrases. The taxonomy consists of 150 concepts arranged into a tree of a maximum depth of four. The annotators were instructed to use the existing concepts from the taxonomy, and introduce new ones only if they could not find a suitable one in the taxonomy. They were also instructed not to use microstructures of order higher than two.

User post	Claim segment	Claim paraphrase	Claim microstructure
Men should fall in love with women that's why they where created and women should get married to men because it makes everything easier.	*Men should fall in love with women.*	*People of opposite sex should fall in love.*	desires(entails(OppositeSex, FallingInLove))
	that's why they where created	*Men and women are created to pair.*	believes(purpose(MenAndWomen, Procreation))
	women should get married to men because it makes everything easier.	*Heterosexual marriages make everything easier.*	believes(entails(HeterosexualMarriage, Normal))

Table 2: An example of a user post segmented into three claim segments, each paraphrased and translated into the corresponding claim microstructure.

Out of 920 claim paraphrases, annotator A1 managed to translate 882 claims into 707 distinct microstructures, while annotator A2 translated 842 claims into 767 distinct microstructures. The average annotation effort was 33 hours. The number of claims for which both annotators provided a microstructure is 819 (89%), while the number of claims for which both provided an identical microstructure is only 58 (6.3%), The annotators introduced a total of 157 new concepts, indicating that the initial taxonomy was of too limited a scope. The low annotator agreement and the relatively large number of newly added concepts suggest that a fair amount of ambiguity exists in translating paraphrases to microstructures. Our analysis revealed that, in the majority of cases, the ambiguity is genuine and in such cases having more candidate microstructures for a single claim can be considered advantageous.

The analysis also revealed that 'believes' is the most frequent modality, used for about 79% of claims. For A1, *entails* is by far the most common relation (61%), while A2 made a more balanced use of relations, with the top two being *has* (21%) and *entails* (15%). The concepts most frequently used by A1 are *homosexuality*, *homosexual people* and *marriage*, while for A2 these are *The Bible*, *homosexual people*, and *government interest*.

4 Stance Classification

4.1 Setup

Annotation. We consider claim stance classification as one potential application of claim microstructures. To this end, we asked two annotators to label the stance of each of 819 claim paraphrases on a five-point scale: *strong favor* (F), *likely favor* (f), *neither* (N), *likely against* (a), and, *strong against* (A). We adopt the definition of F, N, and A stance from Mohammad et al. (2016), with the

		Stance	
Claim paraphrase		**A1**	**A2**
Gay couples should be able to experience parenting.		F	F
Gay couples don't have children.		N	N
By natural means, infertility is wrong.		a	a
A homosexual relationship lacks the ability to procreate.		a	A

Table 3: Claim stance annotations.

	Regression	Classification		
Features	**5-way**	**5-way**	**3-way-N**	**3-way-E**
seg-w2v	0.084	**0.230**	**0.259**	**0.383**
seg-tfidf	**0.133**	0.170	0.248	0.297
par-w2c	0.133	0.170	0.248	0.297
par-tfidf	**0.250**	**0.290**	**0.487**	**0.377**
ms-onehot	0.316	**0.320**	**0.507**	**0.473**
ms-path	**0.331**	0.315	0.501	0.462

Table 4: Stance classification macro-averaged F1-score using segments (*seg*), paraphrases (*par*), and microstructures (*ms*) as features. The best result in each group is shown in boldface.

addition of the in-between options (f and a) for indicating implicit or indirect stance. Table 3 shows some examples. On the five classes, we observe a moderate inter-annotator agreement of 0.53 Cohen's κ (Cohen, 1960). The aggregation was done by first removing 16 instances on which the annotators disagreed in stance polarity, and then averaging and rounding the two labels by treating them as numbers from the $[-2, +2]$ interval.

Baselines. We compare against two baselines, which, to the best of our knowledge, are considered state of the art for stance classification (Sobhani et al., 2016): (1) a sum of skip-gram vectors (Mikolov et al., 2013)[2] for each word and a (2) tf-idf unigram and bigram representation of a claim. For baselines, we use these representations on claim segments (*seg*). For the sake of completeness, we also run the baselines on claim paraphrases (*par*), but note that this serves only as a reference, as obtaining paraphrases is arguably a task that is more difficult to automate than obtaining microstructures.

Microstructures. To represent the claim microstructures (*ms*), we adopted a simple one-hot encoding scheme: we use one one-hot vector for each of the modalities, relations, relation negations, concepts, and opinion holders concatenating the vectors into a single feature vector (*onehot*). In addition, to leverage the taxonomical relations between concepts, we experimented with encoding for each concept its ancestors in the taxonomy, by encoding the nodes along the path leading from the root to the concept (*path*).

Models. We used support vector machine (SVM) classifier and regression models with an RBF kernel, as implemented in the LibSVM library of Chang and Lin (2011). We trained and evaluated the models on 803 claim instances (either segments, paraphrases, or microstructures) using a 5×3 nested cross-validation, using grid search to optimize hyperparameters C and γ.

Tasks. We considered four task: (1) a 5-way regression setup, in which the model is trained to predict the numeric stance score, but afterwards the predictions are rounded and mapped to labels, (2) a 5-way classification task, (3) a 3-way classification task in which the implicit labels (a and f) are mapped to neutral (3-way-N), and a (4) 3-way classification task in which the implicit labels are mapped to explicit for and against labels (3-way-E). The last two tasks are easier, so we expected the models to perform better on these tasks.

4.2 Results

Table 4 shows the classification results in terms of macro-averaged F1-score. As expected, the 3-way classification tasks are easier than 5-way classification tasks. Furthermore, the 5-way regression model performs better than 5-way classifier, suggesting that using distance-sensitive loss is beneficial for this task. In all four tasks, the

---

[2] We use the pre-trained vectors available at
https://code.google.com/p/word2vec/

claim microstructures considerably outperform both segment-based baselines, yielding between 9 and 25 points of improvement in F1-score, depending on the task. All differences between the baseline and the microstructure model are statistically significant at p<0.05 (tested using a two-tailed permutation test (Yeh, 2000)). By comparing with claim paraphrases as a reference, we find that microstructures give comparable performance for 5-way and 3-way-N classification tasks (the differences are not statistically significant at p<0.05), while for 5-way regression and 3-way-E classification tasks the microstructures outperform paraphrase representations. Finally, the performance difference between one-hot encoded microstructures and microstructures with path-encoded concepts are not statistically significant at p<0.05, suggesting that stance classification did not profit from encoding taxonomical relations.

In the above experiments, the results for microstructures were obtained on annotations of A1. The models trained on annotations of A2 gave consistently lower performance, albeit still better (and statistically different) than the baseline.

We conclude the experimental section by noting that microstructures improve claim stance classification performance over a segment-based baseline by a maximum of 50.7% F1-score for a 3-way classification setup.

5 Conclusion and Future Work

We presented a framework for representing the microstructures of claims. A microstructure expresses the relations between domain-specific concepts, and is intended to capture the beliefs, value judgments, and desired policies conveyed by claims. In the proof-of-concept study, we manually annotated microstructures for one debating topic. The annotators were able to translate 89% of claims into microstructures, thus proving the viability of the approach. We next demonstrated the usefulness of microstructures on the task of claim stance classification, where a simple encoding of microstructures yielded notable performance improvements over segment-based baselines. This in turn suggests that a claim microstructure does a good job in capturing the argumentative gist of the claim.

We note, however, that this is a preliminary study, which has left aside some important practical issues. While our results are promising, the major question now is how to automatically extract the microstructures from text. In our study, the claims were segmented and paraphrased by human annotators; an end-to-end system would need to both segment out the claims and extract the corresponding microstructures. We believe that one way to tackle this problem might be to frame it as an information extraction task.

In our preliminary study, the annotators managed to translate most of the claims into microstructures. However, the low agreement rate (6.3%) suggests that the annotation workflow could perhaps be improved.

Another issue worth investigating is the application of the framework to a new domain: the tedious work of deriving a domain-specific taxonomy of concepts and the microstructures could perhaps be alleviated using active learning methods.

Finally, it would of course be interesting to investigate the use of microstructures in other opinion mining and argument mining tasks, including tasks that could profit from analyzing the logical links between claims. We intend to pursue some of these directions in future work.

References

Ehud Aharoni, Anatoly Polnarov, Tamar Lavee, Daniel Hershcovich, Ran Levy, Ruty Rinott, Dan Gutfreund, and Noam Slonim. 2014. A benchmark dataset for automatic detection of claims and evidence in the context of controversial topics. In *Proceedings of the First Workshop on Argumentation Mining*, pages 64–68.

Pranav Anand, Marilyn Walker, Rob Abbott, Jean E Fox Tree, Robeson Bowmani, and Michael Minor. 2011. Cats rule and dogs drool!: Classifying stance in online debate. In *Proceedings of the 2nd workshop on computational approaches to subjectivity and sentiment analysis*, pages 1–9. Association for Computational Linguistics.

Roy Bar-Haim, Indrajit Bhattacharya, Francesco Dinuzzo, Amrita Saha, and Noam Slonim. 2017. Stance classification of context-dependent claims. In *Proceedings of the 15th Conference of the European Chapter of the Association for Computational Linguistics*, pages 251–256. Association for Computational Linguistics.

Filip Boltužić and Jan Šnajder. 2014. Back up your stance: Recognizing arguments in online discussions. In *Proceedings of the First Workshop on Argumentation Mining*, pages 49–58. Association for Computational Linguistics.

Filip Boltužić and Jan Šnajder. 2015. Identifying prominent arguments in online debates using semantic textual similarity. In *Proceedings of the 2nd Workshop on Argumentation Mining*, pages 110–115. Association for Computational Linguistics.

Filip Boltužić and Jan Šnajder. 2016. Fill the gap! Analyzing implicit premises between claims from online debates. In *Proceedings of the 3rd Workshop on Argument Mining*, pages 124–133. Association for Computational Linguistics.

Chih-Chung Chang and Chih-Jen Lin. 2011. LIBSVM: A library for support vector machines. *ACM Transactions on Intelligent Systems and Technology (TIST)*, 2(3):27.

Jérémie Clos, Nirmalie Wiratunga, Joemon Jose, Stewart Massie, and Guillaume Cabanac. 2014. Towards argumentative opinion mining in online discussions. In *Proceedings of the SICSA Workshop on Argument Mining (the Scottish Informatics & Computer Science Alliance)*, page 10.

Jacob Cohen. 1960. A coefficient of agreement for nominal scales. *Educational and psychological measurement*, 20(1):37–46.

Norbert E Fuchs, Kaarel Kaljurand, and Tobias Kuhn. 2008. Attempto controlled English for knowledge representation. In *Reasoning Web*, pages 104–124. Springer.

Trudy Govier. 2013. *A Practical Study of Argument, Enhanced Edition*, 7th edition. Cengage Learning.

Ivan Habernal and Iryna Gurevych. 2015. Exploiting debate portals for semi-supervised argumentation mining in user-generated web discourse. In *Proceedings of the 2015 Conference on Empirical Methods in Natural Language Processing*, pages 2127–2137.

Kazi Saidul Hasan and Vincent Ng. 2013. Stance classification of ideological debates: Data, models, features, and constraints. In *International Joint Conference on Natural Language Processing*, pages 1348–1356.

Kazi Saidul Hasan and Vincent Ng. 2014. Why are you taking this stance? Identifying and classifying reasons in ideological debates. In *Proceedings of the 2014 Conference on Empirical Methods in Natural Language Processing (EMNLP)*, pages 751–762. Association for Computational Linguistics.

Ran Levy, Yonatan Bilu, Daniel Hershcovich, Ehud Aharoni, and Noam Slonim. 2014. Context dependent claim detection. In *Proceedings of COLING 2014, the 25th International Conference on Computational Linguistics: Technical Papers*.

Marco Lippi and Paolo Torroni. 2016. Argumentation mining: State of the art and emerging trends. *ACM Transactions on Internet Technology (TOIT)*, 16(2):10.

Tomas Mikolov, Kai Chen, Greg Corrado, and Jeffrey Dean. 2013. Efficient estimation of word representations in vector space. In *Proceedings of ICLR*, Scottsdale, AZ, USA.

Marie-Francine Moens. 2014. Argumentation mining: Where are we now, where do we want to be and how do we get there? In *Post-proceedings of the forum for information retrieval evaluation (FIRE 2013)*.

Saif M. Mohammad, Svetlana Kiritchenko, Parinaz Sobhani, Xiaodan Zhu, and Colin Cherry. 2016. SemEval-2016 Task 6: Detecting stance in tweets. In *Proceedings of SemEval-2016*, pages 31–41. Association for Computational Linguistics.

Raquel Mochales Palau and Marie-Francine Moens. 2009. Argumentation mining: The detection, classification and structure of arguments in text. In *Proceedings of the 12th International Conference on Artificial Intelligence and Law*, pages 98–107. ACM.

Andreas Peldszus and Manfred Stede. 2015. Joint prediction in mst-style discourse parsing for argumentation mining. In *Proceedings of the 2015 Conference on Empirical Methods in Natural Language Processing*, pages 938–948. Association for Computational Linguistics.

Ruty Rinott, Lena Dankin, Carlos Alzate Perez, Mitesh M Khapra, Ehud Aharoni, and Noam Slonim. 2015. Show me your evidence-an automatic method for context dependent evidence detection. In *Proceedings of the 2015 Conference on Empirical Methods in Natural Language Processing*, pages 440–450. Association for Computational Linguistics.

Parinaz Sobhani, Saif M Mohammad, and Svetlana Kiritchenko. 2016. Detecting stance in tweets and analyzing its interaction with sentiment. In *Proceedings of the Fifth Joint Conference on Lexical and Computational Semantics (*SEM 2016)*, pages 159–168. Association for Computational Linguistics.

Christian Stab and Iryna Gurevych. 2017. Parsing argumentation structures in persuasive essays. *Computational Linguistics*, (in press).

Veselin Stoyanov and Claire Cardie. 2008. Topic identification for fine-grained opinion analysis. In *Proceedings of the 22nd International Conference on Computational Linguistics-Volume 1*, pages 817–824. Association for Computational Linguistics.

Adam Wyner, Tom van Engers, and Anthony Hunter. 2016. Working on the argument pipeline: Through flow issues between natural language argument, instantiated arguments, and argumentation frameworks. *Argument & Computation*, 7(1):69–89.

Adam Wyner and Tom Van Engers. 2010. A framework for enriched, controlled on-line discussion forums for e-government policy-making. In *Proceedings of eGov 2010*, pages 1–11.

Bishan Yang and Claire Cardie. 2013. Joint inference for fine-grained opinion extraction. In *Proceedings of the 51st Annual Meeting of the Association for Computational Linguistics*, pages 1640–1649. Association for Computational Linguistics.

Alexander Yeh. 2000. More accurate tests for the statistical significance of result differences. In *Proceedings of the 18th conference on Computational linguistics-Volume 2*, pages 947–953. Association for Computational Linguistics.

Linguistic Reflexes of Well-Being and Happiness in Echo

Jiaqi Wu, Marilyn Walker, Pranav Anand and **Steve Whittaker**

University of California Santa Cruz
{jwu64,mawalker,panand,swhittak}@ucsc.edu

Abstract

Different theories posit different sources for feelings of well-being and happiness. Appraisal theory grounds our emotional responses in our goals and desires and their fulfillment, or lack of fulfillment. Self-Determination theory posits that the basis for well-being rests on our assessments of our competence, autonomy and social connection. And surveys that measure happiness empirically note that people require their basic needs to be met for food and shelter, but beyond that tend to be happiest when socializing, eating or having sex. We analyze a corpus of private micro-blogs from a well-being application called ECHO, where users label each written post about daily events with a happiness score between 1 and 9. Our goal is to ground the linguistic descriptions of events that users experience in theories of well-being and happiness, and then examine the extent to which different theoretical accounts can explain the variance in the happiness scores. We show that recurrent event types, such as OBLIGATION and IN-COMPETENCE, which affect people's feelings of well-being are not captured in current lexical or semantic resources.

1 Introduction

There has recently been huge interest in well-being, with a recent review arguing that psychological well-being plays a causal role in promoting job success, physical health, and long-term relationships (Lyubomirsky et al., 2005; Kahneman, 1999). In this paper we analyze a corpus of private micro-blogs from a well-being application called ECHO, with the aim to detect, understand, and fur-

RECORDING (*Negative*): I have to clean the kitchen since it's my chore this week, but I really don't want to do it!
REFLECTION (*Positive*): I'm glad I did it!! The kitchen was clean and I watched the kardashians while doing it!

RECORDING (*Positive*): I am having a lovely lunch with my two friends. We are eating at Pacific Thai. Tom yumm!!
REFLECTION (*Negative*): I miss hanging out with friends, I've been so busy lately.

Figure 1: RECORDING and REFLECTION of Echo

ther advance systems that can improve both short and longer-term issues with well-being.

ECHO initiates user-written reactions to daily events, called RECORDINGS, as well as subsequent REFLECTIONS on those events at points in the future (Isaacs et al., 2013).[1] Each reaction is labelled *at the time of recording or reflection* by the *user*, the first-person experiencer, with a *happiness* rating from 1 and 9. Note that all users' posts and ratings are private, distinguishing this corpus from public sources like LiveJournal, where the content of posts might be influenced by considerations of self-presentation. Figure 1 shows a RECORDING and REFLECTION from two users, after binning the happiness ratings into positive and negative.

Our goal is to ground the linguistic descriptions of events that users experience, such as those in Figure 1, in theories of well-being and happiness. Without such a grounding, it is difficult for the ECHO system to make recommendations to users to improve their well-being, or to explain the relationships between different event types and well-being, or to develop a policy that can do a good job of selecting events for targeted reflection (Konrad et al., 2015; Isaacs et al., 2013). That is, for ECHO's purposes, we need techniques that

---

[1] The ECHO corpus is not publicly available because of the ethical agreement with ECHO users. To protect users' privacy, the uploaded images are not stored for analysis.

Proceedings of the 8th Workshop on Computational Approaches to Subjectivity, Sentiment and Social Media Analysis, pages 81–91
Copenhagen, Denmark, September 7–11, 2017. ©2017 Association for Computational Linguistics

not only reliably categorize a user's scalar happiness level, but are explanatory with respect to the sources of that happiness level.

There are two principal challenges to this goal. First, different theories posit different sources for feelings of well-being and happiness. Second, the relevant computational resources for sentiment or mood are primarily lexically based, while many of the events can only be characterized well via their compositional semantics (Reschke and Anand, 2011).

Other research also shares our motivation of understanding the relationship between what people say and their levels of happiness and related moods. Mishne (2005) used a corpus of 340,000 posts from Livejournal that were self-annotated with the 40 most common moods. Lexical features alone improved classification accuracy by 6 to 15% over a balanced baseline. These results were then improved considerably (Keshtkar and Inkpen, 2009). Mihalcea and Liu (2006) experimented with the subset of *happy/sad* posts, and used conditional probability to explore the "happiness factor" of various terms, and the relationship of these terms to well-being categories such as human-centeredness and socialness. Schwartz et al. (2016) extract 5,100 public status updates on Facebook and have Turkers annotate them using Seligman's dimensions for well-being: Positive Emotions, Engagement, Relationships, Meaning, and Accomplish (Seligman et al., 2006; Forgeard et al., 2011). They then predict each dimension with lexical and LDA topic features.

A related line of work builds lexico-semantic resources for sentiment analysis with a focus on how the participants of an event are affected by it. Goyal and Riloff (2013) bootstrap a set of patient-polarity verbs from narratives and Ding and Riloff (2016) extract event-triples from blogs that reliably indicate positive or negative affect on one of the event participants. Reed et al. (2017) take a similar approach. Deng et al. (2013) annotate how participants of an event are affected, and Deng & Wiebe (2014) show that this assists inference about the author's sentiment towards entities or events. Balahur et al. (2012) use the narratives produced by the ISEAR questionnaire (Scherer et al., 1986) for first-person examples of particular emotions ("I felt angry when X and then Y happened") and extract sequences of subject-verb-object triples, which they then annotate for seven

basic emotions. Choi & Wiebe (2014) use WordNet to try to learn similar patterns, and Rupenhofer & Brandes (2015) annotate synsets in GermaNet based on an event decomposition framework. Russo et al. (2015) proposed a shared task for recognition of a set of pleasant and unpleasant events from a clinical framework for well-being (MacPhillamy and Lewinsohn, 1982). Work on AFINN, SentiWordNet and the Connotation Lexicon also aim to refine existing sentiment resources to capture more subtle notions of sentiment (Feng et al., 2013; Kang et al., 2014; Baccianella et al., 2010; Nielsen, 2011).

Here we report an exploratory study where we synthesize theoretical constructs associated with well-being and happiness from different sources. We then develop several methods for characterizing events in terms of these theories. We examine the extent to which different theoretical accounts can explain the variance in the happiness scores in ECHO. We show that each theory explains a part of the variance, but that our event characterizations need to be more fine-grained. We show that several recurrent event types which affect people's feelings of well-being, such as OBLIGATION and INCOMPETENCE, are not captured in current lexical or semantic resources.

2 Background and Motivation

ECHO is designed to encourage users to react to daily events as well as to periodically reflect on past events (Isaacs et al., 2013). Figure 2 depicts the user interface, showing a RECORDING from today, as well as prompts to reflect on events from the past. ECHO has been deployed with 134 users, in three different experiments on well-being (Konrad et al., 2016b,a). The total corpus consists of 10354 posts, where 7573 are RECORDINGS and 2781 are REFLECTIONS. While the corpus could be considered relatively small, these posts provide a window onto users' private thoughts as opposed to what users are willing to make public on social media. In addtion, the annotations for happiness are provided by the user, the first-person experiencer, and not by a third party.

Our aim is to explain users' emotional reactions to different categories of events mentioned in ECHO posts, linking the user reactions directly to theories of well-being as exemplified in Table 1.

Influential accounts such as Appraisal Theory (Scherer et al., 2001, 1986; Ortony et al., 1990)

Row #	Source	Subtype	Affect	Example
1	**Goals**	Achieved	POS	I applied to an scholarship got a large chunk of my reading done and got started cramming for next test .
2		Thwarted	NEG	Wasn't able to get back in time for my class section .
3	**Eudaimonics**	Autonomy	POS	Good day at work had the right support and students were listening and behaving which was awesome.
4		Lack-Autonomy	NEG	Long list of things to do before going out tonight.
5		Competence	POS	After working hard and spending so many countless hours, I finally finished my project for my psych class !
6		Incompetence	NEG	My midterm was really long and I didn't finish.
7		Connection	POS	Having a nice time with my parents watching the Opening Winter Olympic Ceremony.
8		Lack or Neg-Connection	NEG	My friend needs a bone marrow biopsy and chemo.
9	**Hedonics**	Savouring	POS	I love home cooking! Especially if it's Italian.
		Savouring	NEG	The bus was rather packed and had a few people bump into me from where I was sitting.

Table 1: Examples of Theoretical Categories and Instantiations in ECHO

Figure 2: Screenshot of the Echo Interface

argue that success or failure in personal goals directly mediates affect. Rows 1 and 2 in Table 1. Such mediation arises because emotions have an important adaptive signaling function that serves to motivate future behaviors in relation to those goals. Row 1 provides a description from ECHO of successfully achieving goals. Appraisal theory posits that goal achievement promotes positive affect, which then serves to reinforce the relevant behavior. Row 2 provides an example of failing to achieve an important personal goal, which

is posited to promote negative affect, motivating people to modify current behaviors to change that negative outcome.

There are significant critiques of the adaptive goal-based account espoused in Appraisal theory. Appraisal theory focuses on short-term personal goals, but Eudaimonic psychologists instead focus on what determines long-term happiness. Eudaimonic theorists suggest that certain fundamental psychological needs have to be satisfied for people to experience sustained positive long-term emotions. Self-determination theory argues that there are 3 basic psychological needs: AUTONOMY, COMPETENCE and CONNECTION (Deci and Ryan, 2010; Ryan and Deci, 2000; Bandura, 1977). We add these to our inventory in Table 1 in Rows 3 to 8. According to self-determination theory, satisfaction of these basic needs results in positive emotions. Row 3 describes a good day at work. Row 5 describes feeling competent because hard work led to an achievement, and Row 7 describes feeling connected with family. On the other hand, if these basic needs are not satisfied, then negative emotions will regularly arise. For example, obligations to do things one does not feel like doing (Row 4), or a job that does not engage personal decision making or involvement (lack of autonomy) can make one feel unhappy. Similarly, people may feel unhappy due to an experience where the demands of the situation outstrip one's basic abilities, such as doing poorly on a test (lack of competence), as in Row 6. In addition, bad things happening to friends (Row 8) as well as separation from family or friends often reduces happiness (lack of connection).

In addition, there is strong evidence from SAVOURING theory (Jose et al., 2012; Bryant et al., 2011) arguing that people often experience highly positive or negative emotions arising from situations that aren't directly goal-related, and that relate more directly to basic drives (Maslow, 1943; Elson, 2012). For example, experiences such as eating, experiencing nature, sex and physical exercise tend to engender positive emotions, whereas pain, discomfort and inactivity have the opposite effects, and these are documented in results from happiness surveys (Kahneman et al., 2004; Seligman et al., 2006). Thus while experiences such as eating may serve the survival goal of preventing starvation, avoiding starvation is unlikely to be a direct personal goal every time we eat, suggesting that such experiences are not explained by Appraisal theory. Similar arguments have been made by Lewinsohn and colleagues who have shown that encouraging people to engage in certain simple activities (shopping, mowing the lawn, driving, personal hygiene) have quite predictable effects on mood without engaging significant personal goals (MacPhillamy and Lewinsohn, 1982; Lewinsohn et al., 1985; Lewinsohn and Amenson, 1978).

3 Empirical Approach

Dataset	Pos	Neg	Total
Train	4743	3180	7923
Test	810	515	1325

Table 2: Number of Sentences for Train and Test

We start with the 10354 posts from the ECHO corpus and map happiness scores between [1, 4] to negative, and scores between [6, 9] to positive. For posts labelled 5 by the experiencer, we categorize it as negative if its REFLECTION score decreases to lower than 5, and positive if its REFLECTION score increases. We label the rest of the 5s as neutral, and leave them aside. We then have 5997 positive posts and 3573 negative posts. We randomly sample 2868 posts as training data, and 478 as test data. We keep the rest of the 6224 posts untouched for future work. Then we split the posts into sentences. Table 2 shows the splits for each class.

We first test the separability of the positive and negative sentences with an SVM classifier from Weka 3.8, using as baselines only unigrams and LIWC (Pennebaker et al., 2001) as features. Results for these baseline classifiers are in Table 3,

Features	Metric	Pos	Neg	All
UniGram	Prec	0.75	0.66	0.72
	Rec	0.81	0.59	0.72
	F1	0.78	0.62	0.72
LIWC	Prec	0.72	0.72	0.72
	Rec	0.89	0.45	0.72
	F1	0.80	0.55	0.70

Table 3: Weighted Metrics for SVM on Test

Unigram	LIWC
fun	affect,posemo,leisure
good	affect,posemo,drives,reward
we	we,social,drives,affiliation
lunch	bio,ingest
glad	affect,posemo
want	cogproc,discrep
why	interrog,cogproc,cause
need	cogproc,discrep
no	negate
not	negate,cogproc,differ

Table 4: The most informative UniGram features weighted by Information Gain

LIWC	Words
negemo	stress*, sad, sick, hate
posemo	fun, well, great, love
negate	dont, didnt, no, cant, havent
anger	hate, frustrat*, annoying
i	i, my, me, im, myself
differ	but, not, really, didnt
leisure	fun, game*, relax*, family
discrep	want, need, would, should
sad	sad, miss, hurt*, missed
risk	stop, problem*, avoid*
anx	stress*, nervous, worried
ingest	food*, dinner*, lunch*
body	sleep, slept, stomach*
insight	feel, know, think, found
affiliat	we, friends, friend, love
reward	good, got, get, great
feel	feel, feeling, felt, hard
family	family, mom, sister*, dad
we	we, our, us, weve, lets

Table 5: The most informative LIWC features ranked by Information Gain.

illustrating that the positive and negative classes can be separated with F1 above .70, and that both unigrams and LIWC perform worse on the negative class.

However, as discussed above, the word level representations of the features in the baselines do not help us with our goal to understand how linguistic descriptions of events that affect well-being map onto theoretical constructs. Table 4 and Table 5 provide the most informative UniGrams

Well-Being	Frames	Example Lexical Units
Goal	Desiring, Intentionally_Act, Purpose	want, feel like, hope, wanted, wish, do, did, done, doing, does, plan, purpose, in order, intention, goals
Autonomy & Obligation	Being_obligated, Required_event, Avoiding, Inhibit_movement, Have_as_requirement, Complaining	complain, grumble, complaints, have to, had to, should, having to, need, get to, had to, have to, got to, should, avoid , ducking, take, need, needed, requires
Competence	Activity_done_state, Attempt, Capability, Bungling, Difficulty, Practice, Activity_finish, Accomplishment	finished, trying, try, tried, effort, attempt, efforts, can, could, exercise, practice, rehearsal, exercising, able, ability, unable, messed up; ruined; screwed up , ruin, hard, difficult, easy, tough, easier challenging, impossible, a breeze, hardest, finish, finishing, completed, accomplished, achieve
Connection & Lack-of Connection	Death, Forming_relationships, Social_event, Kinship, People, People_by_residence, Telling, Communication_response	birthday, married, divorce, befriend, dinner, social, party, picnic, mom, family, parents, sister, cousin, told, tell, informed, people, girl, man, roommate, reply, answers, answer, reacted
Savouring	Emotions_of_mental_activity, Feeling, Annoyance, Desirability, Food, Chemical-sense description, Ambient_temperature, Emotions-by-stimulus, Stimulus_focus, Intoxicants, Communication_noise, Experiencer_Focus, Perception_experience, Biological_urge, Death	enjoyed, like, hate, glad, annoyed, cry, yelled, whooped, honked, irritated, feel, feeling, yummy, alcohol, weed, drugs, dope, see, felt, seeing, hear, experience, senses, experiences, taste, feel, delicious, tasty, sweet, food, coffee, bread, cheese, good, bad, great, better, best, horrible, worst wonderful, weird, nice, relaxing, annoying, interesting, sad, weird enjoyable, comforting, entertaining, unpleasant, hilarious, rest, relaxation, exhilarating, tiring, nicer, disturbing, disappointing, embarrassing, irritating, upsetting, heartbreaking, consoling, tedious, traumatic, chilling, calming, frightening touching, pleasure, satisfying, fascinating, tired, exhausted, sleepy, hungry, nauseated, horny

Table 6: Frame Categories and Associated Well-Being Classes.

and LIWC categories. We cannot recommend to an ECHO user that they should for example, try to use the word *why* less (Row 7) because it is correlated with negative feelings, or try to use less negation (Rows 9 and 10). It is difficult to associate these features with well-being classes. Even in cases where the words seem to be strongly related to a well-being category, a single word typically fails to provide enough information, e.g., "it was **fun** talking to him" and "worked on a **fun** project" belong to different well-being classes. Moreover, the mapping of LIWC categories to words are many-to-many, e.g. the "discrep" category contains words related to both Goals and Autonomy. We posit that we need compositional semantic features to ground our a Well-Being classification of events.

We thus explore two different methods for mapping these well-being event categories into lexical descriptions, one of which is top-down and the other which is bottom-up. Our top-down method is based on mapping general event types from FrameNet to the theoretical categories enumerated in Table 1. We take frame specific features for each theoretical category from the lexical units for each frame. For example, GOALS are often dis-

cussed in terms of specific frames from the Desiring and the Intentionally_act classes, as shown in the first two rows of Table 6.

We show that FrameNet features do provide an interesting level of generalization but much of the compositional semantics of events is still missing from this characterization (Section 4). Thus, our bottom-up method applies the AutoSlog linguistic-pattern learner to induce lexically-grounded predicate patterns from the ECHO data (Section 5). We show how many light verbs acquire a specific semantics with their arguments, and how common events like "Talking" are separated into positive and negative events depending on whether they are "Talking about" or "Talking with".

4 Frames and Well-Being

Table 6 provides our posited mapping from frame categories to the appraisal category of GOALS as well as to the eudaimonic categories of AUTONOMY, COMPETENCE and CONNECTION, and to the hedonic category of SAVOURING. To develop features related to these frame categories, we apply SEMAFOR (Das et al., 2013) to label the ECHO posts with their corresponding frames using

FrameNet 1.5 (Baker et al., 2015; Baker, 2014). We partition frame features into subsets corresponding to the different theoretical constructs as defined in Table 6. We acknowledge that our mapping may not be perfect, and that some frames could conceivably be categorized as both goal related and eudaimonic.

Features	Metric	Pos	Neg	All
GOALS	Prec	0.62	0.49	0.57
	Rec	0.94	0.09	0.61
	F1	0.75	0.15	0.51
EUDAIMONIC	Prec	0.63	0.58	0.61
	Rec	0.93	0.16	0.63
	F1	0.75	0.25	0.56
SAVOURING	Prec	0.61	0.44	0.55
	Rec	0.97	0.04	0.61
	F1	0.75	0.08	0.49
ALL FRAMES	Prec	0.69	0.74	0.71
	Rec	0.91	0.38	0.70
	F1	0.78	0.50	0.67

Table 7: Coverage of Different Theoretical Categories.

We train an SVM with each feature subset, and evaluate the models on our test set, with results in Table 7. The general ALL FRAME feature is also listed for comparison. The .67 F1 of FRAME is slightly lower than LIWC in Table 3, but in our view, more interpretable. In addition, the average count of FRAME features per sentence is an order of magnitude less than LIWC features (hence, much less than unigram features), suggesting the targeted power of these features. See Table 8. We posit that FRAMES are thus more discriminative than LIWC for well-being classes, and that FRAME features are more naturally categorized into well-being categories at a semantic level.

Features	Dataset	Pos	Neg	Total
UniGram	Train	8.5	9.9	9.1
	Test	8.1	9.8	8.7
LIWC	Train	25.4	31.4	27.8
	Test	23.8	30.6	26.4
ALL FRAMES	Train	2.7	5.2	3.7
	Test	3.3	4.0	3.6

Table 8: Average Feature Counts for Sentence

The Goals section of Table 7 shows that Appraisal theory does well at predicting positive events, but performs poorly for negative events, primarily due to low recall. All features achieve

Features	Metric	Pos	Neg	All
AUTONOMY	Prec	0.0	0.39	0.15
	Rec	0.0	1.0	0..39
	F1	0.0	.56	0.22
COMPETENCE	Prec	0.56	0.58	0.60
	Rec	0.98	0.04	0.61
	F1	0.76	0.07	0.49
CONNECTION	Prec	0.62	0.58	0.60
	Rec	0.97	0.06	0.62
	F1	0.76	0.11	0.49

Table 9: Results for Individual Eudaimonic Categories.

good F1 for the positive class, but not the negative class. This is consistent with the results in Table 3.

The EUDAIMONIC features include Autonomy & Obligation, Competence and Connection. The SVM trained with just eudaimonic features produces the highest F1 score for the negative class, highlighting the role of eudaimonic related events in negative well-being. See Table 7. The results for an breaking eudaimonic into its constituent categories is in Table 9. The results show that most of our autonomy categories are related to negative autonomy, to obligations that cause feelings of negative well-being. On the other hand, the results indicate that competence and connection play a large role in positive well-being.

The top 25 most informative frame features are illustrated in Table 10 (out of 639 instantiated in ECHO). These illustrate general events for well-being, but compositional differences, such as "spending my nights by the side of my textbook" and "spending my nights with friends" are not captured. The first "spend (time)" evokes the theoretical construct of obligation, while "spend (time with)" is related to connection.

5 Linguistic Pattern Learning

We also apply Autoslog-TS, a weakly supervised linguistic-pattern learner as a way of learning some compositional patterns. Autoslog only requires training documents labeled broadly into our two classes of POSITIVE or NEGATIVE. The learner uses a set of syntactic templates to define different types of linguistic expressions. In general, this method tends to produce high precision (and potentially low recall) markers of the particular classes that can seed further hypothesizing.

The left-hand side of Table 11 lists example pattern template and the right-hand side illustrates

Well-Being	Frame	Affect	Example
GOALS	Desiring	POS	I think it went well and I **hope** I did a good job.
	Intentionally_act	NEG	My midterm was really long and I **didn't** finish.
AUTONOMY	Being_obligated	NEG	I'm mad that I **had to** drive all the way to Fresno.
	Required_event	NEG	I **need to** stay awake and listen, but it 's hard.
COMPETENCE	Capability	POS	I feel so empowering whenever I'm **able to** help others.
	Attempt	NEG	**Tried to** chat with some people online, did n't work out.
CONNECTION	Kinship	POS	My **mom** and I hung out and walked around for 6 hours .
	Telling	NEG	I wonder how much they will **tell** me my teeth are bad today.
SAVOURING	Chemical-sense_description	POS	**Yummy** burgers and sides.
	Food	POS	Made homemade ice cream with my husband:...**cookie dough**

Table 10: Top Frame Categories and Associated Well-Being Classes.

a specific lexico-syntactic pattern (**in bold**) that represents an instantiation of each general pattern template for learning well-being patterns in our data.[2]

In order to enable selection of particular patterns, AutoSlog-TS computes statistics on the strength of association of each pattern with each class, i.e. P(POSITIVE $| p$) and P(NEGATIVE $| p$), along with the pattern's overall frequency. We define two tuning parameters for each class: θ_f, the frequency with which a pattern occurs, θ_p, the probability with which a pattern is associated with the given class. AutoSlog lets us systematically explore tradeoffs with precision and recall. Here we select θ_f and θ_p to optimize F1 on our test set. For more detail, see (Riloff, 1996; Oraby et al., 2015).

Our primary interest here is Autoslog's ability to learn compositional patterns. Autoslog can, in principle, provide three kinds of information: i) it can provide supplement the lexical units for a given frame; ii) it can supplement the frames in a well-being category; and iii) it can reveal reliable markers of mood that well-being categories do not capture. Because our interest in frames is ultimately as a way of relating well-being categories with linguistic signals, we will not distinguish (i) and (ii) here.

Here we discuss all patterns with a $\theta_p > .7$ Several lexicosyntactic patterns fit within our well-being categories but are not captured by frames, while as expected there are overlaps between FrameNet and Autoslog as well. Examples are listed in Table 12. One large class includes straightforward lexical patterns: FINISHED, FIN-

ISH, and FINALLY which we associate with feelings of comptence. Verbal patterns with EAT and ATE indicate savouring, with NOT_EAT reliably marking negative sentences. The frames also show many specific types of food (cake), and we use a comprehensive list from DBpedia (Lehmann et al., 2014) to collapse all these to the general type FOOD, allowing us to develop patterns such as MADE_FOOD.

Autoslog also discovers many patterns syntactically linking content (nouns and verbs) and function words (e.g., prepositions and light verbs). It thus furnishes a ready source for multi-word, partially compositional expressions of positivity or negativity. In what follows, we provide some examples (note that in the patterns below, expressions in brackets are used to indicate expressions not part of the pattern that correlate with it in the data).

There are 262 positive patterns of the form Verb/Noun + "with", e.g. TALKED_WITH, DINNER_WITH, BREAKFAST_WITH, STUDYING_WITH, PLAYED_WITH, TIME_WITH, MET_WITH, SHOPPING_WITH, COFFEE_WITH, all of which describe activities that involve connection. There are also 100 negative patterns of this form, which are much more heterogenous, involving both negative social experiences (ARGUMENT_WITH, DRAMA_WITH, INFURIATED_WITH, FIGHT_WITH), but also various problematic events (STRESSED_WITH, DIFFICULTIES_WITH, DISSATISFIED_WITH) and instruments for negative events (STOP_WITH, POISONING_WITH). Moreover, while the positive patterns cover 523 sentences in the data, the negative patterns cover only 133.

There are 62 patterns involving the string

---

[2]The examples are shown as general expressions for readability, but the actual patterns must match the syntactic constraints associated with the pattern template.

	Pattern Template	Example Instantiations
1	<subj> PassVP	**<I> am so relaxed** after getting to sleep in and rest all morning.
2	<subj> ActVP	When it does happen, **<I> feel energized** because IT IS a special experience to me.
3	<subj> ActVP Dobj	**<I> enjoy his efforts** lately to make me happier.
4	<subj> ActInfVP	Found some some stuff but I AM not sure if **<I> want to keep** them.
5	<subj> PassInfVP	2 of **<my housemates> were supposed to clean** on Tuesday and they still haven't.
6	<subj> AuxVP Dobj	We ate and **<We> had a glass of my favorite wine.**
7	<subj> AuxVP Adj	**<All of the colors> are so much more vibrant.**
8	ActVP <dobj>	Cannot wait to study while **eating <this>.**
9	InfVP <dobj>	Just realized I **forgot to turn in <my homework>.**
10	ActInfVP <dobj>	I really **need to start <my hw>** sooner...
11	Subj AuxVP <dobj>	IT IS the Super Bowl today and **THERE IS <a party>** at my house.
12	NP Prep <np>	**Driving in <the rain>** is scary.
13	ActVP Prep <np>	Almost as if I forgot something terribly important or I **messed up <something>** important in my life.
14	PassVP Prep <np>	And I feel like I did but just this once I messed up and I might **be punished for <it>.**
15	InfVP Prep <np>	Felt amazing to be **done with <finals>**!
16	<possessive> NP	**<Her> attitude** is not working anymore.

Table 11: AutoSlog-TS Templates and Example Instantiations

"talk", 32 positive (71 items) and 30 negative (66 items). The positive ones strongly indicate connection (e.g., TALK_WITH, HAVE_TALK, REMEMBER_[TO]_TALK, GOT_[TO]_TALK, TALK_THROUGH). In contrast, the negative index either the obligation to talk (e.g., TRYING_TALK, NEED_TALK, HAVE_[TO]_TALK) or a failure to talk (e.g., NOT_TALK_TO, NOT_WANT_TALK, STOP_TALKING).

There are 36 patterns with the string 'go', 12 positive (16 items) and 24 negative (40 items). There are 34 patterns involving the past tense form "went", which reverses the polarity to 25 positive patterns (273 items) and 9 negative (9 items). Across the two versions of the lemma, the positive patterns provide several expressions for savouring (WENT/GO_ON/FOR [a walk, a hike, a ride], WENT/GO_SHOPPING/SWIMMING, WENT/GO_TO [the mall, a movie]). For the negative, the predominance of 'go' comes from the fact that they are largely negated (NOT_GO_TO [the movies]) or in infinitive contexts that suggest obligation ([HAVE TO]_GO_TO [class], [HAVE TO]_GO_WORK). Similarly, the positive class contains 9 patterns with 'bought' and 1 with 'buy' (ENTICED_[TO]_BUY) and the negative class has 6 patterns with 'bought' and 16 with 'buy', all emphasizing buying necessities (BUY_GROCERIES/TICKET, NEED/WANT_BUY, NOT_BUY) Thus, even though these expressions all involve the same verbs and prepositions, the surrounding environments, as reflected in the form of the verb, split between positive and negative sentence classes.

There are 73 bigram patterns of the form NEW_X, 56 positive (83 items) and 17 negative (21 items). In general, the positive ones describe new objects – SHIRT, SHEETS, COMPUTER, CLOTHES, TEA – and acquaintances (NEW_FRIEND), thus encompassing both Connection and possibly Savouring. In contrast, the negative patterns describe changes to routines – HABITS, school QUARTER, PROFESSOR, LIVING [conditions], or SCHEDULE – which are likely to engender a sense of instability, and hence be Eudaimonically negative.

Thus, these patterns illustrate that Autoslog can serve as a high-precision method of building additional patterns – especially compositional ones – for a given well-being category.

6 Conclusions and Future Work

In this paper, we have advanced a synthetic categorization of the sources for well-being and happiness. We have used a corpus of private microblogs from the ECHO application to explore how well we can map linguistic expressions of well-being to this classification. We have shown that

Prob.	Freq.	Pattern and Text Match	Sample Post
Positive Example Patterns			
1.00	11	ActVp Prep <NP> (WENT ON)	I just **went on** a hike this is the best thing ever.
1.00	7	<subj> ActVP Dobj (MADE FOOD)	**Made a German pancake** for breakfast.
1.00	7	NP Prep <np> (CATCHING WITH)	**Catching up with** old friends!
1.00	7	ActVP <dobj> (USED)	**Used** the Laurel's Kitchen Bread Book recipe.
1.00	6	ActVP Prep <np> (GOT OFF)	**Got off** work.
1.00	4	NP Prep <np> (TALK WITH)	Having a really nice **talk with** my aunt.
0.95	18	ActVP <dobj> (FINISHED)	**Finished** my paper.
0.78	39	ActVP <dobj> (TOOK)	**Took** a walk after class and truly enjoyed the outdoors!
0.78	25	<subj> ActVP (ATE)	We **ate** and had a glass of my favorite wine.
0.73	11	InfVP Prep <np> (SPEND WITH)	Happy to simply **spend time with** friends.
Negative Example Patterns			
1.00	9	InfVP <dobj> (AVOID)	Better buy ... in smaller packaging to **avoid** wasting again.
1.00	8	ActVP <dobj> (USE)	All she did was **use** water and wipe a few corners.
1.00	7	InfVP <dobj> (STOP)	I need to **stop** smoking.
1.00	6	<subj> ActVP Prep <np> (NOT TALK TO)	And now my bf is busy and **can't talk to** me.
1.00	5	<subj> ActVP Dobj (TEXTED ME)	He **texted me** finally but then he randomly stopped.
1.00	5	<subj> ActVP (NOT SLEEP)	Have to get up early and I **can't sleep**.
1.00	4	ActVP <dobj> (NOT FIND)	I **did not find** the time to finish my homework.
0.82	14	<subj> ActVP (REALIZED)	I JUST **realized** that I have to go tomorrow.
0.81	13	<subj> ActVP (TAKE)	Since I **take** around 35 minutes to get ready, I missed ...
0.80	20	ActVP <dobj> (TOLD)	**Told** my mom about my grades.

Table 12: Examples of Characteristic ECHO Patterns using AutoSlog-TS Templates

FrameNet provides useful generalizations, while the linguistic pattern learner AutoSlog illustrates the details and challenges of the compositional nature of user's descriptions of their daily experiences. Moreover, we have demonstrated that, independently, each of these methods can produce performance similar to that of conventional lexical methods with a feature space that is smaller, and, in the case of FrameNet features, psychologically grounded. Our Autoslog exploration moreover reveals a way of exploring the space of patterns that our FrameNet mapping has missed. In future work, we aim to automatically combine these two methods and bring the Autoslog patterns under the well-being categorization we have advocated here. We also plan to investigate new models with the untouched 6224 Echo posts, as well as larger public corpus like LiveJournal.

In addition, we plan to explore the source of the fact that there are more positive patterns (both as types and the tokens they capture) than the negative ones, which directly relates to the lower Neg recall for all classifiers we tested. While we could not find any clear reason in our examination of the data, this asymmetry may indicate that markers of negativity are more syntactically distributed than our current list of patterns looks for, or perhaps less linguistically reliable.

Acknowledgments

This research was partially supported by NSF Robust Intelligence #IIS-1302668-002 and NSF HCC #IIS-1321102.

References

Stefano Baccianella, Andrea Esuli, and Fabrizio Sebastiani. 2010. Sentiwordnet 3.0: An enhanced lexical resource for sentiment analysis and opinion mining. In *LREC*. volume 10, pages 2200–2204.

Colin Baker, Nathan Schneider, Miriam R L Petruck, and Michael Ellsworth. 2015. Getting the roles right: Using framenet in nlp. In *Proceedings of the 2015 Conference of the North American Chapter of the Association for Computational Linguistics: Tutorial Abstracts*. Association for Computational Linguistics, Denver, Colorado, pages 10–12. http://www.aclweb.org/anthology/N15-4006.

Collin Baker. 2014. Framenet: A knowledge base for natural language processing. In *Proceedings of Frame Semantics in NLP: A Workshop in Honor of Chuck Fillmore (1929-2014)*. Association for Computational Linguistics, Baltimore, MD, USA, pages 1–5.

http://www.aclweb.org/anthology/W/W14/W14-3001.

Alexandra Balahur, Jesus M. Hermida, and Andres Montoyo. 2012. Building and exploiting emotinet, a knowledge base for emotion detection based on the appraisal theory model. *IEEE Trans. Affect. Comput.* 3(1):88–101.

A. Bandura. 1977. Self-efficacy: toward a unifying theory of behavioral change. *Psychological review* 84(2):191.

Fred B Bryant, Erica D Chadwick, and Katharina Kluwe. 2011. Understanding the processes that regulate positive emotional experience: Unsolved problems and future directions for theory and research on savoring. *International Journal of Wellbeing* 1(1).

Yoonjung Choi and Janyce Wiebe. 2014. +/-effectwordnet: Sense-level lexicon acquisition for opinion inference. In *EMNLP*. pages 1181–1191.

Dipanjan Das, Desai Chen, André F. T. Martins, Nathan Schneider, and Noah A. Smith. 2013. Frame-semantic parsing. *Computational Linguistics* XX(YY):WW–ZZ.

Edward L Deci and Richard M Ryan. 2010. *Self-determination*. Wiley Online Library.

Lingjia Deng, Yoonjung Choi, and Janyce Wiebe. 2013. Benefactive/malefactive event and writer attitude annotation. In *ACL*. pages 120–125.

Lingjia Deng and Janyce Wiebe. 2014. Sentiment propagation via implicature constraints. In *EACL*. pages 377–385.

Haibo Ding and Ellen Riloff. 2016. Acquiring knowledge of affective events from blogs using label propagation. In *AAAI*.

David K. Elson. 2012. *Modeling Narrative Discourse*. Ph.D. thesis, Columbia University, New York City.

Song Feng, Jun Seok Kang, Polina Kuznetsova, and Yejin Choi. 2013. Connotation lexicon: A dash of sentiment beneath the surface meaning. In *Association for Computational Linguistics (ACL)*.

Marie JC Forgeard, Eranda Jayawickreme, Margaret L Kern, and Martin EP Seligman. 2011. Doing the right thing: Measuring wellbeing for public policy. *International Journal of Wellbeing* 1(1).

Amit Goyal and Ellen Riloff. 2013. A computational model for plot units. *Computational Intelligence* 29(3):466–488.

Ellen Isaacs, Artie Konrad, Alan Walendowski, Thomas Lennig, Victoria Hollis, and Steve Whittaker. 2013. Echoes from the past: how technology mediated reflection improves well-being. In *Proceedings of the SIGCHI Conference on Human Factors in Computing Systems*. ACM, pages 1071–1080.

Paul E Jose, Bee T Lim, and Fred B Bryant. 2012. Does savoring increase happiness? a daily diary study. *The Journal of Positive Psychology* 7(3):176–187.

Daniel Kahneman. 1999. Objective happiness. *Well-being: The foundations of hedonic psychology* 3:25.

Daniel Kahneman, Alan B Krueger, David A Schkade, Norbert Schwarz, and Arthur A Stone. 2004. A survey method for characterizing daily life experience: The day reconstruction method. *Science* 306(5702):1776–1780.

Jun Seok Kang, Song Feng, Leman Akoglu, and Yejin Choi. 2014. Connotationwordnet: Learning connotation over the word+sense network. In *Proceedings of the 52nd Annual Meeting of the Association for Computational Linguistics (Volume 1: Long Papers)*. Association for Computational Linguistics, Baltimore, Maryland, pages 1544–1554. http://www.aclweb.org/anthology/P14-1145.

Fazel Keshtkar and Diana Inkpen. 2009. Using sentiment orientation features for mood classification in blogs. In *Natural Language Processing and Knowledge Engineering, 2009. NLP-KE 2009. International Conference on*. IEEE, pages 1–6.

Artie Konrad, Victoria Bellotti, Nicole Crenshaw, Simon Tucker, Les Nelson, Honglu Du, Peter Pirolli, and Steve Whittaker. 2015. Finding the adaptive sweet spot: Balancing compliance and achievement in automated stress reduction. In *Proceedings of the 33rd Annual ACM Conference on Human Factors in Computing Systems*. ACM, pages 3829–3838.

Artie Konrad, Ellen Isaacs, and Steve Whittaker. 2016a. Technology-mediated memory: Is technology altering our memories and interfering with well-being? *ACM Transactions on Computer-Human Interaction (TOCHI)* 23(4):23.

Artie Konrad, Simon Tucker, John Crane, and Steve Whittaker. 2016b. Technology and reflection: Mood and memory mechanisms for well-being. *Psychology of well-being* 6(1):1–24.

Jens Lehmann, Robert Isele, Max Jakob, Anja Jentzsch, Dimitris Kontokostas, Pablo Mendes, Sebastian Hellmann, Mohamed Morsey, Patrick van Kleef, Sören Auer, and Chris Bizer. 2014. DBpedia - a large-scale, multilingual knowledge base extracted from wikipedia. *Semantic Web Journal* .

Peter M Lewinsohn and Christopher S Amenson. 1978. Some relations between pleasant and unpleasant mood-related events and depression. *Journal of abnormal psychology* 87(6):644.

Peter M Lewinsohn, Robin M Mermelstein, Carolyn Alexander, and Douglas J MacPhillamy. 1985. The unpleasant events schedule: A scale for the measurement of aversive events. *Journal of Clinical Psychology* 41(4):483–498.

Sonja Lyubomirsky, Laura King, and Ed Diener. 2005. The benefits of frequent positive affect: Does happiness lead to success? *Psychological bulletin* 131(6):803.

Douglas J MacPhillamy and Peter M Lewinsohn. 1982. The pleasant events schedule: Studies on reliability, validity, and scale intercorrelation. *Journal of Consulting and Clinical Psychology* 50(3):363–380.

Abraham Harold Maslow. 1943. A theory of human motivation. *Psychological review* 50(4):370.

Rada Mihalcea and Hugo Liu. 2006. A corpus-based approach to finding happiness. In *AAAI Spring Symposium: Computational Approaches to Analyzing Weblogs*. pages 139–144.

Gilad Mishne. 2005. Experiments with mood classification in blog posts. In *Proceedings of ACM SIGIR 2005 workshop on stylistic analysis of text for information access*. volume 19, pages 321–327.

Finn Årup Nielsen. 2011. A new anew: Evaluation of a word list for sentiment analysis in microblogs. *arXiv preprint arXiv:1103.2903* .

Shereen Oraby, Lena Reed, Ryan Compton, Ellen Riloff, Marilyn Walker, and Steve Whittaker. 2015. And thats a fact: Distinguishing factual and emotional argumentation in online dialogue. *NAACL HLT 2015* page 116.

Andrew Ortony, Gerald L Clore, and Allan Collins. 1990. *The cognitive structure of emotions*. Cambridge university press.

J. W. Pennebaker, M. E. Francis, and R. J. Booth. 2001. *LIWC: Linguistic Inquiry and Word Count*.

Lena Reed, Jiaqi Wu, Shereen Oraby, Pranav Anand, and Marilyn Walker. 2017. Learning lexico-functional patterns for first-person affect. In *Proceedings of the 55th Annual Meeting of the Association for Computational Linguistics*.

Kevin Reschke and Pranav Anand. 2011. Extracting contextual evaluativity. In *Proceedings of the Ninth International Conference on Computational Semantics*. Association for Computational Linguistics, pages 370–374.

Ellen Riloff. 1996. Automatically generating extraction patterns from untagged text. In *Proceedings of the national conference on artificial intelligence*. pages 1044–1049.

Josef Ruppenhofer and Jasper Brandes. 2015. Extending effect annotation with lexical decomposition. In *6TH WORKSHOP ON COMPUTATIONAL APPROACHES TO SUBJECTIVITY, SENTIMENT AND SOCIAL MEDIA ANALYSIS WASSA 2015*. page 67.

Irene Russo, Tommaso Caselli, and Carlo Strapparava. 2015. Semeval-2015 task 9: Clipeval implicit polarity of events. In *Proceedings of the 9th International Workshop on Semantic Evaluation (SemEval 2015)*. Association for Computational Linguistics, Denver, Colorado, pages 443–450. http://www.aclweb.org/anthology/S15-2077.

R.M. Ryan and E.L. Deci. 2000. Self-determination theory and the facilitation of intrinsic motivation, social development, and well-being. *American psychologist* 55(1):68.

Klaus R Scherer, Angela Schorr, and Tom Johnstone. 2001. *Appraisal processes in emotion: Theory, methods, research*. Oxford University Press.

Klaus R Scherer, Harald G Wallbott, and Angela B Summerfield. 1986. *Experiencing emotion: A cross-cultural study*. Cambridge University Press.

H Andrew Schwartz, Maarten Sap, Margaret L Kern, Johannes C Eichstaedt, Adam Kapelner, Megha Agrawal, Eduardo Blanco, Lukasz Dziurzynski, Gregory Park, David Stillwell, et al. 2016. Predicting individual well-being through the language of social media. In *Pac Symp Biocomput*. volume 21, pages 516–527.

Martin EP Seligman, Tayyab Rashid, and Acacia C Parks. 2006. Positive psychotherapy. *American Psychologist* 61(8):774.

Forecasting Consumer Spending from Purchase Intentions Expressed on Social Media

Viktor Pekar and **Jane Binner**
Business School, University of Birmingham, Birmingham, UK
{v.pekar, j.m.binner}@bham.ac.uk

Abstract

Consumer spending is a vital macroeconomic indicator. In this paper we present a novel method for predicting future consumer spending from social media data. In contrast to previous work that largely relied on sentiment analysis, the proposed method models consumer spending from purchase intentions found on social media. Our experiments with time series analysis models and machine-learning regression models reveal utility of this data for making short-term forecasts of consumer spending: for three- and seven-day horizons, prediction variables derived from social media help to improve forecast accuracy by 11% to 18% for all the three models, in comparison to models that used only autoregressive predictors.

1 Introduction

Social media is increasingly reflecting many social phenomena that previously could be studied only with traditional surveying techniques such as telephone or face-to-face interviews. Recent research has demonstrated that it can be used to track the spread of epidemics (Culotta, 2010), monitor mass emergency situations (Nguyen et al., 2017), study political preferences during election campaigns (Tumasjan et al., 2010), predict product sales (Elshendy et al., 2017) and stock price changes (Si et al., 2014).

In this paper we examine the idea that social media can provide useful evidence about consumer confidence, a macroeconomic indicator describing the propensity of households to consume goods and services in the near future. Consumer confidence is one of the most crucial indicators of the health of an economy, as consumer spend-

ing constitutes the largest component of GDP in many developed countries. Government institutions and market research agencies compile their consumer confidence indices on a regular basis. Among the best-known ones are the Consumer Sentiment Index produced by University of Michigan for the US and GfK's Income Expectation and Willingness-to-buy indicators for the EU. These measures are obtained using traditional surveys, which have significant drawbacks: they are costly to conduct, based on low-frequency observations and published with substantial delays. Social media data hold the promise to overcome these drawbacks.

Previous research studied models of consumer spending trained on search engine data, based on the intuition that web searches for product names indicate intended purchases (Vosen and Schmidt, 2011; Scott and Varian, 2015; Wu and Brynjolfsson, 2015). Search engine data, however, do not capture the context of the purchase intention, such as the context available on social media in the form of extended coherent text, and thus are more likely to contain noise. A number of studies aimed to estimate a consumer confidence index from social media using sentiment analysis (O'Connor et al., 2010; Daas and Puts, 2014; Igboayaka, 2015). These methods derive a sentiment index from messages related to the economic outlook, which is compared with an official index to detect correlation or to train a model to predict it.

In contrast to this work, our method aims to model future consumer spending from purchase intentions expressed on social media. The method determines phrases referring to intended purchases and creates their condensed semantic representations, which are then used in a regression model alongside autoregressive predictors. Our experiments with time series analysis models (Seasonal Autoregressive Integrated Moving Average) and

Proceedings of the 8th Workshop on Computational Approaches to Subjectivity, Sentiment and Social Media Analysis, pages 92–101
Copenhagen, Denmark, September 7–11, 2017. ©2017 Association for Computational Linguistics

machine-learning regression models (AdaBoost and Gradient Boosting) demonstrate utility of this data for making short-term forecasts of consumer spending. We find that for three- and seven-day horizons the semantic predictors help to improve forecast accuracy by 11% to 18% for all the three models.

The main novel contributions of this paper are (i) a prediction model that uses semantic information obtained from purchase intentions, which allows on the one hand, to abstract from specific lexical data, and on the other, reduce the complexity of the model; (ii) a study of optimal forecast horizons for the model that uses this information; (iii) an investigation of possibilities to incorporate semantic predictors with endogenous variables (i.e., lagged values of the consumer spending index) within the model.

The remainder of the paper is organized as follows. In the next section we review related work. The proposed method is described in Section 3. Section 4 details experimental setup. Results and their discussion are presented in Section 5. Section 6 concludes.

2 Related work

2.1 Sentiment analysis

A popular approach in previous work on modelling economic indicators from textual data has been to use automatically detected sentiment of documents. The study by O'Connor et al. (2010) predicts consumer confidence from sentiment found in Twitter posts that contain pre-defined keywords, such as "economy" or "job". Sentiment is assessed using a lexicon-based method and a daily sentiment index is constructed, which is then used as a predictor in an ordinary least-squares model of the ICS index. Daas and Putz (2014) take a similar approach, using a commercial sentiment analyser and a list of economy-related keywords, to study consumer confidence in Dutch social media. They find their sentiment measure to correlate and co-integrate with an official consumer index. Georgoula et al. (2015) use time-series analysis to study the relationship between Bitcoin prices, fundamental economic variables, and measurements of collective mood derived from Twitter. Using an SVM classifier trained on tweets mentioning Bitcoin, they obtain a sentiment measure which is used as a variable in an OLS and a VECM models. Souza et al. (2016) examine the relationship between Twitter sentiment, on the one hand, and the trade volume, returns, and volatility of selected stocks, on the other. Their method uses a domain-independent SVM classifier to construct a daily sentiment index, which is then used in a VAR framework along with the economic variables. Granger causality tests are used to identify causality links between these variables.

2.2 Lexical analysis

Sentiment analysis is known to be a difficult NLP problem, where accuracy varies greatly depending on domain customization. Therefore, methods that use lexical information instead seem to be an interesting alternative. Dergiades et al. (2015) examined raw counts of Twitter and Facebook posts containing "Grexit"-related words, detecting causality from them to changes in Greek government bonds for the same time period using Granger causality tests. Scott and Varian (2015) use search engine queries as predictors of Consumer Sentiment Index. To deal with the "fat regression" problem (the number of potential predictors is similar or even greater than the number of available observations), they introduce a Bayesian method to select predictor variables.

To deal with a large number of predictors derived from lexical data, various dimensionality reduction techniques have been proposed. Coussement and Van den Poel (2008) predict customer churn from the text of call centre emails. Creating classification features using Latent Semantic Indexing applied to the email corpus, they combined them with features traditionally used to predict customer churn (such as product usage data) in a maximum entropy classifier, and found that the former were helpful in identifying customers prone to churn. Rönnqvist and Sarlin (2015) analyse news articles to predict "bank distress" events, such as government interventions. Their approach constructs para2vec (Le and Mikolov, 2014) representations of news articles which are input into a neural network model to predict a distress score for a bank.

2.3 Combining sentiment and lexical data

Several papers used a combination of sentiment and lexical information in their models. Hansen and McMahon (2016) assess the effect of central bank communications on different market and real economic variables. From a corpus of central bank publications, they estimate an LDA model and manually select those topics that have to do with a discussion of economic outlook. A dictionary-based sentiment analysis is used to obtain a monthly sentiment index, which is input as a variable in a Factor-Augmented VAR framework. Archak et al. (2011) present a hedonic regression model of product sales that uses customer reviews of the products as input. The reviews are analysed to extract nouns as potential references to product features and adjectives related to the nouns as potential evaluative phrases. The noun-adjective co-occurrences are arranged into a matrix which is then transformed using a technique similar to ANOVA decomposition. The reduced dimensionality matrix is input as variables of a regression model, along with non-textual variables such as the price of the product. Si et al. (2014) use a combination of lexicon-based sentiment analysis and LDA topics extracted from Twitter posts containing a stock's ticker symbol, on which the stock's price is regressed using a VAR model.

3 Proposed method

Our method aims to predict an official consumer spending index from the mentions of purchase intentions. Specifically, we expect that the semantics of noun phrases that are stated as intended purchases will be predictive of the official index for a certain number of subsequent days. The method consists of the following steps. First, tweets mentioning a purchase intention are collected from Twitter API. Second, noun phrases referring to the objects of the intended purchases are extracted and their daily counts are obtained to create a noun-by-date matrix. In order to account for semantic similarities between the nouns, a word2vec model is used to create a semantic vector for each date. Finally, a regression model of the consumer index is trained that uses the semantic vectors as well as lagged values of the index. These steps are detailed in the following sections.

3.1 Detecting purchase intention

Prior work on recognizing intentions have used both rule-based (Hamroun et al., 2016) and machine learning approaches (Chen et al., 2013). In this paper we opt for a rule-based method, as it can ensure high precision, while recall is of a less concern considering large volumes of available data. To obtain tweets mentioning purchase intentions, we issue a set of queries to the Twitter Search

API, which are meant to capture common ways to express an intention to buy something. They are created from combinations of (1) first-person pronouns ("I" and "we"), (2) verbs denoting intentions ("will", "'ll", "be going to", "be looking to", "want to", "wanna", "gonna"), and (3) verbs denoting purchase ("buy", "shop for", "get oneself"), thus obtaining queries such as "I will buy" or "we are going to buy".

The text of each tweet is cleaned (any material outside of the grammatical text is removed) and processed with a part-of-speech tagger. PoS tag patterns are then applied to extract the head noun of the noun phrase following the purchase verb (e.g., "headphones" in "I am looking to buy new headphones"). After that, daily counts of the head nouns are calculated.

3.2 Semantic vectors

To represent the semantics of the nouns, we use the word2vec method (Mikolov et al., 2013) which has proven to produce accurate approximations of word meaning in different NLP tasks (Baroni et al., 2014). A word2vec model is a neural network that is trained to reconstruct the linguistic context of words. The model is built by taking a sequence of words as input and learning to predict the next word, using a feed-forward topology where a projection layer in the middle is taken to constitute a semantic vector for the word, after connection weights have been learned. The semantic vector is a fixed-length, real-valued pattern of activations reaching the projection layer. For each word, the input text originally has a dimensionality equal to the vocabulary size of the training corpus (typically millions of words), but the semantic modelling provides reduction to the size of the vector (typically several hundreds). The reduced dimensionality helps to reduce the complexity of the models, prevent overfitting, and is beneficial in computationally intensive classification and regression algorithms.

For each date, we map each noun that was observed on that day to a semantic vector, using word2vec vectors trained on a large corpus of Twitter posts. The semantic vectors of all the nouns for each day are then averaged to obtain a single vector. The components of the vectors will then be used as variables in regression models.

To allow for some time between the stated purchase intention and the actual purchase, we experiment with different numbers of days between the day on which intentions were registered and the day for which the value of the consumer spending index is predicted.

3.3 Combining endogenous and exogenous variables

Our method makes predictions based on endogenous variables (i.e., lagged values of the index itself) and exogenous variables (i.e., semantic vectors obtained from Twitter). Thus, given a target value of the consumer spending index y_t at day t, a lag p, a k-dimensional semantic vector, and allowing for s days between the day when purchase intentions were registered and the day for which spending was reported (i.e., day t), a training instance is composed of endogenous variables $y_{t-1}, y_{t-2}, ..., y_{t-p}$ and exogenous variables $x^1_{t-s}, x^2_{t-s}, ..., x^k_{t-s}$.

We implemented two ways to combine the two types of variables to obtain a prediction. The first is simple concatenation of the variables into one vector of predictors. The second involves first training separate regression models for the endogenous variables and semantic variables separately, and then using the predicted values of each to train a third model that outputs the final predicted value.

3.4 Regression methods

In our experiments we include the following regression methods[1].

SARIMA(X). The Seasonal Autoregressive Integrated Moving Average (SARIMA) is a variety of the general ARIMA model. ARIMA(p,d,q) is defined via terms p, d, and q, where p represents the number of time-lagged variables; d — the number of differences required to remove seasonality and make the forecast variable stationary; and q — the number of time-lagged error parameters to account for an observed moving average. The orders of p and q can be identified using an autocorrelation and a partial autocorrelation function, or using information criteria, such as Akaike IC, or estimated from a validation set. The degree of differencing can be determined using stationarity tests such as the Dickey-Fuller test. Given order values, coefficients of the model can be estimated by least square regression or maximum likelihood estimators.

SARIMA is formed by including additional seasonal terms: SARIMA(p, d, q)$(P, D, Q)_m$, where P, D, and Q are used to represent seasonal autoregressive model, the degree of seasonal differencing, and the seasonal moving average, correspondingly, while m stands for the length of the seasonal period. To identify the P, D, Q, and m terms, the autocorrelation and partial autocorrelation algorithms or information criteria can also be used.

SARIMAX is a SARIMA that allows for one or more exogenous variables to be included into the regression. We input the semantic vector as exogenous variables into SARIMAX.

AdaBoost Regression. AdaBoost (Freund and Schapire, 1996) is a machine-learning ensemble algorithm that uses the entire training data to successively train a series of weak learners, such as decision stumps. After one weak model is trained, the algorithm identifies the most difficult instances and computes their weights to exaggerate their effect on the training of the next model. The objective of this step is to "teach" the next model to correctly predict the test instances on which errors were made. Initially all instances have the same weight and hence have the same impact on training of the initial model. After each iteration, the weights of instances are adjusted, while the weights of instances with accurate predictions are decreased. Furthermore, each model is assigned a weight based on its overall accuracy. During the testing phase, the forecast values and the weights of the models are taken into account to produce a weighted average value.

Gradient Boosting Regression. Gradient Boosting (Friedman, 2001) is a gradient descent ensemble algorithm, which, similar to other boosting methods, operates by sequential training of weak models, which collectively would form a strong model. This is accomplished by training successive regression models on the residuals of the previous model, computed from errors it made. With each training round, Gradient Boosting improves the previous model by adding to it a new model that is trained only on the residuals, thus gradually fixing up errors made in the previous steps. To prevent overfitting, we additionally use an early stopping technique: the training of the model stops, if the validation loss has been increasing in four consecutive iterations.

During evaluation, we experimentally deter-

---

[1]We use the implementations in the `scikit-learn` and `statsmodels` packages.

mine parameters of AdaBoost and Gradient Boosting on a validation dataset using the grid search technique. The model with the best parameter configuration is then evaluated on the test set.

4 Experiment setup

4.1 Data

Consumer Spending Index. As the forecast variable in our model, we use the Gallup Consumer Spending Index (CSI) [2]. The index represents the average dollar amount Americans report spending on a daily basis. The survey is conducted using telephone interviews with approximately 1,500 national adults. Respondents are asked to reflect on the day prior to being surveyed and provide an estimate of how much money they spent on that day. The eventual index is presented as a 3-day and a 14-day rolling averages of these amounts. In our evaluation, we used the 3-day values of CSI, between October 1, 2015 and July 31, 2016, i.e. 297 days in total.

Twitter. For the same period, we collected Twitter posts that originate from the US and that express intentions to buy, obtaining the total of 68,730 messages. Counts of nouns referring to purchases were extracted and rolling averages for each noun for three-day periods were calculated. To eliminate noisy data, we selected the 1000 most common nouns to construct semantic vectors.

Semantic vectors. Considering the amount of available training instances, we use the 25-dimensional vectors pre-trained on a large corpus of Twitter posts from the GloVe project[3].

Train-validation-test split. The available data was divided into the training, validation and test parts, in proportion 60%-20%-20%. The CSI values and their split into the three parts are shown in Figure 1. Because we use seven-day lags to create endogenous variables, there are seven-day gaps between the train and validation sets as well as between the validation and test sets there are seven day gaps, to ensure that no training data is used for validation or testing.

4.2 Evaluation method

Once a model was trained on the training set and its parameters optimized on the validation set, it was evaluated on the test set using dynamic forecasting: given the first day t of the test set, and the forecast horizon h, the model predicted h days in the future, for each day from t_2 to t_h the values predicted by the model for previous days were input as endogenous variables. In the following, we report results for $h = 1$, 3 and 7.

As evaluation metric, we use the Root Mean Squared Error (RMSE):

$$RMSE = \sqrt{\frac{1}{T} \sum_{n=1}^{T} (y_n - \hat{y}_n)^2}$$

where y_n and $\hat{y}_n$ are the actual observation and the predicted value at day t_n, and T is the set of test values.

As the baselines, we use prediction models trained with the same algorithms but only on endogenous variables.

5 Results and discussion

5.1 SARIMA

5.1.1 Parameter identification

To construct a SARIMA$(p, d, q)(P, D, Q)_m$ model, we follow the Box-Jenkins procedure (Box and Jenkins, 1990) for time-series models. First, we establish that the time series being modelled is stationary using both DF-GLS, a version of the Dickey-Fuller test (a unit root hypothesis rejected at α=0.001, for 8 auto-selected lags), and the Kwiatkowski-Phillips-Schmidt-Shin test (a stationarity hypothesis cannot be rejected at α=0.1 for auto-selected lags). Thus, no differencing is required and we select the d parameter of the non-seasonal part to be 0.

Next, we identify the other two non-seasonal parameters using autocorrelation and partial autocorrelation plots (see Figure 2), as the number of lags at which the two functions enter the 95% confidence interval, thus suggesting p=1 and q=1. Examining ACF, we also find indications of seasonality: there are spikes at lags 7 and 8 and at 13 and 14 lags, but these spikes die down fairly quickly. This observation suggests a weekly seasonality ($m = 7$) as well as stationarity at the seasonal level.

Additionally, we tested different values for p and q as well as P and Q using Akaike Information Criterion, Bayesian Information Criterion, and Hannan-Quinn Information Criterion for time-series model selection. The results, shown

[2]http://www.gallup.com/poll/112723/gallup-daily-us-consumer-spending.aspx
[3]Available at https://nlp.stanford.edu/projects/glove/

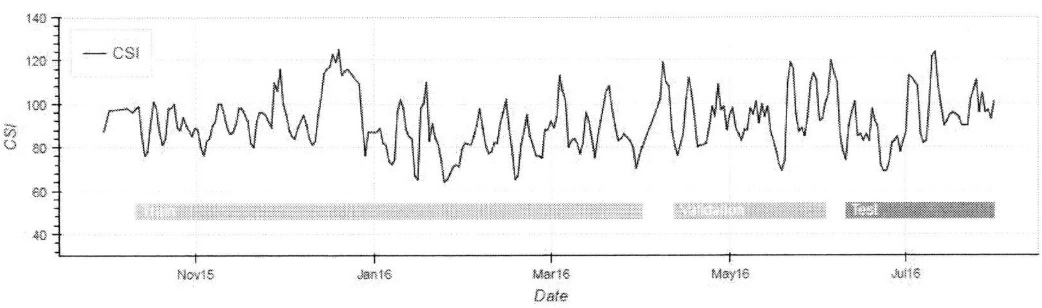

Figure 1: Train-validation-test split in the CSI values.

Figure 2: Auto-correlation and partial autocorrelation functions of CSI.

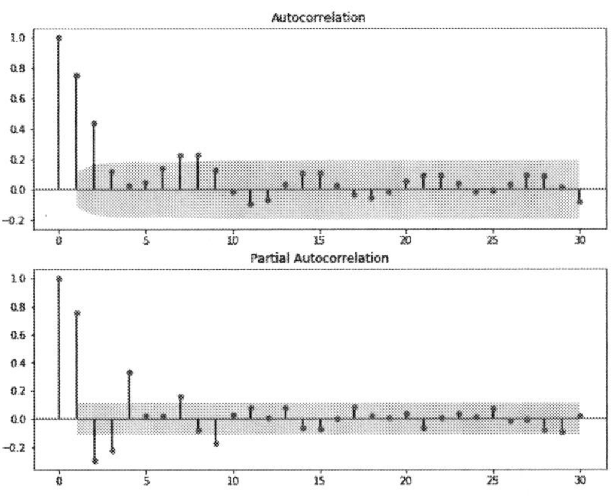

AIC		BIC		HQIC	
(3,0,5)	-245.45	**(0,0,2)**	**-148.88**	**(0,0,2)**	**-203.74**
(0,0,2)	**-241.15**	(0,0,3)	-145.5	(0,0,3)	-202.24
(0,0,3)	-240.95	(1,0,2)	-144.99	(1,0,2)	-201.74
(1,0,2)	-240.45	(0,0,4)	-141.4	(3,0,5)	-200.29
(0,0,4)	-240.04	(2,0,2)	-140.63	(0,0,4)	-200.04

Table 2: Identification of seasonal AR and MA parameters in SARIMA based on Akaike IC, Bayesian IC and Hannan-Quinn IC.

	Horizon=1	Horizon=3	Horizon=7
Lag 0	14.93	13.72	13.74
Lag 1	**14.79**	14.16	**12.61**
Lag 2	15.85	14.57	14.91
Lag 3	14.88	14.37	14.72
Lag 4	16.02	16.28	15.97
Lag 5	15.03	**13.37**	14.07
Lag 6	15.21	14.78	14.7
Lag 7	15.27	14.86	14.12

Table 3: RMSE on the test set of SARIMA at different forecast horizons, for different lags between the day of registered purchase intentions and the forecasted CSI.

in Tables 1 and 2, largely agree with parameter identification based on ACF and PACF, and suggest that the optimal model takes the form SARIMA$(1,0,2)(0,0,2)_7$, which we thus used in further experiments.

AIC		BIC		HQIC	
(1,0,2)	**-267.49**	**(1,0,2)**	**-251.58**	**(1,0,2)**	**-261.03**
(3,0,4)	-267.22	(1,0,3)	-248.02	(1,0,3)	-259.37
(1,0,3)	-267.11	(2,0,2)	-246.76	(2,0,2)	-258.11
(1,0,4)	-266.48	(1,0,4)	-244.2	(1,0,4)	-257.44
(3,0,2)	-266.25	(3,0,2)	-243.98	(3,0,2)	-257.22

Table 1: Identification of non-seasonal AR and MA parameters in SARIMA based on Akaike IC, Bayesian IC and Hannan-Quinn IC.

5.1.2 Lag length between purchase intention and spending index

Having identified the parameters of SARIMA for endogenous variables, we tested its quality with exogenous (i.e., semantic) variables supplied to it. To do that, we varied the number of days between the day of the CSI index and the day on which purchase intentions were registered that were used to forecast the index. These results are shown in Table 3.

The lag of one day seems a good choice: it is the best for the forecast horizons of 1 and 7 days, and

	Train	Validation	Test	Δ, %
Horizon=1				
Endogenous	7.15	13.46	15.09	—
Endog+Semantic	5.77	13.88	**14.79***	-1.9
Horizon=3				
Endogenous	7.15	13.83	15.44	—
Endog+Semantic	6.65	14.26	**13.37***	-13.4
Horizon=7				
Endogenous	7.15	13.46	15.09	—
Endog+Semantic	5.78	13.74	**12.52***	-17.03

Table 4: SARIMAX vs. baseline SARIMA. Improvements on the baseline are in bold, significant improvements (at $p < 0.05$) are indicated with an asterisk.

one of the best settings for the horizon of 3 days. It can be noted that for all the horizons RMSE values are considerably higher for lags greater than 1.

5.1.3 Adding exogenous variables

Table 4 compares SARIMAX with the optimal intention-index lag and the baseline SARIMA, for the three forecast horizons, on the train, validation and test datasets. The last column shows the difference of SARIMAX to the baseline as percentage of RMSE change. Statistical significance of the difference to the baseline was measured using a paired t-test. The results show that the addition of semantic variables leads to significantly improved forecasts, for all the three horizons, and the improvements tend to become greater as the forecast horizon increases: at $h=7$, the reduction in RMSE is 17%.

5.2 AdaBoost

5.2.1 Lag length between purchase intention and spending index

As the first step in experiments with AdaBoost, we examined different lags between the day on which purchase intentions were expressed and the day for which CSI was forecasted. To that end, we trained AdaBoost models on only semantic variables for different lag values. The performance of these models is shown in Table 5. Note that the results are the same for all the three forecast horizons, since the models included only on exogenous variables and past predicted values are not used to forecast the current value. These results suggest that the best lags are between 4 and 6 days, this contrasts with the findings for SARIMA, where the optimal was lag 1.

	AdaBoost	Gradient Boosting
Lag 0	15.34	12.91
Lag 1	14.78	12.98
Lag 2	14.38	**12.71**
Lag 3	14.24	13.59
Lag 4	13.59	13.18
Lag 5	13.8	13.09
Lag 6	**13.38**	12.86
Lag 7	15.21	12.86

Table 5: RMSE on the test set of AdaBoost and Gradient Boosting, for different lags between the day of registered purchase intentions and the forecasted CSI.

	Train	Validation	Test	Δ, %
Horizon=1				
Endogenous	5.94	8.86	9.61	—
Endog+Semantic	6.22	10.38	11.05	+14.9
Ensemble	7.16	10.16	11.92	+24.0
Horizon=3				
Endogenous	5.94	9.38	14.58	—
Endog+Semantic	7.39	12.69	**12.61**	-13.5
Ensemble	9.16	11.39	**14.51**	0.0
Horizon=7				
Endogenous	7.23	9.72	14.33	—
Endog+Semantic	4.73	11.99	**11.69***	-18.4
Ensemble	9.44	11.6	**11.94***	-16.6

Table 6: AdaBoost models with exogenous variables vs. Baseline AdaBoost.

5.2.2 Adding exogenous variables

Table 6 describes evaluation of two ways to introduce exogenous variables to forecast CSI with AdaBoost: the concatenation of endogenous and exogenous variables into one vector of predictors ("Endog+Semantic") and the ensemble method ("Ensemble", see Section 3.3). The last column shows each method's difference to the baseline ("Endogenous"). Because the experiments with SARIMA revealed that the CSI values have weekly seasonality, we use seven lagged values as endogenous variables in the AdaBoost algorithms. Exogenous variables are semantic variables at lag 6, which was found to be the optimal in the previous step.

Similar to the SARIMA results, these results also indicate that exogenous variables become beneficial as forecast horizons increase: at $h=1$, the baseline could not be beaten, but at $h=3$ and $h=7$ both methods which use exogenous variables

	Train	Validation	Test	$\Delta, \%$
Horizon=1				
Endogenous	4.51	9.48	9.52	–
Endog+Semantic	2.47	10.22	10.49	+10.1
Ensemble	6.46	9.04	**9.05**	-4.9
Horizon=3				
Endogenous	4.92	9.72	13.18	–
Endog+Semantic	4.55	10.83	13.28	0.0
Ensemble	8.56	9.43	**11.62**	-11.8
Horizon=7				
Endogenous	2.99	10.6	13.98	–
Endog+Semantic	4.55	10.68	**12.07**	-13.6
Ensemble	9.96	9.56	14.65	+4.7

Table 7: Best Gradient Boosting settings vs. Baseline.

improve on the baseline, often to a statistically significant level. The greatest improvement is achieved at $h=7$ with the concatenation method, which reduced RMSE by 18%.

5.3 Gradient Boosting

5.3.1 Lag length between purchase intention and spending index

As with the other regression methods, we first looked at the effect of the lag between the purchase intentions and the forecasted index on Gradient Boosting: for each lag between 0 and 7, a model was trained using only exogenous variables. The results are shown in Table 5.

While the best lag was found to be the lag of 2, the differences between the lags are not very prominent and tend to stay within 7% of each other. This result is still at odds with what was found for SARIMAX and AdaBoost. In subsequent experiments with Gradient Boosting, exogenous variables were used to forecast CSI at the lag of 2.

5.3.2 Adding exogenous variables

Table 7 describes the performance for Gradient Boosting models when exogenous variables are introduced via concatenation with the endogenous ones ("Endog+Semantic") and via an ensemble regressor that combines separate predictions made with endogenous and exogenous variables ("Ensemble"). The results again suggest that exogenous variables become helpful at longer forecast horizons: while at $h=1$ the concatenation method fails to outperform the baseline, and for the ensemble method the RMSE reduction is only 4.9%,

the improvement on the baseline at $h=3$ and $h=7$ reaches 13.6%. The ensemble method tends to fare better than the concatenation method, but not consistently so: at $h=7$ its forecasts are worse than those of the baseline.

6 Conclusion

In this paper we have presented a new method to forecast consumer spending from purchase intentions found on social media, aiming to approximate responses of participants of traditional consumer surveys. In contrast to previous work that modelled economic confidence from the sentiment of social media posts, we use semantic models of nouns that are stated as intended purchases, which, on the one hand, helps to incorporate richer evidence available in the data, and on the other, creates low-complexity regression models. The utility of the data was evaluated using three popular forecasting methods: Seasonal ARIMA, AdaBoost, and Gradient Boosting regressors.

The key findings of this work can be summarized as follows. Adding information on intended purchases as exogenous variables alongside lagged values of the consumer spending index often yields statistically significant improvements over a baseline that is trained on the lag variables alone. The benefits are greater at longer forecast horizons: while we found little evidence of improvement at one-step ahead forecasts, at the horizons of three and seven days, exogenous variables reduced forecast errors by between 11% and 18% for all the regression methods. Furthermore, we analysed the optimal lag length between the day on which purchase intentions were registered and the day for which spending is forecasted, but could not find any lag values that would be consistently better than others across the regression methods.

As future work, we plan to further explore the proposed method on larger datasets. A particular interesting extension may be a comparison of this method to those that derive a prediction of consumer spending from search engine queries, considering that both approaches aim to capture consumer purchase intentions, but do so using very different types of user-generated content. Another promising extension may study techniques for eliminating the demographic bias present on social media, in order to create models that better approximate real-world data on consumer spending.

References

Nikolay Archak, Anindya Ghose, and Panagiotis G. Ipeirotis. 2011. Deriving the pricing power of product features by mining consumer reviews. *Management Science*, 57(8):1485–1509.

Marco Baroni, Georgiana Dinu, and Germn Kruszewski. 2014. Don't count, predict! a systematic comparison of context-counting vs. context-predicting semantic vectors. *52nd Annual Meeting of the Association for Computational Linguistics, ACL 2014 - Proceedings of the Conference*, 1:238–247.

George Edward Pelham Box and Gwilym Jenkins. 1990. *Time Series Analysis, Forecasting and Control*. Holden-Day, Incorporated.

Zhiyuan Chen, Bing Liu, Meichun Hsu, Malu Castellanos, and Riddhiman Ghosh. 2013. Identifying intention posts in discussion forums. pages 1041–1050.

Kristof Coussement and Dirk Van den Poel. 2008. Integrating the voice of customers through call center emails into a decision support system for churn prediction. *Inf. Manage.*, 45(3):164–174.

Aron Culotta. 2010. Towards detecting influenza epidemics by analyzing twitter messages. In *Proceedings of the First Workshop on Social Media Analytics*, SOMA '10, pages 115–122, New York, NY, USA. ACM.

Piet Daas and Marco Puts. 2014. Social media sentiment and consumer confidence. In *Workshop on using Big Data for forecasting and statistics*.

Theologos Dergiades, Costas Milas, and Theodore Panagiotidis. 2015. Tweets, Google Trends, and sovereign spreads in the GIIPS. *Oxford Economic Papers*, 67(2):406.

Mohammed Elshendy, Andrea Fronzetti Colladon, Elisa Battistoni, and Peter A Gloor. 2017. Using four different online media sources to forecast the crude oil price. *Journal of Information Science*, 0(0):0165551517698298.

Yoav Freund and Robert E. Schapire. 1996. Experiments with a new boosting algorithm. In *International Conference on Machine Learning*, pages 148–156.

Jerome H. Friedman. 2001. Greedy function approximation: A gradient boosting machine. *The Annals of Statistics*, 29(5):1189–1232.

Ifigeneia Georgoula, Demitrios Pournarakis, Christos Bilanakos, Dionisios N. Sotiropoulos, and George M. Giaglis. 2015. Using time-series and sentiment analysis to detect the determinants of bitcoin prices. In *9th Mediterranean Conference on Information Systems*.

Mohamed Hamroun, Mohamed Salah Gouider, and Lamjed Ben Said. 2016. Large scale microblogging intentions analysis with pattern-based approach. *Procedia Comput. Sci.*, 96(C):1249–1257.

Stephen Hansen and Michael McMahon. 2016. Shocking language: Understanding the macroeconomic effects of central bank communication. In *NBER International Seminar on Macroeconomics 2015*. Journal of International Economics (Elsevier), Volume 99, Supplement 1.

Jane-Vivian Igboayaka. 2015. Using social media networks for measuring consumer confidence: Problems, issues and prospects. Master's thesis, University of Ottawa.

Quoc V. Le and Tomas Mikolov. 2014. Distributed representations of sentences and documents. In *Proceedings of the 31th International Conference on Machine Learning, ICML 2014, Beijing, China, 21-26 June 2014*, pages 1188–1196.

Tomas Mikolov, Kai Chen, Greg Corrado, and Jeffrey Dean. 2013. Efficient estimation of word representations in vector space. *CoRR*, abs/1301.3781.

Dat Tien Nguyen, Kamela Ali Al Mannai, Shafiq Joty, Hassan Sajjad, Muhammad Imran, and Prasenjit Mitra. 2017. Robust classification of crisis-related data on social networks using convolutional neural networks. In *Proceedings of 11th International AAAI Conference on Web and Social Media (ICWSM)*.

Brendan T. O'Connor, Ramnath Balasubramanyan, Bryan R. Routledge, and Noah A. Smith. 2010. From tweets to polls: Linking text sentiment to public opinion time series. In *ICWSM*.

Samuel Rönnqvist and Peter Sarlin. 2015. Detect & describe: Deep learning of bank stress in the news. In *IEEE Symposium Series on Computational Intelligence, SSCI 2015, Cape Town, South Africa, December 7-10, 2015*, pages 890–897.

Steven L. Scott and Hal R. Varian. 2015. Bayesian Variable Selection for Nowcasting Economic Time Series. In *Economic Analysis of the Digital Economy*, NBER Chapters, pages 119–135. National Bureau of Economic Research, Inc.

Jianfeng Si, Arjun Mukherjee, Bing Liu, Sinno Jialin Pan, Qing Li, and Huayi Li. 2014. Exploiting social relations and sentiment for stock prediction. In *Proceedings of EMNLP*.

Thársis T. P. Souza, Olga Kolchyna, Philip Treleaven, and Tomaso Aste. 2016. Twitter sentiment analysis applied to finance: A case study in the retail industry. In Gautam Mitra and Xiang Yu, editors, *Handbook of Sentiment Analysis in Finance*, chapter 23.

Andranik Tumasjan, Timm Sprenger, Philipp Sandner, and Isabell Welpe. 2010. Predicting elections with Twitter: What 140 characters reveal about political sentiment. In *International AAAI Conference on Web and Social Media*.

Simeon Vosen and Torsten Schmidt. 2011. Forecasting private consumption: survey-based indicators vs. Google trends. *Journal of Forecasting*, 30(6):565–578.

Lynn Wu and Erik Brynjolfsson. 2015. The future of prediction: How Google searches foreshadow housing prices and sales. In *Economic Analysis of the Digital Economy*, pages 89–118. University of Chicago Press.

Mining fine-grained opinions on closed captions of YouTube videos with an attention-RNN

Edison Marrese-Taylor, Jorge A. Balazs, Yutaka Matsuo
Graduate School of Engineering
The University of Tokyo
Tokyo, Japan
emarrese,jorge,matsuo@weblab.t.u-tokyo.ac.jp

Abstract

Video reviews are the natural evolution of written product reviews. In this paper we target this phenomenon and introduce the first dataset created from closed captions of YouTube product review videos as well as a new attention-RNN model for aspect extraction and joint aspect extraction and sentiment classification. Our model provides state-of-the-art performance on aspect extraction without requiring the usage of hand-crafted features on the SemEval ABSA corpus, while it outperforms the baseline on the joint task. In our dataset, the attention-RNN model outperforms the baseline for both tasks, but we observe important performance drops for all models in comparison to SemEval. These results, as well as further experiments on domain adaptation for aspect extraction, suggest that differences between speech and written text, which have been discussed extensively in the literature, also extend to the domain of product reviews, where they are relevant for fine-grained opinion mining.

1 Introduction

On-line videos have become indispensable to people's daily lives, as traffic statistics showed that by 2010 it accounted for 56.6% of the total global consumer traffic (Siersdorfer et al., 2010). Studies support the notion that on-line reviews can have a strong influence in the decision-making of potential Internet buyers (Chevalier and Mayzlin, 2006), thus becoming a major factor for both consumers and marketers (Hu et al., 2008).

Video reviews are the natural evolution of written product reviews. In fact, people are increasingly turning to platforms such as YouTube to help them shop, looking for product reviews (Lawson, 2015). YouTube unboxing videos have become a growing phenomenon (Lawson, 2015; Insights, 2014). In 2015 alone, people in the U.S. watched 60M hours of them on YouTube, totaling 1.1 B views. The same year, views of product review videos increased by 40% compared to 2014, and more than 1 million channels related to product reviews were counted (Baysinger, 2015). Despite all of this, the most widely used approaches in opinion mining focus only on tweets or written product reviews available on websites like Amazon.

Therefore, in this paper we present the first opinion mining study focusing on *video product reviews*. We take the fine-grained approach, which aims to detect the subjective expressions in text and to characterize their sentiment orientation, and analyze the closed captions of *video product reviews* extracted from YouTube. Fine-grained opinion mining is important for a variety of NLP problems, including opinion-oriented question answering and opinion summarization, having been studied extensively in recent years. In practical terms, this approach defines the tasks of aspect extraction (*AE*), sentiment classification (*SC*) and a joint setting (*AESC*).

While *AE* and *AESC* have often been tackled as sequence labeling problem, where the sentence is a stream of tokens to be labeled using IOB and collapsed or sentiment-bearing IOB labels (Zhang et al., 2015) respectively, *SC* can be regarded as a semantic compositional problem, where the obtained representation is used to predict the sentiment.

Accounting for the patent differences between speech and written text, which have also led linguists to consider them as different domains (Biber, 1991) exhibiting different syntactic (O'Donnell, 1974) and distributional properties, we created the first annotated dataset using closed

Proceedings of the 8th Workshop on Computational Approaches to Subjectivity, Sentiment and Social Media Analysis, pages 102–111
Copenhagen, Denmark, September 7–11, 2017. ©2017 Association for Computational Linguistics

captions of YouTube product review videos, which we named the *Youtubean* dataset.

Motivated by the success of attention-based approaches in multiple NLP problems such as machine translation (Bahdanau et al., 2015), parsing (Vinyals et al., 2015), slot-filling (Liu and Lane, 2016) and others (Luong et al., 2015), we also introduce an attention-augmented RNN model for *AE* and *AESC*. Compared to previous work, the attentional component makes our model specially suitable for *AESC*, since it directly addresses the compositional nature of the sentiment classification task as it allows the model to represent the input sentence as a convex combination of word representations. This is confirmed by our results on the SemEval ABSA dataset (Pontiki et al., 2014), given that our model offers state-of-the-art performance for *AESC* while also performing equivalently to the state-of-the-art for aspect extraction without the need for manually-crafted features.

We also show that our attention-RNN model outperforms the baseline for both *AE* and *AESC* on our dataset. However, we observed that compared to the SemEval corpora, all the tested models decreased their performance on it. As indicated by a descriptive analysis of our corpus and by additional experiments using domain adaptation techniques for *AE*, which did not offer considerable gains, our results seem to support the existence of the aforementioned differences between speech and written text in the context of product reviews and their importance for fine-trained opinion mining. Our code and data are available for download on GitHub[1].

2   Related Work

Our work is related to aspect extraction using deep learning, a task that is often tackled as a sequence labeling problem. In particular, our work is related to Irsoy and Cardie (2014), who pioneered in the field by using multi-layered RNNs on a subset of the MPQA 1.2 dataset (Wiebe et al., 2005). Later, Liu et al. (2015) successfully adapted the architectures by Mesnil et al. (2013), experimenting on the SemEval 2014 dataset (Pontiki et al., 2014). Compared to these, our model is novel since it introduces the usage of attention for *AE*. In this sense, our work is also related to Liu and Lane (2016), who introduced an attention RNN for slot-filling in Natural Language Understanding.

We also find related work on the usage of RNNs for open domain targeted sentiment (Mitchell et al., 2013), where Zhang et al. (2015) experimented with neural CRF models using various RNN architectures on a dataset of informal language from Twitter. In our case, the domain is different since we focus on product reviews.

Regarding target-based sentiment analysis, we find several ad-hoc models that account for the sentence structure and the position of the aspect on it, such as Tang et al. (2016b) and Tang et al. (2016a), who use attention-augmented RNNs for the task. However, these models require the location of the aspect to be known in advance and therefore are only useful in pipeline models. Our work is similar to these since it also makes use of an attentional component to model compositionally in sentiment classification, but we model aspect extraction and sentiment classification as a joint task instead of using a pipeline approach.

AESC has also often been tackled as a sequence labeling problem, mainly using CRFs (Mitchell et al., 2013). To model the problem in this fashion, collapsed or sentiment-bearing IOB labels (Zhang et al., 2015) are used. Pipeline models (i.e. task-independent model ensembles) have also been extensively studied by the same authors. We also find Xu et al. (2014) who performed *AESC* by modeling the linking relation between aspects and the sentiment-bearing phrases.

When it comes to the video review domain, we find related work on YouTube mining, mainly focused on exploiting user comments. For example, Wu et al. (2014) exploited crowdsourced texual data from time-synced commented videos, proposing a temporal topic model based on LDA. However, Schultes et al. (2013) showed that comments with references to video content[2] represent only 2% to 4% of comments in YouTube. Therefore, we think this kind of analysis might be limited. The work of Tahara et al. (2010) introduced a similar approach for *Nico Nico* using time-indexed social annotations to search for desirable scenes inside videos.

On the other hand, Severyn et al. (2014) proposed a systematic approach to mine user comments that relies on tree kernel models. Additionally, Krishna et al. (2013) performed sentiment analysis on YouTube comments related to popular topics using machine learning techniques, show-

---

[1] github.com/epochx/opinatt

[2] Class C7 in the paper

103

Video title	Video id	Length	# of sentences
Sprint Samsung Galaxy S5 Full Review!	jdzbw68mpZE	10:23	97
Samsung Galaxy S5 Review	zV0u2UFwv6E	12:07	147
Samsung Galaxy S5 Review - Phones 4u	1lxAO_YgZ98	5:07	41
Samsung Galaxy S5 Review	_Ihe7jm63kU	3:49	45
Samsung Galaxy S5 "Special "Review & Camera Samples	nayKYv_7b6M	12:00	52
Samsung Galaxy S5 vs Apple iPhone 5s: Which Is Better?	1dvzHyHID0k	3:34	32
Samsung Galaxy S5 review	bRv5JrKnp3M	24:15	164

Table 1: Detail of the reviews used to create the *Youtubean* dataset.

ing that the trends in users' sentiments is well correlated to the corresponding real-world events. Siersdorfer et al. (2010) presented an analysis of dependencies between comments and comment ratings, proving that community feedback in combination with term features in comments can be used for automatically determining the community acceptance of comments.

Finally, we find some papers that have successfully attempted to use closed caption mining for video activity recognition (Gupta and Mooney, 2010) and scene segmentation (Gupta and Mooney, 2009). Similar work has been done using closed captions to classify movies by genre (Brezeale and Cook, 2006) and summarize video programs (Brezeale and Cook, 2006).

3 Dataset

In YouTube, video authors con provide their own closed captions, or they can be generated automatically by the engine. In both cases, these captions can be interpreted as a time-indexed transcript of the speech in the video. Therefore, to minimize the amount of noise in the data, we utilized the user-provided closed captions of seven of the most popular reviews of the Samsung Galaxy S5 and creatd an annotated dataset for fine-grained opinion mining. We obtained, cleaned and processed the data, and annotated the aspects following the guidelines by Pontiki et al. (2014) using *brat*[3] (Stenetorp et al., 2012). We divided the annotation process into two steps.

First, two different annotators tagged aspects independently, obtaining an exact inter-annotation agreement of 0.705 F1-score. This value rose to 0.823 when allowing for partial matches, which we defined as any overlap between the annotated terms. Discrepancies were discussed until a final setting was reached.

With these annotations fixed, we asked the same annotators to tag the sentiment of each extracted

aspect. On this task, the annotators obtained an average agreement of 0.942 F1-score. This time, discrepancies were discussed with a third person who acted as an arbiter, until an agreement was reached. Both aspect extraction and sentiment classification inter-annotator agreements are comparable to the values obtained in similar tasks (Jimenez-Zafra et al., 2015) (Wiebe et al., 2005).

Corpus	R	L	Y
# Sentences	3041	3045	578
# Aspects	1288	1042	525
Mean word/sentence	15.47	16.76	20.71
Mean const. tree depth	9.10	10.16	11.40
Mean word/aspect	1.97	1.83	2.14
Mean aspects/sentence	1.20	0.76	1.38
Sentences with aspects	66.46%	48.87%	66.96%

Table 2: Descriptive corpora comparison.

Table 1 provides some key information about the the source video reviews we have used to build our dataset, which we named the *Youtubean* dataset. Table 2 compares it to the SemEval Laptops and Restaurants corpora, regarded as the de facto datasets for written review mining. Several differences can be observed. A big distinction lies in mean sentence and aspect lengths, both of which are considerably longer in *Youtubean*. We also analyzed sentence syntax complexity in terms of the constituency tree depth, observing that our sentence trees are deeper on average. Furthermore, *Youtubean* exhibits both longer and more frequent aspect mentions.

4 Proposed Model

Our proposed model is a two-pass bidirectional RNN architecture that includes an attentional component. Formally, given an embedded input sequence $x = [x_1, ..., x_n]$ with one-hot encoded labels $y = [y_1, ..., y_n]$, we define the first pass as follows.

$$\bar{x}_i = [x_{i-d}; ...; x_i; ...; x_{i+d}] \tag{1}$$

$$\vec{h}_i = \sigma(\bar{x}_i, \vec{h}_{i-1}) \tag{2}$$

---

[3] http://brat.nlplab.org/

$$\overleftarrow{h}_i = \sigma(\bar{x}_i, \overleftarrow{h}_{i+1}) \qquad (3)$$

$$h_i = [\overrightarrow{h}_i; \overleftarrow{h}_i] \qquad (4)$$

Where σ denotes the sigmoid nonlinearity, $\overrightarrow{h}_i$ and $\overleftarrow{h}_i$ are the forward and backward hidden states of the RNN, which are concatenated, and $\bar{x}_i$ is a context window of ordered word embedding vectors around position i, with a total size of $2d + 1$. This context window is intended to improve the model capabilities to capture short-term temporal dependencies (Mesnil et al., 2013).

The second pass goes through the hidden states h_i and performs sequence labeling token by token. We use the attentional decoder from (Vinyals et al., 2015).

$$u_{i,j} = v^\top \tanh(W_\alpha[h_i; h_j]) \qquad (5)$$

$$\alpha_{i,j} = softmax(u_{i,j}) \qquad (6)$$

$$t_i = \sum_{j=1}^{n} \alpha_{i,j} \cdot h_j \qquad (7)$$

$$\hat{y}_i = softmax(W_s[h_i; t_i; y_{i-1}]) \qquad (8)$$

Where $\hat{y}_i$ is a probability distribution over the label vocabulary for input i. As shown, this is obtained using both the corresponding *aligned* input h_i and the attention distribution over all hidden states t_i, i.e. using a global attention scheme (Luong et al., 2015). While generating the output $\hat{y}_i$, we explicitly model the dependency on the previous label by adding y_{i-1} to the computation. These two components are combined using a feed forward neural network, whose output dimension is the size of the tag label vocabulary for *AE* or *AESC*. To initialize the attention matrix h_n is used so the model does not bypass it. As a loss function we use the minibatch average cross-entropy.

The addition of the attentional component to our model is motivated by two factors. In the first place, in contrast to Mesnil et al. (2013) who directly make use of a window of previous hidden states for AE, the attentional components allows us to access contextual information in a more natural and selective way. For AESC, the attention directly models sentiment compositionality.

5 Experimental setup

For our experiments, in addition to *Youtubean*, we also worked with the SemEval ABSA 2014 Laptops and Restaurants corpora (Pontiki et al., 2014), which can be regarded as the de facto datasets for fine-grained review mining. For *AE* we use the train/test splits provided for Phase B. For *AESC*, since the test data does not have sentiment labels, we worked only with the training data. On the other hand, since the size of *Youtubean* is smaller than the SemEval corpora, we used 5-fold cross validation to make results more robust. For each fold, we used 10% of the development data as a validation set and compare our results using two-sided t-tests.

For evaluation, we used the CoNLL *conlleval* script for evaluation based on F1-score. To perform joint aspect extraction and sentiment classification, we only considered *positive* (+), *negative* (−) and *neutral* (0) as sentiment classes, and the additional *conflict* class is mapped to *neutral*. To gain insights on the output of the models for *AESC*, we decoupled the IOB collapsed tags using simple heuristics to recover the *simple* aspect extraction F1-score as well as classification performances for each sentiment class, but we used the *joint* tagging *conlleval* F1-score to evaluate the models.

As a baseline, we implemented the RNN architectures by Liu et al. (2015), which are the state-of-the-art in fine-grained aspect extraction. We experimented with Jordan-style RNNs (JRNN), Elman-style RNNs (RNN), LSTMs and the bidirectional versions of these last two. We followed Irsoy and Cardie (2014) to merge the forward and backward hidden states, setting $y_t = \sigma(\overrightarrow{U}\overrightarrow{h}_t + \overleftarrow{U}\overleftarrow{h}_t)$, where $\overrightarrow{U}, \overleftarrow{U}$ are output matrices for the forward and backward hidden states $\overrightarrow{h}_t$, $\overleftarrow{h}_t$, respectively. This gives the models more flexibility to capture complex relations in a sentence, making them able to learn how to weight future and past information.

For both our attention-RNN model and the baseline RNNs, we experimented with Senna embeddings (Collobert et al., 2011), GoogleNews embeddings (Mikolov et al., 2013) and WikiDeps (Levy and Goldberg, 2014). The usefulness of working with pre-trained embeddings for the baseline RNNs was already shown by (Liu et al., 2015). However, for comparison when experimenting with our model, we also used randomly initialized embeddings of sizes 50 and 300 to test this hypothesis.

To make our results more transparent, we explicitly experimented with two different preprocessing pipelines. We used Senna (Collobert et al., 2011), which provides both a POS-tagger and a chunker, and CoreNLP (Manning et al., 2014). The latter lacks a chunker so we combined it with the CoNLL *chunklink* script[4]. As Liu et al. (2015), we also experimented adding the same 14 linguistic binary features they used, which are based on POS-tags and chunk IOB-tags. These are concatenated to the hidden layer of the RNN before the final output non-linearity.

To train our baseline models we set a learning rate of 0.01 with decay and early stopping on the validation set. We set a fixed window size of 1 for bi-directional and 3 for unidirectional models, and always train word embeddings. Exploratory experiments showed that most models stop learning after a few epochs —3 or 4— so we only trained for a maximum of 5 epochs.

In the case of our attention-RNN model (ARNN), here we only report results using LSTMs, which outperformed all others cells we tried on preliminary experiments. We explored different hyper-parameter configurations, including context window sizes of 1, 3 and 5 as well as hidden state sizes of 100, 200 and 300, and dropout keep probabilities of 0.5 and 0.8. We also experimented concatenating the RNN hidden states after the first pass with the binary features used by (Liu et al., 2015). Finally, we also experimented with unidirectional versions of the RNNs. For training, we used mini-batch stochastic gradient descent with a mini-batch size of 16 and padded sequences to a maximum size of 200 tokens. We used exponential decay of ratio 0.9 and early stopping on the validation when there was no improvement in the F1-score after 1000 training steps.

6 Results

6.1 Aspect Extraction (*AE*)

6.1.1 Laptops

Table 3 summarizes our best baseline results on the Laptops datasets. For contrast we include the best F1-scores obtained by Liu et al. (2015) (cf. F1* columns). We observed the CoreNLP pipeline outperformed the Senna pipeline, with an average absolute gain of 2.105%, significant at $p = 1.29 \times 10^{-5}$, and binary features proved useful offering average absolute gains of 1.538% ($p = 1.29 \times 10^{-5}$). Finally, note that the best configurations always use SennaEmbeddings, which

---

[4]http://ilk.uvt.nl/team/sabine/homepage/software.html

outperformed others significantly for each case.

Model	Emb.	$|h|$	feat	F1	F1*
JRNN	Senna	50	No	70.81	73.42
LSTM	Senna	100	Yes	70.92	**75.00**
BiLSTM	Senna	50	Yes	69.03	74.03
RNN	Senna	50	No	**71.87**	74.43
BiRNN	Senna	50	Yes	69.45	74.57

Table 3: Results of our implemented baseline RNN models on the Laptops dataset.

Table 4 summarizes the best results of our ARNN model on the Laptops dataset, where we obtained a maximum F1-score of 74.74. Again, the CoreNLP pipeline significantly outperformed Senna, with an average absolute gain of 1.39 ($p = 3.4 \times 10^{-33}$) F1-score. Bidirectionality provided an absolute average gain of 1.15 F1-score ($p = 4.61 \times 10^{-20}$).

Both SennaEmbeddings and GoogleNews provided statistically equivalent results ($p = 0.65$), which were also significantly superior to WikiDeps with p-values 9.54×10^{17} and 2.6×10^{-13} respectively. Pre-trained embeddings outperformed random embeddings on average, comparing across same-sized cases. Linguistic binary features did not statistically contribute to the performance.

Embeddings	$|d|$	$|cw|$	$|h|$	F1
SennaEmbeddings	50	1	100	**74.74**
Random	50	3	300	70.19
WikiDeps	300	3	200	69.53
GoogleNews	300	3	100	71.17
Random	300	3	200	70.03

Table 4: Best results for our ARNN on *AE* for the Laptops dataset.

6.1.2 Restaurants

Table 5 summarizes our best baseline results for the Restaurants dataset, again for contrast we include the best F1-scores obtained by Liu et al. (2015) (cf. F1* columns).

Regarding the usage of the linguistic features, we found that they contributed to increasing performance with an average absolute gain of 1.083% ($p = 1.65 \times 10^{-6}$). This is consistent with previous findings by Liu et al. (2015). The Senna pipeline outperformed CoreNLP with an average absolute gain of 1.161% ($p = 1.02 \times 10^{-8}$). Embeddings caused statistically significant differences, where WikiDeps outperformed both other embeddings on average.

Model	Emb.	$|h|$	feat	F1	F1*
JRNN	WDeps	100	Yes	78.20	79.89
LSTM	WDeps	100	Yes	**78.97**	81.37
BiLSTM	WDeps	200	Yes	74.73	81.06
RNN	Senna	200	Yes	77.13	81.66
BiRNN	WDeps	100	No	74.33	**82.06**

Table 5: Results of our implemented baseline RNN models on the Restaurants dataset.

Table 6 summarizes the best results by our ARNN model on the Restaurants dataset, where we obtained a maximum F1-score of 81.83. All of our best performing models use a bidirectional architecture. In fact, bidirectionality provided an average significant absolute gain of 0.89 F1-score ($p = 1.25 \times 10^{-17}$). Additionally, using CoreNLP as preprocessing pipeline provided an average gain of 0.585 F1-score ($p = 2.98 \times 10^{-21}$) over Senna.

Embeddings	$|d|$	$|cw|$	$|h|$	F1
SennaEmbeddings	50	1	100	**81.83**
Random	50	3	100	78.79
WikiDeps	300	3	100	78.68
GoogleNews	300	3	300	78.73
Random	300	1	100	78.38

Table 6: Best results for our attention-RNNs on *AE* on the Restaurants dataset.

Context windows proved beneficial as confirmed by the significantly different average F1-scores of 76.55, 77.59 and 77.28 for window sizes 1, 3 and 5 respectively. We also observed significant performance differences using SennaEmbeddings, which outperformed all others with an average F1-score of 77.94. GoogleNews and WikiDeps exhibited average F1-scores of 76.93 and 76.55, which are statistically different ($p = 4.08 \times 10^{-6}$) and although they also outperformed random embeddings for $d = 300$, they performed statistically worse than random embeddings for $d = 50$. Linguistic binary features did not statistically contribute to the performance.

6.1.3 *Youtubean*

Table 7 summarizes our results for baseline RNNs on *Youtubean*. Again, we observed that adding linguistic features had a positive effect on the performance, with an average absolute gain of 1.30% ($p = 0.01$). SennaEmbeddings and WikiDeps provided better performance compared to GoogleNews, with average F1-scores of 49.11, 49.64 and 45.37 respectively. The first two values were statistically indistinguishable. We could not observe

significant differences in the performance for different pipelines.

RNN	Pipeline	Emb.	Feat.	$|h|$	F1
RNN	Senna	WDeps	Yes	100	55.82*
RNN	CoreNLP	WDeps	No	200	55.69*
LSTM	CoreNLP	Senna	No	100	**56.13**
BiRNN	CoreNLP	WDeps	No	200	50.15
BiLSTM	Senna	Senna	Yes	100	50.09

Table 7: Results of our implemented baseline RNN models on *AE* for the *Youtubean* dataset.

To further study the relation between written and video product reviews for aspect extraction, a task that has been broadly studied by our community, we complemented our RNNs baseline with two classic domain adaptation methods. Despite their simplicity, they are surprisingly difficult to beat (Daume III and Marcu, 2006). These techniques basically mean using each of the SemEval corpora as a source (SRC) dataset for transfer learning, where *Youtubean* is set as the target (TGT).

Our first domain-adaptation technique was WEIGHTED, a method that trains a model on the union of the SRC and TGT datasets, reweighting examples from SRC (Daume III and Marcu, 2006). We did so by multiplying the input embedding matrix by the given weight w, which we set to 0.2 based on the corpus size ratio. For training, we used 10-fold cross validation, adding all the examples of the SRC dataset to the training part of each fold-based arrangement. Since these model took longer to train we only experimented with the Senna pipeline. We omitted our bidirectional architectures given their poor performance and always included linguistic features, which generally contributed to an improved F1-score in our in-domain models.

RNN	SRC	Emb.	$|h|$	F1
LSTM	L	Google	50	57.17
RNN	L	Google	100	55.12
JRNN	L	WDeps	200	**58.30**

Table 8: Results for the WEIGHTED technique.

As Table 8 shows, using the Laptops dataset as SRC gives the best results in each case. Using this corpus led to an average absolute improvement over Restaurants of 3.79% ($p = 7.76 \times 10^{-11}$.) When it comes to embeddings, GoogleNews provided the best average performance with 53.44 F1-score. However, this value was statistically indistinguishable at $p < 0.08$ from WikiDeps, with an average 52.8 F1-score.

Our second domain adaptation method was PRED, which uses the output of a SRC-trained classifier as a feature in the TGT model. Concretely, we first trained a model using all the examples on SRC. We then fed that model with all the TGT examples, adding its outputs as additional features to the TGT dataset, thus creating a new augmented version of it. Since these features are IOB-tags, we concatenate them with the linguistic features. We trained our models on the augmented TGT dataset, choosing the best performing settings from our previous experiments on *AE*.

RNN	SRC	Emb.	$|h|$	F1
LSTM	L	Senna	100	56.83
BiLSTM	R	WDeps	100	52.81
BiRNN	R	WDeps	100	52.99*
BiRNN	R	WDeps	200	52.90*
RNN	R	WDeps	100	57.70
JRNN	R	WDeps	200	**59.69**

Table 9: Results for the PRED technique.

Table 9 summarizes our results for PRED. We found that using Senna as the pre-processor provided better results in average, with an 0.89% absolute gain significant at $p = 0.01$. The Restaurants dataset provided better results than Laptops in average, with an absolute gain of 3.23%, significant at $p = 8.78 \times 10^{-6}$.

Finally, Table 10 shows our best results for our introduced ARNN in the *Youtubean* dataset. For this case, we omitted random embeddings and binary features as previous experiments showed they did not contribute to increase the performance.

Embeddings	$|cw|$	$|h|$	F1
SennaEmbeddings	3	100	56.28
WikiDeps	3	100	57.21
GoogleNews	3	100	**57.67**

Table 10: Best results for our ARNNs for *AE* on *Youtubean*.

6.2 Joint aspect extraction and sentiment classification (*AESC*)

On our experiments for this task we based our parameter settings on the results for *AE*, so we only used bidirectional ARNN models, and skipped binary features and random embeddings.

6.2.1 Laptops

Table 11 summarizes our best results for the Laptops corpus. Based on the results for *AE*, we only used CoreNLP as a pre-processing pipeline. For the RNN baseline, embeddings also reported significant differences, with SennaEmbeddings offering average absolute gains of 5.78 F1-score ($p = 10^{-4}$) over GoogleNews and 2.47 F1-score ($p = 8 \times 10^{-3}$) over WikiDeps.

For training our ARNN we only used the CoreNLP pipeline, since it significantly outperformed Senna in our experiments for *AE*. All the values in the table were significantly different, although we observed different embeddings provided statistically equivalent results for certain lower performing parameter settings.

Model	Emb.	Tagging F1		Classification F1		
		single	joint	+	−	0
LSTM	Senna	74.30	**47.19**	77.40	12.63	80.00
RNN	Senna	74.08	46.52	77.13	17.70	**80.52**
JRNN	Senna	**76.00**	46.62	**77.97**	**22.86**	80.39
ARNN	Google	68.22	46.69	69.23	62.69	**86.83**
ARNN	Senna	**72.85**	**52.46**	**73.23**	**69.29**	85.59
ARNN	Wiki	71.46	50.85	63.94	61.07	83.23

Table 11: Results for *AESC* on Laptops

6.2.2 Restaurants

Regarding the Restaurants dataset, Table 12 shows a summary of our best results. For this case, we only used the Senna pipeline, as it provided better results for *AE*. We found that in the baseline RNNs SennaEmbeddings outperformed both other embeddings with average absolute gains of 2.37 ($p = 7.2 \times 10^{-4}$) and 3.36 ($p = 1.19 \times 10^{-6}$) F1-score WikiDeps and GoogleNews, respectively.

For our ARNN, as in the previous case, we only used CoreNLP as preprocessing pipeline given that it provided better results for *AE*. All the values in the table were significantly different.

Model	Emb.	Tagging F1		Classification F1		
		single	joint	+	−	0
LSTM	Senna	**69.24**	**44.75**	67.81	**62.40**	87.22
RNN	Senna	67.08	40.64	**70.73**	58.47	**87.39**
JRNN	Senna	66.74	40.65	67.04	49.29	86.47
ARNN	Google	73.80	50.63	78.90	**53.25**	81.08
ARNN	Senna	**79.57**	**54.75**	79.78	46.45	82.70
ARNN	Wiki	74.90	52.74	**81.47**	51.39	**83.22**

Table 12: Results for *AESC* on Restaurants

6.2.3 *Youtubean*

On *Youtubean*, as Table 13 shows, we see important performance drops compared to SemEval. In particular, the baseline models seem to be unable to correctly classify negative aspects. For this dataset, we found out that Senna provides better results than CoreNLP with an average absolute gain of 3.94 F1-score, which was significant at $p = 2.5 \times 10^{-4}$. Embeddings did not provide statistically significant differences. Similarly, binary features did not statistically contribute to the performance either.

Model	Emb.	Tagging F1		Classification F1		
		single	joint	+	−	0
LSTM	Senna	41.32	25.38	**35.83**	**9.59**	72.53
RNN	Senna	**47.59**	30.12	0	0	**76.64**
JRNN	Senna	42.86	**30.45**	23.33	0	62.32
ARNN	Google	52.84	40.58	45.39	**22.07**	79.94
ARNN	Senna	52.43	41.17	48.05	15.58	80.28
ARNN	Wiki	**55.50**	**41.49**	**52.32**	14.85	**81.07**

Table 13: Results for *AESC* on *Youtubean*.

7 Discussion

Results for aspect extraction showed that our implemented RNN baseline performs similarly to the original models by (Liu et al., 2015), although we remained unable to replicate their exact numbers. Despite that, our attention-RNN is able to provide results that are better than our implementation and comparable to the original values for both Laptops and Restaurants datasets. Moreover, we achieved these results without the need to add the linguistic features, which did not offer significant performance differences in our experiments. We think the variable sentence representation introduced by the attentional component is able to model some of the semantics encoded in these binary features.

For aspect extraction in our dataset, we see our model is able to perform better than the baseline, again without the need to add manually-crafted features. However, simple domain adaptation techniques applied to the baseline RNNs managed to obtain the best results, adding a maximum of 3.56 F1-score over the baseline. We think this shows that video reviews and written reviews share some regularities, which could be exploited further to obtain better results. In this sense, it would be interesting to apply these domain adaptations techniques to our attention-RNN model and compare the results. However, regularities among these domains seem to be limited, given that our obtained gains were small and that no domain consistently delivered better performance.

Regarding *AESC*, as shown by our decoupled results, we see all models slowly decreased their performance for aspect extraction, compared with results for *AE*. This seems reasonable given the additional challenges of performing both tasks at the same time.

When it comes to sentiment classification, we see our attention-RNN outperforms the baseline RNNs by a solid margin. However, all models tend to perform poorly for the negative (−) class. We believe this may be related to the imbalanced nature of the datasets, or due to the additional composition challenges negation involves, which seem to be critical in our dataset. Compared to the baseline RNNs, which in some cases seemed basically unable to detect negative sentiment, our attention-RNN model offers increased, although yet limited capabilities to deal with the negative class.

For *AESC*, we also observed that SennaEmbeddings did not always provide top performances, being outperformed by other embeddings, even though the former were previously shown to offer the best performance for aspect extraction in all cases. We think this is related to the nature of the embeddings, since SennaEmbeddings were designed for the tasks in (Collobert et al., 2011) which do not include sentiment, while other embeddings can be regarded as general-purpose.

8 Conclusions

In this paper we presented the first fine-grained opinion mining study focusing on *product video reviews*. We introduced the first annotated dataset for the domain, *Youtubean*, and aspect extraction and *AESC* with a novel attention-RNN. Our model offered state-of-the art performance for *AESC* and results comparable to a strong RNN baseline for aspect extraction. Our descriptive corpus analysis as well as the performance obtained by all the models in our dataset suggest that differences between speech and written text, discussed extensively in the literature, also extend to the domain of product reviews, where they are relevant for fine-grained opinion mining. These findings introduce relevant research challenges and concrete paths for future researchers.

For future work, we plan to increase the size of our dataset and include reviews extracted from different product categories. By doing this, we intend to make our results more robust and to further study the differences between written and video review, ultimately deriving new ways to overcome them. Finally, we also want to exploit the additional data from YouTube, such as the audio, video or specific frames extracted from it, and user comments, to improve our results.

References

Dzmitry Bahdanau, Kyunghyun Cho, and Yoshua Bengio. 2015. Neural machine translation by jointly learning to align and translate. In *Proceedings of the 2015 International Conference on Learning Representations*. San Diego, California. http://arxiv.org/abs/1409.0473.

Tim Baysinger. 2015. YouTube wants viewers to buy directly from product review videos.

Douglas Biber. 1991. *Variation across speech and writing*. Cambridge University Press.

Darin Brezeale and Diane Cook. 2006. Using closed captions and visual features to classify movies by genre. In *Proceedings of the 7th International Workshop on Multimedia Data Mining (MDM/KDD06): Poster Session*. ACM, Washington, DC, USA.

Judith Chevalier and Dina Mayzlin. 2006. The effect of word of mouth on sales: Online book reviews. *Journal of Marketing Research* 43(3):345–354. https://doi.org/10.1509/jmkr.43.3.345.

Ronan Collobert, Jason Weston, Lon Bottou, Michael Karlen, Koray Kavukcuoglu, and Pavel Kuksa. 2011. Natural Language Processing (Almost) from Scratch. *J. Mach. Learn. Res.* 12:2493–2537. http://dl.acm.org/citation.cfm?id=1953048.2078186.

Hal Daume III and Daniel Marcu. 2006. Domain adaptation for statistical classifiers. *Journal of Artificial Intelligence Research* pages 101–126. http://www.jair.org/papers/paper1872.html.

S. Gupta and R.J. Mooney. 2009. Using closed captions to train activity recognizers that improve video retrieval. In *Computer Vision and Pattern Recognition Workshops, 2009. CVPR Workshops 2009. IEEE Computer Society Conference on*. pages 30–37. https://doi.org/10.1109/CVPRW.2009.5204202.

Sonal Gupta and Raymond J. Mooney. 2010. Using closed captions as supervision for video activity recognition. In *Proceedings of the Twenty-Fourth AAAI Conference on Artificial Intelligence (AAAI-2010)*. Atlanta, GA, pages 1083–1088. http://www.cs.utexas.edu/users/ailab/?gupta:aaai10.

Nan Hu, Ling Liu, and Jie Jennifer Zhang. 2008. Do online reviews affect product sales? the role of reviewer characteristics and temporal effects. *Inf. Technol. and Management* 9(3):201–214. https://doi.org/10.1007/s10799-008-0041-2.

YouTube Insights. 2014. The magic behind unboxing on YouTube.

Ozan Irsoy and Claire Cardie. 2014. Opinion Mining with Deep Recurrent Neural Networks. In *Proceedings of the 2014 Conference on Empirical Methods in Natural Language Processing (EMNLP)*. Association for Computational Linguistics, Doha, Qatar, pages 720–728. http://www.aclweb.org/anthology/D14-1080.

Salud M. Jimenez-Zafra, Giacomo Berardi, Andrea Esuli, Diego Marcheggiani, Mara Teresa Martn-Valdivia, and Alejandro Moreo Fernandez. 2015. A Multi-lingual Annotated Dataset for Aspect-Oriented Opinion Mining. In *Proceedings of the 2015 Conference on Empirical Methods in Natural Language Processing*. Association for Computational Linguistics, Lisbon, Portugal, pages 2533–2538. http://aclweb.org/anthology/D15-1302.

Amar Krishna, Joseph Zambreno, and Sandeep Krishnan. 2013. Polarity trend analysis of public sentiment on youtube. In *Proceedings of the 19th International Conference on Management of Data*. Computer Society of India, Mumbai, India, India, COMAD '13, pages 125–128. http://dl.acm.org/citation.cfm?id=2694476.2694505.

Matt Lawson. 2015. 2015 holiday trends - shopping moments are replacing shopping marathons. *https://adwords.googleblog.com/2015/10/2015-holiday-trends-shopping-moments.html*.

Omer Levy and Yoav Goldberg. 2014. Dependency-based word embeddings. In *Proceedings of the 52nd Annual Meeting of the Association for Computational Linguistics*. volume 2, pages 302–308. http://www.aclweb.org/anthology/P14-2050.pdf.

Bing Liu and Ian Lane. 2016. Attention-Based Recurrent Neural Network Models for Joint Intent Detection and Slot Filling. In *Interspeech 2016*. pages 685–689. https://doi.org/10.21437/Interspeech.2016-1352.

Pengfei Liu, Shafiq Joty, and Helen Meng. 2015. Fine-grained Opinion Mining with Recurrent Neural Networks and Word Embeddings. In *Proceedings of the 2015 Conference on Empirical Methods in Natural Language Processing*. Association for Computational Linguistics, Lisbon, Portugal, pages 1433–1443. http://aclweb.org/anthology/D15-1168.

Thang Luong, Hieu Pham, and Christopher D. Manning. 2015. Effective Approaches to Attention-based Neural Machine Translation. In *Proceedings of the 2015 Conference on Empirical Methods in Natural Language Processing*. Association for Computational Linguistics, Lisbon, Portugal, pages 1412–1421. http://aclweb.org/anthology/D15-1166.

Christopher D. Manning, Mihai Surdeanu, John Bauer, Jenny Finkel, Steven J. Bethard, and David McClosky. 2014. The Stanford CoreNLP Natural Language Processing Toolkit. In *Association for Computational Linguistics (ACL) System Demonstrations*. pages 55–60. http://www.aclweb.org/anthology/P/P14/P14-5010.

Grgoire Mesnil, Xiaodong He, Li Deng, and Yoshua Bengio. 2013. Investigation of recurrent-neural-network architectures and learning methods for spoken language understanding. In *INTERSPEECH*. pages 3771–3775.

Tomas Mikolov, Ilya Sutskever, Kai Chen, Greg S Corrado, and Jeff Dean. 2013. Distributed Representations of Words and Phrases and their Compositionality. In C. J. C. Burges, L. Bottou, M. Welling, Z. Ghahramani, and K. Q. Weinberger, editors, *Advances in Neural Information Processing Systems 26*, Curran Associates, Inc., pages 3111–3119.

Margaret Mitchell, Jacqui Aguilar, Theresa Wilson, and Benjamin Van Durme. 2013. Open Domain Targeted Sentiment. In *Proceedings of the 2013 Conference on Empirical Methods in Natural Language Processing*. Association for Computational Linguistics, Seattle, Washington, USA, pages 1643–1654. http://www.aclweb.org/anthology/D13-1171.

Roy C O'Donnell. 1974. Syntactic differences between speech and writing. *American Speech* 49(1/2):102–110.

Maria Pontiki, Dimitris Galanis, John Pavlopoulos, Harris Papageorgiou, Ion Androutsopoulos, and Suresh Manandhar. 2014. SemEval-2014 Task 4: Aspect Based Sentiment Analysis. In *Proceedings of the 8th International Workshop on Semantic Evaluation (SemEval 2014)*. Association for Computational Linguistics and Dublin City University, Dublin, Ireland, pages 27–35. http://www.aclweb.org/anthology/S14-2004.

Peter Schultes, Verena Dorner, and Verena Lehner. 2013. Leave a comment! an in-depth analysis of user comments on youtube. In *11. Internationale Tagung Wirtschaftsinformatik, Leipzig, Germany*. page 42.

Aliaksei Severyn, Alessandro Moschitti, Olga Uryupina, Barbara Plank, and Katja Filippova. 2014. Opinion Mining on YouTube. In *Proceedings of the 52nd Annual Meeting of the Association for Computational Linguistics (Volume 1: Long Papers)*. Association for Computational Linguistics, Baltimore, Maryland, pages 1252–1261. http://www.aclweb.org/anthology/P14-1118.

Stefan Siersdorfer, Sergiu Chelaru, Wolfgang Nejdl, and Jose San Pedro. 2010. How useful are your comments?: Analyzing and predicting youtube comments and comment ratings. In *Proceedings of the 19th International Conference on World Wide Web*. ACM, New York, NY, USA, WWW '10, pages 891–900. https://doi.org/10.1145/1772690.1772781.

Pontus Stenetorp, Sampo Pyysalo, Goran Topić, Tomoko Ohta, Sophia Ananiadou, and Jun'ichi Tsujii. 2012. brat: a web-based tool for NLP-assisted text annotation. In *Proceedings of the Demonstrations Session at EACL 2012*. Association for Computational Linguistics, Avignon, France.

Yasuyuki Tahara, Atsushi Tago, Hiroyuki Nakagawa, and Akihiko Ohsuga. 2010. Nicoscene: Video scene search by keywords based on social annotation. In Aijun An, Pawan Lingras, Sheila Petty, and Runhe Huang, editors, *Active Media Technology*, Springer Berlin Heidelberg, volume 6335 of *Lecture Notes in Computer Science*, pages 461–474.

Duyu Tang, Bing Qin, Xiaocheng Feng, and Ting Liu. 2016a. Effective LSTMs for Target-Dependent Sentiment Classification. In *Proceedings of COLING 2016, the 26th International Conference on Computational Linguistics: Technical Papers*. The COLING 2016 Organizing Committee, Osaka, Japan, pages 3298–3307. http://aclweb.org/anthology/C16-1311.

Duyu Tang, Bing Qin, and Ting Liu. 2016b. Aspect Level Sentiment Classification with Deep Memory Network. In *Proceedings of the 2016 Conference on Empirical Methods in Natural Language Processing*. Association for Computational Linguistics, Austin, Texas, pages 214–224. https://aclweb.org/anthology/D16-1021.

Oriol Vinyals, Lukasz Kaiser, Terry Koo, Slav Petrov, Ilya Sutskever, and Geoffrey Hinton. 2015. Grammar as a foreign language. In *Advances in Neural Information Processing Systems*. pages 2773–2781. http://papers.nips.cc/paper/5635-grammar-as-a-foreign-language.

Janyce Wiebe, Theresa Wilson, and Claire Cardie. 2005. Annotating Expressions of Opinions and Emotions in Language. *Language Resources and Evaluation* 39(2):165–210. https://doi.org/10.1007/s10579-005-7880-9.

Bin Wu, Erheng Zhong, Ben Tan, Andrew Horner, and Qiang Yang. 2014. Crowdsourced time-sync video tagging using temporal and personalized topic modeling. In *Proceedings of the 20th ACM SIGKDD International Conference on Knowledge Discovery and Data Mining*. ACM, New York, NY, USA, KDD '14, pages 721–730. https://doi.org/10.1145/2623330.2623625.

Liheng Xu, Kang Liu, and Jun Zhao. 2014. Joint Opinion Relation Detection Using One-Class Deep Neural Network. In *Proceedings of COLING 2014, the 25th International Conference on Computational Linguistics: Technical Papers*. Dublin City University and Association for Computational Linguistics, Dublin, Ireland, pages 677–687. http://www.aclweb.org/anthology/C14-1064.

Meishan Zhang, Yue Zhang, and Duy Tin Vo. 2015. Neural Networks for Open Domain Targeted Sentiment. In *Proceedings of the 2015 Conference on Empirical Methods in Natural Language Processing*. Association for Computational Linguistics, Lisbon, Portugal, pages 612–621. http://aclweb.org/anthology/D15-1073.

Understanding human values and their emotional effect

Alexandra Balahur
European Commission Joint Research Centre
Directorate I, Unit I3 Text and Data Mining
Via E. Fermi 2749, 21027 Ispra (VA), Italy
alexandra.balahur@ec.europa.eu

Abstract

1 Abstract

Emotions can be triggered by various factors. According to the Appraisal Theories (De Rivera, 1977; Frijda, 1986; Ortony et al., 1988; Johnson-Laird and Oatley, 1989) emotions are elicited and differentiated on the basis of the cognitive evaluation of the personal significance of a situa-tion, object or event based on appraisal criteria (intrinsic characteristics of objects and events, sig-nificance of events to individual needs and goals, individuals ability to cope with the con-sequences of the event, compatibility of event with social or personal standards, norms and val-ues). These differences in values can trigger re-actions such as anger, disgust (contempt), sad-ness, etc., because these behaviors are evaluated by the public as being incompatible with their social/personal standards, norms or values. Such arguments are frequently present both in main-stream media, as well as social media, building a society-wide view, attitude and emotional reac-tion towards refugees/immigrants. In this demo, I will talk about experiments to annotate and de-tect factual arguments that are linked to human needs/motivations from text and in consequence trigger emotion in the media audience and pro-pose a new task for next year's WASSA.

References

A. Ortony, G.L. Clore, and A. Collins, The Cognitive Structure of Emotions. Cambridge Univ. Press, 1988.

J. De Rivera, A Structural Theory of the Emotions, Psychological Issues, vol. 10, no. 4, 1977.

N. Frijda, The Emotions. Cambridge Univ. Press, 1986.

P.N. Johnson-Laird and K. Oatley, The Language of Emotions: An Analysis of a Semantic Field, Cognition and Emotion, vol. 3, pp. 81-123, 1989.

Proceedings of the 8th Workshop on Computational Approaches to Subjectivity, Sentiment and Social Media Analysis, page 112
Copenhagen, Denmark, September 7–11, 2017. ©2017 Association for Computational Linguistics

Did you ever read about Frogs drinking Coffee?
Investigating the Compositionality of Multi-Emoji Expressions

Rebeca Padilla López and **Fabienne Cap**

Abstract

In this work, we present a first attempt to investigate multi-emoji expressions and whether they behave similarly to multiword expressions in terms of non-compositionality. We focus on the combination of the **frog** and the **hot beverage** emoji, but also show some preliminary results for other non-compositional emoji combinations. We use off-the-shelf sentiment analysers as well as manual classifications to approach the compositionality of these emoji combinations.

1 Introduction

Emojis do not only represent faces, but also concepts and ideas such as weather, objects, or activities (Pavalanathan and Eisenstein, 2016). We assume that these "concept" emojis are not always used as literal representations, but that there are many instances of their use as indicators of a certain emotion or intention. In this paper, we focus on two such "concept" emojis: the *frog face* emoji and the *hot beverage* emoji. We want to analyse the sentiment value of these emojis when used together and when used separately. By looking up tweets that contain the emojis and classifying them as positive, neutral or negative, we show that the meaning of the combination of these emojis is non-compositional, and could not be inferred from the meaning of its components. This is in-line with the behaviour of multi-word expressions and motivates for further study of the phe-

nomenon. The choice of emojis is based on what has been observed in social media sites such as Facebook, Twitter and Tumblr. The users of these sites seem to use these emojis with a definite emotion and intention in mind. This is likely to have its origin in a popular internet meme known as *"But That's None of My Business"*.

According to *Know Your Meme*[1], this meme represents *"a sarcastic expression used as a postscript to an insult or disrespectful remark said towards a specific individual or group"*. Thus, this is the kind of sentiment we expect to find in tweets that include both the *frog face* and the *hot beverage* emoji. When analysing tweets that only include the *frog face* emoji, we expect the sentiment to be neutral. For the *hot beverage* emoji, we assume a neutral sentiment too. When it comes to the frequency distribution of words, the separate meanings of the *hot beverage* emoji and the *frog face* emoji are expected to be quite literal. It is expected to find that words related to frogs and beverages are very common in these tweets, but not in tweets where both emojis appear.

2 Background

In recent years, sentiment analysis has found an invaluable source of material and information in social media. Because of their prevalence in social media, emoticons became the focus of many sentiment analysis studies. Kouloumpis et al. (2011) found that, in the microblogging domain, emoticons were more useful than part-of-speech features for training data collection. Research shows that emoticons do not only represent affective stances, but also intention or identity and can be used to strengthen a message (Derks et al., 2008). Because of their similarities, it is likely that this is

Figure 1: Frog face, hot beverage, tropical drink, cocktail glass, teacup without handle, clapping hands sign, nail polish and lipstick.

---

[1] http://knowyourmeme.com/memes/but-that-s-none-of-my-business

Proceedings of the 8th Workshop on Computational Approaches to Subjectivity, Sentiment and Social Media Analysis, pages 113–117
Copenhagen, Denmark, September 7–11, 2017. ©2017 Association for Computational Linguistics

true also of emojis.

Nowadays, emojis have started substituting emoticons for conveying emotions (Pavalanathan and Eisenstein, 2016) and they are becoming an important part of internet language. Chin et al. (2016) have used emojis to expand on positive or negative sentiment and classified tweets into five emotions. This shows that emojis can help us be more precise in our sentiment analysis. Moreover, Kelly and Watts (2015) investigate the "appropriation" of emojis. In other words, appropriation is the usage in a way that was not intended or envisaged by the designer (Dix, 2007). Even though there has not been much previous work on emojis, they have certain interesting characteristics that make them worthy of being investigated and they could become a useful feature when analysing the sentiment of social media text in the future.

3   Methodology

3.1   Collecting tweets

In order to collect tweets, we went through iEmoji's archive of tweets[2] and manually retrieved 1,000 tweets that contained the *hot beverage* emoji and not the *frog face* emoji, 1,000 that had the *frog face* but not the *hot beverage* and 1,000 that had both. All tweets were published between 2013 and 2016 and were chosen randomly from random pages from the archive. They were pre-processed before the analysis: all hash characters, usernames and emojis were deleted.

3.2   Sentiment analysis and frequency distribution

The three tweet sets were analysed using two different analysers: i) TEXTBLOB (Smedt and Daelemans, 2012) and ii) VADER (Hutto and Gilbert, 2014).

TEXTBLOB is based on a pattern library and returns a tweet's polarity and subjectivity. For the present work, we focused on polarity, which goes from -1 (negative) to 1 (positive), 0 being neutral. VADER was trained to be used on social media and microblogging texts. It returns a dictionary such as: "'pos': 0.446, 'neg': 0.0, 'neu': 0.554, 'compound': 0.6166". We used the "compound" value, since it represents the overall sentiment value of the tweet and uses the same scale as TEXTBLOB.

To evaluate their performance, we manually classified the 100 first tweets from each set and

---

[2]http://www.iemoji.com/

compared this manual annotation to the results the analysers gave for them. Then, we calculated their precision and recall for positive, negative and neutral tweets. Finally, we had a look at the frequency distribution of the words in the tweets, focusing on the 15 most common words.

4   Results

We evaluated our hypothesis using three different approaches: off-the-shelf sentiment analysers (4.1), manual classification (4.2) and finally we report on the most frequent words occurring in the context of the investigated emojis and their combination (4.3).

4.1   Sentiment Analysis

	Both	FrogFace	Hot Beverage
TEXTBLOB	0,048	0,11	0,17
VADER	0,011	0,16	0,18

Table 1: Polarity results for each tweet set. Polarity ranges from 1 (positive) over 0 (neutral) to -1 (negative).

After automatically analysing each of the 3000 tweets and obtaining its polarity score, the average score for every 1000 tweet sets was calculated. The results are shown in Table 1. The sentiment analysis shows a small but clear difference between the sentiment that each emoji has separately and the sentiment they have when used together. TEXTBLOB and VADER give very similar scores to the frog face tweets (0,11 and 0,16) and to the hot beverage tweets (0,17 and 0,18), and these two sets are at the same time quite similar to each other in their scores. Since they seem to have a similar sentiment, if their meaning were still literal when combined, we would expect the combination to have the same score, but from our results we can see that the score for the combination is lower. Even though we first assumed a more negative sentiment for the combination, the results make sense: tweets with both emojis are supposed to have a subtle, sarcastic tone, which is not easily recognised by sentiment analysers yet. Nevertheless, the distinction is there, and we will have a closer look at it in an additional evaluation using manual classification.

4.2   Manual Classification

We manually classified 100 tweets for each tweet set as negative, positive or neutral. An overview is given in Table 3. The *frog face* set and the *hot*

		Positive Tweets		Negative Tweets		Neutral Tweets		Average	
		Precision	Recall	Precision	Recall	Precision	Recall	Precision	Recall
TB	Both	0.10	0.26	0.47	0.11	0.15	0.28	0.24	0.21
	FrogFace	0.69	0.68	0.55	0.33	0.62	0.73	0.62	0.58
	HotBeverage	0.70	0.66	0.22	0.25	0.57	0.60	0.49	0.50
VADER	Both	0.20	0.60	0.63	0.26	0.14	0.22	0.32	0.36
	FrogFace	0.73	0.70	0.58	0.46	0.62	0.71	0.64	0.62
	HotBeverage	0.70	0.66	0.00	0.00	0.60	0.68	0.43	0.44

Table 2: Precision and recall for all tweet sets, calculated using the manual classification as gold standard.

beverage set have a similar distribution and are in general fairly positive, but the combination of both is clearly negative, which supports the hypothesis in question. The meaning in this case is non-compositional and non-literal. While classifying the tweets, it was obvious that they had the same sarcastic, disrespectful tone as the *"But That's None of My Business"* meme, and some even used the same words. For example, one Twitter user wrote *"I can solve all your problems, yet you do stupid shit. But that's none of my business."* [3], followed by a *hot beverage* and a *frog face*.

We also used this manual classification to evaluate the performance of both classifiers. The results are given in Table 2. Precision and recall are lower for both analysers when it comes to the combination of emojis. This is not surprising, since they were expected to be more difficult to analyse due to the sarcasm and the subtlety of their sentiment. The analysers performed best when classifying positive tweets. VADER performed sightly better for the *frog face* tweets, and TEXTBLOB performed better for the *hot beverage* tweets. We attribute the overall low performance to the fact that there was a lot of sarcasm in the tweets, and for this to be understood one needs some real-world knowledge which is almost impossible for a classifier to make use of.

	Positive	Negative	Neutral
Both	15	67	18
FrogFace	47	15	38
HotBeverage	54	8	38

Table 3: Manual classification of tweets.

4.3 Word count

For the word count-based evaluation, we looked at the 15 most common words in each set of 1000 tweets. If a word is repeated in the same tweet, it is

	Both	**FrogFace**	**HotBeverage**
1	but (372)	frog (256)	coffee (396)
2	be (132)	emoji (225)	tea (132)
3	the (123)	the (103)	the (124)
4	people (114)	like (102)	a (90)
5	you (99)	I (90)	I (85)
6	like (97)	frogs (85)	morning (73)
7	don't (97)	my (77)	day (72)
8	all (91)	have (66)	my (65)
9	are (88)	a (56)	need (60)
10	a (86)	but (55)	good (59)
11	I (76)	I'm (54)	I'm (59)
12	not (75)	! (52)	be (58)
13	girls (71)	love (52)	cup (57)
14	if (70)	be (49)	hot (56)
15	have (65)	no (48)	starbucks (55)

Table 4: Most common words from each 1,000 tweet set.

counted as many times as it appears. In Table 4 we see the *hot beverage* set's most common word is "coffee", and the second one is "tea". Most of the words are semantically related and show a literal use of the emoji. For the *frog face* tweets, the most common word is "frog", and the plural "frogs" is on 6th place, which also points to a literal use. In the combined set the most common word is "but". Even though it is a function word and would usually be ignored, in this case it is not, because it is the first word in the meme ("But That's None of My Business") and it can indicate an objection. In this last case, the words do not tell us much about the sentiment or meaning of the emoji combination. This suggests that the emojis have a non-literal meaning. The results also show emojis are often used in addition to the concept they represent, without substituting it. This could be an interesting direction for future work.

---

[3] https://twitter.com/rai_close/status/557368926506864640

5 Other emoji combinations

5.1 Frog face plus other beverages

While retrieving tweets we noticed a few tweets that expressed the same sentiment as the *frog face* and *hot beverage* tweets, but had a different beverage emoji, e.g. the *tropical drink, cocktail glass* or *teacup without handle* emojis. We found 18 such tweets. For example, a user wrote *"Got a pic of u that could expose u so keep saying stuff"* [4] and added a *frog face* and a *teacup without handle*. This sample is too small to confirm that the sentiment and meaning of these combinations will remain the same regardless of the drink emoji. However, nothing similar was observed when retrieving tweets containing the *hot beverage*. The *frog face* was never substituted by another face. This might indicate that the *frog face* is the main element of the combination and the one which brings the sarcastic, negative tone to the expression.

5.2 Clapping Hands Sign emoji

For the *clapping hands sign* emoji, we expect a change of meaning whenever it is repeated or placed in certain parts of the sentence. On its own, it is mostly used to show excitement or appreciation. However, when placed between each word in a sentence (sometimes two or three words), the connotation turns negative. In this case, the user is aggressively sharing their opinion, telling off the readers or correcting them.

In order to investigate this hypothesis, we used iEmoji to retrieve 50 tweets in which the emoji appeared several times between the words and 50 tweets where the emoji appeared differently. We found a significant change in meaning and sentiment in all of them. For example, one user wrote *"@Michael_Sanchez I didn't expect this to happen. So happy rn. Good luck sir"* [5], with a *clapping hands sign* at its end. On the other hand, another user wrote *"PLANNED PARENTHOOD DOESN'T JUST DO ABORTIONS"* [6]. After every word, there was a *clapping hands sign* emoji, emphasising the message and seemingly trying to correct a false idea. We investigated only a small sample, but this use of the emojis was consistent throughout all tweets, which indicates there is a pattern worth studying.

5.3 Nail Polish emoji

The *nail polish* emoji shares the sarcastic subtext of the emoji combination we extensively studied in this paper, but its meaning changes and becomes literal when used in combination with the *lipstick* emoji. In this case, the *lipstick* emoji retains its literal meaning and turns the *nail polish* emoji into a literal representation of nail polish. We retrieved 50 tweets with the *nail polish* emoji appearing next to the *lipstick* emoji, and 50 tweets with only the *nail polish* emoji. In 47 out of the 50 tweets, the difference was clear. For example, one user tweeted *"@TAMU sorry my tampons and wallet are so threatening,"* [7] adding a *nail polish* at the end. This tweet is clearly sarcastic and has nothing to do with makeup. A counter example is this tweet: *"I need a makeup advent calendar in my life"* [8] with a *nail polish* next to a *lipstick* and a clearly literal meaning. This is a small sample, but the pattern is found in most of the tweets, which suggests it is not accidental.

6 Conclusion

We showed that there is a distinct change between the literal meaning the frog face and the hot beverage emojis have when used separately and the more subtle, non-literal meaning their combination has. This is shown in the frequency distribution of the words and in the sentiment analysis of the tweets. Both sentiment analysers showed a small yet observable difference in sentiment, and while this was not enough to reach any conclusions, the difference became clearer after the manual classification of the tweets.

This kind of multi-emoji expression is not unique, since there are similar cases that have also been examined, but it is uncommon and each case has its own characteristics. Even though the case that has been studied here is not a widespread phenomenon, emojis are a very recent addition to our communication methods. In the future we expect to see more transformations in the way emoji are used, which would be worth being researched in depth.

---

[4] https://twitter.com/jc00003333/status/525776951966183424

[5] https://twitter.com/BrokenHarmonyML/status/789534743117205504

[6] https://twitter.com/Jeeennnnaa/status/788912245975748608

[7] https://twitter.com/ShelbyLCole/status/800022278679367680

[8] https://twitter.com/sophiaguyy/status/801143183157686272

References

Delenn Chin, Anna Zappone, and Jessica Zhao. 2016. Analyzing Twitter Sentiment of the 2016 Presidential Candidates .

Daantje Derks, Arjan E. R. Bos, and Jasper von Grumbkow. 2008. Emoticons in computer-mediated communication: Social motives and social context. *CyberPsychology & Behavior* 11(1):99–101. https://doi.org/10.1089/cpb.2007.9926.

Alan Dix. 2007. Designing for appropriation. *BCS-HCI '07 Proceedings of the 21st British HCI Group Annual Conference on People and Computers: HCI...but not as we know it* 2:27–30.

Clayton J. Hutto and Eric Gilbert. 2014. Vader: A parsimonious rule-based model for sentiment analysis of social media text. *Eighth International AAAI Conference on Weblogs and Social Media* pages 216–225.

Ryan Kelly and Leon Watts. 2015. Characterising the Inventive Appropriation of Emoji as Relationally Meaningful in Mediated Close Personal Relationships. *Experiences of Technology Appropriation: Unanticipated Users, Usage, Circumstances, and Design* .

Efthymios Kouloumpis, Theresa Wilson, and Johanna Moore. 2011. Twitter sentiment analysis: The good the bad and the omg! *Proceedings of the Fifth International AAAI Conference on Weblogs and Social Media (ICWSM 11)* pages 538–541.

Umashanthi Pavalanathan and Jacob Eisenstein. 2016. Emoticons vs. Emojis on Twitter: A Causal Inference Approach. *AAAI Spring Symposium on Observational Studies through Social Media and Other Human-Generated Content* http://arxiv.org/abs/1510.08480.

Tom De Smedt and Walter Daelemans. 2012. Pattern for Python. *Journal of Machine Learning Research* 13:2063–2067.

Investigating Redundancy in Emoji Use: Study on a Twitter Based Corpus

Giulia Donato
University of Copenhagen
`giulia.dnt@gmail.com`

Patrizia Paggio
University of Copenhagen
University of Malta
`paggio@hum.ku.dk`
`patrizia.paggio@um.edu.mt`

Abstract

In this paper we present an annotated corpus created with the aim of analyzing the informative behaviour of emoji – an issue of importance for sentiment analysis and natural language processing. The corpus consists of 2475 tweets all containing at least one emoji, which has been annotated using one of the three possible classes: *Redundant*, *Non Redundant*, and *Non Redundant + POS*. We explain how the corpus was collected, describe the annotation procedure and the interface developed for the task. We provide an analysis of the corpus, considering also possible predictive features, discuss the problematic aspects of the annotation, and suggest future improvements.

1 Introduction

Nowadays emoji are widespread throughout mobile and web communication both in private conversations and public contexts such as blog entries or comments. In 2015, the Oxford Dictionary declared the emoji *Face with tears of joy* "Word of the year", and since then the academic interest towards the topic, as well as the development of relevant resources, have grown substantially. Emoji are best known to be markers for emotions, and in this sense they can be considered an evolution of emoticons. However, these pictographs can be used to represent a much wider range of concepts than emoticons, including objects, ideas and actions in addition to emotions, and thus they interact with the content expressed in the surrounding text in more complex ways. Furthermore, emoji are used not only at the end of a message, e.g. a tweet, but can occur anywhere and possibly in sequences. Therefore, understanding the seman-

tic relation they have with the surrounding text, in particular whether emoji add independent meaning, is an important step in any approach attempting to process their contribution to the overall content of a given message, both for the purposes of sentiment analysis and natural language processing.

We are interested in investigating to what extent it is possible for a human annotator, and subsequently for an automatic classifier, to determine if emoji in tweets are used to emphasize or add information, which may well be emotional information, but could also have a different semantic flavour. If emoji do add meaning, we also ask how easy it is to understand if they are being used as syntactic substitutes for words. In this paper, we focus on the corpus of English tweets that was collected and annotated to provide training data for a number of classifiers aiming at predicting whether emoji in microblogs are used in a redundant or a non-redundant way.

The classification experiments achieved promising results (F-score of 0.7) for the best performing model, which combined LSA with handcrafted features and employed a linear SVM in a One vs. All fashion. The process and results of the experiments will be described in a future paper (in preparation).

In Section (2) we review related research, then in Section (3) we describe how the tweets were extracted and collected to create the corpus, and give counts of the various represented categories. In Section (4) the annotation process is described, Section (5) presents and discusses the results, and finally in Section (6) we provide a conclusion.

2 Related research

Several studies trace parallels between emoticons and emoji, sometimes using both terms inter-

Proceedings of the 8th Workshop on Computational Approaches to Subjectivity, Sentiment and Social Media Analysis, pages 118–126
Copenhagen, Denmark, September 7–11, 2017. ©2017 Association for Computational Linguistics

changeably, with the purpose of dealing with emotion expression or automatic emotion detection, and thus only considering those pictographs that resemble facial features. Boia et al. (2013) focus on emoticons and their use in tweets. The authors attempted to determine the reliability of emoticon labels in sentiment classification by means of a user study and generated a sentiment lexicon from a corpus of 2.1 million tweets. They found that agreement between the sentiment expressed by emoticons and the sentiment expressed by the surrounding words is only slightly higher than random, showing that emoticons are likely to be used as a means to add emotion to an otherwise neutral text. The experiment based on the sentiment lexicon proved that emoticons are good indicators of sentiment in the tweet, but are less effective in retrieving related sentiment words, thus confirming that emoticons complement the text rather than stressing what is already expressed by the words.

The paper by Hallsmar and Palm (2016) is instead focused on the effectiveness of using emoji to automatically annotate training data for multiclass emotion classification. The researchers employed a training corpus of 400,000 tweets, 100,000 for each of four classes (sadness, anger, fear and happiness), then tested against 80 instances, manually collected and labeled according to their textual content. The results show that emoji can be effectively used to automatically annotate the emotion class in large sets of tweets, thus suggesting that emoji, in contrast with emoticons, may co-occur with semantically related words.

Other works have analyzed the semantics of emoji, mostly by means of distributional semantics. In Barbieri et al. (2016), the authors used the skip-gram model paired with different dataset sizes and different filtering methods to generate emoji embeddings. These were evaluated against a set of 50 emoji pairs manually annotated for *similarity* and *relatedness* scores. The similarity scores obtained by the models were strongly correlated with those in the gold standard, particularly if stop words and punctuation are removed from the dataset. This indicates that surrounding words and other emoji are useful for inferring the meaning of a given emoji, possibly indicating that the emoji is being used in a redundant way.

In Eisner et al. (2016), emoji embeddings were learnt from their description in the Unicode emoji standard, and representations are thus obtained for all represented emoji including those that appear infrequently in online text. In spite of the model being trained on much less data, the authors claim to outperform Barbieri et al. (2016) on the task of Twitter sentiment analysis. These results point to the fact that the emoji descriptions in the Unicode standard are a valid source from which to model their semantics.

The issue whether emoji add content to the text they occur in, particularly in tweets, or whether they are largely redundant, as well as how their specific use in this respect can be predicted, is not investigated directly in any of the studies mentioned so far.

The paper by Zanzotto et al. (2011) addresses the problem of linguistic redundancy within the realm of microblogs. Although this study does not specifically target emoji, it is of particular interest for our work given the formal definitions provided for both redundancy and non redundancy as well as the methodology employed. The authors performed a classification experiment on 1242 pairs of tweets related to news, previously annotated considering four possible relations, i.e. entailment (redundant), paraphrase (redundant), related/unrelated (non-redundant), and contradiction (non-redundant). They used the annotated corpus to test different models in a classification experiment, and obtained the best results with a combination of syntactic and similarity features computed across the word vectors of each pair.

The methodology adopted in our work builds on the Zanzotto et al. (2011) study, both as concerns the fundamental question we ask, and the way we have collected and annotated our training corpus. A crucial difference is, however, that our analysis focuses on the use of emoji.

3   Corpus Preparation

To answer our research questions we set up a corpus of English tweets automatically extracted from Twitter with the aid of specific emoji keywords. The corpus was then annotated by four human coders to be further used in a machine learning experiment. The annotated corpus consists of tweets containing emoji paired with their counterparts where the emoji has been removed, for a total of 2475 pairs.

The purpose of the corpus collection and annotation was twofold. Our primary goal was to pro-

Category	Emoji	Names
Traveling/Commuting		*car, airplane, sailboat*
Events		*party popper, jack-o-lantern, graduation cap*
Places		*school, european castle, home + garden*
Other Activities		*artist palette, books, television*
Feelings		*smiling face with heart eyes, unamused face, crying face*
People		*man and woman holding hands, person walking, person raising one hand*
Eating & Drinking		*pizza, doughnut, hot beverage*
Nature & Animals		*dog, snowflake, maple leaf*
Music		*microphone, guitar, musical notes*
Sport		*trophy, swimmer, basketball and hoop*

Table 1: List of the emoji used to extract tweets for the corpus collection

vide training data to develop classifiers that could predict the relation of emoji in unseen tweets. A secondary goal was to investigate how easy it is for human coders to distinguish different uses of emoji with respect to their semantic contribution. In order to clarify this aspect, we run an inter-annotator agreement test on part of the annotated material.

3.1 Emoji Selection

To select a set of meaningful emoji to use for the data extraction, we start by defining a categorization of the whole emoji set. The Unicode consortium website provides the full emoji dataset, in which every emoji is annotated with a code, fourteen different graphic renderings, the emoji name, the date of addition to the Unicode standard, and a set of keywords that identify the content of each pictograph. Unicode separates groups of emoji according to similar renderings and, possibly, semantic relatedness, but does not provide an official ontology.

Previous studies interested in emoji semantics use different categorizations for their purposes. Cappallo et al. (2015) relied on the categories listed in the MSCOCO (Lin et al., 2014) dataset: *Person & Accessory, Animal, Vehicle, Outdoor Object, Indoor Object, Sport, Kitchenware, Food, Furniture, Appliance, Electronics*. These categories partially overlap the ones in Emojipedia (Burge, 2013): *Smileys & People, Animals & Nature, Food & Drink, Activity, Travel & Places,* *Objects, Symbols, Flags*. Emojipedia categorizes the pictographs considering their graphical properties, while the MSCOCO categories are modeled for object recognition, thus they discriminate more precisely among inanimate objects.

Barbieri et al. (2016) used word embeddings, dimensionality reduction and clustering, to identify 11 clusters labeled as: *Sports & Animals, Nature, Body gestures & Positive, Free Time, Unclear, Love & Parties, Letters, Barber & Symbols, Eating & Drinking, Music, Sad & Tears*. These labels reflect the graphical and conceptual similarity of the data points included in a specific cluster. Nevertheless, some of the labels are claimed to be inconsistent since the relevant clusters include few and apparently unrelated pictographs.

Vidal et al. (2016) used a categorization based on Emojipedia which includes six categories: *Food & Drinks, Non-food objects, Celebrations, Activity, Travel & Places, Nature*.

After having considered the categorizations mentioned above we developed our own including the following labels: *Nature & Animals, Places, Traveling/Commuting, Sport, Events, Other Activities, Music, Eating & Drinking, People, Feelings*. Our intent was to select a small number of relatively broad and easily recognizable categories. Furthermore, we chose to keep events and activities separate from entities, as is done in many linguistically-oriented ontologies.

From each category in our list we have selected three emoji; in order to get clearly distinguishable pictographs we have considered both their frequency of use given by the Emojitracker, thus favouring the most frequent tokens, and their graphical features. The full list of emoji is shown in table 1.

3.2 Data Collection

All the data were collected between the 1st and 2nd of November 2016 by means of the Twitter Streaming API and the Python Tweepy wrapper.

To extract the data we added to the script a filter for the English language and passed the list of the selected emoji as the keywords parameter. Both the possibilities of filtering data by language and keywords are provided as features by the API.

The raw data included 501,342 tweets, subsequently reduced to 196,434 after removing all duplicate entries. A series of common preprocessing steps were applied before the annotation: in particular all the mentions of other users and all the links were replaced with placeholders.

The accepted character length on Twitter is 140; in the cleaned corpus the average length of the tweets was of 50 characters, 555 tweets were longer than 140 characters with a maximum length of 196 characters. Thus, as an additional step, all the tweets below a threshold length of 10 characters and above a threshold length of 140 characters were discarded. We checked again for the presence of duplicates after replacing mentions and links, since tweets may have the same content and differ only for these elements; this lead to a resulting collection of 180,958 instances. In this cleaned version of the corpus the average tweet length is of 52 characters with a standard deviation of 32.

The best represented category is, unsurprisingly, *Feelings* with a total of 99,050 instances. Within *Feelings* the most frequent emoji is *Smiling face with heart shaped eyes* with 60,479 extracted tweets. The least represented category is *Places* with a total of 900 instances. Within this category the least frequent emoji is *School* with 47 extracted tweets.

From these data we created a balanced corpus by sampling 900 instances from each category, since this is the size of the least populated one. From the resulting corpus of 9000 instances we further removed all the tweets containing only the emoji used for the data extraction since this would have resulted in pairs containing one empty tweet and one tweet consisting in an emoji key-

word repeated multiple times. The final collection contained 8985 pairs; from this corpus we randomly sampled 4100 pairs for the annotation. The size was chosen considering the corpus size in the Zanzotto et al. (2011) paper, which we used as a methodological model for our work.

4 Annotation

The annotation of the 4100 tweet pairs took place remotely between the 21st and the 31st of December 2016 and was performed by four annotators, three located in Greece and one in the Netherlands. All the annotators were fluent English speakers. For the annotation we developed an ad-hoc user interface.

We chose a multiclass setup with three classes of interest: *Redundant, Non-redundant*, and *Non-redundant + POS*; we will further define these classes and explain them with examples shortly below. The annotators were asked to assign a class to each pair in the corpus.

4.1 Classes Definition

The general definition of redundancy is *repetition of already expressed information*; to describe the classes for the annotation we relied on Zanzotto et al. (2011), who define as redundant tweet pairs which are in a relation of paraphrase or entailment, while pairs in a relation of contradiction or relatedness are considered non-redundant. We expect an emoji to be considered redundant if it represents an object or an action also expressed by words in the text (the emoji is a synonym of another word) or if it represents an object or action whose presence is directly implied by the text (the emoji is entailed by the words).

The final set of classes includes three labels: *Redundant, Non-Redundant, Non-Redundant + POS*. The Redundant class indicates that the emoji of interest repeats the information present in the text or that its meaning is implied by the text.

On the contrary, we expect the Non-Redundant class to be assigned when the emoji adds information not already present or implied in the text.

Lastly the Non-Redundant + POS class, which can be considered as a subset of the Non Redundant class, indicates the case where the emoji is used with a syntactic function (and can be labeled with its POS), thus replacing a word. We provided a set of examples to the annotators and clarified possible edge cases. An extract from the examples is listed here:

1. *Redundant*

   - "We'll always have Beer. I'll see to it. I got your back on that one. 🍺"
   - "@USER I need u in Paris girls ▮▯"

2. *Non-Redundant*

   - "I wish you were here ✈"
   - "Hopin for the best 🎓"

3. *Non-Redundant + POS*

   - "Thank you so so so so much ily Here's a 🍕 as a thank you gift x"
   - "Good morning 🌍"

An edge case could be represented by:

- "Reading is always a good idea 📚 . Thank you for your sincere support @USER. Happy reading."

In this case the emoji represents books which are related to the verb "reading", however the act of reading does not necessarily imply the presence of books (it is not an entailment) since it is possible to read newspapers, blogs, comments, emails; the emoji is narrowing down the meaning of the verb, therefore it is adding information and we should consider it non-redundant.

Emotions also represent a challenge since we need to rely on symbols or simplifications to depict complex expressions. While a case such as:

- "i'm so proud of myself 😗 *pats my back*"

is clearly non-redundant (here the emoji is used ironically), a tweet like:

- "My forever love 😻 @URL"

represents redundant use.

4.2 Interface

To annotate the tweets we set up a dynamic interface accessible online and hosted - until the completion of the task - on a server at the Demokritos Institute of Research in Athens (http://www.demokritos.gr/); we provided detailed guidelines explaining how to access and use the interface and describing the annotation criteria and the classes with the aid of examples.

Before the annotation started, we tested the interface on the latest versions of Mozilla Firefox and Google Chrome. Since browsers do not always render emoji automatically we provided our interface with a link to the Symbola Font, one of the richest in emoji renderings.

On the first page of the interface each annotator had a welcoming message and a briefer version of the instructions already provided in the guidelines. After the instructions and three examples of tweet pairs with the correspondent class checked, the annotators could move on to the annotation page which presented the pairs, a forced choice form to select the class and a submit button. The pairs were updated dynamically after each submission and the checked value was stored together with the index of the pair and the annotator id. The default value of the form was set to blank; we gave the annotators the possibility to submit a blank value whenever they were undecided about the class to pick; the blank submissions were recorded as *undefined*.

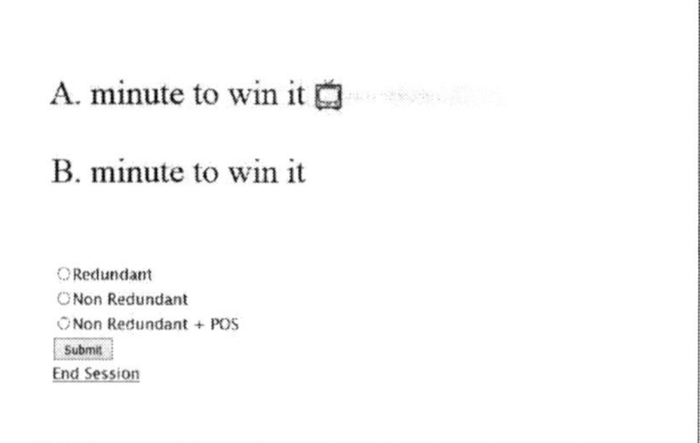

Figure 1: Screen capture of the annotation interface

The first 100 pairs were annotated by all the annotators to measure the inter-annotator agreement; after this set of common pairs the annotators had random access to further 1,000 pairs each among the remaining 4000. On completion of the task the annotators were redirected to a thanksgiving page. Furthermore, we gave them the option to interrupt and restart the annotation process in order to complete the task in multiple sessions. Their work was automatically saved to a csv (comma separated value) file after each session's interruption.

Due to the random access, after the first 100 pairs, some of the 1,000 pairs left were presented and annotated more than once, hence they were discarded from the final corpus. Additionally, one of the annotators reported problems with the interface when saving the last part of her work. Therefore, and also considering the fact that we excluded the 100 pairs used to calculate the agreement, our final corpus consists of 2475 annotated pairs in total.

4.3 Annotation Reliability

To assess the inter-annotator agreement we adopt Cohen's *kappa* coefficient (Cohen, 1960).

Coehn's κ is used to assess agreement between two annotators and it is considered more robust than simple percentage agreement since it corrects for chance agreement. Moreover, this choice allows us to compare our results with those obtained by Zanzotto et al. (2011) for a similar, although more complex, task.

Considering the agreement results described in Zanzotto et al. (2011) we expected to get a κ of 0.6, which is generally considered moderate agreement (Landis and Koch, 1977).

	A1	A2	A3	A4
A1	-	0.76	0.78	0.7
A2	0.76	-	0.81	0.8
A3	0.78	0.81	-	0.71
A4	0.7	0.8	0.71	-

Table 2: Observed agreement

	A1	A2	A3	A4
A1	-	0.57	0.62	0.48
A2	0.57	-	0.66	0.64
A3	0.62	0.66	-	0.5
A4	0.48	0.64	0.5	-

Table 3: Cohen's κ agreement

In tables 2 and 3 we report the results for the percentage and Cohen's κ agreement between each pair of annotators. The average percentage agreement is 76%, while the average Cohen's κ is 0.576, a value only slightly lower than what we were aiming for. A discussion of the difficulties encountered by the annotators is provided in the next section. To comply with the suggestion given by one of the anonymous reviewers, we also calculated agreement using Fleiss' kappa and Krippendorff's alfa. The values we obtained, however, are very similar (0.575 and 0.576, respectively.)

5 Analysis and Discussion

5.1 Corpus Analysis

Our gold standard contains a total of 2475 annotated pairs, as stated in the previous section.

	End	*Not End*	*Total*
R	452	382	834
	(0.357)	(0.316)	(0.337)
Non-R	768	660	1428
	(0.607)	(0.546)	(0.577)
Non-R+POS	37	139	176
	(0.029)	**(0.115)**	(0.071)
Undefined	9 (0.007)	28	37
		(0.023)	(0.015)
Total	1266 (1)	1155 (1)	2475 (1)

Table 4: Conditional frequency of the emoji class given the emoji position: absolute counts and proportions. The largest proportion for each class in each condition is in boldface.

	CD	*NN*	*Other*	Total
R	362	328	144	834
	(0.348)	(0.336)	(0.314)	(0.337)
Non-R	583	565	280	1428
	(0.560)	**(0.580)**	(0.610)	(0.577)
Non-R+POS	73	79	24	176
	(0.070)	**(0.081)**	(0.052)	(0.071)
Undefined	23	3	11	37
	(0.022)	(0.003)	**(0.024)**	(0.015)
Total	1041	975	459	2475
	(1)	(1)	(1)	(1)

Table 5: Conditional frequency of the emoji class given the emoji POS tag: counts and proportions. The largest proportion for each class in each condition is in boldface.

The distribution of the classes is as follows: the *Redundant* class has 834 instances (33.7%), the *Non-Redundant* class has 1428 instances (57.7%), the *Non-Redundant + POS* class has 176 instances (7.1%). Additionally, 37 instances are annotated as *undefined* (1.5%).

Table 4 details how the classes are distributed given the position of the emoji as either close to the end of the tweet or not[1]: 35.7% of the instances are annotated as Redundant (R in the tables), 60.7% as Non-Redundant (Non-R), 2.9% as

---

[1]The emoji position was computed by dividing the index of the emoji in the tokenized tweet by the number of tokens in the tweet. We considered close to the end those emoji with a value equal or above 0.7

Non-Redundant + POS (Non-R+POS), and 0.7% are undefined. In the opposite condition (when the position of the emoji is not close to the end of the tweet) 31.6% instances are Redundant, 54.6% are Non-Redundant, 11.5% are Non-Redundant + POS, and 2.3% are undefined. Interestingly, although not surprisingly, the Non-Redundant + POS class is the only one (leaving the undefined instances out) to show a higher probability of occurrence in the "not close to the end" than the "close to the end" condition.

From the distribution we can see that, at least in a corpus the size of ours, the distinction between close or non close to the end is not a strong indicator of whether the emoji is used to repeat or add information, with the exception of the case in which the emoji not only adds information but also replaces a word. The differences in the distribution are significant, as demonstrated by a χ-squared test of independence (χ-squared = 81.644, df = 3, p-value < 0.001). An analysis of the residuals confirmed that the effect of position is highest in the case of the Non-Redundant + POS class.

We had an intuition that the part-of-speech category of the emoji might be an interesting feature to look for the purposes of training classifiers to predict the relation of the emoji with the content of the rest of the text. Therefore, the corpus was run through the Stanford Tagger. We decided to use the standard Stanford POS Tagger from the Python NLTK wrapper since traditional POS taggers have been reported to achieve satisfactory results when compared with domain specific taggers (Derczynski et al., 2013), and also since Twitter-specific POS taggers do not seem to provide tags for emoji.

In table 5 we report the frequencies for the most frequent tags, which are *CD* or *NN* (cardinal number and noun, respectively). The column *Other* sums the frequencies of the remaining categories. The Stanford POS Tagger considers several features prior to assigning a tag to unknown words. This set of features includes capitalization, context (n-grams), hyphens, numbers, and allcaps (Toutanova et al., 2003). Tokens containing allcaps, a slash or a dash as well as numbers are tagged with NN (since they might be company names). Thus the POS-tag assigned to an emoji may either be the result of these specific features or may be based on the n-gram sequence in which the emoji is embedded.

From the numbers in the table, and again leaving out the undefined instances, it would appear that NN might be used as a predictor of the two Non Redundant classes, while CD seems more predictive of Redundant use. The differences are significant on a χ-squared test of independence (χ-squared = 21.385, df = 6, p-value < 0.01). An analysis of the residuals showed that, if we ignored the undefined instances, the largest contributions to the differences are found in the negative effect of CD on the Non-Redundant class, the negative effect of Other on Non-Redundant + POS and the positive effect of NN on that same class.

To sum up, the analysis shows that position (close to the end or not) and part-of-speech class might be useful features to consider when training a classifier to predict whether emoji in tweets are being used in a redundant or additive way.

5.2 Annotation difficulties

We saw earlier that the inter-annotator results are slightly lower than expected. Some annotators reported difficulty in assigning a class when the tweet content was not meaningful, thus a possible way to improve the annotation design and increase the agreement would be to filter out all the spam and advertisement tweets that contain little or non-informative text and keep only tweets from individual (possibly verified) users, avoiding corporate accounts and bots.

To gain a better understanding of the difficulties of the annotation process we considered a small sample of pairs where two annotators assigned the Non-Redundant class and the other two assigned the Non-Redundant + POS class, some examples are listed here:

- "✈️ 🆚 Legia Warsaw"

- "🍕 - like who comments 'ifb'"

From these examples it can be seen that disagreement emerges when the tweet content is very short and unstructured and the function of the emoji is ambiguous, given also the lack of syntactic cues in the text. Such cases include occurrences where the text of the tweet consists of hashtags only.

We also noted disagreement (mostly among a single annotator and the three others) in cases where the emoji is strongly related to other words in the text. E.g.:

- "I wish I was a pet so I could just stay home,

lounge all day and have no responsibilities "

- "@USER mom, my birthday is coming"

In such cases it is possible that one or more annotator identified a relation of synonymy or entailment (thus, label the instance as "Redundant") while the others consider it as relatedness or similarity (thus, label the instance as "Non Redundant"). This suggests that identifying entailment at token level instead than from pairs of sentences, especially in unstructured and short text, is a hard task. We must also note that even though we balanced the amount of tweets per category in our corpus, we did not further balance the tweets in each category according to the emoji used to retrieve them. Therefore, we cannot exclude a possible effect derived from the most common of these emoji and we should consider to improve this aspect in future research.

Lastly, we cannot exclude that difficulties may have arisen due to renderings of other co-occurring emoji that were missing from the Symbola font we adopted.

6   Conclusion

We have presented an annotated corpus of tweets that was developed with the purpose of training models to classify the informative behaviour of emoji in tweets.

We have described the entire process of retrieving, cleaning, and presenting the data to the annotators through the graphical user interface specifically developed for the task. The interface source code is available at `https://github.com/giuliadnt/Annotation_gui`; the corpus can be provided by the main author on request.

The reliability of the annotation was measured and, although the average κ score was slightly lower than expected, it still showed close to moderate agreement among the annotators, an acceptable result given the difficulty of the task.

We have also provided an analysis of the corpus in terms of the distribution of three classes of emoji behaviour (Redundant, Non-Redundant, and Non-Redundant + POS) given the position of the emoji in the tweet, as well as their part-of-speech category. Both dimensions seem to provide at least some predictive power, and have in fact been used as features to develop classifiers of emoji informative behaviour in tweets (paper in preparation),

There are several aspects we have discussed in this work that may constitute a limitation and are, therefore, open to improvements and changes. The most important is perhaps the fact that the three classes of interest are far from being equally represented. Thus, more data should be collected. Doing so could also reduce the effect of noisy examples, such as those of tweets only consisting of emoji.

Regarding this aspect we could also consider the possibility of using a binary setup, thus merging Non Redundant and Non Redundant + POS into the same class and balancing the amount of instances related to each case within it. Improvements to the annotation interface should also be considered if more data is annotated.

Considering the confusion sometimes made by the annotators between similarity and entailment, more examples should be provided to train them more extensively to categorize such cases correctly.

Furthermore, the agreement can be improved by including additional annotators and removing from the corpus those tweets that result to be particularly problematic

As future work it will be interesting to evaluate emoji's behaviour in the context of specific NLP tasks such as threads summarization. Moreover, it would be important to verify if the redundancy between emoji and words is equivalent or differs from the redundancy among the words alone in the context of the same tweet.

Acknowledgments

We would like to express our gratitude to George Giannakopoulos, the Institute of Informatics and Telecommunications at NSCR Demokritos (Athens, GR) and everybody at Sci.FY for the help and support throughout the whole data collection and annotation process. We would also like to thank Daniela Schneevogt and Michael Schlichtkrull for all their suggestions and the reviewers for the feedback provided.

References

Francesco Barbieri, Francesco Ronzano, and Horacio Saggion. 2016. What does this emoji mean? a vector space skip-gram model for twitter emojis. In *Language Resources and Evaluation conference, LREC*. Portoroz, Slovenia.

Marina Boia, Boi Faltings, Claudiu-Cristian Musat, and Pearl Pu. 2013. A:) is worth a thousand words: How people attach sentiment to emoticons and words in tweets. In *Social Computing (SocialCom), 2013 International Conference on*. IEEE, pages 345–350.

Jeremy Burge. 2013. Emojipedia. `https:// emojipedia.org/`.

Spencer Cappallo, Thomas Mensink, and Cees GM Snoek. 2015. Image2emoji: Zero-shot emoji prediction for visual media. In *Proceedings of the 23rd ACM international conference on Multimedia*. ACM, pages 1311–1314.

Jacob Cohen. 1960. A coefficient of agreement for nominal scales. *Educational and Psychological Measurement* 20(1):37–46. https://doi.org/10.1177/001316446002000104.

Leon Derczynski, Alan Ritter, Sam Clark, and Kalina Bontcheva. 2013. Twitter part-of-speech tagging for all: Overcoming sparse and noisy data. In *RANLP*. pages 198–206.

Ben Eisner, Tim Rocktäschel, Isabelle Augenstein, Matko Bošnjak, and Sebastian Riedel. 2016. emoji2vec: Learning emoji representations from their description. *arXiv preprint arXiv:1609.08359* .

Freferik Hallsmar and Jonas Palm. 2016. Multi-class sentiment classification on twitter using an emoji training heuristic .

J Richard Landis and Gary G Koch. 1977. The measurement of observer agreement for categorical data. *biometrics* pages 159–174.

Tsung-Yi Lin, Michael Maire, Serge Belongie, James Hays, Pietro Perona, Deva Ramanan, Piotr Dollár, and C Lawrence Zitnick. 2014. Microsoft coco: Common objects in context. In *European Conference on Computer Vision*. Springer, pages 740–755.

Kristina Toutanova, Dan Klein, Christopher D Manning, and Yoram Singer. 2003. Feature-rich part-of-speech tagging with a cyclic dependency network. In *Proceedings of the 2003 Conference of the North American Chapter of the Association for Computational Linguistics on Human Language Technology-Volume 1*. Association for Computational Linguistics, pages 173–180.

Leticia Vidal, Gastón Ares, and Sara R Jaeger. 2016. Use of emoticon and emoji in tweets for food-related emotional expression. *Food Quality and Preference* 49:119–128.

Fabio Massimo Zanzotto, Marco Pennacchiotti, and Kostas Tsioutsiouliklis. 2011. Linguistic redundancy in twitter. In *Proceedings of the Conference on Empirical Methods in Natural Language Processing*. Association for Computational Linguistics, pages 659–669.

Modeling Temporal Progression of Emotional Status in Mental Health Forum: a Recurrent Neural Net Approach

Kishaloy Halder, Lahari Poddar, Min-Yen Kan

School of Computing
National University of Singapore
{kishaloy, lahari, kanmy}@comp.nus.edu.sg

Abstract

Patients turn to Online Health Communities not only for information on specific conditions but also for emotional support. Previous research has indicated that the progression of emotional status can be studied through the linguistic patterns of an individual's posts. We analyze a real-world dataset from the *Mental Health* section of healthboards.com. Estimated from the word usages in their posts, we find that the emotional progress across patients vary widely.

We study the problem of predicting a patient's emotional status in the future from her past posts and we propose a Recurrent Neural Network (RNN) based architecture to address it. We find that the future emotional status can be predicted with reasonable accuracy given her historical posts and participation features. Our evaluation results demonstrate the efficacy of our proposed architecture, by outperforming state-of-the-art approaches with over 0.13 reduction in Mean Absolute Error.

1 Introduction

Online mental health forums offer a medium of peer support where individuals who have endured the adversity of mental illness can share their own experiences and offer help to others facing similar conditions. While each individual goes through life, their outlook and emotional state continue to evolve over time.

Understanding the complex patterns in which an individual interacts with an online community can help us understand his or her emotional state. Our hypothesis is that individuals' online forum participation can signal that state. Previous research on social media have established the relation between an individual's psychological state and her linguistic and conversational patterns (Tamersoy et al., 2015; Paul and Dredze, 2011; De Choudhury et al., 2013a). This motivates us to study user participations in online medical communities through a linguistic lens.

We propose a framework for tracking linguistic changes of a user over time for understanding her emotional status. We use our framework to analyze user participation on a large dataset collected from the mental health forums of the website healthboards.com[1]. These forums are dedicated for users discussing mental health issues ranging from anxiety, depression, stress, to even self-injury recovery. We choose this community since it is one of the largest online mental health forums, discussing a wide range of mental health issues. Additionally it has highly active members by not only their number of posts but also by longer periods of time for which they have been participating in the forum.

Models of time-varying user preferences in the recommendation domain (Matsubara et al., 2012; Koren, 2009) generally assume that users evolve according to a 'global clock', whereas patients participating in health forums progress according to his or her own personal timeline. By observing the word usage patterns of users in the site over time, we find that there exist different classes of users. While some users go through an *improvement* over time, lessening their use of negative words in their subsequent posts, some users move on a *deteriorating* slope where increased negative emotions can be observed in their posts. Decreased social interaction and increased negativity could be early indicators of depression, which

---

[1]www.healthboards.com/boards/
mental-health-board

127

Proceedings of the 8th Workshop on Computational Approaches to Subjectivity, Sentiment and Social Media Analysis, pages 127–135
Copenhagen, Denmark, September 7–11, 2017. ©2017 Association for Computational Linguistics

claims the lives of $15 - 20\%$ of its patients (Sadeque et al., 2016). Hence it will be immensely beneficial to detect such users early, to be able to prevent unfortunate life-critical situations.

We make the key observation that people who *improve* over time tend to participate more in the community for the purpose of helping others (by replying to others' posts), than seeking help for themselves (by initiating threads). This indicates a belief in social support system and is reflected through increasing positivity in their posts. On the other hand, one of the major symptoms of depression is withdrawal from social interactions. Users with decreasing levels of forum participation, indicated by the increasing gap between their consecutive posts, tend to have increased negativity in their future posts.

Building on these observations, we show that a user's patterns of participation can be predictive of her emotions in the future posts. Inspired by our empirical analysis, we design features to capture the interaction styles of a user along with the textual contents of her posts. We use these heterogeneous features in a neural architecture to build a time series predictor model.

In recent years, recurrent neural networks (RNN) have achieved remarkable success in a range of sequence modeling tasks (Lipton et al., 2015; Kuremoto et al., 2014; Qiu et al., 2014). Inspired by the success of recurrent neural networks with pre-trained word embeddings for text modeling, we use a stack of RNN layers for encoding the textual content of a post. Given the encoded textual features along with the other participation features of a series of user posts, we employ another set of RNN layers to model the temporal progression of her emotional status. We find that by using a small number of consecutive posts, we can predict the emotional status of the next post with reasonable accuracy.

The main contributions of the paper can be summarized as:

- A systematic investigation of the temporal progression of emotional status across users from a real-world large dataset crawled from an online mental health forum. We identify three different classes of users according to their emotional progress over time.

- Identification of several forum participation and textual features indicative of users' temporal progression of emotional status.

- A proposed recurrent neural network based architecture that uses the identified features to predict the future emotional status of a user.

- A comparative study of the efficacy of our proposed architecture against state-of-the-art methods, and a complementary analysis on sensitivity of the prediction accuracy with respect to history length and variants of the architecture.

To the best of our knowledge, ours is the first work towards modeling the temporal progression of emotional status in online health forums.

2 Related Work

We start with a discussion of research efforts in understanding online textual contents related to mental health issues posted in social media as well dedicated health forums. Then we discuss works on time series forecasting which are relevant for temporal modeling of emotional status.

Detecting emotional crisis from social media outlets (e.g., Twitter) has gained significant attention in recent years (De Choudhury et al., 2013b; Coppersmith et al., 2014; De Choudhury et al., 2013a). They investigate the use of several linguistic features (choice of negative words in tweet, increased medicinal words), as well as other social features (e.g., egonetwork) to accomplish the task. However such social features are often not available in case of online health forums. In the absence of explicit signals by the users (e.g., 'mood'), the textual features can be indicative of one's emotional status.

There have been efforts from the intersection of biomedical, and NLP community to understand and analyze the textual contents users post in online health forums (Rey-Villamizar et al., 2016; Gkotsis et al., 2016; Paul and Dredze, 2011; Sadeque et al., 2016). After studying the patient community of `dailystrength.org`, Rey-Villamizar et al. found that on an average, the anxiety levels of patients in the community lower over time (Rey-Villamizar et al., 2016). Although they spot a global trend at the community level, there is a definite need to model the dynamics of users' emotional status over time. Sadeque et al. consider a user's linguistic and timeline features to predict whether a user will withdraw from the forum completely (Sadeque et al., 2016). In contrast, we are interested in modeling the temporal progression of users' emotional status.

Traditionally for time series prediction deterministic algorithms e.g., k-nearest neighbor (Wei and Keogh, 2006), ARIMA models (Hillmer and Tiao, 1982) have been used in different domains such as stock price forecasting (Pai and Lin, 2005), weather prediction (Cadenas et al., 2016) etc. Machine Learning based approaches have also been used in the literature for temporal modeling tasks in online communities (Matsubara et al., 2012; Danescu-Niculescu-Mizil et al., 2013; Cheng et al., 2015). Recently deep neural networks have shown significant progress due their capability of modeling complex sequential patterns (Ahmed et al., 2010; Lipton et al., 2015; Kuremoto et al., 2014; Qiu et al., 2014).

We propose an architecture using neural networks for modeling the temporal progression of a user using both textual and forum participation features. We believe ours is the first work to use RNNs on online health forum data and demonstrate its effectiveness over traditional machine learning models.

3 Analysis of Mental Health Forum

Online health forums provide a common platform for patients to interact with others suffering from similar diseases. Health forum websites provide a variety of functionalities. Apart from conventional discussion forum, some websites offer social media style features – e.g., "friend", "follow", virtual "hug". Although these could be indicative of a user's emotional status, in this work we focus on the most common setting: the discussion forum[2].

3.1 Dataset Description

We collected data from the *Mental Health* section of healthboards.com, a long running support group website. It comprises of individual forums for mental conditions (24 in total e.g., *Addiction & Recovery, Anger Management, Anxiety, Depression, Hypochondria, Self-injury Recovery,* and *Stress*). The website grants users three forms of participation:

• **Starting a thread:** typically contains a question about her own health.

• **Replying to own thread:** acknowledging others' advice or providing additional context to the

Number of posts	29,708
Number of users	1364
Average number of posts per user	21.7
Average number of words per post	140
Average life span of a user	528 days
90 percentile life span of a user	1515 days
Number of posts initiating a thread	4456
Number of posts Replying to own thread	4159
Number of posts Replying to others' thread	21,093

Table 1: Statistics of our Mental Health Discussion Forum Dataset.

original question.

• **Replying to others' thread:** providing suggestions in others' threads.

Since the objective of this work is to study the progression of emotional status over time, we have selected users who have spent at least 30 days and have posted more than 5 times in any of the above categories (statistics shown in Table 1).

3.2 Capturing Emotional Status

The emotional state a user is going through is manifested by her choice of words in her posts (Park et al., 2012; De Choudhury et al., 2013b; Rey-Villamizar et al., 2016). Coppersmith et al. show that standard polarity lexicons e.g., LIWC[3] can be reliably used to identify emotional crisis in the user posts (Coppersmith et al., 2014). Inspired from their feature design, we define a metric to capture the emotional status of a user from the word usage in her posts. We note that although some websites (e.g., dailystrength.org) let users report their "mood" (e.g., *horrible, okay, good*) along with the posts which could possibly be used as an absolute metric — it is not commonly available in most of the health forum websites. Instead, we rely on a simple metric derived from the polarity word usages in the posts. We thus define the *Negative eMotion Index* (NMI) of a post as:

$$\text{NMI} = \frac{\#\text{negative words} - \#\text{positive words}}{\#\text{total words}}$$

We obtain the list of stemmed polarity words from the MPQA subjectivity lexicon[4]. Note that the NMI score of a post is in the range $\{-1, 1\}$. A high NMI score denotes more emotional crisis in a post and vice versa. Apart from the individual words, we also handle simple negation structures: we account for occurrences like "not feeling well", "not ok" by reversing the polarity of

---

[2]Found in healthboards.com, patientslikeme.com, dailystrength.org, medhelp.org and many others

[3]http://liwc.wpengine.com/
[4]http://mpqa.cs.pitt.edu/lexicons/subj_lexicon/

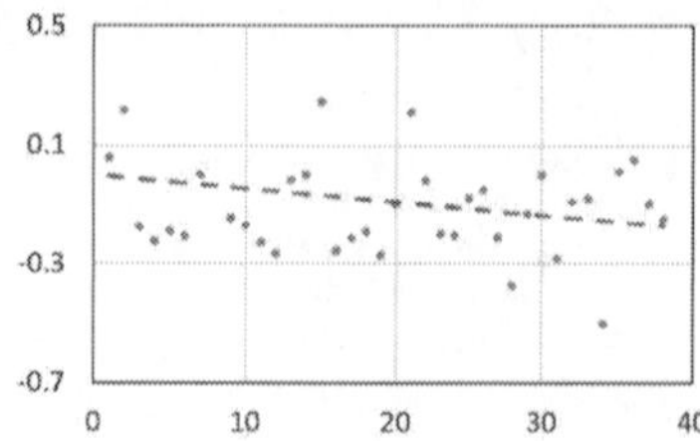

Figure 1: Temporal progression of NMI for a sample user (suffering from depression) from 38 posts made over a period of 90 days. The dashed red line denotes the trend according to linear regression model.

a *positive* word in cases where it is preceded by "not" or "no" (with distance$\leq$ 2). Since writing "n't' instead of "not" is a common practice (e.g., "haven't", "aren't"), we replace them with "not" as a part of pre-processing.

3.3 Temporal Progression of Emotional Status

The NMI progression for a sample user is shown in Figure 1. The posts (in chronological order) are along X-axis and their NMI scores are plotted along Y-axis. The trending line (based on linear regression model), is shown in red. We introduce a metric called NMI differential over time denoted by NMI':

$$\text{NMI}' = \frac{\delta \text{NMI}}{\delta t}$$

where δNMI is the difference in NMI over time period δt. Note that the slope of the trending line is same as NMI'. This admits three possible NMI' trends:

$$\text{NMI}' \begin{cases} < 0 & => \text{NMI is reducing over time} \\ > 0 & => \text{NMI is increasing over time} \\ = 0 & => \text{NMI remains constant over time} \end{cases}$$

The case NMI' < 0 points to those patients who are *improving* with time; > 0 is for those who are *deteriorating*; otherwise it denotes those patients who are *stable*. We present the CDF of NMI' across all the patients in Figure 2.

We find that the patients are Normally distributed among the three classes. Considering a soft boundary of 0.03 for NMI', we find that around 31% are in *improving* (NMI' < -0.03) class, 49% belong to the *stable* ($-0.03 <$ NMI' < 0.03) class. Interestingly, 20% of all the users fall in the *deteriorating* class.

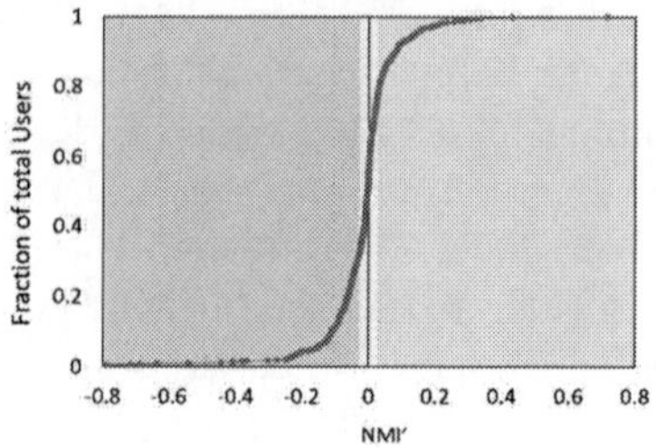

Figure 2: CDF of NMI' across all patients in Mental Health section of HealthBoards. 31% are *improving*, 20% are *deteriorating*, and 49% are *stable* with a soft threshold of NMI' = 0.03.

3.4 Prediction Task

The above study shows that the global trends observed on a community level do not reflect well on an individual basis. Hence we ask the following research question.

RQ: Given a user's history of forum participations, can we model the progression of her emotional status over time?

As we discussed in Section 2, this question is largely unanswered by the existing literature. To this end, we formally define a prediction task. The graphical representation of the task is shown in Figure 3. Given past k post details (text, and other participation metrics), the task is to predict the next NMI score. Note that we do not observe the post text that the user would be writing next, the task focuses on estimating the next NMI for her.

All the posts written by a user within a certain time period are combined into a single *post-block*. In this work, we set this time period to be 24 hours. This is done primarily since a user's emotional status is unlikely to change within a single day. Additionally, individual posts can be short and noisy (e.g. "thank you", "take care") so combining multiple posts of the same day will be a better reflection of a user's emotional health. For a user we consider her last k post-blocks in the forum and predict the NMI score of her next post-block.

4 Method

In this section we discuss our approach towards modeling the temporal progression of a users' emotional status. Our task falls in the guise of time series forecasting. In our case, we have heterogeneous features (e.g., post types, timing of posts) generated as artifact of user participation in the on-

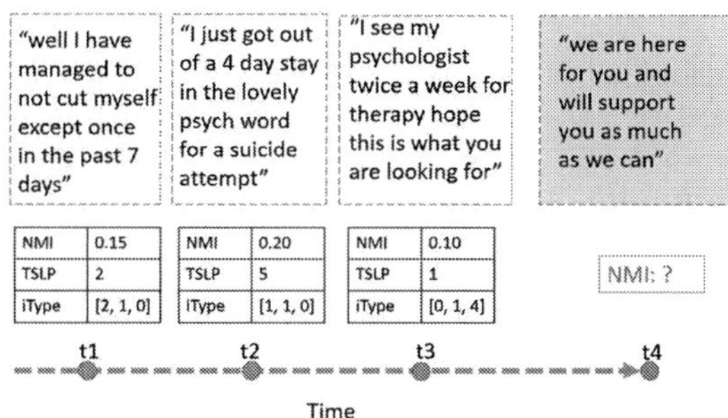

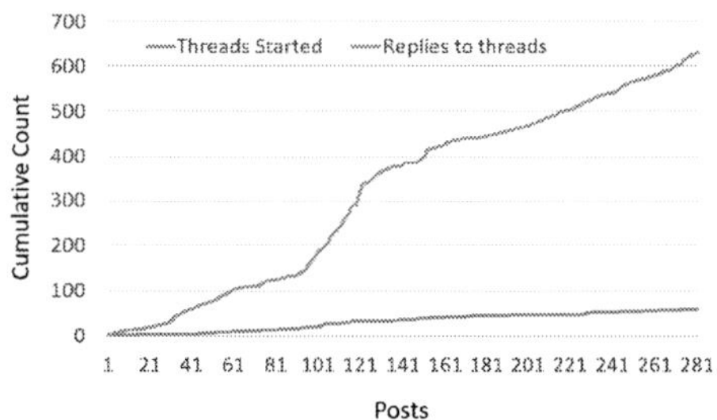

Figure 3: Graphical illustration of the prediction task. The task is to predict the next NMI score given past k posts. The shading on the text block denotes that it is not observed.

Figure 4: Temporal cumulative distribution of interaction types for a sample user in *improving* class. She keeps posting to others' threads instead of starting her own increasingly with time.

line platforms. To this end, we propose an RNN based architecture which not only takes the past NMI scores, but also incorporates other evidences seamlessly in the modeling process.

Our architecture consists of two components, namely, (1) text encoder and (2) time series encoder. The text encoder takes text of a single post-block as input and outputs a feature vector representation for it. We first encode the textual component of each post-block using the text encoder. Overall we build an ensemble style network to account for both textual and other numeric features since both these classes of features are heterogeneous in nature. One component of the network learns from the temporal sequence of feature vectors of text, while the other one from the numeric features. Both of these components consider sequence of feature vectors for the past k post-blocks in order to predict the NMI for the next to come.

In the following subsections we describe the numeric features and the two components in detail.

4.1 Numeric Features

For each post-block we consider the following numeric features.

Time Since Last Post (TSLP): The frequency with which a user engages in the forum can be indicative of her emotional health. Since people with depression often tend to withdraw from social contacts, the time gap between a user's posts can represent her diminishing social interactions (Sadeque et al., 2016). For each post-block of a user, we consider the time difference between the earliest post of the current block and the latest post of the previous block as a feature.

Interaction Type (iType): An individual user post can either be (i) initiating a thread or (ii) re-

plying to someone else's thread or (iii) replying to a self-initiated thread.

The type of interaction a user has on the forum can reflect her current role or purpose in the community. While some users seek answers to their own questions and troubles (by starting discussion threads), some users help other community members overcome theirs (by posting suggestions and advices on other's threads). The distribution of interaction type for a sample patient who has improved over time is shown in Figure 4. As we can see, with time she starts posting more on others' threads rather than starting her own. Similar trends could be observed for other patients as well whose emotional status have improved over time.

To encode this, for each post-block, we count the number of individual posts within the block that belong to the above three categories and use the counts as features.

NMI score: Apart from the participation and textual features, the past NMI scores could also be predictive of the future NMI score. Hence we use NMI scores of the post-blocks as features. Since there are multiple posts within a post-block, we take their mean NMI and consider it as the NMI score of the post-block.

For a post-block we concatenate the above mentioned numeric features to form a single numeric feature vector.

4.2 Text Encoder

For each post-block we first concatenate the raw texts of individual posts and use a text encoder to encode it into a feature vector. In the text encoder we first embed each word using an embedding layer, initialized with 50 dimensional Glove

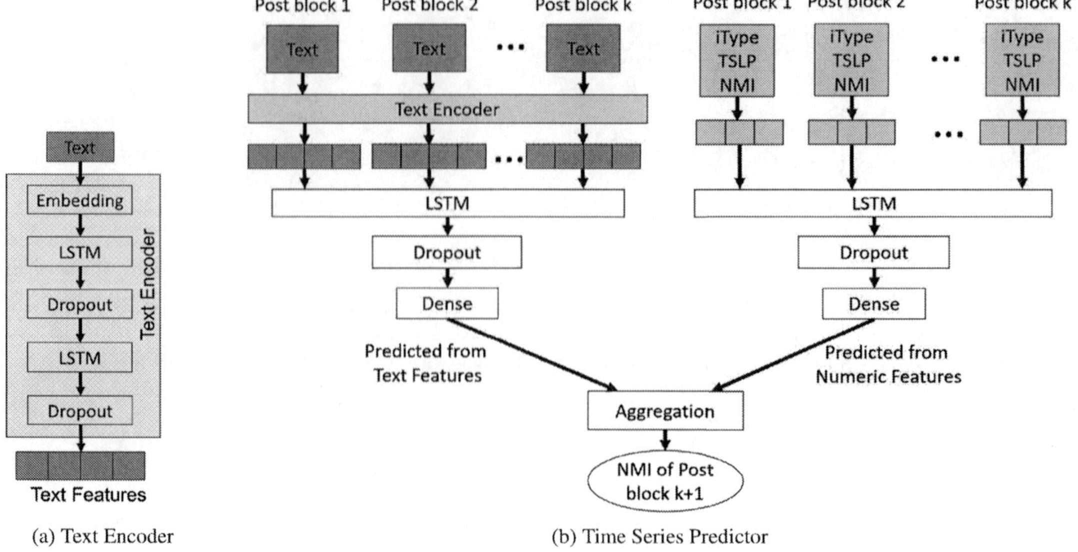

(a) Text Encoder (b) Time Series Predictor

Figure 5: Illustration of model architecture. Each post-block consists of text and numeric features. The encoder for text is shown on the left side. The time series predictor, that combines both text and numeric features to predict NMI score of the next post, is shown on the right.

word embeddings [5]. The embeddings of the words are made trainable so as to reflect the domain and task dependent nature of the words. After embedding the word vectors, the sequence of words go through a stack of two LSTM layers, to encode the text into a vector. In our experiments we find that, using two stacked LSTM layers help in learning the latent representation of a text better than just a single layer. After each LSTM layer we add a Dropout layer so as to prevent overfitting.

Note that, there is only one text encoder component in the network. All the posts are encoded using the same text encoder.

4.3 Time Series Predictor

Now, given the feature vectors of the past k post-blocks we need to predict the NMI score of the next post-block. To tackle this task of time series prediction, we use a recurrent neural network architecture due to its superiority in handling short sequential data. There are two identical RNN components in our network for text, and numeric features respectively as shown in Figure 5b. The input to the RNN at each time-step i is the feature vector representation of the ith post-block – textual feature vector for one and numeric feature vector for the other. The output of the RNN at

the end of k time-steps yields the structural representation of the temporal emotional progression of the user. This is fed through a Dropout layer to prevent over-fitting. Finally a Dense layer is used to make a prediction from the output of the RNN. Given the predictions from both textual and numeric features, we aggregate (by taking mean) these two real-valued numbers to get the final NMI score of the $(k + 1)^{th}$ post-block.

Figure 5 shows an illustration of the architecture of our proposed of model. We also considered different variants of this architecture. The findings are discussed in Section 5.5.

5 Experiments

For our experiments, we consider a dataset from mental health forums of HealthBoards (as described in Section 3.1). In the following, we first describe how we setup the data for our prediction task. Later we describe the competitive baselines and compare our model with them in terms of the prediction accuracy. Finally we conclude with a discussion on the parameter sensitivity and other variants of our model.

5.1 Experimental Setup

Our objective is, given a history of k consecutive post-blocks of a user, predicting the NMI score of

<hr>
[5] nlp.stanford.edu/projects/glove/

her $(k+1)^{th}$ post-block. To this end, for each user we first sort her posts in chronological order. Then we combine all posts made within a 24-hour period by a user to form a single post-block. Thereafter we form tuples of length $(k+1)$ from the sorted list of post-blocks using a sliding window method. For each such tuple of length $(k+1)$, using the features of the first k post-blocks we predict the NMI score of the $(k+1)^{th}$ post-block.

Consider a user with the sequence of post-blocks as shown in Table 2a. For history length $k=3$, we reconstruct the sequence into temporal tuples as shown in Table 2b, where, given a tuple of past 3 posts $(P1, P2, P3)$ we are predicting the NMI score of the next post $(P4)$.

Post	NMI
P1	0.21
P2	0.24
P3	0.27
P4	0.25
P5	0.31

(a) Chronological Post-blocks of a user

Post 1	Post 2	Post 3	NMI
P1	P2	P3	0.25
P2	P3	P4	0.31

(b) Tuples of Post-blocks

Table 2: Temporal dataset construction from posts

We split our dataset in 80% tuples for training and 20% for testing and report five-fold cross validation results. We randomly selected 10% of our training data as the validation set.

To evaluate the performance of our NMI prediction task we employ the commonly used Mean Absolute Error (MAE) as our metric.

5.2 Parameter Settings

The parameters of our model include parameters for history length k, parameters for the text encoder and parameters for the time series encoder. We set the parameters using grid search on the validation set. We set the history length k to 5.

For the text encoder, the max length of a post-block text is set to 100. The embedding dimension for the words is set to 50 and is initialized with Glove embeddings. The sizes of the LSTM hidden layers are set to 64. The output of the LSTM layers go through dropout layers with 70% dropout rate to prevent over fitting.

For the time series encoder the sizes of both LSTM layers are set to 256. They are followed by dropout layers with 60% dropout rate. The predictions are made using a Dense layer with hyperbolic tangent as a non-linearity function.

Mean absolute error is used as loss function and Adam optimizer is used for optimization. Number of epochs is set to 20 but with an early stopping criteria depending on the validation accuracy. The analysis of the sensitivity of the parameters are discussed in Section 5.5.

5.3 Baselines

We compare our proposed model with traditional supervised regression models. We train the baseline models using the same history length and numeric participation features as our model and use Bag-of-Words (BOW) features to represent the textual content of a post. We consider the following models for comparison:

- **Linear Regression :** This is the basic ordinary least squares Linear Regression.

- **SVM Regression :** We experiment with support vector regression with both linear and non-linear RBF kernels.

- **Decision Tree Regression :** Learns a local linear regression approximating a sine curve. We set the max depth of the tree to be 5.

- **Random Forest Regression :** An ensemble learner that averages the predictions of a number of decision trees to improve accuracy and prevent over fitting. We use 100 decision trees to constitute the forest.

We use python's scikit-learn library[6] for the above models.

5.4 Prediction Results

We present a comparison of the results of the proposed method with the competing the state-of-the-art methods. Note that we have three sets of observed signals – text features, participation features, and NMI score. We collectively call the latter two as numeric features in this section. We perform an ablation study with numeric features, and text features across all the competing methods. The results are presented in Table 3.

We observe that our method outperforms other models comfortably. It achieves the best accuracy when it considers both set of features. Interestingly we find that the numeric feature set alone is quite predictive about the future, whereas if we only use the text features – the accuracy degrades. The traditional ML based baseline models yield

---

[6]http://scikit-learn.org/stable/index.html

Model	MAE		
	Numeric Features	Text Features	Numeric + Text Features
Linear Regression	0.2034	8.3553	3.4914
SVM (linear kernel)	0.2022	3.1513	0.2125
SVM (RBF kernel)	0.2724	0.2072	0.2071
Decision Tree	0.2106	0.2078	0.2106
Random Forest	0.2046	0.2032	0.2031
Our Model	0.0788	0.0802	**0.0781**

Table 3: Prediction results of different models

far less accurate results. Specifically we find that both linear regressor model and the SVM regressor with linear kernel model are unable to use the BOW features for the prediction task. Overall we can conclude that our architecture leveraging RNNs, is able to capture the temporal progression of emotional status with reasonable accuracy.

5.5 Parameter Sensitivity Analysis

We now study the sensitivity of our model by varying the history length from 1 to 5. Table 4 presents the accuracy scores obtained by our model with varying history lengths across different feature combinations.

Generally the performance improves with increasing history length, which is intuitive. We also observe that the numeric feature consistently appear to be more predictive compared to text feature alone. However we achieve best score with a combination of both while considering a history length of 5.

History Length	MAE		
	Numeric Features	Text Features	Numeric + Text Features
1	0.0813	0.0824	0.0810
2	0.0813	0.0818	0.0808
3	0.0807	0.0814	0.0803
4	0.0797	0.0806	0.0798
5	0.0788	0.0802	**0.0781**

Table 4: Effect of history length and features on the performance of our model.

Discussion on Model Architecture Variants: Apart from the architecture presented in Section 4, we experimented with a few other variants as mentioned below.

- For the RNN we experimented with both LSTM (Hochreiter and Schmidhuber, 1997) and GRU (Cho et al., 2014) and got similar results. Furthermore, we did not observe any significant improvement by replacing the RNN with a Bidirectional RNN (Schuster and Paliwal, 1997).

- We tried with larger embedding dimensions for words and larger neuron counts in the RNN layers but that led to over-fitting, possibly due to the dataset size.

- Instead of using a simple mean as the aggregation function, we experimented with using another Dense layer for predicting the final score. The Dense layer takes as input the concatenation of the outputs of the previous two Dense layers (from textual and numeric features) and outputs the final NMI score. This increased the number of parameters in the model but did not improve performance.

- Instead of using the textual and numeric features separately in the time series predictor, we also experimented with concatenating all the features into a single post feature vector. Thereafter the sequence of post feature vectors were fed into an RNN followed by a Dense layer to make the prediction. The performance of this model was slightly worse with MAE 0.0787.

6 Conclusion

In this paper we have presented a framework towards understanding temporal progression of users' emotional status in online mental health forums. We identify several forum participation features that are indicative of a user's temporal emotional progression. Our proposed neural network architecture uses textual content as well as participation features from a user's past posts to predict her future emotional status. Empirical evaluations on a large real world dataset of online mental health forum demonstrate the superiority of recurrent neural network for temporal modeling, as our model outperforms state-of-the-art approaches significantly.

In future, we would like to explore how our model can be extended to capture progression of other physical illnesses especially long term ones e.g., ALS, Multiple Sclerosis. Incorporating social features into the model could be another interesting direction. Social media and other online platforms will play an important role in providing healthcare in the 21st century (Dredze, 2012). With the constant influx of users seeking help from online health outlets, we believe our generic framework would be applicable to a wide spectrum of online mental health forums.

References

Nesreen K. Ahmed, Amir F. Atiya, Neamat El Gayar, and Hisham El-Shishiny. 2010. An empirical comparison of machine learning models for time series forecasting. *Econometric Reviews* 29(5-6):594–621.

Erasmo Cadenas, Wilfrido Rivera, Rafael Campos-Amezcua, and Christopher Heard. 2016. Wind speed prediction using a univariate arima model and a multivariate narx model. *Energies* 9(2):109.

Justin Cheng, Cristian Danescu-Niculescu-Mizil, and Jure Leskovec. 2015. Antisocial behavior in online discussion communities. In *ICWSM*.

Kyunghyun Cho, Bart Van Merriënboer, Dzmitry Bahdanau, and Yoshua Bengio. 2014. On the properties of neural machine translation: Encoder-decoder approaches. *arXiv preprint arXiv:1409.1259*.

Glen Coppersmith, Mark Dredze, and Craig Harman. 2014. Quantifying mental health signals in twitter. *ACL 2014* 51.

Cristian Danescu-Niculescu-Mizil, Robert West, Dan Jurafsky, Jure Leskovec, and Christopher Potts. 2013. No country for old members: User lifecycle and linguistic change in online communities. In *Proceedings of the 22nd international conference on World Wide Web*. ACM, pages 307–318.

Munmun De Choudhury, Scott Counts, and Eric Horvitz. 2013a. Social media as a measurement tool of depression in populations. In *Proceedings of the 5th Annual ACM Web Science Conference*. WebSci '13, pages 47–56.

Munmun De Choudhury, Michael Gamon, Scott Counts, and Eric Horvitz. 2013b. Predicting depression via social media. AAAI.

Mark Dredze. 2012. How social media will change public health. *IEEE Intelligent Systems* 27(4):81–84.

George Gkotsis, Anika Oellrich, Tim JP Hubbard, Richard JB Dobson, Maria Liakata, Sumithra Velupillai, and Rina Dutta. 2016. The language of mental health problems in social media. In *Third Computational Linguistics and Clinical Psychology Workshop (NAACL)*. pages 63–73.

Steven C Hillmer and George C Tiao. 1982. An arima-model-based approach to seasonal adjustment. *Journal of the American Statistical Association* 77(377):63–70.

Sepp Hochreiter and Jürgen Schmidhuber. 1997. Long short-term memory. *Neural computation* 9(8):1735–1780.

Yehuda Koren. 2009. Collaborative filtering with temporal dynamics. In *Proceedings of the 15th ACM SIGKDD International Conference on Knowledge Discovery and Data Mining*. KDD '09, pages 447–456.

Takashi Kuremoto, Shinsuke Kimura, Kunikazu Kobayashi, and Masanao Obayashi. 2014. Time series forecasting using a deep belief network with restricted boltzmann machines. *Neurocomputing* 137:47–56.

Zachary C Lipton, David C Kale, Charles Elkan, and Randall Wetzell. 2015. Learning to diagnose with lstm recurrent neural networks. *arXiv preprint arXiv:1511.03677*.

Yasuko Matsubara, Yasushi Sakurai, Christos Faloutsos, Tomoharu Iwata, and Masatoshi Yoshikawa. 2012. Fast mining and forecasting of complex timestamped events. In *Proceedings of the 18th ACM SIGKDD international conference on Knowledge discovery and data mining*. ACM, pages 271–279.

Ping-Feng Pai and Chih-Sheng Lin. 2005. A hybrid arima and support vector machines model in stock price forecasting. *Omega* 33(6):497–505.

Minsu Park, Chiyoung Cha, and Meeyoung Cha. 2012. Depressive moods of users portrayed in twitter. In *Proceedings of the ACM SIGKDD Workshop on healthcare informatics (HI-KDD)*. pages 1–8.

Michael J Paul and Mark Dredze. 2011. You are what you tweet: Analyzing twitter for public health. *Icwsm* 20:265–272.

X. Qiu, L. Zhang, Y. Ren, P. N. Suganthan, and G. Amaratunga. 2014. Ensemble deep learning for regression and time series forecasting. In *2014 IEEE Symposium on Computational Intelligence in Ensemble Learning (CIEL)*. pages 1–6.

Nicolas Rey-Villamizar, Prasha Shrestha, Farig Sadeque, Steven Bethard, Ted Pedersen, Arjun Mukherjee, and Thamar Solorio. 2016. Analysis of anxious word usage on online health forums. *EMNLP 2016* page 37.

Farig Sadeque, Ted Pedersen, Thamar Solorio, Prasha Shrestha, Nicolas Rey-Villamizar, and Steven Bethard. 2016. Why do they leave: Modeling participation in online depression forums. In *Proceedings of the 4th Workshop on Natural Language Processing and Social Media*. pages 14–19.

Mike Schuster and Kuldip K Paliwal. 1997. Bidirectional recurrent neural networks. *IEEE Transactions on Signal Processing* 45(11):2673–2681.

Acar Tamersoy, Munmun De Choudhury, and Duen Horng Chau. 2015. Characterizing smoking and drinking abstinence from social media. In *Proceedings of the 26th ACM Conference on Hypertext & Social Media*. ACM, pages 139–148.

Li Wei and Eamonn Keogh. 2006. Semi-supervised time series classification. In *Proceedings of the 12th ACM SIGKDD international conference on Knowledge discovery and data mining*. ACM, pages 748–753.

Towards an integrated pipeline for aspect-based sentiment analysis in various domains

Orphée De Clercq[1], **Els Lefever**[1], **Gilles Jacobs**[1], **Tijl Carpels**[2] **and Véronique Hoste**[1]
[1] LT[3], Language and Translation Technology Team, Ghent University, Belgium
[2] Hello Customer, Belgium
{orphee.declercq, els.lefever, gillesm.jacobs, veronique.hoste}@ugent.be
tijl@hellocustomer.com

Abstract

This paper presents an integrated ABSA pipeline for Dutch that has been developed and tested on qualitative user feedback coming from three domains: retail, banking and human resources. The two latter domains provide service-oriented data, which has not been investigated before in ABSA. By performing in-domain and cross-domain experiments the validity of our approach was investigated. We show promising results for the three ABSA subtasks, aspect term extraction, aspect category classification and aspect polarity classification.

1 Introduction

With the rise of web 2.0 applications, customers have been given a new platform to express their opinions in the form of reviews on designated websites. At the same time many companies proactively collect direct customer feedback after an interaction, such as a store visit, a client meeting or online purchase. Both information types have in common that besides quantitative data ("How would you rate the overall shopping experience on a scale from one to ten") also qualitative data ("Why did you assign this score") is being collected. A fine-grained analysis of this qualitative textual feedback offers companies valuable detailed insights into the strong and weak aspects of their products and services and allows them to strengthen their offer.

Extracting this information automatically is known as the task of aspect-based sentiment analysis (ABSA). ABSA systems (Pontiki et al., 2014) focus on the detection of all sentiment expressions within a given document and the concepts and aspects (or features) to which they refer. Such systems do not only try to distinguish the positive from the negative utterances, but also strive to detect the target of the opinion, which comes down to a very fine-grained sentiment analysis task and "almost all real-life sentiment analysis systems in industry should be based on this level of analysis" (Liu, 2015, p10).

This fine-grained sentiment analysis task received special attention in the framework of three SemEval shared tasks: SemEval 2014 Task 4 (Pontiki et al., 2014) and SemEval 2015 Task 12 (Pontiki et al., 2015), which focussed on English customer reviews, and SemEval 2016 Task 5 (Pontiki et al., 2016) where seven other languages were also included. Each time the idea was to perform three subtasks: (i) extract all aspect expressions of the entities, (ii) categorize these aspect expressions into predefined categories and (iii) determine whether an opinion on an aspect is positive, negative or neutral.

In this paper, we discuss a fine-grained sentiment analysis pipeline to deal with qualitative Dutch feedback data coming from three different domains: banking, retail, and human resources. This paper presents a collaboration between academia and industry to create a proof-of-concept, the pipeline is currently in production at Hello Customer. In the framework of the SemEval shared tasks, similar methodologies have been investigated, but the research presented here differs in two ways. First, the main focus has always been on customer reviews of experiences (restaurants, hotels, movies) or tangible products (laptops, smartphones). Besides product-oriented data, we move towards more service-oriented data coming from financial institutions and human resources agencies. Second, the various ABSA subtasks have always been tackled and evaluated separately in the framework of SemEval. In reality, however, all steps have to be performed sequen-

Proceedings of the 8th Workshop on Computational Approaches to Subjectivity, Sentiment and Social Media Analysis, pages 136–142
Copenhagen, Denmark, September 7–11, 2017. ©2017 Association for Computational Linguistics

tially, entailing error percolation from one step to the other. In this paper we present such an integrated pipeline for each domain and also perform cross-domain experiments.

The remainder of this paper is organized as follows. Section 2 describes the data we have collected and annotated. Next, in Section 3 we present the pipeline that has been developed for performing this task and in Section 4 we discuss the results. We end this paper with a conclusion and suggestions for future work.

2 Datasets and Annotations

In the past, ABSA datasets have been annotated comprising movie reviews (Thet et al., 2010), reviews for electronic products(Hu and Liu, 2004; Brody and Elhadad, 2010), and restaurant reviews (Brody and Elhadad, 2010; Ganu et al., 2009). As mentioned above, in the framework of three SemEval shared tasks (Pontiki et al., 2014, 2015, 2016), several benchmark review datasets coming from various domains (electronics, hotels, restaurants, and telecom) and languages (English, Dutch, French, Arabic, Chinese, Spanish, Turkish and Russian) have been made publicly available.

For the work presented here, direct customer feedback data written in Dutch was collected in three domains: banking, retail and human resources (HR). The data provider for the first domain, **banking**, is a large Belgian financial institution offering basic financial products (e.g. loans, insurances) and services (e.g. investing or financial advice). The second domain, **retail**, comprises data coming from a large clothing company with offline stores all over Belgium and an online webshop. Data for the third domain, **HR**, comes from two data providers who are active in the recruiting sector, namely employment agencies.

For all domains, data was collected by asking customers two things: (i) assign a NPS score[1] to the company and (ii) provide textual feedback for this score. This feedback is referred to as a *verbatim*, which can vary from one short sentence to various sentences discussing various aspects. Table 1 presents an overview of all data that has been collected and annotated in the three domains, expressed in number of verbatims and tokens.

Domain	# verbatims	# tokens
Banking	1700	15870
Retail	1500	15796
HR	1000	11960

Table 1: Verbatims and tokens in each domain.

For the actual annotations, see Figure 1 for a visualization, we annotated each aspect term and assigned it to a predefined aspect category (CatEx). These aspect categories are domain-dependent and consist of a main category (e.g. Personnel) and subcategory (e.g. quality)[2]. For banking there are 22 such possible combinations, for retail 24 and for HR 23. Table 2 gives an overview of the three largest main categories per domain.

In a next step, sentiment bearing words were selected, assigned a polarity: positive, negative or neutral (OpinEx), and linked to the appropriate aspect term (is_about arrow). All annotations were carried out with the BRAT rapid annotation tool (Stenetorp et al., 2012).

OpinEx [positive] is_about CatEx [PERSONNEL_service]
vriendelijke   bediening

Figure 1: Annotation (*EN: Friendly service*).

For all three domains, we went through the same annotation process to ensure consistency. First, a preliminary aspect category typology was devised after which 50 verbatims were annotated by two annotators independently from each other. These annotations were discussed, inconsistencies were resolved and the typology was altered, if necessary. Next, an inter-annotator agreement study was conducted on 50 new verbatims, which were again annotated by two independent annotators. The annotations were compared to the annotations of a third, more experienced annotator who also received more time to complete the task. Accuracy was calculated on two levels: the consistency of the annotated **category** expressions (cat) and the consistency of the annotated **polarity** expressions (pol).

As can be observed in Table 3, the IAA was high for all three domains. For the remainder of the annotation work, the same two annotators performed all annotations and frequently checked and discussed their work to ensure consistency.

---

[1]Net Promotor Score, a customer loyalty business metric. Customers are asked: How likely is it that you would recommend [company] to a friend or colleague? Trademark of Bain & Company, Inc and Fred Reichheld.

[2]We were inspired by the SemEval ABSA annotation guidelines available at http://bit.ly/2t0EkaB.

Domain	cat	#	cat	#	cat	#
Banking	BANK	317	PERSONNEL	903	PRODUCT	168
Retail	STORE	306	PERSONNEL	682	COLLECTION	1191
HR	HR	129	PERSONNEL	637	SERVICES	230

Table 2: Typology of the three main aspect categories and occurrences per domain.

	Banking		Retail		HR	
	cat	pol	cat	pol	cat	pol
Annot 1	94	94	92	94	94	96
Annot 2	86	98	97	97	93	97

Table 3: IAA, expressed in accuracy (%).

3 Methodology

A pipeline was developed in order to perform the three incremental ABSA subtasks relying on supervised machine learning techniques. For the actual experiments, all datasets were split in a 90% train and a 10% held-out test set.

3.1 Aspect Term Extraction

Approaching the task of aspect term extraction as a sequential IOB labeling task has proven most successful (Liu, 2012). The two systems achieving top performance on English reviews for SemEval 2015 were a classifier using Conditional Random Fields (CRF) (Toh and Su, 2015) and a designated Named Entity Recognizer (San Vicente et al., 2015). Both systems implemented typical named entity features, such as word bigrams, trigrams, token shape, capitalization, name lists, etc. For SemEval 2016, subsequent work by Toh and Su (2016) found that using the output of a Recurrent Neural Network as additional features is beneficial for the labeling tasks.

We relied on a sequential IOB labeling approach using CRF as implemented in CRFSuite (Okazaki, 2007). For each token, and its two neighbouring tokens, the following features were extracted: (1) **token shape features**, based on whether the token contains capitalization, digits, or exclusively alphanumeric characters, as well as the final two and three characters as an approximate suffix; (2) **lemma**, (3) CGN **part-of-speech** (PoS) tag, (4) **syntactic chunk**, and (5) **Named Entity** label as provided by the LeTs preprocessing toolkit (Van de Kauter et al., 2013). Both full labels and coarse super-category for PoS, chunk, and NE labels were included as features.

For the experiments, CRF models with the LBFGS (Nocedal, 1980) optimization function were first trained on each domain separately and, next, all training data was combined, leading to four models in total. Hyper-parameters were optimized by randomized search with 500 iterations in 10-fold cross-validation. The models with winning hyper-parameters as determined by flat F1-score (weighted macro-averaging) were subsequently tested on the held-out test sets in three setups: in-domain (e.g. trained on banking and tested on banking), cross-domain (e.g. trained on banking and tested on retail) and all domain (e.g. trained on all training data and tested on banking).

To evaluate, we calculated flat (i.e. non-sequence) precision, recall, and F1-scores.

3.2 Aspect Category Classification

The aspect category classification subtask requires a system able to label a large variety of classes, in our case 22, 24 and 23 categories. The two systems achieving the best results for SemEval 2015 both used a classification approach (Toh and Su, 2015; Saias, 2015). Furthermore, especially lexical features in the form of bag-of-words have proven successful. The best system (Toh and Su, 2015) also incorporated lexical-semantic features in the form of clusters learned from a large corpus of reference review data, whereas the second-best (Saias, 2015) applied filtering heuristics on the classification output and thus solely relied on lexical information for the classification. For SemEval 2016 Toh and Su (2016) discovered that when the probability output of a Deep Convolutional Neural Network (Severyn and Moschitti, 2015) was added as additional features, the performance increased.

For the experiments presented here, classifiers were built using LibSVM (Chang and Lin, 2011). Our feature space includes lexical information by relying on **bag-of-word** features in the form of token unigrams. Because for Dutch no large reference review datasets are available in the var-

Test Train	Banking			Retail			HR		
	Prec	Rec	F-1	Prec	Rec	F-1	Prec	Rec	F-1
Banking	<u>94.8</u>	<u>95.1</u>	<u>94.9</u>	89.6	90.9	89.2	95.2	95.4	95.0
Retail	93.0	93.9	93.2	<u>95.6</u>	<u>95.5</u>	<u>95.6</u>	94.9	95.1	94.4
HR	93.4	94.2	93.4	91.0	91.4	89.7	<u>96.5</u>	<u>96.8</u>	**96.4**
All training	95.1	95.4	**95.2**	95.8	95.8	**95.8**	95.9	96.2	95.9

Table 4: Precision, recall, and F-1 scores for aspect term extraction on held-out test sets.

ious domains, we were inspired by the work of De Clercq and Hoste (2016) to also include lexical semantic features derived from Dutch **Word-Net** information, viz. Cornetto (Vossen et al., 2013) and **DBpedia** (Lehmann et al., 2013) for the aspect terms available in the training data for each of the domains.

After training our models, these are tested on the held-out test set. Important to note is that for this setup we do not work with gold standard aspect terms, but rely on the output from the aspect term extraction step. Since each verbatim can be labeled with zero, one or more categories that are not mutually exclusive, we decided to use Hamming score, a multi-label evaluation metric that divides the number of correct labels by the union of predicted and true labels.

3.3 Aspect Polarity Classification

Machine learning approaches to sentiment analysis make use of classification algorithms, such as Naïve Bayes or Support Vector Machines trained on a labeled dataset (Pang and Lee, 2008). Current state-of-the-art approaches model a variety of contextual, lexical and syntactic features (Caro and Grella, 2013), allowing them to capture context and the relations between the individual words. Though deep learning techniques have also been applied to this subtask, mainly in the form of word embeddings (Mikolov et al., 2013), for SemEval 2016 the best performing system relied solely on (advanced) linguistic features (Brun et al., 2016).

We followed a supervised approach and built SVM classifiers using LibSVM. As we conceived ABSA as an integrated task, the input for the polarity classification includes the detected aspect term (result of step 1) and category (result of step 2), together with the preprocessed sentence in which the aspect term occurs. As a result, error percolation between the different steps impacts the performance of the polarity classification sys-

tem. As information sources, we implemented the following features: (1) **bag-of-words**: binary token unigram features, (2) **lexicon** lookup features based on domain-specific lexicons extracted from the training data, as well as existing sentiment lexicons for Dutch, i.e. Pattern (De Smedt and Daelemans, 2012) and Duoman (Jijkoun and Hofmann, 2009), (3) **negator**: flips the value of negated lexicon matches and (4) the **predicted** category of the aspect term. For these experiments, we also envisaged the three different setups: in-domain, cross-domain, and all domain. It is important to mention that for sentiment prediction, the entire sentence is considered for the construction of the features. As a result, conflicting sentiments will be ruled out. In future work, we intend to limit the context window of the detected aspect term. As the polarity detection takes into account the output of the previous two steps, this task was also evaluated by means of the hamming score metric (cfr. 4.3).

4 Results

4.1 Aspect Term Extraction

In Table 4 the results are presented for the different experiments training on in-domain data (underlined scores), cross-domain data, and a combination of all training data. We observe good results for aspect term extraction for all three domains. In-domain scores are slightly better than cross-domain scores, except for retail. This might be explained by the fact that retail has very different aspect targets than the other two domains, which are both more services-oriented. In addition, the target extraction scores show that training on all data improves scores slightly for the banking and the retail domain, but decreases for HR.

4.2 Aspect Category Classification

To evaluate, we report hamming scores for (i) a classifier taking the in-domain predictions for aspect terms as input (*In-domain*) and (ii) the predictions of the classifier trained on all training data from the various domains for the aspect term extraction (*All training*).

	In-domain	All training
Banking	58.1	57.4
Retail	67.0	68.5
HR	46.6	46.8

Table 5: Aspect category classification results.

As can be seen in Table 5, the score difference between both setups is small. Overall, we observe that predicting the correct aspect categories is much more challenging for HR than for the other two domains. A qualitative analysis revealed that a lot of errors are caused by error percolation from the previous step. For HR more in particular, there is a lot of confusion between closely-related categories such as PERSONNEL_service and PERSONNEL_availability.

4.3 Aspect Polarity Classification

We report hamming scores for the classifiers taking the aspect terms derived from the aspects terms that were extracted in the *All training* setup[3].

Train \ Test	Banking	Retail	HR
Banking	<u>84.5</u>	83.3	67.1
Retail	**86.8**	**<u>88.9</u>**	**86.7**
HR	86.0	86.1	<u>86.1</u>
All	84.5	86.8	85.4

Table 6: Aspect polarity classification results.

Table 6 shows satisfactory results for polarity classification based on automatically predicted aspect terms. The results show that training polarity classifiers on all domains results in lower classification scores than in-domain training, which confirms the intuition that sentiment expressions are often ambiguous and domain-dependent. Although the HR data set is rather limited (1000 verbatims), cross-domain training on HR also results in consistently good polarity prediction for the other domains. Training on banking, however, results in bad polarity prediction for the HR aspect terms. A qualitative analysis revealed that the HR polarity classification relies on more general

sentiment expressions also occurring in other domains (e.g. *vriendelijk (EN: friendly)*, *super (EN: excellent)*), but also on very HR-specific sentiment words (e.g. *nauwkeurig (EN: accurate)*, *doeltreffend (EN: effective)*). Remarkably, retail has the best cross-domain performance, it even outperforms the in-domain results for banking and HR. This is because the retail model always predicts the positive class for these two test sets, making this a hard to beat majority baseline.

5 Conclusion

In this paper we presented an ABSA pipeline that implements an integrated approach for the three ABSA subtasks, which have been performed and evaluated separately in previous research. We collected and annotated qualitative user feedback in three domains: banking, retail and HR. Especially the banking and HR data are novel in that they comprise service-oriented customer feedback.

By performing in-domain and cross-domain experiments we show promising classification results for all three subtasks. Considering the aspect term extraction task, it seems that training on all available training data is beneficial for the banking and retail domain. The HR domain, however, benefits most from in-domain training data. For the aspect category classification, again the HR domain reveals a different result than the other domains, in that it is much more harder to classify. The polarity classification experiments reveal that for all domains it is better to train on small domain-specific datasets instead of combining training data from different domains. Strikingly, the retail domain generalizes best to the other domains, though these results should be corroborated on larger datasets.

As we address the ABSA task incrementally, we observed error percolation in each step. We believe, however, that only an incremental approach reflects how ABSA is performed in a real-world setting. In future work, we will explore the viability of domain adaptation for ABSA on larger and different datasets and with other languages.

Acknowledgments

We wish to thank the annotators and the anonymous reviewers. This work has been supported by the Flanders Innovation & Entrepeneurship government agency (VLAIO).

---

[3]Experiments revealed no difference in performance when relying on the *in-domain* aspect terms.

References

Samuel Brody and Noemie Elhadad. 2010. An unsupervised aspect-sentiment model for online reviews. In *Proceedings of the 11th Annual Conference of the North American Chapter of the Association for Computational Linguistics (NAACL-2010)*, pages 804–812.

Caroline Brun, Julien Perez, and Claude Roux. 2016. XRCE at SemEval-2016 Task 5: Feedbacked Ensemble Modeling on Syntactico-Semantic Knowledge for Aspect Based Sentiment Analysis. In *Proceedings of the 10th International Workshop on Semantic Evaluation (SemEval-2016)*, pages 277–281.

Luigi Di Caro and Matteo Grella. 2013. Sentiment analysis via dependency parsing. *Computer Standards & Interfaces*, 35(5):442–453.

Chih-Chung Chang and Chih-Jen Lin. 2011. LIBSVM: A library for support vector machines. *ACM Transactions on Intelligent Systems and Technology*, 2:27:1–27:27.

Orphée De Clercq and Véronique Hoste. 2016. Rude waiter but mouthwatering pastries! An exploratory study into Dutch Aspect-Based Sentiment Analysis. In *Proceedings of the Tenth International Conference on Language Resources and Evaluation (LREC 2016)*, pages 23–28.

Tom De Smedt and Walter Daelemans. 2012. Vreselijk mooi! Terribly beautiful: a subjectivity lexicon for Dutch adjectives. In *Proceedings of the 8th International Conference on Language Resources and Evaluation (LREC-2012)*, pages 3568–3572.

Gayatree Ganu, Noemie Elhadad, and Amélie Marian. 2009. Beyond the stars: improving rating predictions using review text content. In *Proceedings of the 12th International Workshop on the Web and Databases (WebDB-2009)*, pages 1–6.

Minqing Hu and Bing Liu. 2004. Mining and summarizing customer reviews. In *Proceedings of the 10th International Conference on Knowledge Discovery and Data Mining (KDD-2004)*, pages 168–177.

Valentin Jijkoun and Katja Hofmann. 2009. Generating a non-English subjectivity lexicon: Relations that matter. In *Proceedings of the 12th Conference of the European Chapter of the Association for Computational Linguistics (EACL-2009)*, pages 398–405.

Marjan Van de Kauter, Geert Coorman, Els Lefever, Bart Desmet, Lieve Macken, and Véronique Hoste. 2013. LeTs Preprocess: The multilingual LT3 linguistic preprocessing toolkit. *Computational Linguistics in the Netherlands Journal*, 3:103–120.

Jens Lehmann, Robert Isele, Max Jakob, Anja Jentzsch, Dimitris Kontokostas, Pablo N. Mendes, Sebastian Hellmann, Mohamed Morsey, Patrick van Kleef, Soren Auer, and Christian Bizer. 2013. DBpedia – A Large-scale, Multilingual Knowledge Base Extracted from Wikipedia. *Semantic Web Journal*, 6:167–195.

Bing Liu. 2012. Sentiment analysis and opinion mining. *Synthesis Lectures on Human Language Technologies*, 5(1):1–167.

Bing Liu. 2015. *Sentiment Analysis - Mining Opinions, Sentiments, and Emotions*. Cambridge University Press.

Tomas Mikolov, Ilya Sutskever, Kai Chen, Greg S Corrado, and Jeff Dean. 2013. Distributed representations of words and phrases and their compositionality. In *Advances in Neural Information Processing Systems*, pages 3111–3119.

Jorge Nocedal. 1980. Updating quasi-Newton matrices with limited storage. *Mathematics of Computation*, 35(151):773–782.

Naoaki Okazaki. 2007. CRFsuite: a fast implementation of Conditional Random Fields (CRFs).

Bo Pang and Lillian Lee. 2008. Opinion mining and sentiment analysis. *Foundations and Trends in Information Retrieval.*, 2(1-2):1–135.

Maria Pontiki, Dimitris Galanis, Haris Papageorgiou, Ion Androutsopoulos, Suresh Manandhar, Mohammad AL-Smadi, Mahmoud Al-Ayyoub, Yanyan Zhao, Bing Qin, Orphée De Clercq, Véronique Hoste, Marianna Apidianaki, Xavier Tannier, Natalia Loukachevitch, Evgeniy Kotelnikov, Núria Bel, Salud María Jiménez-Zafra, and Gülşen Eryiğit. 2016. Semeval-2016 task 5: Aspect based sentiment analysis. In *Proceedings of the 10th International Workshop on Semantic Evaluation (SemEval-2016)*, pages 19–30.

Maria Pontiki, Dimitris Galanis, Haris Papageorgiou, Suresh Manandhar, and Ion Androutsopoulos. 2015. Semeval-2015 task 12: Aspect based sentiment analysis. In *Proceedings of the 9th International Workshop on Semantic Evaluation (SemEval-2015)*, pages 486–495.

Maria Pontiki, Dimitris Galanis, John Pavlopoulos, Harris Papageorgiou, Ion Androutsopoulos, and Suresh Manandhar. 2014. Semeval-2014 task 4: Aspect based sentiment analysis. In *Proceedings of the 8th International Workshop on Semantic Evaluation (SemEval-2014)*, pages 27–35.

José Saias. 2015. Sentiue: Target and aspect based sentiment analysis in SemEval-2015 Task 12. In *Proceedings of the 9th International Workshop on Semantic Evaluation (SemEval-2015)*, pages 767–771.

Iñaki San Vicente, Xabier Saralegi, and Rodrigo Agerri. 2015. EliXa: A Modular and Flexible ABSA Platform. In *Proceedings of the 9th International Workshop on Semantic Evaluation (SemEval-2015)*, pages 748–752.

Aliaksei Severyn and Alessandro Moschitti. 2015. UNITN: Training Deep Convolutional Neural Network for Twitter Sentiment Classification. In *Proceedings of the 9th International Workshop on Semantic Evaluation (SemEval-2015)*, pages 464–469.

Pontus Stenetorp, Sampo Pyysalo, Goran Topic, Tomoko Ohta, Sophia Ananiadou, and Junichi Tsujii. 2012. BRAT: a web-based tool for NLP-assisted text annotation. In *Proceedings of the 13th Conference of the European Chapter of the Association for Computational Linguistics (EACL-2012)*, pages 102–107.

Tun Thura Thet, Jin-Cheon Na, and Christopher S.G. Khoo. 2010. Aspect-based Sentiment Analysis of Movie Reviews on Discussion Boards. *Journal of Information Science*, 36(6):823–848.

Zhiqiang Toh and Jian Su. 2015. NLANGP: Supervised machine learning system for aspect category classification and opinion target extraction. In *Proceedings of the 9th International Workshop on Semantic Evaluation (SemEval-2015)*, pages 496–501.

Zhiqiang Toh and Jian Su. 2016. NLANGP at SemEval-2016 Task 5: Improving Aspect Based Sentiment Analysis using Neural Network Features. In *Proceedings of the 10th International Workshop on Semantic Evaluation (SemEval-2016)*, pages 282–288.

Piek Vossen, Isa Maks, Roxane Segers, Hennie van der Vliet, Marie-Francine Moens, Katja Hofmann, Erik Tjong Kim Sang, and Maarten de Rijke. 2013. Cornetto: a lexical semantic database for Dutch. In Peter Spyns and Jan Odijk, editors, *Essential Speech and Language Technology for Dutch, Theory and Applications of Natural Language Processing*, pages 165–184. Springer.

Building a SentiWordNet For Odia

Gaurav Mohanty and **Abishek Kannan** and **Radhika Mamidi**
Language Technologies Research Center
Kohli Center on Intelligent Systems
International Institute of Information Technology, Hyderabad
{gaurav.mohanty,abishek.kannan}@research.iiit.ac.in
radhika.mamidi@iiit.ac.in

Abstract

As a discipline of Natural Language Processing, Sentiment Analysis is used to extract and analyze subjective information present in natural language data. The task of Sentiment Analysis has acquired wide commercial uses including social media monitoring tasks, survey responses, review systems, etc. Languages like English have several resources which aid in the task of Sentiment Analysis. SentiWordNet and Subjectivity WordList are examples of such tools and resources. With more data being available in native vernacular, language-specific SentiWordNet(s) have become essential. For resource poor languages, creating such SentiWordNet(s) is a difficult task to achieve. One solution is to use available resources in English and translate the final source lexicon to target lexicon via machine translation. Machine translation systems for the English-Odia language pair have not yet been developed. In this paper, we discuss a method to create a SentiWordNet for Odia, which is resource-poor, by only using resources which are currently available for Indian languages. The lexicon created, would serve as a tool for Sentiment Analysis related task specific to Odia data.

1 Introduction

For resource-poor languages, one popular approach is to use readily available resources in English to generate a source lexicon. The source lexicon is then translated using a Machine Translation system or a bilingual dictionary to create the final target lexicon (Bakliwal et al., 2012). In case of the English-Odia language pair, a good Machine Translation system is absent. The online bilingual dictionaries for the same have very few word pairs. Manual translation is expensive in terms of human resource and time. Another approach is to use available parallel corpora for the language pair and use a word-alignment tool in order to get a one-to-one mapping between words. For this method, a sufficiently large corpus is required in order to get an appropriate number of unique word pairs. Such a large corpus is unavailable for the English-Odia language pair. In fact, larger corpora is available for Odia and other Indian language pairs. WordNets developed under the IndoWordNet structure (Bhattacharyya, 2010) do not map words directly but they match synsets instead. These WordNets for Indian languages serve well in translation from source to target lexicon. The SentiWordNets present for such Indian languages helps in assignment of polarity to the final collection of words.

Odia SentiWordNet is built using WordNets and SentiWordNets available for other Indian languages. WordNets include those of Bengali, Tamil, Telugu and Odia itself. SentiWordNets used include those of Bengali, Tamil and Telugu.

The paper is divided into various sections. Section 2 comprises of previous work and progress towards building SentiWordNets for Indian languages. Section 3 describes resources used for creation of Odia SentiWordNet. Section 4 contains a detailed explanation of procedure followed for the same and defines the evaluation scheme for verification of resource thus created. An insight on future work and extensibility of the SentiWordNet is provided in Section 5.

2 Previous Work

Since its introduction in 1961 by IBM, Sentiment Analysis has been a fast growing area in computer

143

Proceedings of the 8th Workshop on Computational Approaches to Subjectivity, Sentiment and Social Media Analysis, pages 143–148
Copenhagen, Denmark, September 7–11, 2017. ©2017 Association for Computational Linguistics

science. Research on Sentiment Analysis began in English. However with increasing demand, several researchers have developed various tools and resources for many other languages. Odia (ISO 639 language code: ori)[1], being a resource-poor language, lacks necessary tools to perform Sentiment Analysis.

Since opinion mining has proved extremely useful in online review and survey systems and since data is more readily available than ever, Sentiment Analysis serves as an effective method to achieve automated scoring of products, movies, etc.

Turney worked on classifying customer reviews (Turney, 2002). They adopt an unsupervised learning technique to predict the semantic orientation of phrases. Hatzivassiloglou (Hatzivassiloglou and R. McKeown, 1997) and Turney (Turney and Littman, 2003) describe methods of using a set of words gathered a priori as a seed list to classify the semantic orientation of phrases. The former method (Hatzivassiloglou and R. McKeown, 1997) was the first to deal with opinion classification in phrases. The approach mainly uses adjectives for Sentiment Analysis. However, sufficient pre-processing was carried out using available tools for English before the phrases were successfully classified.

Even though sentiment depends on context, lexical resources have proven to give a good baseline for further studies. The English language has several lexical resources such as the SentiWordNet as described by Esuli (Esuli and Sebastiani, 2006). It contains over 3 million tokens assigned with polarity and objectivity score. The resource has been improved over the years as demonstrated in literature (Baccianella et al., 2010). Another such important resource is the Subjectivity Lexicon (Wilson et al., 2005) which is a part of OpinionFinder[2].

Languages which have a scarcity of readily available data depend on resource rich languages to build such lexicons. Whalley (Whalley and Medagoda, 2015) describes how the Sinhalese sentiment lexicon was created using the English SentiWordNet 3.0. The SentiWordNet in English was mapped to a Sinhalese dictionary and the scores were copied from one language to another. Another way to achieve this is by linking the WordNets of the source and target language. Joshi proposed a method to create a SentiWordNet for Hindi by linking the English and Hindi WordNets and assigning scores to the synsets in Hindi WordNet (Joshi et al., 2010). Dipankar Das suggested a method to develop WordNet affect lists in Bengali using affect wordlists already available in English. (Das and B, 2010). The method uses a bilingual dictionary to translate words from English to Bengali. Amitava Das (Das and Bandyopadhyay, 2010) (Das and Gambäck, 2012) (Das and Bandyopadhyay, 2011) proposes several ways to generate such lexical resources for other Indian languages. One approach suggests the usage of both English SentiWordNet 3.0 and Subjectivity Lexicon and adopting a translation based approach in order to build the lexicon in three Indian languages (Das and Bandyopadhyay, 2010). A SentiWordNet for Tamil has also been developed using a similar translation based approach for currently available resources in English (Kannan et al., 2016). Due to lack of a sufficiently large parallel corpus or a bilingual dictionary, direct translation techniques from English to Odia could not be applied in-order to build the SentiWordNet in Odia.

3 Prerequisites

For creating Odia SentiWordNet, SentiWordNets of three Indian languages, namely Bengali, Tamil and Telugu are used. Polarity of words for these resources has proved to be reliable (Das and Bandyopadhyay, 2010). Multiple SentiWordNets are used for a better estimate of sentiment for each word and reduction of ambiguities while building the resource. For creation of lexicon for Odia, WordNets for Odia and the other three Indian languages are used. These WordNets have synsets linked via a common synset identification number (ID), without direct word-to-word mapping. The resources used are described below.

3.1 SentiWordNets for Indian Languages

SentiWordNet is a lexical resource explicitly devised for supporting sentiment classification and opinion mining applications. According to Baccianella, SentiWordNet is the result of the automatic annotation of all the synsets of WordNet towards the notions of positivity, negativity, and neutrality (Baccianella et al., 2010). Each synset is associated with three numerical scores : pos(s), neg(s), and obj(s) which indicate positive, negative, and objective i.e., neutral respectively. Senti-

---

WordNets for Bengali, Telugu and Tamil were created using Das's approach (Das and Bandyopadhyay, 2010). Each of these comprises of four lists under the categories of "Positive", "Negative", "Neutral" and "Ambiguous" which contain words of positive, negative, neutral polarity and ambiguous words, respectively. The Parts-of-Speech tag information for each word is also provided. Table 1 gives detailed statistics for each of the SentiWordNets used.

Language	POS	NEG	NEU	AMB
Bengali	1779	3714	359	648
Telugu	2136	4076	359	1093
Tamil	2225	4447	361	1168

Table 1: Statistics for SentiWordNets

3.2 WordNets for Indian Languages

"Wordnets are lexical structures composed of synsets and semantic relations" (Fellbaum, 1998). A synset comprises a set of synonyms. They are linked by semantic relations like hypernymy (is-a), meronymy (part-of), troponymy (manner-of), etc. WordNets for four different languages are used for building the lexicon for Odia SentiWordNet. These WordNets are linked across languages through common synset IDs. They are part of the linked IndoWordNet structure (Bhattacharyya, 2010). WordNets for Bengali, Tamil and Telugu were used for creating the source lexicon. Odia WordNet was used for generating the target lexicon. Table 2 describes the statistics of the number of tokens present in every Part-Of-Speech category for each language.

LANG	Odia	Bengali	Telugu	Tamil
NOUN	27216	27281	12078	16312
VERB	2418	2804	2795	2803
ADJ	5273	5815	5776	5827
RB	377	445	442	477
Total	35284	36346	21091	25419

Table 2: IndoWordNet Statistics.

4 Procedure

A step-by-step procedure to be followed is illustrated in Figure 1. This procedure can be adopted for a different target language, as long as the target language has a WordNet which is linked with other Indian language WordNets. The procedure is divided into three parts:

1. **Creating Source Lexicon:** SentiWordNets from Indian languages are used to assign a polarity to corresponding WordNet synsets. A final list of synsets IDs with the corresponding polarity serves as a source list.

2. **Generating Target Lexicon:** For every synset ID from source, the corresponding words from the target language WordNet are assigned the same polarity as that of the synset ID.

3. **Evaluation of Final Resource:** The created target lexicon needs to be evaluated for errors. This paper adopts manual evaluation by language specific annotators and reports annotator agreement score.

4.1 Creating Source Lexicon

Source Lexicon acquisition begins with SentiWordNets available for the three aforementioned Indian languages. In order to create a reliable baseline for Odia, only words with positive and negative polarity are considered. Currently, ambiguous words or those having neutral polarity are not considered for the creation of source lexicon. For each language, words with positive and negative polarity are extracted from their corresponding SentiWordNets.

The corresponding synset ID of each word is then found from that language's WordNet. This is attained by using a hash-map created over all the words in WordNet for that language. The synset ID for the identified word serves as a key to a dictionary δ. The corresponding value is a list with the polarity of the word as an item. In case δ already has a synset ID as a key, the polarity of the word is appended to the existing list for that key in δ. Such a case would occur when word and its synonym (both part of the same synset) are both present in the SentiWordNet for that language. Such a case can also occur when a word from a different language's WordNet has a synset ID which is already a key in δ. The final dictionary comprises of several synset IDs as key. A total of 6203 synset IDs were identified. For each key the value in δ is a list of polarities (positive or negative) which are observed for words in the sysnet across languages.

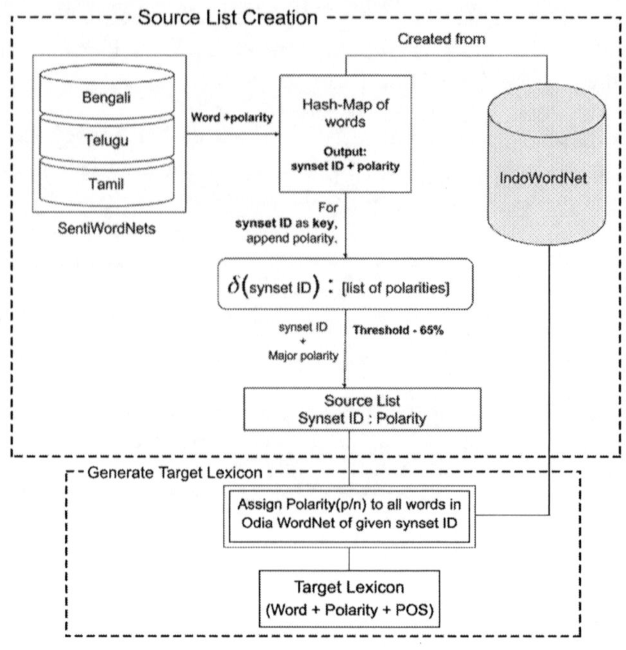

Figure 1: Flow of Design for Odia SentiWordNet

A word and its synonyms should commonly have the same polarity. This should also be true across languages, in an ideal scenario. However, it was observed that in many cases the list of polarities for a given key is not homogeneous. This is because a word with a particular sentiment in one language may not necessarily have the same sentiment in another language. Infact, it was also observed that, in very few cases, a word with a given sentiment in one language sometimes did not have the same sentiment for some of its synonyms in the same language. Every synset ID which exists as a key in δ is to be assigned a single polarity. Any of the synset IDs which have contradicting polarities to a certain degree should be ignored as these will affect the reliability of the Odia SentiWord-Net. For a given key (synset ID), the polarity in its list in δ which holds a majority greater than 65% is considered the final polarity for that synset ID. This results in a list of synset IDs with an assigned major polarity. The list serves as the "Source" to map to synsets in Odia WordNet. The source list comprises of 5661 synset IDs along with their major polarity.

4.2 Generating Target Lexicon

In order to create the Target Lexicon, Odia Word-Net is used. The Odia WordNet is linked to the other three aforementioned WordNets through a common synset ID. A total 5407 synset IDs from the Source List were found to exist in Odia Word-Net. For each synset ID in Source list, the corresponding words are extracted from Odia WordNet. Each of these words is assigned the major polarity (positive or negative) corresponding to that synset ID in the Source list. A total of 13917 tokens were assigned polarity. Table 3 provides details on the total tokens extracted from Odia WordNet. Only adjectives and adverbs are added to the final Target Lexicon. Nouns and verbs were not added to the Target Lexicon because the polarity associated with these words is usually context dependent. These are added to a separate list for future inspection.

No. of observed OWN synsets	5661
Adjectives and Adverbs	4747
Nouns and Verbs	9170
Total number of tokens	13917

Table 3: Target Lexicon Statistics

The final Target Lexicon comprises of words along with their sentiment polarity, Part-of-Speech tag and synset ID corresponding to the language's WordNet. The final lexicon contained 1839 pos-

Word	Meaning	Polarity
ଭାଗ୍ୟଶାଳୀ	fortunate	Positive
ସତ୍ତୋଟପଣିଆ	truthful, honest	Positive
ଆଲୋକିତ	enlightened	Positive
ସୀମିତ	limited	Negative
ଠିକ୍	correct	Positive
ଏକ୍ଲା	alone, deserted	Negative
ଲୋଭୀ	selfish	Negative

Figure 2: Odia words with polarity

itive entries and 2908 negative entries. Figure 2 shows a few examples of Odia words with their corresponding assigned polarity.

4.3 Resource Evaluation

In order to assess the reliability of the Odia Senti-WordNet, a random sampling of 2500 words was created from the Target Lexicon. In order to maintain a balanced sample set, 1250 words were randomly picked from each polarity list. This sample set was provided to three manual annotators to be independently annotated as positive or negative. The manual annotators were native Odia speakers and spoke the language on a daily basis. Each of the three annotators were asked to annotate every token of the sample set with the polarity they deemed appropriate. No annotator had prior information about the assigned polarity to a token. This ensured unbiased annotation of tokens.

In order to capture inter-annotator agreement, Fleiss Kappa[3] score for the annotated sample set was also calculated. Fleiss Kappa is calculated using the following formula:

$$\kappa = \frac{\bar{P} - \bar{P_e}}{1 - \bar{P_e}} \quad (1)$$

$\bar{P}$ represents the sum of observed agreement. The sum of agreement by chance is denoted by $\bar{P_e}$. Fleiss Kappa score is calculated using three raters for two categories (positive/negative). A substantial agreement score of $\kappa = \mathbf{0.76}$ is reported for Odia SentiWordNet.

In order to further improve upon the Target Lexicon, words with sentiment which none of the annotators agreed to, were removed. This was done only for the sample of 2500 words. Table 4 gives metrics for the Odia SentiWordNet thus created. A total of 98 words with incorrect polarity were removed.

Initial Positive Tokens	1839
Initial Negative Tokens	2908
Final Positive Tokens	1803
Final Negative Tokens	2846
Inter-Annotator Agreement (**Fleiss Kappa**)	
0.76	

Table 4: Evaluation Details

5 Conclusion and Future Work

Odia SentiWordNet will serve as a useful resource for Sentiment Analysis on Odia data. The method adopted is generic and can be used to create similar sentiment lexicons for other Indian languages which are part of the IndoWordNet structure. In order to find the accuracy of the created resource, it needs to be tested on actual user generated data. Odia data is readily available online. Currently, a set of 1000 Odia sentences is being manually annotated. The annotated set would serve as gold data. These sentences are taken from online newspaper articles[4]. Odia SentiWordNet will be tested on these 1000 sentences in order to predict the sentiment associated with each sentence. Comparison with results of manual annotation should give a more accurate insight on how reliable the resource is. The resource serves as a baseline and can be improved in the future. Several resource expansion strategies can be used to enrich Odia Senti-WordNet. One particular method involves usage of antonym relations. Antonyms of a word, which are not already present in the resource can be assigned opposite polarity. Antonym creation rules, specific to the language, can be applied to generate antonyms of many words in the resource as suggested previously in literature (Das and Bandyopadhyay, 2010). If a sufficiently large corpus becomes available, SentiWordNet can be used to capture language-specific nuances. The raw corpus can be trained on a word embedding tool (e.g Word2Vec) to create word clusters of similar

---

[3]https://en.wikipedia.org/wiki/Fleiss`kappa

[4]http://thesamaja.in/

words based on the prior and subsequent neighbours of a word in the corpus. Such clusters can be further used to expand the lexicon.

Acknowledgments

The authors would like to thank Pruthwik Mishra, Shastri V. Mohapatra and Ranjita Mohanty for their help in manual annotation and checking the reliability of Odia SentiWordNet. The SentiWordNets for Tamil, Bengali and Telugu were acquired from Amitava Das' website[5]. The IndoWordNet was accessed from CLIFT IIT Bombay website[6].

References

Stefano Baccianella, Andrea Esuli, and Fabrizio Sebastiani. 2010. Sentiwordnet 3.0: An enhanced lexical resource for sentiment analysis and opinion mining. In *Proceedings of the Seventh conference on International Language Resources and Evaluation (LREC'10)*. European Languages Resources Association (ELRA). http://aclweb.org/anthology/L10-1531.

Akshat Bakliwal, Piyush Arora, and Vasudeva Varma. 2012. Hindi subjective lexicon: A lexical resource for hindi adjective polarity classification. In Nicoletta Calzolari, Khalid Choukri, Thierry Declerck, Mehmet Ugur Dogan, Bente Maegaard, Joseph Mariani, Jan Odijk, and Stelios Piperidis, editors, *LREC*. European Language Resources Association (ELRA), pages 1189–1196. http://dblp.uni-trier.de/db/conf/lrec/lrec2012.htmlBakliwalAV12.

Pushpak Bhattacharyya. 2010. Indowordnet. In Nicoletta Calzolari, Khalid Choukri, Bente Maegaard, Joseph Mariani, Jan Odijk, Stelios Piperidis, Mike Rosner, and Daniel Tapias, editors, *LREC*. European Language Resources Association. http://dblp.uni-trier.de/db/conf/lrec/lrec2010.htmlBhattacharyya10.

Amitava Das and Sivaji Bandyopadhyay. 2010. Sentiwordnet for indian languages. In *Proceedings of the Eighth Workshop on Asian Language Resouces*. Coling 2010 Organizing Committee, Beijing, China, pages 56–63. http://www.aclweb.org/anthology/W10-3208.

Amitava Das and Sivaji Bandyopadhyay. 2011. Dr sentiment knows everything! In *Proceedings of the ACL-HLT 2011 System Demonstrations*. Association for Computational Linguistics, Portland, Oregon, pages 50–55. http://www.aclweb.org/anthology/P11-4009.

Amitava Das and Björn Gambäck. 2012. Sentimantics: Conceptual spaces for lexical sentiment polarity representation with contextuality. In *Proceedings of the 3rd Workshop in Computational Approaches to Subjectivity and Sentiment Analysis*. Association for Computational Linguistics, Stroudsburg, PA, USA, WASSA '12, pages 38–46. http://aclweb.org/anthology/W12-3707.

Dipankar Das and Sivaji B. 2010. Developing bengali wordnet affect for analyzing emotion.

A. Esuli and F. Sebastiani. 2006. Sentiwordnet: A publicly available lexical resource for opinion mining. In *Proceedings of the Fifth International Conference on Language Resources and Evaluation (LREC'06)*. European Language Resources Association (ELRA). http://aclweb.org/anthology/L06-1225.

Christiane Fellbaum, editor. 1998. *WordNet: An Electronic Lexical Database*. Language, Speech, and Communication. MIT Press, Cambridge, MA.

Vasileios Hatzivassiloglou and Kathleen R. McKeown. 1997. Predicting the semantic orientation of adjectives. In *8th Conference of the European Chapter of the Association for Computational Linguistics*. http://aclweb.org/anthology/E97-1023.

Aditya Joshi, AR Balamurali, and Pushpak Bhattacharyya. 2010. A fall-back strategy for sentiment analysis in hindi: a case study. *Proceedings of the 8th ICON* .

Abishek Kannan, Gaurav Mohanty, and Radhika Mamidi. 2016. Towards building a sentiwordnet for tamil. In *Proceedings of the 13th International Conference on Natural Language Processing*. NLP Association of India, Varanasi, India, pages 30–35. http://www.aclweb.org/anthology/W16-6305.

Peter D. Turney. 2002. Thumbs up or thumbs down?: Semantic orientation applied to unsupervised classification of reviews. In *Proceedings of the 40th Annual Meeting on Association for Computational Linguistics*. Association for Computational Linguistics, Stroudsburg, PA, USA, ACL '02, pages 417–424. https://doi.org/10.3115/1073083.1073153.

Peter D. Turney and Michael L. Littman. 2003. Measuring praise and criticism: Inference of semantic orientation from association. *ACM Trans. Inf. Syst.* 21(4):315–346. https://doi.org/10.1145/944012.944013.

J Whalley and N Medagoda. 2015. Sentiment lexicon construction using sentiwordnet 3.0. *ICNC'15 - FSKD'15, School of Information Science and Engineering, Hunan University, China* .

Theresa Wilson, Paul Hoffmann, Swapna Somasundaran, Jason Kessler, Janyce Wiebe, Yejin Choi, Claire Cardie, Ellen Riloff, and Siddharth Patwardhan. 2005. Opinionfinder: A system for subjectivity analysis. In *Proceedings of HLT/EMNLP 2005 Interactive Demonstrations*. http://aclweb.org/anthology/H05-2018.

---

[5]http://amitavadas.com/sentiwordnet.php
[6]http://www.cfilt.iitb.ac.in/indowordnet/

Lexicon Integrated CNN Models with Attention for Sentiment Analysis

Bonggun Shin, Timothy Lee, Jinho D. Choi
Math and Computer Science
Emory University
Atlanta, GA 30322
{bonggun.shin,timothy.lee,jinho.choi}@emory.edu

Abstract

With the advent of word embeddings, lexicons are no longer fully utilized for sentiment analysis although they still provide important features in the traditional setting. This paper introduces a novel approach to sentiment analysis that integrates lexicon embeddings and an attention mechanism into Convolutional Neural Networks. Our approach performs separate convolutions for word and lexicon embeddings and provides a global view of the document using attention. Our models are experimented on both the SemEval'16 Task 4 dataset and the Stanford Sentiment Treebank and show comparative or better results against the existing state-of-the-art systems. Our analysis shows that lexicon embeddings allow building high-performing models with much smaller word embeddings, and the attention mechanism effectively dims out noisy words for sentiment analysis.

1 Introduction

Sentiment analysis is a task of identifying sentiment polarities expressed in documents, typically positive, neutral, or negative. Although the task of sentiment analysis has been well-explored (Mullen and Collier, 2004; Pang and Lee, 2005; Wilson et al., 2005), it is still very challenging due to the complexity of extracting human emotion from raw text. The recent advance of deep learning has definitely elevated the performance of this task (Socher et al., 2013; Kim, 2014; Yin and Schütze, 2015) although there is much more room to improve.

In the traditional setting where statistical models are based on sparse features, lexicons consisting of words and their sentiment scores are shown to be highly effective for sentiment analysis because they provide features that may not be captured from training data (Hu and Liu, 2004; Kim and Hovy, 2004; Ding et al., 2008; Taboada et al., 2011). However, since the appearance of word embeddings, the use of lexicons is getting faded away because word embeddings are believed to capture the sentiment aspects of those words. This brought us two important questions:

- Can lexicons be still useful for sentiment analysis when coupled with word embeddings?

- If yes, what is the most effective way of incorporating lexicons with word embeddings?

To answer these questions, we first construct lexicon embeddings that are specifically designed for sentiment analysis and integrate them into the existing Convolutional Neural Network (CNN) model similar to Kim (2014). Three ways of lexicon integration to the CNN model are proposed, which show distinctive characteristics for different genres (Section 3.2). We then incorporate an efficient attention mechanism to our CNN models, which provides a global view of the document by emphasizing (or de-emphasizing) important words and lexicons (Section 3.3). Our models using lexicon embeddings are evaluated on two well-known datasets, the SemEval'16 dataset and the Stanford Sentiment Treebank, and show state-of-the-art results on both datasets (Section 4). To the best of our knowledge, this is the first time that lexicon embeddings are introduced for sentiment analysis.

2 Related Work

The first attempt of sentiment analysis on text was initiated by Pang et al. (2002) who pioneered this field by using bag-of-word features. This work mostly hinged on feature engineering; since then, many kinds of feature learning methods had been introduced to increase the performance (Pang and

149

Proceedings of the 8th Workshop on Computational Approaches to Subjectivity, Sentiment and Social Media Analysis, pages 149–158
Copenhagen, Denmark, September 7–11, 2017. ©2017 Association for Computational Linguistics

Lee, 2008; Liu, 2012; Gimpel et al., 2011; Feldman, 2013; Mohammad et al., 2013b). Aside from pure machine learning approaches, lexicon based approaches had been another trend, which relied on the manual or algorithmic creation of word sentiment scores (Hu and Liu, 2004; Kim and Hovy, 2004; Ding et al., 2008; Taboada et al., 2011).

Since the emergence of the Convolutional Neural Networks (CNN; Collobert et al. (2011)), conventional methods have become gradually obsolete because of the outstanding performance from the CNN variants. CNN based models are distinguished from earlier methods because they do not rely on laborious feature engineering. The first success of CNN in sentiment analysis was triggered by document classification research (Kim, 2014), where CNN showed state-of-the-art results in numerous document classification datasets. This success has engendered an upsurge in deep neural network research for sentiment analysis. Various modified models have been proposed in the literature. One of the famous deep learning methods that models a document is the generalized phrase proposed by Yin and Schütze (2014), which represents a sentence using element-wise addition, multiplication, or recursive auto-encoder.

Endeavors to capture n-gram information bore fruits with CNN, max pooling, and softmax (Collobert et al., 2011; Kim, 2014), which is regarded as the standard methods of the document classification problem these days. Kalchbrenner et al. (2014a) extended this standard CNN model with dynamic k-max pooling, which served as an input layer to another stacked convolution layer. Multichannel CNN methods (Kim, 2014; Yin and Schütze, 2015) are another branch of CNN, where assorted embeddings are considered together when convolving the input. Unlike Kim (2014)'s model that relies on a single type of embedding with different mutability characteristics of the weights of embedding layer, Yin and Schütze (2015) incorporates diverse sort of embedding types using multichannel CNN.

Two notable pioneers in using lexicon for sentiment analysis are Mohammad et al. (2013a); Kalchbrenner et al. (2014b) generated scores with other manually generated sentiment lexicon scores to achieved the state-of-the-art result in SemEval-2013 Twitter sentiment analysis task. In general domain, Hu and Liu (2004) generated a user review lexicon that showed promising result in capturing sentiment in customer product reviews.

Attention based methods have been successful in many application domains, such as image classification (Stollenga et al., 2014), image caption generation (Xu et al., 2015), machine translation (Cho et al., 2014; Bahdanau et al., 2014; Luong et al., 2015), and question answering (Shih et al., 2016; Chen et al., 2015; Yang et al., 2016). However, in the field of sentiment analysis, the attention is applied to only aspect-based sentiment classification (Yanase et al., 2016). To the best knowledge of ours, there is no attention-based model for a general sentiment analysis task.

3 Approach

The models proposed here are based on a convolutional architecture and use naive concatenation (Section 3.2.1), multichannel (Section 3.2.2), separate convolution (Section 3.2.3), and embedding attention (Section 3.3) for the integration of lexicon embeddings to CNN.

3.1 Baseline

Our baseline approach is a one-layer CNN model using pre-trained word embeddings, which is a reimplementation of the CNN model introduced by Kim (2014). Let $s \in \mathbb{R}^{n \times d}$ be a matrix representing the input document, where n is the number of words, d is the dimension of the word embeddings, and each row corresponds to the word embedding, $w_i \in \mathbb{R}^d$, where w_i indicates the i'th word in the document. This document matrix s is fed into the convolutional layer and convolved by the weights $c \in \mathbb{R}^{l \times d}$, where l is the length of the filter.

The convolutional layer can take m-number of filters of the length l. Each convolution produces a vector $v_c \in \mathbb{R}^{n-l+1}$, where elements in v_c convey the l-gram features across the document. The max pooling layer selects the most salient features from each of the m vectors produced by the filters. As a result, the output of this max pooling layer is a vector $v_m \in \mathbb{R}^{(n-l+1) \times m}$. The selected features are passed onto the softmax layer, which is optimized for the score of each sentiment class label.

3.2 Lexicon Integration

Lexicon embeddings are derived by taking scores from multiple sources of lexicon datasets. Each lexicon dataset consists of key-value pairs, where the key is a word and the value is a list of sentiment scores for that word (e.g., probabilities of the word in positive, neutral, and negative contexts). These scores range between -1 and 1, where -1 and 1 being the most negative and positive, respectively. However, some lexicons contain non-probabilistic scores (e.g., frequency counts of the word in sentimental contexts), which are normalized to $[-1, 1]$.

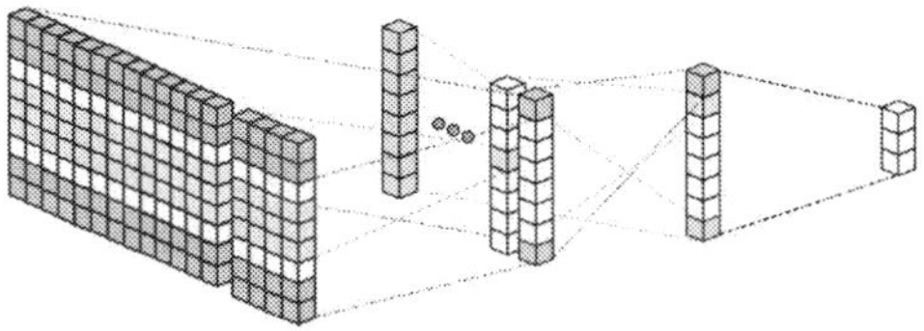

(a) Naive concatenation (Section 3.2.1). The lexicon embeddings (on the right) are concatenated to the word embeddings (on the left).

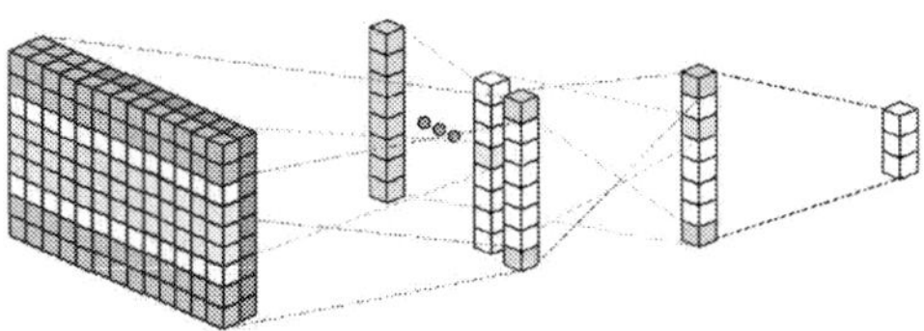

(b) Multichannel (Section 3.2.2). The lexicon embeddings are added to the second channel whereas the word embeddings are added to the first channel.

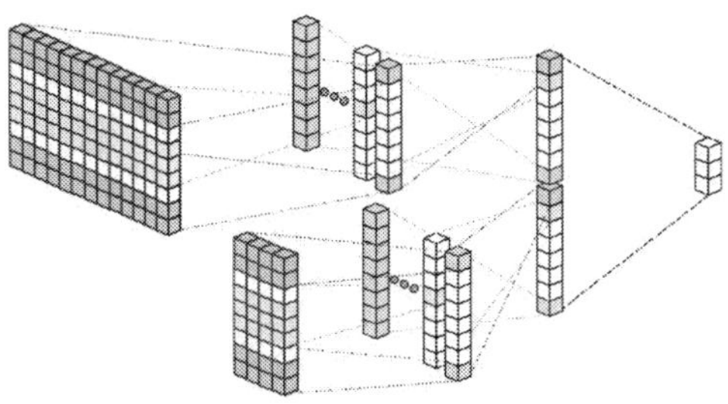

(c) Separate convolution (Section 3.2.3). The lexicon embeddings are processed by a separate convolution (on the right) from the word embeddings (on the left).

Figure 1: Lexicon integration to the CNN model.

For each word $w \in W$, where W is the union of all words in the lexicon datasets, a lexicon embedding is constructed by concatenating all the scores among the datasets with respect to w. If w does not appear in certain datasets, 0 values are assigned in place. The resulting embedding is in the form of a vector $v \in \mathbb{R}^e$, where e is the total number of scores across all lexicon datasets. The following subsections propose three methods for lexicon integration to the baseline CNN model (Section 3.1), which depict different characteristics depending on the peculiarities of each domain.

3.2.1 Naive Concatenation

The simplest way of blending a lexicon embedding into its corresponding word embedding is to append it to the end of the word embedding (Figure 1(a)). In a formal notation, the document matrix becomes $s \in \mathbb{R}^{n \times (d+e)}$. The subsequent process is the same as the baseline approach.

3.2.2 Multichannel

Inspired by Yin and Schütze (2015) who integrated several kinds of word embeddings using multichannel CNN, lexicon embeddings in this approach are represented in another channel along with the word embedding channel where both channels are convolved together (Figure 1(b)). Since the dimension of lexicon embeddings is considerably smaller than that of word embeddings (i.e., $d \gg e$), zeros are padded to the lexicon embeddings so their dimensions match (i.e., $d = e$). The identical shape of these two channels allows multichannel convolution to the input document.

3.2.3 Separate Convolution

Another way of adding lexicon embeddings to the CNN model is to process a separate convolution for them (Figure 1(c)). In this case, two individual convolutions are applied to word embeddings and lexicon embeddings. The max pooled output features from each convolution are then merged together to form an input vector to the softmax layer. Formally, let l_w, l_x be the filter lengths for word embeddings and lexicon embeddings, respectively. Let m_w and m_x be the numbers of filters for word embeddings and lexicon embeddings, respectively. The resulting penultimate layer includes max pooled features from word embeddings and lexicon embeddings of size $[(n - l_w + 1) \times m_w] + [(n - l_x + 1) \times m_x]$.

3.3 Embedding Attention

Section 3.2 describes how lexicon embeddings can be incorporated into the CNN model in Section 3.1. Each CNN model uses several filters with different lengths; given the filter length l, the convolution considers l-gram features. However, these l-gram features account only for local views, not the global view of the document, which is necessary for several transitional cases such as negation in sentiment analysis (Socher et al., 2012). To ameliorate this issue, we introduce the embedding attention vector (EAV), which transforms the document matrix in each embedding space into a vector. For example, the EAV in the word embedding space is calculated as a weighted sum of each column in the document matrix $s \in \mathbb{R}^{n \times d}$, which yields a vector $v \in \mathbb{R}^d$. For each document, two EAVs can be derived, one from the document matrix consisting of word embeddings and the other from the one consisting of lexicon embeddings. All embeddings in the document matrix are used to create the EAV through multiple convolutions and max pooling as follows:

1. Apply m-number of convolutions with the filter length 1 to the document matrix $s \in \mathbb{R}^{n \times d}$. For lexicon embeddings, the document matrix has a dimension of $\mathbb{R}^{n \times e}$.

2. Aggregate all convolution outputs to form an attention matrix $s_a \in \mathbb{R}^{n \times m}$, where n is the number of words in the document, and m is the number of filters whose length is 1.

3. Execute max pooling for each row of the attention matrix s_a, which generates the attention vector $v_a \in \mathbb{R}^n$ (Figure 2(a)).

4. Transpose the document matrix s such that $s^T \in \mathbb{R}^{d \times n}$, and multiply it with the attention vector $v_a \in \mathbb{R}^n$, which generates the embedding attention vector $v_e \in \mathbb{R}^d$ (Figure 2(b)).

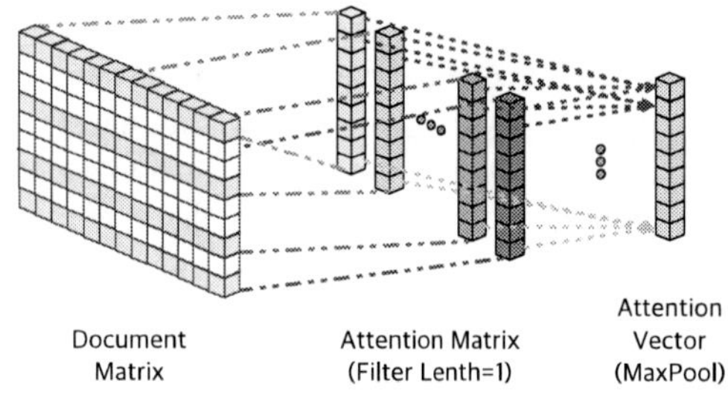

(a) Given a document matrix, the attention matrix is first created by performing multiple convolutions. The attention vector is then created by performing max pooling on each row of the attention matrix.

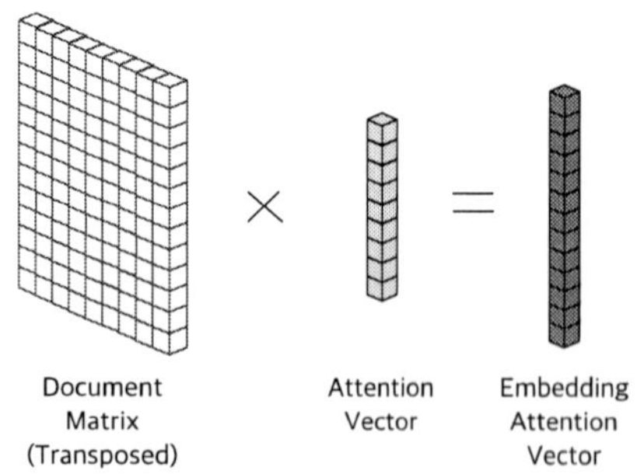

(b) The embedding attention vector is created by multiplying the transposed document matrix to the attention vector.

Figure 2: Construction of the embedding attention vector from a document matrix.

The resulting EAVs are appended to the penultimate layer to serve as additional information for the softmax layer. For our experiments, EAVs are generated from both word and lexicon embedding spaces for all of the three lexicon integration methods in Section 3.2.

4 Experiments

4.1 Corpora

4.1.1 SemEval-2016 Task 4

All models are evaluated on the micro-blog dataset distributed by the SemEval'16 Task 4a (Nakov et al., 2016). The dataset is gleaned from tweets with annotation of three sentiment classes: positive, neutral, and negative. The available dataset contains only tweet IDs and their sentiment polarities; the actual tweet texts are not included in this dataset due to the copyright restrictions. Although the download script provided by SemEval'16 gives a way of accessing the actual texts on the web, a portion of tweets is no longer accessible. To compensate this loss, the dataset also includes tweet instances from the SemEval'13 task.

	+	0	−	All
TRN	6,480	6,577	2,328	15,385
DEV	786	548	254	1,588
TST	7,059	10,342	3,231	20,632

Table 1: Statistics of the SemEval'16 Task 4 dataset. +/0/−: positive/neutral/negative, TRN/DEV/TST: training, development, evaluation sets.

The classification results are evaluated by averaging the F1-scores of positive and negative sentiments as suggested by the SemEval'16 Task 4a.

4.1.2 Stanford Sentiment Treebank

Another dataset consisting of movie reviews from Rotten Tomatoes is used for evaluating the robustness of our models across different genres. This dataset, called the Stanford Sentiment Treebank, was originally collected by Pang and Lee (2005) and later extended by Socher et al. (2013). The sentiment annotation in this dataset is categorized into five classes: very positive, positive, neutral, negative, and very negative. Following the previous work (Kim, 2014), the results are evaluated by the conventional classification accuracy.

	++	+	0	-	−	All
TRN	1288	2322	1624	2218	1092	8,544
DEV	165	279	229	289	139	1,101
TST	399	510	389	633	279	2,210

Table 2: Statistics of the Stanford Sentiment Treebank dataset. ++/+/0/-/−: very positive/positive/ neutral/negative/very negative.

4.2 Embedding Construction

4.2.1 Word Embeddings

To best capture the word semantics in each genre, different corpora are used to train word embeddings for the SemEval'16 (S16) and the Stanford Sentiment Treebank (SST) datasets. For S16, word embeddings are trained on tweets collected by the Archive Team,[1] consisting of 3.67M word types. For SST, word embeddings are trained on the Amazon Review dataset,[2] containing 2.67M word types.

All documents are pre-tokenized by the open-source toolkit, NLP4J.[3] The word embeddings are trained by the original implementation of word2vec from Google using skip-gram and negative sampling.[4] No explicit hyper-parameter tuning is performed. For each genre, four sets of embeddings with different dimensions (50, 100, 200, 400) are trained to observe the impact of the embedding size on each approach.

4.2.2 Lexicon Embeddings

Six types of sentiment lexicons are used to build lexicon embeddings. All lexicons include sentiment scores; some lexicons contain information about the frequency of positive and negative sentiment polarity associated with each word:

- National Research Council Canada (NRC) Hashtag Affirmative and Negated Context Sentiment Lexicon (Kiritchenko et al., 2014).

- NRC Hashtag Sentiment Lexicon (Mohammad et al., 2013a).

- NRC Sentiment140 Lexicon (Kiritchenko et al., 2014).

- Sentiment140 Lexicon (Mohammad et al., 2013a).

- MaxDiff Twitter Sentiment Lexicon (Kiritchenko et al., 2014).

- Bing Liu Opinion Lexicon (Hu and Liu, 2004).

When creating lexicon embeddings, the narrow coverage of vocabulary in lexicons often raises missing scores. If a given word is missing in a specific lexicon, neutral scores of 0 are substituted.

---

[1] archive.org/details/twitterstream
[2] snap.stanford.edu/data/web-Amazon.html
[3] github.com/emorynlp/nlp4j
[4] code.google.com/p/word2vec

Table 3 shows the word type coverage of our word and lexicon embeddings for each dataset. The lexicon embeddings show relatively poor coverage; nevertheless, our experiments show that these lexicon embeddings help sentiment classification in various ways (Section 4.3).

	Word Emb		Lexicon Emb	
	S16	**SST**	**S16**	**SST**
TRN	70.12	97.66	11.53	9.20
DEV	81.90	98.91	3.29	3.32
TST	68.57	98.58	12.40	4.98

Table 3: The percentage of word types covered by our word and lexicon embeddings for each dataset.

4.3 Evaluation

Seven models are evaluated to show the effectiveness of lexicon embeddings to sentiment analysis: baseline (Section 3.1), naive concatenation (NC; Section 3.2.1), multichannel (MC; Section 3.2.2), separate convolution (SC; Section 3.2.3), and the three integration approaches with embedding attention ($*$-EAV; Section 3.3). The comparisons of our proposed models to the previous state-of-the-art approaches are outlined in Table 4. For all experiments, the fixed random seed of 1 is used to avoid performance boost from different randomness (see Section 4.4.1 for more discussions). The following configuration are used for all models:

- Filter size = (2, 3, 4, 5) for both word and lexicon embeddings.

- Number of filters = (64 and 9) for word and lexicon embeddings, respectively.

- Number of filters = (50 and 20) for constructing embedding attention vectors in word and lexicon embedding spaces, respectively.

It is worth mentioning that the performance of our baseline models improved quite a bit when the training corpora for word embeddings and sentiment analysis were tokenized coherently. Unlike several other work, we used the identical tokenization tool, NLP4J, to preprocess all corpora, which gave considerable boost in performance. Comparing the baseline to SC, lexicon embeddings significantly improved accuracy for S16, about 2%, surpassing the previous state-of-the-art result achieved by Deriu et al. (2016). However, SC did not show much improvement for SST where the baseline was already performing well.

Model	S16 (Avg F1 Score)	SST (Accuracy)
Baseline	61.6	47.5
NC	63.4	46.8
MC	61.8	47.0
SC	63.6	47.5
NC-EAV	63.4	**48.8**
MC-EAV	62.1	47.3
SC-EAV	**63.8**	**48.8**
Deriu et al. (2016)	63.3	-
Rouvier and Favre (2016)	63.0	-
Kim (2014)	-	48.0
Kalchbrenner et al. (2014b)	-	48.5
Le and Mikolov (2014)	-	48.7
Yin and Schütze (2015)*	-	**49.6**

Table 4: Evaluation set results (random seed is fixed to 1) of the proposed models in comparison to the state-of-the-art approaches. **Deriu et al. (2016)**: the first place for the SemEval'16 task 4a using an ensemble of two CNN models. **Rouvier and Favre (2016)**: the second place for the SemEval'16 task 4a using various embeddings in CNN. **Kim (2014)**: the state of the art single layer CNN model. **Kalchbrenner et al. (2014b)**: dynamic CNN with k-max pooling. **Le and Mikolov (2014)**: logistic regression on top of paragraph vectors. **Yin and Schütze (2015)**: the state-of-the-art dual layer CNN with five channel embeddings.

Comparing these lexicon integrated models with the ones with embedding attention vectors (∗-EAV), EAV did not help much for S16 but significantly improved the performance for SST, achieving the state-of-the-art result of 48.8% for a single-layer CNN model. The accuracy achieved by our best model is still 0.8% lower than the state-of-the-art result achieved by Yin and Schütze (2015); however, considering their model uses five embedding channels and dual-layer convolutions whereas our model uses a single channel and a single-layer convolution, in other words, our model is much more compact, this is very promising. These results suggest that lexicon embeddings coupled with the embedding attention vectors allow to build robust sentiment analysis models.

Figure 3 illustrates the robustness of our lexicon integrated models with respect to the size of word embeddings. Our baseline produces inconsistent and unstable results as different sizes of word embeddings are used. Furthermore, a larger size of word embeddings tends to significantly outperform a smaller size of word embeddings. Such tendency is reduced with the incorporation of lexicon embeddings. While the standard deviations for the accuracies achieved by the baseline using different sizes of word embeddings are 0.8491 and 1.1909 for S16 and SST, respectively, they are reduced to 0.4208 and 0.5764 respectively for lexicon integrated models. Furthermore, the accuracy achieved by the lexicon integrated model using the word embedding size 50 is higher or equal to the highest accuracy achieved by the baseline using the word embedding size 200, which implies that it is possible to build more compact models using lexicon embeddings without compromising accuracy.

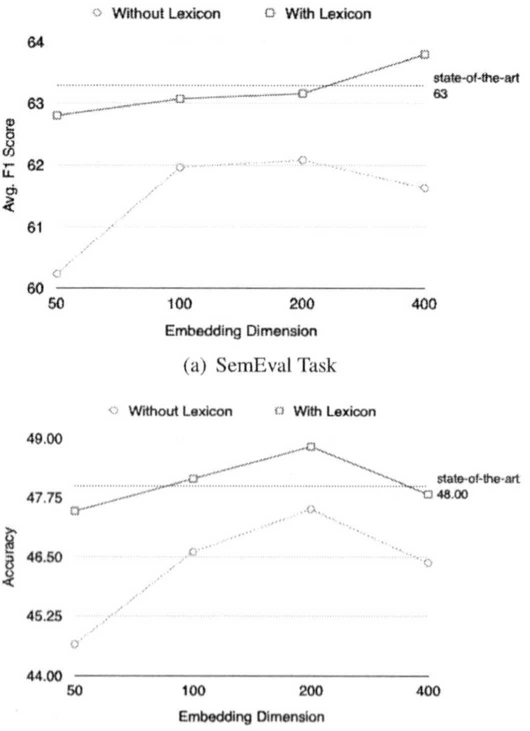

Figure 3: Performance changes across various dimensions of word embeddings.

4.4 Analysis

4.4.1 Randomness in Deep Learning

Different random seeds when training the CNN models could possibly change the behavior of models, sometimes by more than 1%. This is due to the randomness in deep learning, such as the random shuffling the datasets, initialization of the weights and drop-out rate of a tensor. To reduce the impact of random seed on our result and capture the general characteristic of the model, we performed a group analysis by training each model with 10 different random seeds (Figure 4).

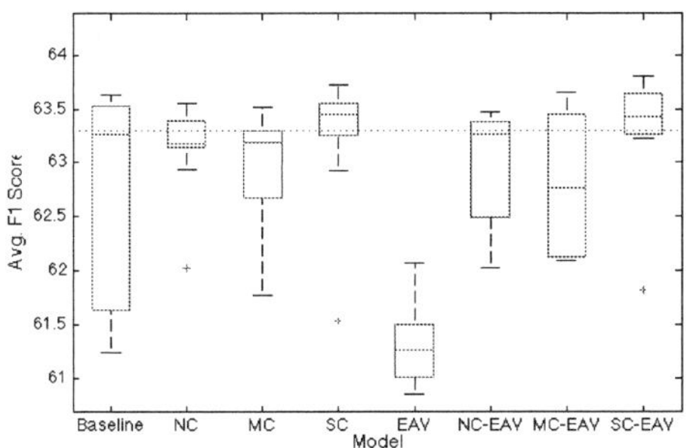

(a) SemEval Task: The baseline model has a higher variance than the proposed models. Adding lexicon information improves the baseline model to be more accurate. In addition, EAV marginally pushes the performance.

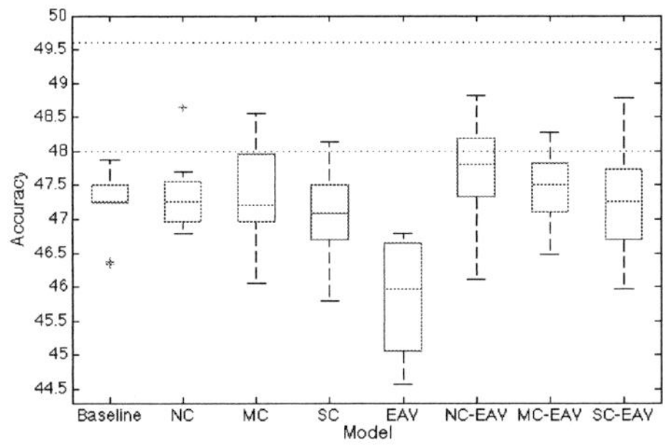

(b) SST Task: The baseline model itself is stable because the vocabulary of the word embedding covers approximately all words in SST, as shown in Table 3. Although adding lexicon information destabilize the model lightly, lexicon information enhance the accuracy. EAV is advantageous in general. This effect is visually shown in this figure, when comparing naive concatenation (NC; (Section 3.2.1) with NC-EAV.

Figure 4: Generalized performance evaluation of the models. Each model is trained 10 times with different random seeds and the results are summarized as a bar plot. In this plot, the central red line indicates the median, and the bottom and top edges of the box indicate the 25th and 75th percentiles, respectively. the '+' symbol represents outliers.

4.4.2 S16: SemEval'16 Task 4

For S16, the lexicon integration tends to reduce the variances, and the introducing embedding attention vectors pushes the accuracy even higher than the models without it across different random seeds. Another notable observation for S16 is that although multichannel method underperforms when the random seed is fixed to a specific number as seen in Table 4, it produces a competitive output in the group analysis setting. Such low performance with a fixed random seed is probably attributed to the well known problem of optimization, trapping in local optima.

4.4.3 SST: Stanford Sentiment Treebank

The problem conditions for SST are different in terms of vocabulary coverage. This difference is caused by the source of the lexicon embeddings, where all of them were constructed from Twitter dataset. Since most of the lexical words are from Twitter, it shows less vocabulary coverage on SST than that of S16 as shown in the right columns of Table 3. Because of this poor relatedness between lexicons and datasets, we hypothesized that adding a lexicon might be less effective on the performance of SST task. However, our models seems to successfully adopt exogenous features enough to push the accuracy marginally higher than the models without lexicons.

On the contrary, the coverage of word embeddings on SST is notably high at around 98%, while only around 70% for S16 (left columns of Table 3). These conditions are well reflected in the group analysis of the model in SST. Since word embeddings themselves are sufficient enough to cover majority of words, the model variance of the baseline is relatively small compared to S16.

4.4.4 Attention

Embedding attention vectors allow to visualize the importance of each word and lexicon for sentiment analysis through a heatmap. In Figure 5, all negative words get higher weights (reds), while non-sentimental words do not (greens and light blues) in EAV. This visualization is especially useful for neural models because it provides an compelling explanatory information about how the models work.

4.4.5 Learning Speed

Another advantage of the proposed model, SC-EAV, is that it accelerates the learning speed (Figure 6). High F1 score can be achieved in the earlier step,

155

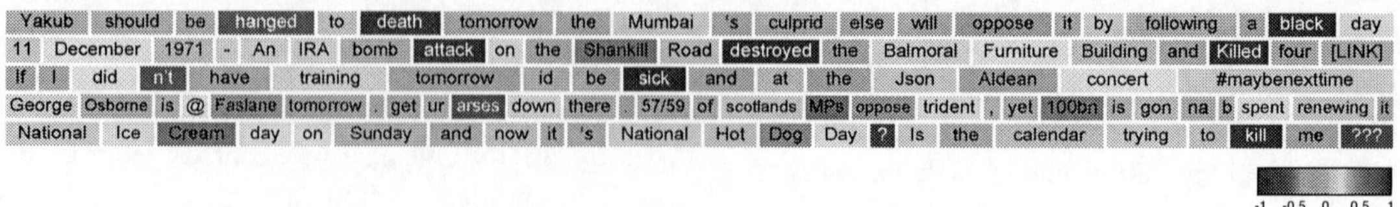

Figure 5: Five selected negative tweets with the attention heatmap. Examples are from the set where the baseline gives wrong answers but SC-EAV predicts correctly. Intensity of each word roughly ranges from -1 to 1. This weights (intensities) are the values of the attention vector of the word embeddings in the SC-EAV model. While negative words get more attention (reds), non-sentimental words such as stop words get less attention (greens and light blues).

if lexicon information is incorporated along with EAV. This statement is general behavior because the learning curves in Figure Figure 6 are the result of averaging ten different learning attempts with different random seeds.

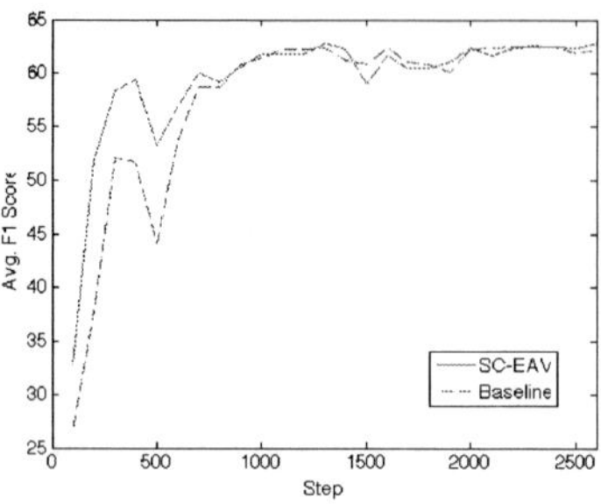

Figure 6: Lexicon information and EAV accelerate the learning speed. High F1 score can be achieved in the earlier step, if lexicon information is incorporated along with EAV.

5 Conclusion

This paper proposes several approaches that effectively integrate lexicon embeddings and an attention mechanism to a well-explored deep learning framework, Convolutional Neural Networks, for sentiment analysis. Our experiments show that lexicon integration can improve accuracy, stability, and efficiency of the traditional CNN model. Multiple training results with different random seeds show the generalization of the effectiveness of using lexicon embeddings and embedding attention vectors. The training curve comparison further shows another benefit of this integration for more robust learning. The attention heatmap analysis confirms that embedding attention vectors endow CNN models with explanatory features, which gives good understanding of how the CNN models work.

Much more future work is left. The proposed attention models are applied to each single word. However, focusing on multiple words could give more promising information. Application of the attention mechanism to multiple words at the same time is a possible direction. Majority of the lexicons in this work are from tweet dataset. More lexicon dataset from general could be used to improve the coverage of our system. We focused on a simple and yet well performing system. In order to maximize the score, ensemble of multi layer CNN models could be applied.[5]

Acknowledgments

We gratefully acknowledge the support of the University Research Committee Grant (URC) from Emory University, and the Infosys Research Enhancement Grant. Any contents expressed in this material are those of the authors and do not necessarily reflect the views of these awards and grants. Special thanks are due to Jung-Hyun Kang for producing the wonderful figures.

References

Dzmitry Bahdanau, Kyunghyun Cho, and Yoshua Bengio. 2014. Neural machine translation by jointly learning to align and translate. *ICLR* .

Kan Chen, Jiang Wang, Liang-Chieh Chen, Haoyuan Gao, Wei Xu, and Ram Nevatia. 2015. Abccnn: An attention based convolutional neural network for visual question answering. *arXiv preprint arXiv:1511.05960* .

Kyunghyun Cho, Bart Van Merriënboer, Caglar Gulcehre, Dzmitry Bahdanau, Fethi Bougares, Holger Schwenk, and Yoshua Bengio. 2014. Learning phrase representations using rnn encoder-decoder for statistical machine translation. *EMNLP,* .

---

[5]All our resources are publicly available
: http://nlp.mathcs.emory.edu

Ronan Collobert, Jason Weston, Léon Bottou, Michael Karlen, Koray Kavukcuoglu, and Pavel Kuksa. 2011. Natural language processing (almost) from scratch. *Journal of Machine Learning Research* 12(Aug):2493–2537.

Jan Deriu, Maurice Gonzenbach, Fatih Uzdilli, Aurelien Lucchi, Valeria De Luca, and Martin Jaggi. 2016. Swisscheese at semeval-2016 task 4: Sentiment classification using an ensemble of convolutional neural networks with distant supervision. *Proceedings of SemEval* pages 1124–1128.

Xiaowen Ding, Bing Liu, and Philip S Yu. 2008. A holistic lexicon-based approach to opinion mining. In *Proceedings of the 2008 international conference on web search and data mining*. ACM, pages 231–240.

Ronen Feldman. 2013. Techniques and applications for sentiment analysis. *Communications of the ACM* 56(4):82–89.

Kevin Gimpel, Nathan Schneider, Brendan O'Connor, Dipanjan Das, Daniel Mills, Jacob Eisenstein, Michael Heilman, Dani Yogatama, Jeffrey Flanigan, and Noah A Smith. 2011. Part-of-speech tagging for twitter: Annotation, features, and experiments. In *Proceedings of the 49th Annual Meeting of the Association for Computational Linguistics: Human Language Technologies: short papers-Volume 2*. Association for Computational Linguistics, pages 42–47.

Minqing Hu and Bing Liu. 2004. Mining and summarizing customer reviews. In *Proceedings of the tenth ACM SIGKDD international conference on Knowledge discovery and data mining*. ACM, pages 168–177.

Nal Kalchbrenner, Edward Grefenstette, and Phil Blunsom. 2014a. A convolutional neural network for modelling sentences. *arXiv preprint arXiv:1404.2188* .

Nal Kalchbrenner, Edward Grefenstette, and Phil Blunsom. 2014b. A convolutional neural network for modelling sentences. In *Proceedings of the 52nd Annual Meeting of the Association for Computational Linguistics (Volume 1: Long Papers)*. Association for Computational Linguistics, Baltimore, Maryland, pages 655–665. http://www.aclweb.org/anthology/P14-1062.

Soo-Min Kim and Eduard Hovy. 2004. Determining the sentiment of opinions. In *Proceedings of the 20th international conference on Computational Linguistics*. Association for Computational Linguistics, page 1367.

Yoon Kim. 2014. Convolutional neural networks for sentence classification. *arXiv preprint arXiv:1408.5882* .

Svetlana Kiritchenko, Xiaodan Zhu, and Saif M Mohammad. 2014. Sentiment analysis of short informal texts. *Journal of Artificial Intelligence Research* 50:723–762.

Quoc V. Le and Tomas Mikolov. 2014. Distributed representations of sentences and documents. In *Proceedings of the 31th International Conference on Machine Learning, ICML 2014, Beijing, China, 21-26 June 2014*. pages 1188–1196. http://jmlr.org/proceedings/papers/v32/le14.html.

Bing Liu. 2012. Sentiment analysis and opinion mining. *Synthesis lectures on human language technologies* 5(1):1–167.

Minh-Thang Luong, Hieu Pham, and Christopher D Manning. 2015. Effective approaches to attention-based neural machine translation. *EMNLP* .

Saif Mohammad, Svetlana Kiritchenko, and Xiaodan Zhu. 2013a. Nrc-canada: Building the state-of-the-art in sentiment analysis of tweets. In *Proceedings of the seventh international workshop on Semantic Evaluation Exercises (SemEval-2013)*. Atlanta, Georgia, USA.

Saif M Mohammad, Svetlana Kiritchenko, and Xiaodan Zhu. 2013b. Nrc-canada: Building the state-of-the-art in sentiment analysis of tweets. *arXiv preprint arXiv:1308.6242* .

Tony Mullen and Nigel Collier. 2004. Sentiment analysis using support vector machines with diverse information sources. In *EMNLP*. volume 4, pages 412–418.

Preslav Nakov, Alan Ritter, Sara Rosenthal, Fabrizio Sebastiani, and Veselin Stoyanov. 2016. Semeval-2016 task 4: Sentiment analysis in twitter. In *Proceedings of the 10th International Workshop on Semantic Evaluation (SemEval-2016)*. Association for Computational Linguistics, San Diego, California, pages 1–18. http://www.aclweb.org/anthology/S16-1001.

Bo Pang and Lillian Lee. 2005. Seeing stars: Exploiting class relationships for sentiment categorization with respect to rating scales. In *Proceedings of the 43rd Annual Meeting on Association for Computational Linguistics*. Association for Computational Linguistics, pages 115–124.

Bo Pang and Lillian Lee. 2008. Opinion mining and sentiment analysis. *Foundations and trends in information retrieval* 2(1-2):1–135.

Bo Pang, Lillian Lee, and Shivakumar Vaithyanathan. 2002. Thumbs up?: sentiment classification using machine learning techniques. In *Proceedings of the ACL-02 conference on Empirical methods in natural language processing-Volume 10*. Association for Computational Linguistics, pages 79–86.

Mickael Rouvier and Benoit Favre. 2016. Sensei-lif at semeval-2016 task 4: Polarity embedding fusion for robust sentiment analysis. In *Proceedings of the 10th International Workshop on Semantic Evaluation (SemEval-2016)*. Association for Computational Linguistics, San Diego, California, pages 202–208. http://www.aclweb.org/anthology/S16-1030.

Kevin J Shih, Saurabh Singh, and Derek Hoiem. 2016. Where to look: Focus regions for visual question answering. *CVPR* .

Richard Socher, Brody Huval, Christopher D Manning, and Andrew Y Ng. 2012. Semantic compositionality through recursive matrix-vector spaces. In *Proceedings of the 2012 Joint Conference on Empirical Methods in Natural Language Processing and Computational Natural Language Learning*. Association for Computational Linguistics, pages 1201–1211.

Richard Socher, Alex Perelygin, Jean Y Wu, Jason Chuang, Christopher D Manning, Andrew Y Ng, and Christopher Potts. 2013. Recursive deep models for semantic compositionality over a sentiment treebank. In *Proceedings of the conference on empirical methods in natural language processing (EMNLP)*. Citeseer, volume 1631, page 1642.

Marijn F Stollenga, Jonathan Masci, Faustino Gomez, and Jürgen Schmidhuber. 2014. Deep networks with internal selective attention through feedback connections. In *Advances in Neural Information Processing Systems*. pages 3545–3553.

Maite Taboada, Julian Brooke, Milan Tofiloski, Kimberly Voll, and Manfred Stede. 2011. Lexicon-based methods for sentiment analysis. *Computational linguistics* 37(2):267–307.

Theresa Wilson, Janyce Wiebe, and Paul Hoffmann. 2005. Recognizing contextual polarity in phrase-level sentiment analysis. In *Proceedings of the conference on human language technology and empirical methods in natural language processing*. Association for Computational Linguistics, pages 347–354.

Kelvin Xu, Jimmy Ba, Ryan Kiros, Kyunghyun Cho, Aaron Courville, Ruslan Salakhutdinov, Richard S Zemel, and Yoshua Bengio. 2015. Show, attend and tell: Neural image caption generation with visual attention. *International Conference for Machine Learning (ICML)* .

Toshihiko Yanase, Kohsuke Yanai, Misa Sato, Toshinori Miyoshi, and Yoshiki Niwa. 2016. bunji at semeval-2016 task 5: Neural and syntactic models of entity-attribute relationship for aspect-based sentiment analysis. *Proceedings of SemEval* pages 289–295.

Zichao Yang, Xiaodong He, Jianfeng Gao, Li Deng, and Alex Smola. 2016. Stacked attention networks for image question answering. *CVPR* .

Wenpeng Yin and Hinrich Schütze. 2014. An exploration of embeddings for generalized phrases. In *ACL (Student Research Workshop)*. pages 41–47.

Wenpeng Yin and Hinrich Schütze. 2015. Multichannel variable-size convolution for sentence classification. In *Proceedings of the Nineteenth Conference on Computational Natural Language Learning*. Association for Computational Linguistics, Beijing, China, pages 204–214. http://www.aclweb.org/anthology/K15-1021.

Explaining Recurrent Neural Network Predictions in Sentiment Analysis

Leila Arras[1], Grégoire Montavon[2], Klaus-Robert Müller[2,3,4], and Wojciech Samek[1]
[1]Machine Learning Group, Fraunhofer Heinrich Hertz Institute, Berlin, Germany
[2]Machine Learning Group, Technische Universität Berlin, Berlin, Germany
[3]Department of Brain and Cognitive Engineering, Korea University, Seoul, Korea
[4]Max Planck Institute for Informatics, Saarbrücken, Germany
{leila.arras, wojciech.samek}@hhi.fraunhofer.de

Abstract

Recently, a technique called Layer-wise Relevance Propagation (LRP) was shown to deliver insightful *explanations* in the form of input space relevances for understanding feed-forward neural network classification decisions. In the present work, we extend the usage of LRP to recurrent neural networks. We propose a specific propagation rule applicable to multiplicative connections as they arise in recurrent network architectures such as LSTMs and GRUs. We apply our technique to a word-based bi-directional LSTM model on a five-class sentiment prediction task, and evaluate the resulting LRP relevances both qualitatively and quantitatively, obtaining better results than a gradient-based related method which was used in previous work.

1 Introduction

Semantic composition plays an important role in sentiment analysis of phrases and sentences. This includes detecting the scope and impact of negation in reversing a sentiment's polarity, as well as quantifying the influence of modifiers, such as degree adverbs and intensifiers, in rescaling the sentiment's intensity (Mohammad, 2017).

Recently, a trend emerged for tackling these challenges via deep learning models such as convolutional and recurrent neural networks, as observed e.g. on the SemEval-2016 Task for *Sentiment Analysis in Twitter* (Nakov et al., 2016).

As these models become increasingly predictive, one also needs to make sure that they work as intended, in particular, their decisions should be made as transparent as possible.

Some forms of transparency are readily obtained from the structure of the model, e.g. recursive nets (Socher et al., 2013), where sentiment can be probed at each node of a parsing tree.

Another type of analysis seeks to determine what input features were important for reaching the final top-layer prediction. Recent work in this direction has focused on bringing measures of feature importance to state-of-the-art models such as deep convolutional neural networks for vision (Simonyan et al., 2014; Zeiler and Fergus, 2014; Bach et al., 2015; Ribeiro et al., 2016), or to general deep neural networks for text (Denil et al., 2014; Li et al., 2016a; Arras et al., 2016a; Li et al., 2016b; Murdoch and Szlam, 2017).

Some of these techniques are based on the model's local gradient information while other methods seek to redistribute the function's value on the input variables, typically by reverse propagation in the neural network graph (Landecker et al., 2013; Bach et al., 2015; Montavon et al., 2017a). We refer the reader to (Montavon et al., 2017b) for an overview on methods for understanding and interpreting deep neural network predictions.

Bach et al. (2015) proposed specific propagation rules for neural networks (LRP rules). These rules were shown to produce better explanations than e.g. gradient-based techniques (Samek et al., 2017), and were also successfully transferred to neural networks for text data (Arras et al., 2016b).

In this paper, we extend LRP with a rule that handles multiplicative interactions in the LSTM model, a particularly suitable model for modeling long-range interactions in texts such as those occurring in sentiment analysis.

We then apply the extended LRP method to a bi-directional LSTM trained on a five-class sentiment prediction task. It allows us to produce reliable explanations of which words are responsible for

Proceedings of the 8th Workshop on Computational Approaches to Subjectivity, Sentiment and Social Media Analysis, pages 159–168
Copenhagen, Denmark, September 7–11, 2017. ©2017 Association for Computational Linguistics

attributing sentiment in individual texts, compared to the explanations obtained by using a gradient-based approach.

2 Methods

Given a trained neural network that models a scalar-valued prediction function f_c (also commonly referred to as a prediction score) for each class c of a classification problem, and given an input vector x, we are interested in computing for each input dimension d of x a relevance score R_d quantifying the relevance of x_d w.r.t to a considered *target* class of interest c. In others words, we want to analyze which features of x are important for the classifier's decision *toward* or *against* a class c.

In order to estimate the relevance of a *pool* of input space dimensions or variables (e.g. in NLP, when using distributed word embeddings as input, we would like to compute the relevance of a word, and not just of its single vector dimensions), we simply sum up the relevance scores R_d of its constituting dimensions d.

In this described framework, there are two alternative methods to obtain the single input variable's relevance in the first place, which we detail in the following subsections.

2.1 Gradient-based Sensitivity Analysis (SA)

The relevances can be obtained by computing squared partial derivatives:

$$R_d = \left(\frac{\partial f_c}{\partial x_d}(x) \right)^2 .$$

For a neural network classifier, these derivatives can be obtained by standard gradient backpropagation (Rumelhart et al., 1986), and are made available by most neural network toolboxes. We refer to the above definition of relevance as Sensitivity Analysis (SA) (Dimopoulos et al., 1995; Gevrey et al., 2003). A similar technique was previously used in computer vision by (Simonyan et al., 2014), and in NLP by (Li et al., 2016a).

Note that if we sum up the relevances of all input space dimensions d, we obtain the quantity $\|\nabla_x f_c(x)\|_2^2$, thus SA can be interpreted as a decomposition of the squared gradient norm.

2.2 Layer-wise Relevance Propagation (LRP)

Another technique to compute relevances was proposed in (Bach et al., 2015) as the Layer-wise Relevance Propagation (LRP) algorithm. It is based on a layer-wise relevance conservation principle, and, for a given input x, it redistributes the quantity $f_c(x)$, starting from the output layer of the network and backpropagating this quantity up to the input layer. The LRP relevance propagation procedure can be described layer-by-layer for each type of layer occurring in a deep convolutional neural network (weighted linear connections following non-linear activation, pooling, normalization), and consists in defining rules for attributing relevance to lower-layer neurons given the relevances of upper-layer neurons. Hereby each intermediate layer neuron gets attributed a relevance score, up to the input layer neurons.

In the case of recurrent neural network architectures such as LSTMs (Hochreiter and Schmidhuber, 1997) and GRUs (Cho et al., 2014), there are two types of neural connections involved: many-to-one weighted linear connections, and two-to-one multiplicative interactions. Hence, we restrict our definition of the LRP procedure to these types of connections. Note that, for simplification, we refrain from explicitly introducing a notation for non-linear activation functions; if such an activation is present at a neuron, we always take into account the *activated* lower-layer neuron's value in the subsequent formulas.

In order to compute the input space relevances, we start by setting the relevance of the output layer neuron corresponding to the target class of interest c to the value $f_c(x)$, and simply ignore the other output layer neurons (or equivalently set their relevance to zero). Then, we compute layer-by-layer a relevance score for each intermediate lower-layer neuron accordingly to one of the subsequent formulas, depending on the type of connection involved.

Weighted Connections. Let z_j be an upper-layer neuron, whose value in the forward pass is computed as $z_j = \sum_i z_i \cdot w_{ij} + b_j$, where z_i are the lower-layer neurons, and w_{ij}, b_j are the connection weights and biases.

Given the relevances R_j of the upper-layer neurons z_j, the goal is to compute the lower-layer relevances R_i of the neurons z_i. (In the particular case of the output layer, we have a single upper-layer neuron z_j, whose relevance is set to its value, more precisely we set $R_j = f_c(x)$ to start the LRP procedure.) The relevance redistribution onto lower-layer neurons is performed in two steps. First, by computing relevance messages

$R_{i \leftarrow j}$ going from upper-layer neurons z_j to lower-layer neurons z_i. Then, by summing up incoming messages for each lower-layer neuron z_i to obtain the relevance R_i. The messages $R_{i \leftarrow j}$ are computed as a fraction of the relevance R_j accordingly to the following rule:

$$R_{i \leftarrow j} = \frac{z_i \cdot w_{ij} + \frac{\epsilon \cdot sign(z_j) + \delta \cdot b_j}{N}}{z_j + \epsilon \cdot sign(z_j)} \cdot R_j$$

where N is the total number of lower-layer neurons to which z_j is connected, ϵ is a small positive number which serves as a stabilizer (we use $\epsilon = 0.001$ in our experiments), and $sign(z_j) = (1_{z_j \geq 0} - 1_{z_j < 0})$ is defined as the sign of z_j. The relevance R_i is subsequently computed as $R_i = \sum_j R_{i \leftarrow j}$. Moreover, δ is a multiplicative factor that is either set to 1.0, in which case the total relevance of all neurons in the same layer is conserved, or else it is set to 0.0, which implies that a part of the total relevance is "absorbed" by the biases and that the relevance propagation rule is approximately conservative. Per default we use the last variant with $\delta = 0.0$ when we refer to LRP, and denote explicitly by LRP_{cons} our results when we use $\delta = 1.0$ in our experiments.

Multiplicative Interactions. Another type of connection is a two-way multiplicative interaction between lower-layer neurons. Let z_j be an upper-layer neuron, whose value in the forward pass is computed as the multiplication of the two lower-layer neuron values z_g and z_s, i.e. $z_j = z_g \cdot z_s$. In such multiplicative interactions, as they occur e.g. in LSTMs and GRUs, there is always one of the two lower-layer neurons that constitutes a *gate*, and whose value ranges between $[0, 1]$ as the output of a sigmoid activation function (or in the particular case of GRUs, can also be equal to one minus a sigmoid activated value), we call it the *gate* neuron z_g, and refer to the remaining one as the *source* neuron z_s.

Given such a configuration, and denoting by R_j the relevance of the upper-layer neuron z_j, we propose to redistribute the relevance onto lower-layer neurons in the following way: we set $R_g = 0$ and $R_s = R_j$. The intuition behind this reallocation rule, is that the *gate* neuron decides already in the forward pass how much of the information contained in the *source* neuron should be retained to make the overall classification decision. Thereby the value z_g controls how much relevance will be attributed to z_j from upper-layer neurons. Thus,

even if our local propagation rule seems to ignore the respective values of z_g and z_s to redistribute the relevance, these are indeed taken into account when computing the value R_j from the relevances of the *next* upper-layer neurons to which z_j is connected via weighted connections.

3 Recurrent Model and Data

As a recurrent neural network model we employ a one hidden-layer bi-directional LSTM (bi-LSTM), trained on five-class sentiment prediction of phrases and sentences on the Stanford Sentiment Treebank movie reviews dataset (Socher et al., 2013), as was used in previous work on neural network interpretability (Li et al., 2016a) and made available by the authors[1]. This model takes as input a sequence of words $x_1, x_2, ..., x_T$ (as well as this sequence in reversed order), where each word is represented by a word embedding of dimension 60, and has a hidden layer size of 60. A thorough model description can be found in the Appendix, and for details on the training we refer to (Li et al., 2016a).

In our experiments, we use as input the 2210 tokenized sentences of the Stanford Sentiment Treebank test set (Socher et al., 2013), preprocessing them by lowercasing as was done in (Li et al., 2016a). On five-class sentiment prediction of full sentences (very negative, negative, neutral, positive, very positive) the model achieves 46.3% accuracy, and for binary classification (positive vs. negative, ignoring neutral sentences) the test accuracy is 82.9%.

Using this trained bi-LSTM, we compare two relevance decomposition methods: sensitivity analysis (SA) and Layer-wise Relevance Propagation (LRP). The former is similar to the "First-Derivative Saliency" used in (Li et al., 2016a), besides that in their work the authors do not aggregate the relevance of single input variables to obtain a word-level relevance value (i.e. they only visualize relevance distributed over word embedding dimensions); moreover they employ the absolute value of partial derivatives (instead of squared partial derivatives as we do) to compute the relevance of single input variables.

In order to enable reproducibility and for encouraging further research, we make our imple-

---

[1]`https://github.com/jiweil/`
`Visualizing-and-Understanding-Neural-`
`Models-in-NLP`

161

mentation of both relevance decomposition methods available[2] (see also (Lapuschkin et al., 2016)).

4 Results

In this Section, we present qualitative as well as quantitative results we obtained by performing SA and LRP on test set sentences. As an outcome of the relevance decomposition for a chosen *target* class, we first get for each word embedding x_t in an input sentence, a *vector* of relevance values. In order to obtain a *scalar* word-level relevance, we remind that we simply sum up the relevances contained in that vector. Also note that, per definition, the SA relevances are positive while LRP relevances are signed.

4.1 Decomposing Sentiment onto Words

In order to illustrate the differences between SA and LRP, we provide in Fig. 1 and 2 heatmaps of exemplary test set sentences. These heatmaps were obtained by mapping positive word-level relevance values to red, and negative relevances to blue. The exemplary sentences belong either to the class "very negative" or to the class "very positive", and the target class for relevance decomposition is always the *true* class. On the left of the Figures, we indicate the *true* sentence class, as well as the bi-LSTM's *predicted* class, whereby the upper examples are correctly classified while the bottom examples are falsely classified.

From the inspection of the heatmaps, we notice that SA does not clearly distinguish between words speaking *for* or *against* the target class. Indeed it sometimes attributes a comparatively high relevance to words expressing a positive appreciation like *thrilling* (example 5), *master* (example 6) or *must-see* (example 11), while the target class is "very negative"; or to the word *difficult* (example 19) expressing a negative judgment, while the target class is "very positive". On the contrary, LRP can discern more reliably between words addressing a negative sentiment, such as *waste* (1), *horrible* (3), *disaster* (6), *repetitive* (9) (highlighted in red), or *difficult* (19) (highlighted in blue), from words indicating a positive opinion, like *funny* (2), *suspenseful* (2), *romantic* (5), *thrilling* (5) (highlighted in blue), or *worthy* (19), *entertaining* (20) (highlighted in red).

Furthermore, LRP explains well the two sentences that are mistakenly classified as "very positive" and "positive" (examples 11 and 17), by accentuating the negative relevance (blue colored) of terms speaking *against* the target class, i.e. the class "very negative", such as *must-see list*, *remember* and *future*, whereas such understanding is not provided by the SA heatmaps. The same holds for the misclassified "very positive" sentence (example 21), where the word *fails* gets attributed a deep negatively signed relevance (blue colored). A similar limitation of gradient-based relevance visualization for explaining predictions of recurrent models was also observed in previous work (Li et al., 2016a).

Moreover, an interesting property we observe with LRP, is that the sentiment of negation is modulated by the sentiment of the subsequent words in the sentence. Hence, e.g. in the heatmaps for the target class "very negative", when negators like *n't* or *not* are followed by words indicating a negative sentiment like *waste* (1) or *horrible* (3), they are marked by a negatively signed relevance (blue colored), while when the subsequent words express a positive impression like *worth* (12), *surprises* (14), *funny* (16) or *good* (18), they get a positively signed relevance (red colored).

Thereby, the heatmap visualizations provide some insights on how the sentiment of single words is composed by the bi-LSTM model, and indicate that the sentiment attributed to words is not static, but depends on their context in the sentence. Nevertheless, we would like to point out that the explanations delivered by relevance decomposition highly depend on the quality of the underlying classifier, and can only be "as good" as the neural network itself, hence a more carefully tuned model might deliver even better explanations.

4.2 Representative Words for a Sentiment

Another qualitative analysis we conduct is dataset-wide, and consists in building a list of the most resp. the least relevant words for a class. To this end, we first perform SA and LRP on *all* test set sentences for one specific target class, as an example we take the class "very positive". Secondly, we order all words appearing in the test sentences in decreasing resp. in increasing order of their relevance value, and retrieve in Table 1 the ten most and least relevant words we obtain. From the SA

true	predicted	N°	Notation: -- very negative, - negative, 0 neutral, + positive, ++ very positive
		1.	do n't waste your money .
		2.	neither funny nor suspenseful nor particularly well-drawn .
		3.	it 's not horrible , just horribly mediocre .
		4.	... too slow , too boring , and occasionally annoying .
		5.	it 's neither as romantic nor as thrilling as it should be .
	--	6.	the master of disaster - it 's a piece of dreck disguised as comedy .
		7.	so stupid , so ill-conceived , so badly drawn , it created whole new levels of ugly .
		8.	a film so tedious that it is impossible to care whether that boast is true or not .
		9.	choppy editing and too many repetitive scenes spoil what could have been an important documentary about stand-up comedy .
--		10.	this idea has lost its originality ... and neither star appears very excited at rehashing what was basically a one-joke picture .
	++	11.	ecks this one off your must-see list .
	-	12.	this is n't a `` friday '' worth waiting for .
	-	13.	there is not an ounce of honesty in the entire production .
	-	14.	do n't expect any surprises in this checklist of teamwork cliches ...
	-	15.	he has not learnt that storytelling is what the movies are about .
	-	16.	but here 's the real damn : it is n't funny , either .
	+	17.	these are names to remember , in order to avoid them in the future .
	-	18.	the cartoon that is n't really good enough to be on afternoon tv is now a movie that is n't really good enough to be in theaters .
	++	19.	a worthy entry into a very difficult genre .
++		20.	it 's a good film -- not a classic , but odd , entertaining and authentic .
	--	21.	it never fails to engage us .

Figure 1: SA heatmaps of exemplary test sentences, using as target class the *true* sentence class. All relevances are positive and mapped to red, the color intensity is normalized to the maximum relevance per sentence. The true sentence class, and the classifier's predicted class, are indicated on the left.

true	predicted	N°	Notation: -- very negative, - negative, 0 neutral, + positive, ++ very positive
		1.	do n't waste your money .
		2.	neither funny nor suspenseful nor particularly well-drawn .
		3.	it 's not horrible , just horribly mediocre .
		4.	... too slow , too boring , and occasionally annoying .
		5.	it 's neither as romantic nor as thrilling as it should be .
	--	6.	the master of disaster - it 's a piece of dreck disguised as comedy .
		7.	so stupid , so ill-conceived , so badly drawn , it created whole new levels of ugly .
		8.	a film so tedious that it is impossible to care whether that boast is true or not .
		9.	choppy editing and too many repetitive scenes spoil what could have been an important documentary about stand-up comedy .
--		10.	this idea has lost its originality ... and neither star appears very excited at rehashing what was basically a one-joke picture .
	++	11.	ecks this one off your must-see list .
	-	12.	this is n't a `` friday '' worth waiting for .
	-	13.	there is not an ounce of honesty in the entire production .
	-	14.	do n't expect any surprises in this checklist of teamwork cliches ...
	-	15.	he has not learnt that storytelling is what the movies are about .
	-	16.	but here 's the real damn : it is n't funny , either .
	+	17.	these are names to remember , in order to avoid them in the future .
	-	18.	the cartoon that is n't really good enough to be on afternoon tv is now a movie that is n't really good enough to be in theaters .
	++	19.	a worthy entry into a very difficult genre .
++		20.	it 's a good film -- not a classic , but odd , entertaining and authentic .
	--	21.	it never fails to engage us .

Figure 2: LRP heatmaps of exemplary test sentences, using as target class the *true* sentence class. Positive relevance is mapped to red, negative to blue, and the color intensity is normalized to the maximum absolute relevance per sentence. The true sentence class, and the classifier's predicted class, are indicated on the left.

SA		LRP	
most relevant	least relevant	most relevant	least relevant
broken-down	into	funnier	wrong
wall	what	charm	n't
execution	that	polished	forgettable
lackadaisical	a	gorgeous	shame
milestone	do	excellent	little
unreality	of	screen	predictable
soldier	all	honest	overblown
mournfully	ca	wall	trying
insight	in	confidence	lacking
disorienting	's	perfectly	nonsense

Table 1: Ten most resp. least relevant words identified by SA and LRP over all 2210 test sentences, using as relevance target class the class "very positive".

word lists, we observe that the highest SA relevances mainly point to words with a strong semantic meaning, but not necessarily expressing a positive sentiment, see e.g. *broken-down, lackadaisical* and *mournfully*, while the lowest SA relevances correspond to stop words. On the contrary, the extremal LRP relevances are more reliable: the highest relevances indicate words expressing a positive sentiment, while the lowest relevances are attributed to words defining a negative sentiment, hence both extremal relevances are related in a meaningful way to the target class of interest, i.e. the class "very positive".

4.3 Validation of Word Relevance

In order to quantitatively validate the word-level relevances obtained with SA and LRP, we perform two word deleting experiments. For these experiments we consider only test set sentences with a length greater or equal to 10 words (this amounts to retain 1849 test sentences), and we delete from each sentence up to 5 words accordingly to their SA resp. LRP relevance value (for deleting a word we simply set its word embedding to zero in the input sentence representation), and re-predict via the bi-LSTM the sentiment of the sentence with "missing" words, to track the impact of these deletions on the classifier's decision. The idea behind this experiment is that the relevance decomposition method that most pertinently reveals words that are important to the classifier's decision, will impact the most this decision when deleting words accordingly to their relevance value. Prior to the deletions, we first compute the SA resp. LRP word-level relevances on the original sentences (with no word deleted), using the *true* sentence

sentiment as target class for the relevance decomposition. Then, we conduct two types of deletions. On initially correctly classified sentences we delete words in decreasing order of their relevance value, and on initially falsely classified sentences we delete words in increasing order of their relevance. We additionally perform a random word deletion as an uninformative variant for comparison. Our results in terms of tracking the classification accuracy over the number of word deletions per sentence are reported in Fig. 3. These results show that, in both considered cases, deleting words in decreasing or increasing order of their LRP relevance has the most pertinent effect, suggesting that this relevance decomposition method is the most appropriate for detecting words speaking *for* or *against* a classifier's decision. While the LRP variant with relevance conservation LRP_{cons} performs almost as good as standard LRP, the latter yields slightly superior results and thus should be preferred. Finally, when deleting words in increasing order of their relevance value starting with initially falsely classified sentences (Fig. 3 right), we observe that SA performs even worse than random deletion. This indicates that the lowest SA relevances point essentially to words that have no influence on the classifier's decision at all, rather that signalizing words that are "inhibiting" it's decision and speaking *against* the true class, as LRP is indeed able to identify. Similar conclusions were drawn when comparing SA and LRP on a convolutional network for document classification (Arras et al., 2016a).

4.4 Relevance Distribution over Sentence Length

To get an idea of which words over the sentence length get attributed the most relevance, we compute a word relevance statistic by performing SA and LRP on all test sentences having a length greater or equal to 19 words (this amounts to 50.0% of the test set). Then, we divide each sentence length into 10 equal intervals, and sum up the word relevances in each interval (when a word is not entirely in an interval, the relevance portion falling into that interval is considered). For LRP, we use the absolute value of the word-level relevance values (to avoid that negative relevances cancel out positive relevances). Finally, to get a distribution, we normalize the results to sum up to one. We compute this statistic by considering

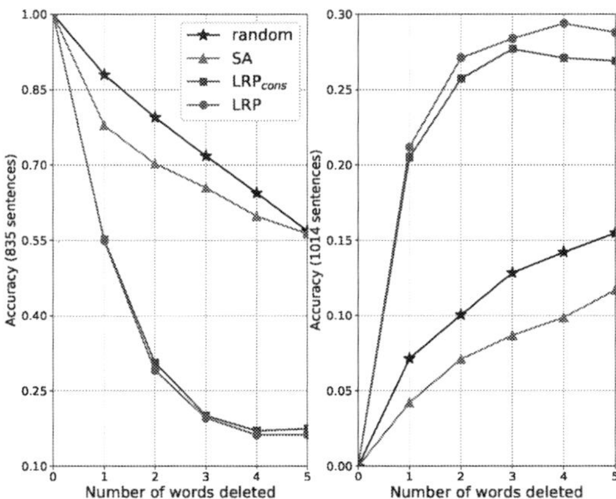

Figure 3: Impact of word deleting on initially correctly (left) and falsely (right) classified test sentences, using either SA or LRP as relevance decomposition method (LRP_{cons} is a variant of LRP with relevance conservation). The relevance target class is the true sentence class, and words are deleted in decreasing (left) and increasing (right) order of their relevance. Random deletion is averaged over 10 runs (std < 0.016). A steep decline (left) and incline (right) indicate informative word relevance.

either the total word relevance obtained via the bi-LSTM model, or by considering only the part of the relevance that comes from one of the two unidirectional model constituents, i.e. the relevance contributed by the LSTM which takes as input the sentence words in their original order (we call it left encoder), or the one contributed by the LSTM which takes as input the sentence words in reversed order (we call it right encoder). The resulting distributions, for different relevance target classes, are reported in Fig. 4. Interestingly, the relevance distributions are not symmetric w.r.t. to the sentence middle, and the major part of the relevance is attributed to the second half of the sentences, except for the target class "neutral", where the most relevance is attributed to the last computational time steps of the left or the right encoder, resulting in an almost symmetric distribution of the total relevance for that class. This can maybe be explained by the fact that, at least for longer movie reviews, strong judgments on the movie's quality tend to appear at the end of the sentences, while the beginning of the sentences serves as an introduction to the review's topic, describing e.g. the movie's subject or genre. Another

particularity of the relevance distribution we notice, is that the relevances of the left encoder tend to be more smooth than those of the right encoder, which is a surprising result, as one might expect that both unidirectional model constituents behave similarly, and that there is no mechanism in the model to make a distinction between the text read in original and in reversed order.

5   Conclusion

In this work we have introduced a simple yet effective strategy for extending the LRP procedure to recurrent architectures, such as LSTMs, by proposing a rule to backpropagate the relevance through multiplicative interactions. We applied the extended LRP version to a bi-directional LSTM model for the sentiment prediction of sentences, demonstrating that the resulting word relevances trustworthy reveal words supporting the classifier's decision *for* or *against* a specific class, and perform better than those obtained by a gradient-based decomposition.

Our technique helps understanding and verifying the correct behavior of recurrent classifiers, and can detect important patterns in text datasets. Compared to other non-gradient based explanation methods, which rely e.g. on random sampling or on iterative representation occlusion, our technique is deterministic, and can be computed in one pass through the network. Moreover, our method is self-contained, in that it does not require to train an external classifier to deliver the explanations, these are obtained directly via the original classifier.

Future work would include applying the proposed technique to other recurrent architectures such as character-level models or GRUs, as well as to extractive summarization. Besides, our method is not restricted to the NLP domain, and might also be useful to other applications relying on recurrent architectures.

Acknowledgments

We thank Rico Raber for many insightful discussions. This work was partly supported by BMBF, DFG and also Institute for Information & Communications Technology Promotion (IITP) grant funded by the Korea government (No. 2017-0-00451 for KRM).

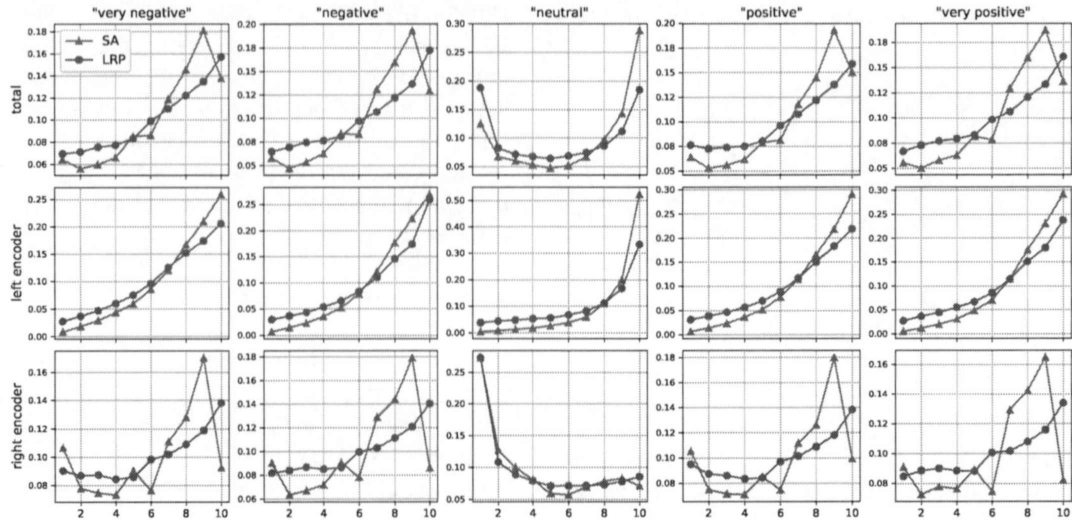

Figure 4: Word relevance distribution over the sentence length (divided into 10 intervals), per relevance target class (indicated on the top), obtained by performing SA and LRP on all test sentences having a length greater or equal to 19 words (1104 sentences). For LRP, the absolute value of the word-level relevances is used to compute these statistics. The first row corresponds to the total relevance, the second resp. third row only contain the relevance from the bi-LSTM's left and right encoder.

References

Leila Arras, Franziska Horn, Grégoire Montavon, Klaus-Robert Müller, and Wojciech Samek. 2016a. Explaining Predictions of Non-Linear Classifiers in NLP. In *Proceedings of the ACL 2016 Workshop on Representation Learning for NLP*. Association for Computational Linguistics, pages 1–7.

Leila Arras, Franziska Horn, Grégoire Montavon, Klaus-Robert Müller, and Wojciech Samek. 2016b. "What is Relevant in a Text Document?": An Interpretable Machine Learning Approach. *arXiv* 1612.07843.

Sebastian Bach, Alexander Binder, Grégoire Montavon, Frederick Klauschen, Klaus-Robert Müller, and Wojciech Samek. 2015. On Pixel-Wise Explanations for Non-Linear Classifier Decisions by Layer-Wise Relevance Propagation. *PLOS ONE* 10(7):e0130140.

Kyunghyun Cho, Bart van Merrienboer, Caglar Gulcehre, Dzmitry Bahdanau, Fethi Bougares, Holger Schwenk, and Yoshua Bengio. 2014. Learning Phrase Representations using RNN Encoder-Decoder for Statistical Machine Translation. In *Proceedings of the 2014 Conference on Empirical Methods in Natural Language Processing (EMNLP)*. Association for Computational Linguistics, pages 1724–1734.

Misha Denil, Alban Demiraj, and Nando de Freitas. 2014. Extraction of Salient Sentences from Labelled Documents. *arXiv* 1412.6815.

Yannis Dimopoulos, Paul Bourret, and Sovan Lek. 1995. Use of some sensitivity criteria for choosing networks with good generalization ability. *Neural Processing Letters* 2(6):1–4.

Felix A. Gers, Jürgen Schmidhuber, and Fred Cummins. 2000. Learning to Forget: Continual Prediction with LSTM. *Neural Computation* 12(10):2451–2471.

Muriel Gevrey, Ioannis Dimopoulos, and Sovan Lek. 2003. Review and comparison of methods to study the contribution of variables in artificial neural network models. *Ecological Modelling* 160(3):249–264.

Sepp Hochreiter and Jürgen Schmidhuber. 1997. Long Short-Term Memory. *Neural Computation* 9(8):1735–1780.

Will Landecker, Michael D. Thomure, Luís M. A. Bettencourt, Melanie Mitchell, Garrett T. Kenyon, and Steven P. Brumby. 2013. Interpreting Individual Classifications of Hierarchical Networks. In *IEEE Symposium on Computational Intelligence and Data Mining (CIDM)*. pages 32–38.

Sebastian Lapuschkin, Alexander Binder, Grégoire Montavon, Klaus-Robert Müller, and Wojciech Samek. 2016. The Layer-wise Relevance Propagation Toolbox for Artificial Neural Networks. *Journal of Machine Learning Research* 17(114):1–5.

Jiwei Li, Xinlei Chen, Eduard Hovy, and Dan Jurafsky. 2016a. Visualizing and Understanding Neural

Models in NLP. In *Proceedings of the 2016 Conference of the North American Chapter of the Association for Computational Linguistics: Human Language Technologies (NAACL-HLT)*. pages 681–691.

Jiwei Li, Will Monroe, and Dan Jurafsky. 2016b. Understanding Neural Networks through Representation Erasure. *arXiv* 1612.08220.

Saif M. Mohammad. 2017. Challenges in Sentiment Analysis. In Erik Cambria, Dipankar Das, Sivaji Bandyopadhyay, and Antonio Feraco, editors, *A Practical Guide to Sentiment Analysis*. Springer International Publishing, pages 61–83.

Grégoire Montavon, Sebastian Lapuschkin, Alexander Binder, Wojciech Samek, and Klaus-Robert Müller. 2017a. Explaining nonlinear classification decisions with deep Taylor decomposition. *Pattern Recognition* 65:211–222.

Grégoire Montavon, Wojciech Samek, and Klaus-Robert Müller. 2017b. Methods for Interpreting and Understanding Deep Neural Networks. *arXiv* 1706.07979.

James Murdoch and Arthur Szlam. 2017. Automatic Rule Extraction from Long Short Term Memory Networks. In *International Conference on Learning Representations Conference Track (ICLR)*.

Preslav Nakov, Alan Ritter, Sara Rosenthal, Fabrizio Sebastiani, and Veselin Stoyanov. 2016. SemEval-2016 Task 4: Sentiment Analysis in Twitter. In *Proceedings of the 10th International Workshop on Semantic Evaluation (SemEval-2016)*. Association for Computational Linguistics, pages 1–18.

Marco Tulio Ribeiro, Sameer Singh, and Carlos Guestrin. 2016. "Why Should I Trust You?": Explaining the Predictions of Any Classifier. In *Proceedings of the 22nd ACM SIGKDD International Conference on Knowledge Discovery and Data Mining*. pages 1135–1144.

David E. Rumelhart, Geoffrey E. Hinton, and Ronald J. Williams. 1986. Learning representations by back-propagating errors. *Nature* 323:533–536.

Wojciech Samek, Alexander Binder, Grégoire Montavon, Sebastian Lapuschkin, and Klaus-Robert Müller. 2017. Evaluating the visualization of what a Deep Neural Network has learned. *IEEE Transactions on Neural Networks and Learning Systems* PP(99):1–14.

Mike Schuster and Kuldip K. Paliwal. 1997. Bidirectional Recurrent Neural Networks. *IEEE Transactions on Signal Processing* 45(11):2673–2681.

Karen Simonyan, Andrea Vedaldi, and Andrew Zisserman. 2014. Deep Inside Convolutional Networks: Visualising Image Classification Models and Saliency Maps. In *International Conference on Learning Representations Workshop Track (ICLR)*.

Richard Socher, Alex Perelygin, Jean Y. Wu, Jason Chuang, Christopher D. Manning, Andrew Y. Ng, and Christopher Potts. 2013. Recursive Deep Models for Semantic Compositionality Over a Sentiment Treebank. In *Proceedings of the 2013 Conference on Empirical Methods in Natural Language Processing (EMNLP)*. Association for Computational Linguistics, pages 1631–1642.

Matthew D. Zeiler and Rob Fergus. 2014. Visualizing and Understanding Convolutional Networks. In *Computer Vision ECCV 2014: 13th European Conference*. pages 818–833.

Appendix

Long-Short Term Memory Network (LSTM)

We define in the following the LSTM recurrence equations (Hochreiter and Schmidhuber, 1997; Gers et al., 2000) of the model we used in our experiments:

$$i_t = \texttt{sigm}\left(W_i\,h_{t-1} + U_i\,x_t + b_i\right)$$

$$f_t = \texttt{sigm}\left(W_f\,h_{t-1} + U_f\,x_t + b_f\right)$$

$$o_t = \texttt{sigm}\left(W_o\,h_{t-1} + U_o\,x_t + b_o\right)$$

$$g_t = \texttt{tanh}\left(W_g\,h_{t-1} + U_g\,x_t + b_g\right)$$

$$c_t = f_t \odot c_{t-1} + i_t \odot g_t$$

$$h_t = o_t \odot \texttt{tanh}(c_t)$$

Here above the activation functions $\texttt{sigm}$ and $\texttt{tanh}$ are applied element-wise, and $\odot$ is an element-wise multiplication.

As an input, the LSTM gets fed with a sequence of vectors $x = (x_1, x_2, ..., x_T)$ representing the word embeddings of the input sentence's words. The matrices W's, U's, and vectors b's are connection weights and biases, and the initial states h_0 and c_0 are set to zero.

The last hidden state h_T is eventually attached to a fully-connected linear layer yielding a prediction score vector $f(x)$, with one entry $f_c(x)$ per class, which is used for sentiment prediction.

Bi-directional LSTM The bi-directional LSTM (Schuster and Paliwal, 1997) we use in the present work, is a concatenation of two separate LSTM models as described above, each of them taking a different sequence of word embeddings as input.

One LSTM takes as input the words in their original order, as they appear in the input sentence. The second LSTM takes as input the same words but in *reversed* order.

Each of these LSTMs yields a final hidden state vector, say $\overrightarrow{h_T}$ and $\overleftarrow{h_T}$. The concatenation of these two vectors is eventually fed to a fully-connected linear layer, retrieving one prediction score $f_c(x)$ per class.

GradAscent at EmoInt-2017: Character- and Word-Level Recurrent Neural Network Models for Tweet Emotion Intensity Detection

Egor Lakomkin,* Chandrakant Bothe* and Stefan Wermter
Knowledge Technology, Department of Informatics,
University of Hamburg,
Vogt-Koelln Str. 30, 22527 Hamburg, Germany
`knowledge-technology.info`
`{lakomkin, bothe, wermter}@informatik.uni-hamburg.de`

Abstract

The WASSA 2017 EmoInt shared task has the goal to predict emotion intensity values of tweet messages. Given the text of a tweet and its emotion category (anger, joy, fear, and sadness), the participants were asked to build a system that assigns emotion intensity values. Emotion intensity estimation is a challenging problem given the short length of the tweets, the noisy structure of the text and the lack of annotated data. To solve this problem, we developed an ensemble of two neural models, processing input on the character. and word-level with a lexicon-driven system. The correlation scores across all four emotions are averaged to determine the bottom-line competition metric, and our system ranks place forth in full intensity range and third in 0.5-1 range of intensity among 23 systems at the time of writing (June 2017).

1 Introduction

Sentiment analysis of a text reveals information on the degree of positiveness or negativeness of the opinion expressed by the writer. Such information can be useful for providing better services for users (Kang and Park, 2014) or preventing potentially dangerous situations (O'Dea et al., 2015). Traditionally the most popular way of sentiment representation is either binary (positive, negative) or multi-class (for example 5 classes: very negative, negative, neutral, positive, very positive). While being simple, such a scheme looses interpretability and a continuous intensity scale might be preferred. Twitter sentiment and emotion intensity detection are still challenging tasks and re-

---

*equal contribution

main active areas of research. These difficulties have several reasons: extensive usage of hashtags, slang, abbreviations, and emoticons. Also, tweets are usually typed on mobile devices which can lead to a substantial amount of typos. As traditional NLP tools are usually trained on datasets containing clean text, which makes it difficult to use them for tweet analysis.

Existing approaches for modeling emotion intensity rely heavily on manually constructed lexicons, which contain information about intensity weights for each available word (Mohammad and Bravo-Marquez, 2017a; Neviarouskaya et al., 2007). The intensity for the whole sentence can be inferred by combining individual scores of words. While being easily interpretable, such models have several limitations. Ignoring word order and compositionality of the language is the first issue, which is critical for modeling sequences. Constructing such lexicons is a labour-intensive process, which needs to be carried out continuously due to the constant development of language. Data-driven approaches like deep neural networks can overcome such limitations, and they have been behind many recent advances in text processing tasks, such as language modeling, machine translation, POS tagging, and classification (Irsoy and Cardie, 2014; Socher et al., 2013). The appealing property of such models is their ability to combine feature extraction and classification stages given a sufficient amount of training data.

In this paper, we augment traditional lexicon-based models with two neural network-based models: one with character and one with word input. Character-level deep neural networks recently showed outstanding results on text understanding tasks such as machine translation (Kalchbrenner et al., 2016) and text classification (Zhang et al., 2015). In a domain-specific task such as predict-

169

Proceedings of the 8th Workshop on Computational Approaches to Subjectivity, Sentiment and Social Media Analysis, pages 169–174
Copenhagen, Denmark, September 7–11, 2017. ©2017 Association for Computational Linguistics

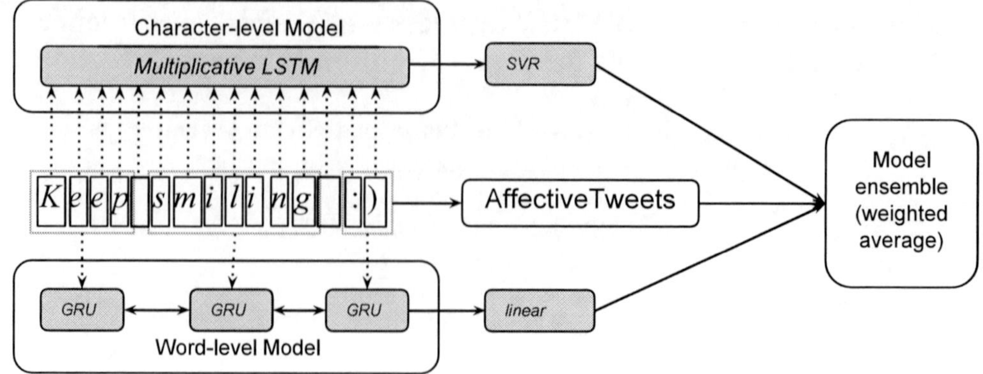

Figure 1: Overall model architecture. It combines a lexicon-based AffectiveTweets model with two neural models: a character and a word-level model via averaging scores with weights tuned on the provided validation set.

ing the emotion intensity of tweets, a character-level model can theoretically capture the notion of hashtags, emoticons, or character repetitions, which all are unique to social media. The intuition is that a character-level model captures common writing patterns such as punctuations and signaling characters. A word-level recurrent neural model can incorporate the order of information using distributed representations of words trained on a large amount of text.

Our final model is a weighted average of the scores provided by the baseline, our character- and word-level model. Our ensemble model achieved forth position in the 0-1 emotion intensity range task and third position in the 0.5-1.0 range task on the public leaderboard (GradAscent team) on CodaLab[1] at the time of writing this paper (June 2017).

2 Approach

Our system is an ensemble of the provided baseline system and two neural network-based models; processing character and word input respectively. Combining the word and character representations we can deal with noisiness of the tweet messages as well as capturing the semantics of the text by using distributed word representations.

2.1 Data pre-processing

We perform only a few preprocessing steps, like striping URLs, user mentions (@username) and leave only the following characters:

`a-zA-Z@-!:(),;?.#'0-9*`. We always convert a message to lowercase before feeding it to the models.

Table 1: WASSA 2017 Emotion Intensity Shared task dataset statistics.

Split	Joy	Anger	Fear	Sadness	Sum
Train	823	856	1147	786	3612
Dev	78	83	109	73	343
Test	714	760	995	673	3142

2.2 Baseline model

The baseline system is a WEKA-based model called AffectiveTweets (Mohammad and Bravo-Marquez, 2017a). This system combines features derived from several lexicons like MPQA (Wilson et al., 2005), Bing Liu (Hu and Liu, 2004), AFINN (Nielsen, 2011), Sentiment 140 (Kiritchenko et al.), NRC Hashtag sentiment lexicon, NRC Word-Emotion Association Lexicon (Mohammad and Turney, 2013), NRC-10 Expanded (Bravo-Marquez et al., 2016), NRC Hashtag Emotion Association (Saif and Kiritchenko, 2015), and SentiWordNet (Baccianella et al., 2010) with traditional NLP features like word- and character n-grams, POS tags (Gimpel et al., 2011), and processing of negations. In addition to those features, AffectiveTweets incorporates SentiStrength values (Thelwall et al., 2012), Brown clusters (Brown et al., 1992) trained on ~53 million tweets[2], combining them with averaged and concatenated first

---

[1] https://competitions.codalab.org/competitions/16380

[2] http://www.cs.cmu.edu/~ark/TweetNLP/

k word embeddings of the tweet. Finally, a support Vector Machine model is used as a regression model for predicting emotion intensity values.

2.3 Character-level RNN model

We extracted character-level sentence representations by encoding the whole tweet text with the pre-trained recurrent neural network model[3]. This model contains a single multiplicative LSTM (Krause et al., 2016) layer with 4,096 hidden units, trained on $\sim$80 million Amazon product reviews as a character-based language model (Radford et al., 2017). We extracted the hidden vector corresponding to the last character of a tweet and also averaged the representations of all hidden vectors. Concatenation of the two vectors is used as a tweet representation. In our experiments, we observed that adding averaged character representations improves the overall performance, especially when evaluating high-intensity tweets.

In addition to the pre-trained character-level language model, we investigate a model trained specifically for tweets. Our observation was that the tweets have a different language structure than product reviews, which might affect the transferability of features between domains. For instance, the extensive use of emoticons, character repetition, and hashtags, which are common for tweet messages, however, significantly different from product reviews which are often longer and grammatically correct.

We trained the character-based language model on the Sentiment 140 corpus comprised of 1.6 million tweets (Go et al., 2009). A single-layer LSTM (Hochreiter and Schmidhuber, 1997) with 1024 hidden units was trained with Adam optimizer (Kingma and Ba, 2014) with 0.0005 learning rate and clipping gradients at norm 1. We used the Support Vector Regressor (SVR) algorithm to classify tweets represented as a fixed-length vector with a character-based recurrent neural network. Results of different setups are reported in Table 2.

2.4 Word-level model

We used distributed representations to model the words in a tweet. We carried out several experiments where we used random initialization for word embeddings and two pre-trained versions of GloVe embeddings (Pennington et al., 2014)

Table 2: Effect of different character-level recurrent neural network representations: last cell vector of the pre-trained model (PT, last) and Twitter-specific character LM (Twit, last). Also, in addition, we tested a concatenation of the last cell vector with the average of all cell vectors for the pre-trained model (PT, last+avg) and Twitter model (Twit, last+avg). Results are reported on the test set, where avg_p corresponds to Pearson coefficient and avg_s to Spearman.

Range	(0.0-1.0)		(0.5-1.0)	
Model	**avg_p**	**avg_s**	**avg_p**	**avg_s**
PT, last	0.470	0.468	0.412	0.404
PT, last+avg	**0.474**	**0.472**	**0.419**	**0.413**
Twit, last	0.312	0.307	0.296	0.288
Twit, last+avg	0.319	0.310	0.298	0.301

Table 3: Effect of different word embedding initializations for the word-level model: randomly initialized, pre-trained GloVe embeddings on Twitter and Wikipedia.

Range	(0.0-1.0)		(0.5-1.0)	
Model	**avg_p**	**avg_s**	**avg_p**	**avg_s**
Random emb.	0.291	0.276	0.250	0.227
GloVe (Twitter)	0.300	0.293	0.231	0.220
GloVe (Wiki)	**0.326**	**0.323**	**0.259**	**0.252**

trained on Wikipedia and Twitter[4], to test if Twitter specific word representations are more suitable to solve the problem. Out-of-vocabulary words were replaced with a special word 'OOV' and initialized as a random vector, which was tuned during the training. We used a 50-dimensional embedding representation in all our experiments.

A bidirectional gated recurrent unit (GRU) network (Chung et al., 2014) with a 32-dimension cell size was used for modeling the tweet as a hidden memory vector. The vector corresponding to the last word was fed to a dense layer with 1 neuron predicting emotion intensity. We used GRUs as they tackle the common vanishing gradient problem of RNNs during the training and they contain fewer parameters than LSTM units. The word-level model is trained on the given EmoInt corpus with Adam optimizer using different embedding setups, the results are presented in Table 3.

---

[3]https://github.com/openai/
generating-reviews-discovering-sentiment

[4]https://nlp.stanford.edu/projects/
glove/

Table 4: Pearson and Spearman correlation coefficients of baseline, character and word-level models and its ensemble for fear, anger, joy and sadness emotions and also average values. Results are calculated on the provided test set labels.

Model	avg_p	avg_s	anger_p	anger_s	fear_p	fear_s	joy_p	joy_s	sad_p	sad_s
Test set results (Intensity range: 0-1)										
Baseline	0.655	0.652	0.631	0.623	0.631	0.622	0.645	0.654	0.712	0.711
Char_LM	0.474	0.472	0.415	0.400	0.575	0.551	0.278	0.299	0.629	0.638
Word_Level	0.326	0.323	0.253	0.258	0.337	0.332	0.201	0.194	0.435	0.395
Char_LM + Word_Level	0.659	0.656	0.580	0.572	0.658	0.638	0.708	0.714	0.688	0.701
Baseline + Char_LM + Word_Level	**0.721**	**0.717**	**0.678**	**0.665**	**0.698**	**0.686**	**0.744**	**0.750**	**0.763**	**0.767**
Test set results (Intensity range: 0.5-1)										
Baseline	0.475	0.449	0.495	0.464	0.476	0.432	0.370	0.363	0.558	0.537
Char_LM	0.419	0.413	0.316	0.327	0.488	0.435	0.416	0.423	0.457	0.467
Word_Level	0.259	0.252	0.237	0.257	0.220	0.226	0.211	0.201	0.451	0.408
Char_LM + Word_Level	0.471	0.467	0.389	0.406	0.488	0.435	0.536	0.547	0.470	0.481
Baseline + Char_LM + Word_Level	**0.562**	**0.543**	**0.565**	**0.545**	**0.531**	**0.494**	**0.528**	**0.531**	**0.624**	**0.601**

3 Experiment

The dataset for the WASSA-2017 competition (Mohammad and Bravo-Marquez, 2017b) is comprised of 7097 annotated tweets, classified into 4 categories: joy, anger, fear, and sadness (dataset statistics are presented in Table 1). For each annotated tweet there is an ID, full text, emotion category, and emotion intensity value. Emotion intensity is a real value in the range from 0 to 1, where higher value correspond to a higher intensity of the emotion conveyed. A sample from the EmoInt corpus:

```
30112 LOVE LOVE LOVE #smile
#fun #relaxationiskey joy 0.740,
```

where 30112 is the ID of a tweet, which is labeled as "*joy*" with an intensity of 0.740.

3.1 Ensembling of the models

Ensembling of several models is a widely used method to improve the performance of the overall system by combining predictions of several classifiers. Several ensembling techniques have been proposed recently: mixing experts (Jacobs et al., 1991), model stacking, bagging and boosting (Breiman, 1996) and a simple weighted average of the scores of individual models, which we used in this work. The main reason for our choice was the limited size of the training data, and using more complex approach like stacking could lead to overfitting. In this work, we output emotion intensity values as a linear combination of individual predictions of three systems: baseline, character and word-level models.

$$emotion_{intensity} = w_b * baseline_{emotion}$$
$$+ w_w * w\_rnn_{emotion} + w_c * c\_rnn_{emotion},$$
$$w_b + w_w + w_c = 1 \quad (1)$$

where $baseline_{emotion}$, $w\_rnn_{emotion}$ and $c\_rnn_{emotion}$ are intensities of the baseline, character and word-level models correspondingly for the emotion (joy, anger, fear or sadness). Ensembling coefficients w_b, w_c and w_w were tuned on the development set to maximize the average Pearson correlation coefficient using grid-search.

4 Results & Conclusion

We report Pearson and Spearman correlation for each emotion class on the provided test data, shown in Table 4. The correlation rank coefficients assess how relevant and similar the two sets of ranking are. The character and word-level neural models achieve lower correlation values than the baseline, which is an indicator that models containing much of external knowledge perform better than end-to-end models on the tasks with a handful amount of samples; however, they bring additional value to the ensemble. Pearson and Spearman correlation coefficients are improved by 0.066 and 0.065 for the intensities in the full range of 0-1, achieving #4 position on the leaderboard. Additionally, the systems were evaluated on the sample with moderate or high emotional intensities with values from 0.5 to 1. Our ensemble model places rank #4 and shows 0.087 ($\sim 18.5\%$ relative) improvement on both correlation coefficients.

Surprisingly, tweet representations obtained with the character-level model show competitive or even better results for fear and joy emotion categories for samples with high-intensity emotions, and overall the Char_LM model shows similar results to the AffectiveTweet baseline model. Given the fact that the Char_LM model did not have any external knowledge or supervision other than the provided data, this demonstrates the effectiveness of the character-level modeling of noisy and short texts.

Acknowledgments

This project has received funding from the European Union's Horizon 2020 research and innovation programme under the Marie Sklodowska-Curie grant agreement No 642667 (SECURE). We would like to thank Dr. Cornelius Weber and Dr. Sven Magg for their helpful comments and suggestions.

References

Stefano Baccianella, Andrea Esuli, and Fabrizio Sebastiani. 2010. Sentiwordnet 3.0: An enhanced lexical resource for sentiment analysis and opinion mining. In Nicoletta Calzolari, Khalid Choukri, Bente Maegaard, Joseph Mariani, Jan Odijk, Stelios Piperidis, Mike Rosner, and Daniel Tapias, editors, *Proceedings of the International Conference on Language Resources and Evaluation, LREC 2010, 17-23 May 2010, Valletta, Malta*. European Language Resources Association.

Felipe Bravo-Marquez, Eibe Frank, Saif M. Mohammad, and Bernhard Pfahringer. 2016. Determining word-emotion associations from tweets by multi-label classification. In *2016 IEEE/WIC/ACM International Conference on Web Intelligence, WI 2016, Omaha, NE, USA, October 13-16, 2016*. IEEE Computer Society, pages 536–539. https://doi.org/10.1109/WI.2016.0091.

Leo Breiman. 1996. Bagging predictors. *Machine learning* 24(2):123–140.

Peter F Brown, Peter V Desouza, Robert L Mercer, Vincent J Della Pietra, and Jenifer C Lai. 1992. Class-based n-gram models of natural language. *Computational linguistics* 18(4):467–479.

Junyoung Chung, Caglar Gulcehre, Kyunghyun Cho, and Yoshua Bengio. 2014. Empirical evaluation of gated recurrent neural networks on sequence modeling. *arXiv: 1412.3555v1* pages 1–9.

Kevin Gimpel, Nathan Schneider, Brendan O'Connor, Dipanjan Das, Daniel Mills, Jacob Eisenstein, Michael Heilman, Dani Yogatama, Jeffrey Flanigan, and Noah A. Smith. 2011. Part-of-speech tagging for twitter: Annotation, features, and experiments. In *The 49th Annual Meeting of the Association for Computational Linguistics: Human Language Technologies, Proceedings of the Conference, 19-24 June, 2011, Portland, Oregon, USA - Short Papers*. The Association for Computer Linguistics, pages 42–47.

Alec Go, Richa Bhayani, and Lei Huang. 2009. Twitter sentiment classification using distant supervision. *CS224N Project Report, Stanford* 1(12).

Sepp Hochreiter and Jürgen Schmidhuber. 1997. Long short-term memory. *Neural computation* 9(8):1735–1780.

Minqing Hu and Bing Liu. 2004. Mining and summarizing customer reviews. In Won Kim, Ron Kohavi, Johannes Gehrke, and William DuMouchel, editors, *Proceedings of the Tenth ACM SIGKDD International Conference on Knowledge Discovery and Data Mining, Seattle, Washington, USA, August 22-25, 2004*. ACM, pages 168–177. https://doi.org/10.1145/1014052.1014073.

Ozan Irsoy and Claire Cardie. 2014. Opinion mining with deep recurrent neural networks. In *the Proceedings of the Conference on EMLNP*. pages 720–728.

Robert A Jacobs, Michael I Jordan, Steven J Nowlan, and Geoffrey E Hinton. 1991. Adaptive mixtures of local experts. *Neural Computation* 3(1):79–87.

Nal Kalchbrenner, Lasse Espeholt, Karen Simonyan, Aaron van den Oord, Alex Graves, and Koray Kavukcuoglu. 2016. Neural machine translation in linear time. *arXiv:1610.10099* .

Daekook Kang and Yongtae Park. 2014. Review-based measurement of customer satisfaction in mobile service: Sentiment analysis and vikor approach. *Expert Systems with Applications* 41(4):1041–1050.

Diederik Kingma and Jimmy Ba. 2014. Adam: A method for stochastic optimization. *arXiv preprint arXiv:1412.6980* .

Svetlana Kiritchenko, Xiaodan Zhu, and Saif M. Mohammad. ???? Sentiment analysis of short informal texts 50:723–762.

Ben Krause, Liang Lu, Iain Murray, and Steve Renals. 2016. Multiplicative lstm for sequence modelling. *arXiv:1609.07959* .

Saif M. Mohammad and Felipe Bravo-Marquez. 2017a. Emotion intensities in tweets. In *Proceedings of the Sixth Joint Conference on Lexical and Computational Semantics (*Sem)*. Vancouver, Canada.

Saif M. Mohammad and Felipe Bravo-Marquez. 2017b. WASSA-2017 shared task on emotion intensity. In *Proceedings of the Workshop on Computational Approaches to Subjectivity, Sentiment and Social Media Analysis (WASSA)*. Copenhagen, Denmark.

Saif M. Mohammad and Peter D. Turney. 2013. Crowdsourcing a word-emotion association lexicon 29(3):436–465.

Alena Neviarouskaya, Helmut Prendinger, and Mitsuru Ishizuka. 2007. Textual affect sensing for sociable and expressive online communication. *Affective Computing and Intelligent Interaction* pages 218–229.

Finn Årup Nielsen. 2011. A new ANEW: evaluation of a word list for sentiment analysis in microblogs. In Matthew Rowe, Milan Stankovic, Aba-Sah Dadzie, and Mariann Hardey, editors, *Proceedings of the ESWC2011 Workshop on 'Making Sense of Microposts': Big things come in small packages, Heraklion, Crete, Greece, May 30, 2011*. CEUR-WS.org, volume 718 of *CEUR Workshop Proceedings*, pages 93–98.

Bridianne O'Dea, Stephen Wan, Philip J Batterham, Alison L Calear, Cecile Paris, and Helen Christensen. 2015. Detecting suicidality on twitter. *Internet Interventions* 2(2):183–188.

Jeffrey Pennington, Richard Socher, and Christopher D Manning. 2014. GloVe: Global vectors for word representation. In *the Proceedings of the Conference on EMLNP*. pages 1532–1543.

Alec Radford, Rafal Jozefowicz, and Ilya Sutskever. 2017. Learning to generate reviews and discovering sentiment. *arXiv: 1704.01444* .

Mohammad Saif and Svetlana Kiritchenko. 2015. Using hashtags to capture fine emotion categories from tweets. *Computational Intelligence* 31(2):301–326. https://doi.org/10.1111/coin.12024.

Richard Socher, Alex Perelygin, Jean Y Wu, Jason Chuang, Christopher D Manning, Andrew Y Ng, and Christopher Potts. 2013. Recursive deep models for semantic compositionality over a sentiment treebank. In *the Proceedings of the Conference on EMLNP*. volume 1631, pages 1631–1642.

Mike Thelwall, Kevan Buckley, and Georgios Paltoglou. 2012. Sentiment strength detection for the social web. *JASIST* 63(1):163–173. https://doi.org/10.1002/asi.21662.

Theresa Wilson, Janyce Wiebe, and Paul Hoffmann. 2005. Recognizing contextual polarity in phrase-level sentiment analysis. In *HLT/EMNLP 2005, Human Language Technology Conference and Conference on Empirical Methods in Natural Language Processing, Proceedings of the Conference, 6-8 October 2005, Vancouver, British Columbia, Canada*. The Association for Computational Linguistics, pages 347–354.

Xiang Zhang, Junbo Zhao, and Yann LeCun. 2015. Character-level convolutional networks for text classification. *arXiv: 1509.01626* .

NUIG at EmoInt-2017: BiLSTM and SVR Ensemble to Detect Emotion Intensity

Vladimir Andryushechkin, Ian David Wood and James O' Neill

Insight Centre for Data Analytics,
National University of Ireland, Galway

{vladimir.andryushechkin,ian.wood,james.oneill}@insight-centre.org

Abstract

This paper describes the entry NUIG in the WASSA 2017[1] shared task on emotion recognition. The NUIG system used an SVR (SVM regression) and BiLSTM ensemble, utilizing primarily n-grams (for SVR features) and tweet word embeddings (for BiLSTM features). Experiments were carried out on several other candidate features, some of which were added to the SVR model. Parameter selection for the SVR model was run as a grid search whilst parameters for the BiLSTM model were selected through a non-exhaustive ad-hoc search.

1 Introduction

The WASSA 2017 shared task on emotion intensity (EmoInt) is a competition intended to stimulate research into emotion recognition from text (Mohammad and Bravo-Marquez, 2017). The task provides a corpus of 3960 English language tweets annotated with a continuous intensity score for each of four basic emotions: anger, fear, joy and sadness. This is a subset of the set of basic emotions proposed by Ekman (Ekman, 1992), which has been widely used as an emotion representation scheme in emotion recognition research (Mohammad, 2016; Poria et al., 2017). An additional 3142 tweets were used for evaluation of competition entries, with annotations withheld during the competition.

The NUIG entry to the task consisted of an ensemble of two supervised models: an SVR (Support Vector Machine Regression[2]) with n-gram and several custom features and a BiLSTM (Bidirectional Long-Short Term Memory[3]) model utilising tweet word embeddings. The models are accessible on DockerHub, GitHub and as a Rest API service (see Section 6).

In Section 2 we briefly overview related work. In Section 3 we discuss the data cleaning and preprocessing steps taken. In Section 4 we describe the model architectures and parameter choices. In Section 5 we discuss some observed issues with the models.

2 Related Research

In this section we briefly describe related work that has attempted to model emotions using machine learning based regressors and classifiers.

Wu et al. (Wu et al., 2006) use a hybrid of keyword search and Artificial Neural Networks (when no emotional keywords are present) to tackle the problem of detecting multiple emotions (anger, fear, hope, sadness, happiness, love and thank) achieving an average test accuracy for all emotions of 57.75 %. In the speech recognition domain, Wllmer et al. (Wöllmer et al., 2008) have applied Long Short Memory Networks (LSTMs) to detect emotions from speech using spectral features and measurements of voice quality, in an attempt to continuously represent emotions as opposed to using discrete classes of valence, arousal and dominance. Schuller et al. (Schuller et al., 2008) in 2008 combined both acoustic models of speech, phonetics and word features on the EMO-DB database[4] which demonstrated the importance of incorporating word models for such emotion recognition tasks.

---

[1] 8th Workshop on Computational Approaches to Subjectivity, Sentiment & Social Media Analysis
[2] http://scikit-learn.org/

[3] keras+theano: https://keras.io/
[4] see here: http://emodb.bilderbar.info/

Proceedings of the 8th Workshop on Computational Approaches to Subjectivity, Sentiment and Social Media Analysis, pages 175–179
Copenhagen, Denmark, September 7–11, 2017. ©2017 Association for Computational Linguistics

3 Preprocessing

Tokenisation for both models was based on the regular expressions and rules provided with Stanford's Glove Twitter Word Vectors (Pennington et al., 2014) with some custom additions and modifications. Notable changes included the removal of hash symbols from tags, and extra emoticon detection patterns.

Removal of hash symbols had noticeable impact on the training accuracy for the BiLSTM model (for SVR it did not have significant impact). One possible explanation is the presence of hash tags in the training data for which the corresponding word is present in the word embedding, but not the tag itself. A concrete example is "#firbromyalgia". Note that stop words were not removed.

The preprocessing steps were as follows:

1. URL's, @mentions are replaced by standard tokens: "<url>" and "<user>"

2. emoticons were replaced by a small set of standard tokens: "<smile>", "<lolface>", "<sadface>", "<neutralface>", "<heart>"

3. hash symbols are removed from #hashtags

4. repeated full stops, question marks and exclamation marks are replaced with a single instance with a special token "<repeat>" added

5. characters repeated 3 times or more are replaced with one instance and a special token "<elong>" is added

6. a special token "<allcaps>" is added for each word in all capitals

7. remaining punctuation characters are treated as individual tokens

8. apostrophes are removed from negative contractions (e.g. "don't" is changed to "dont")[5]

9. other contractions are split into two tokens (e.g.: "it's" is changed to "it" and "'s")

10. tokens are converted to lower case

4 Model Architecture and Training

The overall model is a simple ensemble of an Support Vector Regression (SVR — see Section 4.1) and Bidirectional Long-Short Term Memory neural network (BiLSTM — see Section 4.2). The ensemble is described in Section 4.3.

The BiLSTM model was chosen due to it's recent excellent performance across numerous NLP tasks. The SVR model chosen as a baseline implementation, but found to contribute to the overall performance. Standard Long-Short Term Memory (LSTM) models were also attempted, however were outperformed by our BiLSTM (results not reported here).

Emotion	C	gamma	epsilon	tol
anger	1.0	0.01	0.001	1e-04
fear	1.0	0.01	0.001	1e-04
joy	1.0	0.01	0.001	1e-05
sadness	1.0	0.001	0.001	1e-05

Table 1: Parameters for SVR models

4.1 Support Vector Machine Regression

The core features for the SVR model are a bag of 1,2,3 and 4-grams. N-grams with corpus frequency less than 2 or document frequency greater than 100 were removed. Experiments including words with document frequency up to 1000 showed similar performance, so the more stringent criterion resulting in a much smaller vocabulary was chosen. Note that this will also remove most words commonly considered stop words.

The following extra features were added. Average, min and max word vectors for each token are taken as features due to variation in sentence length[6]. Proportion of Capital symbols and proportion of words with first capital are considered. Finally, average, standard deviation, min and max of cosine similarities between the vector for each emotion name (e.g. "fear") and word vectors of all words in a tweet are added to the experiment.

An RBF (Radial Basis Function) kernel was chosen in preference to a Linear kernel as the classifier's training time is prompt due to the small dataset size. This kernel provided marginally better results.

A grid search of model parameters C, gamma, tolerance and epsilon was applied to find the optimal set parameters. The best combination is stored for each emotion model separately (see Table 1). Other model parameters were left at their default values in the `sklearn.svm.SVR` implementation as those values performed better than alternatives.

4.2 Bidirectional LSTM

Preprocessed and tokenized sentences are converted to 100-dimensional twitter Glove word vectors. We considered also 200–dimensional vectors[7], however performance was slightly worse and memory requirements substantially increased.

Embedding vectors were fed into a BiLSTM network followed by a layer trained with dropout (Srivastava et al., 2014) to reduce over-

---

[5]This transformation was evident from analysis of the word embedding dictionary

[6]Length calculated before removing rare words/n-grams
[7]100d and 200d Glove Twitter 27B word vectors

fitting issues. The output of the dropout layer was inputted to a 2-hidden layer network before a final activation layer.Experiments were carried out on the 2-hidden layers where the number of neurons were varied between 20–60 in the first hidden layer and in the range of 10–20 in the second layer. For the sake of brevity, we only focus on the best performing architecture which is 100–50–25–1 (See Figure 1). Smaller layer sizes are not sufficient to catch the shape of the data and excessively big layer sizes lead to over-fitting and exponential growth of training time.

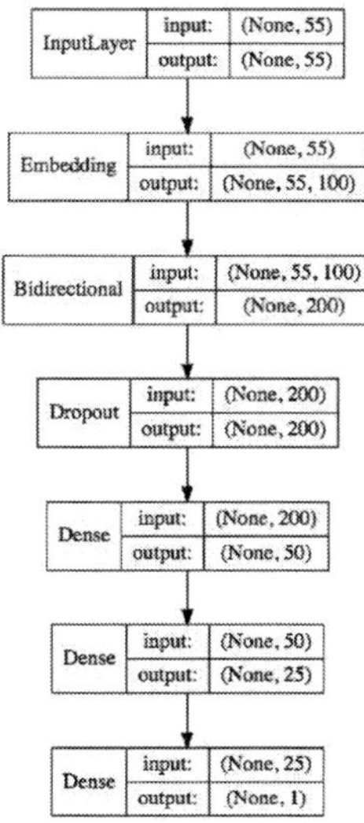

Figure 1: BiLSTM model architecture

For the loss function in training, Mean Absolute Error (MAE) is used in preference to Mean Squared Error (MSE) as it assigns equal weight to the data points and thus emphasizes the extremes. The "Softsign" activation function is found the best for the problem. Spearman and Pearson correlations are used as the main evaluation of network structures and parameter settings, however we also considered R2 scores, as in some cases Spearman and Pearson scores remained the same over training epochs while the R2 score improved.o

To avoid over-fitting, the number of training epochs is chosen through evaluating models after each epoch. The number of epochs at which training did not significantly improve Spearman correlation ρ is chosen for the final model (see Table 2). It is evident that fear takes considerably longer to train, 4 times longer than joy for example.

Emotion	anger	joy	fear	sadness
Training Epochs	12	8	36	18

Table 2: Number of BiLSTM training epochs.

Emotion	Estimator	R2	Pearson	Spearman
anger	svr	0.34	0.60	0.57
	lstm	0.36	0.63	0.61
	averaged	**0.42**	**0.66**	**0.63**
fear	svr	0.44	0.67	0.63
	lstm	0.45	0.68	0.66
	averaged	**0.49**	**0.71**	**0.68**
joy	svr	0.36	0.62	0.63
	lstm	0.35	0.59	0.59
	averaged	**0.41**	**0.65**	**0.65**
sadness	svr	0.43	0.68	0.69
	lstm	0.45	0.70	0.69
	averaged	**0.49**	**0.73**	**0.72**
average	averaged	**0.45**	**0.68**	**0.67**

Table 3: Performance comparison of individual and ensemble models evaluated on the WASSA test set.

4.3 Ensemble

With the limited time available, we attempted three simple approaches: taking the maximum, minimum and average of the predicted intensity between the two models. The best performance was obtained by averaging the LSTM and SVR outputs (see Table 3).

We believe that further investigation of the characteristics that led to a better ensemble model would likely lead to improvements in model design both in the BiLSTM itself and in alternative ensemble strategies.

5 Discussion

Overall, we see that performance in the development data set, used to select model parameters, did not differ substantially from performance on the test set, indicating that overfitting did not occur (see Table 4). Interestingly the difference between development and test set performance varies in line with the number of epochs. Concretely, *fear* and especially *sadness* see a strong performance gain on the test set, whereas the *joy* model degraded in performance, which was trained for the lowest number of epochs for all emotions. Given that our performance relative to the best performing entry also followed this pattern and that a dropout layer was used, which has been shown to control overfitting (Srivastava et al., 2014), it seems likely that choosing a larger number of epochs would have resulted in better models.

Analysis of model prediction errors on test data

Emotion	eval data	R2	Pearson	Spearman
anger	dev	**0.50**	**0.71**	**0.67**
	test	0.42	0.66	0.63
fear	dev	0.45	0.62	0.65
	test	**0.49**	**0.71**	**0.68**
joy	dev	**0.53**	**0.73**	**0.73**
	test	0.41	0.65	0.65
sadness	dev	0.26	0.52	0.56
	test	**0.49**	**0.73**	**0.72**
average	dev	0.43	0.64	0.65
	test	**0.45**	**0.68**	**0.67**

Table 4: Performance comparison between development and test sets.

revealed that extreme values were not modelled well for both SVR and BiLSTM models, with the SVR model performing marginally better, as seen for *anger* in Figure 2 (other emotions were similar). In the case of the BiLSTM model, we attribute this to the choice of L1 error as the loss function, which does not penalise large errors strongly. Overall performance with this loss function was, however, better on the provided data.

We also attempted to use the Emotion Hashtag Corpus (Mohammad, 2012) as training data for the BiLSTM model. This corpus only has category labels, so a model was built providing class probabilities, which were used as a proxy for intensity of the emotion classes. The performance was worse than random however, with an average R2 score of -3.63 (correlation 0.28), and this approach was abandoned. We believe this is due to two main factors: the intrinsic noise associated with emotion hash tags as emotion labels and that emotion probability is not a good analogue for emotion intensity. It would be interesting to experiment in the future with adding a binary feature for each emotion provided by a model trained on the hashtag corpus to our models.

6 Conclusion

The English language datasets provided for the WASSA competition are relatively clean but small, and the annotated labels for four emotions are precise and valuable. We performed experiments on the provided data drawing on our experience in emotion detection. The best built models are developed further and put together as an accessible service / software. The service is now available as part of the MixedEmotions platform[8] as well as the DockerHub as a docker image, on

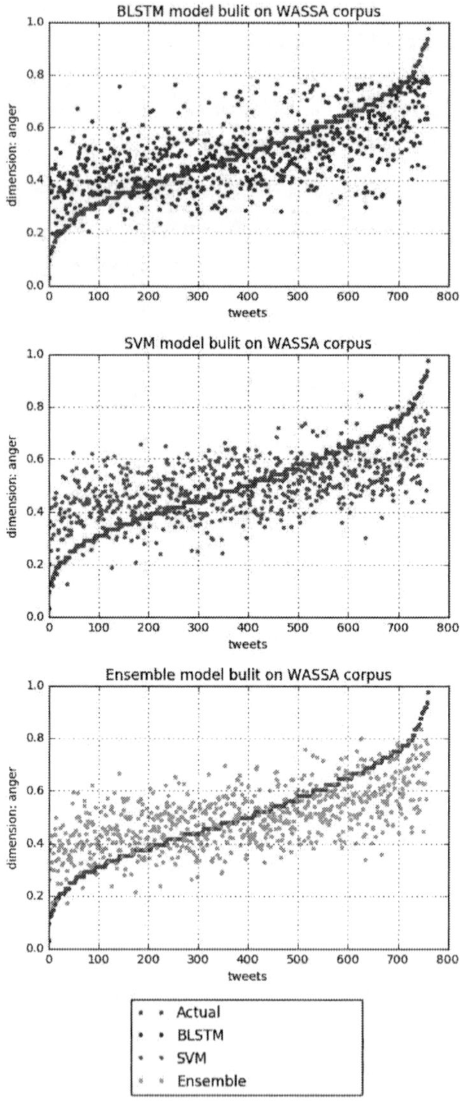

Figure 2: Model Predictions for *anger*. Other emotions follow a similar pattern.

---

[8]http://mixedemotions.insight-centre.org/

GitHub[9] DockerHub[10].

Acknowledgments

This work was supported in part by the European Union supported project MixedEmotions (H2020-644632) and the Science Foundation Ireland under Grant Number SFI/12/RC/2289 (Insight).

References

Paul Ekman. 1992. An argument for basic emotions. *Cognition and Emotion* 6(3-4):169–200.

Saif M. Mohammad. 2012. #emotional tweets. In *Proceedings of the First Joint Conference on Lexical and Computational Semantics*. Association for Computational Linguistics, Stroudsburg, PA, USA, SemEval '12, pages 246–255.

Saif M. Mohammad. 2016. Sentiment analysis: Detecting valence, emotions, and other affectual states from text. In Herbert L. Meiselman, editor, *Emotion Measurement*. Woodhead Publishing, pages 201–237.

Saif M. Mohammad and Felipe Bravo-Marquez. 2017. WASSA-2017 shared task on emotion intensity. In *Proceedings of the Workshop on Computational Approaches to Subjectivity, Sentiment and Social Media Analysis (WASSA)*. Copenhagen, Denmark.

Jeffrey Pennington, Richard Socher, and Christopher D. Manning. 2014. Glove: Global vectors for word representation. In *Empirical Methods in Natural Language Processing (EMNLP)*. pages 1532–1543.

Soujanya Poria, Erik Cambria, Rajiv Bajpai, and Amir Hussain. 2017. A review of affective computing: From unimodal analysis to multimodal fusion. *Information Fusion* 37:98–125.

Bjorn Schuller, Bogdan Vlasenko, Dejan Arsic, Gerhard Rigoll, and Andreas Wendemuth. 2008. Combining speech recognition and acoustic word emotion models for robust text-independent emotion recognition. In *Multimedia and Expo, 2008 IEEE International Conference on*. IEEE, pages 1333–1336.

Nitish Srivastava, Geoffrey Hinton, Alex Krizhevsky, Ilya Sutskever, and Ruslan Salakhutdinov. 2014. Dropout: A simple way to prevent neural networks from overfitting. *The Journal of Machine Learning Research* 15(1):1929–1958.

Martin Wöllmer, Florian Eyben, Stephan Reiter, Björn Schuller, Cate Cox, Ellen Douglas-Cowie, and Roddy Cowie. 2008. Abandoning emotion classes-towards continuous emotion recognition with modelling of long-range dependencies. In *Ninth Annual Conference of the International Speech Communication Association*.

Chung-Hsien Wu, Ze-Jing Chuang, and Yu-Chung Lin. 2006. Emotion recognition from text using semantic labels and separable mixture models. *ACM transactions on Asian language information processing (TALIP)* 5(2):165–183.

---

[9]https://github.com/MixedEmotions/05_emotion_wassa_nuig
[10]https://hub.docker.com/r/mixedemotions/05_emotion_wassa_nuig/

Unsupervised Aspect Term Extraction with B-LSTM & CRF using Automatically Labelled Datasets

Athanasios Giannakopoulos, Claudiu Musat, Andreea Hossmann
and **Michael Baeriswyl**
Artificial Intelligence and Machine Learning Group — Swisscom AG
`firstName.lastName@swisscom.com`

Abstract

Aspect Term Extraction (ATE) identifies opinionated aspect terms in texts and is one of the tasks in the SemEval Aspect Based Sentiment Analysis (ABSA) contest. The small amount of available datasets for supervised ATE and the costly human annotation for aspect term labelling give rise to the need for unsupervised ATE. In this paper, we introduce an architecture that achieves top-ranking performance for supervised ATE. Moreover, it can be used efficiently as feature extractor and classifier for unsupervised ATE. Our second contribution is a method to automatically construct datasets for ATE. We train a classifier on our automatically labelled datasets and evaluate it on the human annotated SemEval ABSA test sets. Compared to a strong rule-based baseline, we obtain a dramatically higher *F-score* and attain precision values above 80%. Our unsupervised method beats the supervised ABSA baseline from SemEval, while preserving high precision scores.

1 Introduction

For many years now, companies are offering users the possibility of adding reviews in the form of sentences or small paragraphs. Reviews can be beneficial for both customers and companies. On the one hand, people can make better decisions by getting insights about available products and solutions. One the other hand, companies are interested in understanding how and what customers think about their products, which helps in employing marketing solutions and correction strategies. To this end, performing an automated analysis of the user opinions becomes a crucial issue.

Performing sentiment analysis to detect the overall polarity of a sentence or paragraph comes with two major disadvantages. First, sentiment analysis on sentence (or paragraph) level does not fulfill the purpose of getting more accurate and precise information. The polarity refers to a broader context, instead of pinpointing specific targets. Secondly, many sentences or paragraphs contain opposing polarities towards distinct targets, making it impossible to assign an accurate overall polarity.

The need for identifying aspect terms and their respective polarity gave rise to the Aspect Based Sentiment Analysis (ABSA), where the task is first to extract aspects or features of an entity (i.e. Aspect Term Extraction or ATE[1]) from a given text, and second to determine the sentiment polarity (SP), if any, towards each aspect of that entity. The importance of ABSA led to the creation of the ABSA task in the SemEval[2] contest in 2014 (Pontiki et al., 2014).

Supervised ATE using human annotated datasets leads to high performance for aspect term detection on unseen data, however it has two major drawbacks. First, the size of the labelled datasets is quite small, reducing the performance of the classifiers. Second, human annotation is a very slow and costly procedure.

The drawbacks of supervised ATE can be tackled using unsupervised ATE. The size of the datasets can be significantly increased using targets from publicly available reviews (e.g. *Amazon* or *Yelp*). Reviews are opinion texts and contain plenty of opinionated aspect terms, which makes them perfect candidates for constructing new datasets for ATE. With respect to the second drawback, an au-

---

[1] Also known as Opinion Term Extraction (OTE).

[2] The SemEval (Semantic Evaluation) contest is an ongoing series of evaluations of computational semantic analysis systems.

180

Proceedings of the 8th Workshop on Computational Approaches to Subjectivity, Sentiment and Social Media Analysis, pages 180–188
Copenhagen, Denmark, September 7–11, 2017. ©2017 Association for Computational Linguistics

tomated data labelling process with high precision can replace the slow and error-prone human annotation procedure.

We innovate by performing ATE starting from opinion texts (e.g. reviews). This is a completely unsupervised task since there are no labels to explicitly pinpoint that certain tokens of the text are aspect terms. Reviews may contain labels (e.g. number of stars in a 1-5 star rating system) which are related to their overall polarity. However, such labels are not useful for ATE.

In this work, we present a classifier, which can be used for feature extraction and aspect term detection for both unsupervised and supervised ATE. We validate its suitability for ATE by achieving top-ranking results for supervised ATE using the SemEval-2014 ABSA task datasets[3]. Then, we use it for unsupervised ATE.

Moreover, we contribute by introducing a new, completely automated, unsupervised and domain independent method for annotating raw opinion texts. Then, we use our classifier to perform unsupervised ATE by training it on the automatically labelled datasets obtained with our method. Against all expectations, our unsupervised method beats the supervised ABSA baseline from SemEval-2014, while achieving high precision scores. The latter is very important for unsupervised techniques since we wish to extract non-noisy aspect terms, i.e. minimize the number of false positives.

The rest of this paper is organized as follows. Section 2 presents the related work for ATE. Our approach for supervised and unsupervised ATE is described in Sections 3 and 4 respectively. Section 5 presents our experiments and results for both supervised and unsupervised ATE. Finally, Section 6 focuses on our conclusions and future work.

2 Related Work

Research in the area of both supervised and unsupervised ATE has flourished after the creation of the SemEval ABSA task in 2014. The winners of the SemEval-2014 ABSA contest (Toh and Wang, 2014) use supervised methods for ATE. They extract features, similar to those used in traditional Name Entity Recognition (NER) systems (Tkachenko and Simanovsky, 2012) using

the provided training sets. Moreover, they exploit external sources, such as the WordNet lexicographer files (Miller, 1995) and word clusters (e.g. Brown clusters (Turian et al., 2010) or K-means[4]). Toh and Su (2015) suggest using gazetteers (Kazama and Torisawa, 2008) and word embeddings (Mikolov et al., 2013) for ATE. Toh and Su (2016) use the probability output of an Recurrent Neural Network (RNN) to further enrich the feature space.

Independently of the feature extraction techniques, supervised ATE is treated as a sequential labelling task. Top-ranking participants in the SemEval ABSA contest use Conditional Random Fields (CRF) or Support Vector Machine (SVM) as sequential labelling classifiers (Toh and Wang, 2014; Toh and Su, 2015; Chernyshevich, 2014; Brun et al., 2014).

There is also related work with respect to unsupervised ATE. Liu et al. (2015) exploit syntactic rules to automatically detect aspect terms. (Garcia-Pablos et al., 2015; Garcia-Pablos and Rigau, 2014) use a graph representation to describe the interactions between aspect terms and opinion words in raw text. Graph nodes are ranked using PageRank and high-ranked nodes are used to create a set of aspect terms. Then, they use this set to annotate unseen data by simply performing exact or lemma matching.

Systems similar to (Hercig et al., 2016; Yin et al., 2016; Soujanya et al., 2016) perform semi-supervised ATE since they use human annotated datasets for training but enrich their feature space using features extracted by exploiting large unlabelled corpora. Pavlopoulos and Androutsopoulos (2015) present a method for constructing new datasets for ATE, however they use non-standard evaluation metrics. Finally, systems like (Garcia-Pablos et al., 2017) focus on classifying the aspect terms into categories. We do not compare against such systems, since they do not perform the same task and are not equivalent to ours.

In all but one[5] aforementioned cases, the evaluation of the model is performed using the *F-score*, as defined in (Pontiki et al., 2014). In case of unsupervised ATE, achieving higher precision is more important than higher recall as highlighted in (Liu et al., 2015).

---

[3]The SemEval ABSA datasets contain human annotation for ATE for both the laptop and the restaurant domains only in 2014.

[4]https://en.wikipedia.org/wiki/
K-means_clustering

[5]Pavlopoulos and Androutsopoulos (2015) use a non-standard definition of precision and recall.

We perform both supervised and unsupervised ATE using a model that utilizes continuous word representations and performs feature extraction and sequential labelling simultaneously while training. In case of supervised ATE, the training datasets are those of the SemEval ABSA task (human annotated). In case of unsupervised ATE, we annotate raw opinion texts (e.g. reviews) with a completely automated and unsupervised process, which we introduce. To the best of our knowledge, we are the first to train a classifier using an automatically labelled dataset and perform evaluation on human annotated datasets.

3 Supervised Aspect Term Extraction

The ATE task can be modelled as a token-based classification task, where labels are assigned to the tokens of a sequence, depending on whether they are aspect terms or not. For supervised ATE, we apply a classification pipeline that consists of 3 steps: (i) data preprocessing, (ii) model training and (iii) model evaluation.

The feature extraction is performed from a two-layer bidirectional long short-term memory (B-LSTM) network while the model is training, similar to the way a Convolutional Neural Network (CNN) extracts features while performing image classification. Therefore, we do not explicitly include this step in the aforementioned pipeline.

3.1 Data Preprocessing

We break down each sentence into tokens using the spaCy parser[6] and follow the traditional IOB format (short for Inside, Outside, Beginning) for sequential labelling. Tokens that represent the aspect terms of the sentence are labelled with B. In case an aspect term consists of multiple tokens, the first token receives the B label and the rest receive the I label. Tokens that are not aspect terms are labelled with O. Given the sentence "The internal speakers are amazing." with target "internal speakers", the labelling would be as follows: (The|O) (internal|B) (speakers|I) (are|O) (amazing|O) (.|O).

3.2 Classifier Architecture

We employ a two-layer B-LSTM to extract features for each token, which are used by a CRF for token-based classification. Features are created by exploiting the word morphology and the structure

of the sentence. The architecture is depicted in Fig. 1 and is inspired by the NER system presented in (Yang et al., 2016). However, we employ LSTM cells and use word embeddings from fastText[7].

First B-LSTM layer: Randomly initialized character embeddings of each token are given as input into the first B-LSTM layer, which aims at learning new word embeddings. The first and second directions (left $\rightarrow$ right and left $\leftarrow$ right) of the first B-LSTM layer are responsible for learning word embeddings by exploiting the prefix and the suffix of each token respectively.

Second B-LSTM layer: For each token of a sentence, we create a feature vector by combining (i) the extracted word embeddings from the first B-LSTM layer and (ii) pre-trained word embeddings using fastText. These feature vectors are given as input to the second B-LSTM layer, which extracts a feature vector for each token by exploiting the structure of the sentence. Similar to the first B-LSTM layer, the first and second directions are responsible for extracting features using the previous and the next tokens of each word.

CRF layer: The final layer uses the extracted feature vectors in order to perform sequential labelling.

4 Unsupervised Aspect Term Extraction

The human annotation process — required to identify aspect terms in small sentences and construct datasets for supervised ATE — comes at a high cost, mainly for two reasons:

1. Human annotated datasets typically consist of a few thousand sentences[8] extracted from large corpora of domain-specific reviews. The **small amount of data** reduces the performance of classifiers.

2. **Human annotation** is very slow, costly and risky. Annotators may introduce noise in the datasets by labelling words incorrectly, either because they are sloppy workers or because they do not know exactly what aspect terms are. For example, given the sentence "Works well, and I am extremely happy to be back to an apple OS.", human annotators may consider the word "works" as a target[9]. However, aspect terms are nouns and noun

---

[7]https://github.com/facebookresearch/fastText

[8]The datasets of the SemEval ABSA task consist of approximately 3000 sentences for English.

[9]Example taken from the golden annotated dataset for laptop reviews of the SemEval-2014 ABSA task.

---

[6]https://spacy.io/docs/

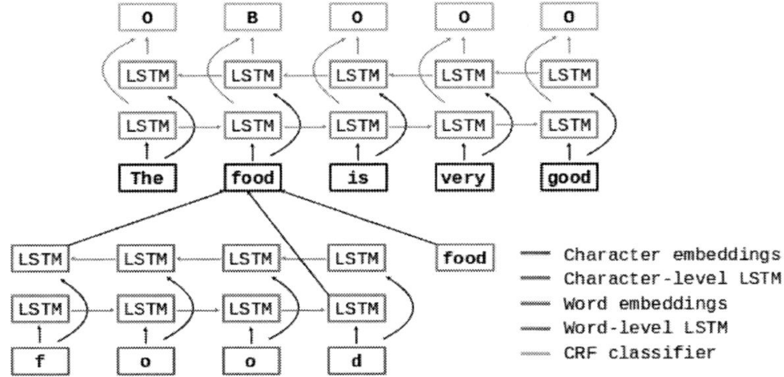

Figure 1: Sequential labelling using B-LSTM & CRF classifier.

phrases (Liu et al., 2015), therefore the verb "works" should not be considered as a target. We employ unsupervised ATE in order to overcome both problems. We tackle the first problem by using large datasets of opinion texts (e.g. reviews). Such datasets are ideal for ATE since they contain a plethora of opinionated aspect terms. In order to tackle the second problem, we introduce and use an automated and unsupervised method for labelling the tokens of the aforementioned datasets using the IOB format. We consider only noun and noun phrases as candidate aspect terms and focus on token labelling with high precision in order to reduce falsely annotated aspect terms. In that way, we minimize the cost, the time and the mistakes introduced by the human annotation process.

We use the publicly available datasets of *Amazon* and *Yelp* for laptop and restaurant reviews respectively and perform some data cleaning such as removing URLs from the reviews.

4.1 Automated Data Labelling

Using raw opinion texts (e.g. reviews) for ATE is a completely unsupervised task since there are no labels to explicitly pinpoint that certain tokens of the text are aspect terms. Reviews frequently contain labels (e.g. number of stars in a 1-5 star rating system) related to their overall polarity but these are not useful for ATE.

Our goal is to label each token of the unlabelled opinion texts in an automated way using the IOB format with unsupervised methods. While labelling aspect terms, we focus on high precision, a property that guarantees that the resulting datasets will contain as little noisy aspect terms as possible. The importance of high precision is also high-

lighted in (Liu et al., 2015), where authors construct syntactic rules primarily by focusing on this criterion.

Algorithm 1 describes the automated data labelling method. First, we create a list of quality phrases and prune it using a desired threshold value. Then, we iterate through all sentences and annotate tokens that obey certain syntactic rules as aspect terms. We repeat this procedure for multiword aspect terms and finally label the tokens using the IOB format.

Algorithm 1 Automated Data Labelling

1: $qual\_phrases = run\_autophrase(corpus)$
2: $candidates = prune(qual\_phrases, q_{th})$
3: **for** sentence **in** corpus **do**
4:     labels = []
5:     **for** token **in** sentence **do**
6:         **if** token **in** candidates **then**
7:             $l = get\_label(token, rules, lexicon)$
8:             $labels.append(l)$
9:     $assign\_iob\_tags(sentence, labels)$

4.1.1 Quality Phrase List

We start by building a sorted list of the form $(quality\,phrase, q)$, where $q \in [0, 1]$ represents the quality value of each phrase. The quality phrases — which we use as candidate aspect terms — are *n-grams* that appear in the raw review corpora and exceed a minimum support threshold[10]. The list of quality phrases is built by applying the AutoPhrase algorithm (Shang et al., 2017) on the review datasets for laptops and restaurants. The quality of each phrase is determined via a

---

[10]Support is an indication of how frequently the *n-gram* appears in the dataset.

classification task with decision trees that takes into account a list of high quality phrases using *Wikipedia*. The values of the features (e.g. *tf-idf*) used in the decision trees to predict the quality of each phrase are more informative when the provided corpora are domain dependent. Therefore, we apply AutoPhrase on each dataset separately, rather than combining the two datasets.

The extracted quality phrases, together with a set of syntactic rules, contribute in the automated data labelling process, which is based on 3 pillars:

1. a sentiment lexicon
2. a pruned list of quality phrases
3. syntactic rules able to capture aspect terms

Existing ATE systems (Garcia-Pablos et al., 2015), although unsupervised, exploit also syntactic rules derived from supervised tools (e.g. parsers). Moreover, they require domain-dependent human input (e.g. seed words) to perform double-propagation. We avoid that by using a sentiment lexicon.

4.1.2 Sentiment Lexicon

In many cases, aspect terms have modifiers (e.g. "This is a great screen") or are objects of verbs (e.g. "I love the screen of this laptop") that express a sentiment. Therefore, we make use of a sentiment lexicon[11], which is necessary in order to perform a look-up on whether modifiers and verbs express a sentiment or not.

4.1.3 Pruned Quality Phrases

We prune our quality phrases since they contain both true and noisy aspect term candidates. More concretely, we filter the list of quality phrases in order to keep *n-grams* with a quality above a certain threshold.

We present an example to show the value of the pruning step. The list of quality phrases extracted using the *Amazon* review dataset on laptops contains the *1-gram* "couch" and the *2-gram* "touch pad" with quality 0.67 and 0.95 respectively. However, the presence of the word "couch" as an aspect term in laptop reviews is completely arbitrary. Therefore, we prune the list of quality phrases using an empirical quality threshold of $q_{th} = 0.7$ and $q_{th} = 0.6$ for the laptop and restaurant domain respectively. We set these thresholds manually after inspecting the lists of qual-

---

[11] We use the sentiment lexicon of Bing Liu:
`https://www.cs.uic.edu/~liub/FBS/`
`sentiment-analysis.html`

ity phrases and detecting the quality value under which a lot of domain-irrelevant candidate aspect terms appear.

While the pruning step removes irrelevant phrases, as shown above, it also means that *n-grams* such as "set up", which are true aspect term candidates are removed from the list due to low quality ($q_{set\ up} = 0.32$). However, reducing noisy aspect term candidates (e.g. "couch" with $q = 0.67$) is more important than keeping all aspect term candidates since we wish to annotate aspect terms with high precision.

We can make the data labelling method completely automated by setting a fixed quality threshold q_{th} for pruning the list of quality phrases. We highlight that a fixed threshold of $q_{th} = 0.7$ leads to a good — but not optimal — trade-off between high precision values and good *F-score* for ATE.

4.1.4 Syntactic Rules for ATE

The pruned quality phrases and the sentiment lexicon are combined with syntactic rules in order to extract aspect terms from sentences. Before applying any syntactic rule, we validate if a token is a potential aspect term by checking if it (i) is not a stopword, (ii) is present in the pruned quality phrases and (iii) has a POS tag that is present in [NOUN, PRON, PROPN, ADJ, ADP, CONJ]. Table 1 tabulates all rules used for ATE and gives examples of reviews with the respective extracted aspect terms. For simplicity, we adopt a syntactic rule notation similar to the one used in (Liu et al., 2015). The functions used in Table 1 have the following interpretation:

- $depends(d, t_i, t_j)$ is true if the syntactic dependency between the tokens t_i and t_j is d.
- $opinion\_word(t_i)$ is true if the token t_i is in the sentiment lexicon.
- $mark\_target(t_i)$ means that we mark the token t_i as aspect term.
- $is\_aspect(t_i)$ is true if the token t_i is already marked as aspect term.

4.1.5 Language and Domain Adaptation

The automated data labelling method requires adaptation in order to be used in different languages. More concretely, we need to adapt (i) the syntactic rules of Table 1, (ii) the sentiment lexicon and (iii) the tools required from Autophrase (e.g. part-of-speech tagger) to the target language. We can use the automated data labelling method for ATE dataset construction in a completely

Rules	Example	Extracted Targets
$depends(dobj, t_i, t_j)$ **and** $opinion\_word(t_j)$ **then** $mark\_target(t_i)$	I like the screen	screen
$depends(nsubj, t_i, t_j)$ **and** $depends(acomp, t_k, t_j)$ **and** $opinion\_word(t_k)$ **then** $mark\_target(t_i)$	The internal speakers are amazing	internal speakers
$depends(nsubj, t_i, t_j)$ **and** $depends(advmod, t_j, t_j)$ **and** $opinion\_word(t_k)$ **then** $mark\_target(t_i)$	The touchpad works perfectly	touchpad
$depends(pobj$ **or** $dobj, t_i, t_j)$ **and** $depends(amod, t_k, t_i)$ **and** $opinion\_word(t_k)$ **then** $mark\_target(t_i)$	This laptop has great price	price
$depends(cc$ **or** $conj, t_i, t_j)$ **and** $is\_aspect(t_j)$ **then** $mark\_target(t_i)$	Screen and speakers are awful	screen speakers
$depends(compound, t_i, t_j)$ **and** $is\_aspect(t_j)$ **then** $mark\_target(t_i)$	The wifi card is not good	wifi card

Table 1: Syntactic rules for aspect term extraction.

domain-independent fashion. To do so, we only need to set the pruning threshold q_{th} of the quality phrase list to a fixed value (Section 4.1.3). Our experiments reveal that setting $q_{th} = 0.7$ results in a good trade-off between high precision and *F-score*, independently of the laptop or the restaurant domain.

4.2 Model Training and Evaluation

We train a B-LSTM & CRF classifier to perform unsupervised ATE for both domains using the automatically labelled datasets constructed in Section 4.1. The classifier is evaluated on the human annotated test datasets of the SemEval-2014 ABSA contest.

5 Experiments and Results

We perform experiments for supervised and unsupervised ATE in the laptop and the restaurant domain and evaluate our classifier using the CoNLL[12] *F-score*. Compared to other supervised learning methods, we reach the performance of SemEval-2014 ABSA winners in the restaurant domain. For laptops, our supervised system exceeds the best *F-score* of the SemEval-2014 ABSA contest by approximately 3%. With respect to unsupervised ATE, our technique achieves (i) very high precision and (ii) an *F-score* that exceeds the supervised baseline of the SemEval ABSA.

5.1 Experiments for Supervised ATE

For supervised learning, we perform experiments using the human annotated training and test sets provided by the SemEval-2014 ABSA contest for

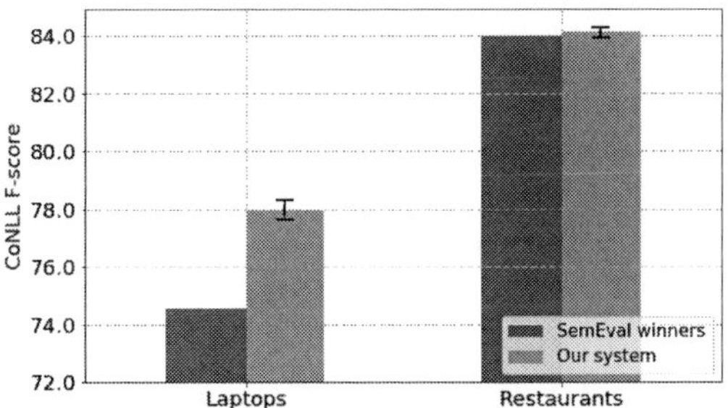

Figure 2: Results for supervised ATE using the B-LSTM & CRF architecture. We compare against the winners of the SemEval-2014 ABSA contest.

the laptop and restaurant domain. Our classifier uses the B-LSTM & CRF architecture presented in Fig. 1 and its implementation is based on (Dernoncourt et al., 2017).

We use a random 80-20% split on the original training set of SemEval-2014 ABSA contest in order to create a new train and validation set. We keep the test set for our final evaluation. For most of the parameters, we use the default values of (Dernoncourt et al., 2017). However, we use the *adam* optimizer with learning rate $\alpha = 0.01$ and a batch size of 64. Moreover, we use the pre-trained word embeddings of fastText.

We train the classifier using the reduced training set for a maximum number of 100 epochs. After each epoch, we evaluate our model using the CoNLL *F-score* on the validation set. Moreover, we use early stopping with a patience of 20 epochs. This means that the experiment terminates earlier if the CoNLL *F-score* of the validation set does not improve for 20 consecutive epochs. At the end of each experiment we choose the model of the epoch that gives the best performance on the

---

[12] http://www.cnts.ua.ac.be/conll2003/

validation set and make predictions on the test set. We repeat the aforementioned procedure for 50 experiments and present the experimental results for both domains in Fig 2.

The *F-score* of the SemEval-2014 ABSA winners is 74.55 and 84.01 for the laptop and the restaurant domain respectively. The B-LSTM & CRF classifier achieves an *F-score* of 77.96 ± 0.38 for laptops and an *F-score* of 84.12 ± 0.2 for restaurants with a confidence interval of 95%. With our performance, we would have surely won in the laptop domain and probably also in the restaurant domain.

5.2 Experiments for Unsupervised ATE

We also perform experiments for ATE with unsupervised learning. For training, we use the automatically labelled datasets (hereafter denoted as ALD) obtained using the methodology described in Section 4.1 with $q_{th} = 0.7$ and $q_{th} = 0.6$ for the laptop and the restaurant domain respectively. For testing, we use the human labelled datasets (hereafter denoted as HLD) of the SemEval-2014 ABSA task.

Our main goal is to evaluate our unsupervised technique on human annotated datasets. To the best of our knowledge, the largest available human annotated datasets for ATE are provided by the SemEval ABSA task and contain laptop and restaurant reviews. Therefore, our analysis focuses only on these two domains.

We start by creating a rule-based baseline model to make predictions for the HLD simply by applying techniques presented in Section 4.1. This baseline (presented in the following section) does not rely on any machine learning techniques for the annotation procedure.

We aim at beating the rule-based baseline by using machine learning. To this end, we use the ALD to train our classifier. For unsupervised ATE, we run two types of experiments. The first one uses the traditional IOB labelling format and is stricter. The second one is more relaxed and uses only B and O labels (i.e. I labels are converted to B). The intuition is that aspect terms can be identified by separating B and I labels from O. Therefore, I and B labels are treated equally against O.

Rule-based Baseline Model

The methodology described in Section 4.1 is used in order to make predictions on the HLD for laptops and restaurants, i.e. the rule-based baseline

	Labels: IOB		Labels: OB		
	P	**F$_1$**	**P**	**F$_1$**	
Rule-based	65.13	24.35	76.65	23.76	
SVM	61.64	37.94	72.02	43.29	Laptops
B-LSTM & CRF	**66.67**	**42.09**	**74.51**	**44.37**	
SemEval		35.64			
Rule-based	84.26	28.74	96.67	27.37	
SVM	67.28	48.08	80.83	57.36	Restaurants
B-LSTM & CRF	**74.03**	**53.93**	**83.19**	**63.09**	
SemEval		47.15			

Table 2: Experiments for unsupervised ATE. We compare B-LSTM & CRF classifier against the rule-based baseline, an SVM classifier and the baseline of the SemEval-2014 ABSA contest.

model does not use any machine learning algorithm. During the annotation process, a token of the HLD is labelled as a target if (i) it belongs in the pruned quality phrases list and (ii) satisfies at least one of the rules in Table 1. A comparison between the predicted and the golden labels of the HLD gives a quality estimation of the syntactic rules we create and acts as a baseline.

SVM

We train a linear SVM classifier[13] in order to create a second baseline model that uses machine learning. For SVM, we use the baseline features presented in (Stratos and Collins, 2015) and build 1-0 feature vectors by exploiting the word morphology and the sentence structure (i.e. adjacent words of each token). The training and the evaluation are done using the ALD and the HLD respectively.

In addition, we wish to show the trade-off between precision and recall for different values of q_{th}. We perform experiments for different values of q_{th} and validate that the higher q_{th} the higher the precision and the lower the recall. For example, an SVM classifier trained on an ALD with $q_{th} = 0.7$ achieves an $F_1 = 39.63$ and $P = 71.54$ (Table 2 shows results for $q_{th} = 0.6$ for restaurants). We choose to keep $q_{th} = 0.6$ for the restaurant domain because we are interested in a good combination of high precision and *F-score*.

---

[13]We use the implementation of LIBLINEAR (Fan et al., 2008).

B-LSTM & CRF

We employ the B-LSTM & CRF classifier using the ALD as training set and the HLD as test set, i.e. the evaluation is performed on the human annotated datasets of SemEval-2014 ABSA task. In addition, we use the ABSA training sets of SemEval-2014 as validation sets.

The maximum number of epochs and the patience are set to 20 and 5 respectively. As stopping criterion, we simply choose the epoch that achieves the best *F-score* on the validation set. In all our experiments, we compare the performance of the B-LSTM & CRF classifier with the respective performance of the rule-based baseline and the SVM model. We do not report any confidence intervals for the B-LSTM & CRF classifier because the training time increases dramatically in the case of unsupervised ATE due to the increased size of the dataset. Conducting one experiment usually takes more than $15h$, which means that a round of at least 20 experiments, that would allow for defining confidence intervals, would be computationally intensive. For this reason, we leave the report of confidence intervals for unsupervised ATE for future work. However, we repeat up to 3 experiments for each case and verify that the CoNLL *F-score* and the precision are always higher compared to SVM. Results for the laptop domain can be visualized in Fig. 3. We do not present any figures for the restaurant domain since the learning curves are very similar to the ones of the laptop domain.

We draw several conclusions by observing the results tabulated in Table 2. First, the B-LSTM & CRF classifier achieves higher *F-score* for both domains compared to the rule-based baseline model and the SVM classifier. The *F-score* relative improvement between the rule-based baseline and the B-LSTM & CRF classifier is 73% and 88% for the laptop and the restaurant domain respectively. At the same time, we preserve high precision and attain values above 80%. Finally, our unsupervised method beats the supervised baseline *F-score* from SemEval ABSA.

6 Conclusion and Future Work

We present a B-LSTM & CRF classifier which we use for feature extraction and aspect term detection for both supervised and unsupervised ATE. We validate this classifier by performing supervised ATE and achieving top-ranking performance

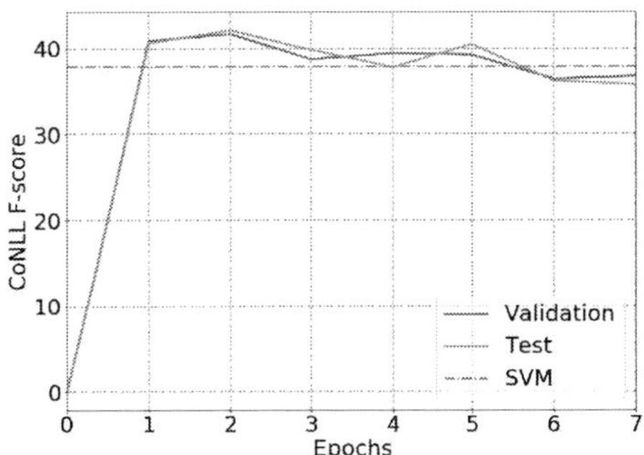

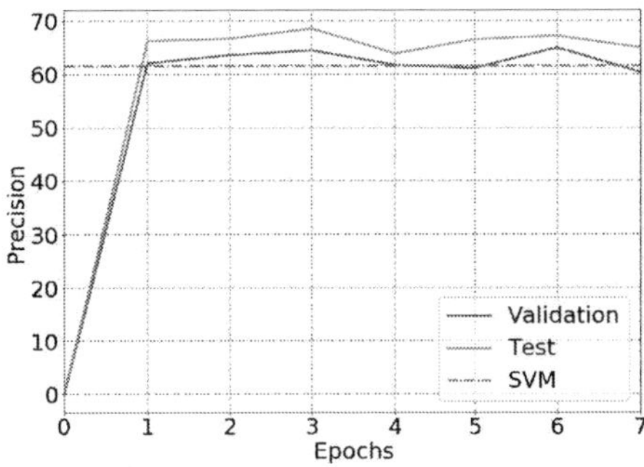

Figure 3: *F-score* (top) and precision (bottom) comparison between B-LSTM & CRF and SVM for unsupervised ATE in the laptop domain. B, I and O labels are used.

on the human annotated datasets of the SemEval-2014 ABSA contest for the laptop and restaurant domain. Moreover, we introduce a new, automated, unsupervised and domain independent method to label tokens of raw opinion texts as aspect terms with high precision. We use the automatically labelled datasets to train the B-LSTM & CRF classifier, which we evaluate on human annotated datasets. Against all odds, our unsupervised method beats the supervised ABSA baseline *F-score* from SemEval, while preserving high precision scores.

As future work, we plan to perform ATE for different domains (e.g. hotels) using our methods. Moreover, we plan to work towards adapting our techniques to multilingual datasets (e.g. French, Spanish, etc.). We would also investigate the idea of exploiting the available ratings (e.g. 1-5 stars) of the review datasets in order to construct new datasets for ATE. This would allow us to perform ATE with distant supervision.

References

Caroline Brun, Diana Nicoleta Popa, and Claude Roux. 2014. Xrce: Hybrid classification for aspect-based sentiment analysis. In *Proceedings of the 8th International Workshop on Semantic Evaluation (SemEval 2014)*.

Maryna Chernyshevich. 2014. IHS R&D Belarus: cross-domain extraction of product features using crf. In *Proceedings of the 8th International Workshop on Semantic Evaluation (SemEval 2014)*.

Franck Dernoncourt, Ji Young Lee, and Peter Szolovits. 2017. NeuroNER: an easy-to-use program for named-entity recognition based on neural networks .

Rong-En Fan, Kai-Wei Chang, Cho-Jui Hsieh, Xiang-Rui Wang, and Chih-Jen Lin. 2008. LIBLINEAR: A library for large linear classification. *Journal of Machine Learning Research* .

Aitor Garcia-Pablos, Montse Cuadros, and German Rigau. 2015. V3: Unsupervised aspect based sentiment analysis for semeval-2015 task 12.

Aitor Garcia-Pablos, Montse Cuadros, and German Rigau. 2017. W2VLDA: Almost unsupervised system for aspect based sentiment analysis .

Aitor Garcia-Pablos and German Rigau. 2014. Unsupervised acquisition of domain aspect terms for aspect based opinion mining.

Tomáš Hercig, Tomáš Brychcín, Lukáš Svoboda, Michal Konkol, and Josef Steinberger. 2016. Unsupervised methods to improve aspect-based sentiment analysis in Czech. *Computación y Sistemas* .

Junichi Kazama and Kentaro Torisawa. 2008. Inducing gazetteers for named entity recognition by large-scale clustering of dependency relations. *Proceedings of ACL-08: HLT* .

Qian Liu, Zhiqiang Gao, Bing Liu, and Yuanlin Zhang. 2015. Automated rule selection for opinion target extraction .

Tomas Mikolov, Ilya Sutskever, Kai Chen, Greg Corrado, and Jeffrey Dean. 2013. Distributed representations of words and phrases and their compositionality. In *NIPS Proceedings*.

George A. Miller. 1995. Wordnet: A lexical database for english. In *Communications of the ACM*.

John Pavlopoulos and Ion Androutsopoulos. 2015. Aspect term extraction for sentiment analysis: New datasets, new evaluation measures and an improved unsupervised method.

Maria Pontiki, Harris Papageorgiou, Dimitrios Galanis, Ion Androutsopoulos, John Pavlopoulos, and Suresh Manandhar. 2014. Semeval-2014 task 4: Aspect based sentiment analysis. In *Proceedings of the 8th International Workshop on Semantic Evaluation (SemEval 2014)*.

Jingbo Shang, Jialu Liu, Meng Jiang, Xiang Ren, Clare R. Voss, and Jiawei Han. 2017. Automated phrase mining from massive text corpora. *CoRR* abs/1702.04457.

Poria Soujanya, Cambria Erik, and Gelbukh Alexander. 2016. Aspect extraction for opinion mining with a deep convolutional neural network. *Knowledge-Based Systems* .

Karl Stratos and Michael Collins. 2015. Simple semi-supervised pos tagging .

Maksim Tkachenko and Andrey Simanovsky. 2012. Named entity recognition: Exploring features .

Zhiqiang Toh and Jian Su. 2015. NLANG: supervised machine learning system for aspect category classification and opinion target extraction. In *Proceedings of the 9th International Workshop on Semantic Evaluation (SemEval 2015)*.

Zhiqiang Toh and Jian Su. 2016. NLANG at semeval-2016 task 5: Improving aspect based sentiment analysis using neural network features. In *Proceedings of SemEval-2016*.

Zhiqiang Toh and Wenting Wang. 2014. DLIREC: aspect term extraction and term polarity classification system. In *Proceedings of the 8th International Workshop on Semantic Evaluation (SemEval 2014)*.

Joseph Turian, Lev Ratinov, and Yoshua Bengio. 2010. Word representations: A simple and general method for semi-supervised learning.

Zhilin Yang, Ruslan Salakhutdinov, and William W. Cohen. 2016. Multi-task cross-lingual sequence tagging from scratch .

Yichun Yin, Furu Wei, Li Dong, Kaimeng Xu, Ming Zhang, and Ming Zhou. 2016. Unsupervised word and dependency path embeddings for aspect term extraction .

PLN-PUCRS at EmoInt-2017:
Psycholinguistic features for emotion intensity prediction in tweets

Henrique D. P. dos Santos, Renata Vieira
Pontifical Catholic University of Rio Grande do Sul
Porto Alegre - Brazil
`henrique.santos.003@acad.pucrs.br, renata.vieira@pucrs.br`

Abstract

Linguistic Inquiry and Word Count (LIWC) is a rich dictionary that map words into several psychological categories such as Affective, Social, Cognitive, Perceptual and Biological processes. In this work, we have used LIWC psycholinguistic categories to train regression models and predict emotion intensity in tweets for the EmoInt-2017 task. Results show that LIWC features may boost emotion intensity prediction on the basis of a low dimension set.

1 Introduction

In Natural Language Processing tasks many techniques rely on statistical methods to classify texts based on word distribution. Sentiment analysis also takes advantage of this kind of approach to detect emotion or polarity in sentences (Liu and Zhang, 2012). Twitter became the main source of data to extract sentiment information in social media because of its data characteristics: huge amount of small sentences distributed in a timeline, which are easily gathered.

In Twitter, sentiment classification intends to extract polarity or emotion with regards to a specific subject. The polarity defines a positive or negative valency and the emotion usually is modeled over Ekman's six basic emotions: joy, anger, sadness, happiness, surprise, fear and disgust (Ekman, 1992).

This work intends to score tweets for emotion intensities, by giving a real value for each tweet (Mohammad and Bravo-Marquez, 2017a), as part of the EmoInt-2017 task. The goal of the task is, given a tweet, to predict the intensity of a specific emotion expressed in it (Mohammad and Bravo-Marquez, 2017b). The intensity score is a real-valued score between 0 and 1. The minimum possible score 0 stands for feeling the least amount of emotion and the maximum possible score 1 stands for feeling the maximum amount of emotion. This shared task analyze the emotion: anger, fear, joy and sadness. We show an approach that can score emotions based on psycholinguistic features.

The rest of this paper is organized as follows. In Section 2 we describe LIWC, the well-known psycholinguistic dictionary used in our experiments, Section 3 covers some previous work that use psycholinguistic features to classify text. Section 4 presents the proposed techniques and their evaluation. In Section 5 we discuss the most informative LIWC categories for each emotion set and finally, we conclude in Section 6 with future work.

2 LIWC Categories

Linguistic inquiry and word count (LIWC), besides being a software, is a psycholinguistic lexicon created by psychologists with focus on studying the various emotional, cognitive, and structural components present in individuals' verbal and written speech samples (Pennebaker et al., 2015). This resource allows non-specialists to retrieve psychological statistics in text, and to search for patterns that are able to detect differences in group of documents.

The first LIWC version was developed as part of an exploratory study of language and disclosure (Pennebaker, 1993). The second (LIWC2001) and third (LIWC2007) versions updated the original with an expanded dictionary and a modern software design (Pennebaker et al., 2001, 2007).The most recent evolution, LIWC2015 (Pennebaker et al., 2015), has significantly altered both the dictionary and software options. LIWC 2007 has been available as a open source dictionary.

LIWC dictionary classifies words in a variety

Proceedings of the 8th Workshop on Computational Approaches to Subjectivity, Sentiment and Social Media Analysis, pages 189–192
Copenhagen, Denmark, September 7–11, 2017. ©2017 Association for Computational Linguistics

Category	Examples
Affective	happy, cried, love, hurt
Social	mate, talk, they, dad
Cognitive	cause, know, ought, think
Perceptual	look, heard, feeling, view
Biological	eat, blood, pain, hand

Table 1: LIWC psychological process examples

of psychological categories based on psychologists studies and observations (Tausczik and Pennebaker, 2010). LIWC assigns words into one of four high-level categories: linguistic processes, psychological processes, personal concerns, and spoken categories. These are further subdivided into a three-level hierarchy. The taxonomy ranges across topics (e.g., health and money), emotional responses (e.g., negative emotion) and processes not captured by either, such as cognition (e.g., discrepancy and certainty). The words carry rich information about the author's personality, sentiments, style, topics, and social relationships.

The main categories in LIWC dictionary are the following:

- Linguistic Dimensions and Other Grammar

- Affective, Social, Cognitive, Perceptual and Biological processes

- Drives, Time orientations and Relativity

- Personal concerns and Informal language

These categories are then specialized in other sub-categories, as in Affective processes sub-categorized as Positive and Negative Emotions, Anxiety, Anger and Sadness.

Some examples of words in such categories can be found in Table 1. These categories were translated to other languages (Balage Filho et al., 2013), and have been used to compare writing styles between languages and countries (Afroz et al., 2012). In this paper we use this dictionary for emotion prediction.

3   Related Work

There has been a lot of research seeking text classification in the scope of social media. Here we focus on the works that use LIWC psycholinguistic features to solve some of those problems.

Nguyen et al. (2013) use the LIWC psychological lexicon to distinguish blog posts of the autism community from others. They analyze the frequency distribution differences in psychological processes between those communities and are able to detect them with 79% of accuracy using machine learning. Mohtasseb and Ahmed (2009) use psychological features to find online diaries in blogs. Iyyer et al. (2014) classifies political ideology between liberal and conservatives in social media. Santos et al. (2017) took advantage of LIWC dictionary to analyze and detect personal stories posts in Brazilian blogs with 81% of precision over thousands of posts.

LIWC Psycholinguistic features are also used to define the writer personality, as Poria et al. (2013) shown in their work. Besides, it can be used to identify mental issues in online forum communities (Cohan et al., 2016).

There is a great potential for psychologically oriented dictionaries and here we use it to score emotions values in tweets together with Support Vector Machines algorithms.

4   Psycholinguistic Features

For evaluating the prediction property of psycholinguistic categories, each tweet is converted to a vector of 64 positions, one for each LIWC category, explained previously. Each LIWC category represents the frequency distribution of this category appearance in the specific tweet. Each word could fit multiples categories, e.g. the word "admits" belongs to categories: Common verbs, Present tense, Social processes, Cognitive processes and Insight.

For our experiments we use Python library Scikit-Learn (Pedregosa et al., 2011) machine learning algorithms. We ran cross-fold validation with 10 folds.

We use Support Vector Regression (SVR) tunning the RBF, Linear, Linear SVR and Sigmoid kernel parameters C (the penalty parameter) and γ (the kernel width hyperparameter) performing full grid search over the 800 combinations of exponentially spaced parameter pairs (C, γ) following (Hsu et al., 2003). For Gradient Boosting Regression we run a simple grid search. Only the best results of each algorithm, using Spearman rank correlation, are shown in Table 2.

The best results were obtained using Gradient Boosting Regression, Linear SVR and SVR with linear kernel, all with default parameters. All three algorithms are highlighted in Table 2 be-

Algorithm	joy	anger	sadness	fear	Avg Score
SVR k=Linear	0.431	0.502	0.557	0.441	**0.483**
Linear SVR	0.428	0.504	0.556	0.443	**0.482**
Gradient Boosting	0.420	0.519	0.565	0.420	**0.481**
SVR k=RBF	0.399	0.445	0.517	0.407	0.442
SVR k=Sigmoid	-0.016	-0.085	-0.108	0.069	-0.035

Table 2: Spearman Score running each algorithm over emotions sets

Joy	Anger	Sadness	Fear
Total function words	Auxiliary verbs	1st pers singular	Anxiety
Negations	Present tense	Social processes	Sadness
Cognitive processes	Negations	Sadness	Feel
Discrepancy	Swear words	See	Ingestion
Tentative	Humans	Ingestion	Space
Exclusive	Relativity	Leisure	Death
Positive emotion			
Negative emotion			
Affective processes			
Anger			

Table 3: Top 10 LIWC most informative features

cause there is no statistical difference in the Spearman rank correlation.

In Scikit-learn library, SVR with linear kernel differs from Linear SVR because the last use *liblinear* rather than *libsvm*. The processing time and prediction score is better using *liblinear* then the generic SVM library, as we see in Table 2.

After defining the regression algorithm and the best parameters, we built the model for each emotion dataset, based on the training set. Then we run each model for the test set and generate the output for evaluation. The LIWC resource, test dataset and scripts can be accessed in author's Github project page [1].

5 Most Informative Features

Using univariate linear regression tests, we tested the effect of a single regressor and listed the most informative LIWC features for each emotion tweet set. In Table 3 we show the top 10 features.

LIWC sub-categories such as *Positive and Negative Emotion, Affective and, Anger* are features with good prediction level for every emotion set. *Sadness* sub-category, as expect, is a good predictor for Sadness emotion intensity. *Positive and Negative Emotion* are categories that range a variety of words in LIWC dictionary, so, for a emotion

regression task, is expect that they have a good regression information. It is important to state that Anger is a subcategory of Negative Emotion.

Another interesting confirmation is *death, sadness* and *anxiety* categories as good predictors for **Fear** emotion set. *Anger* category appears as an informative feature for **Joy** emotion set, we will look further in the details of that to see whether it is informative due to a low feature value or something else. Also, we want to look further to explain *Negations* LIWC category as good predictor in **Joy** emotion set.

6 Conclusion and Further Work

Psycholinguistic features have been used to classify texts and sentences for a variety of tasks. Here we presented our system that makes use of such categories for emotion intensity prediction. Each word was mapped to several psychological categories and used as a feature vector.

In future work, we intend to study these categories with other well-known good predictors like Affective Tweets classifier (Bravo-Marquez et al., 2016). Also, psychological categories could improve the semantic information of word embedding vectors.

Acknowledgments

This work was partially supported by CAPES (Coordenação de Aperfeiçoamento de Pessoal de Nível Superior) Foundation (Brazil), PUCRS (Pontifícia Universidade Católica do Rio Grande do Sul) and UFRGS (Universidade Federal do Rio Grande do Sul).

References

Sadia Afroz, Michael Brennan, and Rachel Greenstadt. 2012. Detecting hoaxes, frauds, and deception in writing style online. In *Security and Privacy (SP), 2012 IEEE Symposium on*. IEEE, pages 461–475.

Pedro P Balage Filho, Thiago AS Pardo, and Sandra M Aluısio. 2013. An evaluation of the brazilian portuguese liwc dictionary for sentiment analysis. In *Proceedings of the 9th Brazilian Symposium in Information and Human Language Technology (STIL)*. pages 215–219.

Felipe Bravo-Marquez, Eibe Frank, Saif M Mohammad, and Bernhard Pfahringer. 2016. Determining word–emotion associations from tweets by multi-label classification. In *WI'16*. IEEE Computer Society, pages 536–539.

Arman Cohan, Sydney Young, and Nazli Goharian. 2016. Triaging mental health forum posts. In *Proceedings of the 3rd Workshop on Computational Linguistics and Clinical Psychology: From Linguistic Signal to Clinical Reality, San Diego, California, USA, June*. volume 16.

Paul Ekman. 1992. An argument for basic emotions. *Cognition & emotion* 6(3-4):169–200.

Chih-Wei Hsu, Chih-Chung Chang, Chih-Jen Lin, et al. 2003. A practical guide to support vector classification. *National Taiwan University* .

Mohit Iyyer, Peter Enns, Jordan Boyd-Graber, and Philip Resnik. 2014. Political ideology detection using recursive neural networks. In *Proceedings of the Association for Computational Linguistics*. pages 1113–1122.

Bing Liu and Lei Zhang. 2012. A survey of opinion mining and sentiment analysis. In *Mining text data*, Springer, pages 415–463.

Saif M. Mohammad and Felipe Bravo-Marquez. 2017a. Emotion intensities in tweets. In *Proceedings of the sixth joint conference on lexical and computational semantics (*Sem)*. Vancouver, Canada.

Saif M. Mohammad and Felipe Bravo-Marquez. 2017b. WASSA-2017 shared task on emotion intensity. In *Proceedings of the Workshop on Computational Approaches to Subjectivity, Sentiment and Social Media Analysis (WASSA)*. Copenhagen, Denmark.

Haytham Mohtasseb and Amr Ahmed. 2009. Mining online diaries for blogger identification. In *Proceedings of the World Congress on Engineering*. volume 1.

Thin Nguyen, Dinh Phung, and Svetha Venkatesh. 2013. Analysis of psycholinguistic processes and topics in online autism communities. In *Multimedia and Expo (ICME), 2013 IEEE International Conference on*. IEEE, pages 1–6.

F. Pedregosa, G. Varoquaux, A. Gramfort, V. Michel, B. Thirion, O. Grisel, M. Blondel, P. Prettenhofer, R. Weiss, V. Dubourg, J. Vanderplas, A. Passos, D. Cournapeau, M. Brucher, M. Perrot, and E. Duchesnay. 2011. Scikit-learn: Machine learning in Python. *Journal of Machine Learning Research* 12:2825–2830.

James W Pennebaker. 1993. Putting stress into words: Health, linguistic, and therapeutic implications. *Behaviour research and therapy* 31(6):539–548.

James W Pennebaker, Roger J Booth, and Martha E Francis. 2007. Linguistic inquiry and word count: Liwc [computer software]. *Austin, TX: liwc. net* .

James W Pennebaker, Ryan L Boyd, Kayla Jordan, and Kate Blackburn. 2015. The development and psychometric properties of liwc2015. Technical report, The University of Texas at Austin.

James W Pennebaker, Martha E Francis, and Roger J Booth. 2001. Linguistic inquiry and word count: Liwc 2001. *Mahway: Lawrence Erlbaum Associates* 71(2001):2001.

Soujanya Poria, Alexandar Gelbukh, Basant Agarwal, Erik Cambria, and Newton Howard. 2013. Common sense knowledge based personality recognition from text. In *Mexican International Conference on Artificial Intelligence*. Springer, pages 484–496.

Henrique D.P. dos Santos, Vinicius Woloszyn, and Renata Vieira. 2017. Portuguese personal story analysis and detection in blogs. In *Web Intelligence (WI), 2017 IEEE/WIC/ACM International Conference on*. IEEE, Leipzig, Germany.

Yla R Tausczik and James W Pennebaker. 2010. The psychological meaning of words: Liwc and computerized text analysis methods. *Journal of language and social psychology* 29(1):24–54.

Textmining at EmoInt-2017: A Deep Learning Approach to Sentiment Intensity Scoring of English Tweets

Hardik Meisheri and **Rupsa Saha** and **Priyanka Sinha** and **Lipika Dey**

`(hardik.meisheri,rupsa.s,priyanka27.s,lipika.dey)@tcs.com`

Abstract

This paper describes our approach to the Emotion Intensity shared task. A parallel architecture of Convolutional Neural Network (CNN) and Long short term memory networks (LSTM) alongwith two sets of features are extracted which aid the network in judging emotion intensity. Experiments on different models and various features sets are described and analysis on results has also been presented.

1 Introduction

Sentiment analysis is an area of active research in the field of natural language processing. It aims to identify the sentiment expressed by the author of some form of textual data. Apart from the entities available in text, identification of opinion, sentiment, nuances, sarcasm etc., provide important contextual clues that help in natural language understanding and more complex information extraction tasks. The strength of the emotions expressed in text help quantify and compare subjective expressions and can be used downstream as well. Traditional fact-based approaches are rule based and prove insufficient for modern-day NLP requirements especially with large amounts of polarized short, noisy text from social media platforms such as Twitter. Twitter has become a rich source of user opinions and spread of information on this social site has far reaching consequences. Emotion Intensity task in WASSA-2016 aims to explore various approaches of determining the intensity of certain emotions expressed by a speaker via a tweet (Mohammad and Bravo-Marquez, 2017). Our approach is to explore the use of a Deep Learning framework for the same.

A significant amount of research in Natural Language Processing focuses on identifying the sentiment polarity of a given text, rather than the degree to which a given emotion is present in a text. A similar task was proposed in SemEval 2016 Task 7, and on a smaller scale in SemEval-2015 Task 10 'Sentiment Analysis in Twitter' Subtask E (Rosenthal et al., 2015).

The data for this task consists of tweets across various domains, classified into four emotions : joy, sadness, anger and fear. The training data additionally carries a real-valued score between 0 and 1 per tweet, indicating the degree of the emotion (that the tweet is classified as) the present in the tweet.

2 Related Work

In SemEval 2016 Task 7 the objective was to attribute an intensity score to English and Arabic phrases (Kiritchenko et al., 2016). Mostly supervised methods were used, with a variety of features, including different sentiment lexicons, word embeddings, point wise mutual information (PMI) scores between terms (single words and multi-word phrases), lists of words which express negation, modifiers etc. Team ECNU (Wang et al., 2016) approached it as a ranking task, using Random Forest algorithm. UWB, iLab-Edinburgh and NileTMRG all treated the task as a regression problem, and had supervised approaches. UWB used Gaussian Regression (Hercig et al., 2016), while iLab-Edinburgh went in for linear regression (Refaee and Rieser, 2016). Team LSIS (Htait et al., 2016) had a completely unsupervised approach, using sentiment lexicons and PMI scores.

Similar approaches, that is, usage of sentiment lexicons in a supervised setup, word embeddings, etc. were also seen in the proposed systems of SemEval 2015 Task 10 (Subtask E) (Rosenthal et al., 2015).

193

Proceedings of the 8th Workshop on Computational Approaches to Subjectivity, Sentiment and Social Media Analysis, pages 193–199
Copenhagen, Denmark, September 7–11, 2017. ©2017 Association for Computational Linguistics

3 Methodology

3.1 Preprocessing

Text from tweets are inherently noisy. They contain twitter specific words along with hashtags and username mentions. Cleaning the text before further processing helps to generate better features and semantics. We employ the following preprocessing steps.

- **Hashtags** are important markers for determining sentiment or user intent. The "#" symbol is removed and the word itself is retained.

- **Username mentions**, i.e.words starting with "@", generally provide no information in terms of sentiment. Hence such terms are removed completely from the tweet. If however, the text contains multiple tweets as part of a single conversation, the user mentions would have been an important aspect.

- **Emoticons** (for example, ':(',':)', ':P' etc) are removed during embedding generation although they are retained while feature extraction.

- Extra spaces are removed.

3.2 Feature Generation

For extracting **Lexicon Features**, we follow the procedure as per the baseline system provided in the WASSA Emotion Intensity Task. The knowledge sources that have been used are: MPQA subjective lexicon (Wilson et al., 2005), Bing Liu lexicon (Ding et al., 2008), AFINN (Nielsen, 2011), Sentiment140 (Kiritchenko et al., 2014), NRC Hashtag Sentiment Lexicon (Mohammad and Kiritchenko, 2015), NRC Hashtag Emotion Association Lexicon (Mohammad et al., 2013), NRC Word-Emotion Association Lexicon (Mohammad and Turney, 2013), NRC-10 Expanded Lexicon (Bravo-Marquez et al., 2016) and the SentiWordNet (Esuli and Sebastiani, 2007). Two more features are calculated on the basis of emoticons (obtained from AFINN (Nielsen, 2011)) and negations present in the text.

Following the baseline system, we generate 45 features for each tweet, which we term as Feature Set A.

In addition to this, we use the **SentiNeuron** model proposed by (Radford et al., 2017) to generate another feature. It is an unsupervised method of generating sentiment signals. LSTM based network with 4096 units have been trained on a 82 million large Amazon reviews dataset to predict next word. Output of 2388th unit, which is sentiment signal is used as feature. This feature is then normalized between 0 to 1, and further referred to as Feature Set B.

Thus for each tweet, we arrive at 46 features generated as above. Parallel architecture of CNN and LSTM layers are used to extract important words as well as the temporal information contained in the sentence. Details of the parallel architecture are presented in subsection 3.6

3.3 Embeddings

The processed text is then converted to word embeddings. Converting text into word embeddings represents each word of the text into a d dimensional vector (Mikolov et al., 2013). We use available pre-trained embeddings which are trained on large data set. The following modules were used:

GloVe Word Embeddings - trained on 2 billion tweets from twitter (Pennington et al., 2014), vectors of 25, 50, 100 and 200 dimensions are provided as part of the pre-trained model. For this work, we use the 200 dimensional vectors. GloVe embeddings are used for the datasets corresponding to anger, fear and joy emotions.

Edinburgh Embeddings - trained on 10 million tweets for sentiment classification, they provide 400 dimensional vectors (Petrovic et al., 2010). We use them for sadness emotion.

Each tweet can further be divided in words, and we assume maximum number of words in any tweet be 35. This assumption is in line with the 140 characters limit on each tweet. Each tweet is thus represented as a $\langle 35 \times d \rangle$ matrix, where d is the output dimension of embeddings of a single word.

3.4 CNN Model

Convolution Neural Network based models have been used extensively in extracting textual features in NLP (Poria et al., 2015) (Kim, 2014). Three parallel CNN layers are employed to get bigrams, trigrams and 4-grams (Johnson and Zhang, 2014). With each of these layers two convolution filters are used to traverse through entire matrix. The width of each filter is fixed to d (the dimension of embeddings for each word), hence one dimensional convolution is used. To get a single value from the outputs of the filters, we use Max Pooling. As mentioned earlier maximum number of words that tweet contains is assumed to be 35, max pooling values for bigrams, trigrams and 4-grams are 34, 33 and 32 respectively. Max pooling layer selects single value from each filter, therefore output of CNN architecture is 6 features for each tweet. Figure 1 shows the CNN architecture with an example sentence.

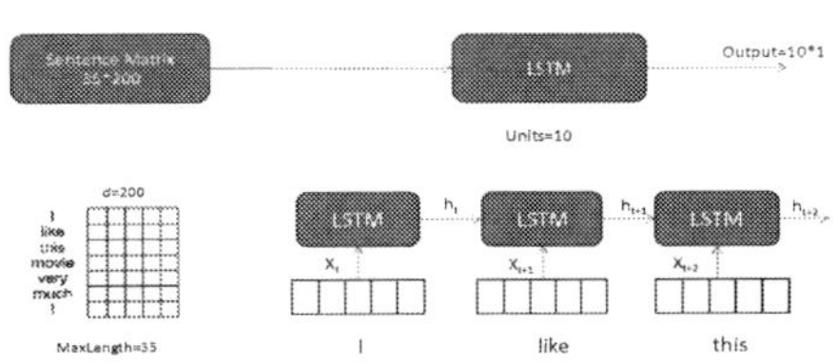

Figure 2: LSTM Architecture

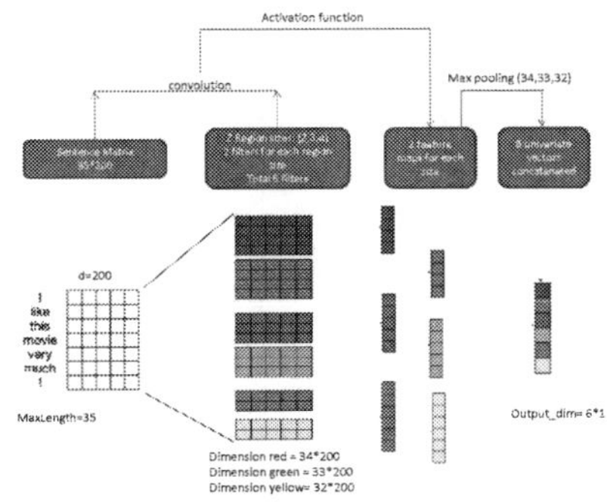

Figure 1: CNN Architecture

3.5 LSTM model

The inherent characteristics of sequence in text makes extraction of textual features a prime candidate for the use of Recurrent Neural Networks. RNNs are suited for capturing temporal relationships, which, in our case, are exhibited by words. Long short term memory networks (LSTMs) are a type of Recurrent Neural Networks which can easily capture long term dependences in a sequence, overcoming the common problem of vanishing gradient (Goldberg, 2016). Figure 2 shows the LSTM architecture with an example. Similar to CNN architecture, LSTM also receives a matrix for a tweet as input. At each step, embeddings of single word is provided. The number of LSTMs is a hyper parameter, fixed at 10 for this task. The model outputs a feature vector of dimension 10.

3.6 Unified Model

Proposed system architecture is presented in Figure 3, which integrates convolutional neural network (CNN) and Long short term memory networks (LSTM). As shown, output of CNN and LSTM is merged, along with feature sets A and B. Before merging output of CNN layer is flatten to match dimension of other features. This is achieved through the Merge layer as shown. Output of merge layer is then propagated to fully connected neural network layer with 10 hidden units. Finally, output layer is defined with single hidden unit.

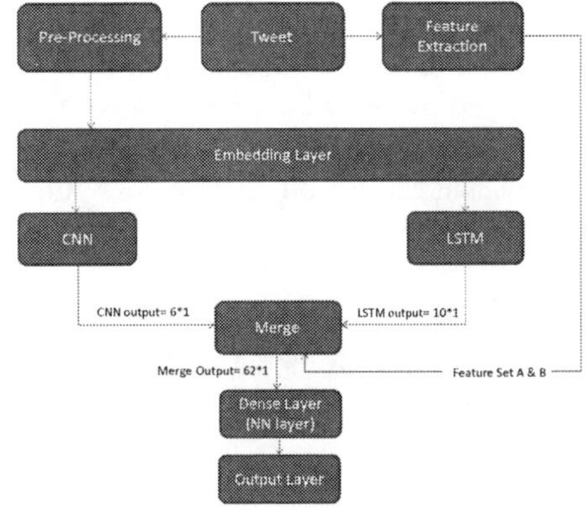

Figure 3: Merged Architecture

4 Results and Discussion

4.1 Results

Training, development and test sets each had individual files for each emotion namely, anger, fear, joy and sadness. We have trained the model separately for each emotion. Final submission for the test set was done with unified model (CNN + LSTM + Features) with joy and anger trained with Mean Square Error as loss function and fear and sadness trained with the custom loss function. This model secured 8th rank in task.

Separate experiments were performed using CNN and LSTM layers, as well as a combination of each with features, followed by our proposed model. Pearson Correlation Coefficient and Spearman's Correlation Coefficient are used as metrics.

- LSTM layer followed by dense layer is trained with mean square error as loss function. RMSProp (Hinton et al., 2012) was used as optimizer as it is effective for Recurrent Neural Networks (RNNs). Two experiments done for this, one with features and one without.

- CNN layer followed by dense layer is trained with mean square error as loss function. Adam (Kingma and Ba, 2014) is used as the optimizer. Two experiments done for this, one with features and one without.

- The unified model, described previously, is also used in two experiments. In one, it is trained with mean square error as loss function, irrespective of emotion, and uses Adam as optimizer. The second experiment with the unified model is the proposed system, where Mean Square Error loss function is used for joy and anger and custom loss function is used for fear and sadness.

Results on the development dataset are shown in Table 1. Along with models defined above baseline results are also shown.

In order to demonstrate the difference brought about by the separate feature sets used, Table 3 shows Pearson Score on the development set with and without different sets.An identical set of experiments are conducted replacing the mean square error function with a custom loss function. Custom loss is defined as

$$loss = 1 - Pearson\ Correlation$$

Table 4 compares the results on the development set for each emotion based on the loss function used.

Table 3: Pearson Correlation results on Development Set

	$SetA\&B$	$SetB$	$SetA$	$None$
Anger	0.690	0.567	0.681	0.390
Fear	0.637	0.542	0.628	0.625
Joy	0.764	0.650	0.738	0.670
Sadness	0.556	0.527	0.573	0.372
Avg	0.661	0.571	0.655	0.514

All the above experiments are replicated on the test set. Figure 5 and Figure 4 shows experiments with different set of features with mean square error as loss function and custom loss function respectively. It is evident that trend which was evident in development set about fear and sadness emotion performing better does not hold true for test set.

Table 4: Results on Development Set

	Custom Loss		MSE	
	$Pearson$	$Spearman$	$Pearson$	$Spearman$
Anger	0.563	0.594	0.690	0.626
Fear	0.690	0.689	0.636	0.592
Joy	0.666	0.671	0.764	0.755
Sadness	0.649	0.658	0.556	0.573
Avg	0.642	0.653	0.661	0.636

Table 2 shows the results of different data on test set. It is observed that LSTM model outperform the unified model on test set. This points to the disparity in test and development data in terms of words. Although vocabulary was expanded to include words in test set, the sentiment relatedness is hard to capture using CNN.

4.2 Analysis

It can be seen that different feature sets play an important role in guiding the model. In Table 3 feature set A provided a significant improvement in the results whereas feature set B alone degraded the performance of the system, albeit when merged with feature set A, the results improve. Table 4 compares the results on the development set for each emotion based on the loss function used. It shows that the custom loss function performs better in fear and sadness emotions.

Table 1: Comparison of different approaches on development data

Model	Avg Pearson	Avg Spearman	Anger		Fear		Joy		Sadness	
			Per.	Spr.	Per.	Spr.	Per.	Spr.	Per.	Spr.
Baseline	0.611	0.601	0.605	0.562	0.574	0.558	0.703	0.689	0.562	0.597
CNN	0.285	0.286	-0.17	-0.08	0.278	0.231	0.636	0.628	0.395	0.361
LSTM	0.582	0.565	0.566	0.528	0.567	0.524	0.733	0.736	0.461	0.473
CNN + Features	0.650	0.641	0.674	0.668	0.539	0.508	0.753	0.728	0.630	0.658
LSTM + Features	0.671	0.653	0.668	0.612	0.638	0.596	**0.77**	**0.762**	0.609	0.642
CNN + LSTM +features	0.661	0.637	**0.690**	**0.626**	0.637	0.592	0.764	0.755	0.556	0.573
Submitted Model	**0.698**	**0.674**	**0.690**	**0.626**	**0.69**	**0.658**	0.764	0.755	**0.649**	**0.658**

Table 2: Comparison of different approaches on test data

Model	Average Pearson	Average Spearman	Anger		Fear		Joy		Sadness	
			Per.	Spr.	Per.	Spr.	Per.	Spr.	Per.	Spr.
CNN	0.384	0.382	0.237	0.255	0.364	0.361	0.391	0.396	0.544	0.516
LSTM	0.621	0.609	0.598	0.583	0.677	0.652	0.567	0.571	0.641	0.631
CNN + Features	0.645	0.630	0.597	0.586	0.651	0.629	0.648	0.639	0.682	0.667
LSTM + Features	**0.703**	**0.691**	**0.669**	**0.652**	**0.723**	**0.705**	**0.71**	**0.705**	**0.711**	**0.702**
CNN + LSTM + features	0.680	0.668	0.646	0.631	0.702	0.684	0.674	0.668	0.697	0.687
Submitted Model	0.649	0.638	0.604	0.593	0.663	0.645	0.66	0.658	0.668	0.657

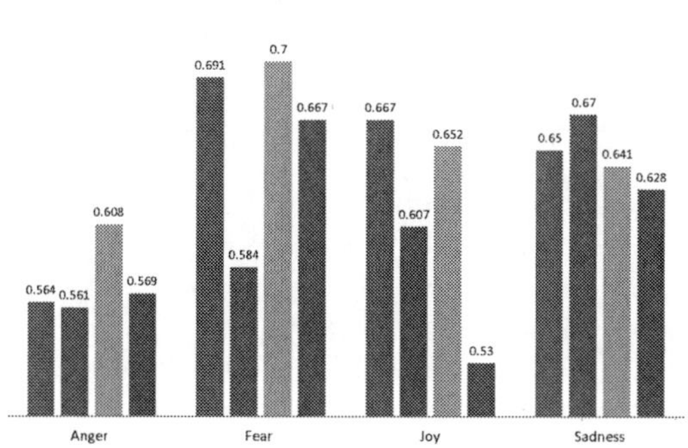

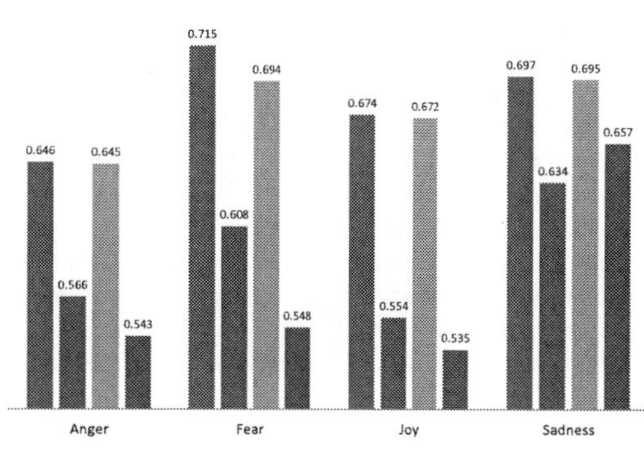

Figure 4: Results on test data using custom loss function

Figure 5: Results on test data using Mean Square Error function

5 Conclusion

We have applied a unified deep learning model to the emotion intensity task on twitter data. Two sets of features have been extracted using traditional NLP methods and recent deep learning based feature generation. LSTM and CNN based models have been implemented for regression task. A mixture of LSTM and CNN has been proposed. Experiments on combination of feature set on models are presented. Results shows that features help as indicated by the higher correlation. In addition to that mixture model performs better on development set while on test set LSTM model proves to be more accurate.

References

Felipe Bravo-Marquez, Eibe Frank, Saif M Mohammad, and Bernhard Pfahringer. 2016. Determining word–emotion associations from tweets by multi-label classification. In *WI'16*. IEEE Computer Society, pages 536–539.

Xiaowen Ding, Bing Liu, and Philip S Yu. 2008. A holistic lexicon-based approach to opinion mining. In *Proceedings of the 2008 international conference on web search and data mining*. ACM, pages 231–240.

Andrea Esuli and Fabrizio Sebastiani. 2007. Sentiwordnet: A high-coverage lexical resource for opinion mining. *Evaluation* pages 1–26.

Yoav Goldberg. 2016. A primer on neural network models for natural language processing. *Journal of Artificial Intelligence Research* 57:345–420.

T Hercig, T Brychcın, L Svoboda, and M Konkol. 2016. Uwb at semeval-2016 task 5: Aspect based sentiment analysis. In *Proceedings of the 10th International Workshop on Semantic Evaluation (SemEval-2016), Association for Computational Linguistics, San Diego, California*. pages 354–361.

Geoffrey Hinton, Nitish Srivastava, and Kevin Swersky. 2012. Neural networks for machine learning lecture 6a overview of mini-batch gradient descent .

Amal Htait, Sebastien Fournier, and Patrice Bellot. 2016. Lsis at semeval-2016 task 7: Using web search engines for english and arabic unsupervised sentiment intensity prediction. *Proceedings of SemEval* pages 469–473.

Rie Johnson and Tong Zhang. 2014. Effective use of word order for text categorization with convolutional neural networks. *arXiv preprint arXiv:1412.1058* .

Yoon Kim. 2014. Convolutional neural networks for sentence classification. *arXiv preprint arXiv:1408.5882* .

Diederik P. Kingma and Jimmy Ba. 2014. Adam: A method for stochastic optimization. *CoRR* abs/1412.6980.

Svetlana Kiritchenko, Saif M Mohammad, and Mohammad Salameh. 2016. Semeval-2016 task 7: Determining sentiment intensity of english and arabic phrases. *Proceedings of SemEval* pages 42–51.

Svetlana Kiritchenko, Xiaodan Zhu, and Saif M Mohammad. 2014. Sentiment analysis of short informal texts. *Journal of Artificial Intelligence Research* 50:723–762.

Tomas Mikolov, Ilya Sutskever, Kai Chen, Greg S Corrado, and Jeff Dean. 2013. Distributed representations of words and phrases and their compositionality. In *Advances in neural information processing systems*. pages 3111–3119.

Saif M. Mohammad and Felipe Bravo-Marquez. 2017. Wassa-2017 shared task on emotion intensity. In *Proceedings of the EMNLP 2017 Workshop on Computational Approaches to Subjectivity, Sentiment, and Social Media (WASSA), September 2017, Copenhagen, Denmark*.

Saif M Mohammad and Svetlana Kiritchenko. 2015. Using hashtags to capture fine emotion categories from tweets. *Computational Intelligence* 31(2):301–326.

Saif M Mohammad, Svetlana Kiritchenko, and Xiaodan Zhu. 2013. Nrc-canada: Building the state-of-the-art in sentiment analysis of tweets. *arXiv preprint arXiv:1308.6242* .

Saif M Mohammad and Peter D Turney. 2013. Crowdsourcing a word–emotion association lexicon. *Computational Intelligence* 29(3):436–465.

Finn Årup Nielsen. 2011. A new anew: Evaluation of a word list for sentiment analysis in microblogs. *arXiv preprint arXiv:1103.2903* .

Jeffrey Pennington, Richard Socher, and Christopher D. Manning. 2014. Glove: Global vectors for word representation. In *Empirical Methods in Natural Language Processing (EMNLP)*. pages 1532–1543.

Sasa Petrovic, Miles Osborne, and Victor Lavrenko. 2010. The edinburgh twitter corpus. In *Proceedings of the NAACL HLT 2010 Workshop on Computational Linguistics in a World of Social Media*. pages 25–26.

Soujanya Poria, Erik Cambria, and Alexander F Gelbukh. 2015. Deep convolutional neural network textual features and multiple kernel learning for utterance-level multimodal sentiment analysis. In *EMNLP*. pages 2539–2544.

A. Radford, R. Jozefowicz, and I. Sutskever. 2017. Learning to Generate Reviews and Discovering Sentiment. *ArXiv e-prints* .

Eshrag Refaee and Verena Rieser. 2016. ilab-edinburgh at semeval-2016 task 7: A hybrid approach for determining sentiment intensity of arabic twitter phrases. *Proceedings of SemEval* pages 474–480.

Sara Rosenthal, Preslav Nakov, Svetlana Kiritchenko, Saif M Mohammad, Alan Ritter, and Veselin Stoyanov. 2015. Semeval-2015 task 10: Sentiment analysis in twitter. In *Proceedings of the 9th international workshop on semantic evaluation (SemEval 2015)*. pages 451–463.

Feixiang Wang, Zhihua Zhang, and Man Lan. 2016. Ecnu at semeval-2016 task 7: An enhanced supervised learning method for lexicon sentiment intensity ranking. *Proceedings of SemEval* pages 491–496.

Theresa Wilson, Janyce Wiebe, and Paul Hoffmann. 2005. Recognizing contextual polarity in phrase-level sentiment analysis. In *Proceedings of the conference on human language technology and empirical methods in natural language processing*. Association for Computational Linguistics, pages 347–354.

YNU-HPCC at EmoInt-2017: Using a CNN-LSTM Model for Sentiment Intensity Prediction

You Zhang, Hang Yuan, Jin Wang and **Xuejie Zhang**
School of Information Science and Engineering
Yunnan University
Kunming, P.R. China
xjzhang@ynu.edu.cn

Abstract

The sentiment analysis in this task aims to indicate the sentiment intensity of the four emotions (e.g. anger, fear, joy, and sadness) expressed in tweets. Compared to the polarity classification, such intensity prediction can provide more fine-grained sentiment analysis. In this paper, we present a system that uses a convolutional neural network with long short-term memory (CNN-LSTM) model to complete the task. The CNN-LSTM model has two combined parts: CNN extracts local n-gram features within tweets and LSTM composes the features to capture long-distance dependency across tweets. Our submission ranked tenth among twenty two teams by average correlation scores on prediction intensity for all four types of emotions.

1 Introduction

Advanced Social Network Services (SNSs) such as Twitter, Facebook, and Weibo provide an online platform, where people share their personal interests, activities, thoughts, and emotions. Sentiment analysis technology is used to automatically draw affective information from text. In recent researches, the majority of existing approaches and works on sentiment analysis aim to complete classification tasks. In contrast, it is often useful to know the degree of an emotion expressed in text for applications such as movies, products, public sentiments and politics.

Such attractive applications provide the motivation for the WASSA-2017 shared task on Emotion Intensity (EmoInt) (Mohammad and Bravo-Marquez, 2017), which is a competition focused on automatically determining the intensity of emotions in tweets. The task involves one-dimensional sentiment analysis, which requires a system for determining the strength (with a real-value score between 0 and 1) of an emotion expressed in a tweet. All tweets are divided into four datasets, each of which expresses an emotion including anger, fear, joy, and sadness. The tweets with higher scores correspond to a greater degree of emotion.

In the relevant research field of sentiment analysis, it has been shown that many models are available for both categorical approaches and dimensional approaches. A categorical approach focuses on sentiment classification, while a dimensional approach aims to predict the intensity of emotions. Recently, many methods have been successfully introduced for categorical sentiment analysis, such as word embedding (Liu et al., 2015), convolutional neural networks (CNN) (Kim, 2014; Jiang et al., 2016; Ouyang et al., 2015), recurrent neural networks (RNN) (Liu et al., 2015; Irsoy and Cardie, 2014), long short-term memory (LSTM) (Hochreiter and Schmidhuber, 1997; Li and Qian., 2016; Sainath et al., 2015), and bi-directional LSTM (BiLSTM) (Brueckner and Schulter, 2014). We have aimed to employ those methods for dimensional sentiment analysis, and the results show that our approach is feasible. In general, CNN can extract local n-gram features within texts but may fail to capture long-distance dependency. LSTM can address this problem by sequentially modeling texts cross messages (Wang et al., 2016).

In this paper (and for this competition), we primarily introduce a CNN-LSTM model combining CNN and LSTM. First, we construct word vectors from pre-trained word vectors using word embedding. The CNN applies convolutional and max-pooling layers, which are then used to extract n-gram features. Finally, LSTM composes those features and outputs the result. By combining CN-

Proceedings of the 8th Workshop on Computational Approaches to Subjectivity, Sentiment and Social Media Analysis, pages 200–204
Copenhagen, Denmark, September 7–11, 2017. ©2017 Association for Computational Linguistics

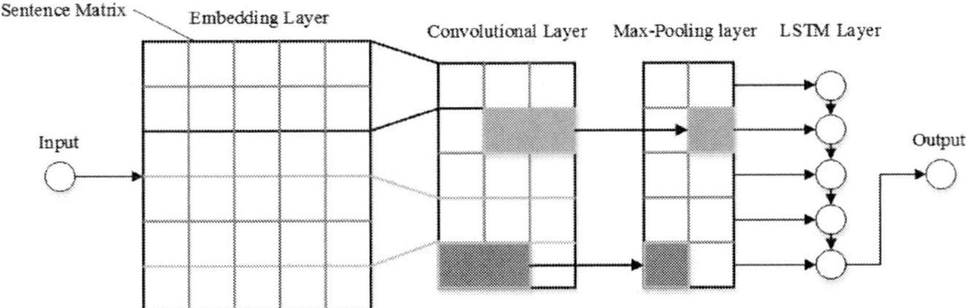

Figure 1: The architecture of CNN-LSTM model.

N and LSTM, the model can extract both local information within tweets and long-distance dependency across tweets. Our experiment reveals that the proposed model has the highest performance with data for anger and joy, while a simple CNN performs best for fear and sadness.

The remainder of this paper is organized as follows. In section 2, we described CNN, LSTM and their combination. The comparative experimental results are presented in section 3. Finally, a conclusion is drawn in section 4.

2 The CNN-LSTM model for Sentiment Intensity Prediction

The dimensional sentiment analysis in this task is intended at producing continues numerical values according to sentiment intensity. Figure 1 shows the overall framework of our model. First, a simple tokenizer is used to transform tweets into an array of tokens, which are the input of the model, and are then mapped in a feature matrix or sentence matrix by an embedding layer. Then, n-gram features are extracted when the feature matrix passes through the convolutional and max pooling layers. LSTM finally composes these useful features to output the final regression results by linear decoder.

2.1 Convolutional Neural Network

In our model, the CNN outputs are used as the inputs for the LSTM. Additionally, a simple CNN model can be produced for our task by directly using a linear regression layer as the output layer. The CNN architecture for the task is described below.

Embedding layer. The embedding layer is the first layer of the model. In this technique, words are encoded as real-valued vectors in a high dimensional space. The layer allows for the initialization of vocabulary words vectors through the pre-trained word vectors matrix. A tweet used as an input is transformed into a sequence of numerical word tokens such as $t_1, t_2, ..., t_N$, where t_N is a number representing a real word and N is the length of the token vector. To keep the size of the results identical for tweets with varying lengths, we limit the maximum value of N to the maximum length of the tweet from all tweets. Any tweet shorter than N will be padded to N using zero.

Convolutional Layer. In a convolutional layer, m filters are used to extract local n-gram features from the matrix of the previous embedding layer. In a sliding window of width w indicating a w-gram feature can be extracted, a filter $F_l(1 \leq l \leq m)$ learns the feature map y_i^l as follows:

$$y_i^l = f(T_{i;i+w-1} \circ W^l + b^l) \tag{1}$$

Where $\circ$ denotes a convolution operation, $W \in \mathbb{R}^{w \times d}$ is the weight matrix from the output of the previous layer, b is a bias, and $T_{i:i+w-1}$ denotes the token vectors $t_i, t_{i+1}, ..., t_{i+w-1}(if k > 0, t_k = 0)$. The result of filter F_l will be $y^l \in \mathbb{R}^d$, where y_i^l is the i-th element of y^l. Here we use ReLU as the activation function for fast calculation.

Max-pooling and Dropout layer. The max-pooling layer is used to down-sample and consolidate the features learned in the previous layer with a common method that takes the maximum of the input value from each filter. First, eliminating non-maximal values can reduce the computation for upper layers. Second, we choose a maximum value, because the salient feature is the most distinguishable trait of a tweet.

CNNs have a habit of overfitting, even with pooling layers. Thus, we introduce a dropout layer (Tobergte and Curtis, 2013) after both a convolution and max-pooling layer.

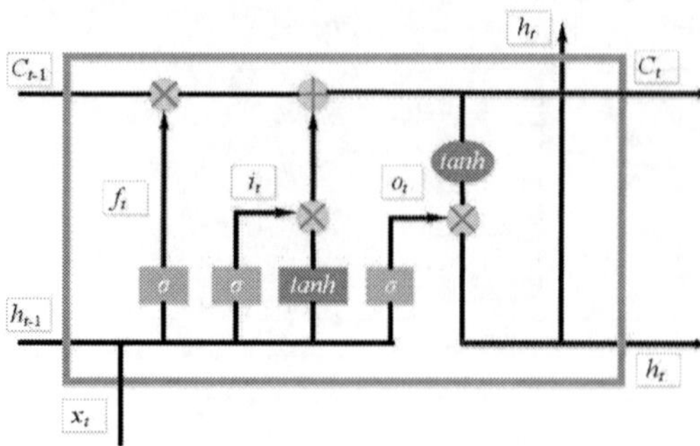

Figure 2: Architecture of LSTM cell.

2.2 Long Short-Term Memory

Recurrent Neural Networks (RNN) are a special type of neural network suitably designed for processing sequence problems. However, in a simple RNN, the gradients can produce very small numbers, which is referred to as the vanishing gradient problem (Bengio et al., 2002). The LSTM network is trained using back propagation (BP) over time and can effectively address this problem. Thus, we consider it to be the second part of our model. In addition, we could use the output of the word embedding layer as an input to the LSTM to obtain a simple LSTM model.

LSTM layer. The LSTM has memory blocks (cells) that contains outputs and gates that manage the blocks for the memory updates. In figure 2, we show how a memory block calculates hidden states h_t and outputs C_t using the following equations:

- Gate

$$f_t = \sigma(W_f \cdot [h_{t-1}, x_t] + b_f)$$
$$i_t = \sigma(W_i \cdot [h_{t-1}, x_t] + b_i) \qquad (2)$$
$$o_t = \sigma(W_o \cdot [h_{t-1}, x_t] + b_o)$$

- Transformation

$$\tilde{C}_t = \tanh(W_c \cdot [h_{t-1}, x_t] + b_C) \qquad (3)$$

- State update

$$C_t = f_t * C_{t-1} + i_t * \tilde{C}_t$$
$$h_t = o_t * \tanh(C_t) \qquad (4)$$

Where x_t is the input vector; C_t is the cell state vector; W and b are cell parameters; f_t, i_t, and o_t are gate vectors; and σ denotes the sigmoid function.

Output Layer. This layer outputs the final regression result, which could be a CNN or CNN-LSTM model. It is a fully connected layer using a linear decoder. A layer output vector defined as,

Content	Example	Pattern
User starts with @	@Bob	<user>
ULRs	http://ie.com	<url>
Numbers	12,345	<number>
Hashtags	#emotions	hashtag

Table 1: The example of pre-processing pattern.

$$y = h(x) = W_d x + b_d \qquad (5)$$

Where x is the text token vector, y is the predicted sentiment intensity of the tweet, and W_d and b_d respectively denote the weights and bias.

The model is trained by the mean absolute error (MAE) between the predicted y and actual y. Given the training set of token matrix $X = \{x_1, x_2, ..., x_n\}$, and their actual degree of the e-motion is $y = \{y_1, y_2, ..., y_n\}$, so the loss function is defined as,

$$L(X, y) = \frac{1}{2n} \sum_{i=1}^{n} \|h(x_i) - y_i\|^2 \qquad (6)$$

3 Experiments and Evaluation

Data pre-processing. The organizers of the competition provided four corpora, each of which corresponds to an emotion (anger, fear, joy and sadness). The training datasets contain tweets along with a real-valued score (between 0 and 1) indicating the degree of the emotion felt by the speaker. Dev sets were provided to help us tune the parameters of the model. Here, we used the Stanford tokenizer to process tweets into an array of tokens. Since the tweets in this task primarily contain English text, all punctuations are ignored and all non-English letters are treated as unknown words. A small part of text contains emojis or emoticons, which perfectly match the conditions for emotional intensity. Therefore, these emojis or emoticons are processed into related words with similar meanings. Patterns are applied to every tweet presented in Table 1. We applied the four patterns and lowed all words to map the known pre-trained tokens. Some words that do not exist in the known tokens are treated as unknown words. In the word vectors, unknown word vectors randomly generated from a uniform distribution $U(-0.25, 0.25)$.

In this experiment, we used pre-trained word vectors including GoogleNews[1] trained by the word2vec toolkit and another one trained by GloVe[2] (Pennington et al., 2014). These programs

---

[1] https://code.google.com/archive/p/word2vec/
[2] https://nlp.stanford.edu/projects/glove/

Model	Metrics							
	Pearson correlation coefficient (r)				Spearman rank coefficient (s)			
	Anger	Fear	Joy	Sadness	Anger	Fear	Joy	Sadness
$\text{CNN}_{word2vec}$	0.628	0.714	0.710	0.630	0.600	0.673	0.716	0.634
$\text{CNN-LSTM}_{word2vec}$	0.591	0.591	0.657	0.551	0.586	0.555	0.662	0.566
$\text{LSTM}_{word2vec}$	0.608	0.554	0.603	0.503	0.569	0.497	0.592	0.498
$\text{BiLSTM}_{word2vec}$	0.544	0.551	0.536	0.500	0.499	0.510	0.511	0.484
CNN_{GloVe}	0.621	**0.687**	0.721	**0.630**	0.623	**0.686**	0.726	**0.639**
CNN-LSTM_{GloVe}	**0.661**	0.644	**0.797**	0.542	0.627	0.607	0.728	0.532
LSTM_{GloVe}	0.642	0.614	0.755	0.539	**0.689**	0.695	**0.772**	0.519
BiLSTM_{GloVe}	0.623	0.657	0.731	0.533	0.598	0.625	0.747	0.544

Table 3: The development data experimentation results on WASSA-2017 shard task on Emotion Intensity (EmoInt).

Parameters	Emotions			
	Anger	Fear	Joy	Sadness
m	64	32	16	32
l	3	3	2	-
n	2	2	2	-
p	0.1	0.8	0.6	0.3
c	2	2	2	-
d	300	100	300	300
b	100	50	60	100
e	30	20	50	30

Table 2: The best-tuned parameters on each dataset.

were used to initialize the weight of the embedding layer in order to build 300-dimension word vectors for all tweets. GloVe is an unsupervised learning algorithm for obtaining vector representations of words.

Implementation. This experiment used Keras with a TensorFlow backend. We use two different pre-trained word vectors and four different datasets. We introduce three other models (CNN, LSTM and BiLSTM) as baseline algorithms. Details of those three models can respectively be found in (Kim, 2014; Jiang et al., 2016; Ouyang et al., 2015), (Hochreiter and Schmidhuber, 1997; Li and Qian., 2016; Sainath et al., 2015) and (Brueckner and Schulter, 2014).

The hyper-parameters were tuned to the performance of training and dev data using the sklearn grid search function (Pedregosa et al., 2012), which can search all possible parameter combinations to evaluate models and find the best one. Different models for different data may have their own optimization parameters. For anger emotion data, the CNN-LSTMs best-tuned parameters are as follows. The number of filters (m) is 64; the length of the filter (l) is 3; the pool length (n) is 2; the dropout rate (p) is 0.1; the LSTM layer count (c) is 2, and the dimension of the LSTM hidden layer (d) is 300. The training runs with a batch size (b) of 100 and 30 epochs (e). The other three emo-

tions shown in Table 2. The results also reveal that the models using pre-trained GloVe vectors and an Adam optimizer achieved the best performance.

Evaluation Metrics. The system is evaluated by calculating the Pearson correlation coefficient (r) and Spearman rank coefficient (s) with gold ratings. Higher r and s values indicate better performance on model prediction.

Results and Discussion. A total of twenty two teams took part in the task. Table 3 shows the detailed results of the proposed CNN-LSTM model against the three baseline models. The averaged r from the four emotions is needed to determine the bottom-line competition metric by witch the submissions will be ranked. Therefore, r is more worth considering for performance than s. The proposed CNN-LSTM model outperformed the baseline models for anger and joy data. Therefore, we chose the CNN-LSTM to create the final system to complete the subtasks of anger and joy, and ranked ninth for both r and s on anger data, eleventh for r, and thirteenth for s on joy data. In contrary, a simple CNN yielded better performance on fear and sadness data from the experimental results. Therefore, for the fear and sadness subtasks, we used a simple CNN that ranked seventh for r and eighth for s on fear data, and sixth for both r and s on sadness data.

4 Conclusion

In this paper, we described the system we submitted to WASSA-2017 Shared Task on Emotion Intensity (EmoInt). The proposed model combines CNN and LSTM to extract both local information within tweets and long-distance dependency across tweets in the regression process. Our introduced model showed good performance in the experimental results. In future work, we will attempt to introduce attention or memory mechanisms, in order to draw more useful sentiment information.

References

Yoshua Bengio, Patrice Simard, and Paolo Frasconi. 2002. Learning long-term dependencies with gradient descent is difficult. *IEEE Transactions on Neural Networks* 5(2):157–166. https://doi.org/10.1109/72.279181.

Raymond Brueckner and Bjorn Schulter. 2014. Social signal classification using deep blstm recurrent neural networks. In *2014 IEEE International Conference on Acoustics, Speech and Signal Processing (ICASSP)*. pages 4823–4827. https://doi.org/10.1109/ICASSP.2014.6854518.

Sepp Hochreiter and Jrgex Schmidhuber. 1997. Long short-term memory. *Neural Computation* 9(8):1735–1780. https://doi.org/10.1162/neco.1997.9.8.1735.

Ozan Irsoy and Claire Cardie. 2014. Opinion mining with deep recurrent neural networks. In *Conference on Empirical Methods in Natural Language Processing*. pages 720–728.

Ming Jiang, Liqiang Jin, Feiwei Qin, Min Zhang, and Ziyang Li. 2016. Network public comments sentiment analysis based on multilayer convolutional neural network. In *2016 IEEE International Conference on Internet of Things (iThings) and IEEE Green Computing and Communications (Green-Com) and IEEE Cyber, Physical and Social Computing (CPSCom) and IEEE Smart Data (SmartData)*. pages 777–781. https://doi.org/10.1109/iThings-GreenCom-CPSCom-SmartData.2016.164.

Yoon Kim. 2014. Convolutional neural networks for sentence classification. *Eprint Arxiv* pages 1746–1751. https://doi.org/10.3115/v1/D14-1181.

Dan Li and Jiang Qian. 2016. Text sentiment analysis based on long short-term memory. In *2016 First IEEE International Conference on Computer Communication and the Internet (ICCCI)*. pages 471–475. https://doi.org/10.1109/CCI.2016.7778967.

Pengfei Liu, Shafiq Joty, and Helen Meng. 2015. Fine-grained opinion mining with recurrent neural networks and word embeddings. In *Conference on Empirical Methods in Natural Language Processing*. pages 1433–1443.

Saif M. Mohammad and Felipe Bravo-Marquez. 2017. WASSA-2017 shared task on emotion intensity. In *Proceedings of the Workshop on Computational Approaches to Subjectivity, Sentiment and Social Media Analysis (WASSA)*. Copenhagen, Denmark.

Xi Ouyang, Pan Zhou, Cheng Hua Li, and Lijun Liu. 2015. Sentiment analysis using convolutional neural network. In *2015 IEEE International Conference on Computer and Information Technology; Ubiquitous Computing and Communications; Dependable, Autonomic and Secure Computing; Pervasive Intelligence and Computing*. pages 2359–2364. https://doi.org/10.1109/CIT/IUCC/DASC/PICOM.2015.349.

Fabian Pedregosa, Gael Varoquaux, Alexandre Gramfort, Vincent Michel, Bertrand Thirion, Olivier Grisel, Mathieu Blondel, Peter Prettenhofer, Ron-Weiss, Vincent Dubourg, Jake Vanderplas, Alexandre Passos, David Cournapeau, Matthieu Brucher, Matthieu Perrot, and Edouard Duchesnay. 2012. Scikit-learn: Machine learning in python. *Journal of Machine Learning Research* 12(10):2825–2830. https://doi.org/10.1007/s13398-014-0173-7.2.

Jeffrey Pennington, Richard Socher, and Christopher D Manning. 2014. Glove: Global vectors for word representation. In *Conference on Empirical Methods in Natural Language Processing*. pages 1532–1543. https://doi.org/10.3115/v1/D14-1162.

Tara N. Sainath, Oriol Vinyals, Andrew Senior, and Hasim Sak. 2015. Convolutional, long short-term memory, fully connected deep neural networks. In *2015 IEEE International Conference on Acoustics, Speech and Signal Processing (ICASSP)*. pages 4580–4584. https://doi.org/10.1109/ICASSP.2015.7178838.

David R. Tobergte and Shirley Curtis. 2013. Improving neural networks with dropout. *Journal of Chemical Information and Modeling* 5(13):1689–1699. https://doi.org/10.1017/CBO9781107415324.004.

Jin Wang, Liang-Chih Yu, K. Robert Lai, and Xuejie Zhang. 2016. Dimensional sentiment analysis using a regional cnn-lstm model. In *Meeting of the Association for Computational Linguistics*. pages 225–230. https://doi.org/18653/v1/P16-2037.

Seernet at EmoInt-2017: Tweet Emotion Intensity Estimator

Venkatesh Duppada and **Sushant Hiray**

Seernet Technologies, LLC

{venkatesh.duppada, sushant.hiray}@seernet.io

Abstract

The paper describes experiments on estimating emotion intensity in tweets using a generalized regressor system. The system combines lexical, syntactic and pretrained word embedding features, trains them on general regressors and finally combines the best performing models to create an ensemble. The proposed system stood 3rd out of 22 systems in the leaderboard of WASSA-2017 Shared Task on Emotion Intensity.

1 Introduction

Twitter, a micro-blogging and social networking site has emerged as a platform where people express themselves and react to events in real-time. It is estimated that nearly 500 million tweets are sent per day [1]. Twitter data is particularly interesting because of its peculiar nature where people convey messages in short sentences using hashtags, emoticons, emojis etc. In addition, each tweet has meta data like location and language used by the sender. It's challenging to analyze this data because the tweets might not be grammatically correct and the users tend to use informal and slang words all the time. Hence, this poses an interesting problem for NLP researchers. Any advances in using this abundant and diverse data can help understand and analyze information about a person, an event, a product, an organization or a country as a whole. Many notable use cases of the twitter can be found here[2].

Along the similar lines, **The Task 1 of WASSA-2017** (Mohammad and Bravo-Marquez, 2017c) poses a problem of finding emotion intensity of

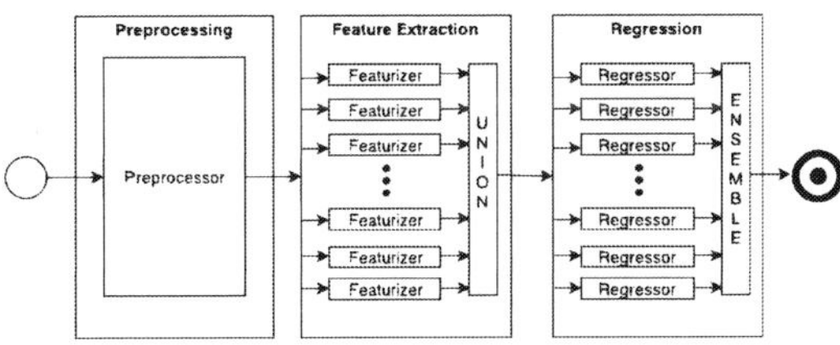

Figure 1: System Architecture

four emotions namely anger, fear, joy, sadness from tweets. In this paper, we describe our approach and experiments to solve this problem. The rest of the paper is laid out as follows: Section 2 describes the system architecture, Section 3 reports results and inference from different experiments, while Section 4 points to ways that the problem can be further explored.

2 System Description

2.1 Preprocessing

The preprocessing step modifies the raw tweets before they are passed to feature extraction. Tweets are processed using **tweetokenize** tool[3]. Twitter specific features are replaced as follows: username handles to USERNAME, phone numbers to PHONENUMBER, numbers to NUMBER, URLs to URL and times to TIME. A continuous sequence of emojis is broken into individual tokens. Finally, all tokens are converted to lowercase.

2.2 Feature Extraction

Many tasks related to sentiment or emotion analysis depend upon affect, opinion, sentiment, sense and emotion lexicons. These lexicons associate words to corresponding sentiment or emotion metrics. On the other hand, the semantic meaning of words, sentences, and documents are preserved

---

[1] https://en.wikipedia.org/wiki/Twitter

[2] https://en.wikipedia.org/wiki/
Twitter_usage

[3] https://www.github.com/jaredks/
tweetokenize

Proceedings of the 8th Workshop on Computational Approaches to Subjectivity, Sentiment and Social Media Analysis, pages 205–211
Copenhagen, Denmark, September 7–11, 2017. ©2017 Association for Computational Linguistics

and compactly represented using low dimensional vectors (Mikolov et al., 2013) instead of one hot encoding vectors which are sparse and high dimensional. Finally, there are traditional NLP features like word N-grams, character N-grams, Part-Of-Speech N-grams and word clusters which are known to perform well on various tasks.

Based on these observations, the feature extraction step is implemented as a union of different independent feature extractors (featurizers) in a light-weight and easy to use Python program EmoInt [4]. It comprises of all features available in the baseline model (Mohammad and Bravo-Marquez, 2017a) [5] along with additional feature extractors and bi-gram support. Fourteen such feature extractors have been implemented which can be clubbed into 3 major categories:

- Lexicon Features
- Word Vectors
- Syntax Features

Lexicon Features: AFINN (Nielsen, 2011) word list are manually rated for valence with an integer between -5 (Negative Sentiment) and +5 (Positive Sentiment). Bing Liu (Hu and Liu, 2004) opinion lexicon extract opinion on customer reviews. +/-EffectWordNet (Choi and Wiebe, 2014) by MPQA group are sense level lexicons. The NRC Affect Intensity (Mohammad, 2017) lexicons provide real valued affect intensity. NRC Word-Emotion Association Lexicon (Mohammad and Turney, 2010) contains 8 sense level associations (anger, fear, anticipation, trust, surprise, sadness, joy, and disgust) and 2 sentiment level associations (negative and positive). Expanded NRC Word-Emotion Association Lexicon (Bravo-Marquez et al., 2016) expands the NRC word-emotion association lexicon for twitter specific language. NRC Hashtag Emotion Lexicon (Mohammad and Kiritchenko, 2015) contains emotion word associations computed on emotion labeled twitter corpus via Hashtags. NRC Hashtag Sentiment Lexicon and Sentiment140 Lexicon (Mohammad et al., 2013) contains sentiment word associations computed on twitter corpus via Hashtags and Emoticons. SentiWordNet (Baccianella et al., 2010) assigns to each synset of WordNet

three sentiment scores: positivity, negativity, objectivity. Negation lexicons collections are used to count the total occurrence of negative words. In addition to these, SentiStrength (Thelwall et al., 2010) application which estimates the strength of positive and negative sentiment from tweets is also added.

Word Vectors: We focus primarily on the word vector representations (word embeddings) created specifically using the twitter dataset. GloVe (Pennington et al., 2014) is an unsupervised learning algorithm for obtaining vector representations for words. 200-dimensional GloVe embeddings trained on 2 Billion tweets are integrated. Edinburgh embeddings (Bravo-Marquez et al., 2015) are obtained by training skip-gram model on Edinburgh corpus (Petrovic et al., 2010). Since tweets are abundant with emojis, Emoji embeddings (Eisner et al., 2016) which are learned from the emoji descriptions have been used. Embeddings for each tweet are obtained by summing up individual word vectors and then dividing by the number of tokens in the tweet.

Syntactic Features: Syntax specific features such as Word N-grams, Part-Of-Speech N-grams (Owoputi et al., 2013), Brown Cluster N-grams (Brown et al., 1992) obtained using TweetNLP [6] project have been integrated into the system.

The final feature vector is the concatenation of all the individual features. For example, we concatenate average word vectors, sum of NRC Affect Intensities, number of positive and negative Bing Liu lexicons, number of negation words and so on to get final feature vector. The scaling of final features is not required when used with gradient boosted trees. However, scaling steps like standard scaling (zero mean and unit normal) may be beneficial for neural networks as the optimizers work well when the data is centered around origin.

A total of fourteen different feature extractors have been implemented, all of which can be enabled or disabled individually to extract features from a given tweet.

2.3 Regression

The dev data set (Mohammad and Bravo-Marquez, 2017b) in the competition was small hence, the train and dev sets were merged to perform 10-fold cross validation. On each fold, a model was trained and the predictions were col-

---

[4]To enable replicability, the code is open sourced at `https://github.com/SEERNET/EmoInt`.

[5]`https://www.github.com/felipebravom/AffectiveTweets`

[6]`http://www.cs.cmu.edu/~ark/TweetNLP/`

lected on the remaining dataset. The predictions are averaged across all the folds to generalize the solution and prevent over-fitting. As described in Section 2.2, different combinations of feature extractors were used. After performing feature extraction, the data was then passed to various regressors Support Vector Regression, AdaBoost, RandomForestRegressor, and, BaggingRegressor of sklearn (Pedregosa et al., 2011). Finally, the chosen top performing models had the least error on evaluation metrics namely Pearson's Correlation Coefficient and Spearman's rank-order correlation.

2.4 Parameter Optimization

In order to find the optimal parameter values for the EmoInt system, an extensive grid search was performed through the scikit-Learn framework over all subsets of the training set (shuffled), using stratified 10-fold cross validation and optimizing the Pearson's Correlation score. Best cross-validation results were obtained using AdaBoost meta regressor with base regressor as XGBoost (Chen and Guestrin, 2016) with 1000 estimators and 0.1 learning rate. Experiments and analysis of results are presented in the next section.

3 Results and Analysis

3.1 Experimental Results

As described in Section 2.2 various syntax features were used namely, Part-of-Speech tags, brown clusters of TweetNLP project. However, these didn't perform well in cross validation. Hence, they were dropped from the final system. While performing grid-search as mentioned in Section 2.4, keeping all the lexicon based features same, choice of combination of emoji vector and word vectors are varied to minimize cross validation metric. Table 1 describes the results for experiments conducted with different combinations of word vectors. Emoji embeddings (Eisner et al., 2016) give better results than using plain GloVe and Edinburgh embeddings. Edinburgh embeddings outperform GloVe embeddings in **Joy** and **Sadness** category but lag behind in **Anger** and **Fear** category. The official submission comprised of the top-performing model for each emotion category. This system ranked 3rd for the entire test dataset and 2nd for the subset of the test data formed by taking every instance with a gold emo-

tion intensity score greater than or equal to 0.5. Post competition, experiments were performed on ensembling diverse models for improving the accuracy. An ensemble obtained by averaging the results of the top 2 performing models outperforms all the individual models.

3.2 Feature Importance

The relative feature importance can be assessed by the relative depth of the feature used as a decision node in the tree. Features used at the top of the tree contribute to the final prediction decision of a larger fraction of the input samples. The expected fraction of the samples they contribute to can thus be used as an estimate of the relative importance of the features. By averaging the measure over several randomized trees, the variance of the estimate can be reduced and used as a measure of relative feature importance. In Figure 2 feature importance graphs are plotted for each emotion to infer which features are playing the major role in identifying emotional intensity in tweets. +/-EffectWordNet (Choi and Wiebe, 2014), NRC Hashtag Sentiment Lexicon, Sentiment140 Lexicon (Mohammad et al., 2013) and NRC Hashtag Emotion Lexicon (Mohammad and Kiritchenko, 2015) are playing the most important role.

3.3 System Limitations

It is important to understand how the model performs in different scenarios. Table 2 analyzes when the system performs the best and worst for each emotion. Since the features used are mostly lexicon based, the system has difficulties in capturing the overall sentiment and it leads to amplifying or vanishing intensity signals. For instance, in example 4 of fear **louder** and **shaking** lexicons imply fear but overall sentence doesn't imply fear. A similar pattern can be found in the 4th example of Anger and 3rd example of Joy. The system has difficulties in understanding of sarcastic tweets, for instance, in the 3rd tweet of Anger the user expressed anger but used **lol** which is used in a positive sense most of the times and hence the system did a bad job at predicting intensity. The system also fails in predicting sentences having deeper emotion and sentiment which humans can understand with a little context. For example, in sample 4 of sadness, the tweet refers to post travel blues which humans can understand. But with little context, it is difficult for the system to accurately estimate the intensity. The performance is

Emotion	Systems	Pearsonr	Spearmanr	Pearsonr ≥ 0.5	Spearmanr ≥ 0.5
Anger	Baseline	0.639583	0.628180	0.510361	0.475215
	Em0-Ed1-Gl0	0.659566	0.628835	0.536701	0.508762
	Em1-Ed1-Gl0	0.660568	0.631893	0.536244	0.511621
	Em0-Ed0-Gl1*	0.675864	0.656034	0.529404	0.512774
	Em1-Ed0-Gl1	0.678214	**0.658605**	0.527375	0.510436
	Ensemble	**0.678477**	0.653964	**0.540919**	**0.518851**
Fear	Baseline	0.631139	0.622047	0.476480	0.432407
	Em0-Ed1-Gl0	0.689571	0.66237	0.539250	0.499864
	Em1-Ed1-Gl0	0.695443	0.670438	0.542909	0.500896
	Em0-Ed0-Gl1	0.691143	0.667255	0.546867	0.510041
	Em1-Ed0-Gl1*	0.697630	0.676379	0.551465	0.510265
	Ensemble	**0.705260**	**0.683536**	**0.55641**	**0.513398**
Joy	Baseline	0.645597	0.652505	0.370499	0.363184
	Em0-Ed1-Gl0	0.696448	0.66237	0.539250	0.499864
	Em1-Ed1-Gl0	0.722115	0.720437	0.519821	0.508484
	Em0-Ed0-Gl1	0.689692	0.689883	0.472973	0.470260
	Em1-Ed0-Gl1*	0.714850	0.713558	**0.551191**	**0.543565**
	Ensemble	**0.728093**	**0.727970**	0.547213	0.537690
Sadness	Baseline	0.711998	0.711745	0.479049	0.452047
	Em0-Ed1-Gl0	0.737805	0.733999	0.547871	0.524843
	Em1-Ed1-Gl0*	0.744550	0.740893	**0.554723**	0.533571
	Em0-Ed0-Gl1	0.731436	0.724570	0.542910	0.536228
	Em1-Ed0-Gl1	0.736081	0.731050	0.553460	**0.548944**
	Ensemble	**0.748901**	**0.743589**	0.547213	0.537690
Average	Baseline	0.657079	0.653619	0.479049	0.452047
	Em0-Ed1-Gl0	0.695847	0.680207	0.51998	0.493755
	Em1-Ed1-Gl0	0.705669	0.690915	0.538424	0.513643
	Em0-Ed0-Gl1	0.69703	0.684436	0.523038	0.507326
	Em1-Ed0-Gl1	0.706694	0.694898	0.545873	0.528303
	Official*	0.708267	0.696801	0.546913	0.526018
	Ensemble	**0.715183**	**0.702265**	**0.55209**	**0.530501**

Table 1: Evaluation Metrics for various systems. Systems are abbreviated as following: For example Em1-Ed0-Gl1 implies Emoji embeddings and GloVe embeddings are included, Edinburgh embeddings are not included in features keeping other features same. Results marked with * corresponds to official submission. Results in **bold** are the best results corresponding to that metric.

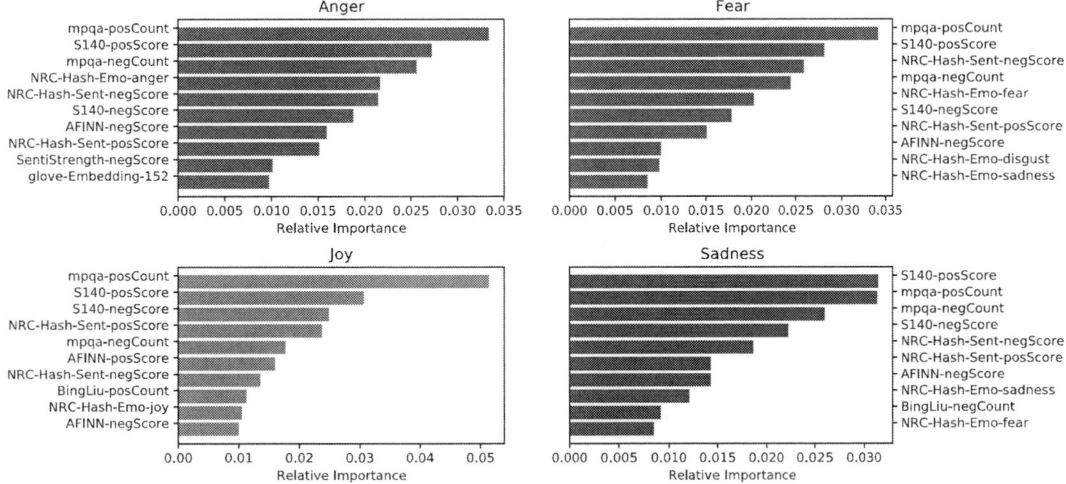

Figure 2: Relative Feature Importance of Various Emotions

poor with very short sentences as there are fewer indicators to provide a reasonable estimate.

4   Future Work & Conclusion

The paper studies the effectiveness of various affect lexicons word embeddings to estimate emotional intensity in tweets. A light-weight easy to use affect computing framework (EmoInt) to facilitate ease of experimenting with various lexicon features for text tasks is open-sourced. It provides plug and play access to various feature extractors and handy scripts for creating ensembles.

Few problems explained in the analysis section can be resolved with the help of sentence embeddings which take the context information into consideration. The features used in the system are generic enough to use them in other affective computing tasks on social media text, not just tweet data. Another interesting feature of lexicon-based systems is their good run-time performance during prediction, future work to benchmark the performance of the system can prove vital for deploying in a real-world setting.

Acknowledgement

We would like to thank the organizers of the WASSA-2017 Shared Task on Emotion Intensity, for providing the data, the guidelines and timely support.

References

Stefano Baccianella, Andrea Esuli, and Fabrizio Sebastiani. 2010. Sentiwordnet 3.0: An enhanced lexical resource for sentiment analysis and opinion mining. In *LREC*. volume 10, pages 2200–2204.

Felipe Bravo-Marquez, Eibe Frank, Saif M Mohammad, and Bernhard Pfahringer. 2016. Determining word–emotion associations from tweets by multilabel classification. In *WI'16*. IEEE Computer Society, pages 536–539.

Felipe Bravo-Marquez, Eibe Frank, and Bernhard Pfahringer. 2015. From unlabelled tweets to twitter-specific opinion words. In *Proceedings of the 38th International ACM SIGIR Conference on Research and Development in Information Retrieval*. ACM, pages 743–746.

Peter F Brown, Peter V Desouza, Robert L Mercer, Vincent J Della Pietra, and Jenifer C Lai. 1992. Class-based n-gram models of natural language. *Computational linguistics* 18(4):467–479.

Tianqi Chen and Carlos Guestrin. 2016. Xgboost: A scalable tree boosting system. In *Proceedings of the 22Nd ACM SIGKDD International Conference on Knowledge Discovery and Data Mining*. ACM, pages 785–794.

Yoonjung Choi and Janyce Wiebe. 2014. +/-effectwordnet: Sense-level lexicon acquisition for opinion inference. In *EMNLP*. pages 1181–1191.

Ben Eisner, Tim Rocktäschel, Isabelle Augenstein, Matko Bošnjak, and Sebastian Riedel. 2016. emoji2vec: Learning emoji representations from their description. *arXiv preprint arXiv:1609.08359* .

Minqing Hu and Bing Liu. 2004. Mining and summarizing customer reviews. In *Proceedings of the tenth*

Emotion	Tweet	Gold Int.	Pred. Int.
Anger	@Claymakerbigsi @toghar11 @scott_mulligan_ @BoxingFa-natic_ Fucker blocked me 2 years ago over a question lol proper holds a grudge old Joe	0.625	0.6245
	We are raging angry.=1/2 bil $ for 2 pro Liars.(Actors) the most useless people in america Where is ours for working 100 X harder? @FoxNews	0.667	0.6665
	dammit @TMobile whays going on!!! 😤😤😤😤😤 lol #smh #mo-bilefails	0.792	0.4062
	People are #hurt and #angry and it's hard to know what to do with that #anger Remember, at the end of the day, we're all #humans #bekind	0.250	0.6040
Fear	Onus is on #Pak to act against #terror groups which find safe havens and all types of support for cross border terror: #MEA	0.667	0.6673
	Ffs dreadful defending	0.479	0.4795
	♪ OLD FISH	0.070	0.5028
	@MannersAboveAll *laughs louder this time, shaking my head* That was really cheesy, wasn't it?	0.083	0.4936
Joy	@headfirst_dom I often imagine hoe our moon would feel meet-ing the jovial moons which are all special	0.500	0.5002
	Your attitude toward your struggles is equally as important as your actions to work through them.	0.340	0.3397
	Oi @THEWIGGYMESS you've absolutely fucking killed me.. 30 mins later im still crying with laughter.. Grindah.. Grindah... 🐨 hahahahahahaha	0.847	0.3726
	@WuffinArts :c You have my most heartfelt condolences. I'm glad it passed with levity and love in it's heart.	0.188	0.5872
Sadness	@nytimes media celebrated Don King endorsing #Obama in 08 and 12 now criticize him for endorsing #Trump who wants new Civil Rights era sad	0.562	0.5623
	@AFCGraMaChroi oh, sorry if I've discouraged you 😢	0.340	0.3397
	oh, btw - after a 6 month depression-free time I got a relapse now... superb #depression	0.917	0.462
	Ibiza blues hitting me hard already wow	0.833	0.4247

Table 2: Sample tweets where our system's prediction is best and worst.

ACM SIGKDD international conference on Knowledge discovery and data mining. ACM, pages 168–177.

Tomas Mikolov, Ilya Sutskever, Kai Chen, Greg S Corrado, and Jeff Dean. 2013. Distributed representations of words and phrases and their compositionality. In *Advances in neural information processing systems*. pages 3111–3119.

Saif M Mohammad. 2017. Word affect intensities. *arXiv preprint arXiv:1704.08798* .

Saif M. Mohammad and Felipe Bravo-Marquez. 2017a. Emotion intensities in tweets .

Saif M. Mohammad and Felipe Bravo-Marquez. 2017b. Emotion intensities in tweets. In *Proceedings of the sixth joint conference on lexical and computational semantics (*Sem)*. Vancouver, Canada.

Saif M. Mohammad and Felipe Bravo-Marquez. 2017c. Wassa-2017 shared task on emotion intensity. EMNLP 2017 Workshop on Computational Approaches to Subjectivity, Sentiment, and Social Media (WASSA), Copenhagen, Denmark.

Saif M Mohammad and Svetlana Kiritchenko. 2015. Using hashtags to capture fine emotion categories from tweets. *Computational Intelligence* 31(2):301–326.

Saif M Mohammad, Svetlana Kiritchenko, and Xiaodan Zhu. 2013. Nrc-canada: Building the state-of-the-art in sentiment analysis of tweets. *arXiv preprint arXiv:1308.6242* .

Saif M Mohammad and Peter D Turney. 2010. Emotions evoked by common words and phrases: Using mechanical turk to create an emotion lexicon. In *Proceedings of the NAACL HLT 2010 workshop on computational approaches to analysis and generation of emotion in text*. Association for Computational Linguistics, pages 26–34.

Finn Årup Nielsen. 2011. A new anew: Evaluation of a word list for sentiment analysis in microblogs. *arXiv preprint arXiv:1103.2903* .

Olutobi Owoputi, Brendan O'Connor, Chris Dyer, Kevin Gimpel, Nathan Schneider, and Noah A Smith. 2013. Improved part-of-speech tagging for online conversational text with word clusters. Association for Computational Linguistics.

F. Pedregosa, G. Varoquaux, A. Gramfort, V. Michel, B. Thirion, O. Grisel, M. Blondel, P. Prettenhofer, R. Weiss, V. Dubourg, J. Vanderplas, A. Passos, D. Cournapeau, M. Brucher, M. Perrot, and E. Duchesnay. 2011. Scikit-learn: Machine learning in Python. *Journal of Machine Learning Research* 12:2825–2830.

Jeffrey Pennington, Richard Socher, and Christopher D Manning. 2014. Glove: Global vectors for word representation. In *EMNLP*. volume 14, pages 1532–1543.

Sasa Petrovic, Miles Osborne, and Victor Lavrenko. 2010. The edinburgh twitter corpus. In *Proceedings of the NAACL HLT 2010 Workshop on Computational Linguistics in a World of Social Media*. pages 25–26.

Mike Thelwall, Kevan Buckley, Georgios Paltoglou, Di Cai, and Arvid Kappas. 2010. Sentiment strength detection in short informal text. *Journal of the American Society for Information Science and Technology* 61(12):2544–2558.

IITP at EmoInt-2017: Measuring Intensity of Emotions using Sentence Embeddings and Optimized Features

Md Shad Akhtar *, **Palaash Sawant** +, **Asif Ekbal** *, **Jyoti Pawar** +, **Pushpak Bhattacharyya** *

* Indian Institute of Technology Patna, India

`[shad.pcs15,asif,pb]@iitp.ac.in`

+ Goa University, India

`palaash77@gmail.com, jdp@unigoa.ac.in`

Abstract

This paper describes the system that we submitted as part of our participation in the shared task on Emotion Intensity (EmoInt-2017). We propose a Long short term memory (LSTM) based architecture cascaded with Support Vector Regressor (SVR) for intensity prediction. We also employ Particle Swarm Optimization (PSO) based feature selection algorithm for obtaining an optimized feature set for training and evaluation. System evaluation shows interesting results on the four emotion datasets i.e. *anger*, *fear*, *joy* and *sadness*. In comparison to the other participating teams our system was ranked 5th in the competition.

1 Introduction

Emotion analysis (Picard, 1997) deals with automatic extraction of emotion expressed in a user written text. Basic emotions expressed by a human being, as categorized by Ekman (1992), are *joy*, *sadness*, *surprise*, *fear*, *disgust* and *anger*. With the growing amount of social media generated text it has become a challenging task to efficiently mine emotions of the user. However, finding only the emotion does not always reflect exact state of mood of a user. Level or intensity of emotion often differs on a case-to-case basis within a single emotion. Some emotions are gentle (e.g *'not good'*) while others can be very severe (e.g. *'terrible'*). Finding the intensity level of the expressed emotion is another non-trivial task that researchers have to face.

The shared task on Emotion Intensity (EmoInt-2015) (Mohammad and Bravo-Marquez, 2017) was targeted to build an efficient system for intensity prediction on a continuous scale of 0 (least intense) to +1 (most intense). There were four datasets collected from Twitter, each reflecting one class of emotion i.e. *anger*, *fear*, *joy* and *sadness*, respectively.

We propose a Long Short Term Memory (LSTM) (Hochreiter and Schmidhuber, 1997) based neural network architecture cascaded with Support Vector Regression (SVR) (Smola and Schölkopf, 2004). We build our system on top of word embeddings along with the assistance of an optimized feature set obtained through Particle Swarm Optimization (PSO) (Kennedy and Eberhart, 1995). A major hurdle in obtaining a good word representation was the noisy and informal nature of text. Therefore, in the preliminary step, we perform a series of normalization heuristics in line with (Akhtar et al., 2015). The word embeddings of the resultant normalized text was more representative than that of the unnormalized text.

The high-dimensionality of feature vector often contributes to high complexity of the system. Also, some features have high degree of relevance towards a particular task/domain than the others. Careful selection of features for any task often leads to improved system performance. However, finding the relevant set of features is cumbersome and time-consuming task. Motivated by this we employ a Particle Swarm Optimization (PSO) based feature selection technique for selecting a subset of features from a feature pool. By utilizing the reduced and pruned feature set for training and evaluation, resultant system often performs considerably well. At the same time complexity of the system also reduces as it requires fewer parameters to learn. Literature survey shows successful application of PSO for various tasks and/or domains (Lin et al., 2008; Akhtar et al., 2017; Yadav et al., 2017).

212

Proceedings of the 8th Workshop on Computational Approaches to Subjectivity, Sentiment and Social Media Analysis, pages 212–218
Copenhagen, Denmark, September 7–11, 2017. ©2017 Association for Computational Linguistics

2 System Description

This section discusses our proposed approach in detail. The subsequent subsections present various components of our system.

2.1 Pre-processing and Normalization

- **Mentions, URLs and Punctuations:**
  In this step we filter out all the user mentions and URLs as they do not have any emotional bondings. Secondly, we strip off all the punctuations from the word boundaries to make it a valid dictionary word, e.g. 'first//' to 'first'. Improper use of punctuation was one of the reasons for data sparsity, when working with distributed word representation. After employing this step we observed that the number of out-of-vocabulary (OOV) words are effectively reduced.

- **Hashtag Segmentation:**
  Here the '#' symbol is stripped off from the hashtags. The resulting token is split into constituent words. For example, '#Spilled-BeerOnFloor' is converted to 'Spilled Beer On Floor'. This is achieved using the *Word-Segment* [1] module for word segmentation available in python. It is to be noted here that the segmented words are required only for obtaining word embeddings. For obtaining lexicon based features (cf. Section 2.3.1) the entire token with the '#' is used.

- **Elongation:**
  User tends to express their state of emotion by elongating a valid word e.g. *'jooooy'*, *'goooodd'* etc. In this step, all such elongated words are identified and converted into valid words by removing the consecutive characters. For example *'jooyyyy'* and *'jooooy'* are converted to *'joy'*.

- **Verb present participle:**
  In Twitter domain, it is observed that user tends to omit the character *'i'* or *'g'* in words ending with 'ing'. For example, *'going'* is written as *'goin'* or *'gong'*. Such errors have been identified and corrected. We apply this rule for all the verbs that ends with either *'ng'* of *'in'*.

- **Frequent noisy term:** We compile a dictionary of frequently used slang terms and abbreviations along with its normal form that are commonly in practice in the Twitter domain. Every token in a tweet is searched in this dictionary. If a match is found then it is replaced with the normal form. The list was compiled utilizing the datasets of WNUT-2015 shared task on Twitter Lexical Normalization (Baldwin et al., 2015).

- **Expand contractions:** Contraction of a multi-word token is formed by making it shorter by dropping some characters and placing an apostrophe between them. For example, the contraction of 'i am' is 'im'. We compile a dictionary of contractions and its normalized forms employing the datasets of (Baldwin et al., 2015). We replace every occurrence of a contraction in a tweet by its expanded form.

2.2 LSTM based Approach

Long short term memory (Hochreiter and Schmidhuber, 1997) network is a special kind of recurrent network that can efficiently learn sequences over a longer period of time. The proposed method utilizes LSTM network to obtain the sentence embedding vector, which is then fed as an input to SVR for prediction. The proposed network comprises of one Bidirectional LSTM (BiLSTM) (Schuster and Paliwal, 1997) layer followed by two dense layers. Hidden layer of the LSTMs consists of 100 neurons whereas the dense layers contain 100 and 50 neurons, respectively.

2.2.1 Word Embeddings

Word embedding (or word vector) is a distributed representation of words that contains syntactic and semantic information (Mikolov et al., 2013; Pennington et al., 2014). For this task, we use GloVe (Pennington et al., 2014) pre-trained word embedding trained on *common crawl* corpus. Each token in the tweet is represented by 300 dimension word vector. The choice of common crawl word embeddings for Twitter datasets is because of the normalization steps (Section 2.1). We observe that the application of normalization has a positive effect on the overall performance of the system.

---

[1] https://github.com/grantjenks/wordsegment

2.3 Particle Swarm Optimization based Feature Selection

Particle swarm optimization (Kennedy and Eberhart, 2001) is an optimization technique build over the social behavior of a flock of birds. Each potential solution, also known as particles, stores its best position attained so far. The global best solution recorded by any particle in the flock is also recorded and shared among the particles. In the search space, each particle moves towards the optimal solution based on its own best position and the global best position. Eventually, particles concentrate on a limited search space dictated by the global best solution found so far. The entire process is governed by three operations namely, *evaluate*, *compare* and *imitate*. Evaluation step quantifies the goodness of each particle, whereas, the comparison step obtains the best solution by comparing the particles. The imitate step produces new particles based on the best solution. A particle is an n-dimensional binary vector, where each element represents one feature. The value of each element (i.e. 0 or 1) signifies the presence or absence of its corresponding feature. Consequently, missing feature in a particle does not participate in training and testing of the system. On termination, PSO yields a particle (encoding a particular feature subset) that represents the best solution. We closely follow PSO based feature selection algorithm of (Akhtar et al., 2017) in the current work.

2.3.1 Feature Set

This section describes the features that we extract to predict the emotion intensity. All these features are fed to the PSO to generate the optimized feature set.

- **VADER Sentiment:** VADER (Gilbert, 2014) stands for Valence Aware Dictionary and Sentiment Reasoner. It is a rule-based sentiment analysis technique designed to work with contents on social media. For every input tweet, it provides positive, negative, neutral and compound sentiment score. We use these four values as features.

- **Lexicon based Features:** For each tweet we extract the following lexicon based features:
    - **Polar word count:** Count of positive and negative words using the *MPQA subjectivity lexicon* (Wiebe and Mihal-

cea, 2006) and *Bing Liu lexicon* (Ding et al., 2008).
    - **Aggregate polarity scores:** Positive and negative scores are obtained from each of the following lexicons: *Sentiment140* (Mohammad et al., 2013), *AFINN* (Nielsen, 2011) and *Sentiwordnet* (Baccianella et al., 2010). It is calculated by aggregating the positive and negative word scores provided by each lexicon.
    - **Aggregate polarity scores (Hashtags):** Aggregate of positive and negative scores of the hashtags in a tweet is calculated from *NRC Hashtag Sentiment lexicon* (Mohammad et al., 2013).
    - **Emotion word count:** Count of the number of words matching each emotion from *NRC Word-Emotion Association Lexicon* (Mohammad and Turney, 2013).
    - **Aggregate emotion score:** Sum of emotion associations of the words present in *NRC-10 Expanded lexicon* (Bravo-Marquez et al., 2016).
    - **Aggregate emotion score (Hashtags):** Sum of emotion associations of the hashtags in tweet matching the *NRC Hashtag Emotion Association Lexicon* (Mohammad and Kiritchenko, 2015).
    - **Emoticons score:** Positive and negative score of the emoticons obtained from *AFINN* project (Nielsen, 2011).
    - **Negation count:** Count of the number of negating words in the tweet.

2.4 Regression Model

An overall schema of the proposed system is depicted in Figure 1. Our proposed regression model consists of LSTM network and Support Vector Regression (SVR). First a LSTM network is trained using word vectors as input with *sigmoid* activation. Upon completion of training, the output of the top most hidden layer is used as *sentence embedding*. The trained sentence embeddings represent the relevant semantic and syntactic features of the tweets. Next, optimized feature set, as obtained by PSO, is concatenated with sentence embeddings for training a SVR model. The idea of cascading SVR with LSTM was motivated by the recent works of (Akhtar et al., 2016; Wang et al., 2016).

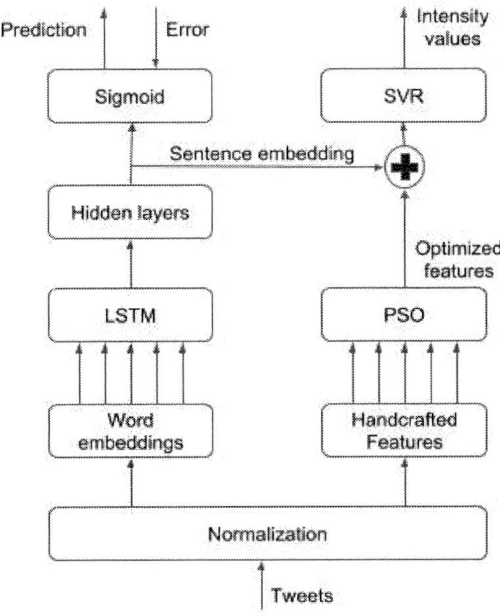

Figure 1: Proposed architecture.

3 Experiments, Results and Analysis

3.1 Dataset

The evaluation dataset (Mohammad and Bravo-Marquez, 2017) comprises of four emotions i.e. *anger*, *fear*, *sadness* and *joy*. The training set contains 857, 1147, 786 & 823 tweets for *anger, fear, sadness* and *joy*, respectively. The development set contains 84, 110, 74 & 79 tweets, while test set comprises of 760, 995, 673 & 714 tweets, respectively for each domain.

3.2 Experimental Results

We use Python based neural network library, i.e. Keras[2], for the implementation. For tokenization of tweets, we utilize CMU ARK tool[3]. The official evaluation metric was Pearson coefficient. We use *tanh* as an activation function at the intermediate layers while at the output layer we utilize *sigmoid*. We employ *Adam* (Kingma and Ba, 2014) optimizer and set the Dropout (Srivastava et al., 2014) as 40%. We train our network for 50 epochs. Table 1 depicts the evaluation results on the development and test sets. We first train a BiLSTM network

---

[2] http://keras.io/
[3] http://www.cs.cmu.edu/~ark/

utilizing GloVe common crawl embeddings. The resultant network produces average Pearson score of merely 0.1877. We observe that a good percentage of tokens (mostly noisy) were missing in the embeddings - thus poses challenge to the network during the learning phase. Subsequently, we try to minimize the effect of noisy tokens by utilizing GloVe Twitter embeddings. Though, the network obtains improved average Pearson score at 0.1921, improvement is not significant. On analysis we find similar issues with Twitter embeddings. To address the problem of data sparsity we employ a series of heuristics (c.f. Section 2.1) in order to normalize the text. Consequently, we obtain average Pearson score of 0.6289 with normalization outperforming the baseline system (0.610) provided by the organizers of the shared task.

We then cascade the LSTM network with SVR for the final predictions (*LSTM+SVR*). On cascading we obtain 0.6641 average Pearson score, reporting a gain of 0.04 points. Finally, to further improve the prediction accuracies we introduce various handcrafted lexicon features (c.f. Section 2.3.1) into the architecture (*LSTM+SVR+Feat*). Although, we see an improvement of 0.01 point in average Pearson score, introduction of same set of lexicons features have contrasting effect on different emotion datasets i.e. *anger, fear, joy* & *sadness*. We observe improvement for *joy* and *sadness*, whereas for *anger* use of this same set of features degrades the system performance. For *fear*, introduction of features to *LSTM+SVR* almost have no effect. Motivated by these results we perform PSO based feature selection algorithm in order to find optimal set of features for different emotions. We get the best average Pearson score of 0.7271 on the development set by utilizing sentence embeddings, optimized feature set and SVR (*LSTM+SVR+PSO*). We also observe improvement in Pearson score for each of the emotion datasets ranging from 0.5-0.7 points over *LSTM+SVR*. It is evident from the obtained results that normalization of tweets is a major factor in obtaining good performance. Also, introduction of the PSO based feature selection in *LSTM+SVR* hybrid model further assists the system in improving the performance.

On final evaluation, i.e. on the test set, our proposed system (*LSTM+SVR+PSO*) scores an average Pearson score of 0.682. In comparison, baseline system produces 0.6470 average Pearson

Models	Descriptions	Pearson score				
		Anger	Fear	Joy	Sadness	Avg

RESULT ON DEV SET

Models	Descriptions	Anger	Fear	Joy	Sadness	Avg
Sentence embeddings - Normalization*	*LSTM*	0.178	0.029	0.462	0.080	0.187
Sentence embeddings - Normalization*#	*LSTM*	0.153	0.050	0.462	0.101	0.192
Sentence embeddings	*LSTM*	0.629	0.645	0.737	0.504	0.628
Sentence embeddings	*LSTM+SVR*	0.669	0.661	0.761	0.563	0.664
Sentence embeddings + All features	*LSTM+SVR+Feat*	0.610	0.663	0.806	0.611	0.673
Sentence embeddings + PSO	***LSTM+SVR+PSO***	**0.719**	**0.732**	**0.826**	**0.632**	**0.727**
Baseline (Mohammad and Bravo-Marquez, 2017)	*LibLinear*	0.599	0.580	0.694	0.569	0.610

RESULT ON TEST SET

Models	Descriptions	Anger	Fear	Joy	Sadness	Avg
Sentence embeddings + PSO	***LSTM+SVR+PSO***	**0.649**	**0.713**	**0.657**	**0.709**	**0.682**
Baseline (Mohammad and Bravo-Marquez, 2017)	*LibLinear*	0.625	0.620	0.635	0.706	0.647

Table 1: Evaluation results on development and test set. *Without normalization step; Other models are with normalization. #With GloVe Twitter word embeddings; Other models utilize GloVe common crawl embeddings.

Lexicons	Datasets			
	Anger	Fear	Joy	Sadness
MPQA			✓	✓
Bing Liu		✓		
SentiWordNET		✓	✓	✓
AFINN			✓	
Sentiment140			✓	✓
NRC Hashtag Sentiment		✓	✓	✓
NRC Hashtag Emotion	anger	anger, anticipation, fear & surprise	anticipation, joy, sadness & surprise	disgust & sadness
NRC10 Expanded	anger, disgust, surprise, positive, anger-ex, fear-ex, positive-ex, negative-ex	anticipation, joy, sadness, surprise, positive, negative, fear-ex, disgust-ex, surprise-ex	anticipation, joy, trust, joy-ex, surprise-ex	anger, anticipation, disgust, fear, surprise, anticipation-ex, disgust-ex, fear-ex, surprise-ex, negative-ex
Emoticons-AFINN		✓		✓

Table 2: Optimized feature set for four datasets.

score, a difference of 4%. For *anger* and *fear* we observe a small performance drop on the test set as compared to the development set while our proposed system performs better in case of *sadness*. Further, we observe that our system does not perform at par (a drop of nearly 17%) for *joy* as compared to the development set. However, similar phenomenon was observed for the baseline system as well i.e. a drop of 6% in *joy*. We also observe that our proposed system is statistically significant over baseline system with *p*-value = 0.03683.

Table 2 shows the optimized set of feature for four datasets i.e. *anger, fear, joy* and *sadness*. It is evident from the table that some of the features have high degree of relevance than others. For example, NRC Hashtag Emotion (Mohammad and Kiritchenko, 2015) & NRC10 Expanded (Bravo-Marquez et al., 2016) lexicons have been utilized by all four of them, whereas Bing Liu (Ding et al., 2008) and AFINN (Nielsen, 2011) lexicons have been employed by only *fear* & *joy*, respectively.

3.3 Error Analysis

We also perform error analysis on the obtained results. Following are the few cases where our system consistently suffers in predicting the intensity values.

- Presence of high intensity emotion words (such as anger, revenge, fury, exciting etc) makes it non-trivial for the system to correctly predicts the intensity values.

Example 1:
Tweet: #Forgiveness might make us look #weak, but the weakest person is the one who holds #anger, #hatred, and #revenge.
Actual: 0.354 **Predicted:** 0.630

Example 2:
Tweet: Police: Atlanta rapper Shawty Lo killed in fiery car crash.
Actual: 0.396 **Predicted:** 0.619

4 Conclusion

In this paper, we have presented a hybrid LSTM-SVR architecture for predicting the intensity level *w.r.t.* to an emotion. We first applied various heuristics for normalizing the tweets. Following this step, the noisiness of tweets is addressed to a great effect and consequently improves the performance of the system. The proposed approach further utilized relevant set of hand-crafted features obtained through a PSO based feature selection technique. Adding optimized features in the proposed architecture (*LSTM+SVR+PSO*) attains significant improvement over the system without it (*LSTM+SVR*) and this phenomenon was observed for all the four emotion datasets i.e. *anger*, *fear*, *joy* and *sadness*.

References

Md Shad Akhtar, Deepak Gupta, Asif Ekbal, and Pushpak Bhattacharyya. 2017. Feature selection and ensemble construction: A two-step method for aspect based sentiment analysis. *Knowledge-Based Systems* 125:116 – 135.

Md Shad Akhtar, Ayush Kumar, Asif Ekbal, and Pushpak Bhattacharyya. 2016. A hybrid deep learning architecture for sentiment analysis. In *COLING 2016, 26th International Conference on Computational Linguistics, Proceedings of the Conference: Technical Papers, December 11-16, 2016, Osaka, Japan*. pages 482–493.

Md Shad Akhtar, Utpal Kumar Sikdar, and Asif Ekbal. 2015. IITP: Hybrid Approach for Text Normalization in Twitter. In *Proceedings of the ACL 2015 Workshop on Noisy User-generated Text (WNUT-2015*. Beijing, China, pages 106–110.

Stefano Baccianella, Andrea Esuli, and Fabrizio Sebastiani. 2010. SentiWordNet 3.0: An Enhanced Lexical Resource for Sentiment Analysis and Opinion Mining. In *LREC*. volume 10, pages 2200–2204.

Timothy Baldwin, Marie Catherine de Marneffe, Bo Han, Young-Bum Kim, Alan Ritter, and Wei Xu. 2015. Shared Tasks of the 2015 Workshop on Noisy User-generated Text: Twitter Lexical Normalization and Named Entity Recognition. In *Proceedings of the ACL 2015 Workshop on Noisy User-generated Text*. Beijing, China, pages 126–135.

Felipe Bravo-Marquez, Eibe Frank, Saif M Mohammad, and Bernhard Pfahringer. 2016. Determining word–emotion associations from tweets by multilabel classification. In *WI'16*. IEEE Computer Society, pages 536–539.

Xiaowen Ding, Bing Liu, and Philip S Yu. 2008. A Holistic Lexicon-based Approach to Opinion Mining. In *Proceedings of the 2008 international conference on web search and data mining*. ACM, pages 231–240.

Paul Ekman. 1992. An argument for basic emotions. *Cognition and Emotion* pages 169–200.

CJ Hutto Eric Gilbert. 2014. Vader: A parsimonious rule-based model for sentiment analysis of social media text. In *Eighth International Conference on Weblogs and Social Media (ICWSM-14)*. *Available at (20/04/16) http://comp. social. gatech. edu/papers/icwsm14. vader. hutto. pdf*.

Sepp Hochreiter and Jürgen Schmidhuber. 1997. Long short-term memory. *Neural computation* 9(8):1735–1780.

James Kennedy and Russell C. Eberhart. 1995. Particle swarm optimization. In *Proceedings of the IEEE International Conference on Neural Networks*. pages 1942–1948.

James Kennedy and Russell C. Eberhart. 2001. *Swarm Intelligence*. Morgan Kaufmann Publishers Inc., San Francisco, CA, USA.

Diederik P. Kingma and Jimmy Ba. 2014. Adam: A method for stochastic optimization. *CoRR* abs/1412.6980. http://dblp.uni-trier.de/db/journals/corr/corr1412.html.

Shih-Wei Lin, Kuo-Ching Ying, Shih-Chieh Chen, and Zne-Jung Lee. 2008. Particle swarm optimization for parameter determination and feature selection of support vector machines. *Expert systems with applications* 35(4):1817–1824.

Tomas Mikolov, Kai Chen, Greg Corrado, and Jeffrey Dean. 2013. Efficient Estimation of Word Representations in Vector Space. *arXiv preprint arXiv:1301.3781* .

Saif Mohammad, Svetlana Kiritchenko, and Xiaodan Zhu. 2013. NRC-Canada: Building the State-of-the-Art in Sentiment Analysis of Tweets. In *Proceedings of the seventh international workshop on Semantic Evaluation Exercises (SemEval-2013)*. Atlanta, Georgia, USA.

Saif M. Mohammad and Felipe Bravo-Marquez. 2017. WASSA-2017 Shared Task on Emotion Intensity. In *Proceedings of the Workshop on Computational Approaches to Subjectivity, Sentiment and Social Media Analysis (WASSA)*. Copenhagen, Denmark.

Saif M Mohammad and Svetlana Kiritchenko. 2015. Using hashtags to capture fine emotion categories from tweets. *Computational Intelligence* 31(2):301–326.

Saif M. Mohammad and Peter D. Turney. 2013. Crowdsourcing a Word-Emotion Association Lexicon 29(3):436–465.

Finn Årup Nielsen. 2011. A new ANEW: Evaluation of a word list for sentiment analysis in microblogs. *arXiv preprint arXiv:1103.2903* .

Jeffrey Pennington, Richard Socher, and Christopher D. Manning. 2014. Glove: Global vectors for word representation. In *Empirical Methods in Natural Language Processing (EMNLP)*. pages 1532–1543. http://www.aclweb.org/anthology/D14-1162.

Rosalind W. Picard. 1997. *Affective Computing*. MIT Press, Cambridge, MA, USA.

M. Schuster and K.K. Paliwal. 1997. Bidirectional Recurrent Neural Networks. *Trans. Sig. Proc.* 45(11):2673–2681.

Alex J. Smola and Bernhard Schölkopf. 2004. A tutorial on support vector regression. *Statistics and Computing* 14(3):199–222. https://doi.org/10.1023/B:STCO.0000035301.49549.88.

Nitish Srivastava, Geoffrey Hinton, Alex Krizhevsky, Ilya Sutskever, and Ruslan Salakhutdinov. 2014. Dropout: A simple way to prevent neural networks from overfitting. *Journal of Machine Learning Research* 15:1929–1958. http://jmlr.org/papers/v15/srivastava14a.html.

Wenya Wang, Sinno Jialin Pan, Daniel Dahlmeier, and Xiaokui Xiao. 2016. Recursive Neural Conditional Random Fields for Aspect-based Sentiment Analysis. *CoRR* abs/1603.06679. http://arxiv.org/abs/1603.06679.

Janyce Wiebe and Rada Mihalcea. 2006. Word Sense and Subjectivity. In *Proceedings of the 21st International Conference on Computational Linguistics and the 44th annual meeting of the Association for Computational Linguistics*. Association for Computational Linguistics, pages 1065–1072.

Shweta Yadav, Asif Ekbal, Sriparna Saha, and Pushpak Bhattacharyya. 2017. Entity Extraction in Biomedical Corpora: An Approach to Evaluate Word Embedding Features with PSO based Feature Selection. In *Proceedings of the 15th Conference of the European Chapter of the Association for Computational Linguistics (EACL)*. Valencia, Spain, page 11591170.

NSEmo at EmoInt-2017: An Ensemble to Predict Emotion Intensity in Tweets

Sreekanth Madisetty and **Maunendra Sankar Desarkar**
Department of Computer Science and Engineering
IIT Hyderabad, Hyderabad, India
{cs15resch11006, maunendra}@iith.ac.in

Abstract

In this paper, we describe a method to predict emotion intensity in tweets. Our approach is an ensemble of three regression methods. The first method uses content-based features (hashtags, emoticons, elongated words, etc.). The second method considers word n-grams and character n-grams for training. The final method uses lexicons, word embeddings, word n-grams, character n-grams for training the model. An ensemble of these three methods gives better performance than individual methods. We applied our method on WASSA emotion dataset. Achieved results are as follows: average Pearson correlation is 0.706, average Spearman correlation is 0.696, average Pearson correlation for gold scores in range 0.5 to 1 is 0.539, and average Spearman correlation for gold scores in range 0.5 to 1 is 0.514.

1 Introduction

Twitter is a popular microblogging platforms in which users share their opinions, feelings on different topics which are happening across the world.

The aim of sentiment analysis is to detect the positive, negative, or neutral feelings from the text, whereas the aim of emotion analysis is to detect the types of feelings in the text, such as anger, fear, joy, sadness, disgust, and surprise. In this paper, we focus on emotion analysis in tweets. Sentiment analysis of Twitter data is very challenging. Users who are posting on Twitter often do not follow grammar rules. This results in noise in the Twitter data. This noisy nature of Twitter data is in the form of spelling mistakes, use of slang words, sentence mistakes, abbreviations,

elongated words, etc. Moreover, the text limit is 140 characters long. In this paper, four emotions are considered. They are anger, fear, joy, and sadness. The task is to predict the emotion intensity of each test instance in a range between 0 and 1. The emotion intensity 1 indicates the maximum emotion whereas 0 indicates the least emotion felt by the author of the tweet.

We use an ensemble of three methods, namely, Support Vector Regression (SVR), Neural Networks, and Baseline to predict the emotion intensity in tweets. The performance of ensemble approach is better than that of the individual methods.

There is a growing interest in sentiment analysis of tweets across variety of domains such as health (Chew and Eysenbach, 2010), stock market (Bollen et al., 2011), disaster management (Mandel et al., 2012), and presedential elections (Wang et al., 2012).

The rest of the paper is organized as follows. Related literature for current work is presented in Section 2. Next in Section 3, problem statement and details of the methods used in this paper are defined. Experimental evaluation of the method is shown in Section 4. We conclude the work by providing directions for future research in Section 5.

2 Related Work

With the increase of user-generated contents in social media, blogs, discussion fora, etc. people are focusing on the problem of analyzing the sentiments expressed in these contents. Go et al. (2009) used emoticons as labels for training data and distance supervision to classify tweets into positive or negative class. Pak and Paroubek (2010) presented a method for automatic collection of a corpus that can be used to train a sentiment classi-

Proceedings of the 8th Workshop on Computational Approaches to Subjectivity, Sentiment and Social Media Analysis, pages 219–224
Copenhagen, Denmark, September 7–11, 2017. ©2017 Association for Computational Linguistics

fier. The authors have classified the tweets into three classes, namely, positive, negative, and neutral using trained classifier. Kouloumpis et al. (2011) used linguistic and lexical features to detect the sentiments of Twitter messages. The authors showed that Part-Of-Speech (POS) features might not be useful for sentiment analysis in the Twitter domain.

Khan et al. (2015) proposed a method for combining lexicon-based and learning-based methods for Twitter sentiment analysis. There has been a lot of work done in the SemEval Twitter sentiment analysis tasks (Rosenthal et al., 2014, 2015; Nakov et al., 2016; Rosenthal et al., 2017).

Combining classifiers has been proved to be very successful for classification problems. A system named Webis achieved top-rank in SemEval-2015 subtask B, task 10 "Sentiment Analysis in Twitter" (Hagen et al., 2015). The authors reproduced four state-of-the-art Twitter sentiment classification methods with diverse feature sets. The predictions of four classifiers are combined by taking the average of classifiers' individual confidence scores for the three classes and predicts the label with the highest score. In the Netflix competition, the winner used an ensemble method to implement a collaborative filtering algorithm (Töscher et al., 2009). In KDD Cup 2009 also, the winner used an ensemble method (Niculescu-Mizil et al., 2009). Zhang et al. (2016) used a classifier fusion based method for polarity classification in Twitter. The authors have used four classifiers in the ensemble method.

3   System Description

In this section, we describe the methodology used for WASSA 2017 shared task on emotion intensity. The WASSA 2017 shared task (Mohammad and Bravo-Marquez, 2017b) problem definition is as follows: *Given a tweet and an emotion E, determine the intensity of the emotion E felt by the author of the tweet.* The intensity is a real-valued score between 0 and 1. The maximum possible emotion intensity 1 stands for feeling the maximum amount of emotion E and the minimum possible emotion intensity 0 stands for feeling the least amount of emotion E. There are four categories of emotion given in the task, namely, anger, fear, joy, and sadness. We combine the three methods (Support vector regression, Neural networks, and Baseline) for predicting the emotion intensity.

3.1   Data Preprocessing

For any machine learning algorithm preprocessing the data is a very important step. As discussed in Section 1 tweets often contain a lot of noise. Before applying the model to the data, preprocessing should be done. Removal of unnecessary tokens from the text will improve the performance of the model. All words are converted to lower case, URLs are removed, numbers, and @ mentions are also removed as these tokens do not contribute in predicting the sentiment of the tweet. Hashtags, emoticons, punctuation marks (?, !) are retained because they will help in predicting the sentiment.

3.2   Support Vector Regression

This is the first method used for predicting emotion intensity in tweets. First, we define the features used in this work.

3.2.1   Features

- No. of hashtags: The number of hashtags present in the tweet.

- Length: Length of the tweet

- Word n-grams: We used word n-grams with n ranging from 1 to 3 i.e., unigrams, bigrams, and trigrams. All these n-grams are word level n-grams.

- Char n-grams: We also used character n-grams. These n-grams include the existence of two, three, four, five, and six consecutive sequence of characters.

- Punctuation: Number of punctuation symbols (?, !) present in the tweet.

- Emoticons: Number of emoticons present in the tweet.

- Elongated words: The number of words with one character repeated more than twice, for example, 'haaapy'.

- Lexicon: NRC Affect Intensity Lexicon (Mohammad, 2017) is used.

All the above features are used for training the model.

3.3 Neural Networks

This is the second method used to determine the emotion intensity in tweets. A multi-layered neural network with two hidden layers is used. These hidden layers consist of 125 and 25 neurons respectively. We used Keras for developing this multi-layered neural network model. Keras is a useful Python library for developing deep learning models. TensorFlow is used as backend for Keras. Word n-grams and character n-grams are used in this model.

3.4 Baseline

This method was given in WASSA 2017 shared task as the baseline method (Mohammad and Bravo-Marquez, 2017a). The authors have created the datasets of tweets annotated for anger, fear, joy, and sadness emotion intensities. They have used the best-worst scaling technique to improve annotation consistency and obtained reliable scores. They created a regression system, *AffectiveTweetsPackage* for the Weka machine learning workbench, to automatically determine emotion intensity and related tasks. The following features are used in this baseline system.

- word n-grams: This feature will check whether the word n-grams are present in the tweet or not, with n values 1, 2, 3, and 4.

- char n-grams: It will check whether the char n-grams are present in the tweet or not, with n values 3, 4, and 5.

- Word Embeddings: *Word2Vec* (Mikolov et al., 2013) is used to create word embeddings with negative sampling skip-gram model. Vector for the tweet is created by averaging the individual word embeddings of the tweet. Word vectors are trained from the Edinburgh Twitter Corpus (Petrovic et al., 2010). Number of dimensions used is 400.

- Lexicons: Lexicons used in this system are AFINN (Nielsen, 2011), BingLiu (Hu and Liu, 2004) , MPQA (Wilson et al., 2005), NRC Affect Intensity Lexicon (Mohammad, 2017), NRC Word-Emotion Association Lexicon (Mohammad and Turney, 2013), NRC10 Expanded (Bravo-Marquez et al., 2016), NRC Hashtag Emotion Association Lexicon (Mohammad and Kiritchenko, 2015), NRC Hashtag Sentiment Lexicon (Mohammad et al., 2013), Sentiment140 (Mohammad et al., 2013), SentiWordNet (Baccianella et al., 2010), SentiStrength (Thelwall et al., 2012).

3.5 Ensemble Combination

Ensemble methods use several learning algorithms to obtain better predictive performance than any other individual method used in the ensemble combination. There are several ways to combine the learning models such as bagging, boosting, majority voting, simple averaging, stacking, etc. Bagging trains each model in the ensemble using a subset of the training data drawn randomly, whereas boosting builds an ensemble in such a way that new model performance will improve for instances that are misclassified by previous models.

In majority voting, each model makes a prediction for the test instance, and the final prediction of the model is the one which is predicted by more models. Simple averaging is also another method for combining predictions of learned models, in which the prediction of the model for each test instance is the average of the predictions of the individual models. Stacking is another approach where the models are combined using another machine learning algorithm. The predictions of the individual model are the input to another learning algorithm (meta-learning algorithm).

We tested different ways of combining the individual regressors to an ensemble method. We observed that each method tries to predict the emotion intensity closer to the actual predictions for some test instances that others fail for. This is because of having different feature sets for different methods which are used in an ensemble. When we combine the individual regression methods, the performance of an ensemble will increase because of individual strengths of the methods. Finally, we observed that simple averaging performs better than other methods.

Our ensemble works as follows: SVR is trained separately for each class, anger, fear, joy, and sadness by considering train and dev data. Testing is performed on test data, and predictions of each class are saved in separate files. These predictions are real-valued scores between 0 and 1. We used all features that are listed in Section 3.2.1 for this method. Next, a multi-layered neural network is trained on the same data as SVR. Two hidden layers are used with 125 and 25 neurons. Num-

Table 1: Number of tweets in each phase.

Emotion	Training	Validation	Testing	All
anger	857	84	760	1701
fear	1147	110	995	2252
joy	823	74	714	1611
sadness	786	74	673	1533
All	3613	342	3142	7097

Table 2: Submitted results for the competition.

Result	Pearson 0to1	Spearman 0to1	Pearson .5to1	Spearman .5to1
Submitted Results	0.525	0.528	0.373	0.369

ber of features is the input to the input layer, and the output is a real value between 0 and 1. For this reason, sigmoid activation function is used in the output layer. Word n-grams and character n-grams are used as features for this model. Then, we directly used the baseline algorithm given in the shared task. It is trained on the same data as SVR and neural network models.

Word embeddings of Edinburgh corpus, lexicons, word n-grams, char n-grams are used as features. Word embeddings are available for 50 dimensions and 400 dimensions. However, we found 400 dimension word embedding to perform better in our experiments. Predictions for each class are obtained from each of the trained models. Finally, the average of individual methods prediction for each test instance is considered as final prediction. The final prediction value is also in between 0 and 1.

4 Experiments

4.1 Data

There are four emotion categories, namely, anger, fear, joy, and sadness in the dataset given in the shared task (Mohammad, 2017). Details of number of tweets in each category for training, validation, and testing are shown in Table 1.

4.2 Results

In this section, we describe the results obtained by our methods. For evaluating the proposed methods, two evaluation metrics Pearson correlation and Spearman correlation are used. Pearson correlation for two sets is equal to 1 if they have a high positive correlation, -1 if they have a high negative correlation, and 0 if there is no correlation.

Table 2 shows our submitted results to the com-

petition before the deadline. Word unigrams, and some limited features (lexicon, hashtags, punctuation) related to the sentiment are used, and SVR is used for learning and predicting the emotion intensities. Later, we improved our method using extra features and using different approaches. Table 3 shows the SVR model using polynomial kernel function. Table 4 shows SVR model using RBF kernel, and Table 5 shows SVR model using linear kernel function. We observe that SVR using linear kernel function is performing better than SVR with RBF and SVR with polynomial kernel function. So, we used SVR with linear kernel in the ensemble. The parameters used in SVR are gamma = 0.1 (kernel coefficient for rbf, poly), and C = 0.001 (penalty term)

Table 6 describes the results using neural networks model with word n-grams and char n-grams as features. The parameters used in this experiment are as follows: loss function is entropy, optimization algorithm is stochastic gradient descent, rectifier activation function is used in the hidden layers whereas sigmoid activation function is used in the output layer. Table 7 presents the results of the baseline method using 50 dimensional word embeddings of Edinburgh corpus whereas baseline method with 400 dimensional word embeddings are presented in Table 8.

The results of ensemble combination of SVR using linear kernel, neural networks, baseline method with 400 dimensional word embeddings are presented in Table 9. We have achieved the following results in the ensemble: average Pearson correlation is 0.706, average Spearman correlation is 0.696, average Pearson correlation for gold scores in range 0.5 to 1 is 0.539, and Spearman correlation for gold scores in range 0.5 to 1 is 0.514. Comparison of proposed method with baseline methods is presented in Table 10. We observe that our proposed method correlation values are higher than two variations of baselines (50d, 400d). We also observe that ensemble method is performing better than any other individual method used in combination. This is due to different feature sets used in the methods mentioned in Section 3.

5 Conclusion

We created two methods Support Vector Regression and Neural Networks and used baseline method from the shared task to detect the emotion

Table 3: SVR with polynomial kernel. Table 4: SVR with rbf kernel. Table 5: SVR with linear kernel.

Emotion	Pearson 0to1	Spearman 0to1	Pearson .5to1	Spearman .5to1	Pearson 0to1	Spearman 0to1	Pearson .5to1	Spearman .5to1	Pearson 0to1	Spearman 0to1	Pearson .5to1	Spearman .5to1
anger	0.405	0.455	0.278	0.276	0.591	0.583	0.431	0.422	0.601	0.590	0.426	0.416
fear	0.333	0.466	0.239	0.250	0.606	0.571	0.491	0.428	0.617	0.589	0.491	0.425
joy	0.416	0.487	0.283	0.354	0.572	0.580	0.374	0.396	0.603	0.621	0.377	0.399
sadness	0.482	0.552	0.438	0.465	0.656	0.656	0.543	0.533	0.665	0.679	0.535	0.531
Average	0.409	0.490	0.310	0.336	0.606	0.597	0.460	0.445	0.622	0.620	0.457	0.443

Table 6: Neural Networks.

Emotion	Pearson 0to1	Spearman 0to1	Pearson .5to1	Spearman .5to1
anger	0.570	0.557	0.432	0.436
fear	0.601	0.567	0.492	0.451
joy	0.571	0.565	0.350	0.329
sadness	0.642	0.630	0.499	0.491
Average	0.596	0.580	0.443	0.427

Table 7: Baseline with 50d word embeddings.

Emotion	Pearson 0to1	Spearman 0to1	Pearson .5to1	Spearman .5to1
anger	0.631	0.620	0.502	0.469
fear	0.622	0.606	0.477	0.431
joy	0.635	0.641	0.368	0.354
sadness	0.710	0.713	0.537	0.521
Average	0.649	0.645	0.471	0.444

Table 8: Baseline with 400d word embeddings.

Emotion	Pearson 0to1	Spearman 0to1	Pearson .5to1	Spearman .5to1
anger	0.636	0.627	0.502	0.472
fear	0.633	0.621	0.484	0.441
joy	0.650	0.654	0.379	0.365
sadness	0.713	0.714	0.555	0.534
Average	0.658	0.654	0.480	0.453

Table 9: Ensemble model combining Support Vector Regression using linear kernel, Neural Networks, Baseline method.

Emotion	Pearson 0to1	Spearman 0to1	Pearson .5to1	Spearman .5to1
anger	0.687	0.672	0.548	0.523
fear	0.703	0.676	0.574	0.517
joy	0.693	0.696	0.435	0.429
sadness	0.739	0.741	0.601	0.587
Average	**0.706**	**0.696**	**0.539**	**0.514**

Table 10: Comparison of proposed method with baseline method. The number in the brackets is the percentage difference with closest competitor (Baseline2).

Method	Pearson 0to1	Spearman 0to1	Pearson .5to1	Spearman .5to1
Baseline1 (50d)	0.649	0.645	0.471	0.444
Baseline2 (400d)	0.658	0.654	0.480	0.453
Ensemble	**0.706** (**7.29%**)	**0.696** (**6.42%**)	**0.539** (**12.29%**)	**0.514** (**13.47%**)

intensity in tweets. The predictions of these three methods are averaged to get the final prediction of each test instance for each class. The results of ensemble method show that average Pearson correlation, average Spearman correlation values are higher than the baseline method, SVR, neural networks.

For future work, we would like to see other learning methods which can improve the performance of the ensemble, and also we want to identify additional features for predicting the emotion intensity. We would like to use different Twitter word embeddings other than Edinburgh corpus in future.

References

Stefano Baccianella, Andrea Esuli, and Fabrizio Sebastiani. 2010. Sentiwordnet 3.0: An enhanced lexical resource for sentiment analysis and opinion mining. In *LREC*. volume 10, pages 2200–2204.

Johan Bollen, Huina Mao, and Xiaojun Zeng. 2011. Twitter mood predicts the stock market. *Journal of computational science* 2(1):1–8.

Felipe Bravo-Marquez, Eibe Frank, Saif M Mohammad, and Bernhard Pfahringer. 2016. Determining word–emotion associations from tweets by multi-label classification. In *WI'16*. IEEE Computer Society, pages 536–539.

Cynthia Chew and Gunther Eysenbach. 2010. Pandemics in the age of twitter: content analysis of tweets during the 2009 h1n1 outbreak. *PloS one* 5(11):e14118.

Alec Go, Richa Bhayani, and Lei Huang. 2009. Twitter sentiment classification using distant supervision. *CS224N Project Report, Stanford* 1(12).

Matthias Hagen, Martin Potthast, Michel Büchner, and Benno Stein. 2015. Webis: An ensemble for twitter sentiment detection .

Minqing Hu and Bing Liu. 2004. Mining and summarizing customer reviews. In *Proceedings of the tenth ACM SIGKDD international conference on Knowl-*

edge discovery and data mining. ACM, pages 168–177.

Aamera ZH Khan, Mohammad Atique, and VM Thakare. 2015. Combining lexicon-based and learning-based methods for twitter sentiment analysis. *International Journal of Electronics, Communication and Soft Computing Science & Engineering (IJECSCSE)* page 89.

Efthymios Kouloumpis, Theresa Wilson, and Johanna D Moore. 2011. Twitter sentiment analysis: The good the bad and the omg! *Icwsm* 11(538-541):164.

Benjamin Mandel, Aron Culotta, John Boulahanis, Danielle Stark, Bonnie Lewis, and Jeremy Rodrigue. 2012. A demographic analysis of online sentiment during hurricane irene. In *Proceedings of the Second Workshop on Language in Social Media*. Association for Computational Linguistics, pages 27–36.

Tomas Mikolov, Ilya Sutskever, Kai Chen, Greg S Corrado, and Jeff Dean. 2013. Distributed representations of words and phrases and their compositionality. In *Advances in neural information processing systems*. pages 3111–3119.

Saif M Mohammad. 2017. Word affect intensities. *arXiv preprint arXiv:1704.08798* .

Saif M. Mohammad and Felipe Bravo-Marquez. 2017a. Emotion intensities in tweets. In *Proceedings of the sixth joint conference on lexical and computational semantics (*Sem)*. Vancouver, Canada.

Saif M. Mohammad and Felipe Bravo-Marquez. 2017b. WASSA-2017 shared task on emotion intensity. In *Proceedings of the Workshop on Computational Approaches to Subjectivity, Sentiment and Social Media Analysis (WASSA)*. Copenhagen, Denmark.

Saif M Mohammad and Svetlana Kiritchenko. 2015. Using hashtags to capture fine emotion categories from tweets. *Computational Intelligence* 31(2):301–326.

Saif M Mohammad, Svetlana Kiritchenko, and Xiaodan Zhu. 2013. Nrc-canada: Building the state-of-the-art in sentiment analysis of tweets. *arXiv preprint arXiv:1308.6242* .

Saif M Mohammad and Peter D Turney. 2013. Crowdsourcing a word–emotion association lexicon. *Computational Intelligence* 29(3):436–465.

Preslav Nakov, Alan Ritter, Sara Rosenthal, Fabrizio Sebastiani, and Veselin Stoyanov. 2016. Semeval-2016 task 4: Sentiment analysis in twitter. *Proceedings of SemEval* pages 1–18.

Alexandru Niculescu-Mizil, Claudia Perlich, Grzegorz Swirszcz, Vikas Sindhwani, Yan Liu, Prem Melville, Dong Wang, Jing Xiao, Jianying Hu, Moninder Singh, et al. 2009. Winning the kdd cup orange challenge with ensemble selection. In *Proceedings of the 2009 International Conference on KDD-Cup 2009-Volume 7*. JMLR. org, pages 23–34.

Finn Årup Nielsen. 2011. A new anew: Evaluation of a word list for sentiment analysis in microblogs. *arXiv preprint arXiv:1103.2903* .

Alexander Pak and Patrick Paroubek. 2010. Twitter as a corpus for sentiment analysis and opinion mining. In *LREc*. volume 10.

Sasa Petrovic, Miles Osborne, and Victor Lavrenko. 2010. The edinburgh twitter corpus. In *Proceedings of the NAACL HLT 2010 Workshop on Computational Linguistics in a World of Social Media*. pages 25–26.

Sara Rosenthal, Noura Farra, and Preslav Nakov. 2017. Semeval-2017 task 4: Sentiment analysis in twitter. In *Proceedings of the 11th International Workshop on Semantic Evaluation (SemEval-2017)*. Association for Computational Linguistics, Vancouver, Canada, pages 493–509.

Sara Rosenthal, Preslav Nakov, Svetlana Kiritchenko, Saif M Mohammad, Alan Ritter, and Veselin Stoyanov. 2015. Semeval-2015 task 10: Sentiment analysis in twitter. In *Proceedings of the 9th international workshop on semantic evaluation (SemEval 2015)*. pages 451–463.

Sara Rosenthal, Alan Ritter, Preslav Nakov, and Veselin Stoyanov. 2014. Semeval-2014 task 9: Sentiment analysis in twitter. In *Proceedings of the 8th international workshop on semantic evaluation (SemEval 2014)*. Dublin, Ireland, pages 73–80.

Mike Thelwall, Kevan Buckley, and Georgios Paltoglou. 2012. Sentiment strength detection for the social web. *Journal of the American Society for Information Science and Technology* 63(1):163–173.

Andreas Töscher, Michael Jahrer, and Robert M Bell. 2009. The bigchaos solution to the netflix grand prize. *Netflix prize documentation* pages 1–52.

Hao Wang, Dogan Can, Abe Kazemzadeh, François Bar, and Shrikanth Narayanan. 2012. A system for real-time twitter sentiment analysis of 2012 us presidential election cycle. In *Proceedings of the ACL 2012 System Demonstrations*. Association for Computational Linguistics, pages 115–120.

Theresa Wilson, Janyce Wiebe, and Paul Hoffmann. 2005. Recognizing contextual polarity in phrase-level sentiment analysis. In *Proceedings of the conference on human language technology and empirical methods in natural language processing*. Association for Computational Linguistics, pages 347–354.

Zhengchen Zhang, Chen Zhang, Fuxiang Wu, Dong-Yan Huang, Weisi Lin, and Minghui Dong. 2016. I2rntu at semeval-2016 task 4: Classifier fusion for polarity classification in twitter. *Proceedings of SemEval* pages 71–78.

Tecnolengua Lingmotif at EmoInt-2017: A lexicon-based approach[*]

Antonio Moreno-Ortiz
University of Málaga
Spain
`amo@uma.es`

Abstract

In this paper we describe Tecnolengua Group's participation in the shared task on emotion intensity at WASSA 2017. We used the Lingmotif tool and a new, complementary tool, Lingmotif Learn, which we developed for this occasion. We based our intensity predictions for the four test datasets entirely on Lingmotif's TSS (text sentiment score) feature. We also developed mechanisms for dealing with the idiosyncrasies of Twitter text. Results were comparatively poor, but the experience meant a good opportunity for us to identify issues in our score calculation for short texts, a genre for which the Lingmotif tool was not originally designed.

1 Introduction

For this shared task on emotion intensity we have used the Lingmotif (Moreno-Ortiz, 2017a) sentiment analysis software. This tool is not specifically built to classify texts, although it offers this feature. It is designed more as a general text analysis tool with a focus on sentiment analysis. It offers several text metrics and displays a detailed view of the analysis results, where specific text segments are marked and annotated with their valence and other data.

For sentiment analysis, it relies on its rich lexical sources rather than on sophisticated machine learning algorithms. We undertook this shared task as an evaluation of the performance of our tool for short texts,[1] and as a good opportunity to learn about the linguistic features and issues that such texts raise in a strictly lexicon-based sentiment analysis tool. It also meant a first attempt to use Lingmotif's sentiment data as features in classification and regression algorithms.

1.1 Task Description and datasets

Unlike most shared tasks on sentiment analysis, the EmoInt Shared Task at WASSA-2017 (Mohammad and Bravo-Marquez, 2017b) focused on sentiment intensity rather than classification. Several annotated Twitter datasets were provided for system training, development and testing. Tweets were classified as belonging in one of three negative emotions (*anger*, *fear*, and *sadness*) and one positive emotion (*joy*).

The training datasets were labeled for sentiment intensity. The annotation system to obtain these datasets is described in Mohammad and Bravo-Marquez (2017a). Basically, they polled the Twitter API to extract tweets that contained representative words for each of the four emotions, which they selected using Roget's Thesaurus. They collected over 7,000 tweets, differentiating between those that contained the query term in hashtag form and those that included them in non-hashtag form. Then they crowdsourced the annotation for this dataset using a Best-Worst Scaling system, whose details we will not reproduce here.

In our experience with the datasets, we believe this procedure offers very reliable results, although we have come across a number of questionable annotations and some obvious errors.[2]

1.2 Lexicon-based Sentiment Analysis

Within Sentiment Analysis it is common to distinguish corpus-based approaches from lexicon-

---

[*]This research was supported by Spain's MINECO through the funding of project Lingmotif2 (FFI2016-78141-P).

[1]We use the term *short text* to refer specifically to under 140 characters, such as those used in Twitter and other social networks.

[2]The authors themselves (Mohammad and Bravo-Marquez, 2017a) warn about the cognitve load that is placed on the respondents during the annotation process.

Proceedings of the 8th Workshop on Computational Approaches to Subjectivity, Sentiment and Social Media Analysis, pages 225–232
Copenhagen, Denmark, September 7–11, 2017. ©2017 Association for Computational Linguistics

based approaches. Generally speaking, lexicon-based approaches are preferred for sentence-level classification (Andreevskaia and Bergler, 2007), whereas corpus-based, statistical approaches are preferred for document-level classification. Of course, these methods can be combined (for example, Riloff et al. (2006)).

Using sentiment dictionaries has a long tradition in the field. WordNet (Fellbaum, 1998) has been a recurrent source of lexical information (Kim and Hovy, 2004; Hu and Liu, 2004; Adreevskaia and Bergler, 2006) either directly as a source of lexical information or for sentiment lexicon construction. Other common lexicons used in English sentiment analysis research include The General Inquirer (Stone and Hunt, 1963), MPQA (Wilson et al., 2005), and Bing Liu's Opinion Lexicon (Hu and Liu, 2004). Yet other researchers have used a combination of existing lexicons or created their own (Hatzivassiloglou and McKeown, 1997; Turney, 2002). The use of lexicons has sometimes been straightforward, where the mere presence of a sentiment word determines a given polarity. However, negation and intensification can alter the valence or polarity of that word.[3] Modification of sentiment in context has also been widely recognized and dealt with by some researchers (Kennedy and Inkpen, 2006; Polanyi and Zaenen, 2006; Choi and Cardie, 2008; Taboada et al., 2011).

One disadvantage on relying solely on a sentiment lexicon is that different domains may greatly alter the valence of words, a fact well recognized in the literature (Aue and Gamon, 2005; Pang and Lee, 2008; Choi et al., 2009). A number of solutions have been proposed to these, mostly using ad hoc dictionaries, sometimes created automatically from a domain-specific corpus (Tai and Kao, 2013; Lu et al., 2011).

Our approach to using a lexicon takes some ideas from the aforementioned approaches. We describe it in the next section.

2   The Lingmotif SA tool

The Tecnolengua group started work on lexicon-based sentiment analysis with the development of Sentitext, a linguistically-motivated sentiment analysis system for Spanish, and evolved within the Lingmotif project to integrate English, French, Italian, and German.[4]

Lingmotif is based on the same principles as Sentitext: a reliance on wide-coverage lexical resources rather than a complex set of algorithms. It utilizes a number of lexical sources and analyzes context, by means of sentiment shifters, in order to identify sentiment-laden text segments and produce a number of scores that qualify a text from a SA perspective, as well as other various text analytics.

Analysis is produced by the identification of words and phrases that are stored in its lexicon. The overall score for a text is computed as a function of the accumulated negative, positive and neutral scores. Specific domains can be accounted for by applying user-provided dictionaries, which can be imported from CSV files, and used along with the application's core dictionary.

Lingmotif was not designed as a sentiment classifier, but as a user-focused text analysis tool. It offers a visual representation of the *sentiment profile* of texts, which allows users to compare the profile of multiple documents side by side, and can process ordered document series. Such features are useful in discourse analysis tasks, where sentiment changes are relevant, whether within or across texts, such as political speeches and narratives, or to track the evolution in sentiment towards a given topic (in news, for example). It uses a simple, easy-to-use GUI that allows users to select input and options, and launch the analysis. Details of the GUI's capabilities can be found in Moreno-Ortiz (2017b).

Results are generated as an HTML/Javascript document, which is saved locally to a predefined location and automatically sent to the user's default browser for immediate display. Internally, the application generates results as an XML document containing all the relevant data; this XML document is then parsed against one of several available XSL templates, and transformed into the final HTML.

2.1   Lexical data

Lingmotif's main asset is its comprehensive lexical sources. For each language, Lingmotif uses the following resources:

---

[3]The use of the terms *valence* and *polarity* is used inconsistently in the literature. We use *polarity* to refer to the binary distinction positive/negative sentiment, and *valence* to a value of intensity on a scale.

[4]The current version of Lingmotif supports English and Spanish. Version 1.2 will include initial support for French. Italian and German will be added in future versions.

- A wide-coverage core sentiment lexicon that contains both unigrams and multiword expressions, from bigrams to 6-grams.

- A set of context rules, where sentiment shifters are defined using a template approach.

- Optionally, a plugin lexicon can be used to account for domain-specific sentiment expression.

A part of speech tagger and lemmatizer are also used. Lingmotif's lexicons are still under development. For this shared task, version 1.2 was used.[5]

2.2 The Lingmotif lexicon

Lexicon entries have the structure `<form>,<part-of-speech>,<valence>`, where valence is an integer from -5 to 5, 0 being neutral. All single-word entries have a non-zero valence. Unigrams can be entered as literals or as lemmas (expressed by angled brackets), in which case they will be inflected during import and expanded into their possible forms. Examples are: `<safe>, JJ, 2`; `<fallacy>, ALL, -3`; `insolent, ALL, -3`[6]

Multi-word expressions are a big asset of Lingmotif. No other sentiment lexicon, to our knowledge, contains a significant amount of, or any at all, multi-word expressions. Avoiding MWEs has practical advantages; first, it obviously makes lexicon construction much simpler, as it does the identification process of sentiment words during analysis, thus facilitating bag-of-words approaches. However, it also ignores the fact that idiomaticity plays a huge role in the expression of sentiment. While it is true that many MWEs contain individual words of the same polarity as the overall expression, for example "turn a blind eye", "raise the alarm", "smear campaign", many do not contain any sentiment words at all ("raise the bar", "silver lining", "lose ground", "peanut gallery"), or even words with the opposite polarity ("smile at danger", "penny wise and pound foolish"). Finally, many zero-valence MWEs do contain individual

words with some valence: "vanity bag", "proper fraction", "fancy dress".

This is the reason why MWEs in Lingmotif can have a 0 valence; the aim is to block detection of individual words which are part of a MWE and whose valence may or may not be the same as that in the MWE. Other zero-valence MWEs are included because they are valence shifters used in the CVS system, mostly intensifiers such as "kind of", "a fair bit of", "through and through".

In version 1.2 multiword expressions can also contain variables that act as placeholders for any word, such as `<fall>_into_2_hands`, which will match any sequence of any form of the lemma "fall" followed by "into", then 0 to 2 words (e.g., "the" "his", "the wrong"), then "hands". This allows flexible representation and identification of variable MWEs and collocations.

Version 1.2 of the English Lingmotif lexicon contains 13,250 unigram lemmas (which expand to 21,300 forms, 12,300 MWE lemmas (which expand to 37,700 forms), and 720 context rules (sentiment shifters).

As for its origin, the Lingmotif lexicon was initially compiled from a lexicographic perspective, aiming at comprehensiveness. The core single-word lexicon was jumpstarted using existing sentiment lexicons, namely, the Harvard General Inquirer (Stone and Hunt, 1963), MPQA (Wilson et al., 2005), and Bing Liu's Opinion Lexicon (Hu and Liu, 2004). These resources were expanded by using a thesaurus and derivational generation rules. The lexicon has been subsequently refined manually using corpus analysis techniques as well by qualitative techniques.

2.3 Sentiment shifters

A sentiment word or expression can change its valence in context. It can be intensified or downtoned, by means of quantifiers, for example, or its valence may be inverted altogether (negation being the most obvious case), thus altering the polarity.

Lingmotif implements a contextual valence shifter (CVS) system based on the matching of a number of context rules that define how a sentiment item changes its polarity in context. Such approach has been used by Polanyi and Zaenen (2006), Kennedy and Inkpen (2006), and Taboada et al. (2011), among others. In our implementation, we use simple addition or subtraction of in-

---

⁵At the time of editing this document version 1.0 can be downloaded from the Tecnolengua website (http://tecnolengua.uma.es/lingmotif). Version 1.2 will be made available during 2017.

⁶The "ALL" notation simplifies acquisition and avoids matching problems derived from bad part-of-speech tagging at run-time.

Inversion		
`NN,-,avoid*,LR,5,INV0`		
`JJ,+-,not,L,2,INV0`		
Intensification		
`NN,-,avoid*,LR,5,INV0`		
`JJ,+-,not,L,2,INV0`		
Downtoning		
`NN,-,avoid*,LR,5,INV0`		
`JJ,+-,not,L,2,INV0`		

Table 1: Sentiment shifters

tegers to modify the original valence, as specified by a set of patterns in which certain features are matched, namely, the part of speech and polarity of the sentiment word, the form, location (left or right), and span (in number of words) of the shifter, and the result of the rule application. Version 1.2 contains over 700 such rules for English. These are some examples:

When a context rule is matched, the resulting text segment is marked as a single unit and assigned the calculated valence, as specified by the rule. New in version 1.2 is multiple rule matching, where results are aggregated. Thus the sequences "really interesting" and "really really interesting" produce different results. This is an experimental feature that we have yet to improve, as it can produce some unexpected results.

2.4 Lingmotif Learn

For this task we created a new tool, still under development, tentatively called "Lingmotif Learn". This is a GUI-enabled convenience tool that manages datasets and uses the Python-based scikit-learn (Pedregosa et al., 2011) machine learning toolkit. This tool facilitates loading and preprocessing of datasets, getting the text run trough the Lingmotif SA engine, and feeding the resulting data into one of several machine learning algorithms.

It makes it easy to compare the performance of different combinations of the available Lingmotif data as features and classification/regression algorithms. After the optimal features and algorithm have been selected, the model is trained and saved; then it can be loaded to classify the development and test datasets.

Table 2 lists the features available for each text after the Lingmotif analysis.

As we will discuss in section 4 below, for this shared task we used only TSS as a predictor. TSS attempts to summarize the overall sentiment of a

ID	Name	Description
1	tss	Text Sentiment Score
2	tsi	Text Sentiment Intensity
3	lex_items	Number of lexical Items
4	pos_score	Positive score
5	neg_score	Negative score
6	pos_items	Number of positive items
7	neg_items	Number of negative items
8	crules	Number of sentiment shifters
9	V0	Number of items with valence 0
10	V-1	Number of items with valence -1
11	V-2	Number of items with valence -2
12	V-3	Number of items with valence -3
13	V-4	Number of items with valence -4
14	V-5	Number of items with valence -5
15	V1	Number of items with valence 1
16	V2	Number of items with valence 2
17	V3	Number of items with valence 3
18	V4	Number of items with valence 4
19	V5	Number of items with valence 5
20	x_marks	Number of exclamation marks
21	q_marks	Number of question marks
22	pmarks	Number of punctuation marks
23	handles	Number of user handles
24	hashtags	Number of hashtags
25	urls	Number of exclamation URLs

Table 2: Set of available features

text on a 0-100 scale. It is arrived at by calculating a *sentiment weight*, which is dependent on text length, and is encapsulated in the TSI feature, which, in turn, is calculated by combining the *pos_score* , *neg_score*, and *lex_items* features. A more detailed description of these scores can be found in Moreno-Ortiz (2017a).

3 Dealing with social media text

It is only recently that we have begun experimenting with social media content analysis. Our focus so far has been on longer texts (user reviews, political debates and speeches, narratives). We undertook this task as a challenge that would give us a first glimpse of the potentiality of our system to analyze tweets and other social media short texts, which certainly show certain specific characteristics, such as the intensive use of emoticons and emojis, hashtags, repetitions, etc. As a first approach to this type of texts, we adapted our system as described below.

3.1 Emoticons and emojis

Emoticons are a well known source of emotion expression, and very common in social media in general and Twitter in particular. Even though the relationship between emoticons and the sentiment conveyed in the overall message is not always unambiguous (Wang and Castanon, 2015), they clearly play an important role in the expression of sentiment, and, relevant to this task, they have been found to have a strong impact in the intensity of the emotions expressed in the message. Accordingly, they have recurrently been used as features for machine learning classifiers in sentiment analysis tasks, even from the first efforts to classify Twitter data, e.g., Go et al. (2009).

Further, the generalization of emoji keyboards in mobile devices in the recent years has no doubt contributed to the proliferation of emojis. If (text) emoticons display certain ambiguity, the sentiment conveyed by emojis is obviously more sophisticated, as is its relation to the text.

This shared task gave us an opportunity to improve on the management of emoticons and emojis we have used so far in Lingmotif. In the current version (1.0), emoticons are dealt with during preprocessing and are converted to a placeholder lexical item with a certain polarity. Emojis are simply ignored.

For this task we implemented support for emojis by including them in the lexicon just like any other sentiment word. Currently, the list of emojis is limited to 126 positive and negative items, which were selected as these and other English and Spanish Twitter datasets. All these emojis are more or less consistent in their usage in terms of their polarity. Emojis denoting surprise, and others which exhibit a high degree of variability in their denoted polarity were not included. At this stage, all emojis in our lexicon have the same level of intensity, i.e., 3/-3 (medium). This is of course far from ideal, and our intention is to provide better intensity ratings, for which we intend to use Novak et al. (2015)'s results, which provide reliable polarity and intensity data for 970 emojis in 13 European Languages.

3.2 Treatment of hashtags

Hashtags have been shown to be excellent cues of the sentiment conveyed in tweets (Mohammad, 2012; Mohammad and Kiritchenko, 2015). Making sense of hashtags is not an easy task, however, since users can be extremely creative in their use. Efforts have been made to process and normalize their content, some of them quite sophisticated (Declerck and Lendvai, 2015).

As a first approach, we introduced in Lingmotif a simple system to process hashtags. Our strategy consisted of trying to match substrings in the hashtag against our single-word lexicon, either as the whole string (minus the hash symbol) or in CamelCase. Simple as it is, this system turned out to be able to decode the content of a significant proportion of hashtags,

4 Analysis and results

We approached the task by running a Lingmotif analysis of each emotion dataset as a single document. Since training datasets were provided already sorted by emotion intensity, this was straightforward and could give us a rough idea of the performance. We used Lingmotif's "Sentiment Profile" feature to quickly check if there was a viable correlation. The Sentiment Profile is a line graph whose data points are obtained by breaking the input text into segments of varying lengths (dependent on the text's overall length), and computing the valence for each segment by averaging the valences of the lexical words and phrases (after the sentiment shifters system discussed above has been applied) contained in the segment. Figure 1 shows the sentiment profile obtained for the anger training dataset.

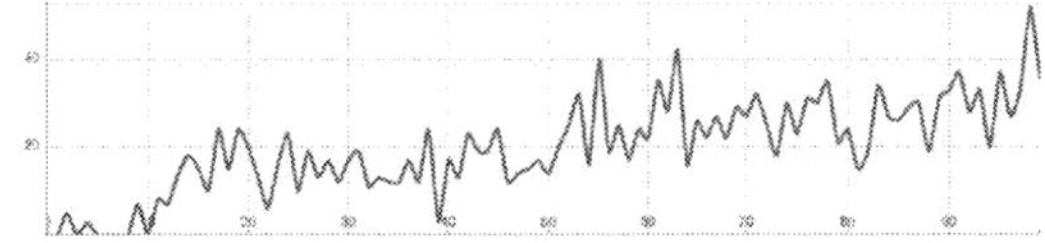

Figure 1: Sentiment Profile for the "anger" training dataset

Higher scores in this graph indicate more positive sentiment. Tweets in the dataset were sorted in decreasing order of intensity, so, as we are using a negative emotion, a higher TSS indicates a lower intensity, and therefore a correlation between TSS and the scores in the dataset. This gave us the impression that average to good performance could be achieved simply by using the TSS data of each individual tweet. Our approach to building the statistical model then consisted of using a simple linear regression (best fit with least squares), using Lingmotif's Text Sentiment Score (TSS) as the independent variable.

For the analysis, we decided to include the emotion word as part of the text to be analyzed. This would ensure that at least one word of the same polarity was included in every tweet. This turned out not to be a good solution, as we will discuss in section 5 below.

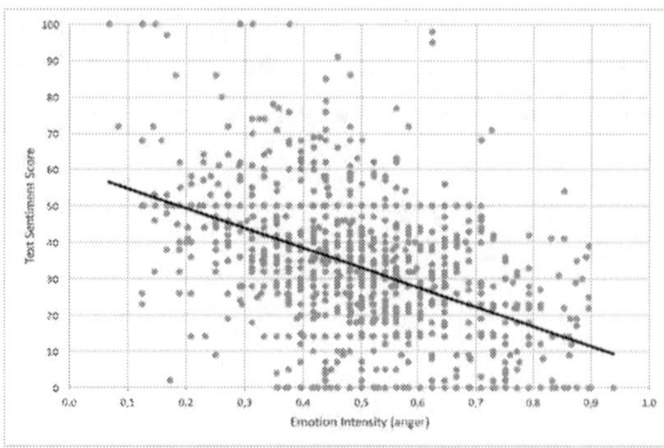

Figure 2: Lingmotif TSS vs. intensity in the anger training dataset

Dataset	Pearson	Spearman
Anger	0.324	0.324
Fear	0.466	0.454
Sadness	0.436	0.449
Joy	0.408	0.393
Average	0.409	0.405

Table 3: Official results.

This first impression, however, turned out no to be too accurate. Figure 2 shows the scatter plot of the anger training dataset in terms of intensity vs Lingmotif's TSS. As the figure shows, it is a relatively poor predictor. The final results obtained are detailed in Table 3.

5 Discussion

We believe these comparatively poor results were due to the fact that Lingmotif's TSS is not well suited to extremely short texts. Even though identification of sentiment words (or hashtags) and expressions is fairly good, thanks to the wide coverage of the Lingmotif Lexicon and sentiment shifters, the intensity reflected by TSS does not seem to finely reflect the intensity as perceived by human annotators of tweets.

As expected, there were also a number of analysis errors, many of them related to the nature of social media text. An analysis of the annotated text, which Lingmotif produces, allowed us to discover certain recurrent problems:

- Unaccounted/bad shifters: "**zero** tolerance for honesty her alliance"

- Overreaching of shifters: ""Why are people that do [**not have iPhones so bitter**] about iPhones????"

- Bad spelling and/or grammar: "These guys **dcan not get nothing right**"

- Irony and sarcasm: "**thanks** or saying My wife and I were getting our iphones today and then losing both of them with no eta **thanks**"

- Complex wording: "You will never find someone who loved you like I did. And that my love, will be my revenge."

Obviously, some of these issues are harder to fix than others. Irony and sarcasm are possibly the hardest cases to deal with automatically, and are very common in social media short texts.[7] Others, however, are of a more practical nature and easier to tackle.

Since the EmoInt organizers allowed participants in the shared task to keep uploading results after the competition was over, we took this opportunity to tackle some of these issues. We started by removing the emotion tag from the tweets, which, in retrospect, we consider a bad decision. We then reduced the range of far-reaching sentiment shifters to avoid overreaching and adapt to the simpler syntactic structures found in tweets.

Another recurrent issue we found is repetitions of emojis. As explained in section **??** above, Lingmotif's current TSS uses text length, in terms of number of lexical items to determine intensity. In "regular" texts, for the same text length, the number of lexical items falls within consistent ranges. However, repetition of emojis as an intensification of emotion is very common in social media text, and, when emojis are treated as lexical items, as we have experimented here for the first time, we obtain some cases where the number of lexical items exceeds by far the average frequency in texts of that length. The result is that the tweet is treated by Lingmotif as a longer text, thus calculating the wrong intensity. We avoided this problem by controlling character repetition during preprocessing, and limiting it to three consecutive same emojis.

Even after this, we realized that our current thresholds for binning texts in terms of their length was too fine, and resulted in tweets falling in one one of three categories according to their length. We fixed this by defining fewer (broader) categories in the lower end of the range, thus making sure that all tweets fall within the same categories in terms of text length. The new text length

---

[7]Wallace et al. (2014) report that 10-15 percent of messages on reddit.com exhibit some form of irony or sarcasm.

Dataset	Pearson	Spearman
Anger	0.423	0.425
Fear	0.524	0.524
Sadness	0.490	0.470
Joy	0.492	0.490
Average	0.482	0.477

Table 4: Results after adjustments

threshold (25 lexical items) is based on the maximum number of lexical items found on the EmoInt datasets.[8]

After applying the above-mentioned adjustments and fixes, we ran the system again to measure their effect, if any. Results were significantly improved, as is reflected in Table 4.

It would have been interesting to experiment with multiple regression using other sentiment features provided by our system, something we were unable to do for this task due to time limitations. In particular, we feel that using the raw *pos_score* and *neg_score* features would have produced better results. Another possibility would be to use *pos_items* and *neg_items*. The difference being that the valence values assigned in the lexicon are ignored, and only polarity is taken into account.

6 Conclusions

This work has been extremely useful to us. We now have a clearer picture of what it means to deal with social media short texts, and the difficulties they pose. This task gave us the chance to adapt our analysis system in a number of ways, at least in terms of form (emojis, character repetitions, etc.).

From a linguistic perspective, we have also found clear evidence that dealing with short texts of the type commonly found in social media call for specific adaptations of our system than the merely superficial ones we have described in this paper. Not only are there a number of formal differences, but the message itself is expressed in extremely condensed ways.

Our most relevant conclusion is that Lingmotif's present sentiment score may not be a good predictor because it does not encapsulate the features it is based on optimally, and we think better results would be achieved by combining such features (*pos_score*, *neg_score*, *lex_items*, and others) using more sophisticated statistical learning meth-

ods, a path that we will explore in future developments.

References

Alina Adreevskaia and Sabine Bergler. 2006. Mining wordnet for fuzzy sentiment: Sentiment tag extraction from wordnet glosses. In *11th Conference of the European Chapter of the Association for Computational Linguistics*. pages 209–216.

Alina Andreevskaia and Sabine Bergler. 2007. Clac and clac-nb: Knowledge-based and corpus-based approaches to sentiment tagging. In *Proceedings of the 4th International Workshop on Semantic Evaluations*. Association for Computational Linguistics, Stroudsburg, PA, USA, SemEval '07, pages 117–120.

Anthony Aue and Michael Gamon. 2005. Customizing sentiment classifiers to new domains: A case study. Borovets, Bulgaria.

Yejin Choi and Claire Cardie. 2008. Learning with compositional semantics as structural inference for subsentential sentiment analysis. In *Proceedings of the Conference on Empirical Methods in Natural Language Processing*. Stroudsburg, PA, USA, EMNLP '08, page 793.

Yoonjung Choi, Youngho Kim, and Sung-Hyon Myaeng. 2009. Domain-specific sentiment analysis using contextual feature generation. In *Proceeding of the 1st international CIKM workshop on Topic-sentiment analysis for mass opinion*. ACM, Hong Kong, China, pages 37–44.

Thierry Declerck and Piroska Lendvai. 2015. Processing and normalizing hashtags. In Galia Angelova, Kalina Bontcheva, and Ruslan Mitko, editors, *Proceedings of RANLP 2015*. INCOMA Ltd, pages 104–110.

Christiane Fellbaum, editor. 1998. *WordNet An Electronic Lexical Database*. The MIT Press, Cambridge, MA; London.

Alec Go, Richa Bhayani, and Lei Huang. 2009. Twitter sentiment classification using distant supervision. *Processing* pages 1–6.

Vasileios Hatzivassiloglou and Kathleen R. McKeown. 1997. Predicting the semantic orientation of adjectives. In *Proceedings of the eighth conference on European chapter of the Association for Computational Linguistics*. Association for Computational Linguistics, Madrid, Spain, pages 174–181.

Minqing Hu and Bing Liu. 2004. Mining and summarizing customer reviews. In *Proceedings of the tenth ACM SIGKDD international conference on Knowledge discovery and data mining*. ACM, Seattle, WA, USA, pages 168–177.

---

[8] After rounding it up. The actual highest number of lexical items found in the EmoInt datasets was 22. The average number of lexical items per tweet was 9.18.

Alistair Kennedy and Diana Inkpen. 2006. Sentiment classification of movie reviews using contextual valence shifters. *Computational Intelligence* 22(2):110–125.

Soo-Min Kim and Eduard Hovy. 2004. Determining the sentiment of opinions. In *Proceedings of the 20th international conference on Computational Linguistics*. Association for Computational Linguistics, Geneva, Switzerland, page 1367.

Yue Lu, Malu Castellanos, Umeshwar Dayal, and ChengXiang Zhai. 2011. Automatic construction of a context-aware sentiment lexicon: An optimization approach. In *Proceedings of the 20th International Conference on World Wide Web*. ACM, New York, NY, USA, WWW '11, pages 347–356.

Saif Mohammad. 2012. #emotional tweets. In *Proceedings of the First Joint Conference on Lexical and Computational Semantics*. Association for Computational Linguistics, Montreal, Canada, pages 246–255.

Saif Mohammad and Felipe Bravo-Marquez. 2017a. Emotion intensities in tweets. In *Proceedings of the sixth joint conference on lexical and computational semantics (*Sem)*. Vancouver, Canada.

Saif Mohammad and Felipe Bravo-Marquez. 2017b. Wassa-2017 shared task on emotion intensity. In *Proceedings of the EMNLP 2017 Workshop on Computational Approaches to Subjectivity, Sentiment, and Social Media*. Copenhagen, Denmark.

Saif M. Mohammad and Svetlana Kiritchenko. 2015. Using hashtags to capture fine emotion categories from tweets. *Computational Intelligence* 31(2):301–326.

Antonio Moreno-Ortiz. 2017a. Lingmotif: A user-focused sentiment analysis tool. *Procesamiento del Lenguaje Natural* 58(0):133–140.

Antonio Moreno-Ortiz. 2017b. Lingmotif: Sentiment analysis for the digital humanities. In *Proceedings of the 15th Conference of the European Chapter of the Association for Computational Linguistics*. Association for Computational Linguistics, Valencia, Spain, pages 73–76.

Petra Kralj Novak, Jasmina Smailovi, Borut Sluban, and Igor Mozeti. 2015. Sentiment of emojis. *PLOS ONE* 10(12):e0144296.

Bo Pang and Lillian Lee. 2008. Opinion mining and sentiment analysis. *Foundations and Trends in Information Retrieval* 2(12):1–135.

Fabian Pedregosa, Gal Varoquaux, Alexandre Gramfort, Vincent Michel, Bertrand Thirion, Olivier Grisel, Mathieu Blondel, Peter Prettenhofer, Ron Weiss, Vincent Dubourg, Jake Vanderplas, Alexandre Passos, David Cournapeau, Matthieu Brucher, Matthieu Perrot, and douard Duchesnay. 2011. Scikit-learn: Machine learning in python. *J. Mach. Learn. Res.* 12:2825–2830.

Livia Polanyi and Annie Zaenen. 2006. Contextual valence shifters. In *Computing Attitude and Affect in Text: Theory and Applications*, Springer, Dordrecht, The Netherlands, volume 20 of *The Information Retrieval Series*, pages 1–10. Shanahan, james g., qu, yan, wiebe, janyce edition.

Ellen Riloff, Siddharth Patwardhan, and Janyce Wiebe. 2006. Feature subsumption for opinion analysis. In *Proceedings of the 2006 Conference on Empirical Methods in Natural Language Processing*. Association for Computational Linguistics, Stroudsburg, PA, USA, EMNLP '06, pages 440–448.

Philip J. Stone and Earl B. Hunt. 1963. A computer approach to content analysis: Studies using the general inquirer system. In *Proceedings of the May 21-23, 1963, Spring Joint Computer Conference*. ACM, New York, NY, USA, AFIPS '63 (Spring), pages 241–256.

Maite Taboada, Julian Brooks, M. Tofiloski, K. Voll, and M. Stede. 2011. Lexicon-based methods for sentiment analysis. *Computational Linguistics* 37(2):267–307.

Yen-Jen Tai and Hung-Yu Kao. 2013. Automatic domain-specific sentiment lexicon generation with label propagation. In *Proceedings of International Conference on Information Integration and Web-based Applications & Services*. ACM, New York, NY, USA, IIWAS '13, pages 53:53–53:62.

Peter D. Turney. 2002. Thumbs up or thumbs down? semantic orientation applied to unsupervised classification of reviews. In *Proceedings of the 40th Annual Meeting of the Association for Computational Linguistics (ACL)*. Philadelphia, USA., pages 417–424.

Byron C. Wallace, Do Kook Choe, Laura Kertz, and Eugene Charniak. 2014. *Humans require context to infer ironic intent (so computers probably do, too)*, Association for Computational Linguistics (ACL), volume 2, pages 512–516.

Hao Wang and Jorge A. Castanon. 2015. Sentiment expression via emoticons on social media. In *2015 IEEE International Conference on Big Data (Big Data)*. IEEE Computer Society, Washington, DC, USA, BIG DATA '15, pages 2404–2408.

Theresa Wilson, Janyce Wiebe, and Paul Hoffmann. 2005. Recognizing contextual polarity in phrase-level sentiment analysis. In *Proceedings of the Conference on Human Language Technology and Empirical Methods in Natural Language Processing*. Association for Computational Linguistics, Stroudsburg, PA, USA, HLT '05, pages 347–354.

EmoAtt at EmoInt-2017: Inner attention sentence embedding for Emotion Intensity

Edison Marrese-Taylor and **Yutaka Matsuo**

Graduate School of Engineering

The University of Tokyo

Tokyo, Japan

{emarrese,matsuo}@weblab.t.u-tokyo.ac.jp

Abstract

In this paper we describe a deep learning system that has been designed and built for the WASSA 2017 Emotion Intensity Shared Task. We introduce a representation learning approach based on inner attention on top of an RNN. Results show that our model offers good capabilities and is able to successfully identify emotion-bearing words to predict intensity without leveraging on lexicons, obtaining the 13th place among 22 shared task competitors.

1 Introduction

Twitter is a huge micro-blogging service with more than 500 million tweets per day from different locations in the world and in different languages. This large, continuous, and dynamically updated content is considered a valuable resource for researchers. In particular, many of these messages contain emotional charge, conveying affectemotions, feelings and attitudes, which can be studied to understand the expression of emotion in text, as well as the social phenomena associated.

While studying emotion in text it is commonly useful to characterize the emotional charge of a passage based on its words. Some words have affect as a core part of their meaning. For example, *dejected* and *wistful* denote some amount of sadness, and are thus associated with sadness. On the other hand, some words are associated with affect even though they do not denote affect. For example, *failure* and *death* describe concepts that are usually accompanied by sadness and thus they denote some amount of sadness.

While analyzing the emotional content in text, mosts tasks are almost always framed as classification tasks, where the intention is to identify one emotion among many for a sentence or pas-

sage. However, it is often useful for applications to know the degree to which an emotion is expressed in text. To this end, the WASSA-2017 Shared Task on Emotion Intensity (Mohammad and Bravo-Marquez, 2017b) represents the first task where systems have to automatically determine the intensity of emotions in tweets. Concretely, the objective is to given a tweet containing the emotion of joy, sadness, fear or anger, determine the intensity or degree of the emotion felt by the speaker as a real-valued score between zero and one.

The task is specially challenging since tweets contain informal language, spelling errors and text referring to external content. Given the 140 character limit of tweets, it is also possible to find some phenomena such as the intensive usage of emoticons and of other special Twitter features, such as hashtags and usernames mentions —used to call or notify other users. In this paper we describe our system designed for the WASSA-2017 Shared Task on Emotion Intensity, which we tackle based on the premise of representation learning without the usage of external information, such as lexicons. In particular, we use a Bi-LSTM model with intra-sentence attention on top of word embeddings to generate a tweet representation that is suitable for emotion intensity. Our results show that our proposed model offers interesting capabilities compared to approaches that do rely on external information sources.

2 Proposed Approach

Our work is related to deep learning techniques for emotion recognition in images (Dhall et al., 2015) and videos (Ebrahimi Kahou et al., 2015), as well as and emotion classification (Lakomkin et al., 2017). Our work is also related to Liu and Lane (2016), who introduced an attention RNN

233

Proceedings of the 8th Workshop on Computational Approaches to Subjectivity, Sentiment and Social Media Analysis, pages 233–237
Copenhagen, Denmark, September 7–11, 2017. ©2017 Association for Computational Linguistics

for slot filling in Natural Language Understanding. Since in the task the input-output alignment is explicit, they investigated how the alignment can be best utilized in encoder-decoder models concluding that the attention mechanisms are helpful.

EmoAtt is based on a bidirectional RNN that receives an embedded input sequence $x = \{x_1, ..., x_n\}$ and returns a list of hidden vectors that capture the context each input token $\{h_1, ..., h_n\}$. To improve the capabilities of the RNN to capture short-term temporal dependencies (Mesnil et al., 2013), we define the following:

$$\bar{x}_i = [x_{i-d}; ...; x_i; ...; x_{i+d}] \tag{1}$$

Where $\bar{x}_i$ can be regarded as a context window of ordered word embedding vectors around position i, with a total size of $2d + 1$. To further complement the context-aware token representations, we concatenate each hidden vector to a vector of binary features b_i, extracted from each tweet token, defining an augmented hidden state $\bar{h}_i = [h_i; b_i]$. Finally, we combine our n augmented hidden states, compressing them into a single vector, using a global intra-sentence attentional component in a fashion similar to Vinyals et al. (2015). Formally,

$$u_j = v^\top \tanh(W_a[\bar{h}_n; \bar{h}_j]) \tag{2}$$
$$\alpha_j = \mathrm{softmax}(u_j) \tag{3}$$
$$t = \sum_{j=1}^{n} \alpha_j \cdot \bar{h}_j \tag{4}$$

Where t is the vector that compresses the input sentence x, focusing on the relevant parts to estimate emotion intensity. We input this compressed sentence representation into a feed-forward neural network, $\hat{y} = W_s t$, where $\hat{y}$ is the final predicted emotion intensity. As a loss function we use the mini-batch negative Pearson correlation with the gold-standard.

3 Experimental Setup

To test our model, we experiment using the training, validation and test datasets provided for the shared task (Mohammad and Bravo-Marquez, 2017a), which include tweets for four emotions: joy, sadness, fear, and anger. These were annotated using Best-Worst Scaling (BWS) to obtain very reliable scores (Kiritchenko and Mohammad, 2016).

Dataset	Tweet Length (tokens)			Vocab. in GloVe
	Mean	Min	Max	
Fear	17.849	2	37	60.8 %
Joy	17.480	2	42	65.0 %
Sadness	18.285	2	38	65.5 %
Anger	17.438	1	41	65.8 %
Average	17.776	1.75	39.5	64.3 %

Table 1: Data summary.

We experimented with GloVe[1] (Pennington et al., 2014) as pre-trained word embedding vectors, for sizes 25, 50 and 100. These are vectors trained on a dataset of 2B tweets, with a total vocabulary of 1.2 M. To pre-process the data, we used Twokenizer (Gimpel et al., 2011), which basically provides a set of curated rules to split the tweets into tokens. We also use Tweeboparser (Owoputi et al., 2013) to get the POS-tags for each tweet.

Table 1 summarizes the average, maximum and minimum sentence lengths for each dataset after we processed them with Twokenizer. We can see the four corpora offer similar characteristics in terms of length, with a cross dataset maximum length of 41 tokens. We also see there is an important vocabulary gap between the dataset and GloVe, with an average coverage of only 64.3 %. To tackle this issue, we used a set of binary features derived from POS tags to capture some of the semantics of the words that are not covered by the GloVe embeddings. We also include features for member mentions and hashtags as well as a feature to capture word elongation, based on regular expressions. Word elongation is very common in tweets, and is usually associated to strong sentiment. The following are the POS tag-derived rules we used to generate our binary features.

- If the token is an adjective (POS tag = A)

- If the token is an interjection (POS tag = !)

- If the token is a hashtag (POS tag = #)

- If the token is an emoji (POS tag = E)

- If the token is an at-mention, indicating a user as a recipient of a tweet (POS tag = @)

- If the token is a verb (POS tag = V)

- If the token is a numeral (POS tag = $)

---

[1]`nlp.stanford.edu/projects/glove`

- if the token is a personal pronoun (POS tag = O)

While the structure of our introduced model allows us to easily include more linguistic features that could potentially improve our predictive power, such as lexicons, since our focus is to study sentence representation for emotion intensity, we do not experiment adding any additional sources of information as input.

In this paper we also only report results for LSTMs, which outperformed regular RNNs as well as GRUs and a batch normalized version of the LSTM in on preliminary experiments. The hidden size of the attentional component is set to match the size of the augmented hidden vectors on each case. Given this setting, we explored different hyper-parameter configurations, including context window sizes of 1, 3 and 5 as well as RNN hidden state sizes of 100, 200 and 300. We experimented with unidirectional and bidirectional versions of the RNNs.

To avoid over-fitting, we used dropout regularization, experimenting with keep probabilities of 0.5 and 0.8. We also added a weighed L2 regularization term to our loss function. We experimented with different values for weight λ, with a minimum value of 0.01 and a maximum of 0.2.

To evaluate our model, we wrapped the provided scripts for the shared task and calculated the Pearson correlation coefficient and the Spearman rank coefficient with the gold standard in the validation set, as well as the same values over a subset of the same data formed by taking every instance with a gold emotion intensity score greater than or equal to 0.5.

For training, we used mini-batch stochastic gradient descent with a batch size of 16 and padded sequences to a maximum size of 50 tokens, given the nature of the data. We used exponential decay of ratio 0.9 and early stopping on the validation when there was no improvement after 1000 steps. Our code is available for download on GitHub [2].

4 Results and Discussion

In this section we report the results of the experiments we performed to test our proposed model. In general, as Table 2 shows, our intra-sentence attention RNN was able to outperform the Weka baseline (Mohammad and Bravo-Marquez, 2017a)

on the development dataset by a solid margin. Moreover, the model manages to do so without any additional resources, except pre-trained word embeddings. These results are, however, reversed for the test dataset, where our model performs worse than the baseline. This shows that the model is not able to generalize well, which we think is related to the missing semantic information due to the vocabulary gap we observed between the datasets and the GloVe embeddings.

To validate the usefulness of our binary features, we performed an ablation experiment and trained our best models for each corpus without them. Table 3 summarizes our results in terms of Pearson correlation on the development portion of the datasets. As seen, performance decreases in all cases, which shows that indeed these features are critical for performance, allowing the model to better capture the semantics of words missing in GloVe. In this sense, we think the usage of additional features, such as the ones derived from emotion or sentiment lexicons could indeed boost our model capabilities. This is proposed for future work.

On the other hand, our model also offers us very interesting insights on how the learning is performed, since we can inspect the attention weights that the neural network is assigning to each specific token when predicting the emotion intensity. By visualizing these weights we can have a clear notion about the parts of the sentence that the model considers are more important. As Figure 1 shows, we see the model seems to be have learned to attend the words that naturally bear emotion or sentiment. This is specially patent for the examples extracted from the Joy dataset, where positive words are generally identified. However, we also see some examples where the lack of semantic information about the input words, specially for hashtags or user mentions, makes the model unable to identify some of these the most salient words to predict emotion intensity. Several pre-processing techniques can be implemented to alleviate this problem, which we intend to explore in the future.

4.1 Anger Dataset

For the anger dataset, our experiments showed that GloVe embeddings of dimension 50 outperformed others, obtaining an average gain of 0.066 correlation over embeddings of size 25 and of 0.021

[2]github.com/epochx/emoatt

Corpus	Dropout	Embeddings	λ	h	EmoAtt		Baseline	
					ρ_{dev}	ρ_{test}	ρ_{dev}	ρ_{test}
Sadness	0.8	GloVe Twitter 50	0.20	50	0.586	0.520	0.562	0.648
Joy	0.8	GloVe Twitter 50	0.20	100	0.790	0.537	0.703	0.654
Anger	0.5	GloVe Twitter 50	0.01	100	0.734	0.470	0.605	0.639
Fear	0.9	GloVe Twitter 50	0.05	100	0.644	0.561	0.574	0.652
Average					0.689	0.522	0.611	0.648

Table 2: Summary of the best results.

Dataset	w/features	w/o features
Sadness	0.586	0.543
Joy	0.790	0.781
Anger	0.734	0.662
Fear	0.644	0.561

Table 3: Impact of adding our binary features.

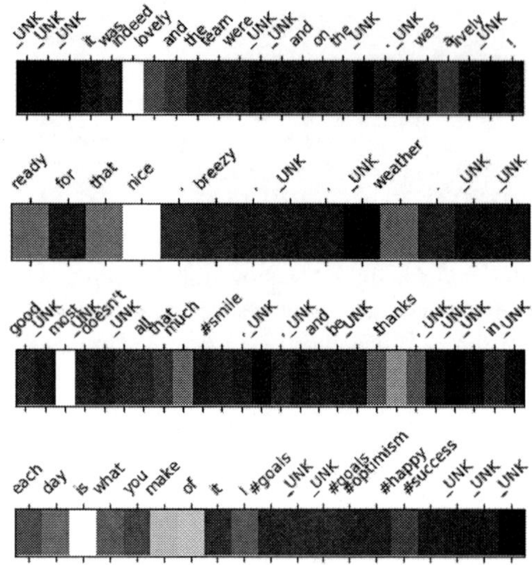

Figure 1: Example of attention weights for the Joy dataset. White denotes more weight.

for embeddings of size 100. However on ly the first of these values was significant, with a p-value of 3.86×10^{-5}. Regarding the hidden size of the RNN, we could not find statistical difference across the tested sizes. Dropout also had inconsistent effects, but was generally useful.

4.2 Joy Dataset

In the joy dataset, our experiments showed us that GloVe vectors of dimension 50 again outperformed others, in this case obtaining an average correlation gain of 0.052 ($p = 5.6 \times 10^{-2}$) over embeddings of size 100, and of 0.062 ($p =$ 3.1×10^{-2}) for size 25. Regarding the hidden size of the RNN, we observed that 100 hidden units offered better performance in our experiments, with an average absolute gain of 0.052 ($p = 6.5 \times 10^{-2}$) over 50 hidden units. Compared to the models with 200 hidden units, the performance difference was statistically not significant.

4.3 Fear Dataset

On the fear dataset, again we observed that embeddings of size 50 provided the best results, offering average gains of 0.12 ($p = 7 \times 10^{-4}$) and 0.11 ($p = 1.9 \times 10^{-3}$) for sizes 25 and 100, respectively. When it comes to the size of the RNN hidden state, our experiments showed that using 100 hidden units offered the best results, with average absolute gains of 0.117 ($p = 9 \times 10^{-4}$) and 0.108 ($p = 0.002.4 \times 10^{-3}$) over sizes 50 and 200.

4.4 Sadness Dataset

Finally, on the sadness datasets again we experimentally observed that using embeddings of 50 offered the best results, with a statistically significant average gain of 0.092 correlation points ($p = 1.3 \times 10^{-3}$) over size 25. Results were statistically equivalent for size 100. We also observed that using 50 or 100 hidden units for the RNN offered statistically equivalent results, while both of these offered better performance than when using a hidden size of 200.

5 Conclusions

In this paper we introduced an intra-sentence attention RNN for the of emotion intensity, which we developed for the WASSA-2017 Shared Task on Emotion Intensity. Our model does not make use of external information except for pre-trained embeddings and is able to outperform the Weka baseline for the development set, but not in the test set. In the shared task, it obtained the 13th place among 22 competitors.

References

Abhinav Dhall, O.V. Ramana Murthy, Roland Goecke, Jyoti Joshi, and Tom Gedeon. 2015. Video and image based emotion recognition challenges in the wild: Emotiw 2015. In *Proceedings of the 2015 ACM on International Conference on Multimodal Interaction*. ACM, New York, NY, USA, ICMI '15, pages 423–426. https://doi.org/10.1145/2818346.2829994.

Samira Ebrahimi Kahou, Vincent Michalski, Kishore Konda, Roland Memisevic, and Christopher Pal. 2015. Recurrent neural networks for emotion recognition in video. In *Proceedings of the 2015 ACM on International Conference on Multimodal Interaction*. ACM, New York, NY, USA, ICMI '15, pages 467–474. https://doi.org/10.1145/2818346.2830596.

Kevin Gimpel, Nathan Schneider, Brendan O'Connor, Dipanjan Das, Daniel Mills, Jacob Eisenstein, Michael Heilman, Dani Yogatama, Jeffrey Flanigan, and Noah A. Smith. 2011. Part-of-speech tagging for twitter: Annotation, features, and experiments. In *Proceedings of the 49th Annual Meeting of the Association for Computational Linguistics: Human Language Technologies*. Association for Computational Linguistics, Portland, Oregon, USA, pages 42–47. http://www.aclweb.org/anthology/P11-2008.

Svetlana Kiritchenko and Saif M. Mohammad. 2016. Capturing reliable fine-grained sentiment associations by crowdsourcing and best–worst scaling. In *Proceedings of the 2016 Conference of the North American Chapter of the Association for Computational Linguistics: Human Language Technologies*. Association for Computational Linguistics, San Diego, California, pages 811–817. http://www.aclweb.org/anthology/N16-1095.

Egor Lakomkin, Cornelius Weber, and Stefan Wermter. 2017. Automatically augmenting an emotion dataset improves classification using audio. In *Proceedings of the 15th Conference of the European Chapter of the Association for Computational Linguistics: Volume 2, Short Papers*. Association for Computational Linguistics, Valencia, Spain, pages 194–197. http://www.aclweb.org/anthology/E17-2031.

Bing Liu and Ian Lane. 2016. Attention-Based Recurrent Neural Network Models for Joint Intent Detection and Slot Filling. In *Interspeech 2016*. pages 685–689. https://doi.org/10.21437/Interspeech.2016-1352.

Grgoire Mesnil, Xiaodong He, Li Deng, and Yoshua Bengio. 2013. Investigation of recurrent-neural-network architectures and learning methods for spoken language understanding. In *INTERSPEECH*. pages 3771 –3775.

Saif M. Mohammad and Felipe Bravo-Marquez. 2017a. Emotion intensities in tweets. In *Proceedings of the sixth joint conference on lexical and computational semantics (*Sem)*. Vancouver, Canada.

Saif M. Mohammad and Felipe Bravo-Marquez. 2017b. WASSA-2017 Shared Task on Emotion Intensity. In *Proceedings of the EMNLP 2017 Workshop on Computational Approaches to Subjectivity, Sentiment, and Social Media (WASSA)*. Copenhagen, Denmark.

Olutobi Owoputi, Brendan O'Connor, Chris Dyer, Kevin Gimpel, Nathan Schneider, and Noah A. Smith. 2013. Improved part-of-speech tagging for online conversational text with word clusters. In *Proceedings of the 2013 Conference of the North American Chapter of the Association for Computational Linguistics: Human Language Technologies*. Association for Computational Linguistics, Atlanta, Georgia, pages 380–390. http://www.aclweb.org/anthology/N13-1039.

Jeffrey Pennington, Richard Socher, and Christopher D. Manning. 2014. Glove: Global vectors for word representation. In *Empirical Methods in Natural Language Processing (EMNLP)*. pages 1532–1543. http://www.aclweb.org/anthology/D14-1162.

Oriol Vinyals, Lukasz Kaiser, Terry Koo, Slav Petrov, Ilya Sutskever, and Geoffrey Hinton. 2015. Grammar as a foreign language. In *Advances in Neural Information Processing Systems*. pages 2773–2781. http://papers.nips.cc/paper/5635-grammar-as-a-foreign-language.

YZU-NLP at EmoInt-2017: Determining Emotion Intensity Using a Bi-directional LSTM-CNN Model

Yuanye He[2,3,4], Liang-Chih Yu[1,3], K. Robert Lai[2,3] and Weiyi Liu[4]
[1]Department of Information Management, Yuan Ze University, Taoyuan, Taiwan
[2]Department of Computer Science & Engineering, Yuan Ze University, Taoyuan, Taiwan
[3]Innovation Center for Big Data and Digital Convergence, Yuan Ze University, Taoyuan, Taiwan
[4]School of Information Science and Engineering, Yunnan University, Kunming, P.R. China
Contact: lcyu@saturn.yzu.edu.tw

Abstract

The EmoInt-2017 task aims to determine a continuous numerical value representing the intensity to which an emotion is expressed in a tweet. Compared to classification tasks that identify 1 among n emotions for a tweet, the present task can provide more fine-grained (real-valued) sentiment analysis. This paper presents a system that uses a bi-directional LSTM-CNN model to complete the competition task. Combining bi-directional LSTM and CNN, the prediction process considers both global information in a tweet and local important information. The proposed method ranked sixth among twenty-one teams in terms of Pearson Correlation Coefficient.

1 Introduction

Categorical and dimensional representations are two major approaches to representing emotional states (Calvo and Kim, 2013; Gunes and Schuller, 2013). The categorical approach represents emotional states using several discrete classes such as positive and negative (binary) or Ekman's (1992) six basic emotions (anger, happiness, fear, sadness, disgust, and surprise), which have been successfully adopted in various sentiment applications (Pang and Lee 2008; Liu, 2012; Feldman, 2013). Based on this representation, application tasks focus on classification (i.e., identify 1 among n emotions for a given text). The dimensional approach provides a more fine-grained (real-valued) sentiment analysis. Knowing the intensity or degree to which an emotion is expressed in text is useful for more intelligent sentiment appli-

cations (Thelwall et al., 2012; Paltoglou et al., 2013; Malandrakis et al., 2013; Kiritchenko and Mohammad, 2016; Wang et al., 2016a; 2016b, Yu et al., 2016).

The EmoInt-2017 task (Mohammad and Bravo-Marquez, 2017b) seeks to automatically determine a continuous numerical value representing the intensity or degree to which an emotion is expressed in a tweet. That is, given a tweet and an emotion X, determine the intensity of emotion X felt by the speaker ranging from 0 (feeling the least amount of emotion X) to 1 (feeling the maximum amount of emotion X). The proposed system uses word embeddings (Mikolov et al., 2013a; 2013b) and a bi-directional LSTM-CNN model to complete the competition task.

Word embeddings can capture both semantic and syntactic information of selected words and provide a low dimensional and continuous vector representation for them. Convoluational neural network (CNN) (Kim, 2014; Kalchbrenner et al., 2014) is effective for extracting features in texts without considering the global information of that text. Long short-term memory (LSTM) (Tai et al., 2015) can capture long-distance dependencies by sequentially modeling texts across words. The proposed bi-directional LSTM-CNN model combines LSTM and CNN to model texts, encoding global information captured by LSTM in the most principal features extracted by CNN.

We first use word vectors to transform tweets into text matrices. The bi-directional LSTM is applied to these matrices to build new text matrices. CNN is applied to the output of the bi-directional LSTM to obtain text vectors for emotion intensity prediction. LSTM, CNN and their combination are described in detail in the following section.

Proceedings of the 8th Workshop on Computational Approaches to Subjectivity, Sentiment and Social Media Analysis, pages 238–242
Copenhagen, Denmark, September 7–11, 2017. ©2017 Association for Computational Linguistics

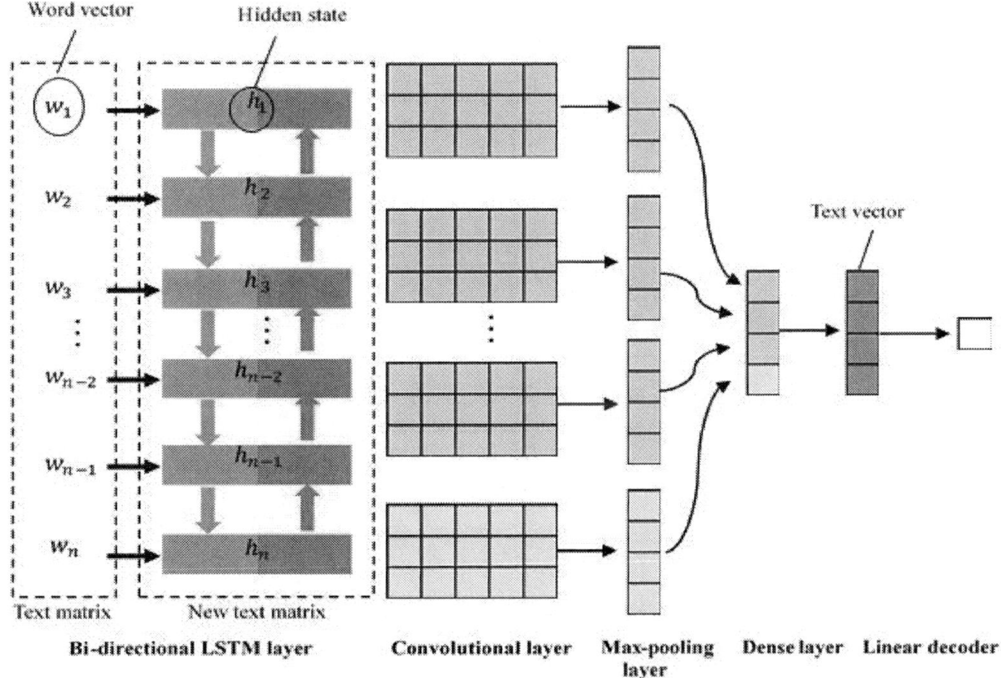

Figure 1: System architecture of the proposed Bi-directional LSTM-CNN model.

2 Bi-directional LSTM-CNN Model

Figure 1 shows the overall framework of the proposed Bi-directional LSTM-CNN model. For a given sentence, the system's input is a sentence matrix composed of the word vectors of all words and punctuation in the sentence. The sentence matrix is further transformed into a new sentence matrix by the Bi-directional LSTM model. The new sentence matrix is then sequentially passed through a convolutional layer and a max pooling layer for feature extraction. The extracted features are then passed through a dense layer to build a sentence vector for emotion intensity prediction.

2.1 Long Short-Term Memory (LSTM)

The LSTM (Hochreiter et al., 1997) uses a gating mechanism to track the state of sequences. There are three gates and a memory cell in the LSTM architecture. The LSTM transition functions are defined as follows:

$$i_t = \sigma(W^i x_t + U^i h_{t-1} + b^i)$$
$$f_t = \sigma(W^f x_t + U^f h_{t-1} + b^f)$$

$$o_t = \sigma(W^o x_t + U^o h_{t-1} + b^o)$$
$$g_t = \tanh(W^g x_t + U^g h_{t-1} + b^g)$$
$$c_t = f_t \circ c_{t-1} + i_t \circ g_t \tag{1}$$
$$h_t = o_t \circ \tanh(c_t)$$

Here W^j, U^j, b^j for $j \in \{i, f, o, g\}$ are the parameters to be learned. h_t is the hidden state to be produced in time step t. The input vector x_t and the hidden state h_{t-1} are the input in time step t. $\sigma(\cdot)$ and $\tanh(\cdot)$ are the logistic sigmoid and hyperbolic tangent functions, $\circ$ is the element-wise multiplication operator, and i_t, f_t, o_t whose values are in (0, 1) are respectively called the input, forget and output gates. c_t is the internal memory cell. i_t controls how much new information will be stored in the current memory cell, f_t controls how much information from the old memory cell will be maintained and o_t controls how much information will be output as the hidden state in the current time step.

LSTM is theoretically powerful in language modelling due to its capability of representing a sentence or text with sequence order information. The last hidden state of the LSTM layer can be

	Anger	Fear	Joy	Sadness
Training set	857	1147	823	786
Development set	84	110	79	74
Test set	760	995	714	673
Max-length in training set	37	42	43	46

Table 1: Summary of data statistics.

	LSTM	CNN	BiLSTM-CNN
LSTM hidden state size	200	-	64
Filter windows	-	2	3
Feature maps	-	128	128
Convolutional layer activation	-	ReLU	ReLU
Dense layer size	-	64	64
Dense layer activation	-	ReLU	ReLU
Dense layer dropout	-	0.3	-
Loss function	MSE	MSE	MSE
Optimizer	adam	adam	adam
Mini-batch size	10	10	10

Table 2: Hyper-parameters Used

regarded as the text representation containing the contextual information of the text. However, LSTM is a biased model, where the words in the tail of a text are more dominant than the words in the header. Thus, prediction performance could be reduced when it is used to capture the emotion intensity of a whole text, since the key components could appear anywhere in the text.

To avoid this problem, we maintain the hidden states of all time steps, and sequentially use the hidden state to replace the original word vector input. Then we build a new text matrix.

In addition, we replace the LSTM layer with a bi-directional LSTM layer consisting of two LSTMs running in parallel: one on the input sequence and the other on the reverse of the input sequence. At each time step, the hidden state of the bi-directional LSTM is the concatenation of the forward and backward hidden states. The hidden state can thus capture both past and future information.

2.2 Convolutional Neural Network (CNN)

The CNN architecture consists of a convolutional layer and a max pooling layer. The convolutional layer's input is the bi-directional LSTM layer's output which is a new text matrix. Once the new text matrix sequentially passes through the convolutional layer, the local n-gram features can be extracted.

The max-pooling layer subsamples the output of the convolutional layer. Pooling is conducted by maintaining the max value of the result of each filter. The max-pooling layer can reduce the dimension of the extracted feature vector and extract the local dependency to maintain the most important information for prediction.

The obtained vectors are then fed to a dense layer to build a text representation. Since emotion intensity is a continuous value, a linear decoder layer uses a linear regression to transform the text representation into a real value.

3 Experiments and Evaluation

This section evaluates the performance of the proposed bi-directional LSTM-CNN model by submitting the results to the EmoInt-2017 task.

Dataset. The statistics of the official dataset (Mohammad and Bravo-Marquez, 2017a) used in this competition are summarized in Table 1. Each tweet was rated with a real-value (emotion intensity) in the range of (0, 1). Training, development and test datasets are provided for four emotions: joy, sadness, fear, and anger. We trained four models corresponding to four emotions using their respective training sets without their development sets. The anger, joy and fear models used the architecture of the proposed bi-directional LSTM-CNN model. To improve results, the sadness model used the architecture of CNN model which excludes the bi-directional LSTM layer shown in Fig.1. For word embeddings, we used GloVe pre-trained word vectors for Twitter (glove.twitter.27B) with 200 dimensions (Pennington et al., 2014).

Implementation details. The hyper-parameters of the network are chosen based on the performance on the development set. In our experiments, we set the length of all tweets in the training set to be

	Anger	Fear	Joy	Sadness	**Avg**
Pearson	0.666	0.677	0.658	0.709	**0.677**
Rank	5	8	6	5	**6**
Spearman	0.641	0.655	0.652	0.713	**0.665**
Rank	5	8	7	5	**6**

Table 3: Results of the proposed BiLSTM-CNN model.

	Anger	Fear	Joy	Sadness	**Avg**
CNN	0.645	0.662	0.617	0.709	**0.658**
LSTM	0.503	0.590	0.585	0.567	**0.561**
BiLSTM-CNN	0.666	0.677	0.658	0.706	**0.677**

Table 5: Comparative results of different methods.

the maximum length in the training set. A linear activation function is used in the output layer. Other hyper-parameters are presented in Table 2.

Evaluation metrics. The EmoInt-2017 task published the results for all participants using the Pearson and Spearman correlation coefficient.

Results. A total of twenty-one teams participated in the task. Table 3 shows the results of the proposed bi-directional LSTM-CNN model. Table 4 shows the results over the subset of the test data with a gold emotion intensity score greater than or equal to 0.5. Table 5 shows the experimental results for CNN, LSTM and their combineations after the release of test set ratings. LSTM used the last hidden state as the text vector, which caused the worse performance than CNN and BiLSTM-CNN. In addition, BiLSTM-CNN performed a little better than CNN and performed well for the subset with higher emotion intensity scores (>=0.5).

4   Conclusions

This study presents a deep learning approach to determine the emotion intensity of tweets. The proposed model combines long short-term memory networks and the convolutional neural networks to encode the global information cap-

	Anger	Fear	Joy	Sadness	**Avg**
Pearson	0.544	0.552	0.471	0.495	**0.516**
Rank	3	5	5	7	**4**
Spearman	0.528	0.520	0.460	0.493	**0.500**
Rank	3	5	5	8	**4**

Table 4: Results of the proposed BiLSTM-CNN model over a subset of the test data with a gold emotion intensity score greater than or equal to 0.5.

tured by LSTM among the most principal features extracted by CNN. Experimental results show that the proposed method archived good performance. Future work will focus on other deep learning approaches such as the attention-based model and tree-LSTM to improve performance, and adopt an additional sentiment corpus to allow the system to capture more sentiment information.

Acknowledgments

This work was supported by the Ministry of Science and Technology, Taiwan, ROC, under Grant No. MOST 105-2221-E-155-059-MY2 and MOST 105-2218-E-006-028. The authors would like to thank the anonymous reviewers and the area chairs for their constructive comments.

References

Rafael A. Calvo and Sunghwan Mac Kim. 2013. Emotions in text: dimensional and categorical models. *Computational Intelligence*, 29(3):527-543.

Paul Ekman. 1992. An argument for basic emotions. *Cognition and Emotion*, 6:169-200.

Ronen Feldman. 2013. Techniques and applications for sentiment analysis. *Communications of the ACM*, 56(4):82-89.

Hatice Gunes and Björn Schuller. 2013. Categorical and dimensional affect analysis in continuous input: Current trends and future directions. *Image and Vision Computing*, 31(2):120-136.

Sepp Hochreiter and Jürgen Schmidhuber. 1997. Long short-term memory. *Neural computation*, 9(8), 1735-1780.

Yoon Kim. 2014. Convolutional neural networks for sentence classification. In *Proceedings of the 2014 Conference on Empirical Methods on Natural*

Language Processing (EMNLP-14), pages 1746-1751.

Nal Kalchbrenner, Edward Grefenstette, and Phil Blunsom. 2014. A convolutional neural network for modelling sentences. In *Proceedings of the 52nd Annual Meeting of the Association for Computational Linguistics (ACL-14)*, pages 655-665.

Svetlana Kiritchenko and Saif M. Mohammad. 2016. The effect of negators, modals, and degree adverbs on sentiment composition. In *Proceedings of the 7th Workshop on Computational Approaches to Subjectivity, Sentiment and Social Media Analysis at NAACL-HLT 2016*, pages 43-52.

Bing Liu. 2012. Sentiment Analysis and Opinion Mining. Morgan & Claypool, Chicago, IL.

Nikos Malandrakis, Alexandros Potamianos, Elias Iosif, Shrikanth Narayanan. 2013. Distributional semantic models for affective text analysis. *IEEE Trans. Audio, Speech, and Language Processing*, 21(11): 2379-2392.

Tomas Mikolov, Kai Chen, Greg Corrado, and Jeffrey Dean. 2013a. Efficient estimation of word representations in vector space. In *Proceedings of International Conference on Learning Representations (ICLR-13): Workshop Track*.

Tomas Mikolov, Ilya Sutskever, Kai Chen, Greg Corrado, and Jeffrey Dean. 2013b. Distributed representations of words and phrases and their compositionality. In *Advances in Neural Information Processing Systems 26*, pages 3111-3119.

Saif M. Mohammad and Felipe Bravo-Marquez. 2017a. Emotion Intensities in Tweets. In *Proceedings of the sixth joint conference on lexical and computational semantics (*Sem)*.

Saif M. Mohammad and Felipe Bravo-Marquez. 2017b. WASSA-2017 Shared Task on Emotion Intensity. In *Proceedings of the EMNLP 2017 Workshop on Computational Approaches to Subjectivity, Sentiment, and Social Media (WASSA)*.

Georgios Paltoglou, Mathias Theunis, Arvid Kappas, and Mike Thelwall. 2013. Predicting emotional responses to long informal text. *IEEE Trans. Affective Computing*, 4(1):106-115.

Bo Pang and Lillian Lee. 2008. Opinion mining and sentiment analysis. *Foundations and trends in information retrieval*, 2(1-2):1-135.

Jeffrey Pennington, Richard Socher, and Christopher D. Manning. 2014. Glove: Global Vectors for Word Representation. In *Proceedings of the 2014 Conference on Empirical Methods on Natural Language Processing (EMNLP-14)*, pages 1532-1543.

Kai Sheng Tai, Richard Socher, and Christopher D. Manning. 2015. Improved semantic representations from tree-structured long short-term memory networks. In *Proceedings of the 52nd Annual Meeting of the Association for Computational Linguistics (ACL-14)*, pages 1556-1566.

Mike Thelwall, Kevan Buckley, and Georgios Paltoglou. 2012. Sentiment strength detection for the social web. *Journal of the Association for Information Science and Technology*, 63(1):163-173.

Jin Wang, Liang-Chih Yu, K. Robert Lai, and Xuejie Zhang. 2016a. Community-based weighted graph model for valence-arousal prediction of affective words. *IEEE/ACM Trans. Audio, Speech and Language Processing*, 24(11):1957-1968.

Jin Wang, Liang-Chih Yu, K. Robert Lai, and Xuejie Zhang. 2016b. Dimensional sentiment analysis using a regional CNN-LSTM model," in *Proceedings of the 53th Annual Meeting of the Association for Computational Linguistics (ACL-16)*, pages 225-230, 2016.

Liang-Chih Yu, Lung-Hao Lee, and Kam-Fai Wong. 2016. Overview of the IALP 2016 shared task on dimensional sentiment analysis for Chinese words. In *Proceedings of the 20th International Conference on Asian Language Processing (IALP-16)*, pages 156-160.

DMGroup at EmoInt-2017: Emotion Intensity Using Ensemble Method

Xiaotian Han[1][*] and **Song Jiang**[2][*]

[1]Department of Computer Science and Technology, Beijing University of Posts and Telecommunications

[2]Department of Microelectronic, Tsinghua University

stentor@163.com, jiangson15@mails.tsinghua.edu.cn

Abstract

In this paper, we present a novel ensemble learning architecture for emotion intensity analysis, particularly a novel framework of ensemble method. The ensemble method has two stages and each stage includes several single machine learning models. In stage1, we employ both linear and nonlinear regression models to obtain a more diverse emotion intensity representation. In stage2, we use two regression models including linear regression and XGBoost. The result of stage1 serves as the input of stage2, so the two different type models (linear and non-linear) in stage2 can describe the input in two opposite aspects. We also added a method for analyzing and splitting multi-words hashtags and appending them to the emotion intensity corpus before feeding it to our model. Our model achieves 0.571 Pearson-measure for the average of four emotions.

1 Introduction

Social media has evolved into a data source that is massive and growing rapidly. Analyzing the emotion of a user's tweet can be helpful to the tasks from personalized advertising to public health monitoring and surveillance. Emotion analysis is a warm area of Natural Language Processing (NLP) dealing with the intensity of emotion in tweets. (An.Y, et al., 2017) Traditional emotion analysis problems are usually classification tasks such as emotion classification (Bandhakavi, et al., 2017). Some of the methods of this task usually use manually designed semantic lexicon. However, these semantic lexicons usually are not general to different corpus and targets and it will take much time to build the

semantic lexicon. And some researchers establish the models using signal machine learning algorithms such as Support Vector Machine (SVM) and naive Bayes (Tang B et al., 2016) However, such signal model just describes the corpus in only one aspect, which will lead to inaccuracy of the emotion analysis since every single model has its own disadvantages. In recent KDD CUPs, winner solutions are not signal models. (Sandulescu, et al 2016, Kadam et al 2015)

Ensemble based methods are among the most widely used techniques for data science problems. Their popularity is because of their good performance compared with strong single learners while being quite easy to arrange in real-world applications. It has been proved in many competitions such as Kaggle competitions (Zou et al 2017) and KDD CUPs mentioned above. Ensemble algorithms usually perform well in the data learning tasks as they can be integrated with different signal algorithms and the strategy of ensemble can be adjusted according to each task.

In this paper, we present a novel ensemble

---

*Song Jiang and Xiaotian Han contributed equally to this article.

Proceedings of the 8th Workshop on Computational Approaches to Subjectivity, Sentiment and Social Media Analysis, pages 243–248
Copenhagen, Denmark, September 7–11, 2017. ©2017 Association for Computational Linguistics

learning architecture for emotion intensity analysis, particularly a novel framework of ensemble method. Our model participated in the WASSA-2017 shared task emotion intensity analysis in tweets. (Mohammad, S.M, et al2017) The goal of the task was to automatically determine the intensity or degree of emotion X when given a tweet and an emotion X. We treat this task as a regression problem. Our ensemble method includes two stages and each stage includes several single regression models. The method can obtain a diverse emotion intensity representation of the corpus. In stage1, we employ three models containing both linear and non-linear regression models and the result of stage1 serves as the input of the stage2. Stage2 has two regression models including linear regression and XGBoost. And finally, the results of the two models in stage2 are added with weights. Meanwhile, we analyze and split multi-words hashtags and this result is also in the algorithm. Our average Pearson-measure score for the average of four emotions is 0.571(shown in Table7).

2 Related Work

A large amount of work related to analyzing emotion have been done. A very broad overview of the existing work was presented in (Pang and Lee, 2008). Meanwhile, there are lots of related work using deeply models (Majumder et al, 2017). In their survey, the authors described existing techniques and approaches for the sentiment analysis and information retrieval. In the paper (Pang et al. 2002) which used machine learning models to predict sentiments in text, the approach showed that SVM classifiers trained using bag-of-words features produced hopeful results. In the paper (Yang et al., 2007), the authors used emotion icons in the blog posts as significant indicators of users sentiment. The authors applied SVM classifier to classify sentiments at the sentence level and then study the overall sentiment of the document. However, social media sources, such as Twitter posts, presented many unsolved natural language processing (NLP) tasks and machine learning challenges. As the intensive study of machine learning in the NLP task, some of the key challenges including data imbalance, noise, and feature sparseness may be solved.

3 System Description

Fig 1 shows the architecture of our ensemble learning model. The core framework of our ensemble models includes the two stages. The ensemble model is an improved version of stacking (Wolpert, 1992; Zhou, 2012). After data processing and feature engineering, the features are sent to the stage1. We test various kinds of regression models. Finally, we find the four regression models can achieve satisfying performance on these features. (Table 6) In stage1, including Linear Regression, Huber Regression, Gradient Boost Decision Trees and XGBoost. The former two models are linear models and the latter two are non-linear. The output of the two different models will be gotten by linear and non-linear algorithms based on raw features, which guarantees the diverse representation of the raw features. With the output of stage1 serves as the input, stage2 also has both linear and non-linear models, including Huber Regression and XGBoost, which are covered by Ensemble block in the figure1.According to the characteristics of data, we carefully tune these models and find some tricks (such as 'emoji' expression) to achieve better performance than raw data. The tuning work will be discussed in following single model sections.

3.1 XGBoost

XGBoost (Chen, T et al,2016) is an open-source software library which provides the gradient boosting framework. From the project description, it aims to provide a Scalable, Portable and Distributed Gradient Boosting (GBM, GBRT, GBDT) Library. In this work, we use XGBoost to as one of the four signal models of stage1 and ensemble model in stage2.

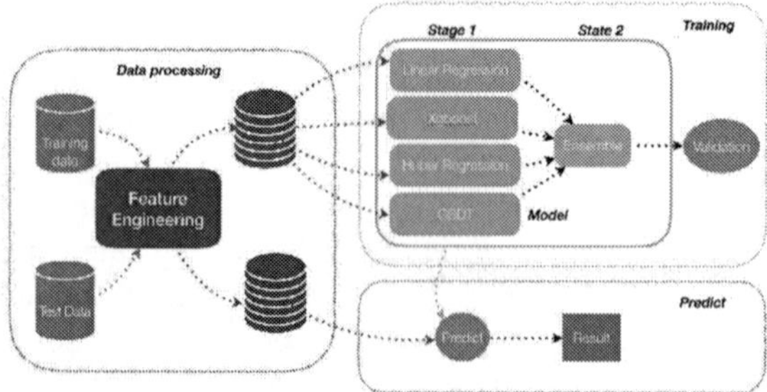

Figure 1: Architecture of the ensemble learning model. Note that "Ensemble" in stage2 contains linear regression and XGBoost models.

XGBoost has gained much popularity and attention recently as it was the algorithm of choice for many winning teams of a number of machine learning competitions. For example, in all the 29 winning solutions published at Kaggle's blog during 2015, 17 teams used XGBoost.

3.2 Gradient Boosting Decision Tree

Gradient Boosting Decision Tree (GBDT) uses decision trees as base learners and combines them into a single strong learner. (Drucker,1996) The final prediction of GBDT is the weighted sum of outputs from each tree. In Stage 1, the model is implemented by scikit-learn package (Pedregosa.F et al, 2011). There are some specific parameters in GBDT: the number of trees (iterations), learning rate, the maximum depth of each tree and the minimum number of samples in a leaf. The last two parameters control the size of each tree. Empirical results show that small values of learning rate favor better test error (Zeiler et al 2012), so we set it as 0.03 in both Stage 1. In Stage 1, we train 500 trees with no less than 50 samples in each leaf, since the data set is much larger.

3.3 Linear Regression

We use the implementation of regularized linear regression from scikit-learn (Pedregosa, F et al 2011) package, with liblinear library solver, to train learner. L2 regularization is chosen to avoid overfitting. We have done tuning work in the training dataset and tried to find the best set of parameters. Finally, the regularization strength is set to 50. Since the distribution of labels in training dataset is not uniform just like class imbalance in classification problem, the weight of positive samples is set to 100, while the weight of negative samples is 1. In addition, the values of all features are normalized to the range of [0,1] with the minimum-maximum scaler.

3.4 Huber Regression

The Huber Regressor (Jeng J et al 2009)optimizes the squared loss for the samples where $|(y - X^0 w)/sigma| < epsilon$ and the absolute loss for the samples where $|(y - X^0 w)/sigma| > epsilon$, where w and sigma are parameters to be optimized. In Huber Regression, the parameter *sigma* is an adjustment factor to guarantee the robustness. In other word, if y is scaled up or down by a certain factor, we do not need to rescale the *epsilon*. The

model we trained to achieve the best average Pearson-measure score 0.554.

4 Feature Engineering

4.1 Data Processing and Feature Extraction

All the data used for training the emotion intensity regression model undergoes the following preprocessing algorithm. Firstly, to determine the importance of word in an emotion, we use a tokenize to separate the corpus into a series of single word. The TfidfVectorizer in the open source sickit-learning (Sklearn) is used to complete this. Secondly, the URL text and other useless specific symbols such as '/' and '_' should be removed from the features because this type of text may mislead the regression model. Then the context information is supposed to be considered since a word may not cover enough information in short texts. Finally consider the following two tweet, *"Sometimes I get mad over something so minuscule I try to ruin somebodies life not like lose your job like get you into federal prison"and "Sometimes I get mad over something so minuscule I try to ruin somebodies life not like lose your job like get you into federal prison #anger "*. The two tweets are nearly same except the last expression tags #anger, which leads to a different intensity. However, the symbol # is removed by TfidfVectorizer, and so is emoji expressions. As a result, these expression texts should be added into the features. Totally, the raw data is processed to features in following steps:

1. Using Scikit-learn TfidfVectorizer to tokenize each tweet.

2. Remove the useless text data including URL and specific symbol.

emotions	train numbers	dev numbers
anger	857	84
sadness	786	74
joy	823	110
fear	1147	110

Table 1: The numbers of instances training dataset and dev datasets

3. Using N-gram (Brown, P. F et al 1992) to import the context information. In this work, N=2.

4. Since default model TfidfVectorizer will remove the emoji and tweet tags, these key expressions need to be recalled.

4.2 Feature Selection

The number of features for the four emotions is from 3722 to 3945 by methods of feature extraction mentioned above. However, some of them are redundant. To improve the efficiency, we design a feature selection strategy to further select the features. Specifically, to avoid overfitting and remove useless features, we design three different

positive	intensity	negative	intensity
fucking	0.609	love	-0.504
fuming	0.568	follow	-0.402
outrage	0.554	heart	-0.367
fuck	0.522	incense	-0.349
angry	0.501	fast	-0.344
furious	0.477	better	-0.329
boiling	0.412	live	-0.309
put	0.406	pray	-0.301
offended	0.403	laughing	-0.290
raging	0.385	best	-0.292

Table 2: anger's words analysis

validation sets (each one 10% of training dataset) and make sure that each feature has performance improvement on all of three validation sets, and then we choose it as an effective feature. This selection process is very important because we can detect if a feature is useful. Finally, 3010 features out of more than 3722 are obtained.

5 Experiments and Analysis

To train and validate our models for this task, we used the dataset provided for Shared Task on Emotion Intensity. (Mohammad, S.M, et al2017) We obtained 857 instances from the training datasets and 84 instances from the Development datasets for the anger intensity, and others show in Table1.We build four different models for the four Emotions: anger, sadness, joy and fear. Table 1 shows the distribution of datasets about all subtasks. All the experiments have been developed using scikit-learn. The models were trained using the default parameters. All our experiments were performed on a machine with Intel Core i5 CPU @ 2.00GHz (4 cores), 8GB of RAM.

5.1 Four Emotion Models

The single model with best score is Huber Regressor, which gets the Pearson of 0.682 in anger task. In the training process of Huber Regressor, every word gets a score of intensity of anger. For example, the word "fucking" gets the 0.609, which is the highest score of intensity of

positive	intensity	negative	intensity
nervous	0.883	terrific	-0.446
panic	0.852	excited	-0.334
anxiety	0.789	refuse	-0.320
nightmare	0.670	wrong	-0.318
die	0.524	love	-0.313
shudder	0.514	serious	-0.308
scared	0.470	year	-0.303
gonna	0.462	walking	-0.300
comments	0.449	yes	-0.299
cry	0.442	kissed	-0.295

Table 3: fear's words analysis

anger. In fact, the word "fucking" mostly means anger. So, the model can represent the intensity of the emotion precisely. Table 2,3,4,5 show the top positive and negative words in four subtasks. As the tables show, the words in the table can reflect the intensity of each emotions.

Table 6 shows our results of the four models on the development datasets for anger emotion intensity prediction. The other three emotions` results are similar to this (not listed here).

5.2 Ensemble Results

Table 7 shows our results on the development datasets and the test datasets for all four subtasks. According to the scores and our ranking in leaderboard, we noticed that our model was not as we expected, which might mainly due to the following reasons:

1. Recently most of teams in many competitions use Neural Networks. As we know, deep learning needs plentiful training dataset(Goodfellow,2016).

positive	intensity	negative	intensity
hilarious	0.612	pity	-0.458
laughter	0.461	hate	-0.448
thanks	0.444	barmy..	-0.420
happy	0.428	tears	-0.383
gets	0.426	bit	-0.382
myahris..	0.423	fucking	-0.379
meant	0.420	sad	-0.365
lol	0.414	say	-0.335
exhilar..	0.406	last	-0.327
nick_off..	0.372	stop	-0.319

Table 4: joy's words analysis

positive	intensity		negative	intensity
depressing	0.723		pine	-0.458
depression	0.672		serious	-0.336
sad	0.603		issues	-0.334
sadness	0.558		moment	-0.331
unhappy	0.517		single	-0.321
despair	0.392		long	-0.320
sulk	0.381		why	-0.313
sick	0.378		look	-0.294
hard	0.367		love	-0.292
swp_roads	0.357		chill	-0.284

Table 5: sadness's words analysis

models	Pearson
LinearRegression	0.55061
HuberRegressor	0.68261
XGBoost	0.64796
GBDT	0.63017
Ensemble	0.68459

Table 6: results of different models of anger

However, our model did not use the Neural Networks and Word Embedding, because the number of training data is not abundant, but we will have try to apply the neural network method to this task in the future.

2. We did not use grid-search to find the best set of parameters of each single model. So, our model can be improved. And we did not use complicated ensemble methods compared with ensemble methods described in (Dietterich, 2002).

3. We did not use the extra information of the emotion intensity of every word which means that we learning the emotion intensity just from the datasets provided. The training datasets and development datasets all the information that we used in the task.

Although our model has a gap with the top teams, we have some advantages as following:

1. we did not consume excessive computing resources, and our training time is ms-level which is fast enough for this task. And our model is suitable for all the subtask while all the subtask has the same model and all the emotions intensity predicted is stable enough, which is robust in train set, development set and test set.

2. After training, we can obtain an extra emotion lexicon which can be used for other

Unsupervised learning task, such as obtain a unlabeled sentence emotion intensity as the scores of four subtask in dev and test datasets have no big difference.

emotions	dev Pearson	test Pearson
anger	0.68459	0.550
sadness	0.47009	0.603
joy	0.66913	0.556
fear	0.56406	0.576
average	0.59697	0.571

Table 7: The results of dev datasets and test datasets (5% lower than baseline)

6 Conclusion and Further Work

Our model achieved moderate performance on the emotion intensity sentiment analysis task with very basic settings include the default setting of the parameters of the methods. Considering that the performance of our model was achieved by a sample settings, there is big achievement of better performance by adopting the more exquisite methods and the more feature engineering. We have several planned works to improve the performance in this task, including the more fusion of the methods and the statistical feature. We will also attempt to optimize our models further and use the word embedding which may provide additional information to improve our performance.

Acknowledgments

We would like to acknowledge the support of the Beijing University of Posts and Telecommunications and Tsinghua University.

References

An, Y., Sun, S., & Wang, S. 2017. Naive Bayes classifiers for music emotion classification based on lyrics. In Computer and Information Science (ICIS), *2017 IEEE/ACIS 16th International Conference on (pp. 635-638). IEEE.*

Bandhakavi, A., Wiratunga, N., Padmanabhan, D., & Massie, S. 2017. Lexicon based feature extraction for emotion text classification. *Pattern Recognition Letters*, 93, 133-142.

Tang, B, Kay, S., & He, H. 2016. Toward optimal feature selection in naive bayes for text categorization. *IEEE Transactions on Knowledge & Data Engineering, 28*(9), 2508-2521.

Sandulescu, Vlad, and Mihai Chiru. 2016."Predicting the future relevance of research institutions-The winning solution of the KDD Cup 2016." *arXiv preprint arXiv:*1609.02728 .

Kadam, Priti, et al. 2015."KDD CUP 2015-Predicting Dropouts in MOOC'S." *Imperial Journal of Interdisciplinary Research* 2(5).

Zou, Haosheng, Kun Xu, and Jialian Li. 2017 "The YouTube-8M Kaggle Competition: Challenges and Methods." *arXiv preprint arXiv*:1706.09274.

Mohammad, Saif M. and Bravo-Marquez, Felipe. September 2017. "WASSA-2017 Shared Task on Emotion Intensity". *In Proceedings of the EMNLP 2017 Workshop on Computational Approaches to Subjectivity, Sentiment, and Social Media (WASSA)* Copenhagen, Denmark.

Pang, Bo, Lee, & Lillian. 2008. Opinion mining and sentiment analysis. *Foundations & Trends in Information Retrieval, 2*(1–2), 1-135.

Majumder, N., Poria, S., Gelbukh, A., & Cambria, E. 2017. Deep Learning-Based Document Modeling for Personality Detection from Text. *IEEE Intelligent Systems, 32*(2), 74-79.

Pang, B., Lee, L., & Vaithyanathan, S. July 2002,. Thumbs up?: sentiment classification using machine learning techniques. In *Proceedings of the ACL-02 conference on Empirical methods in natural language processing-Volume 10* (pp. 79-86). Association for Computational Linguistics.

Yang, C., Lin, K. H. Y., & Chen, H. H. November 2007. Emotion classification using web blog corpora. In *Web Intelligence, IEEE/WIC/ACM International Conference on* (pp. 275-278). IEEE.

Wolpert, D. H. 1992. Stacked generalization .*Neural networks, 5*(2), 241-259.

Zhou, Z. H. 2012. *Ensemble methods: foundations and algorithms*. CRC press.

Chen, T., & Guestrin, C. August 2016. Xgboost: A scalable tree boosting system. In *Proceedings of the 22Nd ACM SIGKDD International Conference on Knowledge Discovery and Data Mining* (pp. 785-794). ACM.

Drucker, H., & Cortes, C. 1996. Boosting decision trees. *In Advances in neural information processing systems* (pp. 479-485).

Pedregosa, F., Varoquaux, G., Gramfort, A., Michel, V., Thirion, B., Grisel, O., ... & Vanderplas, J. 2011. Scikit-learn: Machine learning in Python. *Journal of Machine Learning Research, 12*(Oct), 2825-2830.

Zeiler, M. D. 2012. ADADELTA: an adaptive learning rate method. *arXiv preprint arXiv*:1212.5701.

Jeng, J. H., Tseng, C. C., & Hsieh, J. G. 2009. Study on Huber fractal image compression. *IEEE Transactions on Image Processing*,18(5), 995-1003.

Pedregosa, F., Varoquaux, G., Gramfort, A., Michel, V., Thirion, B., Grisel, O., ... & Vanderplas, J. (2011). Scikit-learn: Machine learning in Python. *Journal of Machine Learning Research, 12*(Oct), 2825-2830.

Brown, P. F., Desouza, P. V., Mercer, R. L., Pietra, V. J. D., & Lai, J. C. 1992. Class-based n-gram models of natural language *Computational linguistics, 18*(4), 467-479.

Goodfellow, I., Bengio, Y., & Courville, A. 2016. *Deep learning*. MIT press.

Dietterich, T. G. 2002. Ensemble learning. *The handbook of brain theory and neural networks*, 2, 110-125.

UWat-Emote at EmoInt-2017: Emotion Intensity Detection using Affect Clues, Sentiment Polarity and Word Embeddings

Vineet John
Cheriton School of Computer Science
University of Waterloo
vineet.john@uwaterloo.ca

Olga Vechtomova
Department of Management Sciences
University of Waterloo
ovechtom@uwaterloo.ca

Abstract

This paper describes the UWaterloo affect prediction system developed for EmoInt-2017. We delve into our feature selection approach for affect intensity, affect presence, sentiment intensity and sentiment presence lexica alongside pretrained word embeddings, which are utilized to extract emotion intensity signals from tweets in an ensemble learning approach. The system employs emotion specific model training, and utilizes distinct models for each of the emotion corpora in isolation. Our system utilizes gradient boosted regression as the primary learning technique to predict the final emotion intensities.

1 Introduction

The goal of this EmoInt task is to predict the intensity of affect expressions in a selection of tweets. The intensity scores are floating point values between 0 and 1, representing low and high intensities of the emotion being expressed, respectively. The emotions analyzed in this shared task are anger, fear, joy and sadness (Mohammad and Bravo-Marquez, 2017b) (Mohammad and Bravo-Marquez, 2017a).

This paper describes the techniques used to clean tweets, build lexical features, find optimal combinations of features to produce a final vector representation of a tweet and train generalized regression, gradient boosted regression and neural-network computed regression models to fit the vector representations to the intensity scores.

The following sections describe each of these processes, followed by an enumeration of the parameters that worked in favor of the best-performing models, a discussion of the results and

potential approaches to boost model accuracy.

2 Related Work

A majority of the existing literature on emotion/affect analysis on text focuses on classification tasks which aim to predict the probability distribution of a pre-defined set of emotions in bodies of text (Alm et al., 2005) (Aman and Szpakowicz, 2007) (Strapparava and Mihalcea, 2007). The VAD (valence, arousal and dominance) model as a way of visualizing multiple aspects of each known emotion was proposed by (Schlosberg, 1954), which has subsequently been adopted by other studies in quantifying emotion (Bradley and Lang, 1999).

This shared task is designed with the purpose of detecting intensity of a tweet given an emotion, which is comparable to detection of arousal to stimulus in the VAD model. The immediate difference that is noted compared to emotion classification tasks is that the training data can be annotated with cross-emotional intensity scores. The annotated scores for the tweets is obtained using Best-Worst Scaling, which increases the reliability of continuous valued scores (Kiritchenko and Mohammad, 2017).

3 Data Cleaning

Tweets, in general, are not always syntactically well-structured and the language used doesn't always strictly adhere to grammatical rules (Barbosa and Feng, 2010). Our feature extraction approach doesn't depend on syntactic features, relying solely on the presence of lexical features.

The grammatically incorrect use of language in many published tweets also makes it a necessity to clean the raw text in order to filter noisy data including special characters, alphanumeric strings, etc. The letter case for each tweet is standard-

Proceedings of the 8th Workshop on Computational Approaches to Subjectivity, Sentiment and Social Media Analysis, pages 249–254
Copenhagen, Denmark, September 7–11, 2017. ©2017 Association for Computational Linguistics

ized by converting all tweets to lowercase. Stopwords are removed using NLTK (Bird, 2006). The hashtags in the tweets are stripped of the # symbol, and each of the hashtags are treated as regular unigrams in the corpus. The twitter handles are stripped away under the hypothesis that they are entity references that aren't correlated with affect.

All of the annotated lexica are also cleaned in the exact same way as the tweets are, to ensure that lexical pattern matching does not suffer as a result of the cleaning.

4   Feature Extraction

We used two primary methods for feature extraction from the tweets' raw text, namely annotated lexicons (Section 4.1) and pre-trained word embeddings (Section 4.2)

4.1   Annotated lexicons

Our system utilizes curated lexicons for emotion intensity/presence and sentiment intensity/presence. We include sentiment lexicons with the hypothesis that positive sentiment-polarity lexicon features would be positively correlated with some emotions and negatively correlated with others and vice-versa, since the emotion classes themselves possess an inherent sentiment polarity.

- **NRC Affect Intensity Lexicon (AI):** This lexicon assigns distinct emotion labels to unigrams, and provides the intensity at which the emotion is expressed. Each of the emotions evaluated in the EmoInt shared task are represented in this lexicon, and a floating point intensity score is assigned to each unigram-emotion pair (Mohammad, 2017).

- **NRC Emotion Lexicon (EL) & NRC Hashtag Emotion Lexicon (HE):** These lexicons contain the association of unigrams and Twitter hashtags with eight emotions (inclusive of the four emotions evaluated in this EmoInt task). EL is manually annotated on Amazon's Mechanical Turk (EL) and is scored either 0 or 1 implying whether or not the unigram is associated with any of the lexicon's eight emotion categories (Mohammad and Turney, 2010). HE is generated automatically from tweets with emotion-word hashtags and the features are floating point scores ranging from 0 to 2.24, indicating the intensity of the emotion category (Mohammad and

Turney, 2013).

- **NRC Emoticon Lexicon (EC), NRC Hashtag Sentiment Lexicon (HS), NRC Emoticon Affirmative Context Lexicon and NRC Emoticon Negated Context Lexicon (EAN) & NRC Hashtag Affirmative Context Sentiment Lexicon and NRC Hashtag Negated Context Sentiment Lexicon (HSAN):** The first two lexicons associate words with positive/negative sentiment and the other two associate words with similar sentiment labels in affirmative or negated contexts generated automatically from tweets with sentiment-emoticons and sentiment-word hashtags. The terms in these lexicons can be unigrams, bigrams or pairs of unigrams and bigrams. The features are three-fold: a real-valued sentiment score denoted by the point-wise mutual information between a term and the positive/negative class, the number of times the term appears in each positive and negative contexts (Kiritchenko et al., 2014) (Mohammad et al., 2013) (Zhu et al., 2014).

- **SentiWordNet (SWN):** SentiWordNet is an opinion mining resource available through NLTK. Words in this lexicon are related in terms of synonymy. For each word present in the WordNet lexicon, three floating point sentiment scores are given: positive, negative and objective, such that

$$\sum_{i \in pos,neg,obj} word\_score_i = 1$$

The positive and negative scores are extracted as features for each of the individual words present in the cleaned tweets. If a word does not have an entry or synonym in SentiWordNet, the positive and negative sentiment scores are assumed to be zero (Esuli and Sebastiani, 2007).

- **Emoji Valence (EV):** This is a hand-classified lexicon of Unicode emojis, rated on a scale of -5 (negative) to 5 (positive)[1].

- **Depeche Mood (DM):** This is a lexicon comprised of about 37,000 unigrams annotated with real-valued scores for the emotional states *afraid, amused, angry, annoyed, don't*

---

[1] https://github.com/wooorm/emoji-emotion

Emotion	Features	P	Sp	P (> 0.5)	Sp (> 0.5)
anger	W2V-GN, W2V-T, GV-T, AI, EL, EC, HS	0.705	0.686	0.521	0.507
fear	W2V-GN, W2V-T, GV-T, AI, SWN, EL, EC, EAN	0.713	0.694	0.558	0.525
joy	W2V-GN, GV-T, SWN, EC, HE, HS	0.728	0.705	0.619	0.599
sadness	W2V-T, GV-T, AI, SWN, EL, EC, EAN, HE, HS	0.679	0.668	0.507	0.468

Table 1: Training Cross-validated Accuracy

Emotion	Features	P	Sp	P (> 0.5)	Sp (> 0.5)
anger	W2V-GN, W2V-T, GV-T, AI, EC, HSL, GV-CC1, GV-CC2	0.691	0.670	0.581	0.556
fear	W2V-GN, W2V-T, GV-T, AI, SWN, EL, EC, EAN, HE, GV-WG, GV-CC2, EV	0.716	0.696	0.558	0.523
joy	W2V-GN, GV-T, AI, EC, HSL, HSAN, GV-WG, GV-CC1, EV	0.728	0.733	0.567	0.556
sadness	W2V-GN, W2V-T, GV-T, AI, SWN, EAN, HE, HSAN, GV-CC2, EV	0.729	0.723	0.550	0.535

Table 2: Testing Accuracy - Features + ML

care, *happy*, *inspired* and *sad* (Staiano and Guerini, 2014).

4.2 Word Embeddings

In addition to the features extracted from annotated lexica, vector representations of each of the tweets are generated from pre-trained word embeddings using large corpora. For our system, we utilize six distinct word embedding sources including two Word2Vec models, and four GloVe models.

- **Word2Vec Model - Google News (W2V-GN), Tweets (W2V-T):** Word2Vec is a technique for learning low-dimensional word embeddings for words in a corpus, based on the continuous bag-of-words (CBOW) and skip-gram models (Mikolov et al., 2013). W2V-GN is trained on the Google News corpus containing over 100 billion words. It is a skip-gram model containing 300-dimensional embeddings for 3 million distinct words and phrases[2]. W2V-T is a similar skip-gram model trained on tweets (Godin

et al., 2015) and the embeddings produced are 400-dimensional and real-valued[3].

- **GloVe Model - Tweets (GV-T), Wikipedia + Gigaword (GV-WG), Common Crawl 42B tokens (GV-CC1), Common Crawl 840B tokens (GV-CC2):** GloVe is similar to Word2Vec, in that it obtains dense vector representations of words. GloVe builds a word co-occurrence matrix for the entire corpus prior to training. This matrix is then utilized to produce word and phrase vectors based on their context of appearance in the corpus (Pennington et al., 2014). The embeddings used in the system are 200- to 300-dimensional and real-valued[4].

The tweet vector representations using each of these word embeddings could be obtained either by averaging or summing up the real-valued word vectors for each of the words that had a corresponding trained vector representation from the pre-trained embeddings. Our system averages the word vectors, to avoid introducing a tweet length bias.

---

[2]https://code.google.com/archive/p/word2vec/

[3]http://www.fredericgodin.com/software

[4]https://nlp.stanford.edu/projects/glove

Emotion	**P**	**Sp**	**P** (> 0.5)	**Sp** (> 0.5)
anger	0.692	0.678	0.529	0.519
fear	0.713	0.701	0.553	0.531
joy	0.676	0.680	0.422	0.423
sadness	0.704	0.711	0.556	0.554

Table 3: Testing Accuracy: Pre-trained Embedding Features + Shallow Neural Network

5   Model Learning

Since the task requires the computation of a real-valued emotion intensity score for the tweets in the test set, we explored several regression methods.

The models initially tested including simple linear regression and generalized linear models like Gaussian process regression and Bayesian ridge regression.

We also conducted experiments using two feed-forward neural network (NN) architectures implemented in Keras[5]. The shallow NN architecture (Fig.1) uses a hidden layer densely connected to a sigmoid output neuron, while the deep NN architecture (Fig.2) uses iteratively smaller dense hidden layers culminating in a sigmoid output neuron.

The first layer for the shallow NN as well as all layers for the deep NN were comprised of densely connected ReLU activation units. The learning method used is stochastic gradient descent (SGD).

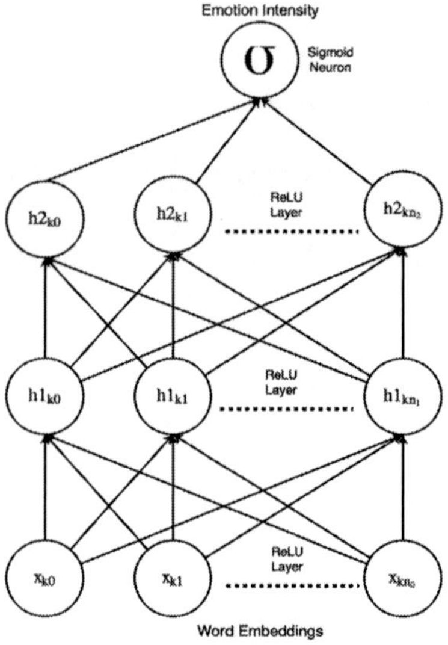

Figure 2: Deep NN Architecture

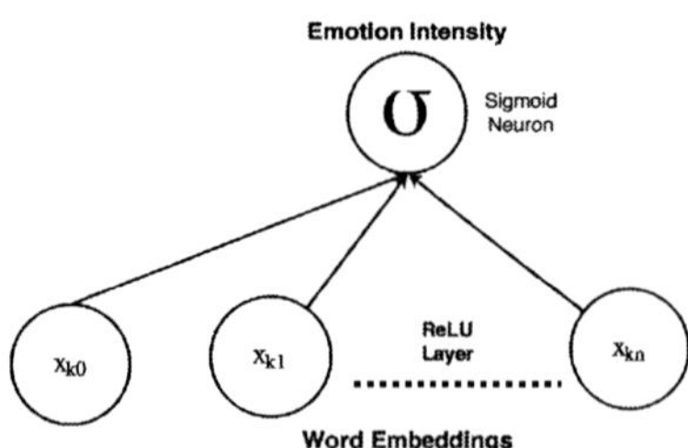

Figure 1: Shallow NN Architecture

However, all of these models were outperformed by gradient boosted regression models. The final system implementation uses the boosted regression implementation provided by the XGBoost library[6] (Chen and Guestrin, 2016).

6   System Tuning

The system was tuned with respect to feature selection by performing an exhaustive grid search in the space of different possible combinations for the features. Consequently, the emotion intensity scores for each of the four emotions' test sets are predicted using models that have been trained on different subsets of the features, the accuracy results of which are discussed in Section 7.

Polynomial transformations of the features extracted from the annotated lexicons described in Section 4.1 were used to introduce non-linearity into the final feature space. The hyper-parameters of the gradient boosted regression model, namely tree-depth and number of boosted trees[7], were tuned using a randomized search strategy. The tree-depth retained it's library-default value of 3, and the number of boosted trees was set to 30,000.

Each of the feature sets was determined using 10-fold cross-validated evaluation on the combination of the training and development datasets.

---

[5]https://github.com/fchollet/keras
[6]http://dmlc.cs.washington.edu/ xgboost.html

[7]http://xgboost.readthedocs.io/en/ latest/python/python_api.html

7 Results

The systems in this shared task are evaluated using the Pearson correlation coefficient, which computes a bivariate linear correlation, and the Spearman rank correlation coefficient, which is a non-parametric version of the Pearson correlation coefficient, and relies on rank/ordering rather than absolute values (Mohammad and Bravo-Marquez, 2017b). These scores are denoted by **P** and **Sp**, respectively, in the results tables.

We present the results of the system submitted to the competition leaderboard in Table 1. The average scores of the system were 0.685 (Pearson) and 0.671 (Spearman). Post-competition evaluation on the gold labels of the test set are presented in tables 2 and 3. The correlation scores improved to 0.716 (Pearson) and 0.705 (Spearman) after grid-search testing including new features (EV & DM) using gradient boosted regression, as shown in table 2. Table 3 presents accuracy scores obtained using the Shallow NN architecture using only word embeddings as features.

Our system ranked 4th overall, and 3rd for the intensity range 0.5 to 1, on the task leaderboard.

8 Discussion

The results demonstrate that there is a different set of features that works best for each emotion in the task. It is observed that pre-trained word embeddings learned using Word2Vec and GloVe dominate the set of best performing features for nearly every emotion.

From experimental observations on the NN architectures in Keras, it was determined that increasing the depth of the network did not significantly improve its prediction accuracy. It was also noticed that the inclusion of regular & polynomial versions of the annotated lexicon features as features severely hampered the network's predictive accuracy. This could potentially be addressed by scaling each feature's values into a standard Gaussian distribution, or by clamping gradients to predetermined boundary values.

It is also worth noting that sentiment polarity lexicons boosted predictive accuracy for all four models, corroborating our hypothesis to justify their inclusion in the feature set.

9 Conclusion

We have described UWat-Emote, used at EmoInt to predict the emotion intensity of tweets. Our best system utilizes a combination of lexical resources and word embeddings to obtain vector representations of tweets, and uses gradient boosted regression to predict real-valued emotion intensities.

The system utilizes separate models for each emotion and achieves average Pearson and Spearman correlation scores of 0.716 and 0.705 respectively. Our implementation is fully open-sourced for replicability[8].

In the future, we would like to explore aspect based affect intensity for larger bodies of text, such as customer reviews for products and services. We would also like to evaluate normalized polynomial-kernel features and integrate the annotated lexicon features into convolutional and recurrent neural-network architectures.

Acknowledgments

We would like to acknowledge the organizers of this shared task, Saif M. Mohammad and Felipe Bravo-Marquez for their support.

We would also like to thank Saif M. Mohammad and Pierre Charron for permitting access to the NRC emotion and sentiment lexicons for this task.

References

Cecilia Ovesdotter Alm, Dan Roth, and Richard Sproat. 2005. Emotions from text: Machine learning for text-based emotion prediction. In *Proceedings of the Conference on HLT/EMNLP*. Association for Computational Linguistics, HLT '05.

Saima Aman and Stan Szpakowicz. 2007. Identifying expressions of emotion in text. In *Text, speech and dialogue*. Springer, pages 196–205.

Luciano Barbosa and Junlan Feng. 2010. Robust sentiment detection on twitter from biased and noisy data. In *Proceedings of the 23rd CICLing: Posters*. Association for Computational Linguistics, pages 36–44.

Steven Bird. 2006. Nltk: the natural language toolkit. In *Proceedings of the COLING/ACL on Interactive presentation sessions*. Association for Computational Linguistics, pages 69–72.

Margaret M Bradley and Peter J Lang. 1999. Affective norms for english words (anew): Instruction manual and affective ratings. Technical report, Technical report C-1, the center for research in psychophysiology, University of Florida.

---

[8] `https://github.com/v1n337/wassa-emoint-2017`

Tianqi Chen and Carlos Guestrin. 2016. Xgboost: A scalable tree boosting system. In *Proceedings of the 22Nd ACM SIGKDD International Conference on Knowledge Discovery and Data Mining*. ACM, pages 785–794.

Andrea Esuli and Fabrizio Sebastiani. 2007. Sentiwordnet: A high-coverage lexical resource for opinion mining. *Evaluation* pages 1–26.

Fréderic Godin, Baptist Vandersmissen, Wesley De Neve, and Rik Van de Walle. 2015. Multimedia lab@ acl w-nut ner shared task: named entity recognition for twitter microposts using distributed word representations. *ACL-IJCNLP* 2015:146–153.

Svetlana Kiritchenko and Saif M Mohammad. 2017. Best–worst scaling more reliable than rating scales: A case study on sentiment intensity annotation. In *Proceedings of The Annual Meeting of the Association for Computational Linguistics (ACL). Vancouver, Canada.*

Svetlana Kiritchenko, Xiaodan Zhu, and Saif M Mohammad. 2014. Sentiment analysis of short informal texts. *Journal of Artificial Intelligence Research* 50:723–762.

Tomas Mikolov, Ilya Sutskever, Kai Chen, Greg S Corrado, and Jeff Dean. 2013. Distributed representations of words and phrases and their compositionality. In *Advances in neural information processing systems.* pages 3111–3119.

Saif M Mohammad. 2017. Word affect intensities. *arXiv preprint arXiv:1704.08798* .

Saif M. Mohammad and Felipe Bravo-Marquez. 2017a. Emotion intensities in tweets. In *Proceedings of the sixth joint conference on lexical and computational semantics (*Sem).* Vancouver, Canada.

Saif M Mohammad and Felipe Bravo-Marquez. 2017b. Wassa-2017 shared task on emotion intensity. In *In Proceedings of the EMNLP 2017 Workshop on Computational Approaches to Subjectivity, Sentiment, and Social Media (WASSA).* pages 26–34.

Saif M Mohammad, Svetlana Kiritchenko, and Xiaodan Zhu. 2013. Nrc-canada: Building the state-of-the-art in sentiment analysis of tweets. *In Proceedings of the seventh International Workshop on Semantic Evaluation Exercises (SemEval-2013)* page 321.

Saif M Mohammad and Peter D Turney. 2010. Emotions evoked by common words and phrases: Using mechanical turk to create an emotion lexicon. In *Proceedings of the NAACL HLT 2010 workshop on computational approaches to analysis and generation of emotion in text*. Association for Computational Linguistics, pages 26–34.

Saif M Mohammad and Peter D Turney. 2013. Crowdsourcing a word–emotion association lexicon. *Computational Intelligence* 29(3):436–465.

Jeffrey Pennington, Richard Socher, and Christopher D. Manning. 2014. Glove: Global vectors for word representation. In *Empirical Methods in Natural Language Processing (EMNLP)*. pages 1532–1543.

Harold Schlosberg. 1954. Three dimensions of emotion. *Psychological review* 61(2):81.

Jacopo Staiano and Marco Guerini. 2014. Depechemood: A lexicon for emotion analysis from crowd-annotated news. *arXiv preprint arXiv:1405.1605* .

Carlo Strapparava and Rada Mihalcea. 2007. Semeval-2007 task 14: Affective text. In *Proceedings of the 4th International Workshop on Semantic Evaluations*. Association for Computational Linguistics, pages 70–74.

Xiaodan Zhu, Svetlana Kiritchenko, and Saif M Mohammad. 2014. Nrc-canada-2014: Recent improvements in the sentiment analysis of tweets. In *Proceedings of the 8th international workshop on semantic evaluation (SemEval 2014)*. Citeseer, pages 443–447.

LIPN-UAM at EmoInt-2017:
Combination of Lexicon-based features and Sentence-level Vector Representations for Emotion Intensity Determination

Davide Buscaldi
LIPN, Université Paris 13,
Villetaneuse,
France
buscaldi@lipn.univ-paris13.fr

Belem Priego
UAM
Atzcapotzalco,
Mexico
belemps@gmail.com

Abstract

This paper presents the combined LIPN-UAM participation in the WASSA 2017 Shared Task on Emotion Intensity. In particular, the paper provides some highlights on the system that was presented to the shared task, partly based on the Tweetaneuse system used to participate in a French Sentiment Analysis task (DEFT2017). We combined lexicon-based features with sentence-level vector representations to obtain a random forest model.

1 Introduction

Nowadays, an important quantity of the textual information that is produced everyday on the Web originates from social media and commercial sites with crowd-sourced reviews. These data include beliefs, opinions and judgments, expressed in various forms, sometimes resorting to the use of figurative language, such as irony, which makes an automated analysis of these texts even more difficult. Therefore, there is an increased interest by academia and industry towards the field of Sentiment Analysis (SA). This research activity has been mainly focused to extract and characterize opinions by recognizing the attitude (positive, negative or objective) of an opinion holder on a certain topic, or determine the global polarity of a given text.

A more recent and emerging field consists of studying the opinions in a more detailed way, revealing the underlying emotions, such as anger, fear, joy and disgust. One of the pioneer works in this sense is the one by (Strapparava and Mihalcea, 2008), in which they proposed for the first time a dataset dedicated to emotion analysis and some knowledge and corpus-based approach.

Their proposal included texts annotated with six emotions: anger, disgust, fear, joy, sadness and surprise. More recently, (Cambria et al., 2014) proposed Sentic.net[1], a resource for concept-level sentiment analysis, containing word senses annotated with weighted emotions.

The Shared Task proposed at WASSA2017 (Mohammad and Bravo-Marquez, 2017) aims to steer research about sentiments and emotions in text towards the intensity of the expressed emotions, and not only on binary polarity values or assigning an emotion to the texts. This paper describes the system submitted to the WASSA 2017 shared task by the joint LIPN-UAM team, in part based on the "Tweetaneuse" system that participated to the French Sentiment Analysis task DEFT 2017 (Benamara et al., 2017). The rest of the paper is structured as follows: in Section 2 we describe the features used and the machine learning approach; in Section 3 we show the results obtained on the official data together with some experiments to verify the effectiveness of the proposed features. Finally, in Section 4 we draw some conclusion about our participation.

2 System Description

The system that we built for our participation in the Shared Task at WASSA2017 is based on a set of 8 features derived from lexicons and various textual clues, and 600 features derived from word embeddings. These features are used to train a random forest regressor. These features are inspired by those previously used for our participation in the French sentiment analysis task at DEFT2017. The basic textual clues were the following ones:

- *smi*: presence of a smiley;

---

[1] http://sentic.net/

Proceedings of the 8th Workshop on Computational Approaches to Subjectivity, Sentiment and Social Media Analysis, pages 255–258
Copenhagen, Denmark, September 7–11, 2017. ©2017 Association for Computational Linguistics

- *shout*: number of uppercase words (to detect the fact that the writer is shouting);

- *excl*: number of exclamation marks;

- *int*: number of interrogation marks.

We used 4 different lexicons: sentic.net (Cambria et al., 2014), labMT (Dodds et al., 2011), the NRC Affect Intensity lexicon (Mohammad, 2017), and the emojis sentiment ranking by (Novak et al., 2015). We already talked about sentic.net in Section 1. We limited the use of sentic.net to the polarity values since the shared task did not involve determining which emotion was contained in the sentence but only its intensity. LabMT is a lexicon obtained via Mechanical Turk that is currently used in the hedonometer.org project to measure average happiness in Twitter. We thought that this lexicon would be particularly useful for the joy and sadness categories. The emojis sentiment ranking is a lexicon obtained from a set of 1.6 million tweets manually annotated with their polarity strength, and is currently, to our knowledge, the only available resource providing the polarity and the intensity for emojis. The features extracted from these lexicons were the following ones:

- *pol*: average of sentic.net polarity values in the sentence;

- *happiness*: average of happiness values according to labMT;

- *nrc_ai*: average of scores from the NRC affect intensity lexicon (according to the emotion being tested);

- *emoji*: sum of scores from the emojis sentiment ranking.

The scores for all dictionaries have been modified to take into account the position where the score is detected. This modification reflects the idea that affective words towards the end of the sentence are more important than those at the beginning or the middle of the sentence. This is particularly true in the case of tweets where there may be affective hashtags at the end of the message, such as in the case *"All I want to do is watch some netflix but I am stuck here in class. #depressing"* (we normalized hashtags by removing the leading #). The formula used is the following one:

$$\hat{s}(w) = s(w) * (1 + 0.15 * rpos(w))$$

Where $rpos(w)$ is the relative position of word w within the sentence (i.e. $pos(w)/len(sentence)$) and $s(w)$ is the original score from the lexicons. The 0.15 weight was arbitrarily chosen.

These features are completed with sentence-level vector representations based on word embeddings. Word embeddings, as introduced by (Bengio et al., 2006), are vector representations of words that capture a certain number of syntactic and semantic relationships, generated with neural networks. One of the problems with word embeddings is how to compose them to obtain a representation of a sentence, knowing that sentences may have variable sizes. (De Boom et al., 2016) showed that it's possible to exploit the properties of embeddings to represent sentences with the average or a combination of the max and the min (per dimension) of the vectors of the composing words. We chose to use the second method since it is the one that achieved the best results in their experiments.

In our work, we used the pre-trained vectors trained on 100 billion words from the Google News dataset used for word2vec (Mikolov et al., 2013). The vocabulary size is 3 million words and the vector length is 300. Therefore, in our system each sentence is represented by a vector of size 600.

The advantages of this representation are two: on one hand, it is more concise than the bag-of-words representation (600 dimensions while a typical BOW vector has thousands of components); on the other, it compensates for the words that are not observed in the training set (since the vocabulary size for embeddings is $>>$ than the vocabulary size for the task training corpora).

3 Results

The official results are listed in Table 1. The system ranked slightly below the baseline system, except on the 'sadness' test set, where our system was better. The results obtained for the emotion intensities in the range $0.5 - 1$ (shown in Table 2) are also very close to the baseline system, with the exception of the results obtained on the 'sadness' test set. This evaluation scenario highlights some problems that our system had on the 'joy' dataset.

Test Set	Pearson	Spearman
anger	0.580	0.575
fear	0.639	0.630
joy	0.583	0.601
sadness	0.676	0.686
average	0.619	0.623
baseline	0.648	0.641

Table 1: Results obtained at the WASSA2017 Shared Task.

Test Set	Pearson	Spearman
anger	0.435	0.439
fear	0.496	0.463
joy	0.366	0.347
sadness	0.489	0.503
average	0.446	0.438
baseline	0.477	0.442

Table 2: Results obtained at the WASSA2017 Shared Task, for intensity values in the range $[0.5, 1.0]$.

We already observed during the development phase that the system was quite 'cautious' in the output scores, providing scores in the range $(0.3, 0.7)$, with some exceptions. We impute this behaviour to two factors: the scarcity of extreme examples in the training set, and the use of random forests. However, we tried to use a Support Vector Regressor but the results were significantly worse (from 5 to 10% less depending on the test set).

Table 3 shows the results we obtained with different configurations of the system, in particular using only vectors, or only dictionary and text-based features. This experiment highlights the fact that on the 'joy' dataset, lexicons and text clues alone were able to beat the vector representations. On the other hand, we can observe that when the vector representations worked, the system was able to perform well. This is difficult to explain, but we suspect it to be related to the data used to train the vectors. We expect newswire data to contain more details about negative events, such as wars, natural disasters or accidents, which contains more words related to fear and sadness. This bias may result in modelling negative words better than positive ones.

Finally, we carried out Correlation Feature Selection (CFS) to test which features were most related to the intensity values. The CFS showed that *nrc_ai* and *emoji* were among the best features for all datasets. Among the base features, the CFS indicates that *excl* was important for 'joy' and 'anger', while *shout* was one of the best features for 'joy' and 'fear'.

Test Set	All features	Vectors	Lexicons+base
anger	0.580	0.547	0.388
fear	0.639	0.632	0.439
joy	0.583	0.524	0.555
sadness	0.676	0.651	0.615
average	0.619	0.588	0.499

Table 3: Pearson correlation obtained with different configurations of the system: *Vectors* - only the max/min of word embeddings are used; *Lexicons+base* - only text-based clues and lexicon-based features are used.

4 Conclusions

In this participation we combined the use of word embeddings with lexicon-based features and simple text clues. According to the low complexity of the system created, the obtained results were close to the baseline system. Further analysis of the results allowed us to detect a possible problem with the news corpus used to train the word embeddings: news language does not necessarily use emotions, and when it does, the emotions are often related to negative events such as wars, natural disasters, etc. We plan to carry out the experiments with a different set of pre-trained vectors, in particular those extracted from Twitter by (Godin et al., 2013).

Feature analysis indicates that the NRC affective intensity dictionary (Mohammad and Turney, 2013) and the Emojis dictionary by (Novak et al., 2015) were particularly useful. As a future work, we plan to add a classification layer to the system to detect whether the emotion expressed is extreme or not, in order to improve the results on the most polarizing messages. Finally, we would like to test the effectiveness of the positional weighting for lexicon scores.

Acknowledgements

This work is part of the program "Investissements d'Avenir" overseen by the French National Research Agency, ANR-10-LABX-0083 (Labex EFL).

References

Farah Benamara, Cyril Grouin, Jihen Karoui, Véronique Moriceau, and Isabelle Robba. 2017. Analyse d'opinion et langage figuratif dans des tweets : présentation et résultats du Défi Fouille de Textes DEFT2017 (In French). In *Actes de l'atelier DEFT2017 associé la conférence TALN*. Orleans, France. To appear.

Yoshua Bengio, Holger Schwenk, Jean-Sébastien Senécal, Fréderic Morin, and Jean-Luc Gauvain. 2006. *Neural Probabilistic Language Models*, Springer Berlin Heidelberg, Berlin, Heidelberg, pages 137–186. https://doi.org/10.1007/3-540-33486-6_6.

Erik Cambria, Daniel Olsher, and Dheeraj Rajagopal. 2014. Senticnet 3: a common and common-sense knowledge base for cognition-driven sentiment analysis. In *Twenty-eighth AAAI conference on artificial intelligence*.

Cedric De Boom, Steven Van Canneyt, Thomas Demeester, and Bart Dhoedt. 2016. Representation learning for very short texts using weighted word embedding aggregation. *Pattern Recogn. Lett.* 80(C):150–156. https://doi.org/10.1016/j.patrec.2016.06.012.

Peter Sheridan Dodds, Kameron Decker Harris, Isabel M Kloumann, Catherine A Bliss, and Christopher M Danforth. 2011. Temporal patterns of happiness and information in a global social network: Hedonometrics and twitter. *PloS one* 6(12):e26752.

Fréderic Godin, Viktor Slavkovikj, Wesley De Neve, Benjamin Schrauwen, and Rik Van de Walle. 2013. Using topic models for twitter hashtag recommendation. In *Proceedings of the 22nd International Conference on World Wide Web*. ACM, pages 593–596.

Tomas Mikolov, Ilya Sutskever, Kai Chen, Greg S Corrado, and Jeff Dean. 2013. Distributed representations of words and phrases and their compositionality. In *Advances in neural information processing systems*. pages 3111–3119.

Saif M Mohammad. 2017. Word Affect Intensities. *arXiv preprint* arXiv:1704.08798.

Saif M. Mohammad and Felipe Bravo-Marquez. 2017. WASSA-2017 shared task on emotion intensity. In *Proceedings of the Workshop on Computational Approaches to Subjectivity, Sentiment and Social Media Analysis (WASSA)*. Copenhagen, Denmark.

Saif M Mohammad and Peter D Turney. 2013. Crowdsourcing a word–emotion association lexicon. *Computational Intelligence* 29(3):436–465.

Petra Kralj Novak, Jasmina Smailović, Borut Sluban, and Igor Mozetič. 2015. Sentiment of emojis. *PloS one* 10(12):e0144296.

Carlo Strapparava and Rada Mihalcea. 2008. Learning to identify emotions in text. In *Proceedings of the 2008 ACM Symposium on Applied Computing*. ACM, New York, NY, USA, SAC '08, pages 1556–1560. https://doi.org/10.1145/1363686.1364052.

deepCybErNet at EmoInt-2017: Deep Emotion Intensities in Tweets

Vinayakumar R and **Premjith B** and **Sachin Kumar S** and **Soman K P**
Center for Computational Engineering and Networking,
Amrita School of Engineering, Amrita Vishwa Vidyapeetham,
Amrita University, India
`vinayakumarr77@gmail.com`

Prabaharan Poornachandran
Center for Cyber Security Systems and Networks,
Amrita School of Engineering, Amrita Vishwa Vidyapeetham,
Amrita University, India

Abstract

This working note presents the methodology used in deepCybErNet submission to the shared task on Emotion Intensities in Tweets (EmoInt) WASSA-2017. The goal of the task is to predict a real valued score in the range [0-1] for a particular tweet with an emotion type. To do this, we used Bag-of-Words and embedding based on recurrent network architecture. We have developed two systems and experiments are conducted on the Emotion Intensity shared Task 1 data base at WASSA-2017. A system which uses word embedding based on recurrent network architecture has achieved highest 5 fold cross-validation accuracy. This has used embedding with recurrent network to extract optimal features at tweet level and logistic regression for prediction. These methods are highly language independent and experimental results shows that the proposed methods is apt for predicting a real valued score in than range [0-1] for a given tweet with its emotion type.

1 Introduction

Internet has become an essential platform to carry out daily activities to our lives. People use social media resources like Twitter, Facebook, WhatsApp, Hike, WeChat etc. to share their language such as views or emotions, stance over issues, reviews related to products, services, blogs etc. In recent days, the amount of language sharing through the internet is ubiquitous. This necessitates the need of analyzing reviews to identify the emotions including estimating the degree to which an emotion is expressed in text. Unlike natural language, the user reviews are small; rich information is represented through nonstandard language such as emoticons, emojis, creatively spelled words (happee), and hash-tagged words (#happy). These factors can make a high influence on the social and economic behavior worldwide like real-world applications such as marketing, e-Governance, business intelligence, social analysis and applications in Natural Language Processing (NLP) - information extraction, question answering, textual entailment, etc. Many methods have been introduced by researchers for emotion annotation work. This gives binary labels for the given text (Alm et al., 2005), (Aman and Szpakowicz, 2007; Brooks et al., 2013),(Neviarouskaya et al., 2009), (Bollen et al., 2011), (Summa et al., 2016). only one annotation work exists for providing a real valued score as annotation for a given text (Strapparava and Mihalcea, 2007). This was a task included in the SemEval-2007 shared task. Many methods devised for automatic emotion classification (Werbos, 1990), (Summa et al., 2016), (Mohammad, 2012), (Bollen et al., 2011), (Aman and Szpakowicz, 2007), (Brooks et al., 2013). However, only less amount work exists on emotion regression other than SemEval-2007 shared task (Strapparava and Mihalcea, 2007).

In this paper, we use Bag-of-Words (BOW) and a Bag-of-Words (BOW) based recurrent embedding system for predicting a real valued score in the range [0-1]. In first case, BOW is used to obtain the feature representation for the tweets and classification is done using logistic regression. We also employed an RNN and LSTM based method for mining the features at tweets level. These methods are language independent. So irrespective of the language, we can use these approaches for finding the stance of micro blogging posts.

The rest of the paper is organized as follows. Section 2 discusses information of shared task. Section 3 discusses the proposed methodology.

Proceedings of the 8th Workshop on Computational Approaches to Subjectivity, Sentiment and Social Media Analysis, pages 259–263
Copenhagen, Denmark, September 7–11, 2017. ©2017 Association for Computational Linguistics

Dataset	Anger	Fear	Joy	Sadness
Training	857	1147	823	786
Development	84	110	79	74
Testing	760	995	714	673

Table 1: Statistics of Tweet Emotion Intensity dataset

Section 4.2 provides experimental analysis and results and at last conclusion is placed in Section 5.

2 Task description

The Emotion Intensity Task is a shared task of 8th Workshop on Computational Approaches to Subjectivity, Sentiment & Social Media Analysis (WASSA 2017) in conjunction with the EMNLP 2017 conference (Mohammad and Bravo-Marquez, 2017). The aim of the task is to obtain a real valued score in the range [0-1] for the given tweet including an emotion type . The tweets in training, validation and testing are from four different categories such as anger, fear, joy, sadness. Each tweet has an emotion type with its score in the range [0-1], where 0 denotes that the tweet has maximally away from its emotion and 1 denotes that the tweet has maximally closer to its emotion . The detailed statistics of the data set is described in Table 1.

3 Methodology

This section provides the information of the proposed approach for predicting a real valued score in the range [0-1] for a given twee with an emotion type . We used two approaches; (1) Bag-of-words (BoW) based word embedding(2) Recurrent Neural Network (RNN) based word embedding

3.1 Bag-of-words based system for Emotion Intensities in Tweets

The embedding size was set to 256 so that each word is now represented using a 256 dimension vector and word length to 70. Anger, Fear, Joy and Sadness have $857, 1147, 823$ and 786 instances. We constructed matrix of shape $857X70, 1147X70, 823X70$ and $786X70$ for training instances and $84X70, 110X70, 79X70$ and $74X70$ for development instances. Next, we replace each word with their corresponding word embedding and this forms an input tensor of shape $857X70X256, 1147X70X256, 823X70X256$ and $786X70X256$ for training instances and $84X70X256, 110X70X256, 79X70X256$ and

$74X70X256$ for development instances. At last, an input tensor is transformed to matrix of shape $857X256, 1147X256, 823X256$ and $786X256$ for training instances and $84X256, 110X256, 79X256$ and $74X256$ for development instances using max-pooling approach. These matrices are passed to logistic regression and a real valued score is chosen for a given tweet with an emotion type using argmax function.

3.2 Recurrent neural network (RNN) based system for Emotion Intensities in Tweets

Recurrent neural network is largely used deep learning architecture for sequence data modeling. This has achieved significant results in various tasks exists in the field of natural language processing (LeCun et al., 2015). It generally looks same as feed forward networks (FFN), additionally contains self-recurrent connection in units (Elman, 1990). This cyclic loop carries out information from one time-step to another. Consequently, RNN are able to learn the temporal patterns by considering the past information in estimating the present states. Generally, RNN takes input as $x_t \in R^n$ and $hi_{t-1} \in R^m$ of arbitrary length to compute succeeding hidden state vector hi_t by using the following formulae recursively.

$$h_t = f(w_{xh}x_t + w_{hh}h_{t-1} + b) \tag{1}$$

$$o_t = sf(w_{oh}h_t + b_{ot}) \tag{2}$$

Where f is the nonlinear activation function, particularly logistic sigmoid function (σ) applied on element wise, hi_0 is usually initialized to 0 at timestep $t0$ and $w_{xh} \in R^{m \times n}$, $w_{hh} \in R^{m \times m}$ and $b \in R^m$ are arguments of affine transformation. Here o is the output at time step t.

Using RNN approach, a system was implemented for predicting a real valued score in the range [0-1] for emotional intensities in tweets. By following the aforementioned mechanism, we constructed an input tensor of shape $857X70X256, 1147X70X256, 823X70X256$ and $786X70X256$ for training instances and $84X70X256, 110X70X256, 79X70X256$ and $74X70X256$ for development instances. So the embedding matrix for the tweets of size $70X256$ in both training and development are now reduced to 256 dimensional vectors. So, embedding matrices of size $857X256, 1147X256, 823X256$ and $786X256$ were used as training samples and

$84X256, 110X256, 79X256$ and $74X256$ were taken as development instances and then fed into the RNN layer followed by logistic regression for prediction.

3.3 Long short-term memory based system for Emotion Intensities in Tweets

RNN issues vanishing and exploding gradient issue in memorizing long-term dependencies (Bengio et al., 1994). To reduce, (Hochreiter and Schmidhuber, 1997) has introduced long short-term memory (LSTM). Unlike RNN simple units in recurrent hidden layer, LSTM has introduced a memory block. A memory block is a complex processing unit that contains one or more memory cell, adaptive gates such as input gate and output gate and Constant Error Carousel (CEC). A memory block stores an information and updates them across time-steps based on the input and output gates. Input and output gate controls the input and output flow of information to a memory cell. Additionally, it is has a built-in value as 1 for constant Error carousel (CEC). This value will be activated when in the absence of value from the outside the signal. Moreover, (Gers et al., 1999) introduced forget gate, (Gers et al., 2002) introduced peephole connections to the memory block in LSTM. A forget gate facilitates to forget or reset the values across time steps and peephole connections helps to learn precise timing of the outputs. The newly proposed architecture has performed well in learning long-range temporal dependencies in various artificial intelligence (AI) tasks (LeCun et al., 2015). Generally, at each time step an LSTM network considers the following 3 inputs; x_t, h_{t-1}, c_{t-1} and outputs h_t, c_t through the following equations

$$i_t = \sigma(w_i x_t + U_i h_{t-1} + V_i m_{t-1} + b_i) \quad (3)$$

$$f_t = \sigma(w_f x_t + U_f h_{t-1} + V_f m_{t-1} + b_f) \quad (4)$$

$$o_t = \sigma(w_o x_t + U_o h_{t-1} + V_o m_{t-1} + b_o) \quad (5)$$

$$\tilde{m}_t = \tanh(w_m x_t + U_m h_{t-1} + b_m) \quad (6)$$

$$m_t = f_t^i \odot m_{t-1} + i_t \odot \tilde{m} \quad (7)$$

$$h_t = o_t \odot \tanh(m_t) \quad (8)$$

Where x_t is the input at time step t, σ is sigmoid non-linear activation function, $\tanh$ is hyperbolic tangent non-linear activation function,$\odot$ denotes element-wise multiplication. Concretely, at $t = 0$

Method	Emotion	Pearson	Spearman
	Anger	0.677	0.697
Bow	Fear	0.675	0.685
	Joy	0.601	0.621
	Sadness	0.657	0.647
	Anger	0.718	0.707
RNN	Fear	0.715	0.75
	Joy	0.601	0.721
	Sadness	0.707	0.71
	Anger	0.721	0.736
LSTM	Fear	0.72	0.753
	Joy	0.621	0.725
	Sadness	0.737	0.724

Table 2: 5-fold cross validation with embedding vector size 128

hidden and memory cell state vectors such as h_0 and c_0 are initialized to 0.

We followed subsections 3.1 and 3.2 to develop a LSTM based system for predicting a real valued score in the range [0-1] for a given emotion including its emotion type. This system is constructed by simple replacing RNN layer with LSTM.

4 Experiments

All deep learning architecture are trained using GPU enabled TensorFlow (Abadi et al., 2016) with backpropagation through time (BPTT) (Werbos, 1990).

4.1 Parameter Selection

To choose optimal parameter for embedding size, the LSTM model is trained with embedding size 128 and 256 and the performance of them is evaluated on the development data set. The detailed evaluation results are displayed in Tables 2 and 3. We didn't use any hyper parameter tuning mechanism for tweet length instead we used static length 70 in all our experiments.

4.2 Evaluation results

We have submitted one run based on LSTM based recurrent embedding system to WASSA2017 and the detailed results is displayed in Tables 4 and 5

Analysis of training results and testing results showed that there is a significant difference in the performance measure. This is due to the overfitting of the model to the training data because, a deep learning framework requires huge amount of data to learn the features. Unavailability of such

Method	Emotion	Pearson	Spearman
BoW	Anger	0.681	0.71
	Fear	0.682	0.695
	Joy	0.611	0.632
	Sadness	0.661	0.654
RNN	Anger	0.721	0.714
	Fear	0.724	0.761
	Joy	0.613	0.742
	Sadness	0.714	0.721
LSTM	Anger	0.731	0.741
	Fear	0.741	0.764
	Joy	0.634	0.732
	Sadness	0.739	0.731

Table 3: 5-fold cross validation with embedding vector size 256

sufficient training data samples caused the overfitting of the system. This in turn affected the accuracy of prediction.

5 Conclusion

This working note has presented a language independent approach based on BoW and recurrent based embedding for predicting a real valued score in the range [0-1] for a given tweet with an emotion type. LSTM network has outperformed both bag-of-words embedding and recurrent based embedding mechanism. This is primarily due to the fact that LSTM has capability to learn long-temporal dependencies across time steps. Due to less number of instances in training data, the accuracy of the proposed mechanism is less. Though, the efficacy of embedding's of RNN and LSTM is considerable and paves the manner in future to use for predicting real valued score in the range [0-1] with more training instances including its emotion type. To justify that the proposed deep learning mechanism has capability to perform better with large amount of instances will be remained as one direction towards future work.

References

Martín Abadi, Paul Barham, Jianmin Chen, Zhifeng Chen, Andy Davis, Jeffrey Dean, Matthieu Devin, Sanjay Ghemawat, Geoffrey Irving, Michael Isard, et al. 2016. Tensorflow: A system for large-scale machine learning. In *Proceedings of the 12th USENIX Symposium on Operating Systems Design and Implementation (OSDI). Savannah, Georgia, USA*.

Cecilia Ovesdotter Alm, Dan Roth, and Richard Sproat. 2005. Emotions from text: machine learning for text-based emotion prediction. In *Proceedings of the conference on human language technology and empirical methods in natural language processing*. Association for Computational Linguistics, pages 579–586.

Saima Aman and Stan Szpakowicz. 2007. Identifying expressions of emotion in text. In *International Conference on Text, Speech and Dialogue*. Springer, pages 196–205.

Yoshua Bengio, Patrice Simard, and Paolo Frasconi. 1994. Learning long-term dependencies with gradient descent is difficult. *IEEE transactions on neural networks* 5(2):157–166.

Johan Bollen, Huina Mao, and Alberto Pepe. 2011. Modeling public mood and emotion: Twitter sentiment and socio-economic phenomena. *ICWSM* 11:450–453.

Michael Brooks, Katie Kuksenok, Megan K Torkildson, Daniel Perry, John J Robinson, Taylor J Scott, Ona Anicello, Ariana Zukowski, Paul Harris, and Cecilia R Aragon. 2013. Statistical affect detection in collaborative chat. In *Proceedings of the 2013 conference on Computer supported cooperative work*. ACM, pages 317–328.

Jeffrey L Elman. 1990. Finding structure in time. *Cognitive science* 14(2):179–211.

Felix A Gers, Jürgen Schmidhuber, and Fred Cummins. 1999. Learning to forget: Continual prediction with lstm .

Felix A Gers, Nicol N Schraudolph, and Jürgen Schmidhuber. 2002. Learning precise timing with lstm recurrent networks. *Journal of machine learning research* 3(Aug):115–143.

Sepp Hochreiter and Jürgen Schmidhuber. 1997. Long short-term memory. *Neural computation* 9(8):1735–1780.

Yann LeCun, Yoshua Bengio, and Geoffrey Hinton. 2015. Deep learning. *Nature* 521(7553):436–444.

Saif M Mohammad. 2012. # emotional tweets. In *Proceedings of the First Joint Conference on Lexical and Computational Semantics-Volume 1: Proceedings of the main conference and the shared task, and Volume 2: Proceedings of the Sixth International Workshop on Semantic Evaluation*. Association for Computational Linguistics, pages 246–255.

Saif M Mohammad and Felipe Bravo-Marquez. 2017. Emotion intensities in tweets.

Alena Neviarouskaya, Helmut Prendinger, and Mitsuru Ishizuka. 2009. Compositionality principle in recognition of fine-grained emotions from text. In *ICWSM*.

Emotion	Pearson	Spearman	Average Pearson	Average Spearman
Anger	0.176	0.155		
Fear	0.023	0.011	0.076	0.071
Joy	-0.019	0.008		
Sadness	0.124	0.108		

Table 4: Test results in range [0-1]

Emotion	Pearson	Spearman	Average Pearson	Average Spearman
Anger	0.19	0.164		
Fear	0.077	0.061	0.14	0.134
Joy	-0.057	0.071		
Sadness	0.235	0.238		

Table 5: Test results in range [0.5-1]

Carlo Strapparava and Rada Mihalcea. 2007. Semeval-2007 task 14: Affective text. In *Proceedings of the 4th International Workshop on Semantic Evaluations*. Association for Computational Linguistics, pages 70–74.

Anja Summa, Bernd Resch, Geoinformatics-Z GIS, and Michael Strube. 2016. Microblog emotion classification by computing similarity in text, time, and space. In *Proceedings of the Workshop on Computational Modeling of Peoples Opinions, Personality, and Emotions in Social Media*. pages 153–162.

Paul J Werbos. 1990. Backpropagation through time: what it does and how to do it. *Proceedings of the IEEE* 78(10):1550–1560.

Author Index